A PRACTICAL APPROACH TO
CONVEYANCING

A PRACTICAL APPROACH TO
CONVEYANCING

TWENTIETH EDITION

Professor Robert M. Abbey

BA (HONS), SOLICITOR

Judge of the First-tier Tribunal (Property Chamber)
(previously Deputy Adjudicator to HM Land Registry) and formerly
Professor of Legal Education and Practice, University of Westminster

Mark B. Richards

LLB (HONS), SOLICITOR

Visiting Lecturer in Law, University of Westminster

OXFORD
UNIVERSITY PRESS

OXFORD

UNIVERSITY PRESS

Great Clarendon Street, Oxford, OX2 6DP,
United Kingdom

Oxford University Press is a department of the University of Oxford.
It furthers the University's objective of excellence in research, scholarship,
and education by publishing worldwide. Oxford is a registered trade mark of
Oxford University Press in the UK and in certain other countries

Seventeenth edition 2015
Eighteenth edition 2016
Nineteenth edition 2017

Impression: 1

Published in the United States of America by Oxford University Press
198 Madison Avenue, New York, NY 10016, United States of America

British Library Cataloguing in Publication Data

Data available

ISBN 978-0-19-882308-7

Printed in Great Britain by
Bell & Bain Ltd., Glasgow

MH18766638422132

For

Emily, Abby, Harriet, and Robin

and

Daniel, Lauren, Alexander, and Thomas

ACKNOWLEDGEMENTS

In Appendix 4, the Standard Conditions of Sale (5th edition) are reproduced for educational purposes only by kind permission of Oyez Professional Services Limited and the Law Society of England and Wales.

In Appendix 5, the Law Society's Standard Form of Contract is reproduced for educational purposes only by kind permission of Oyez Professional Services Limited and the Law Society of England and Wales.

In Appendix 12, Part 1 of the *UK Finance Mortgage Lenders' Handbook for England and Wales* is reproduced by kind permission of the Council of Mortgage Lenders.

Crown Copyright material is reproduced under Class License C2006010631 with the kind permission of the Controller of HMSO.

Land Registry material is Crown copyright and is reproduced with kind permission of the Land Registry.

PREFACE

I am one of those . . . lawyers who never addresses a jury, or in any way draws down public applause; but in the cool tranquillity of a snug retreat, do a snug business among rich men's bonds, and mortgages, and title deeds. All who know me, consider me an eminently safe man.

Bartleby by Herman Melville

Our aim in writing this book is to provide a clear, succinct, and practical guide to conveyancing law and practice. If this aim is achieved, we hope that the reader will be served in acquiring a better understanding and appreciation of a much undervalued skill, namely, the 'art of conveyancing'. We trust that the book will prove beneficial to all solicitors involved in property law as well as their support staff, trainee solicitors, licensed conveyancers, legal executives, law students, and indeed anyone else interested in the transfer of land.

In this edition we have incorporated the latest developments in conveyancing practice and procedure.

We would like to thank former Assistant Land Registrar David Ellison at Land Registry for his helpful comments and guidance on Land Registry practice, as well as Patrick Milne. Our thanks go also to Robert's former colleagues at Russell Jones & Walker, especially Peter Klim, Debbie Valentine, and Robert's assistant, Ajda Ali. We also wish to thank the staff and directors at OUP.

This will be the last edition to be edited by Robert Abbey. He has reached the age where he has more in common with unregistered land than e-conveyancing and so it is time for him to depart. He would like to thank all those who have helped him on the way to this twentieth edition but in particular his co-author Mark, as well as the practitioners and students who have read and hopefully found this book useful in their coming to terms with the delights of conveyancing. He hopes he has been 'an eminently safe man'.

As always we have provided, for quick and easy reference, regular key points summaries and practical checklists.

Robert Abbey
Mark Richards
London
May 2018

CONTENTS SUMMARY

CONTENTS

ONLINE RESOURCE CENTRE CONTENTS

STUDENT AND PRACTITIONER RESOURCES

Multiple-choice questions

Test your knowledge of the topics in the book and receive immediate feedback

Additional appendices

Providing useful further information

Forms

Links to key specimen forms commonly encountered in practice

Interactive conveyancing timelines

Two interactive timelines to help put the conveyancing process in context—one specific to residential conveyancing, and one for commercial conveyancing

Example of compulsory clauses in registered leases

Guidance on completing prescribed clauses

Note on the SRA Code of Conduct 2011

Plus a link to the Code

Law Society practice note on conflicts of interest

Link to the note from August 2011

Further reading and web links

Links to key sites and supplementary resources for students and practitioners in conveyancing

Additional resources from Abbey & Richards: *Property Law*

Free access to the resources for Robert Abbey and Mark Richards' other book, Property Law, *including:*

- documentation in support of the commercial and residential case studies featured in the book
- further multiple-choice questions
- an additional chapter on Commonhold

LECTURER RESOURCES

Figures from the book

Diagrams from the book available to download in electronic format

TABLE OF CASES

TABLE OF LEGISLATION

TABLE OF SECONDARY LEGISLATION

TABLE OF SOLICITORS' RULES

1

INTRODUCTION

A AN INTRODUCTION TO CONVEYANCING

OUR APPROACH IN THIS BOOK

Introduction

This book has been written by two legal academics and solicitors who between them have **1.01**
over 70 years' experience of conveyancing practice. Consequently we believe we have written a book which effectively highlights a practical approach to the process of conveyancing. But it is not a book which just looks backwards. We believe that the future for
conveyancing practitioners lies in greater efficiency and in a deeper understanding of the
conveyancing process, including the system of land registration. With these aims in mind
we have produced a book which we believe addresses these objectives as well as offering an
understanding to practitioners and law students of the process as a whole.

Property law and practice

Conveyancing is not a frozen topic. It is presently a fast-moving and fast-changing area **1.02**
of law and practice. Statute, information technology (IT), case law, and market forces all
represent current factors pressing change upon conveyancing practitioners. Indeed, the title
'conveyancing' itself is turning into 'property law and practice'. As a result, practitioners
have an even greater need for signposts through this maze of changing paths. Therefore, we
have adopted the signpost heading method for all the chapters. You, the reader, will find at
the start of each chapter a list of contents for that particular chapter and the topics within
it. This method has been adopted to help the busy practitioner (or student) find the relevant

area of interest as quickly as possible. We appreciate from our own experience of practice that there is nothing worse than wasting hours fruitlessly searching through untitled sub-chapter sections trying to locate the desired subject. Each paragraph is separately numbered so that you can navigate quickly throughout the text.

Key point summaries and checklists

1.03   Within each chapter there are also two further elements designed to assist the busy reader. First, where appropriate, we have included key points, summaries highlighting important elements within a particular topic. These are provided as reminders of important points that should never be overlooked, even in the hurly-burly of the busy, modern legal office. Second, we have included, at the end of most chapters, checklists for the busy practitioner who may be seeking a quick overview of the important elements or the procedures in any particular topic. Our overall aim is to provide a clear, useful, and, in particular, practical approach to conveyancing which will help all those who use the book. In this way we hope to assist in the pursuit of an understanding of how conveyancing can be a stimulating and, at times, even an exciting legal skill.

AN INTRODUCTION TO CONVEYANCING

1.04   Conveyancing is the process by which legal title to property is transferred. As a consequence, over time a conveyance has become the description for the document making such a transfer. In many ways conveyancing is like Shakespeare's character Autolycus in *The Winter's Tale*, a 'snapper-up of unconsidered trifles'. Like this amiable rogue, conveyancing takes from here, there, and everywhere, from within the full range of the law. Conveyancing rests and has been built upon the three foundations of land law, contract law, and equity and trusts. Because of this, a confident appreciation of land law is crucial for success in conveyancing. Land law sets out the estates and interests that will form the subject matter of all conveyancing transactions, and without an understanding of these details no practitioner will cope. You will also need to have a prior knowledge and understanding of the details concerning the formation of contracts, the formalities of written contracts, misrepresentation, and remedies for breach of contract. When you consider that conveyancing is about the transfer of title, and that these transfers are in the main made by contract, you will readily appreciate why contract law plays such an important part. Each conveyance on sale will involve preparing a written agreement. Moreover, your land law will tell you that without a written contract containing all the terms of the agreement there is no deal (see the Law of Property (Miscellaneous Provisions) Act 1989).

The influence of equity

1.05   A detailed understanding of the influence of equity as well as trust law will always be a prerequisite for a successful conveyancer. This important foundation to conveyancing is not so obviously relevant as land law and contract law, but it is nevertheless a pervasive element in conveyancing. You need to know, for example, all about third-party rights and co-ownership. You will need to understand the differences between tenants in common and joint tenants and their relevance to joint ownership in conveyancing. You will need to be absolutely clear on the law relating to trusts. You will need to remind yourself about the equitable remedies that are available. It is one thing to understand their availability in theory but it is another to apply them to a practical situation (see Chapter 9).

So, the key to understanding the nature of conveyancing is to appreciate how it calls upon **1.06** various disparate areas of the law. It means that you must abandon a discrete approach to applying the separate elements of the law. Conveyancing requires you to blend your knowledge. Conveyancing does not relate just to the transfer of ownership of residential properties. It covers the transfer of title to both houses as well as flats, new and second-hand properties, and commercial property of all kinds. (We look at leaseholds, which will include flats, in Chapter 10, new properties in Chapter 11, and the basics of commercial property in Chapter 12.)

Registered and unregistered conveyancing

The history of land transactions has dictated two parallel conveyancing systems. The sys- **1.07** tem of unregistered conveyancing has for centuries been the method by which the transfer of title has been made. It worked satisfactorily when land ownership was limited to a privileged few, but with the growth of home ownership (along with the population) in the nineteenth century it started to exhibit major pitfalls. Moves to reform the system grew in the direction of the registration of land. Accordingly, the traditional system is considered first, but in outline only, and a more detailed consideration of the reforming land registration system follows.

On 26 February 2002, the Land Registration Act 2002 received the Royal Assent and came **1.08** into force on 13 October 2003. This Act made detailed changes to the present-day system of registered land conveyancing, and indeed to registered land law. This is discussed in Section B below. The Act and subsequent rules make extensive changes to the way registered land is conveyed. How practitioners cope with these changes will demonstrate their ability to handle these alterations to the way they work. We hope this book will assist you in coping with this ongoing revolution in property law and practice.

A CONVEYANCING TIMELINE

We set out in Figure 1.1 a timeline of a typical conveyancing transaction. This shows the vari- **1.09** ous stages in such a transaction and is placed at this early point in the book so that you can familiarize yourself with these stages as you read through the text. You can then look back at the timeline to contextualize what you are reading in relation to the transaction as a whole.

CONVEYANCING OF UNREGISTERED LAND

Introduction

The traditional system of conveyancing of unregistered land has been in existence for **1.10** centuries, although it was overhauled by the Law of Property Act 1925. (This was accompanied initially by the Land Registration Act 1925, which fully put in place the reforming system of land registration. This is continued by the Land Registration Act 2002.) The entire unregistered system relies on the existence of written documents, or deeds, to show to a buyer a period of unchallenged ownership which will substantiate the seller's ownership. At present, statute stipulates a minimum period of unchallenged ownership of 15 years (Law of Property Act 1969, s 23). This will be considered in detail in Chapter 5. It is mentioned here to highlight the different approach taken in registered land. The major problem of the unregistered system is that there is an almost total reliance on the integrity of the title deeds. If they are, either in part or in whole, lost, damaged, or forged, severe problems will inevitably arise

4

Figure 1.1 A conveyancing timeline

Pre-exchange					Exchange and pre-completion				Completion and post-completion		
Stage 1	Stage 2	Stage 3	Stage 4	Stage 5	Stage 6	Stage 7	Stage 8	Stage 9	Stage 10	Stage 11	Stage 12
Taking instructions and advising client	Draft contract	Pre-contract searches, enquiries, & planning	Title	Mortgage (applies throughout process)	Exchange of contracts	Purchase deed	Pre-completion searches and requisitions	Financial statements	Completion	SDLT and registration	Delays and remedies

Note: Refer to the interactive timelines on the Online Resource Centre for details of the issues to be considered at each stage of the process.

for the owner seeking to prove title. (It was reported in the *Observer* (10 January 1999), that deeds to the homes of 60,000 customers of the then Bradford & Bingley Building Society—nearly 15 per cent of their borrowers—were burnt to ashes by a fire in a storage depot. It is just this kind of incident which highlights a major weakness in the system of unregistered conveyancing.) Furthermore, the mere existence of deeds does not guarantee any title, though buyers may take comfort from the existence of deeds stretching back over time along with the actual occupation of the property by the seller. However, these mounting difficulties added momentum to the nineteenth-century calls for reform.

1.11 Many of the different elements of the traditional system are considered at several relevant points throughout the book. In particular, readers are referred to Chapter 3 concerning the draft contract, and Chapter 5 regarding deducing and investigating title.

B CONVEYANCING OF REGISTERED LAND

CONVEYANCING OF REGISTERED LAND

1.12 The preamble to the Land Registry Act 1862 states that 'it is expedient to give certainty to the title to real estates and to facilitate the proof thereof and also to render the dealing with land more simple and economical'. It remains true, 156 years later, that the aims of the system for the conveyancing of registered land should be reliability and simplicity, and that the process be economic. These are the objectives that underpin the drive for the complete registration of land throughout England and Wales. However, above all else the major difference between the traditional system and registered land is that registered land is accompanied by a State guarantee of title that is guaranteed by and through Land Registry.

1.13 As was noted in 1.08, the Land Registration Act 2002 received the Royal Assent on 26 February 2002. This came into force on 13 October 2003, and introduced wholesale changes to the conveyancing of registered land. See 1.14 and 1.185 for further details. The Land Register comprises just over 24.8 million titles, and more than 12.7 million hectares, or almost 85 per cent of the land in England and Wales, is now registered (see the Land Registry *Annual Report and Accounts 2016–2017*).

First registration

1.14 Section 4 of the Land Registration Act 2002 contains an extended list of activities which will induce first registration. These are listed at 1.15. Part 2 of the Land Registration Act 2002 ('the 2002 Act') covers first registration of title. Part 2, Chapter 1 is entitled 'First Registration' and deals with voluntary registration (s 3) as well as compulsory registration (ss 4–8). One of the main aims of the 2002 Act is to make the register of title as comprehensive as possible. The 2002 Act builds on the foundations laid by the Land Registration Act 1997 by extending the triggers for compulsory registration of unregistered land.

Compulsory first registration

1.15 Section 4(1) of the 2002 Act lists the events that trigger compulsory registration. These largely replicate the old law as laid down in the Land Registration Act 1925, and the Land Registration Act 1997. In line with the old law, mines and minerals held apart from the surface are excluded from registration (s 4(9)).

1.16 The events which induce compulsory first registration under the 2002 Act are as follows. (All these requirements came into force on 13 October 2003.)

Transfers of a qualifying estate

1.17 A 'qualifying estate' is either a legal freehold estate in land, or an existing legal lease that has more than seven years to run. Registration is compulsory if the transfer is made:

(a) for valuable or other consideration;
(b) by way of gift;
(c) in pursuance of an order of any court; or
(d) by means of an assent (including a vesting assent).

1.18 For the avoidance of doubt, s 4 also makes it clear that the following events will *not* induce compulsory registration:

(a) transfer by operation of law, for example where a deceased's property vests in his personal representatives (s 4(3));
(b) assignment of a mortgage term, i.e. where the mortgage is by demise or sub-demise (these are very rare and the 2002 Act prohibits any more being created that affect registered property) (s 4(4)(a));
(c) lease merger, i.e. assignment or surrender of a lease to the immediate reversion where the term is to merge in that reversion (s 4(4)(b)).

1.19 Practitioners should also be aware that leases for the grant of a mortgage term—i.e. a mortgage by demise or sub-demise—are not compulsorily registrable (s 4(5)). Accordingly, only charges by way of legal mortgage can be used for mortgages of registered land. In effect, mortgages by demise for registered land only are abolished.

Reversionary leases

1.20 A new category of lease that is subject to compulsory registration is the reversionary lease. This is a right to possession under a lease that takes effect at a future date. A reversionary lease of any term granted to take effect in possession more than three months after the date of grant is required to be registered (s 4(1)(d)). Under the old law, a buyer of land affected by such a reversionary lease might not have discovered it because the tenant was not in possession. However, the buyer might still have been bound by it as an overriding interest under s 70(1)(k) of the Land Registration Act 1925. The change in the law overcomes this conveyancing problem. It should be noted that reversionary leases taking effect within three months are not required to be registered.

Grant of a 'right-to-buy' lease under Part V of the Housing Act 1985

1.21 Section 4(1)(e) replicates the old law found in s 154 of the Housing Act 1985. The grant of a 'right-to-buy' lease under the Housing Act 1985 is subject to compulsory registration, regardless of whether the lease would otherwise be registrable because of its length.

Protected first legal mortgages of a qualifying estate

1.22 The Land Registration Act 1997 introduced first mortgages of unregistered land as an additional trigger for compulsory registration. This is confirmed in s 4(1)(g) of the 2002 Act, which refers to 'the creation of a protected first legal mortgage of a qualifying estate'.

Crown land

1.23 Special provision is made for compulsory registration after the Crown has made a grant of a freehold estate out of demesne land (s 80). Demesne land is land which the Crown holds as feudal lord paramount and in which it has no estate.

Transfers to which s 171A of the Housing Act 1985 applies

A transfer falls within s 171A where a person ceases to be a secure tenant of a dwelling **1.24**
house because his landlord disposes of an interest in that house to a private-sector landlord.
In such circumstances, the tenant's right to buy under Part V of the Housing Act 1985 is
preserved. Such a transfer is subject to compulsory registration even if it would not otherwise be (s 4(1)(b)).

Leases granted for a term of more than seven years from the date of grant

The reduction in the length of leases subject to compulsory registration is an important **1.25**
change in the law, especially as it will bring many business leases onto the register and thus
enable third parties to inspect the lease and its title, and allow parties to discover rental
values. Section 4(1)(c) provides that registration is compulsory if a lease is granted out of a
qualifying estate of an estate in land:

(a) for a term of more than seven years from the date of grant; and
(b) for valuable or other consideration, by way of gift, or in pursuance of an order of any
    court.

Two additional first registration triggers

Two additional triggers for first registration came into effect on 6 April 2009 as a result of **1.26**
the Land Registration Act 2002 (Amendment) Order 2008. They are:

1. the appointment of a new trustee of unregistered land held in trust where the land vests
   in the new trustee by deed—this will include a memorandum executed as a deed to
   which s 83 of the Charities Act 1993 applies, or by a vesting order under s 44 of the
   Trustee Act 1925;
2. the partitioning of unregistered land held in trust among the beneficiaries of that trust.

The consequence of this Order is that if unregistered land is owned by a trust (be it charitable or otherwise) and then it vests in a new trustee by virtue of a deed in the manner set
out above, the trustees must apply for first registration of that land.

Accordingly, and in summary form, first registration will normally arise where an unregis- **1.27**
tered title has been:

• purchased (either as a freehold or as a lease with more than seven years left to run);
• received in exchange for other land or property;
• newly leased for a term of more than seven years;
• passed over in the form of a gift;
• transferred to your client to hold as trustee on the creation of a trust;
• transferred to your client under a court order;
• received by assent from executors or administrators;
• mortgaged.

Compulsory registration does not apply to most leases granted for seven years or less. The
exceptions are:

• when the lease is granted to take effect in possession more than three months after the
  date of the grant, unless the landlords themselves only own a lease that has less than
  seven years to run;
• when the lease has been granted under the right-to-buy provisions of Part V of the
  Housing Act 1985;
• when the lease is subject to a preserved right to buy under the provisions of s 171A of
  the Housing Act 1985.

Reforms made by the 2002 Act

1.28 Although the changes made by the 2002 Act relating to first registration are not as extensive as those made by the 1997 Act, five additional reforms are worth highlighting.

Leases

1.29 The length of leases which are subject to compulsory registration is reduced from more than 21 years to more than seven years (s 4(1)(c)). Similarly, the assignment of an unregistered lease which has more than seven years unexpired at the time of the assignment will have to be registered (s 4(1)(a) and (2)(b)). Most business leases are granted for less than 21 years and therefore many will now become compulsorily registrable. The intention in the future is to reduce the seven-year period to three.

Profits à prendre *in gross and franchises*

1.30 *Profits à prendre* in gross (e.g. fishing or shooting rights) and franchises (e.g. the right to hold a market) may now be voluntarily registered with their own titles. They must, however, be held for an interest equivalent to a freehold or under a lease of which there are still seven years to run (s 3). Fishing rights in particular can be very valuable and so these may now be traded in registered titles. Previously these rights could only be noted on the register.

Crown land

1.31 The Crown may for the first time register land held in demesne, i.e. held in its capacity as ultimate feudal overlord. The 2002 Act enables the Crown to grant itself a freehold estate so that it can register it (s 79).

Submarine land

1.32 The territorial extent of land which can be registered is increased so that some submarine land will become registrable. As before, the 2002 Act applies to land covered by internal waters of the UK that are within England and Wales (s 127(a)). Additionally, however, s 127(b) includes land covered by internal waters *adjacent* to England and Wales which are specified for the purposes by order made by the Lord Chancellor.

'Events' not 'dispositions'

1.33 Whereas the Land Registration Act 1925 listed 'dispositions' which triggered compulsory first registration, the 2002 Act refers to 'events'. This is wider in its ambit and will permit greater flexibility in the future (see s 5, which permits new events to be added afterwards). Recently Land Registry has introduced two new triggers for first registration and these are considered at 1.26.

Time limit for first registration

1.34 Since 1 December 1990, all of England and Wales is an area of compulsory registration, so that if any of the registrable events mentioned above takes place, the title concerned must be submitted for compulsory first registration within the statutory two-month period (2002 Act, s 6(4)). It is possible to apply for voluntary first registration; and there is now an incentive for voluntary registration in that the Land Registration Fees Order 1998, which came into force on 1 April 1999, brought in a 25 per cent reduction for fees payable on voluntary first registration. This has continued into the current Fee Order, the Land Registration Fee Order 2013 (SI 2013/3174).

1.35 Section 6(5) also gives to the Chief Land Registrar power to extend the two-month period for first registration. This will assist late applicants who will, however, be required to furnish the

Registrar with an explanation of the reasons for the delayed application. If a late application is accepted (and such applications normally are), title vests in the new proprietor, but only from the date of registration. If a late application must be made, Land Registry will require up-to-date search results along with those made at the time of completion.

The effect of non-registration

Unless the Registrar extends the two-month period, failure to register within the statutory **1.36** time limit will result in the transfer becoming void. In this event, the transferor will hold the legal estate on a bare trust for the transferee (s 7(2)(a)). Similarly, any grant of a lease or creation of a protected mortgage will become void and take effect instead as a contract for valuable consideration to grant or create the lease or mortgage concerned (s 7(2)(b)). If it becomes necessary to repeat the transfer, lease, or mortgage (because the previous one was void), the transferee, grantee, or mortgagor is liable to the transferor, grantor, or mortgagee for the proper costs involved (s 8(a)). They must also indemnify them for any other liability reasonably incurred as a result of the failure to register (s 8(b)). Of course, the seller will also hold the title as a bare trustee in trust for the buyer, pending completion of the application for first registration (see *Pinekerry Ltd v Kenneth Needs (Contractors) Ltd* (1992) 64 P & CR 245). The deed is not void for all purposes. Enforcement of covenants contained within it will be possible even though registration has not taken place or been applied for. Furthermore, failure to submit an application on behalf of a client is a clear-cut case of professional negligence, and if your client suffers loss, you will have to look to your professional indemnity insurance policy. Finally, there remains the danger that later registration could mean that the subject property is eventually registered subject to interests that might not have affected the property had the registration taken place in the correct period: see *Sainsbury's Supermarkets Limited v Olympia Homes Limited* [2005] EWHC 1235 (Ch). (In this dispute Mr Justice Mann had to consider how to square the interests of a party that had purchased land in good faith and another party who had been granted an option by a former owner who had failed to register their property in time.)

Classes of registered title

On receipt of an application for first registration the Land Registrar will investigate the **1.37** title, and in the light of that investigation will allocate to the property one of the following classes of title:

(a) freehold absolute title (see 1.39);
(b) freehold possessory title (see 1.42);
(c) freehold qualified title (see 1.43);
(d) leasehold absolute title (see 1.44);
(e) leasehold possessory title (see 1.47);
(f) leasehold qualified title (see 1.48);
(g) good leasehold title (see 1.49).

The 2002 Act maintains all the above classes, and does not change the substance of what **1.38** amounts to these different classes of title.

Freehold absolute title

An absolute title is the best class of title available, be it freehold or leasehold. So far as the **1.39** freehold estate is concerned, it is the registered equivalent of the classic fee simple absolute in possession. Almost all freehold titles are registered with absolute title. Section 9(2) of the 2002 Act provides that a person may be registered with absolute freehold title if the Registrar considers that the title is such as a willing buyer could properly be advised by a competent professional adviser to accept. Even if the title is defective, the Registrar may still grant absolute title if he considers that the defect will not cause the holding under the title to be disturbed (s 9(3)).

1.40   The effect of registration with an absolute title is somewhat different from the earlier registered land law. As far as benefits are concerned, the legal estate is vested in the proprietor together with all the interests subsisting for the benefit of the estate, for example easements (s 11(3)). As far as burdens are concerned, the proprietor takes subject only to the interests set out in s 11(4) affecting the estate at the time of first registration.

These are:

(a) interests which are the subject of an entry in the register in relation to the estate (these can be registered charges, notices, and restrictions, and pre-13 October 2003 cautions and inhibitions);

(b) unregistered interests which fall within any of the paragraphs of Schedule 1 (i.e. interests which override first registration);

(c) interests acquired under the Limitation Act 1980 of which the proprietor has notice.

1.41   In determining whether the proprietor has 'notice' under s 11(4)(c), the word will have its usual meaning of actual, constructive, or imputed notice. This will cover matters which ought to have been discoverable from reasonable inspections and enquiries.

Freehold possessory title

1.42   In practice, a possessory title will be given either where the applicant's title is based on adverse possession, or where title cannot be proven because the title deeds have been lost or destroyed. The 2002 Act provides that possessory title will be appropriate where the applicant is either in actual possession, or in receipt of rents and profits, and there is no other class of title with which he may be registered (s 9(5)). Registration with a possessory freehold title has the same effect as registration with an absolute title, except that it does not affect the enforcement of any estate, right, or interest adverse to, or in derogation of, the proprietor's title subsisting at the time of registration or then capable of arising (s 11(7)).

Freehold qualified title

1.43   A qualified title is very rare—indeed, the authors cannot recall having seen more than two such titles during all their many years of conveyancing practice. It will be given where the Registrar considers that the applicant's title can only be established for a limited period, or subject to certain reservations that are such that the title is not a good holding title (s 9(4)). An example of this might be where the transfer to the applicant was made in breach of trust. Registration with a qualified freehold title has the same effect as registration with an absolute title except that it does not affect the enforcement of any estate, right, or interest which appears from the register to be excepted from the effect of registration (s 11(6)). Another example could be where the estate was vested in the first proprietor as a result of the registration of that proprietor as owner of the land under s 8 of the Commons Registration Act 1965.

Leasehold absolute title

1.44   In practice, an absolute leasehold title will be given only if the superior title is either registered with absolute title or, if unregistered, has been deduced to the Registrar's satisfaction. The 2002 Act provides that an absolute leasehold title will be given if the Registrar considers that the title is one that a willing buyer could properly be advised by a competent professional adviser to accept, and the Registrar also approves the lessor's title to grant the lease (s 10(2)). As with absolute freehold, even if the leasehold title is defective, the Registrar may still grant absolute title if he considers that the defect will not cause the holding under the title to be disturbed (s 10(4)).

Registration with an absolute leasehold title has the same effect as registration with an **1.45** absolute freehold title, except that the estate is vested in the leaseholder subject to implied and express covenants, obligations, and liabilities incident to the estate (s 12(3), (4)). These will be apparent from an inspection of the lease (e.g. lessee's covenants). Generally, a lease that is granted or assigned with seven years or less to run is not registrable, and will be an unregistered interest which overrides registered dispositions (Schedule 1, para 1 and Schedule 3, para 1).

When the Registrar issues an absolute leasehold title the State is thereby guaranteeing **1.46** not just that there is a legal leasehold, but also that the lease has been validly granted out of the reversionary title. Clearly the Registrar can do this only if the reversionary title has been disclosed to the Registry to confirm that the lessor has the power to grant the lease. Where the superior title, usually the freehold, is already registered with an absolute class of title, this is sufficient to confer the same class of title on the leasehold. The position where the superior title is not seen is dealt with at 1.49 in relation to good leasehold titles.

Leasehold possessory title

In practice, a possessory title will be given either where the applicant's title is based on **1.47** adverse possession, or where title cannot be proven because the title deeds have been lost or destroyed. The 2002 Act provides that possessory title will be appropriate where the applicant is either in actual possession, or in receipt of rents and profits and there is no other class of title with which he may be registered (s 10(6)). Registration with possessory leasehold title has the same effect as registration with absolute title, but subject to the exceptions and qualifications explained at 1.42 in relation to possessory freehold titles (s 12(8)).

Leasehold qualified title

Like a qualified freehold title, a qualified leasehold title is very rare. It will be given where **1.48** the Registrar considers that the applicant's title (or the lessor's title) can be established only for a limited period, or subject to certain reservations that are such that the title is not a good holding title (s 10(5)). An example of this might be where the grant to the applicant was made in breach of trust. Registration with qualified leasehold title has the same effect as registration with absolute title, but subject to the exceptions and qualifications explained at 1.43 in relation to freehold qualified titles (s 12(7)).

Good leasehold title

A proprietor of this class of title is in the same position as a proprietor of an absolute lease- **1.49** hold title, save as to one major factor. The registration is such that there is no guarantee that the lease has been validly granted. The Registry will issue this class of title when the superior title, the reversionary title, has not been seen and approved by the Registrar. If the lessor was not entitled to grant the lease in the first place, then clearly the Registry would not have all the details to enable it to guarantee the validity of the lease. Consequently, a good leasehold title will be issued in place of the more desirable absolute leasehold title. Some mortgagees will not accept a good leasehold title as a security, and the lender's requirements should always be considered and dealt with if a good leasehold title is offered for sale to a person who requires a loan for the purchase. The problem for the lender is, of course, that if the lease is held to be invalid, the lender will lose its security. (See Chapter 7 and especially 7.88 in relation to the requirements of a lender.)

1.50 This class of title is therefore appropriate where the superior title is neither registered, nor deduced, to the Registrar's satisfaction. The 2002 Act provides that a good leasehold title may be given if the Registrar considers that the title is such as a willing buyer could properly be advised by a competent professional adviser to accept (s 10(3)). A good leasehold title may be given even if the title is open to objection, provided the Registrar considers that the defect will not cause the holding under it to be challenged (s 10(4)). Registration with good leasehold title has the same effect as registration with absolute title, except that it does not affect the enforcement of any estate, right, or interest affecting, or in derogation of, the title of the lessor to grant the lease (s 12(6)).

Title upgrade (conversion)

1.51 The different grades of registered title found under the old law are preserved in the 2002 Act. Section 11 of the Land Registration Act 1986 amended and simplified the original conversion of title provisions of s 77 of the Land Registration Act 1925. Section 62 of the 2002 Act replicates the previous law with some amendments. First, there is new vocabulary. The 2002 Act refers to 'quality of title', and titles are not converted to a different grade, they are subject to an 'upgrade'. It effectively empowers the Registrar to upgrade a class of title if certain conditions are met, and these are now considered:

(a) A freehold possessory title may be upgraded to an absolute title in two situations:
  (i) if the Registrar is satisfied as to the title to the estate (s 62(1)). This might occur where a person was initially registered with possessory title because his or her title deeds were missing. If, subsequently, those deeds come to light, the Registrar can upgrade the title to absolute if he is otherwise satisfied with them;
  (ii) if the title has been registered with possessory title for 12 years and the proprietor is still in possession. The Registrar can then upgrade the title to absolute (s 2(4)).
(b) A qualified title can be upgraded to absolute if the Registrar is satisfied as to the title to the estate (s 62(1)), for example where the cause of the Registrar's original objections is subsequently no longer shown to threaten the holding under that title.
(c) There is provision for upgrading qualified leasehold titles as well (s 62(3)).
(d) A good leasehold title can be upgraded to an absolute title if the Registrar is satisfied as to the superior title (s 62(2)), for example where the superior title is itself registered for the first time.
(e) A possessory leasehold title can be upgraded to good leasehold if the Registrar is satisfied as to the title to the estate (s 62(3)(a)), or if the title has been registered as possessory for 12 years and the proprietor is in possession (s 62(5)).
(f) A possessory leasehold title can be upgraded to absolute if the Registrar is satisfied both as to the title to the estate and as to the superior title (s 62(3)(b)).

1.52 Section 62(7) of the 2002 Act lists the following persons who may apply to upgrade a title:

(a) the proprietor of the estate to which the application relates;
(b) a person entitled to be registered as the proprietor of that estate (e.g. an executor in respect of the testator's land prior to sale);
(c) the proprietor of a registered charge affecting that estate (i.e. prior to exercising its power of sale); and
(d) a person interested in a registered estate which derives from that estate (e.g. a sub-tenant).

1.53 The effect of upgrading a title is set out in s 63 of the 2002 Act. Where a freehold or leasehold title is upgraded to absolute, the proprietor ceases to hold the estate subject to any estate, right, or interest the enforceability of which is preserved by virtue of the previous entry about the class of title (s 63(1)). This principle also applies where leasehold is upgraded from possessory or qualified title to good leasehold. However, the upgrade does not affect or prejudice the enforcement of any estate, right, or interest affecting, or in derogation of, the lessor's title to grant the lease (s 63(2)).

The title certificate and the three registers

The title certificate is an assembly of three separate registers, but each title will have a **1.54** unique title number. This is the reference number that practitioners must always quote to Land Registry in all dealings with the title. The three registers are the property, proprietorship, and charges registers. The title is completed by the addition of a site plan called the title plan. An example of a complete register with a title plan is set out in Appendix 15 and is shown with the kind permission of Land Registry.

Register details

The register comprises three parts: **1.55**

(a) The property register provides a description of the property, including a statement of estate, i.e. whether it is a freehold or leasehold property. If leasehold, the statement of estate will also include the date of the registered lease, its term, parties, and start date. Rights of way and all other easements for the benefit of the property can also be detailed in this register. For all properties reference will also be made in this first register to the title plan of the registered property. The title plan shows the location of the property together with adjoining property. All registered titles will have a title plan.

(b) The proprietorship register includes the class of title followed by the name and address of the registered proprietor. Restrictions and notices will appear within this register (see 1.91–1.97).

(c) The charges register lists the registered charges affecting the property and these are listed in order of priority. The charges register also includes adverse interests, such as restrictive covenants, to which the property may be subject. Furthermore, leases that do not comprise overriding interests will also be noted within the charges register of the superior title.

Land registration and deeds

In the Land Registration Act 1925 registered land deeds were called land or charge certifi- **1.56** cates. However, the 2002 Act abolished these land or charge certificates. The Registry will issue a Title Information Document only (now usually official copies of the registers) after registering a dealing. It may not be proof of title if it is not expressed to be an official copy but merely serves to confirm completion of that application for registration. Title can only be proved by official copies of the registers issued by Land Registry.

Overriding interests

Overriding interests are one of a number of interests in land which bind a proprietor of **1.57** registered land, but they differ in a substantial way from the other categories of interests in that they bind the owner of the legal estate, regardless of whether they are entered on the register. It is for this reason that they have caused uncertainty.

The 2002 Act and interests which override

This Act has reduced the circumstances in which overriding interests can exist. The policy **1.58** behind the 2002 Act is that interests should have overriding status only where protection against buyers is needed, but where it is neither reasonable to expect nor sensible to require any entry on the register. The 2002 Act also contains provisions which are designed to ensure that when overriding interests come to light, they are protected on the register.

1.59 The 2002 Act adopts four ways of dealing with the problems associated with overriding interests. In brief they are:

(a) the abolition of certain rights which can exist as overriding interests—these include the rights acquired by squatters under adverse possession;

(b) the phasing out after ten years of several existing categories of overriding interest, including the ancient rights of franchises, manorial rights, Crown rents, rights concerning embankments and sea walls, and corn rents, and the liability to repair the chancel of a church;

(c) the narrowing and clarification of the scope of some previous categories which remain as overriding interests—the most important of these are easements and profits under the old s 70(1)(a) of the Land Registration Act 1925, and the rights of persons in actual occupation or in receipt of rents and profits under the old s 70(1)(g) of the 1925 Act;

(d) a requirement that when overriding interests come to light they are, as far as possible, entered on the register.

1.60 In addition, a new requirement exists in which a person applying for registration must disclose any overriding interests known to him or her.

1.61 The 2002 Act provides for the continued existence of 14 categories of overriding interest and creates one new category, the Public Private Partnership (PPP) Lease that relates to London Underground transport arrangements. Five of the 14 categories were time limited and disappeared after ten years, i.e. after 13 October 2013. For three categories (legal easements and profits, the rights of persons in actual occupation, and short leases, i.e. for seven years or less) the substantive requirements for what amounts to an overriding interest will be different, depending on whether it is a first registration or a subsequent registrable disposition for valuable consideration. The 2002 Act recognizes this distinction by listing those interests which override first registration in Schedule 1, and those interests which override registered dispositions in Schedule 3.

Unregistered interests which override first registration

1.62 These are set out in Schedule 1 to the 2002 Act. When a person becomes the first registered proprietor of land on first registration, he or she takes the estate subject to certain interests, including 'interests the burden of which is entered on the register' (s 11(4)(a)) and 'interests the burden of which is not so entered but which fall within any of the paragraphs of Schedule 1' (i.e. overriding interests) (s 11(4)(b)). The 14 interests in Schedule 1 are listed below. There is also a fifteenth interest provided for in s 90. This is the PPP Lease that takes effect as if it were included in Schedule 1.

Short leases

1.63 Subject to limited exceptions, most leasehold estates granted for a term not exceeding seven years from the date of the grant override first registration (Schedule 1, para 1). This replicates the position under s 70(1)(k) of the Land Registration Act 1925, save for the reduction in the duration of short leases from 21 years to seven. In future it is likely that the Lord Chancellor will reduce the period still further to three years. A notice of the short lease should be entered on the register of the title out of which it has been granted.

Interests of persons in actual occupation

1.64 This section of the book deals with the overriding status of occupiers' rights on *first registration*. In relation to unregistered interests which override first registration, Schedule 1, para 2 defines the interests of persons in actual occupation as: 'An interest belonging to a person in actual occupation, so far as relating to land of which he is in actual occupation, except for an interest under a settlement under the Settled Land Act 1925'.

Unlike the old law, it should be noted that the 2002 Act does not give overriding status to **1.65** persons who are merely in receipt of rents and profits, i.e. not in actual occupation. This is a change from the old s 70(1)(g). It is often very difficult for a buyer to discover the existence of an intermediate landlord from an inspection of the property.

Another point to note concerning the new law is the wording in Schedule 1, para 2 'so far as **1.66** relating to land of which he is in actual occupation'. Again, this is new. It means that where someone is in actual occupation of part of the land but has rights over the whole of the land purchased, his rights protected by actual occupation are confined to the part that he occupies.

A further change in the law, in relation to an occupier's rights on first registration, is the **1.67** absence of the qualification in the old law contained in s 70(1)(g) which says, 'save where enquiry is made of such person and the rights are not disclosed'. These words are excluded because they can have no relevance to overriding interests on first registration. Whether a purchaser has made enquiries of a person in actual occupation is irrelevant on first registration, because the question of whether or not the first registered proprietor is bound by the rights of an occupier will have been decided at an earlier stage under the unregistered conveyancing rules; that is to say, on completion, when the legal title became vested in the purchaser.

Legal easements and profits à prendre

Here there is an important change. Under the previous law, *equitable* easements that were **1.68** openly exercised and enjoyed by the dominant owner as appurtenant to his land could take effect, on first registration, as overriding interests (see Land Registration Act 1925, s 70(1)(a); *Celsteel Ltd v Alton House Holdings Ltd* [1985] 1 WLR 204, 219–21; *Thatcher v Douglas* (1996) 146 NLJ 282). Under the new law, only *legal* easements and *profits à prendre* can do so (Schedule 1, para 3). Thus, in preventing unregistered equitable easements from acquiring overriding status, the decision in *Celsteel* is reversed. This is in line with the general principle underlying the 2002 Act that rights which are expressly created over land should be completed by registration. It also reflects the established view in un registered land that equitable easements should bind a purchaser only if they are registered as Class D(iii) land charges under the Land Charges Act 1972.

Customary and public rights

Both customary and public rights remain as overriding interests under the 2002 Act **1.69** (Schedule 1, paras 4 and 5; previously Land Registration Act 1925, s 70(1)(a)). Public rights are those which are exercisable by anyone, whether they own land or not, by virtue of the general law. Customary rights, on the other hand, are those which were enjoyed by inhabitants of a particular locality, many of which still survive. Examples of customary rights being upheld include holding a fair or wake on wasteland in Wraysbury (see *Wyld v Silver* [1963] Ch 243) and grazing beasts on common land in Huntingdon (see *Peggs v Lamb* [1994] Ch 172).

Local land charges

There is no change for this category of overriding interest. Local land charges are governed **1.70** by the Local Land Charges Act 1975 and are being computerized together with other local searches as part of the National Land Information Service (NLIS).

Mines and minerals

There is no change to these categories of overriding interest. The overriding status of cer- **1.71** tain mining and mineral rights previously found in s 70(1)(l) and (m) of the Land Registration Act 1925 is preserved in Schedule 1, paras 7–9 to the 2002 Act.

1.72 Lastly, five categories of overriding interest are grouped together under a miscellaneous heading (Schedule 1, paras 10–14). Often onerous, they are rare, of ancient origin, and sometimes very difficult to discover. They all had overriding status under the Land Registration Act 1925 and are:

(a) a franchise;

(b) a manorial right;

(c) a right to rent which was reserved to the Crown on the granting of any freehold estate (whether or not the right is still vested in the Crown) ('Crown rents');

(d) a non-statutory right in respect of an embankment, or sea or river wall; and

(e) a right to payment in lieu of tithe ('corn rents').

Unregistered interests which override registered dispositions

1.73 These are set out in Schedule 3 to the 2002 Act and are in effect overriding interests which affect titles which are already registered. Of these 15 interests, 12 are identical to those that override first registration and have been considered at 1.62. The three categories of overriding interest that differ from those that apply on first registration are short leases, interests of persons in actual occupation, and easements and profits.

Short leases

1.74 Most leasehold estates granted for a term not exceeding seven years from the date of the grant override first registration (Schedule 3, para 1). This replicates the position under s 70(1)(k) of the Land Registration Act 1925, save for the reduction in the duration of short leases from 21 to seven years. In future it is likely that the Lord Chancellor will reduce the period still further to three years. A notice of the short lease should be entered on the register of the title out of which it has been granted. For leases of this type that were in existence at 13 October 2003, Schedule 12, para 12 provides, in effect, that leases that were previously granted for a term of more than seven but not more than 21 years would remain as overriding interests after that date. However, any assignment of such leases will trigger compulsory registration if the term has more than seven years to run at the time of the assignment (s 4(1)(a), (2)(b)).

Interests of persons in actual occupation

1.75 Schedule 3, para 2 provides that an interest belonging at the time of a registered disposition to a person in actual occupation is an overriding interest, so far as it relates to land of which he or she is in actual occupation. So actual occupation protects a person's occupation only so far as it relates to land of which he or she is in actual occupation. Any rights that person has over *other* registered land must be protected by an appropriate entry in the register for that title. This reverses the Court of Appeal decision in *Ferrishurst Ltd v Wallcite Ltd* [1999] Ch 355, in which an overriding interest was held to extend to the whole of a registered title, not merely the part in occupation.

1.76 An exception to this rule is an interest of a person of whom enquiry was made before the disposition and who failed to disclose the right when he or she could reasonably have been expected to do so. This is very similar to the wording of s 70(1)(g) of the Land Registration Act 1925 ('save where enquiry is made of such person and the rights are not disclosed'). The exception operates as a form of estoppel.

1.77 Another exception will be the rights of persons whose occupation is not apparent. An interest will not be protected as an overriding interest if:

(a) it belongs to a person whose occupation would not have been obvious on a reasonably careful inspection of the land at the time of the disposition; and

(b) the person to whom the disposition is made does not have actual knowledge at that time.

Practitioners should note that it is the occupier's occupation that must be apparent, not the occupier's interest. The test is not one of constructive notice of the occupation. It is the less exacting one applicable to an intending purchaser, namely that it should be obvious on a reasonably careful inspection of the land; and even if the person's occupation is not apparent, the exception does not apply where a purchaser has actual knowledge of the occupation. **1.78**

If the occupant is in occupation at the time of completion, the buyer will take subject to the rights of that occupant. However, *City of London Building Society v Flegg* [1988] AC 54 makes it clear that the rights of persons in actual occupation can be overreached. If there are two trustees of the legal estate and if the consideration is properly payable to them, the interest of a beneficiary under a trust is overreached on sale (see 5.91 for a more detailed discussion of overreaching). **1.79**

Practitioners should always be on their guard against the danger of an undisclosed occupier. When acting for a buyer, enquiries should always be made of the seller about who is in actual occupation and what, if any, their interest might be in the property. In particular, if only one spouse is selling, enquiries should be made about the whereabouts of the other spouse and the existence of any family disputes. The property should be physically inspected and enquiries made about occupiers. This is really a matter of common sense. If the property is meant to be empty but there are signs of occupation, then further enquiries must be made of the seller. Similarly, if the seller is meant to be single but again there are signs of another person living at the property, further enquiries must be directed to the seller. **1.80**

Legal easements and profits à prendre

A purchaser of registered land may find it very difficult to discover easements and profits which are not otherwise noted on the register. This is compounded by the fact that non-user of an easement or profit, even for many years, will fail to raise any presumption of abandonment (*Benn v Hardinge* (1992) 66 P & CR 246). The 2002 Act effectively provides that no easements or profits expressly granted or reserved out of registered land after the 2002 Act comes into force can take effect as overriding interests (although there are some transitional arrangements—see 1.85). This is because such rights will not take effect at law until they are registered, i.e. they are registrable dispositions (s 27(1). This is in line with a principal aim of the 2002 Act, which is to ensure that it is possible to investigate title to land almost entirely online with the minimum of additional enquiries. In addition, no equitable easements or profits, however created, are capable of overriding a registered disposition (reversing the decision in *Celsteel Ltd v Alton House Holdings Ltd* [1985] 1 WLR 204). **1.81**

It follows that only a *legal* easement or profit can be overriding in relation to a registered disposition (Schedule 3, para 3(1)). Moreover, the only legal easements and profits that will be capable of being overriding interests are: **1.82**

(a) those already in existence when the 2002 Act came into force (that have not been registered);

(b) those arising by prescription (which is not reformed by the 2002 Act); and

(c) those arising by implied grant or reservation, for example under s 62 of the Law of Property Act 1925.

Moreover, to circumvent the non-abandonment presumption, under Schedule 3, para 3(1), certain categories of legal easement and profit are excluded from overriding status altogether. These cannot be overriding interests unless they either have been registered **1.83** under the Commons Registration Act 1965, or have been exercised within one year prior to the registered disposition in question. They are:

(a) those that are not within the actual knowledge of the person to whom the disposition was made; and
(b) those that would not have been obvious on a reasonably careful inspection of the land over which the easement or profit is exercisable.

1.84 Importantly, it therefore follows that a buyer of registered land for valuable consideration will be bound by an easement or profit that is an overriding interest only if:

(a) it is registered under the Commons Registration Act 1965/Commons Act 2006; or
(b) the buyer actually knows about it; or
(c) it is patent, i.e. obvious, from a reasonable inspection of the land over which the easement or profit is exercisable, so that no seller would be obliged to disclose it; or
(d) it has been exercised within one year before the date of purchase.

Overriding interests and pre-contract enquiries

1.85 As a result of the above, buyers' pre-contract enquiries should request sellers to disclose (a) any unregistered easements and profits affecting the land of which they are aware; and (b) any easements or profits that have been exercised in the previous 12 months. This makes good practical sense for all conveyancers. There will be those with the benefit of unregistered easements and profits that have not been exercised for more than a year. These persons should immediately protect their rights either by lodging a caution against first registration if the servient land is unregistered, or by registering them if the servient land is registered. These are important practical steps of which conveyancers should be aware.

1.86 The 2002 Act contains a transitional provision to allow existing easements or profits which were overriding interests at the time the 2002 Act came into force but which would not qualify under the new provisions to retain their overriding status (Schedule 12, para 9). This is something that buyers should be made aware of, and appropriate enquiry made of the seller at the pre-contract stage.

1.87 There is also a further temporary arrangement limited in time for the protection of easements. A further transitional provision effectively stated that for three years after the 2002 Act came into force *any* legal easement or profit that was not registered would be an overriding interest (Schedule 12, para 10). This meant that until 13 October 2006 the conditions referred to above (e.g. requiring an easement to be either within the knowledge of the buyer, or obvious on a reasonably careful inspection, or exercised within the previous year) did not apply. However, the transitional period having expired, these provisions now apply without regard to these limited transitional arrangements. This three-year period allowed time for persons with the benefit of easements to register them.

1.88 As has been stated previously, some overriding interests lost their overriding status at midnight on 12 October 2013. The interests concerned were:

(a) a franchise;
(b) a manorial right;
(c) a right to rent that was reserved to the Crown on the granting of any freehold estate (whether or not the right is still vested in the Crown);
(d) a non-statutory right in respect of an embankment or sea or river wall;
(e) a right to payment in lieu of tithe;
(f) a right in respect of the repair of a church chancel. (This is considered in Chapter 4 regarding pre-contract searches.)

Third-party protection: notices and restrictions, the new regime

The 2002 Act decreases from four to two the entries that can be made for the protec- **1.89** tion of third-party interests over registered land. They are notices and restrictions, with cautions and inhibitions being abolished. The Law Commission was critical of the old law because it felt it was unduly complicated. The Law Commission said: 'there are four different methods of protecting minor interests. These overlap with each other and it is often possible to protect a right by more than one means.' The 2002 Act therefore abolished inhibitions and cautions (although there are transitional provisions in Schedule 12 relating to inhibitions and cautions against dealings, for example existing cautions will remain on the register pursuant to paras 1 and 2(3) of Schedule 12). Notices and restrictions remain but in a different format. Notices will be used to protect incumbrances on land that are intended to bind third parties. Typical incumbrances that will be protected by notices are easements or restrictive covenants. Restrictions regulate the circumstances in which a disposition of a registered estate or charge may be the subject of an entry in the register.

The major change in the law introduced by the 2002 Act is that either notices or restric- **1.90** tions can be applied for without the permission of the registered proprietor. However, the registered proprietor must be informed of the application and will be at liberty to seek the cancellation of the notice, or to object to an application for a restriction. Interests that are to be protected by an entry in the register have the mouthful of a title 'interests protected by an entry on the register'. Finally, it is worth repeating that cautions registered before 13 October 2003 will remain on the register and will continue to have effect.

Notices

Sections 32–39 of the 2002 Act cover notices that can be one of two types: agreed or uni- **1.91** lateral. Section 33 of the 2002 Act lists interests that cannot be protected by a notice. They are called excluded interests. The most important of these are:

(a) a trust of land;
(b) a settlement under the Settled Land Act 1925;
(c) a lease for a term of three years or less from the date of the grant and which is not required to be registered;
(d) a restrictive covenant made between a lessor and lessee so far as it relates to the property leased;
(e) an interest which may be registered under the Commons Registration Act 1965.

The first two excluded interests are included to prevent notices being used to protect benefi- **1.92** cial interests behind a trust. They are better suited to the protection of a restriction.

If the application is to proceed on the basis of an agreed notice, then it must fall within one **1.93** or more of the three types listed in s 34(3)(a)–(c). They are where:

(a) the applicant is either the registered proprietor, or the person entitled to be registered as proprietor of the estate or charge that is burdened by the interest to be noted;
(b) either the registered proprietor, or the person entitled to be registered as proprietor of the estate or charge consents to the entry of the notice; and
(c) the Registrar is satisfied as to the validity of the applicant's claim.

If the notice is by way of a unilateral notice, then ss 35 and 36 specifically apply. This **1.94** form of notice will take over where the abolished cautions left off. Because all notices, whether consensual or unilateral, will protect the priority of an interest, if valid, as against a subsequent registered disposition, this gives more protection to an applicant than was the case with cautions, which gave no priority at all. If the Registrar enters a unilateral notice in the register, notice of the entry must be given to the proprietor of the registered title or charge to which the entry relates.

Restrictions

1.95   Section 40(1) of the 2002 Act provides that '[a] restriction is an entry in the register regulating the circumstances in which a disposition of a registered estate or charge may be the subject of an entry in the register'. A restriction can be used for many purposes, for example to ensure that where consent is required for a particular transaction, it is obtained. The most frequently encountered example of this kind of restriction will occur when there is a management company, and there is a restriction in the register indicating that no registration of a transfer may be made without the consent of an officer of the management company. This is entered in the register to make sure that other arrangements are completed with the transferee, such as a deed of covenant to pay management charges, and to comply with repairing obligations, before the transfer of ownership can be concluded, i.e. by registration.

1.96   The 2002 Act makes it possible to either enter a notice or apply for a restriction without the consent of the registered proprietor. However, in such a situation, the proprietor will be notified of the application, to which the proprietor may then object. Section 77 of the 2002 Act imposes a duty of reasonableness. A person must not exercise the right to apply for the entry of a restriction without reasonable cause. The duty is owed to any person who suffers damage should there be a breach of this duty to act reasonably. There are new standard forms of restriction set out in Schedule 4 to the Land Registration Rules 2003. A non-standard restriction will only be approved if it appears reasonable and not onerous to the Registrar.

1.97   The Land Registration (Amendment) Rules 2005 came into force on 24 October 2005 and introduced four new standard forms of restriction, one of which (Form II) is of particular importance. This restriction was introduced to address concerns that another standard restriction, a Form A restriction, does not provide sufficient protection for a beneficiary's interest. Accordingly, a person who has a claim regarding a registered property out of a trust of land may apply for a restriction in Form II. The Land Registration (Amendment) Rules 2008 revised the wording of most standard restrictions and introduced four new additional restrictions. Land Registry revised the wording, punctuation, and layout of existing forms of restriction and standardized the use of italics and brackets in the hope that this improved clarity for applicants. Of the four new restrictions, three relate to dispositions where consent or a certificate is required to that disposition (restrictions NN, OO, and PP). Land Registry has issued Practice Guide 19 to assist practitioners with notices, restrictions, and the protection of third-party interests on the register. (All the available Land Registry Practice Guides can be found at **https://www.gov.uk/topic/ land-registration/practice-guides.**)

Cautions against first registration

1.98   Sections 15–22 of the 2002 Act deal with cautions against first registration. A caution against first registration is different from the former type of mainstream cautions in that it exists only in relation to unregistered titles. A party who wishes to advance a claim against an unregistered title may wish to object to that title being submitted for first registration, as registration could adversely affect that party's interest in the land in question. An example would be someone claiming an interest under an implied trust, which cannot be protected by the registration of a land charge. Section 15 deals with the right to lodge these cautions.

Cautions against first registration have of course been with us for a long time, but some innovations are made under the 2002 Act. The principal changes are as follows: **1.99**

(a) **Cautions register** In addition to cautions being recorded in the index map, the 2002 Act creates a new cautions register (s 19(1)).
(b) **One cannot register a caution against one's own land** Persons are prevented from lodging a caution against first registration of their own estate. (Developers sometimes do this as a precaution against incursions from neighbouring landowners.) This should act as an inducement for voluntary registration. Therefore, a caution cannot be used as a substitute for first registration; instead, a person should register his or her estate.

The effect of a caution

This is contained in s 16 and the effect is that: **1.100**

(a) the Registrar must give notice to the cautioner of any subsequent application for first registration and the cautioner's right to object to it (s 16(1));
(b) the Registrar must not deal with the first registration application until the end of that notice period, unless the cautioner has previously objected or advised the Registrar that he will not object (s 16(2)). If the cautioner objects, the Registrar must refer the matter to the adjudicator, unless the objection is groundless or agreement can be reached (s 73(6), (7));
(c) the caution has no effect on the validity or priority of any interest that the cautioner may have in the legal estate to which the caution relates (s 16(3)).

The Land Registry Property Alert system

In 2014 the Land Registry launched Property Alert, a free service to allow homeowners who might be concerned about fraud to be notified of significant changes to their registered title such as the third-party registrations mentioned above (**https://propertyalert.landregistry. gov.uk/**). Once a person has signed up to the service, they will receive e-mail alerts when activity occurs on monitored properties. This should allow participants to take action, if necessary, to protect their property interests. You can monitor up to ten properties. **1.101**

Rectification and indemnity

If a person is registered as proprietor of a registered title, then the State guarantees that the legal estate is indeed vested in the registered proprietor. Moreover, if that is proved to be wrong—i.e. that the registers are wrong—any innocent party suffering loss will be compensated for the loss of any estate or interest in a registered title. As a consequence, Land Registry is most careful in vetting titles submitted for first registration. Rectification can occur and would involve an amendment to the registers or filed plan to put right a substantive error or any claim that has been given legal recognition. The 2002 Act now covers indemnity by s 103, which states that Schedule 8 to the 2002 Act has effect and makes provision for the payment of indemnities by the Registrar. **1.102**

Whereas the Land Registration Act 1925 talks about 'rectification' of the register, the 2002 Act provides for 'alteration', both of the register of title (Schedule 4, s 65) and (this is new) of the register of cautions (ss 20–21). Under the 2002 Act, rectification is just one kind of alteration, and is defined as one which involves the correction of a mistake *and* which prejudicially affects the title of a registered proprietor (Schedule 4, para 1). As a result of the latter, a right to indemnity will naturally flow from rectification. **1.103**

1.104 The 2002 Act sets out eight circumstances in which a person who suffers loss is entitled to be indemnified (Schedule 8, para 1(1)). A claimant can recover any loss which flows from the particular ground, whether that loss is direct or consequential.

1.105 The eight circumstances for indemnity are loss by reason of:

(1) rectification of the register;
(2) a mistake whose correction would involve rectification of the register;
(3) a mistake in an official search;
(4) a mistake in an official copy (formerly 'office copy');
(5) a mistake in a document kept by the Registrar which is not an original and is referred to in the register;
(6) the loss or destruction of a document lodged at the Registry for inspection or safe custody;
(7) a mistake in the cautions register; or
(8) failure by the Registrar to perform his duty under s 50. This is a new duty—when the Registrar registers a statutory charge which has priority over a prior charge on the register, he has a duty to notify the prior charge of that statutory charge.

1.106 No indemnity is payable on account of any mines or minerals, or the existence of any right to work or get mines or minerals unless (rarely) it is noted on the register of title that the title includes the mines or minerals (Schedule 8, para 2).

Indemnity payments

1.107 An indemnity will now be paid to a claimant who has suffered loss as a result of an error or omission in the register whether or not the register is in fact rectified. This is of course subject to the proper care provisions, etc. mentioned at 1.109. No indemnity will be paid for costs and expenses without the Registrar's prior approval. This will be available if there is loss suffered as a result of rectification, or indeed non-rectification. An indemnity payment may also be available as a result of an error made by the Registry, for example in an official search result or as a result of the Registry losing a deed or document.

1.108 The indemnity will be available only if the claimant has suffered actual loss. For example, if rectification is ordered so that an overriding interest can be recognized, the court has held that there is no loss for indemnity purposes: see *Re Chowood's Registered Land* [1933] Ch 574. (This example should now fall within the indemnity provisions set out in Schedule 8.)

1.109 There is one particularly important exclusion affecting the right to indemnity. Schedule 8, para 5 stipulates that no indemnity is available where the applicant has caused, or substantially contributed to, the loss by fraud or lack of proper care. This will also be true if the applicant derives title through a person who contributed to the loss by fraud or lack of proper care, unless the applicant was entitled by reason of a disposition for valuable consideration that has been registered or is protected by an entry within the registers.

Indemnity amounts

1.110 The amount of the indemnity will depend on the nature of the case and will fit one of two templates. First, if rectification is not ordered, the amount of the indemnity will not exceed the value of the claimed estate, charge, or interest at the time of making the error or omission. Second, if rectification is ordered, the amount of the indemnity will not exceed the value of the claimed estate, charge, or interest at the time just before rectification took place.

1.111 Schedule 8, para 10 allows the Registrar to seek recovery of all or part of any indemnity paid out from any person who caused or substantially contributed to the loss by his or her fraud. The Registrar can also assume any right of action the claimant would have been entitled to had the indemnity not been paid. Furthermore, where the register has been rectified, the Registrar may enforce any right of action that the persons in whose favour the register was rectified would have been entitled to enforce if the register had not been rectified.

There are time limits for indemnity claims. For the purposes of the Limitation Act 1980, **1.112** a liability to pay an indemnity under this schedule is a simple contract debt. The claim will therefore be barred six years after the cause of action arose. During 2016–2017, 995 claims were recognized and £6,957,904 paid including costs (compared to £8,020,798 paid in the previous year: *Land Registry Annual Report 2015–2016*). (The 2016–2017 Report also mentions that £308,388 was recovered under Land Registry's statutory right of recourse, compared to £231,298 in the previous year.) Land Registry saw a continuing high number of claims arising out of fraud, with 53 claims in total (such as fraudulent transfers or charges), paying out over £3.8 million for claims of this kind.

The future for conveyancing of registered land: the Land Registration Act 2002

The shape of conveyancing is changing, and the pace of change is certain to quicken. The **1.113** Law Commission, Land Registry, and the present Government all support this process, which really got going back in 1998 with a Law Commission Report. The 2002 Act came into force on 13 October 2003. We have incorporated details of, and commentary on, the reforms introduced by the 2002 Act throughout the text. However, to assist practitioners, we set out in this section a summary of the main changes and reforms.

Land Registration Act 2002

Of the 2002 Act at the time of its Royal Assent, Michael Wills, Parliamentary Secretary at **1.114** the Lord Chancellor's Department, said:

> This piece of legislation marks an important step towards the fulfilment of the Government's commitment to develop a modern basis for land registration to make conveyancing faster and cheaper. Most importantly, it will make possible the development of an electronic conveyancing system, so that land and property transactions can be completed electronically. The Act will bring more information about rights over property onto the register. This will make the property transaction process more open, improving the efficiency of the property market.
> By providing additional benefits for registered landowners, such as greater protection against squatters, the Act will encourage unregistered landowners to register the land, bringing more information about land into the public domain and increasing the transparency of the property market. I am pleased to say that there has been broad cross-party support for the Act in both Houses of Parliament. Credit for this is in large measure due to the excellent drafting and preparatory work of the Law Commission and Land Registry, who undertook an immense project to deliver this reform. This was the single largest law reform project undertaken in the Law Commission since its foundation in 1965.

Over 85 per cent of titles are now registered, and the vast majority of the three million **1.115** property dealings each year relate to registered property. (Indeed, Land Registry, in its 2016–2017 Annual Report, indicated that the Land Register comprises over 24.5 million titles, and more than 12.7 million hectares, or more than 84 per cent of the land in England and Wales, is now registered.) However, the previous legislation governing registration of title was said to be complex, confusing, and badly out of date. The Land Registration Act 1925 was considered to be largely based on an earlier Act of 1875, and also drafted on the basis that conveyances of land would be paper based.

1.116 To correct these perceived faults, the 2002 Act:

(a) allows for the process of dealing with registered land to move from a paper-based system to an all-electronic system within a few years;

(b) completely replaces the existing legislation to allow land registration to be faster and simpler;

(c) establishes a register which will give buyers more certainty by giving fuller information about the rights and responsibilities which the registered proprietor has;

(d) improves the security of property rights in and over registered land by providing better means of protecting them;

(e) provides better protection for the owners of registered land against claims of adverse possession.

1.117 By paving the way for e-conveyancing, it was hoped that the 2002 Act would bring greater transparency to chains of transactions. While the new system will take some time to introduce fully, it should lead to quicker ways of buying and selling land, as well as providing greater security of title.

Main provisions of the 2002 Act

1.118 There are helpful explanatory notes available at **http://www.legislation.gov.uk/ukpga/ 2002/9/contents,** and the following details and account rely heavily on these notes prepared by the Lord Chancellor's Department.

1.119 **Objective of the 2002 Act** The fundamental objective of the 2002 Act is that, under the system of electronic dealing with land that it seeks to create, the register should be a complete and accurate reflection of the state of the title of the land at any given time, so that it is possible to investigate title to land online, with the absolute minimum additional enquiries and inspections. More details about e-conveyancing are given at 1.182.

1.120 **Registration triggers** The intention of the 2002 Act is to extend the registration of land to as many legal estates as is possible. The effect of this is to allow and extend voluntary first registration, as well as to extend compulsory first registration triggers to include leases with more than seven years to run. (Indeed, the clear intention is to reduce this period down to leases with more than three years to run, and the 2002 Act contains a power to give effect to this intention.) Section 4 of the 2002 Act sets out the triggers to first registration and consolidates the position under the Land Registration Act 1997: see 1.17 for details. Section 5 enables the Lord Chancellor to add new compulsory first registration trigger events by way of statutory instrument. Section 6 imposes a requirement on the estate owner to register within two months of the date of the conveyance or transfer to the new estate owner. Should an estate owner fail to comply with s 6, s 7 provides that a transfer will become void. Should this occur, then the transferor would hold the legal estate on a bare trust on behalf of the transferee. If failure to register arises from the grant of a lease or mortgage, they too will be void. They will, however, take effect as an agreement to grant the lease or mortgage.

1.121 The one major area of concern for practitioners must relate to the reduction in the length of leases inducing first registration. This is because, until now, commercial leases in particular have been granted for terms lasting between five and 21 years, but typically ten to 15 years. They have not required registration but have operated as overriding interests. The 2002 Act changes the position by requiring all leases of more than seven years in duration to be subject to compulsory first registration.

1.122 **Overriding interests** These are discussed at 1.57. Under the Land Registration Act 1925, these interests included all the incumbrances, interests, rights, and powers which were not entered on the register but which overrode registered dispositions under the Act. Such interests create a number of problems, since it is possible for a buyer to purchase a registered estate that is subject to adverse interests that are not apparent from the registers. In the 2002 Act, the categories of interests that are not registrable and which exist as overriding interests appear in two distinct lists. The first is relevant to first registration of title; the second to dealings with registered land. It is clear that the legislators want to limit the scope and effect of overriding interests. Consequently, in both lists the types of overriding interest are reduced in scope. The range of particular categories is lessened, with some categories being abolished altogether, while others were phased out after ten years. The guiding principle for the provisions in the 2002 Act reforming the law relating to overriding interests is that interests should be overriding only where it is unreasonable to expect them to be protected in the register.

In its Report of 2001, the Law Commission summarized the extent of overriding interests **1.123** that would be binding on a registered disponee of registered land after the 2002 Act came into force. They mostly comprise:

- most leases granted for three years or less (although currently the limit is at seven years but can be reduced to three);
- the interests of persons in actual occupation where (a) that actual occupation is apparent; and (b) the interest (i) is a beneficial interest under a trust; or (ii) arose informally (such as an equity arising by estoppel);
- legal easements and *profits à prendre* that have arisen by implied grant or reservation or by prescription;
- customary and public rights;
- local land charges; and
- certain mineral rights.

This is a much-reduced list of interests from that covered by s 70 of the 1925 Act, and clearly **1.124** there is an intention to ensure that the registers accurately portray the position that may exist for any particular property with little or no regard for overriding interests.

Third-party rights: protective entries These are discussed at 1.89. The 2002 Act reduces **1.125** to two the methods of protecting the interests of third parties over registered land. Cautions and inhibitions are abolished, *but not retrospectively*, while notices and restrictions are retained. Notices may be used to protect incumbrances affecting land that are intended to bind third parties. A typical example of the kind of incumbrance that could be protected by a notice would be a restrictive covenant. Restrictions regulate the circumstances in which a transaction affecting a registered estate may be the subject of an entry in the register. For example, a restriction might be used where any consents are required to a disposition. The restriction will give notice of the requirement that they be obtained. This will typically arise where a management company is involved, and requires a new estate owner to enter into covenants with it before the transfer of the legal estate can be registered, with the prior approval of the company.

Either form of protective entry can be sought without the consent of the registered propri- **1.126** etor, who nevertheless must be notified and who will be able to apply for cancellation of the notice, or object to an application for a restriction. If a person or company applies for either form of protective entry, they are required by the 2002 Act to act reasonably when exercising rights granted by the statute. There is, therefore, a duty of reasonableness that is owed to any person who suffers damage as a consequence of a breach. No doubt damages will be awarded where an applicant has not acted reasonably.

Adverse possession The stated aim of the 2002 Act is to ensure that registration *and noth-* **1.127** *ing else* should guarantee title and ownership as well as all the details of matters affecting the title. The logical extension of this aim is the limitation of title claims by adverse possession. The Act reforms the law of adverse possession so far as it relates to registered land. In effect there are now two methods by which a party can claim adverse possession. Which method will apply to what property will depend on whether or not the property is registered. The old law (the 12-year rule) will remain in place for all unregistered titles. For registered land, the 2002 Act introduces a new scheme for protecting the interests of registered proprietors against the acquisition of title by persons in adverse possession. A person claiming adverse possession of registered land will be able to apply to be registered as proprietor after ten years' adverse possession. This, on the face of it, seems a liberalization of the previous position. Nothing could be further from the reality of the reforms. This is because the registered proprietor will be notified of that application and will, in most cases, be able to object to it. Where the proprietor does object, the application will be rejected unless the 'squatter' can meet one of three limited exceptions. The whole basis of many successful claims for adverse possession rests on the lack of any need to notify the paper title owner of the squatter's occupation. The new law for registered land changes all of that and will thereby dramatically reduce the number of successful claims.

1.128 The proprietor will have to take steps to evict the squatter, or otherwise regularize the position within two years. Should the registered proprietor fail to do so and the squatter remains in adverse possession, after two more years (making 12 years in total) the squatter will be entitled to be registered as proprietor.

1.129 It should be noted that the new law places the onus on the squatter to take the initiative. If he or she wants to acquire the land, he or she must apply to be made the registered proprietor of the subject property. This is because the registered proprietor's title will not be barred by mere lapse of time; the ownership must be ousted by an act of registration.

1.130 **E-conveyancing** This topic is treated in depth in 1.182. Suffice it to say that one of the main purposes of the 2002 Act was to guide in e-conveyancing within the two to four years after the passing of the Act. Needless to say this was not achieved and may not be fully achieved for some time. The new legislation aims to create the necessary legal framework that will allow registered land conveyancing to be conducted electronically. It is, therefore, worth repeating that the main aim of the 2002 Act is that, under the system of electronic dealing with land that it seeks to create, the register should be a complete and accurate reflection of the state of the title of the land at any given time, so that it is possible to investigate title to land online, with the absolute minimum of additional enquiries and inspections. In the *Land Registry Annual Report 2016–2017*, it was stated that 'Not only will we be digitising our existing services but we will also be testing the future of digital conveyancing through our "Digital Street" pilot which will allow us to safely explore the use of new technologies such as Blockchain and Artificial Intelligence.' It is clear from this that Land Registry remains committed to digitizing its service as soon as possible.

1.131 This is all predicated on a system of electronic dealings making possible online title investigation. However, practitioners need to note that:

(a) e-conveyancing is to be introduced in stages, with the simplest transaction first. As a result, the 2002 Act authorizes the Lord Chancellor to regulate by rules transactions that can be effected electronically;

(b) the 2002 Act also gives the Lord Chancellor power to make e-conveyancing compulsory. While the 2002 Act contemplates a transitional period where paper-based conveyancing will co-exist alongside e-conveyancing, there is a clear intention to terminate paper-based conveyancing sooner rather than later;

(c) Land Registry will control permitted access to the e-conveyancing network. This means that conveyancers will in practice need the continued approval of the Registry to be able to effect e-conveyances. Let us hope that the Registrar exercises this control on a practical and reasonable basis, having regard to the demands of the modern, cost-effective conveyancing practice;

(d) Land Registry will be required to make the necessary arrangements to allow parties to carry out their own conveyancing, i.e. there will still be a place for the 'do-it-yourself' conveyancer. In principle this seems sensible, but quite how it will be carried out in practice is unclear;

(e) at present the e-conveyancing proposals fail to accommodate auction contracts. Changes will be needed to cover conveyancing that involves auction sales;

(f) Land Registry has now for the first time registered a mortgage to be signed electronically. The mortgage, or e-charge, in favour of Coventry Building Society was signed electronically by the borrower and registered at 11.20 a.m. on 24 March 2009;

(g) Land Registry has now introduced e-DRS, an electronic document registration service. With e-DRS, you can send and receive applications to change the register electronically, attaching scanned copies of supporting documents. Details of this facility can be found in Chapter 9. (The Land Registry receives approximately 17,000 applications per day, more than 80 per cent electronically.)

(h) Digital or paperless mortgages are being trialed. In the *Land Registry Annual Report 2016–2017*, it was stated that:

> 'In June 2016 we began operating a pilot version of our digital mortgage service. As it does not yet create a legal deed, borrowers still need to sign a paper deed, but the pilot service has allowed us to check that what we have built will work in the real world . . .. This will be one of the first of a new breed of digital services which enable customers and citizens to update the register digitally. The first truly digital mortgage can be created, signed and registered without the need for any paperwork or emailing and without the need for our colleagues to be involved in the process. Land Registry is planning to launch a new digital mortgage service in 2018 (see 7.155).

Other matters The 2002 Act makes other important changes. Land and charge certificates were abolished. Mortgages by demise were also abolished. The 2002 Act made an important management change applicable to land registration. Initially it created a new office, that of Adjudicator to Land Registry. The Adjudicator was appointed by the Lord Chancellor and was independent of Land Registry. The Adjudicator's duty was to determine objections that are made to any application to the Registrar that cannot be determined by agreement. However, this responsibility has since 1 July 2013 passed to the First-tier Tribunal Property Chamber (Land Registration Division), where such disputes will now be heard by Tribunal Judges. **1.132**

Section 64 of the 2002 Act contains important new requirements to record on the register certain defects in title where such defects would not previously have been recorded. It provides that if the Registrar becomes aware that the right to determine (i.e. end) a registered estate has become exercisable, he may enter this fact on the register. The most obvious example of this would be in a leasehold context where the lessee has breached a lease covenant and the lessor has become entitled to forfeit the lease. Another example would be where a rent charge is unpaid in respect of a freehold estate and the rent charge owner is able to exercise a right of re-entry. If the Registrar notes the defect on the register, a prospective buyer will be alerted to the problem at a much earlier stage of his or her investigations, instead of finding out from replies to enquiries. **1.133**

Section 112 of the Land Registration Act 1925 (as substituted by the Land Registration Act 1988) opened up the register to the public for the first time. This meant that it was no longer necessary for a registered landowner to give consent before his or her title could be inspected. Building on this, s 66 of the 2002 Act extends the scope of the open register. A person may inspect and make copies of, or of any part of, the following: **1.134**

(a) the register of title;

(b) any document kept by the Registrar which is referred to in the register of title;

(c) any other document kept by the Registrar which relates to an application to him; or

(d) the register of cautions against first registration.

1.135 Rules restrict access to documents of a commercially sensitive nature to those who have a good reason to see them. Protection of private information follows the scheme laid down in the Freedom of Information Act 2000. Documents can be exempt and thus kept private: see Chapter 12 for further details of Exempt Information Documents. Finally, the term 'office copies', familiar to conveyancers for decades, is replaced by the term 'official copy'. Section 67(1) provides that an official copy of the items listed above ((a)–(d)) is admissible in evidence to the same extent as the original.

1.136 The 2002 Act is considered in depth in *Blackstone's Guide to the Land Registration Act 2002* (OUP, August 2002), which we wrote to introduce the detailed provisions of the statute to both practitioners and students of conveyancing. At the time of going to press of this book, the Law Commission is reviewing the Land Registration Act 2002 in the Law Commission's Twelfth Programme of Work. Its project is designed to update the Land Registration Act 2002, in light of the experience of its operation since it came into force in October 2003. Its project is not designed to fundamentally reformulate the Act, but to improve specific aspects of its operation within the existing legal framework. A consultation process was undertaken in 2016 and the Law Commission is presently analysing the responses that were received. The consultation paper considers a wide range of issues, including:

- the interests that can be registered;
- how interests are protected on the register;
- the effect of registration;
- the extent of the guarantee of title that registration provides; and
- the development of electronic conveyancing.

Following an analysis of the responses to the consultation, the Law Commission aims to publish its report and draft bill in spring 2018.

KEY POINTS SUMMARY

REGISTERED LAND CONVEYANCING PROCEDURES

1.137 All of England and Wales is now an area of compulsory registration. Consequently, all purchases of unregistered land will be potentially subject to first registration, but not new leases of seven years or less, or longer existing unregistered leases where the remaining term is seven years or less. The Land Registration Act 2002 includes assents, gifts, and mortgages (including remortgages) as events that give rise to registration.

- An application for first registration must be lodged within two months of completion, failing which the legal title will revert back to the previous owner, who will in effect hold the property on a bare trust. The transfer will be void.

- The following title conversions are available to proprietors of registered property: qualified to absolute; qualified to good leasehold; possessory to absolute; possessory to good leasehold; good leasehold to absolute leasehold. The last is perhaps the most important title conversion and probably the most frequently sought. A good leasehold title can be upgraded to absolute so long as an applicant is able to produce to the Registrar the freehold title.

- Always remain vigilant about the major effects of a person in actual occupation pursuant to the provisions of Schedules 1 and 3 to the Land Registration Act 2002. Make full enquiries and searches.

- If you have an interest that requires a protective entry on the title, use a notice or restriction if the owner cooperates or a unilateral notice or restriction if the proprietor's assistance is not forthcoming.

- The State guarantees registered titles and that the legal estate is vested in the registered proprietor. If that is proved to be wrong, then any innocent party suffering loss will be compensated for the loss of any estate or interest in a registered title. An indemnity will now be paid to a claimant who has suffered loss, whether or not the register is in fact rectified. This is subject to the proper care provisions mentioned in 1.107.

- Land and charge certificates are abolished. The Registry will not require old certificates to be returned to it.

- Advise your clients of the existence of Property Alert, a free service to allow homeowners who might be concerned about fraud to be notified of significant changes to their registered title, such as third-party registrations.

C DEFENSIVE LAWYERING IN CONVEYANCING

DEFENSIVE LAWYERING AND THE CONVEYANCING PROCESS

In March 1997, the managing director of the Solicitors' Indemnity Fund wrote that conveyancing 'accounts for over half of all claims against the fund over all years, by both number and value'. Clearly this is a reflection both of the pressure on practitioners to expedite transactions at all costs and also of inappropriate working practices that provoke negligence claims. It is our view that conveyancers, like medical professionals, must practise defensively. By this we mean that in our daily conveyancing routine we must build in working practices that protect us from negligence claims as well as looking after the best interests of the client. If doctors can practise in this way, so can conveyancers. **1.138**

At the same time as the managing director wrote the above, the Risk Improvement Unit of the Solicitors' Indemnity Fund issued a fact sheet entitled *Claims Prevention for Conveyancers*. It is an excellent basis for all practitioners to develop a defensive lawyering methodology. We believe this is such an important area of concern to all conveyancing practitioners that we are considering it here. We hope you will bear in mind this crucial section when working through the subsequent elements of the book. Indeed, some ingredients of this section may initially be unclear without the information that follows in the rest of the book. Even then, we hope you will turn back to this section to underpin your knowledge of the conveyancing process with a defensive lawyering methodology, once you have read through the following parts of the book. Much of what we set out below rests heavily on the claims prevention fact sheet issued by the Indemnity Fund, and we acknowledge the benefits of this document. **1.139**

The problems linger, even after the land registration reforms mentioned earlier. It was stated in the *Law Society Gazette* that 34 per cent of all claims against indemnity insurers Zurich Professional in 2003 concerned conveyancing. Practitioners must remain vigilant, and we therefore hope that the following will assist (see LSG 101/12, 25 March 2004, p 3). The trend continues. On 4 August 2005, it was reported (LSG 102/31) that residential conveyancing continues to give rise to the highest number of negligence claims among two-to-ten-partner firms. This was highlighted in research carried out by the broker Aon. Almost half (43 per cent) of all claims notifications by such firms have been related to conveyancing, more than double those for personal injury claims (14 per cent). The article ended: 'Most residential negligence claims—both by number and value—stem from procedural issues such as a failure to undertake sufficient property searches or a failure to advise the client **1.140** on points of law.' Indeed, it was reported in the *Solicitors Journal* (see *Legal News* 15, April 2013) that '[a] quarter of conveyancing firms have been hit by negligence claims in the past two years' according to Solicitors Regulation Authority researchers. The researchers were quoted as saying: 'These figures suggest service levels could be improved and lessons learnt. Two thirds of firms stated that they pass on lessons learned from complaints and negligence claims to the rest of the firm. Ideally, this should be standard practice across all firms.'

Your duties as a conveyancing practitioner and your client

Fraud

1.141 The worst mistake a practitioner can make is to fail to spot something fraudulent. You should be fully aware of the pitfalls in practice when fraud occurs. As a form of basic guidance, you should read through the Law Society's Practice Note on Mortgage Fraud issued on their website and dated 31 July 2014, at **http://www.lawsociety.org.uk/support-services/advice/practice-notes/mortgage-fraud/**. This practice note highlights the warning signs of mortgage fraud. It highlights the latest criminal methodologies and outlines how conveyancing practitioners can protect themselves and their firm from being used to commit mortgage fraud. Practitioners need to be aware that individual purchasers can commit mortgage fraud by obtaining a higher mortgage than they are entitled to by providing untrue or misleading information or failing to disclose required information. This may include providing incorrect information about any of the following elements: identity, income, employment, the sources of funds other than the mortgage for the purchase, and the value of the property. If you become aware of any such circumstances, you need to investigate them and if necessary take further steps if you think a fraud has been perpetrated. One point that can be overlooked is the need to verify if the practitioner on the other side is real. It has been known recently for fictitious firms to appear and disappear with money to which they were not entitled. If in doubt, telephone the Law Society Records Centre or the Council for Licensed Conveyancers to make sure the firm you are dealing with is listed on either of their records. Online checks can also be made at **http://solicitors.lawsociety.org.uk/**.

1.142 The recent decision in *Purrunsing v A'Court & Co.* [2016] EWHC 789 (Ch) is another important case in the context of property fraud. In this case it was held that conveyancers on both sides of a transaction were liable for the actions of a rogue seller who committed a £470,000 property fraud. A solicitor who acted for the fraudulent seller was found jointly liable along with the buyer's solicitor, to the buyer for breaches of trust which took place when completion of monies were transferred to the fraudster on completion.

1.143 If you become aware of a change in the price or of other information that a lender might reasonably consider would affect the terms of the loan, then you should advise the lender. You act for the lender and there is, as a consequence, a clear obligation on your part to so inform the lender. If you knew something material, but did nothing to advise the lender, this could involve you in a civil claim in negligence. See also the *UK Finance Mortgage Lenders' Handbook (formerly the Council of Mortgage Lenders' Handbook)* on what other information a lender might be entitled to receive. Of course, practitioners do have a duty of confidentiality to their private clients, but this cannot be invoked to the detriment of another client. There is an obligation to act in the best interests of each client. The lender should be told about the variation in the price, but if the client will not agree to this step, then there is a conflict and you should cease to act (see also 2.94).

Cases

1.144 There have been several cases in the courts which impact heavily on working practices in the modern law office. You need to be aware of them and to change how you conduct transactions to meet the new standards required. To assist, we set out in this section some of the more important decisions that need to be considered by any conveyancing practitioner:

(a) If you know that your client is in arrears with a current mortgage but has instructed you to act on a remortgage, you may be under an obligation to report the arrears to the potential new lender before completing the new mortgage (see *National Home Loans Corporation plc v Giffen Couch and Archer* (1996) *The Times*, 31 December 1996 and *Birmingham Midshires Mortgage Services Ltd v David Parry and Co.* [1996] PNLR 494). The *National Home Loans* case was appealed and on 18 June 1997 the Court of Appeal reversed the decision, finding in favour of the firm of solicitors. However, what is clear is that each case is decided on the facts and it may well be that the extent of the duty of a solicitor will depend on the instructions and the extent to which the client appears to require advice. If you know of arrears, this should be reported to your client lender or you should decline to act for the mortgagee.

(b) You must not release the mortgage advance on completion until you have in your possession a properly completed—i.e. executed—mortgage deed. If you do, you risk being in breach of trust (see *Target Holdings Ltd v Redferns* [1996] AC 421). If there is a breach of trust, the liability to the client could be substantial.

(c) In *Royal Bank of Scotland v Etridge (No. 2)* [2001] 4 All ER 449, the House of Lords laid down guidelines for solicitors advising a spouse being asked to agree to a husband's (or wife's) business debts being secured on the matrimonial home. These guidelines also apply to cases where anyone in a non-commercial relationship has offered to guarantee the debts of another, for example a parent and child. The House of Lords adopted a somewhat commercially realistic approach. Detailed guidance on the correct approach is to be found in 7.106; it should be adhered to in circumstances that are the same as, or similar to the facts set out above.

(d) In the context of mortgage fraud, in *Santander UK plc V RA Legal Solicitors* [2014] EWCA Civ 183 the Court of Appeal decided that a solicitor's departure from best practice played a material part in the loss suffered by a lender, and therefore it would not be fair to grant the law firm any relief from liability for breach of trust under s 61 of the Trustee Act 1925. Section 61 gives the court power to relieve from liability a trustee who has committed a breach of trust, if he: (i) acted honestly and reasonably; and (ii) ought fairly to be excused for the breach. The lender had commenced an action for breach of trust against the solicitor for releasing funds to another firm of solicitors whom they had believed to be acting for the seller in a conveyancing transaction. After the transfer of £200,000, of which £150,000 represented the mortgage advance, it became apparent that the other firm of solicitors had not been instructed by the seller, and that a fraud had been committed.

Your client

Always verify your client's identity for the purposes of the Money Laundering, Terrorist **1.145** Financing and Transfer of Funds (Information on the Payer) Regulations 2017. Practitioners should refer to the details in the anti-money-laundering practice note issued by the Law Society on 22 October 2013 and which is available from the Law Society's website. (The Proceeds of Crime Act 2002 created a single set of money laundering offences applicable throughout the UK to the proceeds of all crimes. It also created a disclosure regime, which makes it an offence not to disclose knowledge or suspicion of money laundering.) If you have not acted for the client before, you need to be sure that the client is not seeking to launder money through the conveyancing transaction in respect of which you have received instructions. The major concern in this area for a conveyancing practitioner is that any failure to report a client where there is a reasonable suspicion of money laundering can lead to the practitioner being prosecuted by the authorities for not informing them about the suspicious activities of the client. Because of this onerous obligation on practitioners, always be most careful in verifying the identity of any new client. Furthermore, if a client insists on paying large sums of cash in relation to a purchase this will amount to a suspicious act for money laundering purposes. The Money Laundering, Terrorist Financing and Transfer of Funds (Information on the Payer) Regulations 2017 are detailed and require practitioners to put in place procedures to prevent money laundering and to provide staff training in respect of such procedures. If you do have any suspicion about money laundering involving your client, you should report your concern to the National Crime Agency, Units 1–6 Citadel Place, Tinworth Street, London SE11 5EF or online at **http://www.nationalcrimeagency.gov.uk**. As a form of basic guidance, you should read through the Law Society's anti-money-laundering practice note, which issues guidance and warnings to assist solicitors.

1.146 Be sure there are no conflicts of interest, and also that you have proper instructions from all clients. In effect, despite whatever family relationship exists, you have to be aware of the interests of each individual client, be it a lender, spouse, or child. Always confirm your instructions in writing at each stage of the transaction and especially just before exchange. If you write to confirm instructions, then there can be no dispute at a later stage if the client becomes disillusioned with your assistance. Keep full and detailed attendance notes recording telephone conversations, as well as meetings in the office, with the client. Adopt checklists such as those that permeate this book. Make diary entries of important dates such as completion dates or search priority periods (see Chapter 8).

Crucial time limits

1.147 Conveyancing practitioners are constantly up against crucial time limits. The problem is, in a busy modern legal office, these can easily get overlooked. Your professional negligence insurers will not look kindly on simple errors like overlooked time limits. The use of diaries—either written or electronic—is strongly recommended by us, and we set out below some of the more important time limits to look out for. However, in all cases, we suggest you use the early-warning date system. This puts in your diary a date warning at least a week before the actual deadline. In this way you will have a full five working days' early warning of the final deadline in which to make sure you take the necessary steps required in the particular transaction. You should always use the early warning date system in the cases outlined below.

1.148 **Land Registry search priority periods**   When buying a registered title, the pre-completion Land Registry search is of fundamental importance. First, it will highlight undisclosed incumbrances. Second, it will provide a priority period during which no other registration can obtain precedence over your client's application. It is therefore imperative that you submit your registration application at such time that the Registry receives it within the priority period. The dates and period are clearly stated on the search result and final deadlines for the application should be entered in your diary on receipt of the search result. Make no mistake, if you do not make the application within the priority period and a third party gets in an application for registration, to the detriment of your client, you will be held clearly responsible in negligence for any consequential loss your client suffers. (See Chapter 8 on pre-completion searches for further details of these important Land Registry searches.)

1.149 **Company mortgage registration period**   If you act for a limited company client, any mortgage that it takes out—i.e. where the company is borrowing money—*must* be registered at Companies House within 21 days of the completion date. Remember, courts almost never extend the time limit. Failure to register within the 21-day period will inevitably mean that you will be held liable in negligence to your client for any loss it may suffer as a consequence of your inaction. To ensure that the application gets to the appropriate department within Companies House without delay, we recommend you mark the envelope 'for the attention of the Mortgage Section'; it should then go straight there. If there are any queries on the form submitted with the mortgage, you will have sufficient time to deal with the problem so as to allow the actual registration to take place within the 21-day period. Alternatively you can file online using the 'WebFiling' facility at Companies House; details can be seen at **https://www. gov.uk/government/organisations/companies-house/about/about-our-services#webfiling**.

Stamping deadline After completion of a purchase where the consideration exceeds cur- **1.150** rently £125,000 for most residential properties, Stamp Duty Land Tax (SDLT) of a varying percentage of the consideration must be paid to the Revenue & Customs within 30 days of completion. SDLT is charged at increasing rates for each part of the price. If you fail to pay within this 30-day period, late payment will be possible only on payment of a penalty fee. On the assumption that you were in funds to pay the tax, there can be no excuse for not paying on time and the penalty fee will almost certainly come out of your own funds as the amount will be insufficient to warrant a claim on your indemnity policy. (See Chapter 9 regarding post-completion matters, including SDLT and the varying rates for residential and commercial property.)

Landlord and Tenant Act 1954 deadlines Part II of this Act covers the statutory renewal **1.151** of business leases. This is a particularly fertile area for negligence claims as the statute can require strict time limits. Some conveyancers will say that this is an area best left to litigators. However, it is also the case that many conveyancers deal with commercial lease renewals, which necessitates a secure knowledge of the Act and the time limits concerned. (See Chapter 13, which deals with commercial lease renewals generally.)

Keep a claims record

Learn from your mistakes. Keep a record of all claims and complaints and see if any pat- **1.152** tern is emerging. In this way you can quickly expose any weak links within your firm which require immediate attention. Keep your procedures under constant review and introduce change quickly whenever required. Keep all your staff fully trained and up to date in all aspects of the law, practice, and procedure.

Undertakings

Undertakings given by a conveyancing practitioner can lead to liability that was not con- **1.153** templated when giving the business. To ensure that this does not happen to you, always carefully consider the wording and effect of an undertaking before you actually enter into the particular obligation. Furthermore, wherever practicable, instruct all members of staff that letters of undertaking must be seen and signed by the partner in charge of the department. This, it is hoped, will emphasize to all members of staff the crucial nature of a professional undertaking and that your firm will not issue an undertaking without critical appraisal of all its terms by a practitioner at partner level.

Rejection of applications for registration

Land Registry can reject applications for registration which are found to be substantially **1.154** defective, for example where a transfer is drawn on an incorrect form. Land Registry has therefore drawn up a set of criteria for the early rejection of applications for registration that came into operation on 22 April 2002. This is a policy called early completion. In this regard, early completion is a policy governing applications to discharge mortgages that Land Registry has applied since 3 August 2009. The policy applies to all situations where an application for a discharge of whole has been made with another application but proof of satisfaction (evidence of the discharge of the charge) has not been provided. In essence, if there is no DS1 or other satisfactory proof of the mortgage discharge, Land Registry will reject the application for discharge but complete any other accompanying applications where it is possible to do so, such as a transfer of title. See 9.50 for further details of Land Registry policy governing early completion.

1.155 When the Registry rejects an application, it returns to the sender all the papers and documents originally enclosed. It will also state in writing the reason for rejection, so that this can be resolved before the application is sent back to the Registry. *A rejected application loses its priority.* Any fee sent with the application will be returned, refunded, or credited to the application when it is relodged after the defect has been put right. Land Registry lists the kind of errors that will give rise to rejection in its leaflet Practice Guide 49, dated 1 October 2013. These include but are not limited to:

(a) where an application form is required but none is used;
(b) where a form prescribed by the Land Registration Rules 2003 has not been used;
(c) if a mortgage discharge, the DS1, is not lodged, regardless of any undertaking of any copy DS1 lodged;
(d) where a deed refers to a plan but no plan is lodged;
(e) where proof of payment of SDLT is required but not lodged.

1.156 There are several other reasons for rejection, all of which can arise through administrative errors which may occur in a conveyancing practice. Accordingly, it is clear that this policy will lead to many applications being rejected and, as a result, priority for those applications being lost. The clear moral is to check all applications before they are sent to the Registry to make sure that they are correct and contain all the required information.

KEY POINTS SUMMARY

DEFENSIVE LAWYERING AND THE CONVEYANCING PROCESS

1.157 Always make detailed file notes of telephone conversations with your client and with the practitioner for the other party, and always confirm decisions and instructions in writing.

- Be on your guard against fraud, particularly money laundering. Verify your client's identity.
- Ensure all date-sensitive cases are carefully diarized using early-warning date systems where you have a week's warning before the final deadline.
- Regularly review your working procedures. Issue internal guidelines to all conveyancing staff covering the areas that are particularly sensitive, for example when giving undertakings.
- Learn from your mistakes. Do not ignore previous claims. Keep a claims record and make sure you do not repeat history.

D CONVEYANCING AND INFORMATION TECHNOLOGY

1.158 In January 1993, Professor R. W. Staudt wrote that 'lawyers for the twenty-first century must learn to use electronic information tools to find the law, interact with governmental agencies, prepare their own work and communicate with courts, other lawyers and their clients' ('The Electronic Law School: A 1992 Snapshot of the Centre for Law and Computers at Chicago-Kent College of Law', *Computer & Law*, 3(6) (1993), 33). We believe that Staudt neatly summed up the demands that will be made of conveyancing practitioners in this twenty-first century, and he also set out several critical areas where IT must develop in the future.

1.159 The pressure for innovation and change is already upon us. In the context of conveyancing, the section in this chapter concerned with the future of this legal specialty shows how, if conveyancers are to survive, they will need to adapt and change to meet the needs and demands of society. IT must help in this respect. As far as conveyancing and the storage of legal data on computer are concerned, the core elements of conveyancing will soon be computerized, with Land Registry aiming to hold computer records for all titles recorded at the Registry.

What this means is that the involvement of IT in the legal workplace is now irreversible. It   **1.160**
also indicates that there is a stark need to involve trainee lawyers, and indeed all new conveyancing practitioners, at the earliest opportunity if conveyancing is to survive as a profitable source of income. This will be possible only if those who are to be the future lawyers of this country are trained to expect IT in the office (and the courts) as an integral part of the conveyancing process, rather than being surprised by its presence. With e-conveyancing on the near horizon, this need is all the more pressing (see 1.182 for details). It is our view that modern legal conveyancing practice can only survive and develop with the support of IT.

The Land Registry Portal

One of these developments is now well established within the conveyancing industry. This   **1.161**
is the immediate availability of the Land Registry Portal, an online service which provides instant access to the land register and, in particular, to the more than 24 million computerized registers of title. With regard to their e-services, as at March 2016 the Land Registry confirmed that 99 per cent of service requests (e.g. searches, etc.), 73 per cent of registration applications, and 80 per cent of mortgage discharges are lodged electronically. This is a secure website platform from which to launch all existing and future electronic services. The Land Registry Portal is an electronic gateway that will enable all Registry customers to access systems from a single central point. The Portal can be adjusted to the needs of an individual customer. Registered organizations can control their own access permissions. These permissions are administered and maintained by a designated person called an administrator. It is therefore a web browser-enabled Portal which provides Land Registry services to users electronically, including the online viewing of title plans and title registers.

The attractions of the system are immediate for conveyancing practitioners and include: **1.162**

- online official searches of complete titles with immediate priority;
- online land charges searches;
- online official title copy applications;
- immediate access to computerized registers with the ability to print working copies of on-screen information;
- online Homes Rights searches; and
- the facility to apply for a search of the index map.

In this way the conveyancing process is more streamlined and thereby ready to meet the   **1.163**
challenges of the twenty-first century. To do this the Land Registry Portal came on-stream at the start of 2010. The Registry has said on its website that:

> Land Registry services will be delivered through a variety of channels, one being the new Land Registry Portal (which acts as a gateway to our electronic services, including e-conveyancing). This access channel will be segmented as follows:

Customer type	Customer categories
Licensed conveyancers/Solicitors	Legal services
Banks	Lenders
Building societies	
Government departments	Government services
Estate agents	Property investors/Services
Property professionals	
Local authorities	Other customers

Customer type	Customer categories
Building companies/developers	
Finance houses/credit services	
Insolvency services	
Insurance companies	
Privatized utilities	
Chartered surveyors	
Communications and media	
Others	
Registered citizen	General public
Unregistered citizen	

Customer categories are defined according to the roles they perform, so a lender or utility company undertaking conveyancing activities would fit into the legal services row as a conveyancer. Different segments have different access permissions within the portal and therefore access to different services.

USEFUL WEBSITES

1.164 A list of useful websites can be found in Appendix 2.

KEY POINTS SUMMARY

- Consider using the Land Registry Portal system direct to your own computers as well as the NLIS for online searching.

- Legal on-screen forms are essential for conveyancers. These enable you to call up on-screen any form you require, for example a Land Registry search request, transfer, Land Charges Registry search request, SDLT form or whatever, which you can then complete on-screen. This means that mistakes can be corrected without the expense of a new pre-printed form, as would be necessary if you did not have on-screen forms.

- Conveyancers must communicate to operate. PCs can run software that will allow that communication by fax direct from your PC (and thereby cutting out the expense of a dedicated fax machine) as well as by e-mail. Video conferencing using PCs is becoming an increasingly popular means of communication as well. The use of faxes will wane bearing in mind that faxed applications are no longer accepted by Land Registry.

- Access to government records via the Internet is possible, as well as details of statutes. It is an invaluable source of detail to all conveyancers. However, the real importance lies in the conducting of conveyancing transactions over the Internet (see Section E for progress in this regard). A web browser is required. The most popular browsers are Google Chrome, Mozilla Firefox, and Microsoft Internet Explorer. Obtain the latest version, as they are constantly rewritten to correct security problems. Presently they are free of charge.

- There are transaction management software packages available that purport to conduct each conveyancing transaction for you by producing diaries, letters, checklists, and precedents. They seek to make the conveyancing process quicker and cheaper for the practitioner and client.

- PCs can also be used to hold databases, i.e. lists of important data. These could include a Registry of all the client deeds that you are holding in your fireproof safe, or the details of your clients for future reference. Databases are becoming easier to use and more versatile, and offer practitioners assistance in the smooth operation of their office records systems.

- Online searches are now commonplace. It is possible to arrange access from your computer to Land Registry, so that you can obtain copy deeds and search results. In effect your computer will talk direct to the Land Registry computer. Access to land and property information held by local authorities and other agencies responsible for searches (see 4.55) is also available via the NLIS.

- Four out of five registration applications are now made online using the e-DRS system.

E THE FUTURE OF CONVEYANCING

INTRODUCTION

Following on from the discussion set out above concerning the integral use of IT by con- **1.165** veyancing practitioners, we believe that much of the success in the future will lie in a reconstruction of the way in which many conveyancers presently work. We advocate the full integration of all the facilities that legal IT can offer. However, there are other external influences at work that may dictate to conveyancing practitioners what the future will hold.

In the light of declining profit costs and increasing competition in the conveyancing mar- **1.166** ketplace, many solicitors have decided to change their own working practices, in particular in two different patterns: first, to try to make the process of buying and selling a house all-inclusive: the one-stop approach, in which solicitors will sell property in the style of estate agents and also offer the conveyancing of the property; second, to set up conveyancing call centres. These areas are examined in 1.173. In the near future, futher changes will alter conveyancing practice in a very substantial way and will bring about e-conveyancing. This will mean that the whole process will take place online using the Internet. Deeds will not need to be in a printed format and contracts will be exchanged electronically. Section 8 of the Electronic Communications Act 2000 gives statutory recognition to digital signatures. In a Land Registry press release issued on 20 March 2002, the Registry stated that 'the aim of the electronic conveyancing programme is to introduce, over the next five to ten years, a radical overhaul of the systems for buying, selling and registering property in England and Wales'. This has not taken place within the timescale envisaged, but the opportunity that technology provides is being used to re-engineer the process so as ultimately to replace the present paper-based system of conveyancing with a paperless system of e-conveyancing (see 1.188 for details).

GAZUMPING AND CONVEYANCING REFORM

On 28 July 1997, *The Times* ran an article with the headline 'House selling system to be **1.167** overhauled'. This made clear that the Government was examining how radical changes could be made and that '[i]ts aim will be to cut costs, uncertainty, delay and unhappiness'. It seems that top of the list of targets for change was the 'resurgent menace of gazumping'. Two Ministers, for Housing and for Consumer Affairs, and a Parliamentary Secretary in the Lord Chancellor's Department, were all charged with the responsibility for this examination. Individual case studies were considered to see where changes could be made to the role of solicitors as well as other integral elements of the conveyancing process, including the involvement of lenders, costs, charges, and delays. However, it is the scourge of gazumping that has come in for most scrutiny. When house prices are on the increase, gazumping occurs frequently. An article in *The Telegraph* of 3 October 2013 entitled 'Five dirty tricks in today's rising housing market' stated:

> Dirty trick no. 4 Gazumping: Gazumping is an especially nasty by-product of a booming housing market. It describes a situation where an unreliable—and probably greedy—seller accepts a higher price on their property despite already having accepted an offer from another buyer. The original buyer either has to improve their offer or lose the property—and often they have already spent hundreds of pounds on conveyancing fees and a survey.

1.168 The Government clearly signalled that an end to gazumping was a core element within its proposals for streamlining the system of buying and selling properties in England and Wales. Following the Government examination of the system, it issued a Consultation Paper 'The Key to Easier Home Buying and Selling' (DETR Publications 1999, ISBN 1 85112 134). It contains details of the research carried out by the Department of the Environment, Transport and the Regions as well as its package of proposals.

1.169 The Government research showed that by international standards our conveyancing system was apparently cheap but slow. As a result, proposals were made to try further to refine and streamline the system.

1.170 Current suggestions to stop gazumping include two frontrunners, namely, the Scottish system or a forfeitable preliminary deposit. In Scotland, the buyer and seller enter into a binding agreement as soon as an offer has been accepted. However, this apparently sensible system is not without its own problems, as before an offer can be made, the buyer must still pay for, and have in place, a mortgage facility and a survey result. If the offer is then rejected, the fees for the offer and survey are wasted. It would therefore seem that the adoption of forfeitable deposits could find favour.

1.171 In the circumstances where a deposit system is to be preferred, a sizeable deposit would be payable by both the proposed buyer and the seller. The size of the deposit would have to be at least 0.5 per cent or a full 1 per cent of the proposed purchase price. In the context of an average-priced property this could amount to somewhere in the region of between £850 and £1,700 per transaction. Indeed, if this arrangement is to operate as a true sanction, a deposit of £1,000 would seem more appropriate. If subsequently, but before the creation of a binding agreement between them, either party withdrew, that deposit would be forfeited to the innocent party. The intention is to make sure that the innocent party is not out of pocket as a result of the other party withdrawing. Anti-gazumping deposits are not a perfect solution as they would involve the preparation of additional conditions listing when there would be no forfeiture, such as when the buyer's survey was adverse. Perhaps the best solution is to find another way to speed up the whole process in order to avoid long delays during which the seller might be tempted to decide to sell to another, higher, bidder. One other alternative is to adopt lock-out agreements (see the precedent available on the Online Resource Centre). However, the courts have not helped in their widespread adoption. In *Tye v House* [1997] 45 EG 144, it was held that no injunction would be granted to enforce a lock-out agreement. While they remain valid and enforceable, a breach of the agreement will only find a remedy in damages.

1.172 Ultimately, we anticipate that, in the future, the following will all amount to viable methods of improving the system:

(a) Financial penalties could be imposed on all agencies and authorities responsible for issuing search results where they are dilatory in sending out the result.

(b) Pre-contract lock-out agreements could be adopted in all cases, backed up with statutory support and with complete remedies in default.

(c) The requirement could be imposed for forfeitable deposits of not less than £1,500 to £2,000, again backed up by statutory authority.

(d) The Scottish system could be adopted in all aspects, including solicitors selling property.

(e) All organizations and professions involved in conveyancing could make better use of IT and electronic communication to streamline and speed up the process.

ONE-STOP CONVEYANCING AND CONVEYANCING CALL CENTRES

'An attempt to take the pain out of house buying through a network of one-stop services **1.173** was announced yesterday by the Law Society.' So read a headline to an article in *The Guardian* on 1 August 1997 outlining a new scheme for Solicitors' Property Centres. These centres intend to provide 'consumers with all the services needed to buy and sell a home, including estate agents, solicitors and financial advisers'. The intention was to set up a chain of franchised centres covering the whole of the country. Inevitably, at the core of the service to be provided by the Solicitors' Property Centres, was easily accessible IT. The proposal was that this would speed up the flow of information through the estate agency stage as well as when the conveyancing itself is in progress.

However, this has really become a possibility only as a consequence of changes made by **1.174** the Law Society. Rules inhibiting the work of solicitors in selling property were, in July 1997, earmarked for relaxation by the Law Society Council. It recommended that changes to the rules should be made to 'deregulate' estate agencies separately operated by solicitors. Further recommendations would enable a solicitor acting as an estate agent to work also as a solicitor for the seller and in certain circumstances a buyer, as well as to provide financial and mortgage advice. However, this clearly raises potential problems of conflict of interest (see Chapter 2).

In April 1997, a large countrywide company of estate agents opened the first-ever seven- **1.175** day conveyancing call centre in southern England. This was quickly followed by two more such centres, opened this time by two large firms of solicitors. They all work on a telephone-based approach to the conveyancing process and appeal in particular to direct lenders rather than those that deal with proposed borrowers from their high-street locations. Teams of conveyancers function on a shift basis, with particular teams dealing with discrete elements of the transaction as it develops. This approach seems to appeal to the public as it mimics what many have come to expect, namely, the buying of services from home over the phone. A mortgage can be organized over the phone, as can house insurance, so why not conveyancing representation? This could be the way ahead for the conveyancing market. It is of course impersonal and does not help with the verification of your client's identity (see 1.145). 'But house-buying can never be reduced to that of the simplicity and efficiency of buying baked beans, precisely because houses are large, complex things and the amounts of money involved are so big' (*The Independent*, 7 December 1998, leader section, p 3). Clearly the approach must be considered, in whole or in part, by conveyancing practitioners if they wish to continue to work profitably in the future.

However, this method of handling conveyancing may have its difficulties. A leading article **1.176** has stated: 'One of the country's leading bulk conveyancing firms has quit residential conveyancing, saying the factory concept neither works for the client nor makes any money' (LSG 98/01, 5 January 2001). The firm's view was that this system fails to provide local knowledge and connections. The individual nature of each transaction made it hard to keep costs down, thus making the process of bulk conveyancing uneconomic. And yet in the same publication in the next edition it was reported that a network of solicitors and conveyancers was to invest over £3 million in an effort to increase its share of the bulk conveyancing market (LSG 98/02, 11 January 2001). The aim was for the network to increase the number of conveyances conducted by them from 30,000 to 60,000 in three years (and thus handle approximately 10 per cent of the market). Conveyancers have also turned to the Internet in an attempt to offer a quick and competitive system for electronic property transfers. Bulk conveyancing solicitors use the Internet to obtain initial instructions and thereafter clients are allowed to access the firm's case management system (**http://www.legalmove.com/**).

1.177   Solicitors have also tried to expand via property shops, offering conveyancing services alongside an estate agency. For example, it was reported in April 2000 that in the North East there were 55 branches of a chain of property shops with yearly sales of £20 million (NLJ, 28 April 2000, p 603). However, in April 2004, it was also reported that one of the two original Solicitors' Property Centres from the 1980s had closed. The centre in Wrexham was initially run by eight firms; since 1990 that number was down to three firms of solicitors. An Internet search made in March 2014 for property centres run by solicitors showed only results for Scotland, a sign that the expansion in England and Wales has withered away to nothing.

1.178   Nevertheless, we suggest that the future conveyancing practitioner could work in a dedicated property centre where all types of properties are bought and sold, where the practitioner will offer mortgage and financial advice and will of course convey property for sellers and buyers. Practitioners will use IT as a core element of the working day for all aspects of their work, be it the giving of advice, making searches, the production of documents, letters, e-mails, faxes, or indeed sales documentation for properties on their sales lists. The present somewhat limited horizons for the high-street conveyancers must be broadened if their work and profit costs are to survive. Without this wholesale adoption of a generic approach to the process of buying and selling property, the future will be bleak. It is our view that with it the future will be assured.

1.179   In October 2017, the Government issued a consultation paper '*Improving the Home Buying and Selling Process*'. Views were sought on gazumping, building trust, and confidence, including looking at 'lock-out agreements', as well as digital innovation.

ENERGY PERFORMANCE CERTIFICATES

1.180   The Energy Performance Certificate (EPC)/Predicted Energy Assessment (PEA), which give homeowners, tenants, and buyers information on the energy and carbon emission efficiency of a property, are required to be available to buyers and need to be available prior to marketing a property.

1.181   **The Energy Performance Certificate**   This certificate tells you how energy-efficient a home is on a scale of A–G. The most efficient homes—which should have the lowest fuel bills—are in band A. The certificate also tells you, on a scale of A–G, about the impact the home has on the environment. Better-rated homes should have less impact through carbon dioxide (CO_2) emissions. The average property in the UK is in bands D–E for both ratings. The certificate includes recommendations on ways to improve the home's energy efficiency to save money and help the environment. Sellers of newly built homes will have to provide a predicted assessment of the energy efficiency of the property, but a full EPC should be provided to the buyer when the home is completed. Therefore there is a new duty on a seller to commission an EPC before marketing a property and to make reasonable efforts to secure an EPC within 28 days. If there is a pre-existing EPC it remains valid for ten years. Listed buildings are exempt from these requirements.

E-CONVEYANCING

Introduction

In England and Wales contracts for the sale or creation of interests in land must be made in **1.182** writing and signed by the parties. Similarly, deeds must be in writing and the signature of the party or parties making the deed must be witnessed. All conveyances, transfers, leases, mortgages, and legal charges must be deeds. Thus, notwithstanding the growing use of electronic communication at all the other stages of a conveyancing transaction, the two key stages of making the contract and completion must be achieved by using paper documents.

The Electronic Communications Act 2000 gives Ministers the power to change the law **1.183** to authorize or facilitate the use of electronic communication and electronic storage. This power will improve the conveyancing process by permitting the creation of e-conveyancing documents such as contracts, transfers, conveyances, leases, and mortgages.

E-conveyancing documents will have to be electronically signed with a certificated electronic **1.184** signature and will have to specify when they are intended to take effect. Electronic documents, other than contracts, will also have to be made in a form prescribed by Land Registry. The format of the e-conveyancing documentation will be issued as the processes are prescribed.

E-conveyancing arising from the Land Registration Act 2002

The fundamental objective of the 2002 Act is focused closely on making e-conveyancing **1.185** a distinct reality. The objective is to enable an effective system of electronic dealing with land as a result of the register being a complete and accurate reflection of the state of the title of the land at any given time. This is so that it is possible to investigate title to land online, with the absolute minimum of additional enquiries and inspections. From this fundamental aim flows the entire framework for e-conveyancing that has been constructed by the 2002 Act.

The 2002 Act constructs a framework in which it will be possible to generate and trans- **1.186** fer estates and/or interests in registered land by e-conveyancing. The statute does this by authorizing the execution of formal deeds and documents electronically. The 2002 Act also contemplates the formation of a secure electronic computer network within which to carry out e-conveyancing. It is envisaged that the execution of all such deeds and documents together with their registration will be simultaneous. To achieve this, the process of registration will be initiated by conveyancing practitioners. However, there is State control. Access to the computer network is to be controlled by Land Registry, which will also exercise control over the changes that can be made to the land register. The 2002 Act also provides for the Lord Chancellor to regulate by rules those transactions that can be carried out electronically. Furthermore, it gives the Lord Chancellor power to make the use of e-conveyancing compulsory. Compulsory e-conveyancing will arise only after a period of consultation and after a transitional period when conveyancers will move from the existing paper-based system to an electronic system. Consequently, there will of necessity be a period of time when the two systems co-exist.

The 2002 Act is intended to make it impossible to create or transfer many rights in or over **1.187** registered land except by registering them. Investigation of title should be effected entirely online. It was originally intended that the Registry would also provide a means of managing a chain of transactions by monitoring them electronically. This was meant to enable the cause of delays in any chain to be identified. Once identified, steps would no doubt be taken to put pressure on the delaying party to make sure that the bottleneck to progress was removed. Despite a chain management pilot being processed by the Registry (see

1.190), it seems that they have drawn back from this aspect of the scheme and it may be for others to arrange chain management. The Law Commission anticipated that, because of this supervision by the Registry (or others), far fewer chains will break and conveyancing will be considerably expedited. The involvement of chain management is expected at a very early stage in most, if not all, registered land transactions, as will be highlighted in 1.189.

Anticipated model of e-conveyancing

1.188   The computer e-conveyancing network will be accessible only by contractually authorized professionals, whether those are solicitors, licensed conveyancers, estate agents, or mortgagees. The e-conveyancing network will not be used just for the several stages of each transaction, but also for the provision of property information and to coordinate and manage chains of registered land dealings.

1.189   We originally anticipated that Land Registry would be made responsible for managing chains of transactions in order to smooth their progress. When a buyer or a seller instructs a conveyancing practitioner to act on his or her behalf where there is likely to be a chain of transactions, that practitioner was to be required to notify the Land Registry 'chain manager' of those instructions. Thereafter the practitioner was also to be obliged to advise the Registry of the completion of the several stages in the conveyancing procedure so that the chain manager could log them. In this way each step can be shown in a matrix, thereby building up a complete picture of where in the chain each transaction is. This process should enable all those involved in a transaction to identify bottlenecks within the chain that can be addressed so as to try to expedite the process. This information will be made available via the secure intranet to all parties in the chain. This will be by way of the chain matrix, a grid setting out the steps taken or to be taken in a transaction.

1.190   Land Registry announced a trial of a prototype 'Chain Matrix' service, one of the key elements of its e-conveyancing system, between autumn 2006 and spring 2007. The prototype chain matrix allowed conveyancers, their clients, and selected estate agents to view the progress of property transactions in chains on a dedicated website. This meant that they could see if there were any delays in particular transactions, what was causing them, and when exchange and completion had taken place. Bristol, Portsmouth, and Fareham were chosen for the initial six-month trial. Conveyancers in those areas, dealing with the sale and purchase of properties, were able to update details of the progress of the transactions in the matrix and, using the notepad facility, leave messages for other participants in the chain. Following the trial, Land Registry offered to support developers and commercial enterprises that want to develop chain-matrix-type services. The Chief Executive of Land Registry said of this development that '[t]his decision is both in keeping with our policy of concentrating our resource on enhancing and expanding e-registration services and in line with the research findings. It enables us to carry on doing what we do best, while supporting the commercial market to develop entrepreneurial or innovative new services which will meet the needs of conveyancers in the future.' It would seem, however, that Land Registry has for the moment abandoned the chain matrix in favour of developing e-documents and electronic applications. Land Registry is introducing an enhanced facility to lodge documents electronically, for registration or noting by Land Registry, through the new portal. The e-documents system currently provides for the introduction of the following applications.

Business e-services customers can automatically register:

- e-CON (registration of change of name by marriage/deed poll/registration or civil partnership);

- e-CST (statutory charge (applies to Legal Services Commission applications only)); and
- e-DJP (remove the name of a deceased joint proprietor from the register).

They can lodge electronically:

- e-AN1 (enter an agreed notice);
- e-CCD (cancel a caution against dealing)
- e-CN1 (cancel a notice (other than unilateral notice));
- e-COA (change of address);
- e-CPD (change of property description);
- e-HR1 (registration of a notice of home rights);
- e-HR4 (cancel an existing HR notice);
- e-RX1 (enter a restriction);
- e-RX3 (cancel a restriction);
- e-RX4 (withdraw a restriction);
- e-UN1 (enter a unilateral notice);
- e-UN2 (removal of a unilateral notice);
- e-UN4 (cancellation of a unilateral notice);
- e-WCT (withdraw a caution).

They cannot submit:

- more than one registered title in the same application;
- an application in respect of part only of a registered title, unless provided for in the schedule;
- a title the registration of which is pending;
- a title the individual register of which is not held in electronic form;
- a title to a freehold estate in commonhold land;
- a title to a profit a prendre in gross;
- a title to a franchise;
- a title which has been registered with a qualified title; and

An new document registration service introduced in December 2012 is e-DRS. With e-DRS, you can send and receive applications to change the register electronically, attaching scanned copies of supporting documents. Details of this new facility can be found in Chapter 9).

1.191 In the original e-conveyancing proposals, when the seller and buyer have agreed the terms of the contract, they will send a copy in electronic form to Land Registry, where it will be checked electronically. This is meant to enable any inconsistencies in the agreement on factual matters, such as property address, title number, and seller's name, to be identified and corrected before the contract is made binding. The contract will be made in electronic form and signed using a digital signature, i.e. electronically by the seller and buyer. As is the case now, estate contracts should be protected in the register by the entry of a notice (currently a caution). This noting in the register should be made electronically at the same time as the establishment of the binding contract.

1.192 The draft transfer and any mortgage will be prepared in electronic format and in relation to the transfer agreed between the seller and buyer. As was the case for the contract, the draft will be submitted to the Registry for scrutiny. The particulars of the transfer will be checked electronically against the contract to ensure that there are no inconsistencies. The Registry, in consultation with the seller and buyer, will indicate the form that the land register will take when the transaction is completed by assembling a pre-completion draft register.

1.193 Completion will entail the concurrent happening of the following events:

(a) the execution of the transfer and any charges in electronic form, and their transmission to the Registry, where they will be stored;

(b) the registration of the dispositions so that the register conforms with the notional register previously agreed with the Registry; and

(c) the appropriate (and automatic) movement of funds and the payment of SDLT and Land Registry fees.

1.194 The beneficial effect of this system of e-conveyancing is that the time lag between completion and registration that arises in the paper-based system will be eradicated. Changes to the register will be made automatically as a consequence of electronic deeds and documents and applications created by conveyancing practitioners on behalf of their client sellers and buyers. Land Registry previously issued additional notes about the possible new e-conveyancing system website and these are set out below:

E-conveyancing will comprise a certain amount of re-engineering of the process and is expected to incorporate the following new features:

- At the time the seller's conveyancer uses the e-conveyancing service to transmit the draft contract from their computer to the buyer's conveyancer, automatic validation checks will compare contract data with Land Registry data and electronic messages will indicate any discrepancies and/or omissions. It is anticipated that these will be resolved online. At this time, a new 'notional' register will be built on the system indicating, as each document is prepared, what the new register would look like.

- Conveyancers will also record on the system the stage reached on each transaction by adding data to a 'chain matrix' available in the central service. This will enable conveyancers and Land Registry to see the progress of all the transactions linked together in a chain. Chains will therefore become more transparent. The conveyancer's task in synchronizing exchange and completion dates should be simplified, with any blockage points being immediately identifiable to facilitate enquiries.

- There will also be a facility for conveyancers to view Land Registry's day list (a log of all pending applications) prior to exchange of contracts, in order to ascertain whether or not there is such an application which may adversely affect the transaction—for example a bankruptcy notice.

- At the contract stage, there will be an electronic equivalent of contracts. Contracts will be exchanged electronically when the buyer's and seller's conveyancers have signalled that agreement has been reached and contracts have been signed and released for electronic exchange. The central service will provide for automatic exchange of contracts relating to all transactions in a property chain. For this and other purposes, conveyancers will need to have electronic signatures. Land Registry has initiated a project to determine an effective and affordable e-signature ('document authentication') solution. Payment of deposits on exchange will be accounted for in the central service and paid by the electronic funds transfer (EFT) service.

- A substantive register entry will be made to note the contract. This would also provide, automatically, a priority protection period in respect of any competing application and during which completion with registration would normally be expected to take place. Provision to extend the priority protection period may be necessary for delayed completion.

- During this period the draft electronic transfer and any draft electronic legal charges will be agreed and finalized. These documents will then be signed electronically in anticipation of completion just as they are in the existing paper system. Shortly before completion the parties to the transaction (and all parties in the chain) will signal their readiness to complete in accordance with the terms of the contract. They will do so by using an extension of the chain matrix, which will indicate, first, that all necessary documentation is signed and, second, that all the financial arrangements are in place. Registration will take place with completion.

- All financial obligations, including SDLT and Land Registry fees as well as payments between buyers, sellers, lenders, and conveyancers, will be settled through the EFT service.

With the help of e-technologies, the amounts of SDLT and Land Registry fees will be correct in virtually all cases. This will contrast with the present high incidence of errors.

- Post-completion—it is envisaged that no further action would be needed for transfers relating to registered land. When the purchase of unregistered land is included in a chain of transactions, it will only be possible to achieve simultaneous completion and conditional registration for that transaction. The reason for this is that the unregistered title needs to be examined by Land Registry.

A comparison between paper-based conveyancing and e-conveyancing

It may assist practitioners to see how stages in a conveyance compare as between the present paper-based system and its likely successor, e-conveyancing. The comparison will follow the five stages in a normal conveyance for a purchaser (see Table 1.1): **1.195**

1. estate agent/marketing stage;
2. pre-contract stage;
3. contract stage;
4. post-contract but pre-completion stage; and
5. completion and post-completion stage.

Table 1.1 Paper-based conveyancing and e-conveyancing

Paper-based conveyancing	E-conveyancing
Estate agent/marketing stage	**Estate agent/marketing stage**
Traditional marketing methods used by private sellers or their agents, e.g. adverts, boards, signs, lists, etc.	Traditional marketing methods used by private sellers or their agents, e.g. adverts, boards, signs, lists, etc. There could be additional e-marketing on the Internet through agents or possibly the NLIS.
Pre-contract stage	**Pre-contract stage**
1. Buyer makes an offer which the seller accepts. Their respective conveyancers are instructed.	1. Buyer makes an offer which the seller accepts. Their respective conveyancers are instructed. There may be a requirement to notify Land Registry of a potential transaction so that the chain matrix can be formed, the notification made by the seller, or the estate agent by e-mail.
2. Several searches required, all requested by post.	2. Several searches required, all requested electronically via the NLIS.
3. Paper-based enquiries issued and answers reviewed.	3. Enquiries made by e-mail and answers received by e-mail and reviewed.
4. Survey commissioned.	4. Survey commissioned.
5. Mortgage arrangements made.	5. Mortgage arrangements made online.
6. Paper contract approved and signed by the hand of the contracting party and held by practitioners.	6. E-contract approved by the practitioners and then by Land Registry and electronic signatures arranged.
7. Where a chain of transactions exists, practitioners acting for buyers and sellers in the chain arrange a proposed completion date and seek to make a series of coordinated exchanges.	7. Guided by Land Registry chain manager and by reference to the online chain matrix, a completion date is agreed and contracts are ready to be electronically concluded. Before exchange the Registry may enter the proposed new title entries in draft form on the register in readiness for exchange—the notional register.

Table 1.1 (continued)

Paper-based conveyancing	E-conveyancing
Contract stage	**Contract stage**
Contracts exchanged usually following one of the Law Society formulae (A, B, or C) and usually by telephone between practitioners involved in the chain of transactions.	Electronic exchange based on electronic signatures and the approved e-documentation based on the online matrix information. Deposits paid by EFT system. Completion of financial e-settlement arrangements to be prepared. A note of the contract is entered on the relevant title at the time of exchange and the title freezes. The Registry after exchange will enter the proposed new title entries in draft form on the register in readiness for completion—the notional register.
Post-contract but pre-completion stage	**Post-contract but pre-completion stage**
Requisitions on title.	No need for requisitions on title.
Drafting and approval of transfer deed.	The e-transfer will be approved by the practitioners and Land Registry and draft changes to be made to the register are approved by the Registry.
Final searches.	No need for final Land Registry search; the title is frozen and there is an entry protecting the contract, but a bankruptcy search will be required against the borrowers to protect any lenders. (A company search will still be required if the seller is a company—it can be completed online at Companies House.)
The seller signs the transfer in readiness for completion.	No further signatures required.
Completion and post-completion stage	**Completion and post-completion stage**
Completion	*Completion*
The transfer deed is signed, dated, and delivered to effect completion and the deeds passed over to the buyer's practitioner with undertakings to pay off mortgages and to pass over forms DS1 and END1. Payments are made either by bank transfer, banker's draft, or cheque.	There is no need for a transfer and there are no deeds. Once all parties are advised, Land Registry will complete the change of ownership by making the draft entries of the formal details of title and ownership on the e-register. Payments are made by e-settlement, including redemption monies, fees, SDLT, and costs—the EFT system.
Post-completion	*Post-completion*
SDLT paid. Land registration application made, it is hoped, in the priority period. The Registry updates the title and issues a Title Information Document.	Unless the title is for first registration, there is nothing further to be done. The title has been instantly updated at completion. The title can be accessed electronically on the open-to-the-public land register.

E-conveyancing and first registration

1.196 The effect of e-conveyancing on the practice of first registration is unlikely to be of any great consequence. We assume that the transfer inducing first registration will be possible in electronic format. In essence, while the transaction will be conducted on a paper-based system, the transfer deed will be prepared electronically so that it can then be adopted for the purposes of the first registration application to the Registry. Second, where first registration is voluntary, it will be possible to make the application for electronic voluntary first registration. In both cases the supporting title deeds will have to be physically delivered to the Registry to enable it to approve and first register the newly registered title.

State control of conveyancers and conveyancing

Substantial State control of the conveyancing process and those who conduct that process **1.197** is put firmly in place by this intended model of e-conveyancing. Only those solicitors or licensed conveyancers who have been authorized to do so will be permitted to conduct e-conveyancing. The relationship with the Registry will be contractual, under a 'network access agreement', and the Registry will be obliged to contract with any solicitor or licensed conveyancer who meets specified criteria.

Those specified criteria will be the subject of wide consultation and discussion with the **1.198** relevant professional and other interested bodies. It may be that the intention of the 2002 Act is to raise the standards of conveyancing. It may achieve that; but what it certainly achieves is the State control of conveyancers and conveyancing. Presumably, if an authorized e-conveyancer starts to be identified as a regular producer of bottlenecks in matrices, he or she could be at risk of losing his or her authority. Perhaps such a conveyancer would then have to limit his or her work to unregistered transactions.

Pitfalls of e-conveyancing

E-conveyancing is not without potential difficulties. Several have been anticipated in legal **1.199** and computing journals. Two relevant articles looked at the potential abuse and misuse of digital signatures by unauthorized third parties. See 'The cost of e-conveyancing' (LSG 99/11, 14 March 2002, p 43) and 'The perils of non-repudiation' (LSG 98/39, 11 October 2001, p 45). Practitioners should also consider the warnings about security and computer-virus attacks set out in 'The BadTrans virus and e-conveyancing' *Computers & Law*, December 2001/January 2002, p 8. In that article the author, Raymond Perry, says: 'The Government has already given an indication that in cases where a solicitor is negligent in protecting his digital signature as a result of which the register is altered then Land Registry may look to the solicitor for an indemnity if compensation has to be paid.' This means that solicitors will need to be sure that they have taken all reasonable steps to protect their IT systems from third-party attack and misuse of their digital signatures. Failure to do so could be expensive. The future will clearly require conveyancing practitioners to be experts in 'software updates and virus warnings' as well as in the law and practice of conveyancing.

In the *Law Society Gazette* of 13 December 2012, the Chief Land Registrar was reported **1.200** as saying: 'Electronic conveyancing remains on the agenda of the Land Registry despite proving more difficult to realize than anyone had thought.' This appears to underline the reasons for the slow progress to full e-conveyancing. In February 2017, the Land Registry announced new steps towards digital conveyancing. It released a consultation to amend the 2003 Land Registration Rules to facilitate e-conveyancing. Proposals include:

- accepting documents signed electronically through the government's GOV.UK. Verify system, under which third parties certify citizens' identity when interacting with the government online. Such signatures do not need witnessing because the identity assurance takes place before the e-signature can be used;
- enabling wholly electronic mortgages, at first when there is no change in ownership of the property. Conveyancers will create electronic mortgage deeds online, giving the borrowers a link through which they can sign electronically; and

- revoking rules requiring certain documents to be retained and amending the definition of 'working day' to take into account changes in working practices as well as the 'proper office' order stating where applications should be lodged.

(See the article 'Registry announces new steps to digital conveyancing' in the Law Society Gazette, 10 February 2017.) The proposals are out for consultation.

THE LAW SOCIETY CONVEYANCING QUALITY SCHEME

1.201 The Law Society has designed and is now actively promoting a Conveyancing Quality Scheme (CQS) the aim of which is to provide a recognized quality standard for residential conveyancing practices. This new scheme was introduced from the start of 2011. The Law Society says that the scheme will enhance the reputation of conveyancing solicitors, provide reassurance about integrity and practice standards, and that it will create a trusted conveyancing community that will deter fraud whilst providing a more effective service for clients.

1.202 The scheme utilizes the transaction Protocol and adopts four guiding principles:

1. Probity: application for membership focuses on identity and status checks for individual conveyancers and firms to create a trusted conveyancing community.
2. Practice quality standards: consistent processes and standards are central.
3. Client/stakeholder service: a new client charter aims to ensure quality of service delivery.
4. Quality assurance: monitoring and enforcement are robust and members may be subject to spot checks and audits.

Practices must have three years' conveyancing experience to apply. Membership is annual, with re-accreditation at the end of each 12-month period. Applicants will have to produce evidence that they have vetted and identified key conveyancing staff in the firm. As a minimum all partners connected with residential conveyancing within the firm must have had a Criminal Records Bureau check within the last 12 months. The Law Society further advise that all members of staff involved in residential conveyancing or in a position to handle financial transactions should also have an up-to-date Criminal Records Bureau check.

Changes to the CQS accreditation scheme were announced in 2015. However, the accreditation period of 12 months remains the same. The way in which participants re-apply for the scheme is changing, as is the information collected. The application process will now follow a three-year assessment cycle. Mandatory training will be separated into core training for new starters and update training for existing staff. Finally, the introduction of a desk-based assessment is to be introduced to monitor and enforce the adoption of the Law Society Conveyancing Protocol. This assessment is designed to review key areas in a conveyancing transaction which may indicate whether a practice is complying with the CQS protocol.

1.203 The firm will also be required to produce procedures for practice management focusing on financial management, supervision, file auditing, client care, and complaints. It should also be noted that the application process will include the mandatory training for a new post required by the scheme called the Senior Responsible Officer (SRO). The SRO must be nominated by the firm as being responsible for the scheme. Other staff will also require training on how to comply with the scheme requirements. The Law Society provides courses that are being designed to meet the requirements of the accreditation process and are currently the only ones authorized to do so.

1.204 There are fees payable on applying and for membership. When the scheme was introduced a sole practitioner was required to pay £150 plus VAT to apply (now £165 plus VAT) and a

£200 membership fee (now £220 plus VAT), while a 50+ partnership had fees of £950 plus VAT (now £1,045 plus VAT) and £1,000 plus VAT (now £1,100 plus VAT), respectively. Members can display the scheme logo on their stationery and in their offices.

To coincide with the promotion of this Scheme the Law Society also issued the fifth edition **1.205** of the Standard Conditions of Sale (see Chapter 3), and a 2011 Law Society Code for Completion by Post (see Chapter 8). The Law Society have also issued a revised Conveyancing Protocol—see Chapter 2 for more details.

It was reported in February 2015 that all solicitors on the Nationwide Building Society **1.206** conveyancing panel would have to be accredited under the CQS. This requirement of the largest building society in the country was put in place during the summer of 2015. The Nationwide stated: 'We see CQS as best practice and a valuable indication of firms' commitment to providing a quality service to their clients', *The Law Society Gazette*, 23 February 2015, p 3.

2

TAKING INSTRUCTIONS AND OTHER INITIAL MATTERS

A INTERVIEWING THE CLIENT

GENERAL CONSIDERATIONS

2.01 Right from the start of any transaction it is important to establish a good working relationship with the client. The first interview marks the perfect time to do this, for it gives you the opportunity to instil confidence in the client of your abilities as a conveyancer. The first interview will of course enable you to gather essential facts, but it should also be used, where necessary, to furnish the client with important advice on how to proceed.

2.02 Always try to see the client in person. Too many firms cut corners by relying on the telephone or e-mail for obtaining instructions (some cut-price conveyancers will say they cannot afford to see clients at all), but in the long run this may be a false economy, for clients will normally prefer to meet their solicitor at an early stage. It is our view that, ultimately, it is still the high level of service that impresses clients more, not the low level of fees; and a satisfied client is one who will return to you with future instructions. If a personal interview is impossible, at least ensure that the instructions received and advice given over the telephone are clear, and backed up with a letter of confirmation to the client. The Money Laundering, Terrorist Financing and Transfer of Funds (Information on the Payer) Regulations 2017 require you to obtain satisfactory evidence of the client's identity when you establish a business relationship with the client, for example at the first interview. Strictly speaking, you should not even open a file or prepare a client-care letter until the client's identity has been verified (see 2.95).

Checklists

2.03 It can be helpful to have a checklist of items which will or which may be relevant in the first interview. Consider the practical checklists at the end of this chapter (see 2.117). It is worth obtaining all the information you need from the client at this early stage. This will avoid the need to contact the client for information later on, which is frustrating for you and often annoying to the client. One word of warning on checklists, though: never be a slave to the checklist to the possible exclusion of other relevant matters. Always consider carefully the client's circumstances and ask yourself: 'Is there anything else I need to know from the client? Is there any further advice the client needs from me?'

ESTATE AGENTS

Generally

As you are aware, most sellers will use an estate agent to market their properties and to **2.04** negotiate on the sale price. The agent normally charges the seller a percentage of the selling price as commission. This becomes due on exchange of contracts but is paid out of the sale proceeds on completion. By the time the seller first contacts the conveyancer, the seller usually will have secured a buyer at an agreed price, the agent's work having been done. Some clients will, however, wish to consult their conveyancer much earlier for advice concerning their contractual arrangements with the estate agent (and you should encourage this). Estate agents' terms of business vary, so it is worth advising the client to 'shop around'. Some agents charge a lower percentage but add an extra charge to cover advertising costs. Your firm will probably be able to recommend a reputable agent whose terms are acceptable.

Types of agency contracts

You should be able to advise the client of the different types of agency which are currently **2.05** available and which is the most suitable. Depending on how difficult the property is to sell, your advice is likely to be to use either a sole agency or a multiple agency (see 2.06 and 2.07). Always read the written terms of the proposed agency agreement carefully before giving any express advice regarding the agent's entitlement to commission.

Sole agency

Here the appointed agent is the only agent with the right to sell the property. As the seller is **2.06** not an agent, if the seller finds a buyer personally then the agent is not entitled to any commission. The client may still have to pay for advertising or a 'For Sale' board. If the client appoints more than one agent under a sole agency, each agent is entitled to claim their fee when the property is sold (so the client ends up paying more than one commission). Some agents offer a 'joint sole agency' contract in which two agents agree to share one commission.

Multiple agency

Here the client is free to instruct several agents but only the agent who introduces the **2.07** eventual buyer will be entitled to a commission. It follows that the rate of commission for a multiple agency is generally higher than for a sole agency.

Sole selling rights

You should warn your client to avoid this arrangement because the agent is the only person **2.08** with the right to sell the property. Even if the client finds a buyer personally or through another source, the agent with sole selling rights is entitled to commission (see *Dashwood v Fleurets* [2007] EWHC 1610 (QB)). As with a sole agency, if the client appoints more than one agent under a sole selling rights agreement, each agent is entitled to claim his or her fee when the property is sold.

Ready, willing, and able purchaser agreement

This should also be avoided. The client pays the agent commission if the agent finds a buyer **2.09** who is prepared and able to buy the property and exchange unconditional contracts. The seller still has to pay commission even if the seller withdraws from the sale and contracts are not exchanged.

Estate agents and preliminary deposits

2.10   Once an offer has been accepted (subject to contract), the estate agent frequently asks the buyer for a small preliminary deposit of say £200–£300. You would generally advise the buyer not to pay this deposit because it does not legally secure the property and serves primarily to assist the estate agent's cash flow. Of course, some clients may have paid it already before they instruct you. If this is the case, you should note the amount on your file so that it can be deducted from the deposit paid on exchange. It is also sensible to ask the client for a copy of the agent's receipt for the deposit. The receipt should make it plain that the deposit is fully refundable if the transaction does not proceed. Under the Estate Agents Act 1979, the agent is not obliged to pay interest on preliminary deposits of £500 or less.

CLIENT CARE AND ADVICE ON COSTS

2.11   Caring for the client's needs is always of paramount importance to the competent practitioner, who should be naturally concerned to ensure that the client is happy with the service provided. As part of the continuing drive towards client satisfaction, client-care outcomes are a formal requirement of the SRA Code of Conduct 2011 (the Code), which came into force on 6 October 2011. It is important that practitioners give their clients information about costs and other matters, and operate a complaints-handling procedure. The Code can be found on the Solicitors Regulation Authority (SRA) website (**http://www.sra.org.uk**) and is considered further at 2.89.

Costs

2.12   Outcome 1.13 of the Code requires practitioners to give clients the best possible information, both at the time of engagement, and when appropriate as their matter progresses, about the likely overall cost of their matter. This should include a breakdown between fees, VAT, and disbursements. At the start of a conveyancing transaction, it should be possible to agree an estimate for the whole transaction. Remember that this will also have to include your fee for acting for the client's lender (if any). You should also advise the client of VAT payable on top of your profit costs together with other expenses such as possible Stamp Duty Land Tax (SDLT), Land Registry fees, search fees, and bank transfer fees. If you forget to mention VAT, the client may assume that the quoted figure is inclusive of it (s 89, Value Added Tax Act 1994).

2.13   Once you have settled an estimated figure, it is sensible to inform the client that you reserve the right to increase your charges should the transaction prove to be unduly complicated or protracted. In this way you are not binding yourself to a fixed, unalterable fee. You may reassure the client, however, by saying that in the vast majority of cases, no increase is usually necessary. You should also discuss how and when the costs are to be met (normally at the conclusion of the transaction). You should confirm the estimate to the client in writing, and you must also advise the client immediately in writing if the figure is to be revised. Care is needed here because if you go further than giving an estimate—by committing yourself to a fixed (or 'agreed') fee—then you will not be permitted to charge more even if circumstances arise which make the work unremunerative at that figure.

Complaints-handling and client care generally

Outcome 1.9 of the Code requires clients to be informed in writing at the outset of the mat- **2.14** ter of their right to complain and how complaints can be made. Outcome 1.11 requires you to deal with clients' complaints promptly, fairly, openly, and effectively. Firms should there- fore operate a written complaints procedure, and ensure that all staff are made aware of it. This policy will tend to show that the Outcomes have been achieved and the Principles adhered to. In particular, the Indicative Behaviours in Chapter 1 of the Code recommend that the firm's written complaints procedure should:

- be brought to the clients' attention at the outset of the matter;
- be easy for clients to use and understand, allowing for complaints to be made by any reasonable means;
- be responsive to the needs of individual clients, especially those who are vulnerable;
- enable complaints to be dealt with promptly and fairly, with decisions based on a suf- ficient investigation of the circumstances;
- provide for appropriate remedies; and
- not involve any charges to clients for handling their complaints.

Clients should be provided with a copy of the written complaints procedure upon request and, in the event that a client makes a complaint, the client should be provided with all necessary information concerning the handling of the complaint. Outcome 1.10 requires clients to be informed in writing, both at the time of engagement and the conclusion of the solicitors' complaints procedure, of their right to complain to the Legal Ombudsman, the time frame for doing so, and full details of how to contact the Legal Ombudsman. The Law Society has issued a useful complaints management practice note to help solicitors achieve good practice in this area (**http://www.lawsociety.org.uk/advice/practice-notes/ handling-complaints/**).

In relation to client care generally, the following Indicative Behaviours will tend to show **2.15** that the practitioner has achieved the Outcomes in Chapter 1 of the Code and therefore complied with the Principles:

- agreeing an appropriate level of service with your client, for example the type and fre- quency of communications;
- explaining your responsibilities and those of the client; and
- ensuring that the client is told, in writing, the name and status of the person(s) dealing with the matter and the name and status of the person responsible for its overall supervision.

Remember that the Indicative Behaviours in the Code provide examples of the informa- tion practitioners should be providing in order to meet the Outcomes. However, unlike the Outcomes, the Indicative Behaviours are not mandatory, and a practitioner must decide what is appropriate for an individual client taking into account the client's particular needs and circumstances. For example, it may be inappropriate to give full information in certain cases, such as when acting for a regular client for whom repetitive work is done where the client has already been provided with the relevant information. It follows that the Indica- tive Behaviours are of particular importance when taking instructions from a new or non- established client.

At some stage during the first interview, you should advise the client of the future action **2.16** to be taken to progress the matter, the likely timescale of the transaction, and when you will next contact the client. If the client is unfamiliar with the conveyancing process it is good practice to offer a brief explanation of the procedures involved and to estimate when exchange of contracts and completion are likely to take place. All relevant client-care infor- mation, including advice on costs, must be confirmed to the client in writing.

Stamp Duty Land Tax (SDLT)

2.17 Where the price for the property exceeds a threshold figure (currently £125,000 for residential properties and £150,000 for non-residential and mixed-use properties), the buyer is required to pay a government tax known as Stamp Duty Land Tax (SDLT). In Wales, it is simply known as Land Transaction Tax (LTT). Before 4 December 2014, SDLT was charged at a single rate for the entire price of the property. Since 4 December 2014, SDLT has been charged at increasing rates for each part of the price.

For residential properties the purchaser will pay:

- nothing on the first £125,000;
- 2% on the next £125,000;
- 5% on the next £675,000;
- 10% on the next £575,000;
- 12% on the rest (above £1.5 million).

Example

If the purchaser buys a residential property for £325,000, he will pay SDLT of £6,250. This is calculated as follows:

- nothing on the first £125,000;
- £2,500 on the next £125,000;
- £3,750 on the remaining £75,000.

Since 1 April 2016 there has been a 3 per cent SDLT surcharge when an additional residential property in England, Wales, or Northern Ireland is bought by someone who already owns a home, i.e. second homes and 'buy-to-let' properties. The higher rates are 3 per cent above the current SDLT residential rates. They are charged on the portion of the value of the property that falls into each band, i.e.

- £0–£125,000 0% becomes 3%;
- £125,000–£250,000 2% becomes 5%;
- £250,000–£925,000 5% becomes 8%;
- £925,000–£1.5 million 10% becomes 13%;
- above £1.5 million 12% becomes 15%.

To assist people moving home, if a purchaser buys an additional dwelling before selling their main dwelling they will have 36 months after buying the new property in which to dispose of their previous main residence and claim a repayment of the 3 per cent SDLT surcharge.

From 22 November 2017, first-time buyers paying £300,000 or less for a residential property will pay no SDLT. First-time buyers paying between £300,000 and £500,000 will pay SDLT at 5 per cent on the amount of the purchase price in excess of £300,000, a reduction of £5,000 compared to the amount of SDLT they would have previously paid. A first-time buyer is defined as an individual or individuals who have never owned an interest in a residential property in the United Kingdom or anywhere else in the world and who intends to occupy the property as their main residence. First-time buyers purchasing property for more than £500,000 will not be entitled to any relief and will pay SDLT at the normal rates.

The HM Revenue & Customs calculator for SDLT is a useful resource to help work out how much your client will pay—**http://www.hmrc.gov.uk/tools/sdlt/land-and-property.htm**.

If the price is just over the threshold for SDLT, you should consider apportioning the price between the land and any contents included in the sale (e.g. carpets and curtains). This could reduce the price for the land below the threshold and thus reduce or avoid SDLT altogether. However, you should take care that the price for the contents is a proper reflection of their value. Any overvaluation in these circumstances may constitute a fraud against HM Revenue & Customs (by both you and the client) and could also make the contract for sale unenforceable by action (see *Saunders v Edwards* [1987] 1 WLR 1116). You will also be in breach of the Principles in the SRA Handbook, namely acting with integrity and behaving in a way that maintains the trust the public places in you.

2.18 HM Revenue & Customs has issued guidance as to items it regards as chattels, where apportionment is allowable, and items it regards as fixtures, where apportionment is not allowable:

- **Chattels:**   carpets, curtains, light shades, pot plants, free-standing kitchen white goods, and portable electric or gas fires.
- **Fixtures:**   fitted bathroom sanitary ware, central-heating systems, plants growing in the soil, and gas fires connected to a piped gas supply.

2.19 Any reduction in the purchase price of the property should also be reported to and first approved by the client's prospective mortgagee (if any). The mortgagee may possibly decide to reduce the amount it is prepared to lend.

2.20 To assist you in filling out the SDLT return following completion, ask the buyer for his or her national insurance number when taking instructions and keep it on file.

2.21 For non-residential and mixed-use properties the purchaser pays the following rates of SDLT:

- property price, premium or value up to £150,000 (annual rent no greater than £1,000) = 0%;
- properties between £150,001 and £250,000 = 2%;
- properties over £250,000 = 5%.

ADVICE ON CO-OWNERSHIP

2.22 Where two or more persons are proposing to buy property, it is important to obtain instructions from all intending buyers, and to advise them clearly on the different ways in which the property can be jointly held. The legal estate ought properly to be transferred into the names of all buyers who are contributing to the purchase price (subject to a maximum of four: Trustee Act 1925, s 34(2)). This is now a standard requirement of most lending institutions. Remember that the *legal* estate can only be held as a joint tenancy, not as a tenancy in common. The Law Society has issued a practice note on joint ownership guidance, which is available from its website, **https://www.lawsociety.org.uk/support-services/advice/practice-notes/joint-ownership/**.

Joint tenancy or tenancy in common?

2.23 As far as the equitable estate is concerned, the co-purchasers have to decide whether to hold as joint tenants or tenants in common, and for this they will need your advice.

Joint tenancy

2.24 Under a joint tenancy, the purchasers own collectively the whole of the equitable estate with each other—they do not own individual shares. Accordingly, a 'share' in the property cannot be left by will, because upon death the deceased's 'share' passes automatically to the survivor(s). This is known as the right of survivorship. A joint tenancy is normally suitable for a married couple, civil partners, or co-habitees in a stable relationship, but not for those who have children from a previous relationship (see 2.25). An express declaration of joint tenancy will result in the joint owners being given equal shares in the event of a later severance of the joint tenancy (*Goodman v Gallant* [1986] Fam 106). Practitioners should make prospective joint tenants aware that either co-owner may sever the joint tenancy in the future, in which case the joint tenancy would convert to a tenancy in common (the same would occur if one of the joint tenants became bankrupt). A severance would mean that the other co-owner would not automatically inherit the whole of the property (see *Boycott v Perrins Guy Williams & Ors* [2011] All ER (D) 113, a case concerning former test cricketer Geoffrey Boycott).

Tenancy in common

2.25 A tenancy in common is the opposite to a joint tenancy in that the buyers do own separate shares which may be left by will, or pass on intestacy in the event of no will, or may even be disposed of *inter vivos*. A tenancy in common should be recommended where the buyers are neither married nor in a stable relationship, where they have contributed in unequal proportions to the purchase price, or where they are business partners. It would also be appropriate for couples where one or both have children from a previous relationship, so that those children (and possibly any grandchildren) can be provided for.

2.26 Failure to give proper advice in this area may result in a negligence claim against the solicitor if a client suffers loss as a result. The classic mistake is for a conveyancer to advise a joint tenancy where a tenancy in common is clearly appropriate, for instance where unmarried co-purchasers contribute in unequal shares to the purchase price (see *Ahmed v Kendrick* (1988) 56 P & CR 120).

Establishing whether owners are joint tenants or tenants in common

2.27 You may need to know whether clients who already own property are joint tenants or tenants in common, for instance if one owner dies, or if the property is to be sold and the proceeds split. You can find out by the means outlined in the following paragraphs.

Registered land

2.28 If the title is registered you should consult the proprietorship register of the title to see whether a joint proprietorship restriction has been entered in the following terms: 'No disposition by a sole proprietor of the registered estate (except a trust corporation) under which capital money arises is to be registered unless authorized by an order of the court' (you may come across earlier versions).

2.29 The presence of such a restriction tells you that the owners are tenants in common. The absence of such a restriction tells you that they are joint tenants.

Unregistered land

2.30 If the title is unregistered, you should consult the most recent conveyance to the present owners, which should state whether they (i.e. the purchasers in the conveyance) are joint tenants or tenants in common.

Trust declaration and making wills

2.31 Where purchasers buy as tenants in common you should, on or before completion of the purchase, prepare a declaration of trust, signed by the parties, setting out their respective financial contributions and agreeing their share of the beneficial interest in the property. The declaration can also deal with other matters, such as the proportions each will pay towards the mortgage (if any) and other household expenditure, and the procedures for a later sale if one wishes to sell and the other does not. The declaration of trust should be kept safely and referred to in the event of any later dispute. Its express terms are unlikely to be overturned by a court (see *Pankhania v Chandegra* [2012] EWCA Civ 1438). Land Registry Form JO may be used by joint owners to declare their interests. Without a trust declaration, uncertainty may arise in the event of a later dispute between the co-owners over the distribution of future sale proceeds. The court has a wide discretion to assess their shares in the property having regard to the conduct and contributions of each party (see *Oxley v Hiscock* [2004] EWCA Civ 546) but a purchase of domestic property in the joint names of cohabitants will establish a *prima facie* case of joint and equal beneficial interests until the contrary is proved (see *Stack v Dowden* [2007] UKHL 17). This assumption of joint and equal ownership can be displaced by showing (a) that they had a different common intention at the time of acquisition; or (b) that they later decided on a common intention that their shares would change. If it is clear that either (a) the parties did not intend that there should be an equal division of the beneficial interest at the outset; or (b) they had changed their original intention, but it is not possible to ascertain (even by inference) what their actual intention was, then each party is entitled to the share which the court considers fair having regard to the whole course of dealing between them in relation to the property (see *Jones v Kernott* [2011] UKSC 53). Because the survivorship rule does not apply to a tenancy in common, tenants in common should also be advised to make wills.

ADVICE ON FINANCE

General considerations

It is helpful for the client if, while taking instructions, you can prepare a brief financial statement, showing the expected payments and receipts on the sale and/or purchase. In this way, you can calculate how much extra money the client may need to find, either from the client's own resources or by mortgage loan, in order to complete the transaction(s). **2.32**

Before proceeding with the conveyancing process, it is important to check that: **2.33**

(a) the client understands all the financial implications and can afford to go ahead; and
(b) sufficient funds are or will be available to finance the total expenditure.

If the client has a related sale and purchase, the net proceeds of sale will normally be used to assist the funding of the purchase price: **2.34**

(a) **Calculating the net sale proceeds** You can calculate roughly how much will be available from the sale by deducting from the total sale price the following:
  (i) amount to be repaid under any existing mortgage(s) on the sale property (the client should be able to guide you on this, and you can verify the exact figure direct with the mortgagee);
  (ii) if estate agents are involved, their commission fee including VAT;
  (iii) your costs on the sale, plus VAT and disbursements; and
  (iv) rarely, any Capital Gains Tax (CGT) payable on the sale.

  You should also consider whether any person other than your client has a claim to any part of the sale proceeds which would reduce the amount available to your client, for example someone who contributed towards the purchase price when the property was bought.

(b) **Calculating the full cost of purchase** You will add to the purchase price the following:
  (i) the price agreed for any chattels or other extras included in the purchase;
  (ii) any SDLT payable; and
  (iii) your costs on the purchase, plus VAT and disbursements (including search fees).

To calculate how much the client must find either from the client's own resources or by mortgage loan, simply deduct the net sale proceeds ((a) above) from the full cost of **2.35** purchase ((b) above). Examples of financial statements are set out in Appendix 9 and more fully explained in 8.79.

2.36   If the client is only selling (without a related purchase), you should confirm to the client calculation (a) above. If the client is just buying (without a related sale) you should confirm to the client calculation (b) above.

2.37   It is also prudent to remind the client of other possible expenditure which the client will have to settle personally before completion, for example the surveyor's fee on a purchase (see 2.68), and furniture removal costs.

2.38   Advice may be required on potential liability to capital gains tax (CGT) (see 2.60).

Deposits

Deposit payable on exchange of contracts

2.39   A buyer will normally be required to pay a deposit on exchange of contracts. The deposit acts as part-payment as well as a guarantee, which the seller can forfeit if the buyer defaults on the contract. The deposit is usually 10 per cent of the purchase price, although sometimes the parties agree less. Your client buyer will need to place you in funds for the deposit before exchange and you should advise the client of this now. Many clients believe mistakenly that their mortgage advance will cover the deposit, but the advance is of course not available until shortly before completion (i.e. after exchange).

2.40   **Financing the deposit**   If the client does not have funds available, you will need to explore other ways of financing the deposit. If the client has a related sale, it may be possible to utilize the deposit you receive on the sale towards the purchase deposit. This will depend on the terms of the contract. Alternatively, the deposit guarantee scheme could be considered (see 3.89), or, if the client has a related sale, short-term bridging finance (see 3.87). The last two methods will incur cost for the client and these should be explained.

Mortgages

2.41   Upon taking instructions, it is common for the client to inform you that the mortgage has already been arranged. It is your duty to ensure that these arrangements are satisfactory according to the needs and wishes of the particular client. For instance, someone without dependants who wishes to secure the lowest monthly outlay would generally be advised to have an ordinary repayment mortgage. Yet it is surprising the number of clients who seem to think (or who have been told by commission-hungry brokers) that another type of mortgage is the best option for them.

2.42   You should also warn clients about the dangers of attractive-looking fixed-rate mortgages. Although they can be beneficial when interest rates are rising, they may not be as appealing when mortgage rates start to fall and they often contain hidden penalties for early redemption. Always check the small print of the mortgage conditions as well as the special conditions relating to the particular mortgage. (For a discussion of typical mortgage conditions, including retentions and indemnity guarantee policies, see 6.04.)

Tax relief on mortgages

2.43   Tax relief on private dwelling-house mortgages was abolished on 6 April 2000. However, where a loan is taken out for the purchase or improvement of business premises, interest on that loan may qualify as an allowable expense of the business for tax purposes.

Common types of mortgage

Repayment mortgage   This is generally the cheapest mortgage in terms of monthly outlay. **2.44**
The loan is repaid over the mortgage term (normally 25 years) and each monthly repayment by the borrower to the mortgagee comprises part interest and part capital (in the
early years of the mortgage the capital element is very small). The mortgagee will usually
insist that a separate mortgage protection term assurance policy is arranged so that if (and
only if) the borrower dies during the lifetime of the mortgage, the debt is repaid by the sum
assured. The monthly premium on the mortgage protection policy is typically just a few
pounds. A client without dependants who is looking for the lowest monthly mortgage cost
would be well advised to consider this type of mortgage.

Endowment mortgage   An endowment mortgage is generally more expensive than an **2.45**
ordinary repayment. The mortgage is linked to a life assurance policy which matures at the
end of the mortgage term. None of the capital loan is repaid during the life of the mortgage,
the monthly payments to the mortgagee being interest only. In addition, the borrower pays
monthly premiums on the life policy to a life company.

The maturity value of the policy should in theory be sufficient to repay the capital loan; **2.46**
there may even be surplus funds available if the investment has performed well. However,
returns on endowment policies have suffered over recent years and there is no guarantee
that the proceeds will repay the loan (especially for 'low-cost endowments' where initial
premium contributions are even lower). Any shortfall on the mortgage debt will ultimately
have to be funded by the client, who should be warned of this possibility. The risk of shortfall together with the abolition of tax relief on endowment policy premiums has reduced
the attraction of this type of mortgage.

Existing endowment policies may be surrendered or sold (privately or by auction), but **2.47**
clients should be warned that their value in the early years will be minimal because the
first few years' premiums are normally absorbed by commission charges. Many borrowers have been disappointed to learn that the surrender value of their endowment policy is
substantially less than the total premiums they have contributed. Values on sale to a trader
in second-hand policies can exceed surrender values, and consequently clients thinking of
surrender should also be advised to consider a sale.

Pension mortgage   This is similar to an endowment mortgage but, instead of the loan **2.48**
being linked to a life policy, it is linked to a personal pension policy. The proceeds of the
policy on maturity are used to discharge the loan. This type of mortgage is likely to suit a
self-employed person who has (or should be advised to have) a personal pension. Unlike
an endowment policy the contributions to the pension policy are tax deductible, which is
attractive, particularly for higher-rate taxpayers. On retirement, a tax-free payout of 25 per
cent of the pension fund can be taken as a lump sum to pay off the mortgage loan.

ISA mortgage   In this case, the mortgage is linked to a specific form of savings arrangement. **2.49**
The ISA is normally linked to a unit trust which invests in a spread of stock market investments.
Clients should take a long-term view and aim for an ISA which gives consistently good performance
broadly in line with the various indices of stock market performance. If the ISA performs well,
the proceeds of the savings plan should be enough to repay the mortgage loan. Unlike the
pension mortgage, contributions to an ISA do not qualify for tax relief at the point money is
invested. However, there is no income tax on the dividend income and no CGT when the ISA is
sold. If practitioners intend to give specific (i.e. non-generic) advice concerning a particular type
of ISA, this would constitute investment business, for which authorization would be required
under the Financial Services and Markets Act 2000 (see 2.55). Clearly, many practitioners will
have insufficient expertise in this field and clients would normally be referred to an authorized

independent financial adviser. There are caps on annual contributions into an ISA, making an ISA potentially unsuitable for borrowers with larger mortgages.

2.50   **Interest-only mortgage**   This is the cheapest for the client in terms of monthly outlay because 'interest only' means exactly that—no capital is repaid and the mortgage is not linked to any life policy, pension, or savings plan. Clients must be advised that they will need to find a method of paying off the loan eventually. Lenders should offer interest-only loans exclusively to borrowers who can demonstrate that they have other arrangements in place for repayment of the loan, for example out of an existing pension fund or ISA. However, this is not always the case and you should make your client aware of the risks involved.

Shariah-compliant mortgage

2.51   Islamic law—known as shariah—forbids Muslims from paying interest and this excludes many Muslims from the conventional mortgage products that are on offer. Specialist Muslim lenders such as the Islamic Bank of Britain offer shariah-compliant alternatives. These usually involve the lender initially buying the subject property and then selling it on to the Muslim purchaser at a higher price (known as the *Murabaha*).

2.52   A typical scenario would be:

(a) the client chooses a property and agrees a price;
(b) the bank enters into a contract to buy the property from the seller;
(c) the bank sells the property to the client at a higher price;
(d) the client pays the higher price to the bank in equal instalments over a fixed term of up to 25 years.

2.53   Further information regarding shariah-compliant mortgages can be obtained from **http://www.islamic-bank.com/** and the Islamic Banking and Insurance Institute (020 7245 0404). See also Land Registry Practice Guide 69 (Islamic Financing).

Mortgage guarantee scheme and 'Help to buy'

2.54   In an attempt to boost the housing market, a Government-funded mortgage guarantee scheme was introduced on 1 January 2014 in which loans on residential property from high-street lenders were partly underwritten by the Government. This ended on 31 December 2016. The scheme covered new or old homes up to £600,000 and the Government guaranteed 15 per cent of the value of the mortgage. Lenders taking part were therefore more willing to accept smaller deposits from borrowers and so lend a higher percentage of the value of the property. The Government has also launched a 'Help to buy' equity loan scheme aimed at buyers of brand-new houses and flats, including apartments in converted commercial buildings. This will continue until 2020. For more information on this, see 11.01 in the chapter on New Properties. A 'Help to buy' shared ownership scheme is also available for first-time buyers. This allows individuals or couples earning less than £80,000 (or less than £90,000 in London) to buy a share of a home at 25–75 per cent of its value. They then pay rent to a housing association, which owns the remaining share of the property, but have the option of increasing their ownership later.

Financial Services and Markets Act 2000

2.55   When advising on mortgages you must have regard to the Financial Services and Markets Act 2000 (the Act). Solicitors who conduct 'mainstream' investment business (e.g. advising on specific investments) must be authorized to do so by the Financial Conduct Authority (FCA). Only about 300 firms in England and Wales are currently authorized to conduct mainstream investment business. Solicitors who conduct 'non-mainstream' investment business which is incidental to their legal services (e.g. conveyancing) are regulated by the

SRA, which is a Designated Professional Body (DPB) under the Act. This will cover the overwhelming majority of firms.

The Scope Rules

The Law Society has issued 'Scope Rules' which limit and define the scope of what solici- **2.56** tors can and cannot do as members of the DPB. These are called the Solicitors' Financial Services (Scope) Rules 2001. The aim of the Rules is to ensure that in providing services to clients, solicitors carry on only regulated activities which *arise out of or are complementary to*, the provision of services to their clients, for example conveyancing, corporate work, matrimonial, probate, and trust work. Essentially, non-mainstream investment business falls within the Scope Rules, but mainstream investment business falls outside the Rules and requires authorization from the FCA.

The Scope Rules include: **2.57**

(a) a list of prohibited activities (r 3);
(b) basic conditions which must be satisfied; and
(c) other restrictions relating to particular types of activities and investments.

So if firms consider that their activities will go beyond the Scope Rules, i.e. into mainstream **2.58** investment business, they will need authorization directly from the FCA, otherwise they will be committing a criminal offence.

Generic advice only

If you offer the client generic mortgage advice about the different types of mortgage and their **2.59** suitability for the client (e.g. 'in your circumstances I would recommend a repayment mortgage'), this will fall outside the Act as it is not a regulated activity. However, arranging or giving specific advice about different mortgage providers and mortgage products is a regulated activity and would require prior authorization from the FCA. Unless a regulated mortgage is arranged by a person who is authorized under the Act or with a (properly authorized) financial institution, it will be unenforceable without the leave of the court. Similarly, offering specific advice on an investment product (e.g. a particular pension company in connection with a pension mortgage) would constitute a regulated activity, for which the firm would require prior authorization. If your client is seeking non-generic (i.e. specific) advice, you should refer him or her to a reputable independent financial adviser who is authorized by the FCA.

Capital Gains Tax (CGT)

Principal private dwelling-house exemption

CGT is *prima facie* payable on the disposal of an interest in land. The disposal for tax purposes **2.60** occurs at exchange of contracts (when the beneficial interest passes to the buyer), not on completion. Nevertheless, CGT is rarely payable in the context of residential conveyancing because of the availability of the principal private dwelling-house (PPD) exemption. Section 222 of the Taxation of Chargeable Gains Act 1992 provides that the disposal (i.e. sale) of an individual's PPD, including grounds of up to 0.5 hectare, is exempt from CGT. Although this will apply in most domestic transactions, the practitioner should always check the client's situation carefully to ensure that the exemption does in fact apply in each case.

Only or main residence In the first place, one should establish whether the seller has lived **2.61** anywhere else since the subject property was acquired, because the exemption states that the seller must have lived in the house as his or her only or main residence throughout the period of ownership. Certain periods of absence are disregarded (see Taxation of Chargeable Gains Act 1992, s 223), in particular, the following cumulative periods:

(a) non-residence during the last 18 months of ownership;

(b) the first 12 months of ownership;

(c) any period of absence in employment overseas;

(d) up to four years' absence if a condition of employment; and

(e) any period up to three years in total throughout the period of ownership.

2.62 **Exclusive business use** Second, one should obtain the client's confirmation that no part of the PPD has been used *exclusively* for business purposes; otherwise a proportion of the exemption may be lost in respect of the business use area. The word 'exclusively' is emphasized because if the business room (or rooms) is shared with other members of the household, this should qualify as 'duality of user', enabling the full exemption to apply.

2.63 **Half-ai-hectare limit** The practitioner should establish how much land is being sold along with the PPD. If the grounds exceed half a hectare (5,000 square metres or 1.235 acres) there could be a tax liability on the excess unless the excess is proved to be necessary for the reasonable enjoyment of the house, for example if a large house with a large garden is being sold. Where ownership of the house is retained but land alone is sold, the land enjoys the benefit of the PPD exemption provided the land sold does not exceed half a hectare.

2.64 **Other matters** Check whether the client owns another house. Married couples are only entitled to one PPD exemption. If a married couple own more than one house then they should elect which house is to take the benefit of the exemption. This election is revocable if they wish to change their mind. Finally, check that the client's house was not originally purchased in the name of a company, otherwise the PPD exemption will not apply.

2.65 If there is *prima facie* a charge to tax, how is the chargeable gain calculated? This is done by deducting from the current sale price (or market value if the sale was not at arm's length or was a gift):

(a) the original purchase price, known as the acquisition cost (if the property was acquired before 31 March 1982 this will be the market value on that date);

(b) the incidental costs of acquisition and disposal, for example solicitors' fees, stamp duty, surveyor's fees, estate agents' commission, etc.; and

(c) any expenditure incurred to enhance the value of the property, for example building an extension.

2.66 **Losses and allowances** Even if the PPD does not apply, either in full or in part, any chargeable gain on the sale of the property could be reduced or possibly wiped out altogether if certain allowable deductions are available and taken into account (see the Taxation of Chargeable Gains Act 1992, ss 2(2) and 3(1)). For example, losses from previous assessment years can be carried forward and set off against gains. Also, each individual has an annual allowance for CGT, which is £11,300 for tax year 2017–2018. Chargeable gains are treated as the top slice of an individual's combined gains and income. Any part of a taxable gain on residential property which is not a main residence exceeding the upper limit of the income tax basic rate band (£33,500 for 2017–2018) is taxed at 28 per cent. Below that, the rate is 18 per cent.

2.67 **Advising buyers** Advice on CGT is of course primarily of importance to a client who is selling a property. However, a client who is intending to buy a property which will not be a PPD should be advised of any potential liability for CGT on a subsequent disposal.

ADVICE ON SURVEY

General considerations

2.68 A purchaser should always be advised to have a survey of the property carried out before exchange of contracts because of the *caveat emptor* principle ('Let the buyer beware').

It is for the buyer to discover any physical defects in the property and these may not be apparent from the client's own inspection. A client is sometimes reluctant to incur the additional expense of a survey fee so it is your job to reassure the client that this is money well spent. Failure on your part to give this advice could amount to negligence. For a case on the dangers of not having a survey, see *Hardy v Griffiths* [2014] EWHC 3947.

A physically defective property may of course be unsafe to occupy, but there are financial **2.69** implications for the purchaser as well. The market value of a property will be reduced if it is in poor condition and so the purchaser may be paying more than he should for it. It may also adversely affect the purchaser's ability to mortgage the property or sell it at a later date. These are all considerations which must be drawn to the client's attention.

Different types of survey

There are currently three types of survey widely available, each of which is considered in **2.70** the following paragraphs.

Basic valuation

This is the simplest and cheapest form of survey but it does no more than establish the **2.71** property's value on the open market. A prospective mortgagee will normally commission this type of survey in order to verify whether the property being charged is adequate security for the proposed loan. The mortgagee's surveyor owes a duty of care not only to the lender but also to the borrower, who relies on the report (see *Smith v Eric S Bush* [1990] 1 AC 831). A copy of the report should be made available to the borrower.

Unless the property has been built within the last ten years and has the benefit of National **2.72** House-Building Council (NHBC) guarantee (see 11.55), clients should be advised to seek a survey which is more detailed than the basic valuation. Even for new properties, a basic survey should be recommended.

Home buyer's valuation and survey report

This is more detailed than the basic valuation but not as comprehensive as the full struc- **2.73** tural survey (see 2.75). It is popular among house buyers who, reluctant to incur the costs of a full structural, seek a compromise which gives more information than a basic valu- ation. The small print should be read carefully though; the conditions will often reveal just how superficial the report can be. Invariably, the surveyor will not inspect unexposed or inaccessible areas, for instance, the roof space or below floorboards.

A buyer who opts for this type of survey should be advised to contact the buyer's mort- **2.74** gagee to request that the mortgagee's surveyor carries it out instead of—not in addition to—the basic valuation. This will generally be acceptable to the mortgagee and means that the client will avoid incurring two survey fees.

Full structural survey

A full survey ought in theory to reveal the true state and condition of the property, but this **2.75** is not always the case and the small print of the conditions of survey should be checked for exclusions. You would generally advise the client to have a full structural survey if the property is old (say, more than 80 years), or is of high value, or if the client has plans to alter the property structurally. The survey fee is obviously more (usually in excess of £750), but for this the client should at least get peace of mind (as long as the survey is favourable). If physical defects are revealed, then the client should be advised either to withdraw from the transaction, or to seek from the seller a reduction in the purchase price.

Special considerations

Neighbouring property

2.76   There will be occasions when a survey of neighbouring property will be necessary, for example on the purchase of a flat or property which is structurally attached to neighbouring property. In this case the surveyor should be instructed to inspect the main structure of the building and the adjoining property (if possible), as well as the subject property. The poor physical condition of the building of which a flat forms part will inevitably lead to increased levels of service charge payable by the occupiers of the flats (see Chapter 10 regarding service charges in leases).

Drainage

2.77   You should consider whether the subject property is served by mains drainage, maintainable at the public expense (this will be revealed by the water search, see 4.50). If not, and the drainage system is privately owned, it would be prudent to commission an expert's report on its condition, because your client buyer may incur future costs of maintenance.

Electric wiring

2.78   If the electric wiring in the property has not been checked for many years, then an inspection by an expert should be considered.

Commercial premises

2.79   The acquisition of commercial premises will usually necessitate a thorough inspection and survey, the extent of which will depend on the nature and location of the property and the terms of any relevant lease. This is considered again in Chapter 12. One particular area of concern today is the potential liability for expensive 'clean-up costs' under the Environmental Protection Act 1990, and the Environment Act 1995. The detail of these statutes is outside the scope of this book, but the point must be stressed that any purchaser (and mortgagee) of land for development should consider the desirability of an environmental survey to check for contamination by hazardous substances (e.g. industrial waste).

2.80   Under the Environment Act 1995, local authorities are required to identify contaminated land within their areas and to serve a remediation notice requiring clean-up works to be carried out where necessary. The 'appropriate person' upon whom the notice is served is the original polluter, but if that person cannot be found, then the appropriate person will be the 'owner or occupier' of the land.

2.81   For further information concerning the important topic of contaminated land, please refer to the companion volume to this book, Abbey and Richards, *A Practical Approach to Commercial Conveyancing and Property* (5th edn, OUP, 2016).

LAW SOCIETY CONVEYANCING PROTOCOL

General considerations

2.82   In 1990, the Law Society introduced the Conveyancing Protocol to help speed up the process of residential conveyancing. In the eyes of many of the public, those responsible for the delays in conveyancing were the conveyancers themselves. This of course was largely unfair because other factors played a major part, such as the excessive lengths of time many local authorities were taking to process local searches during the 'boom' years of the 1980s. However, there was clearly a case for some kind of standardization of procedures and documentation among conveyancers and, with this aim in mind, the Conveyancing Protocol was launched.

Practitioners acting for buyer and seller respectively should, at the start of a domestic **2.83** conveyancing transaction, decide between them whether they intend to use the Protocol. It should be noted that there is no obligation to use the Protocol, but use of it is considered preferred practice. In reality, the decision is usually taken by the seller's solicitor, and the buyer's solicitor normally goes along with it. The Protocol has been made compulsory for solicitors' practices that are part of the Conveyancing Quality Scheme. If one party will not adopt it, this does not prevent it being used by the other party. However, the obligation to act in the best interests of the client takes precedence over the Protocol.

Reference will be made to the Protocol throughout this book as the various stages in the **2.84** conveyancing process unfold—see the website address at Appendix 3. It is worth consulting at regular intervals during the transaction to refresh one's memory of what exactly is required under the Protocol.

Advising the client about the Protocol

You should explain the use and purpose of the Protocol to the client when taking instruc- **2.85** tions. Its use will generally be beneficial to the client but there is one area which may cause difficulty—the requirement to keep the other side informed of the client's situation in any related sale or purchase. This should be discussed with the client because it could be contrary to the client's best interests to disclose this information. For instance, if you tell the client's seller that your client has not found a buyer for his own property, the seller may decide to sell to someone else who is in a better position to proceed (e.g. buyer found or no property to sell). If the client declines to offer information about a related sale or purchase, the practitioner must of course respect this wish in accordance with the duty of confidentiality to the client.

Property Information Form

If your client is selling and you have decided to use the Protocol, you can save time by ask- **2.86** ing the client to complete the Property Information Form during the first interview. This Form raises standard questions about the property, such as whether the owner is aware of any boundary disputes, or whether the owner has received any notices concerning the property from the local authority. The Property Information Form is discussed in more detail in Chapter 4.

Commercial transactions

The full terms of the Protocol are generally not appropriate in the context of commer- **2.87** cial conveyancing for the simple reason that the standard forms adopted by the Protocol contemplate the sale of a dwelling. Nevertheless, the spirit behind the Protocol is usually adopted in that the seller will provide the buyer with a pre-contract package which will include a draft contract, replies to pre-contract enquiries, and evidence of title (see Chapter 12 regarding commercial conveyancing).

A commercial developer selling new houses on an estate should also provide a comprehen- **2.88** sive pre-contract package to the individual purchaser's solicitors. Although the properties are dwellings, the full terms of the Protocol are generally inappropriate because the properties very often have not been physically completed before contracts are exchanged (see Chapter 11 regarding new properties).

PROFESSIONAL CONDUCT

SRA Code of Conduct 2011

2.89   The Code came into force on 6 October 2011 and can be found at **http://www.sra.org.uk**. The Code is intended to make it clear to consumers what outcomes they should expect from their legal service providers. The term 'legal service provider' is used because the Legal Services Act 2007 sees the emergence of Alternative Business Structures in which the market for legal services is opened up to anyone deemed 'fit or proper'. This could be a bank, insurance company, or supermarket; hence the widely heard term 'Tesco Law'. As the Code is concerned with outcomes-focused requirements, practitioners need to consider how best to achieve the right outcomes for their clients, taking into account the way that the firm works and its client base. The Code forms part of the SRA Handbook in which ten mandatory principles are all-pervasive, applying to all aspects of legal practice. In addition, there are mandatory Outcomes and non-mandatory Indicative Behaviours. These are now considered.

Principles

2.90   The ten mandatory Principles define the fundamental ethical and professional standards expected of all firms and individuals providing legal services. They are to:

1. uphold the rule of law and the proper administration of justice;
2. act with integrity;
3. not allow your independence to be compromised;
4. act in the best interests of each client;
5. provide a proper standard of service to your clients;
6. behave in a way that maintains the trust the public places in you and in the provision of legal services;
7. comply with your legal and regulatory obligations and deal with your regulators and ombudsmen in an open, timely, and cooperative manner;
8. run your business or carry out your role in the business effectively and in accordance with proper governance and sound financial and risk management principles;
9. run your business or carry out your role in the business in a way that encourages equality of opportunity and respect for diversity;
10. protect client money and assets.

Outcomes

2.91   In addition to the Principles, there are mandatory Outcomes which describe what the practitioner is expected to achieve in order to comply with the Principles in specific contexts. If necessary, a practitioner may need to prove to the SRA how he has achieved the relevant Outcomes.

Indicative Behaviours

2.92   To support the mandatory Outcomes there are non-mandatory Indicative Behaviours (IBs). These provide examples of the kinds of behaviour which may establish whether the practitioner has achieved the relevant Outcomes and complied with the Principles. They are not exhaustive so there may be other and more appropriate ways of achieving the Outcomes, depending on the type of firm and the needs of the clients.

A failure to achieve the Outcomes in the Code or a breach of the Principles is a serious matter and may lead to disciplinary proceedings brought by the SRA.

Many conduct issues will arise during the course of a conveyancing transaction. On **2.93** exchange of contracts and completion, professional undertakings will be given; there are rules governing practitioners' handling of clients' money; there are special provisions regarding contract races, which will be discussed later in the book (see 3.153). In this chapter we will consider client confidentiality, money laundering, acting for more than one party, and guidance on the use of e-mail.

Client confidentiality and money laundering

Confidentiality

Chapter 4 of the Code deals with confidentiality and disclosure. Outcome 4.1 provides **2.94** that a practitioner must keep the affairs of clients confidential except where disclosure is required or permitted by law or the client consents. Outcome 4.3 provides that where your duty of confidentiality to one client comes into conflict with your duty of disclosure to another client, your duty of confidentiality takes precedence. Thus client affairs are confidential and must never be disclosed to a third party without the client's consent, even where the practitioner is no longer acting for the client. Suppose you act for borrower and lender and your borrower client tells you that he or she intends to run a business from the premises, in breach of a mortgage condition. You cannot continue to act because there is a conflict of interest, but neither can you tell the lender the reasons why you can no longer act—this would be a breach of confidentiality to the borrower.

Money laundering

One exception to the confidentiality rule which is of importance in the context of convey- **2.95** ancing concerns money laundering. The National Crime Agency (NCA) has highlighted the prevalence of property transactions as a means of laundering criminal funds, and the high risk of exposure of professionals offering conveyancing services to the public. The Criminal Justice Act 1993, and the Proceeds of Crime Act 2002, introduced criminal offences for *failing to disclose* to the authorities (i.e. to the NCA), knowledge or suspicion of others who are involved in laundering the proceeds of a crime, drug trafficking, or terrorism. Thus, if you have such knowledge or suspicion, you must report it to your firm's Nominated Officer (see 2.99) as soon as practically possible prior to the transaction taking place (subject to any legal professional privilege, see 2.98). For a case where a firm of solicitors failed to perform its anti-money-laundering obligations, see *Purrunsing v A'Court & Co (a firm) & Anor* [2016] EWHC 789 (Ch).

The Law Society has issued an anti-money-laundering practice note (obtainable from the **2.96** Law Society's website, **https://www.lawsociety.org.uk/support-services/advice/practice-notes/aml/**) alerting solicitors to likely circumstances which could amount to assisting in money laundering. These include:

(a) clients who ask you to hold large sums of cash and who then ask for a cheque or bank transfer from your firm;
(b) secretive clients who will not disclose their identity;
(c) unusual instructions, for example clients instructing you from the other end of the country when they could be using a local firm; and
(d) unusual settlement requests, for example paying for a property with large sums of cash.

'Tipping off'

It is an offence to 'tip off' the client that you have made a disclosure to the authorities, or **2.97** that the authorities are investigating a possible laundering offence. This rule is also contrary to the normal solicitor–client relationship of confidentiality. The duty of disclosure extends to any party (not just your client) suspected of being involved, so this covers the other side's client as much as suspicion about your own client.

Legal professional privilege

2.98 The case of *Bowman v Fells* [2005] EWCA Civ 226 has altered how conveyancers should approach reporting issues and careful attention should be paid to the Law Society guidance on its website about the implications of this decision. Essentially, if a conveyancer forms knowledge or suspicion of money laundering, he or she should first consider whether the information on which that knowledge or suspicion is based was received in legally privileged circumstances. If it was, he or she cannot make a report to the NCA without the client's authority. In these circumstances conveyancers should consider whether they would prefer not to act for the client. Advice on a case-by-case basis can be obtained from the Law Society's Professional Ethics helpline (0370 606 2577), and in 2017 the Law Society issued a useful practice note on Legal Professional Privilege at **http://www.lawsociety.org. uk/support-services/advice/practice-notes/legal-professional-privilege/**.

The Money Laundering, Terrorist Financing and Transfer of Funds (Information on the Payer) Regulations 2017

2.99 The Money Laundering, Terrorist Financing and Transfer of Funds (Information on the Payer) Regulations 2017 apply (*inter alia*) to all legal professionals acting in any real property transaction and extend to the proceeds of any criminal activity. There is a useful Treasury-approved Law Society guidance document (please refer to the anti-money-laundering practice note web address at 2.96). The matters outlined in the following paragraphs should be noted in particular:

(a) All staff who handle investment business must be trained to recognize and deal with suspicious transactions (e.g. a large cash sum received from a client for a deposit on a purchase should be treated as suspicious).

(b) Each firm must appoint a reporting officer and establish internal reporting procedures.

(c) There must be procedures for obtaining satisfactory evidence of the client's identity where necessary.

(d) A record of each transaction must be maintained for at least five years.

(e) Evidence of clients' identity obtained must be kept for at least five years after the relationship with the client has ended.

Acting for buyer and seller

2.100 The Outcomes in Chapter 3 of the Code require practitioners to have effective systems and controls in place to help identify and assess conflicts of interest. Accordingly, it is for the practitioner to decide whether acting for both buyer and seller in a particular conveyancing transaction would amount to a client conflict. Outcome 3.3 requires a practitioner to consider factors such as whether:

• the clients' interests are different;
• your ability to give independent advice to the clients may be fettered;
• there is a need to negotiate between the clients;
• there is an imbalance in bargaining power between the clients; and
• any client is vulnerable.

2.101 Clearly, acting for buyer and seller in the same matter carries a high risk of conflicts of interest and the SRA has indicated that it would not expect solicitors to act routinely for buyer and seller. This is supported by Indicative Behaviour (IB) 3.14, which states that acting for a buyer (including a lessee) and seller (including a lessor) in a transaction relating to the transfer of land for value may tend to show that a solicitor has not achieved the Outcomes in Chapter 3 and therefore not complied with the Principles.

Outcome 3.6 states that you can act for more than one party even if there is a client conflict **2.102** where the clients have a substantially common interest in relation to a matter or a particular aspect of it. However, IB 3.11 provides that acting for two or more clients under Outcome 3.6 where a seller is transferring property to a buyer may tend to show that you have not achieved the Outcomes in Chapter 3 and have therefore not complied with the Principles.

In the light of this, best practice is to decline to act for buyer and seller in the same transac- **2.103** tion where the land is being transferred for value. However, it may be possible to act for both parties where the land is being gifted, or being transferred between parties who are related by blood, adoption, marriage, civil partnership, or living together. Similarly, in a commercial context, it may be possible to act where the parties are associated companies (e.g. subsidiaries of the same holding company). However, if a conflict were to arise during the course of the transaction, you would have to cease acting for at least one of the clients and could only continue to act for the other client if the duty of confidentiality to the former client were not put at risk.

Any decision to act for both buyer and seller should be of benefit to both clients, rather **2.104** than in the practitioner's own commercial interests. This accords with Principle 2, which requires the practitioner to act with integrity. You should also bear in mind Principle 3 (not allowing your independence to be compromised) and Principle 5 (providing a proper standard of service to your clients).

Confidentiality may also become an issue in relation to acting for both parties. For example, **2.105** a seller may want certain information kept confidential, but this information may be material to the buyer. As the duty of confidentiality takes precedence over the duty of disclosure (Outcome 4.3), you would have to consider ceasing to act for the buyer.

Acting for joint buyers or joint sellers

You can act for joint buyers or joint sellers provided no conflict of interest exists or is likely **2.106** to arise between them. In most cases, the interests of the joint buyers or sellers are the same, so there is rarely a problem. You should obtain instructions (or verification of instructions) directly from each client, not simply rely on the word of the other(s). This allows you to clarify the client's exact requirements and to ensure that the instructions are not tainted by undue influence or duress.

Acting for lender and borrower

A practitioner must not act for both lender and borrower in a conveyancing transaction **2.107** if there is a client conflict or a significant risk of a client conflict. However, Outcome 3.6 contains an exception where a practitioner may act for two clients even where there is a client conflict provided the clients have a substantially common interest. The Code defines 'substantially common interest' as 'a situation where there is a clear common purpose in relation to a matter or a particular aspect of it between the clients and a strong consensus on how it is to be achieved and the client conflict is peripheral to this common purpose'.

In the case of lender and borrower, the substantially common interest is that both parties **2.108** will want to ensure that the subject property has a good and marketable title free from matters that would adversely affect the property's value. IB 3.7 provides that acting for lender and borrower in relation to a mortgage may tend to show that you have achieved the Chapter 3 outcomes provided:

- the mortgage is a standard mortgage (see below) of property to be used as the borrower's private residence;
- you are satisfied that it is reasonable and in the client's best interests for you to act; and
- the certificate of title required by the lender is in the form approved by the Law Society and the Council of Mortgage Lenders.

A standard mortgage is defined in IB 3.7 as a mortgage provided in the normal course of the lender's activities, where a significant part of the lender's activities consists of lending and the mortgage is on standard terms. In other words, the material terms of the mortgage documentation are not negotiated between the lender's and borrower's solicitors—they are standard terms.

2.109   It follows that a practitioner will normally be able to act for both lender and borrower in a straightforward mortgage of residential property where the lender is an institutional bank or building society lending on standard terms. However, if the mortgage is not on standard terms (e.g. in a commercial transaction), the lender and borrower will most likely need to be separately represented.

2.110   Where you are acting for both lender and borrower and a conflict occurs during the transaction, you must cease acting for both parties unless you can, with the consent of one party, continue to act for the other. The same would apply if, acting under Outcome 3.6, the client conflict ceases to be peripheral to the common purpose. Examples of a conflict occurring would be where the borrower misrepresents to the lender that the purchase price is in fact higher than the price agreed with the seller, or where the terms of the mortgage offer are clearly unfair to the borrower, or where the solicitor becomes involved in negotiations regarding the loan agreement.

2.111   Care must be exercised to ensure that no conflict of interest exists or arises between borrower and lender. In most cases, however, the interests of lender and borrower will coincide, namely, to acquire a good and marketable title to the property (see *Mortgage Express Ltd v Bowerman and Partners* [1996] 2 All ER 836, CA). This important area is considered further at 7.100.

2.112   If the practitioner or a member of the practitioner's immediate family is the borrower, the practitioner should notify the lender in writing of this fact. A similar notification would apply if a practitioner accepts instructions to act for the seller, buyer, and lender. The lender may in these circumstances decide to instruct another firm.

2.113   Reference should also be made to the *UK Finance Mortgage Lenders' Handbook*, which sets out standardized instructions to conveyancers from lenders and forms the contract between conveyancer and lender where the lender has agreed to adopt the *Handbook* (see 7.95 and Appendix 12). Most of the well-known institutional lenders adopt the *Handbook*.

Use of e-mail

2.114   Without proper management and guidance the use of e-mail can cause loss for which solicitors may be held liable. There are also professional conduct implications. Solicitors are therefore encouraged to formulate a best-practice policy for staff when communicating by e-mail.

2.115   The following matters should be considered:

- E-mails should include the firm's name and address and a statement about where the names of the partners can be found.

- For ease of use, adopt a standard template for e-mails incorporating the above information (an alternative template should be used for private e-mails, if permitted).
- Because of the risk that an e-mail may be sent to the wrong person, consider an automated confidentiality warning, for example 'Information in this message is confidential and may be legally privileged. It is intended solely for the person to whom it is addressed. If you are not the intended recipient, please notify the sender, and please delete the message from your system immediately.'
- Incoming e-mails should receive a timely and appropriate response. This may include automated out-of-office responses when staff are away from the office for a day or more.
- A secretary and colleague should have access to an absent person's e-mail to check incoming messages and to deal promptly with urgent enquiries.
- Unless they have no legal significance, e-mails should be printed off and kept on file.
- If a professional undertaking is received by e-mail, check that the context in which it was given provides reasonable assurance of its authenticity. Alternatively, check by telephone/fax that it came from the purported sender.
- Make staff aware that 'deleted' e-mails are capable of being retrieved and can be subject to disclosure in the event of a dispute.
- Make staff aware that the Internet is an insecure medium and vulnerable to hackers and viruses. In particular, staff should be aware that e-mail attachments may contain viruses. Up-to-date virus-scanning software is essential.
- Before downloading a file sent by e-mail, ensure that there will be no breach of copyright.
- The professional conduct principle to 'know your client' applies equally to receiving instructions via e-mail. Make the same checks and enquiries as you would for any other prospective client.
- Do not include confidential information in non-encrypted e-mails without the informed consent of the client, who should be advised of the risks. Unless the e-mail is encrypted, i.e. has a code, there is a risk that it could be accessed by third parties (see 2.116 below).
- Firms should consider monitoring private e-mails sent between staff in order to maintain professional standards. Because of privacy issues, staff should be asked to give their prior consent to such monitoring.

Conveyancing and cyber-crime

Conveyancing firms must be alert to the risk of cyber-crime, in particular fraudsters hacking into their e-mail accounts and intercepting e-mails between practitioners and clients, or between practitioners and their counterparts in conveyancing transactions. There have been cases where sellers have e-mailed their solicitor to ask for the sale proceeds to be transmitted to a named account, but in fact the client's e-mail account had been hacked by fraudsters and the sale monies ended up going into the fraudsters' account. This has happened in reverse too—clients being duped into sending money to fraudsters who had hacked into the solicitor's e-mail account. **2.116**

Always advise your clients of the potential risk of e-mail fraud and the importance of their e-mail accounts being made secure (e.g. regular password changes). Any confidential information, such as bank details, should not be sent by e-mail unless the e-mail is encrypted, or alternatively a password-protected portal is used. Bank account details should also be confirmed in person or by telephone (including a security question). Be especially cautious if, partway through a transaction, you are asked to send money to a different bank account.

ACTING FOR EITHER SELLER OR BUYER

2.117 Has your firm acted for the client before (relevant to client-care advice)?

- Confirm the client's full names, address, and contact telephone numbers.
- Is it necessary to check the client's identity (relevant to money laundering and mortgage fraud)?
- Confirm the address of the property and tenure.
- Confirm details of any estate agents involved. Obtain a copy of the agents' particulars. Has any preliminary deposit been paid to agents?
- Confirm details of the solicitors acting for the other side.
- Is the price agreed?
- Are other terms agreed, for example sale of chattels, likely completion date?
- Which fixtures will remain or be removed?
- Does the client have a related sale or purchase which has to be synchronized with this transaction?
- Who occupies the property (relevant to third-party rights and vacant possession)?
- Is the property near a river or railway, or in an unusual location (relevant to searches and enquiries)?
- Advise on costs and prepare a brief financial statement. Remind the client about other expenses, for example removal fees.
- How much deposit will be paid or received on exchange?
- Is there anything additional you need to know from the client, or upon which the client requires your advice, which may be relevant to this particular transaction?
- Always be on your guard for possible money laundering. Comply with the Money Laundering Regulations 2017.
- Beware of possible cyber-crime, especially through e-mail hackers.

ACTING FOR SELLER—ADDITIONAL CONSIDERATIONS

2.118 Did you act for the client when the property was bought? If so, it may be helpful to get the old file from store.

- Where are the title deeds? If the property is mortgaged, obtain the full name and address of the first mortgagee plus mortgage account number, so you can write to the mortgagee requesting deeds on loan.
- Are there any second or subsequent mortgages? Obtain details of all outstanding mortgages on the property, including names and addresses of lenders and amounts outstanding.
- What are the client's instructions regarding sale proceeds?
- If the Protocol is being used, the client should complete Property Information Form.
- Advise the client not to stop mortgage repayments, or cancel buildings insurance until completion.
- Will CGT be payable on sale proceeds? Confirm whether principal private dwelling-house exemption applies.

ACTING FOR BUYER—ADDITIONAL CONSIDERATIONS

Confirm proposed use of the property (relevant to planning and any restrictions in the title). **2.119**

- How will the purchase price be financed? If the client requires a mortgage, consider mortgage advice.
- How will the deposit payable on exchange be financed?
- Advise on a survey.
- If there is more than one buyer, advise on co-ownership.
- If the client is presently in rented accommodation, advise on giving the landlord notice to end tenancy.
- Advise the client whether SDLT is payable. Can you apportion the price between land and chattels to reduce or eradicate SDLT?

ACTING FOR BUYER AND LENDER

Only act for buyer and lender when the mortgage is by an institutional lender on standard **2.120** terms.

- When acting for a buyer and an institutional lender, have regard to IB 3.7 of the SRA Code of Conduct.
- A set of standard mortgage instructions is contained in the *UK Finance Mortgage Lenders' Handbook* (see 7.95 and Appendix 12).
- Do not act for a buyer and a lender in any circumstances where there is a conflict of interest.

3

THE DRAFT CONTRACT

A PREPARATORY STEPS BY SELLER'S PRACTITIONER

EVIDENCE OF SELLER'S TITLE

3.01 The contract for the sale of the property is drafted by the seller's practitioner and forwarded to the buyer's practitioner in duplicate. The seller's practitioner should keep a copy of the draft contract on file so that any amendments proposed by the buyer's practitioner can if necessary be dealt with over the telephone. Before drafting the contract, you will need to consider the client's existing title to the property.

Registered land

3.02 In registered land, you will examine your client's title by applying for and inspecting official copies of the registered title from Land Registry. But before you can apply for official copies you will preferably need to know the property's title number. If your firm acted on the client's purchase of the property, the old purchase file will probably still be in storage. If so, you can retrieve the old file from store to find out the title number. The old file may also contain other useful pieces of information, such as replies to previous pre-contract enquiries and search results. If the title number is unknown you can apply using the full postal address for the property. In registered land before 13 October 2003, the 'title deeds' constituted a charge certificate if the property was mortgaged, or a land certificate if the property was unmortgaged. Since 13 October 2003, Land Registry no longer issues a land or charge certificate, merely a Title Information Document. However, many land and charge certificates are still in existence and are held as part of 'the deeds'. If the property is leasehold, the original lease will also be with the deeds. There may be other important documents with the deeds as well, such as planning consents and woodworm or damp guarantees. Accordingly, even for registered land, you should as a matter of good practice obtain the deeds, as well as apply for official copies.

Unregistered land

In unregistered land, you consider the title by obtaining and inspecting the title deeds, i.e. the conveyances and other documents of title (e.g. an assent) dealing with earlier dispositions of the legal estate.

3.03

Obtaining the deeds

The title deeds of a mortgaged property will be held by the mortgagee as security for its loan. If there is more than one mortgage, the deeds will be held by the first mortgagee (although in registered land, if the charge certificate still exists, each mortgagee has its own charge certificate). If the property is not mortgaged, the client will either hold the deeds personally, or will have deposited them in safe keeping, perhaps with a bank or solicitor (they may be in your own firm's strongroom). While taking instructions you will have ascertained from the seller the whereabouts of the deeds.

3.04

Seller's solicitor acting for mortgagee

The most likely scenario is that the property is mortgaged to a well-known bank, building society, or other institutional lender. In this case, the lender will usually instruct the seller's solicitor to act for it on the redemption of the mortgage. You should therefore write to the mortgagee quoting the account number of the mortgage (having obtained this from the client) and request the deeds to be forwarded to your firm on loan for the purposes of the intended sale and redemption. The lender will expect from you an undertaking to hold the deeds on the usual terms, namely, to be held to order pending redemption of the mortgage. Effectively the lender is seeking assurance that the practitioner will either return the deeds on demand, or redeem the mortgage. You should always ensure that the terms of your undertaking are absolutely within your control. Do not give an unqualified undertaking that the mortgage will be repaid, as this is something you cannot guarantee.

3.05

Mortgagee separately represented

If, less commonly, the seller's mortgagee instructs its own solicitors to act on the mortgage redemption, you will need to write to them, having obtained their name and address from the mortgagee. Mortgagees' solicitors are often reluctant to part with the original deeds, so the most you are likely to get from them are photocopies. Before doing anything, however, the mortgagee's solicitors will invariably insist on an undertaking from your firm to be responsible for its costs in relation to the mortgage redemption whether or not the redemption actually proceeds. You should try to agree a reasonable upper limit on these costs (ideally no more than £200 + VAT) and consider whether you should ask your client to put you in funds for the appropriate amount.

3.06

Requesting outstanding balance

When requesting the title deeds—either from the mortgagee directly or from its solicitors—it is prudent to request confirmation of the current outstanding balance of the mortgage

3.07

debt. The client may have given you instructions on the point, but you should always obtain verification from the lender, because you must be sure that there will be sufficient proceeds from the sale of the property to redeem the mortgage.

Applying for official copies of the title

3.08 The seller should, at its own expense, supply to the buyer official copies of title (note where the Protocol and/or the Standard Conditions of Sale are being used, official copies are compulsory). The official copies should be as up to date as possible.

3.09 The application for official copies is made on Land Registry Form OC1 to the Land Registry office for the area in which the property is located, and as soon as you (the seller's practitioner) know the title number of the property or the full postal address, you can make the application. Copies of documents referred to on the title and held by Land Registry can be obtained by an application on Form OC2. A small fee is payable for both Forms OC1 and OC2. Practitioners can apply online via the Land Registry website and print off the official copies on their own water-marked paper. This is becoming increasingly popular.

3.10 Initially you may not know the title number because your client cannot recall it, or there may be delay in receiving the deeds. One course of action is to apply for an index map search at Land Registry (see 4.26) and attach to it your application for official copies. Unless the property is easily identifiable from its postal address, the Registry will usually insist on a plan. It will then process both applications together and, assuming the land is registered, send you the relevant official copies.

3.11 Official copies show a time of issue as well as a date, for example 1 June 2018, 12:34:56. The need for a time of issue arises as a result of Land Registry searches and applications acquiring priority on a 'real-time' basis. Thus it is possible for different versions of the register to exist on the same day.

INVESTIGATING THE SELLER'S TITLE

3.12 Once you have obtained the title deeds and if the title is registered official copies from Land Registry, you should check the title carefully before drafting the contract. This is to ensure primarily that the seller's duty of disclosure is satisfied because you have to disclose any incumbrances in the contract (see 3.28). In addition, you must also check that the seller actually owns the legal estate and/or is otherwise entitled to sell it. Lastly, an investigation at this stage will enable you to identify any defects in the title and to anticipate (and, it is hoped, remedy) the questions (or requisitions) which the buyer's practitioner is likely to raise. If there is an error in the title, for example a name change has not been recorded on the register, then the Protocol requires that the seller's solicitor should rectify this rather than wait for the buyer's solicitor to raise it.

3.13 How do you investigate title? You are referred to Chapter 5, where title investigation is examined in depth, but essentially the answer may be summarized as set out in the following paragraphs.

Unregistered land

(a) Decide which document will be your root of title and check that it satisfies the criteria for a 'good' root (see 5.07 for an explanation of what constitutes a good root of title).

(b) Check whether any incumbrances (including those created pre-root) bind the property. These have to be disclosed to the buyer in the contract.

(c) Follow the chain of transactions from the root document down to the present day, ensuring there is no break in the chain of ownership. If there has been a death or change of name, obtain documentary evidence of it.

(d) Examine each document in the chain to ensure there are no specific defects (e.g. incorrect stamping or execution).

(e) Check that the title should not already have been registered. Verify when the compulsory registration order for the locality came into force and confirm that no dealings have taken place since which would have induced first registration.

(f) If the title is leasehold, is the freehold title registered? If not, is an examined copy of the freehold title available? Check the lease to see whether the lessor's consent is required to the proposed sale.

(g) Conduct a land charges search against the seller's name to check for any incumbrances (e.g. restrictive covenants) which may not be revealed by the title deeds.

Following investigation of an unregistered title, the seller's practitioner should prepare an epitome of title (see 5.13) in readiness to send to the buyer's conveyancer with the draft contract.

Registered land

(a) Read carefully the official copies you have received from Land Registry. Check for any **3.14** adverse entries (e.g. cautions (entered before 13 October 2003), notices, or restrictions) which may restrict the seller's right or ability to sell.

(b) Identify from the official copies any incumbrances on the title which have to be disclosed in the contract. These will be itemized in the property and charges registers (note: mortgages which are to be paid off on completion are not incumbrances for this purpose).

(c) Since 1 January 1993, Land Registry has on first registration noted positive as well as restrictive covenants. Accordingly, if the current seller was registered as first proprietor before this date, you should check the deed inducing first registration for any positive (including indemnity) covenants. If these are present, your client seller will now require an indemnity covenant from the buyer. For a full discussion of indemnity covenants see 3.99. (Before 1 January 1993, positive covenants, including indemnity covenants, were generally omitted on first registration unless intermixed with restrictive covenants. Although there is no statutory authority for noting positive covenants, Land Registry's policy change was a helpful initiative for practitioners.)

(d) Since 1 April 2000, the price paid or the value stated on a disposition has been entered on the register. Thus the price paid for the property when the seller bought it may be revealed. However, no entry will be made if it would be misleading, for example if the price paid was only for a part-share of the property's value.

Defects in title

Wherever possible, defects in title should be remedied immediately. For example, in **3.15** unregistered land:

(a) if a previous conveyance has been incorrectly executed, then a reconveyance should be prepared and executed by the appropriate parties;

(b) if a previous conveyance has included or omitted something in error, then a confirmatory conveyance should be made; or

(c) if a previous conveyance has not been stamped, then the duty must be paid (together with the penalty) and a correct stamp obtained.

Indemnity insurance

3.16 If a defect is not capable of remedy, then consideration should be given to obtaining defective title indemnity insurance, normally on payment of a single premium. If the defect constitutes a breach of covenant which cannot or will not be waived by the person with the benefit of the covenant, then restrictive covenant indemnity insurance should also be considered. However, where the defect or breach is recent (i.e. within the last 15 years), such insurance can be very difficult to obtain, or the premiums prohibitively expensive.

Financial Services and Markets Act 2000 (FSMA)

3.17 Solicitors who advise clients about obtaining defective title insurance could become involved in activity regulated by the FSMA. Solicitors may advise upon, and arrange indemnity policies, where the activity is incidental to the conveyancing transaction, but they must comply with the Solicitors' Financial Services (Scope) Rules 2001. These Rules require solicitors who wish to undertake insurance mediation services to appoint a compliance officer and be registered in the register maintained by the Financial Conduct Authority (FCA). The Law Society has negotiated a policy through Countrywide Legal Indemnities but it would be sensible for solicitors to obtain quotations from more than one company. The policy will be a single-premium policy the benefit of which will attach to the land.

Land Registry help

3.18 One helpful area of Land Registry practice can be mentioned here. The Land Registry employs solicitors to deal with difficult legal issues arising from title defects, and it is perfectly acceptable to ask for the Land Registry's view on a particular problem before exchanging contracts. However, bear in mind that it will only offer factual information and impartial advice about its procedures, not advice on the law. There is no fee payable for this service but the Registry requests that your enquiries be as precise as possible and relate only to real cases, not hypothetical circumstances.

CHECKING FOR ANY OTHER OCCUPIERS

3.19 To fulfil a contractual obligation to give vacant possession on completion, the seller must be satisfied before contracts are exchanged that all occupiers will vacate the property on or before the contractual completion date. This is a matter that the seller's practitioner will have raised when taking instructions: who, apart from the seller, occupies the property?

Non-owning spouse or civil partner

3.20 A spouse or civil partner who does not own the legal estate is given a statutory right of occupation under the Family Law Act 1996, amended by the Civil Partnership Act 2004. This applies irrespective of whether the spouse or civil partner has acquired an equitable interest in the property, for instance, through a contribution to the purchase price.

3.21 The statutory right is only binding on a purchaser for value of the legal estate if it is registered, either as a class F land charge in respect of unregistered land or as a Home Rights notice in respect of registered land. Thus in a situation where the practitioner is acting for a sole seller who is married or in a civil partnership, the onus is on the seller's practitioner to check that no such registration has occurred. The importance of this is reinforced by Schedule 4, para 4 to the Family Law Act, which implies a condition in the sale contract that any registered Home Rights will be removed before completion. Accordingly, the practitioner should, with unregistered land, carry out a land charges search against the name of the legal owner or, with registered land, examine the up-to-date official copies.

Releasing rights

Even if the non-owning spouse or civil partner has taken no steps to protect Home Rights, **3.22** there is no guarantee that he or she will not do so before completion. The prudent course therefore is always to obtain a written release from the non-owning spouse or civil partner of all rights in the property together with an agreement to vacate. Otherwise, the seller risks being in breach of contract. A professional conduct point also arises here. The spouse or civil partner must be informed that his or her rights may be affected by giving such consent, and that he or she should obtain independent advice from another practitioner before signing the release.

Where the Law Society's Standard Form of Contract is being used, the pre-printed special **3.23** condition 7 reads as follows:

> Each occupier identified below agrees with the seller and the buyer, in consideration of their entering into this contract, that the occupier concurs in the sale of the property on the terms of this contract, undertakes to vacate the property on or before the completion date and releases the property and any included fixtures and contents from any right or interest that the occupier may have.
>
> **Note:** this condition does not apply to occupiers under leases or tenancies subject to which the property is sold.
>
> Name(s) and signature(s) of the occupier(s) (if any):
>
> Name
>
> Signature

Equitable interests and overriding interests

In addition to statutory rights of occupation, a non-owning spouse or civil partner may **3.24** have acquired an equitable interest arising under a resulting or constructive trust, for example the spouse or civil partner may have contributed to the purchase price when the seller originally bought the property. Even a person not married or civil partner to the seller, such as a cohabitee or house sharer, may have acquired an equitable interest through a financial contribution. If the land is registered, a person with an equitable interest who is in actual occupation may have an overriding interest by virtue of Schedule 3, para 2 to the Land Registration Act 2002.

Releasing rights

There is the technical possibility that the occupier's equitable interest may be overreached **3.25** if the purchase price is paid to at least two trustees of the legal estate. This will also help to nullify any overriding interest (see *City of London Building Society v Flegg* [1988] AC 54). Consideration could be given to the appointment of a second trustee to effect an overreaching, but the practical difficulty remains that the seller has to ensure that vacant possession is given on completion. The wisest course for the seller's conveyancer is therefore always to check the status of each occupier and to obtain a written release from adult occupiers of any rights, together with an agreement to vacate on or before completion. As in 3.22, the occupier should be advised to seek independent advice before signing the release. Since the enactment of the Family Law Act 1996, it is possible for a non-owning 'cohabitant' to obtain an occupation order of the property (s 33). This is a matter which should also be checked.

Tenants

If the property to be sold is subject to and has the benefit of existing leases or tenancy **3.26** agreements, details of these will have to be disclosed in the contract. This aspect is discussed more fully in Chapter 12. If there are tenants but the property is to be sold with vacant possession, then the seller must take steps to terminate the tenancies. To fulfil a contractual obligation to give vacant possession, the seller must be sure that the tenants will physically leave. It follows that early consideration should be given to whether any of the tenants have security of tenure and thus a legal right to remain in possession.

SELLER'S DUTY OF DISCLOSURE

Open contract rules

3.27 The open contract rules are the rules of property law which have been created over time by common law or statute. The rules will apply where the provisions of the contract for sale make no reference to a particular matter, for example if the date for completion is not inserted in the contract, the open contract rule is that completion shall take place within a reasonable period.

Disclosure rule

3.28 Under an open contract the seller is obliged to disclose in the contract all latent incumbrances and defects in title (see *Faruqi v English Real Estates Ltd* [1979] 1 WLR 963). This duty does not extend to physical defects in the property, to which *caveat emptor* (let the buyer beware) applies. However, wilful concealment of a physical defect may give rise to a claim in the tort of deceit (see *Gordon v Selico Co. Ltd* [1986] 1 EGLR 71, which concerned the covering up of dry rot). A breach of the seller's duty of disclosure will normally permit the buyer to rescind the contract and claim damages. This is discussed more fully in Chapter 9.

Latent incumbrance

3.29 A latent incumbrance is one which is not apparent from an inspection of the property (a restrictive covenant is an example of a latent incumbrance). However, there is some doubt about the precise meaning of 'latent'. In *Yandle and Sons v Sutton* [1922] 2 Ch 199, a right of way across land was held to be a latent incumbrance which the seller should have disclosed. The prudent practitioner will therefore ensure that all non-physical defects and incumbrances which are known to the seller are disclosed in the contract. This includes matters apparent from an inspection of the title deeds, thus underlining the importance of a full title investigation by the seller's practitioner (see 3.12).

Disclosure of occupiers

3.30 Is the seller required to disclose another person's occupation of the property? It could be argued that the buyer has a duty to make separate enquiries and should find out for himself (see the rule in *Hunt v Luck* [1902] 1 Ch 428 in unregistered land and Schedule 3, para 2 to the Land Registration Act 2002, in registered land). The difficulty with this argument is that the buyer's duty of inspection really has to do with a different question, namely is the buyer bound by the third-party occupier's interest? A potential cause of action by the buyer against the seller for non-disclosure is a separate matter altogether (see *Caballero v Henty* (1874) LR 9 Ch App 447, supported in *Rignall Developments Ltd v Halil* [1988] Ch 190). As before, the safest practical solution is for the seller to avoid the argument and make a full disclosure.

Impact of Standard Conditions on seller's duty of disclosure

Standard Conditions of Sale

3.31 The Standard Conditions (SCs) are set out in Appendix 4. SC 3.1 dilutes the seller's common law duty of disclosure, as the seller is not obliged to disclose the incumbrances listed in SC 3.1.2 (which include incumbrances discoverable by inspection and 'entries made before the date of the contract in any public register except those maintained by Land Registry or its Land Charges Department or by Companies House'). However, care must be exercised because some of the wording is vague and could be widely interpreted. For instance, incumbrances the seller 'could not reasonably know about' imports constructive knowledge (i.e. *should* the seller have known about them?). The safest practice, even when the SCs are being used, is to disclose all known defects and incumbrances and to include a condition in the contract preventing the buyer from raising any requisition or objection to them. Indeed, SC 4.2.1 provides that the buyer may not raise requisitions on the title shown by the seller taking the steps described in SC 4.1.1. SC 4.1.1 provides that without cost to the buyer, the seller is to provide the buyer with proof of the title to the property and of his ability to transfer it, or to procure its transfer. So, clearly, if the buyer has any concerns about the title, he should raise these with the seller before exchange of contracts. SC 3.1.2(a) provides that the property is sold subject to those incumbrances specified in the contract. The front page of the Law Society Standard Form of Contract includes space for specifying these incumbrances (see Appendix 5).

SC 7.1 purports to restrict the seller's liability for non-disclosure. However, this may be **3.32** ineffective in a non-commercial context, because of the possible contravention of the reasonableness test in the Unfair Contract Terms Act 1977. For example, on a new housing development, it could be argued that the SCs in the seller/developer's contract for sale represent written standard terms of business and are thus subject to the 1977 Act.

Standard Commercial Property Conditions (SCPCs)

The provisions concerning the seller's duty of disclosure in SCPCs are based on those in the **3.33** SCs, but with important differences. There is the same premise that the property is sold free from incumbrances other than those set out in SC 4.1.2, but the provisions of SC 4.1.2 are not the same. Standard Condition 4.1.2(d) is wider than in the SCs by making the sale subject to 'matters, other than monetary charges or incumbrances, disclosed or which would have been disclosed by the searches and enquiries which a prudent buyer would have made before entering into the contract'.

SELLER'S CAPACITY TO SELL

The seller's practitioner should always check the seller's capacity to sell, and ensure that **3.34** any conditions attached to such capacity are fulfilled. Generally, no conditions will attach to sales by a single beneficial owner, i.e. a single estate owner who owns the whole legal and beneficial interest in the property.

Joint owners

Where two or more persons hold the legal estate, they hold on a trust of land, either as **3.35** tenants in common or as joint tenants. On the death of one of two tenants in common, a second trustee will need to be appointed in order to overreach any beneficial interests (see *City of London Building Society v Flegg* [1988] AC 54). Conversely, a sole surviving joint tenant acquires the deceased's beneficial share by survivorship and can sell as beneficial owner (although in unregistered land note that the provisions of the Law of Property (Joint Tenants) Act 1964 must be satisfied; see 5.97 for a discussion of this Act). For the difference between joint tenants and tenants in common and establishing whether co-owners are one or the other, see 2.27.

Other sellers

3.36 If personal representatives (PRs) are selling, then all of the deceased's PRs must be made parties to the contract and purchase deed. As with trustees, overreaching applies, but here even if the seller is a *sole* PR. If a practitioner is acting for a mortgagee exercising its power of sale, the practitioner should ensure that the power of sale exists, has arisen, and is exercisable. Companies regulated by the Companies Acts can sell land, provided the transaction is within the scope of the objects clause of the company's memorandum of association. Sales by charities are governed by the Charities Act 2011. All these matters and others will be considered more fully in Chapter 5, as part of the process of investigating the seller's title.

B FORMATION OF THE CONTRACT

3.37 It is now appropriate to consider the legal formalities for a contract for the sale of land to come into existence. Of course normal contractual principles apply to land contracts just as they do to other legal contracts. There must be:

(a) an intention by the parties to create legal relations;
(b) offer and acceptance; and
(c) consideration.

IMPACT OF SECTION 2 OF THE LAW OF PROPERTY (MISCELLANEOUS PROVISIONS) ACT 1989

3.38 In addition to the above, contracts for the sale or other disposition of land or an interest in land are governed by statute. Section 2 of the Law of Property (Miscellaneous Provisions) Act 1989 lays down the requirements for the creation of land contracts created on or after 27 September 1989. For land contracts created before this date, the relevant statutory provision was s 40 of the Law of Property Act 1925 (now repealed by the 1989 Act).

In writing

3.39 Section 2 prescribes that a contract for the sale or other disposition of land or an interest in land must be made in writing, otherwise it is void. The section abolishes the equitable doctrine of part performance, and the court now has no jurisdiction to allow the enforcement of a 'contract' that does not comply with s 2. However, the innocent party may request a court to invoke the equitable doctrine of proprietary estoppel. In essence, this enables a court to refuse to enforce a right to land, if the person seeking enforcement behaved unfairly (but note there are strict criteria, especially in commercial transactions, see *Yeoman's Row Management Ltd v Cobbe* [2008] UKHL 55 and compare *Thorner v Major & Ors* [2009] WTLR 713 in relation to a family dispute).

Incorporate all agreed terms

3.40 Section 2 further provides that the written contract must incorporate all the agreed terms, either in one document or by reference to another document, and the written contract must be signed by or on behalf of each party to the contract. Where contracts are to be exchanged, both sides need sign only their respective parts, not both parts. In this way the standard exchange of contracts in a conveyancing transaction remains unaffected by s 2, provided both parts of the contract are identical and incorporate all the agreed terms. Exchange of contracts is considered in detail in Chapter 6.

The requirement for the incorporation of all agreed terms is significant because it means **3.41** that if a term is omitted the whole contract becomes invalid. An example would be on the sale of a dwelling where the price is to include chattels. A term to this effect should be included in the contract, otherwise the validity of the entire contract is conceivably at risk (see *Wright v Robert Leonard Development Ltd* [1994] NPC 49, CA). Similarly, ancillary agreements recorded in correspondence between the parties' solicitors should be expressly incorporated by reference in the contract in order to satisfy s 2. The practice of using side letters, once common in commercial conveyancing, now potentially endangers the whole land contract unless the precise terms of the correspondence are properly incorporated in the formal contract.

Variation of contract terms

The impact of s 2 is also felt where the parties wish to vary the terms of a land contract. **3.42** No longer can material variations simply be chronicled in correspondence; they must be recorded in a document which satisfies s 2. This can be achieved by an exchange of documents, signed by the parties, referring to the original contract and the subsequent variation. In *McCausland v Duncan Lawrie Ltd* [1997] 1 WLR 38, two solicitors exchanged letters varying the completion date, but the Court of Appeal held that this did not amount to an effective variation of the contract because it did not satisfy s 2. The court enforced the terms of the original contract.

Mortgages

Section 2 has also had an impact on mortgagees. Before the enactment of s 2, a mortgagee **3.43** could create an equitable mortgage by deposit of title deeds. This took effect as an agreement to create a legal mortgage, and could be enforced by part performance. Now, a lender in these circumstances cannot claim an equitable mortgage because the absence of a written document means there can be no valid disposition of an interest in land. Consequently the prudent lender will now always insist on a legal charge.

'Subject to contract'

Another effect of s 2 is that conveyancers can probably now dispense with the words 'sub- **3.44** ject to contract' in their letters. The phrase was designed to avoid creating what could be regarded as a memorandum, sufficient to satisfy s 40 of the Law of Property Act 1925, of an oral contract that may already have been in existence. As s 2 of the 1989 Act has superseded s 40 of the 1925 Act, there is no danger of this occurring other than in exceptional circumstances, but conveyancers generally still prefer for comfort to use the words in their pre-exchange correspondence.

Intervention by equity

Two cases show that equity will intervene to prevent an injustice by enforcing a contract **3.45** even if the strict requirements of s 2 have not been met. In *Yaxley v Gotts* [2000] Ch 162, an agreement that was merely oral was held to be enforceable on the basis that the claimant had spent money on converting a ground-floor flat in the belief that he owned it. In this case the claimant was able to argue proprietary estoppel and a constructive trust.

Similarly, in *Gillett v Holt* [2001] Ch 210 equity intervened to prevent the repudiation of a repeated promise even though the claimant could not show that he had acted to his detriment in relying on the defendant's promise. However, the Court of Appeal has expressed dislike for the concept that a collateral contract could save a contract that omitted terms from the written agreement. Chadwick LJ has indicated quite clearly that if the parties agree that a contract is conditional on the purchaser also buying carpets and curtains, then a land agreement that does not mention that provision would be invalid (see *Grossman v Hooper* [2001] EWCA Civ 615; [2001] EG 181). In 2008, the House of Lords took a more restrictive approach to the application of proprietary estoppel, especially in a commercial context (see *Yeoman's Row Management Ltd v Cobbe* [2008] UKHL 55). One possibility that remains open to this stricter approach would be a challenge to s 2 under the Human Rights Act 1998. It is arguable that a deprivation of valuable property rights due to a minor failure to comply with a statutory requirement is incompatible with the 1998 Act. However, proceedings under the Human Rights Act would be the last thing your client would want. Clearly, to avoid problems, you must make sure that you and your clients do not use side letters or agreements. Insist that all agreed terms are incorporated in a single contract. (For another House of Lords' decision on proprietary estoppel, see *Thorner v Major & Ors* [2009] WTLR 713.)

Exceptions

3.46   Section 2 does not apply to the following contracts: a lease granted for a term not exceeding three years taking effect in possession without a fine; a contract made at public auction (for auction contracts, see 3.132); and a contract regulated under the Financial Services and Markets Act 2000.

IMPACT OF THE CONTRACTS (RIGHTS OF THIRD PARTIES) ACT 1999

3.47   The Contracts (Rights of Third Parties) Act 1999 (the Act) came into force on 11 November 1999. It amends the law of privity of contract by enabling a third party to sue to enforce a contractual term if:

(a) the contract expressly provides that the third party should have the right to do so; or

(b) the term of the contract purports to confer a benefit on the third party unless, on a proper construction of the contract, it appears that the parties did not intend the contract to be enforceable by the third party.

3.48   The third party must be expressly identified in the contract. This can be done either by reference to a name, description, or a member of a class (e.g. 'successors in title' or 'occupiers of the premises'). The third party need not be in existence at the date of the contract. Thus a third party may include a company not yet incorporated, or a sub-tenant or assignee of a lease. The Act gives that third party the same remedies as would have been available to it if it had been a party to the contract.

Leases

3.49   The Act has very little impact on an ordinary freehold sale and purchase contract but is of more importance in a leasehold context. For example, consider the impact of the Act on mutual enforceability of leasehold covenants. If the tenant's covenants are worded so as to benefit every other tenant in the block, then those tenants should be able to take direct action against the offending tenant without the need for mutual enforceability by the landlord. Sub-leases will also be affected. A covenant by a head landlord in a head lease to insure the premises or provide services will clearly benefit a sub-tenant. Under the Act the sub-tenant is able to enforce the covenant against the head landlord even though there is no privity of estate between the sub-tenant and head landlord. Similarly, the head landlord may be able to enforce a breach of covenant by the sub-tenant in the sub-lease.

Variation of contract

Section 2 of the Act provides that any variation of a contract may also require the consent **3.50** of a third party. Such consent will be necessary if the third party has communicated his or her assent to the contract to the promisor, or if the promisor is aware that the third party has relied on the term, or should reasonably have foreseen that he or she would rely on it where the third party has in fact done so. Thus it may be necessary to obtain the consent of any sub-tenant before any variations are made to a head lease. As a result of this provision, many practitioners drafting leases expressly exclude the operation of the Act to obviate the need to obtain third parties' consent in the future before agreeing a variation of the lease. Moreover, if your client does not wish third parties to take the benefit of the lease covenants then the lease should expressly exclude third parties from taking the benefit. This will put the contracting parties in the position they would have been in before the Act came into force. A suitable clause will read:

> The parties hereto agree and declare that the Contracts (Rights of Third Parties) Act 1999 shall not apply to this lease.

As already mentioned, the Act generally will not apply to ordinary domestic conveyancing **3.51** contracts, and therefore the Act is typically excluded. This is confirmed by SC 1.6, which states that, unless otherwise expressly stated, nothing in the contract will create rights pursuant to the Act in favour of anyone other than the parties to the contract.

LOCK-OUT AGREEMENTS

Either party is free to withdraw from negotiations at any time until contracts are formally **3.52** exchanged. This gives the parties the opportunity to take advice and make proper searches and enquiries before committing themselves to the sale or purchase. A criticism of our system of conveyancing (which differs from the Scottish system, where the parties are bound much earlier when the initial offer is accepted) is that it allows the seller to sell to another buyer at a higher price ('gazumping'). Gazumping is discussed at 1.167. Alternatively a prospective buyer might say to the seller just before exchange, 'I will only proceed if you lower the price' ('gazundering').

An accepted method of preventing gazumping is for the parties at the negotiation stage to **3.53** enter into a 'lock-out agreement'. Here, the seller agrees not to consider any other offers on the property for an agreed period of time. Such an arrangement was upheld in *Pitt v PHH Asset Management Ltd* [1994] 1 WLR 327, in which the court held that the lock-out agreement was outside the ambit of s 2 of the Law of Property (Miscellaneous Provisions) Act 1989. The seller will usually agree to immediately terminate discussions with any third parties and not to provide any information about the property to any other prospective buyer. Naturally a prudent seller might feel reluctant to enter into a lock-out agreement unless the buyer correspondingly promises that he will definitely exchange! (A precedent for a lock-out agreement is available at the Online Resource Centre.)

3.54 The only remedy for breach of a lock-out agreement is likely to be a claim for damages, so it may be sensible for the buyer to include in the agreement a 'liquidated damages' clause, being a fixed sum that would be payable by the seller to the buyer in the event of a breach. No similar method has been judicially endorsed to circumvent the practice of 'gazundering'.

C CONTENTS OF THE CONTRACT

3.55 The contract will plainly include the names and addresses of the parties, their signatures, and of course a date for the contract and a date for completion (although the dates are not inserted until the contract comes into force on exchange). The remainder of the contract comprises the particulars of sale and the conditions of sale, which are now considered.

PARTICULARS OF SALE

3.56 The particulars describe the physical extent of the property being sold and its tenure, i.e. freehold or leasehold. The particulars also refer to any incumbrances subject to which the property is being sold.

3.57 The property may be described using a simple postal address, provided the land is easily identifiable from it. If not, a more detailed description is necessary, referring to a scale plan and/or measurements. This applies particularly on a sale of part of an existing title where a new description will be required (see 3.109 and 3.110).

3.58 For registered land the description in the property register of the title can be used and the title number quoted, together with the class of title (absolute, good leasehold, etc.). The practitioner will of course locate this information in the official copies. For unregistered land, the description in the previous conveyance to the seller can usually be used, although its accuracy should always be verified (see *Gordon-Cumming v Houldsworth* [1910] AC 537). A misdescription may of course entitle the buyer to rescind the contract or seek an abatement in the purchase price (see remedies in Chapter 9).

Contents

3.59 If any contents are to be included in the sale, it is good practice to have a separate list of them which can be attached to the final form of contract (e.g. a copy of the fixtures, fittings, and contents form). Special condition 3 on the Law Society's Standard Form of Contract (see Appendix 5) provides as follows:

    (a) the sale includes those contents which are indicated on the attached list as included in the sale and the buyer is to pay the contents price for them;

    (b) the sale excludes those fixtures which are at the property and are indicated on the attached list as excluded from the sale.

At common law, contents would otherwise be excluded from the sale and fixtures, forming part of the property, would be included in the sale.

CONDITIONS OF SALE

3.60 The conditions of sale set out the terms on which the land is sold. There are general conditions and special conditions.

General conditions

The open contract rules (explained in 3.27) are acknowledged to be unduly complex and **3.61** onerous on sellers. Over time, conveyancers have therefore adopted their own standard-ized general conditions designed to replace the complexities of the open contract rules. The general conditions are periodically updated, and the current edition is the 5th edition of the Standard Conditions of Sale (SCs). These are reproduced in Appendix 4.

The general conditions cover a variety of areas, such as time limits for submission and **3.62** approval of the draft purchase deed, proof of title, and remedies. Many of the general con-ditions will be discussed within the context of other parts of the book. In the vast majority of cases, however, where the transaction proceeds smoothly, there is no need to refer to the general conditions at all—they are simply there as a fall-back in case problems arise. Prac-titioners should be aware that if the Protocol is being used, the Law Society Standard Form of Contract incorporating the current SCs (reproduced in Appendix 5) must be adopted.

In 1999, the Law Society introduced general conditions for commercial transactions and **3.63** the current edition is the Standard Commercial Property Conditions (3rd edition) (SCPCs). Although they are based on the SCs, there are differences to meet the needs of a commercial transaction. Detailed commentary on them can be found at 12.92.

Special conditions

The special conditions are specific to the transaction in question. If the parties agree to **3.64** delete or modify a general condition, this is done by an appropriate special condition. Some special conditions typically apply in many transactions and for convenience they are printed on the last page of the Law Society Standard Form of Contract (see Appendix 5). It should be noted that one of the alternatives in special condition 4 must be deleted depend-ing on whether the property is to be sold with vacant possession or subject to tenancies. Special condition 6 states that neither party can rely on any representation made by the other, unless made in writing by the other or his conveyancer, but this does not exclude liability for fraud or recklessness. This is a sensible provision which effectively prevents reliance on oral statements, which are difficult to prove. It also takes into account the requirements of s 3 of the Misrepresentation Act 1967, which provides that these clauses must be reasonable (see *Morgan v Pooley* [2010] EWHC 2447).

In every transaction the practitioner must consider whether any additional special conditions **3.65** are necessary, over and above those on the printed form. This is particularly so in sales of part of an existing title where the parties often agree to create new easements and covenants, the precise terms of which should properly be expressed in the special conditions (see Section D of this chapter for a detailed discussion of sales of part). Importantly, the 2011 Protocol states that additional special conditions should not be added unless it is necessary to accord with current law or specific and informed instructions have been given by the seller that inclusion of such clauses are necessary and are required for the purposes of the particular transaction.

Void conditions

Certain conditions are deemed to be too harsh on buyers and are made void by statute. **3.66** Knowledge of these is particularly useful for buyers who find themselves negotiating with sellers attempting to restrict the buyer's rights to raise requisitions of any kind. The void conditions of key importance are:

(a) restricting the buyer's choice of solicitor or providing that the seller's solicitors will prepare the conveyance at the buyer's expense (Law of Property Act 1925, s 48);

(b) preventing the buyer from examining a power of attorney under which a document of title has been executed (Law of Property Act 1925, s 125(2)); and

(c) preventing the buyer from objecting to any stamping defect on a document of title, or requiring the buyer to pay for any stamping fee (Stamp Act 1891, s 117).

SOME IMPORTANT AREAS COVERED BY CONDITIONS OF SALE

Vacant possession and completion

Open contract rule on vacant possession

3.67 Under an open contract it is an implied term that the seller must give vacant possession to the buyer on completion. This is rebutted if the contract discloses tenancies, or if the buyer has knowledge before entering the contract of subsisting tenancies (see *Cook v Taylor* [1942] 2 All ER 85 and *Timmins v Moreland Street Property Co. Ltd* [1958] Ch 110).

Vacant possession

3.68 As mentioned in 3.64, special condition 4 contains two alternatives dealing with the question of vacant possession, one of which the seller's practitioner must delete when drafting the contract. SCs 6.1.2 and 6.1.3 also cover vacant possession indirectly. SC 6.1.2 provides for completion by 2 p.m. on the day of completion, otherwise completion is treated as taking place on the next working day. SC 6.1.3 says that 6.1.2 does not apply if the seller has not vacated by 2 p.m., in which case the seller is in default for the purpose of calculating compensation under SC 7.2.1. Thus even if the buyer has not paid the balance of the completion money by 2 p.m., the seller should at least be in a position to offer vacant possession as soon as the balance is paid.

Bringing forward the 2 p.m. deadline

3.69 The parties may of course vary the SCs by special condition, and this is often done in respect of the 2 p.m. deadline for completion. Where the seller has a related purchase completing on the same day as the sale, the seller will inevitably need the sale proceeds to finance the balance to be paid on the purchase. If both sale and purchase contracts set a 2 p.m. deadline, and the sale monies are received only a few minutes before 2 p.m., there may be insufficient time to complete the purchase before the 2 p.m. deadline expires. This will result in the client having to pay compensation to the seller for the delay (see 3.74).

3.70 Consequently, to avoid a potential breach of contract, the practitioner should ensure that the time for completion in the sale contract is set at least half an hour earlier than the time for completion in the purchase contract. This is done by a simple special condition in the sale contract and special condition 5 in the Law Society's Standard Form of Contract allows for this:

> Conditions 6.1.2 and 6.1.3 shall take effect as if the time specified in them were *[insert time required e.g. 1.30 pm]* rather than 2 pm.

Date of completion

3.71 The open contract rule is that completion shall take place within a reasonable period (see *Johnson v Humphrey* [1946] 1 All ER 460). This creates uncertainty and is clearly unsatisfactory. SC 6.1.1 therefore provides for completion to be 20 working days after the date of the contract. However, SC 6.1.1 is in practice never used; when contracts are exchanged the conveyancers simply insert on the front page of the contract a completion date which is mutually agreeable to both parties (the situation differs where the client is purchasing a property in the course of construction and the developer does not wish to be committed to a fixed completion date—see 11.08).

Related sale and purchase   Where the client has a related sale and purchase, the practitioner should seek to ensure that the agreed completion dates for both transactions are the same. If synchronization is not possible, the client must be advised in writing of the implications, financial or otherwise. By completing the sale first, the client may have to move into temporary accommodation and incur other expenses such as furniture storage fees. By completing the purchase first, the client will almost certainly require a bridging loan and the consent of the buyer's mortgagee.   **3.72**

KEY POINTS SUMMARY

VACANT POSSESSION AND COMPLETION

Is the sale with vacant possession or subject to tenancies? Draft the contract accordingly. If the client has a dependent sale and purchase: **3.73**

(a) synchronize the two completion dates or advise the client of the drawbacks of not doing so;

(b) ensure that the time for completion in the sale contract is at least half an hour earlier than the time for completion in the purchase contract.

The 'contract rate': interest on late completion

Late completion is dealt with fully in Chapter 9. Stated simply, the normal effect of SC 7.2 is as follows. If the seller has met all deadlines during the transaction and the buyer fails to pay the balance of the purchase price on the contractual completion date, the buyer will be liable to pay the seller interest on the amount outstanding. Interest is calculated at the 'contract rate' specified in the contract and there is space on the front page of the Law Society contract to insert this. Four per cent above the base rate of a high-street bank is the norm, being seen as sufficiently penal to encourage the buyer not to delay. A higher rate than 4 per cent above base is widely seen as excessive. If the parties forget to insert the contract rate, SC 1.1.1(e) defines it as the Law Society's interest rate from time to time in force (currently 4 per cent above the base rate of Barclays Bank plc).   **3.74**

Related sale and purchase

Care must be exercised where the client has a related sale and purchase. The practitioner should ensure that the contract rate in the purchase contract is no higher than the contract rate in the sale contract. Imagine a situation in which the contract rate on the sale is 4 per cent above base while the contract rate on the purchase is 5 per cent above base. If the client is dependent on the sale proceeds to finance the purchase but the client's buyer completes late, the client will as a consequence be forced to complete the purchase late. The compensation the client has to pay under the purchase contract will be 1 per cent more than the compensation receivable under the sale contract; the client will therefore be out of pocket.   **3.75**

Deposit

Generally

Deposits are traditionally paid on exchange of contracts as part-payment of the purchase price and a guarantee that the buyer will complete. If the buyer defaults on the contract,   **3.76** the seller will generally be entitled to forfeit the whole deposit, even though the seller has suffered no loss.

3.77   The buyer is not obliged to pay a deposit under the open contract rules and so it is important to specify in the contract that a deposit is payable. If the SCs are used, SC 2.2.1 provides for a deposit of 10 per cent of the purchase price to be paid or sent no later than the date of the contract. In calculating the exact amount payable on exchange, one could deduct any preliminary deposit paid to the estate agents.

3.78   The deposit is customarily paid on exchange by the buyer's practitioner to the seller's practitioner. Under SC 2.2.4, payment must be made either by electronic means from an account held in the name of a conveyancer at a clearing bank to an account in the name of a conveyancer, or by cheque drawn on a solicitor's or licensed conveyancer's client account. The buyer's practitioner should therefore ensure that he or she receives the buyer's own cheque in sufficient time for it to be cleared through the buyer's practitioner's account. Alternatively, the buyer could simply remit the deposit to the buyer's practitioner's account by electronic means. Practitioners should be mindful of a buyer who apparently pays a deposit direct to the seller. This should alert you to the possibility of mortgage fraud, and you are referred to the Law Society's guidance on mortgage fraud and a full explanation in 7.157.

Negotiating a reduced deposit

3.79   The buyer's practitioner should consider negotiating a reduced deposit in certain circumstances. The deposit is designed to recompense the seller for loss as a result of the buyer not completing. Accordingly, if the purchase price is high, the seller may be persuaded to accept less on the basis that 10 per cent would be more than enough compensation. Two other instances should also be considered: (a) where the buyer's mortgage exceeds 90 per cent of the purchase price and the buyer has insufficient funds to finance a 10 per cent deposit; and (b) where the buyer is financing the deposit out of deposit monies receivable on a related sale, and the sale price is less than the purchase price—again the buyer will have insufficient funds.

3.80   Correspondingly, the seller's practitioner should be careful not to accept less than 10 per cent without first considering whether the seller will be adequately compensated for any loss. Ask yourself: 'Will the deposit offered cover the cost of bridging finance if my client requires this to complete a related purchase? Will it also cover abortive costs and the costs of a resale?' You should note that as a seller's practitioner you are at risk of being negligent if you accept a reduced deposit without explaining the consequences to the client and without obtaining the client's express authority to do so (see *Morris v Duke Cohan* (1975) 119 SJ 826).

3.81   SC 6.8.3 provides that if less than 10 per cent has been paid on exchange and the seller subsequently serves on the buyer notice to complete (discussed in 9.86), the balance of the 10 per cent immediately becomes payable.

Deposit to be held as agent or stakeholder?

3.82   The open contract position is that the deposit paid on exchange to the seller's conveyancer is held as agent for the seller (see *Ellis v Goulton* [1893] 1 QB 350). This means that once exchange has taken place the seller's conveyancer is free to release the deposit to the seller. But if this occurs, there is inherent risk for the buyer if the seller defaults. This is because although the buyer will be legally entitled to the return of the deposit if the seller defaults, the buyer may have practical difficulty in actually recovering the deposit from the seller (for instance, because the seller is bankrupt or cannot be traced). It follows therefore that a buyer's practitioner should not agree to the deposit being held as agent for the seller unless the buyer is first advised of this risk.

Of course, the safer approach for the buyer is for the deposit to be paid to the seller's prac- **3.83** titioner as stakeholder. In this capacity the practitioner is a custodian of the deposit for *both* parties. The deposit cannot be released to the seller until completion and if the buyer rescinds the contract as a result of the seller's default, the deposit must be returned to the buyer, with interest.

Agent for the buyer

Practitioners should be aware that it is also possible for the deposit to be held as agent for **3.84** the buyer. For obvious reasons this is rarely agreed, but a buyer's practitioner might wish to contemplate it where the seller is acting in person or is represented by someone who is unqualified.

Position under the SCs and SCPCs

The SCs provide for the deposit to be held as stakeholder except where the seller before **3.85** completion agrees to buy another property in England or Wales for his residence (i.e. the seller has a related purchase). In this situation the seller may use all or any part of the sale deposit as a deposit on the related purchase provided it is used only for this purpose (SC 2.2.5). Effectively this permits a deposit to be passed along a chain of transactions and assists the operation of a telephonic exchange under Law Society Formula C (see 6.44). There is no equivalent provision in the SCPCs, which simply provide that the deposit is to be held by the seller's conveyancer as stakeholder on terms that on completion it is paid to the seller with accrued interest (SCPC 3.2.2).

Interest on the deposit

Traditionally the solicitor as stakeholder retained the interest on the deposit as due reward **3.86** for looking after it (see *Harrington v Hoggart* (1830) 1 B & Ad 577). This is no longer the case and the matter is now governed by the SRA Accounts Rules 2011. Where the deposit is held as agent for the seller, then the seller is entitled to the interest. Where the deposit is held as stakeholder, SC 2.2.6 provides that the seller is entitled to 'accrued interest'. Accrued interest is defined in SC 1.1.1(a) and the reader is referred to the full text of the SCs in Appendix 4. If the seller defaults and the buyer rescinds, the buyer is entitled to recover the deposit with accrued interest (SC 7.5.2).

Alternative means of funding the deposit

Bridging loan   If the client buyer has a related sale, it should be possible to borrow the **3.87** deposit (or any shortfall) from the client's bank (or another lender) on a short-term bridging loan. Most banks are happy to help their customers in this way, especially where the loan is only for a short period. However, before releasing any funds, the bank will normally require from the borrower's solicitors an undertaking to repay the bridging loan from the net proceeds of the related sale. The proposed terms of that undertaking will have to be considered carefully (see 6.10).

The practitioner should advise the buyer that the bank will invariably charge an arrange- **3.88** ment fee for the bridging loan. Moreover, the client should be informed that the interest charges on the loan may be high and, in the unlikely event of a delay on completion of the sale, the bridging loan could ultimately prove to be expensive.

Deposit guarantee scheme   Instead of offering the seller a 'cash' deposit, the buyer could **3.89** offer a deposit guarantee from an insurance company. If this is agreed, then an appropriate provision must be inserted in the contract. The scheme operates in the following way. The buyer pays a single premium to the insurance company, which in turn provides a guarantee to the seller for the amount of the deposit. If the buyer defaults under the purchase contract entitling the seller to forfeit the 'deposit', the insurance company pays the seller the amount of the deposit. The insurance company would then exercise its right of recovery against the buyer.

3.90 The deposit guarantee scheme is intended for use where a buyer enters into a simultaneous exchange of contracts on a related sale. It is therefore generally unavailable for first-time purchasers. Understandably, many sellers would prefer to have the security of a 'cash' deposit rather than a claim against an insurance company. It should also be borne in mind that the seller may have a dependent purchase, the deposit for which is to be financed from the buyer's cash deposit.

KEY POINTS SUMMARY

DEPOSIT

3.91 Is the deposit being held as stakeholder or agent for the seller? Stakeholder is safer for the buyer. Warn the buyer of the risks of accepting agent.

- Can the seller be persuaded to accept less than 10 per cent? The seller must ensure there is sufficient deposit to cover any potential losses.
- How will the buyer fund the deposit? Can the deposit on a related sale be utilized? (SC 2.2.5 permits this.)
- Will a bridging loan be required? This is normally the case only if the client has a related sale. Explain the financial consequences to the client. Solicitors' undertaking to lender will be required.
- The buyer perhaps might consider a deposit guarantee scheme as an alternative to a cash deposit, but note the limitations of the scheme.
- As buyer's practitioner, you must ensure that you have cleared funds for the deposit before you exchange contracts.

Title guarantee

3.92 Since the Law of Property (Miscellaneous Provisions) Act 1994 came into force on 1 July 1995, it is no longer necessary to state the seller's capacity in the contract (e.g. beneficial owner, trustee, PR, etc.). Instead, the seller must decide whether to give a full title guarantee, a limited title guarantee, or no title guarantee at all. The importance of the title guarantee is that covenants for title on the part of the seller are implied into the purchase deed. By definition, a limited guarantee will imply less extensive covenants for title than a full guarantee, and no guarantee will imply none at all. For a discussion of the implied covenants, see 9.114.

Full title guarantee

3.93 This is normally given where the seller owns the whole legal and equitable interest in the property and would, before July 1995, have sold as 'beneficial owner'. In the absence of any express provision in the contract, SC 4.6.2 provides that the seller will sell with full title guarantee. This is also the position under the SCPCs (SCPC 6.6.2).

Limited title guarantee

3.94 This is normally given where the legal owner/seller is a PR, or a trustee holding on trust for others. Before July 1995 such a seller would have sold as 'personal representative' or 'trustee', respectively.

No title guarantee

The seller has the option of giving no title guarantee at all, and this is often done in circum-   **3.95**
stances where the seller has little or no knowledge of the property or the title history, or if
the disposition is by way of gift. A mortgagee exercising its power of sale may offer no title
guarantee, but as a buyer's practitioner you should be wary of accepting this, especially
where you are also acting for the buyer's mortgagee, who might insist on a title guarantee.
A seller would generally not wish to give any title guarantee where selling only a possessory title.

Some sellers' practitioners, without going as far as to give no title guarantee, may wish   **3.96**
to protect a client by drafting a special condition in which the seller gives no statutory
covenant for title save to confirm that the seller has not made any prior disposition of or
created any incumbrances affecting the property. Faced with such a draft condition the
practitioner for the buyer and the mortgagee could reasonably seek to reject it, insisting on
a full or limited title guarantee.

If the seller agrees to give a title guarantee (full or limited), s 2(1)(b) of the Law of Prop-   **3.97**
erty (Miscellaneous Provisions) Act 1994 provides that the seller will at his own cost do
all that he reasonably can to give the buyer the title he purports to give. A prudent seller
may take the view that, as the buyer should have satisfied himself on all such matters from
a full investigation of title before exchange, it is for the buyer to bear such cost, not the
seller. Accordingly, the seller should consider the following special condition in the draft
contract:

> The transfer or conveyance to the buyer shall contain the following clause:
>
> In the covenant implied by s 2(1)(b) of the Law of Property (Miscellaneous Provisions) Act
> 1994 the words 'at the Buyer's cost' shall be substituted for the words 'at his own cost'.

In practice, the buyer will rarely choose to sue under the implied covenants for title. The   **3.98**
buyer will instead prefer, should the need arise, to claim against the seller for breach of
contract. (This will be possible if the contract does not merge with the purchase deed on
completion, as is the case under SC 7.3, and SCPC 9.4.) The importance of the implied
covenants for title in practice is therefore limited.

Indemnity covenants

As a result of the doctrine of privity of contract, an owner of land may continue to be   **3.99**
liable under a covenant affecting the land even after the control of the land has passed to
someone else, namely the buyer or buyer's successor in title. In this situation the seller's
practitioner must ensure that the buyer gives the seller an indemnity covenant against any
future breaches of the covenant because the seller could in future be sued for breach of
contract. However, a covenant limited to seisin (i.e. possession) will generally not bind the
covenantor after disposal of the land. So in this situation an indemnity covenant from the
buyer would be inappropriate.

In the sale of leasehold land, where the lease was granted prior to 1 January 1996 the   **3.100**
buyer's indemnity is implied by statute. Section 77(1)(c) of the Law of Property Act 1925
applies to unregistered land (provided the assignment is for value) and Schedule 12, para
20 to the Land Registration Act 2002 applies to registered land (whether or not the assignment is for value). For leases granted on or after 1 January 1996 there is no implied indemnity because of the changes introduced by the Landlord and Tenant (Covenants) Act 1995
(see 7.54 for further details). In respect of freehold land, the contract should deal with
indemnity expressly.

Chain of indemnity covenants

3.101　Your client seller was probably once a buyer too, and when the property was acquired your client may have given an indemnity covenant to the previous owner. If so, your client will still continue to be bound by the indemnity covenant even after disposal of the land. Your client will therefore require an indemnity (for the indemnity) from the present buyer. As the property continues to change hands, a chain of indemnity covenants will be built up between successors in title.

3.102　If the SCs are used, SC 4.6.4 protects the seller. It provides that if, after completion, the seller will remain bound by any obligation affecting the property, the buyer will indemnify the seller against any future breach as well as perform the obligation. The SCPCs contain a similar provision (SCPC 6.6.4). The indemnity covenant itself is given in the purchase deed and indemnity covenants are considered again in the purchase deed chapter (chapter 7).

3.103　To determine whether your client seller requires an indemnity from the buyer, you need to ask yourself two questions:

(a) Did your client previously give any new covenants (not limited to seisin)?
(b) When your client acquired the land, did he or she give the previous owner an indemnity covenant?

3.104　You can discover the answers to these questions as follows: if the land is unregistered, simply read the covenants (if any) given by your client in the most recent conveyance, namely the one to your client. If the land is registered, inspect the charges register for details of any covenants given by the proprietor (i.e. your client) and inspect the proprietorship register for evidence of any indemnity covenant given by the proprietor. (If the proprietor is the first registered proprietor, it may be necessary to inspect the last pre-registration conveyance, i.e. the one to the present proprietor: see 3.13.)

3.105　If the answer to either of the two questions is yes, your client seller will require an indemnity covenant from the current buyer. So when you later approve the draft purchase deed after exchange, you will have to check that the buyer's practitioner has included the indemnity covenant in the draft. For a recent case illustrating the importance of ensuring there is a complete chain of indemnity covenants, see *Stratford on Avon Council v David Wilson Homes Ltd & Ors* [2011] EWHC 3548 (Ch).

D　SALES OF PART

3.106　A sale of part occurs when the owner of land sells off part of an existing title. It may be a house owner selling off part of the garden, or a developer selling plots on a new estate (see Chapter 11), or a landlord granting new leases of flats or offices within a large block (see Chapter 10).

3.107　Obviously the issues we have considered generally in relation to the draft contract apply equally to sales of part. Now we examine the special conveyancing considerations which apply in relation to sales of part; in particular, whether any lender's consent is required, the description of the land in the contract, the grant and reservation of new easements, and the imposition of new covenants.

LENDER'S CONSENT

3.108　If the seller's land is mortgaged, the seller's practitioner must check before exchange that the mortgagee will release from the mortgage the part being sold off. The mortgagee will often insist that the proceeds of sale, or a sufficient part of them, are sent to the mortgagee on completion of the sale as part repayment of the mortgage debt. In addition, under the terms of the mortgage the lender's consent may be required if it is proposed to grant easements over the land being retained by the seller or impose covenants on the retained land. So check the mortgage conditions carefully.

DESCRIPTION IN THE CONTRACT

On sale of whole it is normally possible in the case of registered land to use the exist- **3.109** ing description in the property register together with the title number. Alternatively, if the land is unregistered, you can use the existing description in the last conveyance, provided it is satisfactory. On a sale of part, however, it will be necessary to draft an entirely new description of the land being sold off, and for this purpose reference to a plan is essential. It can also be helpful if the seller (or seller's surveyor) pegs out the new boundaries. This will assist Land Registry's surveyor when the land is surveyed after completion but before the Registry issues a new title number. Initially the new title plan will be plotted from the transfer plan and this may be updated later from the survey information.

IMPORTANCE OF A GOOD PLAN

It is not always appreciated by practitioners just how many disputes arise from poor- **3.110** quality plans, more perhaps than from any other aspect of conveyancing. Conveyancers were subject to judicial criticism in *Scarfe v Adams* [1981] 1 All ER 843, where Cumming-Bruce LJ expressed strong disapproval of conveyancers using small-scale plans in their documents.

Scale plan

Ideally the plan in a sale of part contract and purchase deed should be of sufficient size and **3.111** scale to enable the boundaries to be easily identified. A Land Registry plan is not usually satisfactory because the boundaries on it are only very general. Unless the transaction is simple, such as the sale of part of a garden, use is recommended of a scale plan of at least 1:1,250 (which is the standard urban Ordnance Survey (OS) scale), and the scale itself should be marked on the plan. A scale plan larger than this will probably be required for sales of flats or other lettings of parts of buildings. Practitioners should be aware that all OS maps have limitations of accuracy.

Markings on plan

Convention dictates that the land being sold should be edged red, while the land being **3.112** retained by the seller (normally defined in the contract as 'the retained land') should be edged blue. Other features should also be clearly marked so that, for instance, if a right of way is being granted or reserved, the route would be shown by a broken line of a different colour or, if appropriate, by hatching. Boundary ownership should be shown by inward-facing 'T' marks. It can also be useful to have a north arrow and a key to define the different colours and features. Since 1 October 1995, all measurements on plans should be metric (Unit of Measurement Regulations 1995 (SI 1995/1804)). If a plan prepared after this date is submitted to Land Registry in imperial measurements, it will be returned with a request for it to be recalibrated with metric measurements.

Conflict between plan and verbal description

3.113   Where an accurate scale plan is used, the verbal description in the contract should refer to the property as being 'more particularly delineated on the plan annexed'. The effect of this is that should any discrepancy arise between the verbal description and the plan, the plan will prevail. Where the plan is not to scale the contract should refer to the property as being 'shown for identification purposes only on the plan annexed'. The effect of this in the event of inconsistency between plan and verbal description is that the latter will prevail (see *Eastwood v Ashton* [1915] AC 900). Practitioners should be aware that on a transfer of part of registered land, plans 'for identification purposes only' or anything similar (e.g. 'Do not scale from this drawing') will be rejected by Land Registry. A helpful practice leaflet on plans and their use is available from Land Registry offices or online at **http://www.landregistry.gov.uk**.

NEGATING IMPLIED GRANT OF EASEMENTS IN FAVOUR OF BUYER

3.114   On a sale of part the buyer may acquire certain rights over the seller's retained land by virtue of s 62 of the Law of Property Act 1925 and the rule in *Wheeldon v Burrows* (1879) 12 ChD 31. As the nature and extent of these implied rights is not always clear, it is prudent for the seller's practitioner to exclude the effect of the rules and set out expressly the rights and reservations required by the parties. If implied rights of light or air were granted to the buyer, this could hinder any future plans of the seller to develop the retained land.

3.115   A recommended special condition in the contract negating implied rights would be as follows:

> The Transfer to the Buyer shall contain an agreement and declaration that the Buyer shall not by implication or otherwise become entitled to any rights of light or air which would restrict or interfere with the free use of the Retained Land for building or other purposes.

GRANT AND RESERVATION OF NEW EASEMENTS

3.116   New easements created in favour of the buyer are called 'grants'; new easements created in favour of the seller are called 'reservations'. When acting for a seller wishing to create reservations, reliance should never be placed upon s 62 of the Law of Property Act 1925 or the rule in *Wheeldon v Burrows* (1879) 12 ChD 31, because both of these relate to implied *grants*, not implied reservations.

CREATING NEW COVENANTS

3.117   The seller's practitioner should always consider the covenants, if any, that the seller may wish to impose on the buyer, for instance, regarding the future use of the land being sold off. The buyer's practitioner in turn must determine whether the seller should enter into any new covenants, for example not to obstruct access to the property being sold or possibly a fencing obligation.

Drafting considerations

3.118   Ideally a covenant should be drafted so as to be restrictive (i.e. negative) in nature. This is because generally the burden of a positive covenant will not run with the land (see *Tulk v Moxhay* (1848) 2 Ph 774). So, for instance, rather than say 'The buyer will build only a single-storey dwelling', say 'The buyer shall not erect any building save for a single-storey dwelling.' However, it is not always the drafting *per se* which determines whether a covenant is positive or restrictive in nature; a court would consider the substance of the covenant as well as form.

Fencing covenants

3.119 For fencing covenants it is beneficial to stipulate a time limit for construction, a minimum height in metres, and to specify the type of fence required. An obligation to fence is positive in character and the burden of it generally will not run, but it may be enforced indirectly through a chain of indemnity covenants (see 3.101).

3.120 The benefit of the covenants should be expressly annexed to the whole or any part of the seller's retained land. This is to ensure that the benefit of the covenant will run with the seller's land (see *Federated Homes Ltd v Mill Lodge Properties Ltd* [1980] 1 WLR 594 and *Roake v Chadha* [1984] 1 WLR 40).

A WORKED EXAMPLE OF A SALE OF PART

3.121 Set out below in 3.122 is an imaginary set of instructions from a client who is selling part of a registered title. These instructions are followed by recommended clauses for inclusion in the draft contract.

Instructions

3.122 You act for the owner of 24 Bromley Crescent, Blakey, registered with title absolute under title number BT12345. Your client is selling part of the garden as a building plot with planning permission to a property developer and has given you the following instructions:

(a) Access to the building plot will be along the client's driveway, which runs along the side of the garden. The client will share the use of the driveway with the buyer.

(b) The buyer can lay new drains and sewers and connect them into the client's existing drains and sewers ('the existing services'). The existing services in turn connect into the mains drainage and sewage systems in Bromley Crescent.

(c) Once the buyer's connection is made, the buyer can share the use of the existing services and come on to the seller's retained land to carry out any necessary maintenance or repairs to the services.

(d) There is a greenhouse on the building plot. Once the sale is legally binding on the buyer, the seller will relocate it in the part of the garden he is keeping.

(e) The client does not want to be overlooked, so the new building must be no more than one storey high. The seller will also want to see and approve the plans for the new property before it is built.

(f) The buyer will put up a suitable fence along the boundary between the plot and the land the seller is keeping, and the buyer will maintain the fence.

Recommended clauses for inclusion in the draft contract (with commentary)

3.123 The following 'new' description of the land being sold is suggested:

> All that freehold land ('the Property') more particularly delineated and shown edged red on the plan annexed ('the Plan') forming part of 24 Bromley Crescent, Blakey registered at HM Land Registry with Title Absolute under title number BT12345. The land being retained by the Seller is more particularly delineated and shown edged blue on the Plan ('the Retained Land').

3.124 The following special condition is suggested regarding the grant of easements:

> The Transfer to the Buyer shall contain the following rights in favour of the Buyer and the Buyer's successors in title:
>
> (a) A free and uninterrupted right of way at all times and for all purposes with or without vehicles over the accessway shown hatched black on the Plan ('the Accessway') leading across the Retained Land subject to the Buyer paying a fair proportion according to user of the cost of maintaining repairing and renewing the Accessway;
>
> (b) A right to lay maintain and use for all proper purposes connected with the Property a new drain and sewer ('the New Services') under the Retained Land along the route marked with a broken orange line on the Plan;
>
> (c) A right to connect into the Seller's existing drain and sewer ('the Existing Services') on the Retained Land and to use the Existing Services in common with the Seller subject to the Buyer paying a fair proportion of the cost of maintaining repairing and renewing the Existing Services and making good any damage caused to the satisfaction of the Seller;
>
> (d) A right on giving reasonable notice and at reasonable times (except in the case of emergencies) to enter the Retained Land for the purpose of inspecting maintaining and repairing the New Services and the Existing Services the person exercising such right causing as little damage as possible and making good any such damage caused.

3.125 The seller has been protected by the provision for the buyer to make good any damage caused to the seller's retained land and for repairs to be carried out only upon prior notice, save in the case of an emergency. The route of the new services has also been specified so as to avoid any unnecessary intrusion on to the seller's retained land.

3.126 A special condition highlighting the negation of implied grants of easements would also be appropriate and the clause in 3.115 can be used for this purpose.

3.127 From the instructions, it appears that the only reservation that the seller will require is the right to remove the greenhouse. The following special condition would cover the point:

> The Seller reserves the right to remove the greenhouse on the Property provided that the Seller shall exercise this right before completion and shall cause no unnecessary damage to the Property.

3.128 If the Protocol is being used, the right to remove the greenhouse could be taken care of by mentioning it on the Fixtures, Fittings, and Contents Form.

3.129 The seller has imposed some specific conditions and each one will be the subject of a new covenant imposed on the buyer. Although not mentioned in our instructions, it would be prudent in addition to:

(a) restrict the use of the new property to residential only (this is probably a condition of the planning permission anyway);

(b) prohibit the buyer from obstructing the driveway; and

(c) impose a general covenant against causing a nuisance or annoyance to the owners and occupiers of the seller's retained land.

3.130 The following special condition is suggested:

> The Buyer shall in the Transfer enter into a covenant with the Seller to the intent that the burden of such covenant shall run with and bind the Property and every part thereof and that the benefit of such covenant shall be annexed to and run with the Retained Land and every part thereof to observe and perform the following:
>
> (a) Not to erect on the Property any building or other structure other than one bungalow and garage for residential use and occupation by one family in accordance with plans previously approved in writing by the Seller or the Seller's successors in title;

(b) Within three months from the date of completion to erect and forever thereafter maintain a close-boarded fence not less than two metres in height along the boundary between the Retained Land and the Property between the points marked A and B on the Plan;

(c) Not to park vehicles on or otherwise obstruct or cause or permit to be obstructed the Accessway;

(d) Not to do or permit to be done on the Property anything which may be or grow to be a nuisance or annoyance to the owners or occupiers of the Retained Land.

At the end of this chapter there is a sale of part checklist.   **3.131**

E SPECIAL CONSIDERATIONS

AUCTION CONTRACTS

Contracts made at auction are not governed by s 2 of the Law of Property (Miscellaneous **3.132** Provisions) Act 1989 and thus a binding and enforceable auction contract arises immediately the auctioneer's hammer has fallen. Confirmatory written contracts are then signed at the end of the auction.

As a consequence, a prudent buyer will ensure that a survey is carried out and financial **3.133** arrangements, including the deposit to be paid if the buyer's bid is successful, are in place before the auction. If the contract provides for the risk in the property to pass to the buyer once the contract is in force (SC 5.1.1), then the buyer must also make arrangements for the property to be insured immediately the buyer's bid is accepted.

Before the auction, the buyer's conveyancer should inspect and approve the title, draft **3.134** contract, answers to standard enquiries and all requisite searches. The seller's practitioner will usually produce these items for prior inspection, often at the auction itself (beware of out-of-date local searches). The buyer's conveyancer should raise any additional enquiries which are considered to be relevant. The seller's practitioner should also be present at the auction to deal with questions of a legal nature which may arise.

The contract will comprise the particulars, the conditions of sale, and a memorandum of **3.135** sale. The particulars—which describe the property—are usually prepared by the auctioneer and approved by the seller's conveyancer. The conditions of sale are usually prepared by the seller's conveyancer (although auctioneers often have their own printed conditions which they ask the conveyancer to approve). A memorandum of sale is then attached to the particulars and conditions of sale which the parties sign after the auction.

Conditions of sale in auction contract

The principal concern for the seller's practitioner is of course to ensure that the conditions **3.136** of sale in the contract adequately protect the seller. SC 2.3 incorporates provisions which assist in the contract complying with the Sale of Land by Auction Act 1867:

(a) SC 2.3.2—the sale is subject to a reserve price, i.e. an undisclosed price below which the property will not be sold. Without a reserve price the auctioneer is bound to sell to the highest bidder;

(b) SC 2.3.3—the seller or a person on the seller's behalf (known as a 'puffer') may bid up to the reserve price. Given this option the seller is more likely to achieve the reserve price;

(c) SC 2.3.4—the auctioneer may refuse any bid;

(d) SC 2.3.5—if there is any dispute about a bid, the auctioneer may resolve the dispute or restart the auction at the last undisputed bid;

(e) SC 2.3.6—the deposit is to be paid to the auctioneer as agent for the seller.

3.137 SCPC 2.3 contains the same provisions but with an additional provision 2.3.7. This states that if any cheque tendered in payment of all or part of the deposit is dishonoured when first presented, the seller may, within seven working days of being notified that the cheque has been dishonoured, give notice to the buyer that the contract is discharged by the buyer's breach.

3.138 In addition to SC 2.3 and SCPC 2.3, the seller's practitioner will need to consider whether any additional special conditions are appropriate. The following is a summary of the special conditions that are recommended for use when acting for a seller at auction:

(a) no entitlement by the buyer to withdraw a bid once made;

(b) full disclosure of any tenancies subject to which the property is sold;

(c) reservation of the right by the seller to withdraw the property from sale at any time during the auction;

(d) no right of the buyer to raise any enquiries, objection, or make any requisition after the auction;

(e) no sub-sales permitted by the buyer (for more information on sub-sales, see 3.167); and

(f) buyer to reimburse seller for any search fees and any purchase deed engrossment charges.

3.139 Occasionally last-minute alterations may be necessary to the auction particulars or conditions. If so, an oral statement can be made just before the auction begins, advising prospective bidders of the changes. Successful bidders should produce identification sufficient to enable money laundering checks to be carried out on them by the auction house. Indeed some auction houses insist on pre-registration by prospective bidders in any event before the auction. Seller identification checks are also important to counter the possibility of fraudulent sales (see *Greenglade Estates Ltd v Chana and Strettons Ltd* [2012] EWHC 1913).

CONDITIONAL CONTRACTS

3.140 A conditional contract may be proposed (usually by the buyer) where the parties are ready to exchange but an important matter is still outstanding, for example where the buyer is still waiting for a satisfactory local search, mortgage offer, or planning permission. If the contract is created conditional upon the buyer's receipt of a satisfactory local search, this is a condition precedent to the performance of the contract. It means there can be no binding contract unless and until the condition is satisfied. Accordingly, a seller would normally be advised to resist such a condition for the obvious reason that it would allow the buyer to walk away from the contract if the condition remained unfulfilled.

3.141 We are of the opinion that conditional contracts are generally not to be recommended because they create an element of uncertainty concerning the parties' rights and obligations. In particular, sellers should resist pressure from buyers to enter into conditional contracts. Why not simply delay exchange until the buyer is ready to exchange unconditionally?

3.142 Conditional contracts should *never* be used where either party has a related *unconditional* sale or purchase. For example, suppose your client is buying and selling, with each transaction being dependent on the other in the normal way. You exchange on the purchase as usual (i.e. an unconditional contract) and contemporaneously you exchange a conditional contract on the sale (e.g. subject to the buyer receiving a satisfactory mortgage offer). If the buyer's mortgage offer is not forthcoming, your client will end up with two properties.

Likewise, consider the sale of a lease where the lease stipulates that the landlord's prior **3.143** consent to the sale is required. If the SCs are adopted, SC 8.3 makes the contract conditional on the landlord's consent being given, failing which either party may rescind the contract. Beware of this if your client is buying or selling a lease and your client has a related transaction.

Another danger with conditional contracts is that the law in this area is complex and **3.144** unless great care is taken in drafting the conditions a court may declare the condition void for uncertainty. In *Lee-Parker v Izzett (No 2)* [1972] 1 WLR 775, a contract expressed to be 'subject to the purchaser obtaining a satisfactory mortgage' was held to be void for uncertainty because the condition was too imprecise. Limitations of space do not permit a detailed consideration of the law in this area, or the reproduction of lengthy precedent clauses. However, to assist practitioners we have set out, in the Online Resource Centre, a suggested special condition where completion of the contract is to be conditional upon receipt of a satisfactory local search (one of the most common conditions).

KEY POINTS SUMMARY

CONDITIONAL CONTRACTS

In general terms the following principles of good practice should be noted when drafting **3.145** conditional contracts:

- Define the condition precisely:

  (a) If it relates to the buyer obtaining satisfactory planning permission, specify the exact nature of the permission required and what conditions annexed to the consent would entitle the buyer to withdraw.

  (b) If the condition relates to the buyer's mortgage offer, specify the amount required, details of the proposed lender, and acceptable interest rates.

  (c) If the condition relates to the buyer's local search, specify those adverse replies which would entitle the buyer to withdraw.

  (d) If the condition relates to the buyer's survey, specify the type of survey, the name of the surveyor, and the defects revealed by the survey which would entitle the buyer to withdraw.

- Set time limits for fulfilment of the condition. For example, by which date must the mortgage offer, local search or planning consent be received? It is important to get this right because time for the performance of the condition is of the essence and cannot be extended (see *Aberfoyle Plantations Ltd v Cheng* [1960] AC 115).

- Rather than make up the condition yourself, find a precedent (e.g. from the *Encyclopaedia of Forms and Precedents*) and adapt it carefully to suit your client's needs (see the Online Resource Centre for precedent clause on satisfactory local search).

OPTION AGREEMENTS

In simple terms, a typical option agreement is a contract in which the grantee of the option **3.146** (the buyer) is able, within a fixed period, to serve notice on the owner requiring the latter to transfer the land to the buyer. The option is a particularly useful tool for developers wishing to acquire several pieces of land from different owners in order to develop a larger site. Once the developer has secured options over all the pieces of land, it has effectively gained control of the development site and can safely apply for planning permission. Once planning permission is obtained, the developer can exercise all the options to ensure that it owns every part of the proposed development site. Note that the grant of an option to purchase a new freehold commercial building which is less than three years old is standard-rated for VAT purposes. A more collaborative arrangement, known as a 'Promotion Agreement', has become increasingly popular in recent years. This involves all the various landowners entering into a single joint venture agreement with the developer which sets out the rights and obligations of the owners and how the sale proceeds will ultimately be distributed.

Formalities

3.147 When the option is exercised a binding contract for the sale and purchase of the land comes into existence at that point. The exercise of the option does not have to satisfy s 2 of the Law of Property (Miscellaneous Provisions) Act 1989 and thus only requires the signature of the grantee of the option (see *Spiro v Glencrown Properties Ltd* [1991] Ch 537). However, the original option agreement itself is a land contract and must satisfy s 2 of the Law of Property (Miscellaneous Provisions) Act 1989. In other words, the option agreement must be in writing, incorporate all the agreed terms, and be signed by both parties.

3.148 The courts will construe time limits in option agreements strictly, i.e. time is of the essence (see *Hare v Nicoll* [1966] 2 QB 130).

Option fee

3.149 In return for the grant of the option, the grantee will normally pay the owner an option fee as consideration. The fee may be nominal but is more likely to be substantial if the owner recognizes the development potential of his land. The option fee is sometimes deducted from the purchase price if and when the option is exercised, and the land transferred. The method of calculating the purchase price for the land will normally be agreed at the time the option is granted. It will be either a fixed price, the market value at the time the option is exercised, or the development value to be determined by a valuation formula in the option agreement.

Other terms

3.150 The grantee of the option will normally be expected to investigate title before entering into the option. The option agreement will record this by stating that title having been deduced, the grantee shall not raise any requisition or objection to it. The agreement should provide for a completion date for the purchase, for example ten working days after service of the buyer's notice exercising the option. The method of service of the notice should also be made clear, for example 'notice in writing served on the grantor on or before . . .'. As with ordinary contracts, the agreement should also provide for the incorporation of general conditions of sale, for example the latest SCPC. This avoids an 'open' contract and the consequent complexities of consulting common law and statute if there is a dispute. The grantee may require a warranty from the owner that it will not encumber the land without the grantee's consent.

Registration of option

3.151 Owners who grant options must of course appreciate that the land will be tied up for the length of the option period and any sale of the land by the owner will be subject to the rights under the option (provided the option is registered). Consequently, an option is an estate contract and as such the grantee must protect it by registration. In registered land this is done by lodging either an agreed or unilateral notice on the grantor's title. In unregistered land, this is done by registering a class C(iv) land charge against the name of the grantor. Only registration of the option will make it binding on any subsequent purchaser of the land; actual notice of the option by a subsequent purchaser will be irrelevant (*Midland Bank Trust Co. Ltd v Green* [1981] AC 513).

Put option

The classic form of option described in 3.146 is known as a 'call option'. There is, however, another rarer form of option, which is the reverse of this, known as a 'put option'. This is where the grantor is the prospective buyer and the grantee the prospective seller. In a put option it is the seller who is able to require the buyer to purchase the land. This may occur, for example, where the seller wants the buyer to be locked in to a fixed price in a potentially falling market. The remaining terms of the put option will be substantially the same as those of a call option, for example establishing price, setting completion date, prior deduction of title, etc.   **3.152**

CONTRACT RACES

A contract race arises when a seller decides to deal with more than one prospective buyer, thus creating a 'race' by the buyers to see who can secure the property by being first to exchange contracts. A contract race raises an issue of professional conduct for the seller's conveyancer, who must achieve Outcome 11.3 of the Code of Conduct. A seller's conveyancer who fails to disclose a contract race may also be liable in negligence.   **3.153**

Outcome 11.3 of the Code of Conduct

Where the seller instructs you to deal with more than one prospective buyer, you must inform all buyers immediately of the seller's intention to deal with more than one buyer. Telephone conversations should be confirmed by letter or e-mail. However, in line with your duty of confidentiality to the client (Outcome 4.1) the seller's confirmatory instructions should be obtained *before* such disclosure is made. If the seller refuses to consent to the disclosure, you must immediately cease to act for the seller.   **3.154**

It is a misconception among some practitioners that a contract race must have rules (e.g. first buyer to present signed contract and deposit cheque wins). This is not so—the only obligation is to tell the other side of your client's decision to deal with more than one buyer. In fact if you do nothing more, it allows the seller greater flexibility in deciding with whom he wishes to exchange. It can also avoid disputes about who actually won according to the rules. Conversely, if you are acting for a buyer in a contract race, it is worth trying to establish the ground rules. In any event, if you do decide to set rules (e.g. first party ready to exchange unconditionally will win), ensure that they are recorded clearly and unambiguously in writing.   **3.155**

Meaning of 'deal with more than one buyer'

Essentially this includes providing any documentation or information in order to facilitate the conveyancing process (e.g. the title number, plan, or draft contract). It does not cover activities normally undertaken by an estate agent, such as negotiating the price or showing people round the property.   **3.156**

3.157 Note that the seller's conveyancer must satisfy Outcome 11.3 in a situation where he knows that his client is dealing with another prospective buyer, either directly or through another conveyancer. Because of an unavoidable conflict of interest, Indicative Behaviours 3.13 and 3.14 in the Code effectively prevent a practitioner from acting for more than one of the prospective buyers, or (in any circumstances) both the seller and one of the prospective buyers.

SELLER NOT YET REGISTERED AS PROPRIETOR

3.158 In times of sharply rising property values, the property trader will of course often buy and sell land to realize a gain. It follows that a trader who has recently acquired property may then immediately decide to sell for quick profit. If so, the trader now selling may not yet be registered at Land Registry as the registered proprietor. The implications of this for conveyancers are now considered in relation to both registered and unregistered land.

Registered land

3.159 The Land Registration Act 2002 imposes no restrictions on the rights of the parties to make their own arrangements as to the steps that a seller who is not the registered proprietor should be required to take to perfect his title. Instead, the Lord Chancellor has power to make rules specifying such steps, and such rules would override the terms of any agreement between the parties (2002 Act, Schedule 10, para 2).

3.160 At the time of writing, no such rules have been published. Accordingly, in a situation where a buyer wishes to complete before the seller is registered as proprietor, the buyer's practitioner would be advised to safeguard the buyer's position by examining the following:

(a) official copies of the registered title, showing the seller's predecessor as registered proprietor;
(b) a clear Land Registry search against the title;
(c) a copy of the completed transfer from the registered proprietor to the seller; and
(d) evidence that the seller has lodged a correct application for registration within the priority period of the Land Registry search.

3.161 In addition, the buyer should insist that the seller agrees in the contract to expedite the seller's own Land Registry application (which may involve payment of an expedition fee), and to help answer any requisitions raised by Land Registry in connection either with the seller's or the buyer's application for registration. Always ensure that these contractual provisions will remain in existence after completion (i.e. that they do not merge on completion). SC 7.3 (or SCPC 9.4) provides that completion does not cancel liability to perform any outstanding obligation under the contract.

3.162 When electronic conveyancing is introduced, the 'registration gap' will disappear, because a buyer will be registered as proprietor of the property simultaneously with completion taking place. Until then, the buyer will need to continue to take the safeguards mentioned.

Unregistered land

3.163 Where the seller's pending application is for first registration of title, the buyer's practitioner should examine the unregistered title, including the conveyance to the seller, and be satisfied that the title is good and marketable and that Land Registry will grant absolute title. As with registered land, it is advisable to see evidence that the seller has lodged a correct application for registration (in this case, first registration) and that the seller agrees to assist with any Land Registry requisitions.

The turnaround of registration applications by Land Registry is now much quicker than it **3.164** used to be before computerization. Many offices pride themselves on a turnaround measured in days rather than weeks or months, and it is always worth checking with the Registry as it may be simpler just to wait for the seller to become registered.

SUB-SALES

Generally

A sub-sale occurs where A contracts to sell to B who, before completion, contracts to sell **3.165** the same property to C, usually at a higher price. The sub-sale contract is between B and C. After the two contracts are exchanged, one purchase deed will transfer the legal estate from A to C at the direction of B. The benefit for B in having a single purchase deed is that B need not apply to be registered as proprietor (while on completion receiving the difference in price between the two contracts).

Preliminary matters

Before preparing the sub-sale contract (B–C) the practitioner acting for B must ensure that **3.166** the terms of the A–B contract do not prohibit a sub-sale. SC 1.5.1 and SCPC 1.5 provide that the buyer is not entitled to transfer the benefit of the contract. SC 1.5.2 states that the seller cannot be required to transfer the property in parts or to any person other than the buyer. This effectively prevents a sub-sale unless SC 1.5.1 and 1.5.2 or SCPC 1.5 is excluded by a special condition (see *Pittack v Naviede* [2010] EWHC 1509).

Sub-sale contract special conditions

When drafting the sub-sale contract (B–C), the practitioner for B should consider the fol- **3.167** lowing matters (which can be covered in the special conditions):

(a) Consider the points mentioned in 3.158 in relation to someone (B) seeking to sell before registered as proprietor.
(b) The provisions of the B–C contract should be consistent with the provisions of the A–B contract, for example same completion date, same contract rate, etc.
(c) Importantly, B must be able to serve notice to complete on C even if the A–B contract has not been completed. SC 6.8.1 (or SCPC 8.8.1) provides that a party cannot serve notice to complete without being 'ready able and willing' to complete. On a proper construction of this phrase in the context of a sub-sale, B would not be ready, able, and willing to complete until the A–B contract is completed (see *Cole v Rose* [1978] 3 All ER 1121). Accordingly, SC 6.8.1 (or SCPC 8.8.1) should be amended by an appropriate special condition.
(d) Expressly provide that the transfer or conveyance will be from A to C at the direction of B. This enables B to transfer his equitable interest in the property (acquired when the A–B contract is exchanged) to C.
(e) C will normally be paying more for the property than B. Accordingly, B must ensure he receives the difference in price. The contract should therefore provide that the purchase deed will apportion the purchase price between A and B, with each giving a receipt for his share.

Registration of the sub-sale contract

3.168 Once the sub-sale contract (B–C) has been exchanged, C is at risk because completion of the sub-sale contract is dependent upon completion of the A–B contract. The practitioner for the sub-buyer (C) should therefore protect C's interest under the sub-sale contract by registration. For unregistered land a C(iv) land charge (estate contract) should be registered against the legal estate owner, A (as the legal estate owner is A, not B). For registered land, a notice should be lodged against A's title.

PRACTICAL CHECKLISTS

PRE-DRAFTING

3.169 **Acting for seller**

Obtain the deeds from the mortgagee or seller. The mortgagee will require your undertaking to hold the deeds to order pending redemption:

- If the property has registered title, apply for official copies of title online or on Form OC1 plus copies of other documents referred to on the title (Form OC2).
- Investigate the seller's title and, if title is unregistered, carry out the necessary land charges searches against previous estate owners (unless valid searches are already with the deeds).
- Check that the contract implies that the seller is selling free from incumbrances. It is important to disclose in the draft contract all latent incumbrances and defects in title.
- Obtain details of occupiers of the property. In particular, is there a non-owning spouse or civil partner? The contract will imply that Home Rights are released. Obtain from the occupiers release of any rights of occupation and an agreement to vacate on completion.
- Check the seller's capacity to sell. What conditions, if any, need to be satisfied before the seller can deal with the property?

3.170 **CONTENTS OF CONTRACT**

If the Protocol is being used, the contract should be drafted on the Law Society Standard Form of Contract incorporating the current edition of Standard Conditions of Sale (SCs):

- Ensure that the contract contains all agreed terms to satisfy s 2 of the Law of Property (Miscellaneous Provisions) Act 1989.
- Check that the description of property is accurate and any plan is to scale.
- Consider which SCs or SCPCs should be amended by special condition.
- Consider special conditions generally.
- Where the sale is dependent on a related purchase, ensure that the terms of the two contracts are consistent and protect your client.
- Will the deposit be held as agent or stakeholder? Under the SCs, a sale deposit can be utilized towards a related purchase deposit.
- What title guarantee will be given by the seller, if any?
- Check whether the seller will need an indemnity covenant from the buyer.
- Do any of the special situations discussed in this chapter apply to the present transaction? If so, take appropriate action.

SALE OF PART

The seller must obtain consent of any existing mortgagee. How much money will the mortgagee require on completion?

- Draft the new accurate description of the part being sold by reference to a scale plan; define the seller's retained land.

- Draft any new easements and covenants expressly as special conditions (do not rely on SCs, SCPCs, or implied rights under common law or statute).

- What express easements will the buyer wish to be granted over the land being retained by the seller? (The seller should negate any implied rights in favour of the buyer.)

- What express easements will the seller wish to reserve over the land being sold to the buyer? (Remember that, unlike for buyers, no implied rights are reserved in favour of the seller.)

- Possible easements to consider:

  - Are there any rights of way? With or without vehicles? At certain times only? Who will be responsible for repairs and maintenance? Specify the route on the contract plan.

  - Is there a right to lay new drains, pipelines, cables? Is there a right to connect into and use existing drains, pipelines, cables? Who will be responsible for repairs and maintenance?

  - Is there a right to enter adjoining land to inspect and repair above? If so, when? Is there any notice to be given? Do you need to make good any damage caused? Specify the route on the contract plan.

  - The seller should negate any implied grant of easements in favour of the buyer.

  - What new covenants do the parties wish to impose? If possible, express them as negative restrictions (not positive) so that the burden will pass to successors.

- Possible covenants to consider:

  - use of the land;

  - restriction on new buildings;

  - avoiding nuisance;

  - maintenance and repair of buildings;

  - restriction against parking on or blocking right of way; and

  - fencing.

- For precedent clauses, see the worked example from 3.121 to 3.130.

- Remember that sale of part contract issues are relevant on the sale of a new property on a new estate (see Chapter 11).

4

PRE-CONTRACT SEARCHES AND ENQUIRIES, TOWN AND COUNTRY PLANNING

In this chapter, we will consider what searches need to be made before exchange of contracts, what preliminary enquiries (in their various forms) should be asked, and conclude with a concise look at planning issues as they may affect a subject property.

A PRE-CONTRACT SEARCHES

WHY DO SEARCHES?

4.01 'Let the buyer beware' *(caveat emptor)* remains a cornerstone of conveyancing in England and Wales. As such, a buyer will need to find out as much as possible about the subject property before contracts are exchanged. This is true for both commercial and residential transactions. The simple yet compelling reason for this is that the buyer must take the property in whatever condition it is in, at the point when there is a binding contract for the purchase. The law imposes a clear obligation on the buyer to find out about the property, in that the common law recognizes that the seller has only a limited duty of disclosure. (However, see *Rignall Developments Ltd v Halil* [1987] 3 Ch 170, in which it was made clear that there is a duty of disclosure if a seller is aware of a subsisting local land charge.) Because of this, a prudent buyer needs to discover as much as possible about the property being purchased. Usually, this will be by both pre-contract searches and preliminary enquiries, also called pre-contract enquiries. Therefore, the buyer must carry out all appropriate searches and enquiries before entering into a binding contract to purchase the subject property.

4.02 However, Parliament and the courts have confirmed that a buyer has notice of incumbrances that are registered under various statutes. For example, many matters of major concern to an owner of property involve the local authority. These matters will be discussed later in this chapter, but it is important to realize that they will bind a buyer whether or not a search is carried out. This is true for all searches normally made before contracts are exchanged and is of course the reason for making such searches before a binding contract is in place. Accordingly, it is essential that a buyer makes all necessary searches and not just the usual search with the local authority.

Practitioners must bear in mind that if they fail to carry out every appropriate search, they **4.03** will be liable in negligence for any loss suffered by their client as a result of their negligent conveyancing. The moral of the story for prudent practitioners is to carry out as many searches as they can, even if some of them seem obscure or unlikely to apply. The point is that any one of them might just throw up an onerous registration which could be of material consequence to the buyer (see *Cooper v Stephenson* (1852) Cox M & H 627). Surely it is better from a practical point of view to err on the side of caution by making searches that may at first seem inappropriate. It might just mean that an outlay of £25–£50 on an obscure search could avoid a claim in negligence costing thousands of pounds.

WHAT SEARCHES SHOULD YOU DO, AND WHEN?

The following searches will be considered, all of which may be required prior to an **4.04** exchange of contracts and can be relevant to both commercial and residential transactions:

(a) Local authority search and enquiries (see 4.06).
(b) Commons registration search—Part II Optional Enquiry 22 (see 4.23).
(c) Coal mining search (see 4.24).
(d) Index map search (see 4.26).
(e) Land charges search (see 4.29).
(f) Company search (see 4.31).
(g) Other searches dependent upon the location of the property (see 4.32).
(h) Physical search or inspection of the property (see 4.34).
(i) Environmental searches (including flooding) (see 4.44).
(j) Water and drainage search (see 4.50).

A prudent practitioner will carefully consider this list to decide which search or searches **4.05** will be required in each transaction. The selection will vary depending on the location and nature of the subject property.

Local authority search and enquiries

No conveyance, transfer, mortgage, or remortgage should proceed without (1) a search **4.06** of the local land charges registry; together with (2) enquiries of the local authority. Such is the importance of these two that the search application should come up automatically at the start of any new purchase. The search is made at the local authority, accompanied by a plan if the land is not easily identifiable from the postal address. A fee is charged for the search and since 1 April 2017 VAT is payable on the search fee.

The Land Registry is to become the sole registering authority for Local Land Charges (LLC) in England and Wales and the sole provider of official search results. The Infrastructure Act 2015 provides for the transfer of responsibility for LLC from local authorities to Land Registry. Preparatory work on the new service began in April 2015. Unofficial searches of the LLC register will continue, as now, to be provided by personal search companies where required. Changes to the Land Registration Act 2002 and Local Land Charges Act 1975 are necessary to enable the Registry to offer the service. A pilot for CON29 searches (the questions asked of the local authority: see 4.18) will be developed with a number of local authorities and the private sector at the same time. Eventually it may be that the proposed reform leads to a situation in which the Land Registry provides search results from the LLC register but replies to CON29 requests will still be dealt with by the local authority; in effect, this means that for any conveyancer there will be two search requests, as against one currently. On the other hand, Land Registry says that with the passage of the Infrastructure Bill, which gained Royal Assent in February 2015, this will allow it to develop a single digital LLC service. The implementation of the LLC project will support wider Government priorities to facilitate land and property conveyancing and to make public data more easily accessible for the benefit of the wider economy. Land Registry says that there are over 20 million records to be put on the LLC database and this will be done by one local authority after another, i.e. area by area. Accordingly, the intention is that through the Local Land Charges programme, the Land Registry will deliver a single, digital Local Land Charges Register, standardizing the cost, speed, and format of results. The Registry will do this by centralizing and digitizing the current 326 Local Land Charges Registers in England, held in a range of formats, and replacing them with a single digital register, available online. According to the Law Society Gazette 'Local land charges data in England is currently held by 326 local authorities: 10 handle paper data only; 99 handle paper and digital data; 217 are fully digital', (Gazette website, 8 December 2017). HM Land Registry is hoping to complete building work on a digital register for local land charges by 2023 after confirming that City of London Corporation has begun migrating its data to the central system in December 2017.

The search also directs important enquiries to the local authority concerned with subjects within their control such as road schemes, notices, or planning matters. A local search should be seen and approved by every purchaser before exchange of contracts. It will disclose public charges, many of which are not matters of title and so not within the seller's duty of disclosure (see 3.27–3.33 for further details). These charges will be registered by the local authority whose obligation it is to record them as required by the Local Land Charges Act 1975. Standard Condition 3 of the Standard Conditions of Sale makes a sale subject to local land charges. Accordingly, the buyer must have a search to make sure full details are obtained from the council of all relevant information affecting the property concerned. The search and enquiries are usually sent by post, but if the matter is urgent you can carry out a personal search of the local land charges register. Unfortunately not all councils will answer all the enquiries on a personal basis. If a complete set of answers is not going to be available, a personal search should be avoided because there will be no official search result upon which a buyer can seek to rely. (For a detailed consideration of personal searches, see 4.16.) Detailed consideration will therefore be given to the two elements of the process, namely a search of the local land charges register and then enquiries to be made of the local authority.

The local land charges register

4.07 This search is of such consequence and importance that it must be made in every conveyancing transaction. This is because of the effect of statute. The Local Land Charges Act 1975 requires each district, metropolitan borough, and London borough council to maintain a register of local land charges, being matters or burdens registered with them and disclosed on the public registers. From a practical point of view, the importance of the register to the practitioner is that these matters or burdens are registrable within the local land charges (LLC) register and nowhere else. Furthermore, an owner of property affected by such a registration is deemed to have full knowledge of it. Accordingly, a buyer must see a local land charges search result to be fully informed about these matters or burdens before exchanging contracts.

4.08 Before considering the various parts of the register, two points of confusion should be clarified. First, while LLC registers were originally established by the Land Charges Act 1925 practitioners must not confuse this search result with the land charges search, the details of which will be examined at 4.29. Land charges searches of this nature will also feature later when consideration is given to pre-completion searches. Second, practitioners will habitually refer to a local land charges search result, but this will also include replies to standard or 'additional' enquiries included with the form of local land charges search. These enquiries are answered by the local authority when issuing the result of the search in the LLC registry. Indeed, in many search results there are no entries to disclose in the register but there are fundamentally important answers to enquiries that will be of major concern to a buyer. These will be considered later in this chapter at 4.18.

To begin with, we will examine the LLC register. The important matters or burdens in the **4.09** register are identifiable and set out in the search within 12 constituent parts of the register. They are generally of a financial nature or relate to the use of the land. The 12 parts are:

1. General financial charges;
2. Specific financial charges;
3. Planning charges;
4. Miscellaneous charges;
5. Fenland ways maintenance charges;
6. Land compensation charges;
7. New towns charges;
8. Civil aviation charges;
9. Open-cast coal mining charges;
10. Listed buildings charges;
11. Light obstruction notices;
12. Drainage scheme charges.

As will be immediately apparent from the list, some parts of the register are more commonly **4.10** encountered than others. Indeed, in some ways, because of the different types of charges, results affecting rural properties will be different from urban properties, and results affecting commercial properties will be different from residential properties.

The distinction between registered and unregistered land is irrelevant for the LLC register; **4.11** such charges apply across the board. The local authority can enforce all these charges save for part 11, which remains the concern of the individuals concerned, and parts 8 and 9, which are predictably enforceable by the relevant statutory authority.

The list of the 12 parts highlights the kind of information that will be disclosed in the **4.12** search result. This includes various financial charges that will affect the property, planning consents concerning the property, and compulsory purchase orders, as well as tree preservation orders. Additionally, other registrations of consequence will be revealed, such as whether or not the property is within a conservation area or smoke control zone. In the case of this last kind of restriction the client will need to be advised of the restrictive nature of the registration and how it might affect the property and its neighbourhood.

Once the search result is issued, it should be appreciated that there is no priority period **4.13** for the result, or indeed any other form of protection given by the search. Clients should be made aware of the fact that if an adverse entry is made the day after the search result is issued there is absolutely no protection available. In effect, all the search result gives is an indication of the entries in the register at the time of the issue of the search result, and nothing else. However, s 4 of the Local Land Charges Act 1975 does provide a limited form of protection. Should an error or omission be made in the search result there are limited rights to claim compensation. An entry in the register remains lawful notwithstanding the error or omission and an owner of the subject property will still be subject to it. To address this difficulty, search validation schemes have arisen. These exist to offer protection to a buyer so that on payment of a premium, insurance cover will be available against onerous entries being made after the date of the search result and before exchange. The compensation available is for the loss in value as a result of the registration. Because buyers prefer a 'clean' situation—that is to say, where there is a clear search result rather than the possibility of compensation—these schemes have not been particularly successful.

4.14 For the busy conveyancing practitioner the following entries should in particular raise some concern and require further action. However, this is not an exhaustive list and all entries disclosed in the search result should be read carefully and considered before the result is put away in the client's file.

(a) **Compulsory purchase orders**   This speaks for itself. The buyer cannot proceed as the local authority intends to purchase the property compulsorily.

(b) **Conservation areas**   This topic is complex and is therefore considered further at 4.22 in the context of question 10 raised in the enquiries directed to the local authority.

(c) **Financial charges**   A typical financial charge is one arising out of the local authority having made up the road abutting the property and where there are outstanding monies payable by the owner for this road-making. These are of major consequence, as a buyer will not want to proceed with a purchase where there is money due to the local authority. If the purchase does proceed, either the seller must contract to pay off the council or an allowance should be made in the contract, with the buyer then taking over the liability.

(d) **Listed building registration**   Buildings can be deemed to be of special historical or architectural merit. If one falls into this category the Planning (Listed Buildings and Conservation Areas) Act 1990 controls the use and alteration of the property. These controls can be significant and a buyer must be informed of these details from the search result.

(e) **Tree preservation orders**   Buyers must be informed of such an order as it prohibits the felling or lopping of specific trees without the permission of the local authority. Failure to obtain consent may lead to a heavy fine.

(f) **Various planning entries**   These include planning consents containing conditions. A pitfall for practitioners here can be that on seeing an appropriate consent the practitioner assumes that the consent is acceptable without checking the conditions. The trap is that the conditions could preclude the buyer from benefiting from the consent. Always check conditions attaching to planning consents.

(g) **Assets of community value**   Part 5, Chapter 3 of the Localism Act 2011 provides for a scheme called 'Assets of community value' whereby local councils are required to maintain a list of 'community assets'. Assets are nominated to the local authority by parish councils or groups with a connection with the community, but not individuals. Once listed, owners must be informed and the asset must be registered in the LLC register (and as a restriction in registered land). If the nomination is accepted, the relevant group will be given time to come up with a bid for the asset when sold. However, bidding only arises when the owner decides to dispose of it; there is no compulsion to sell and no right of first refusal. The scheme does not create a community right to buy the asset, just to bid for it on sale. It should be noted that residential property is exempt from being on the register. This scheme has been effective from 21 September 2012. Owners of land placed on the register may appeal against its listing and owners can claim compensation if they can demonstrate its value has been reduced by the listing process. It should be noted that the asset must be a building or land and must further the well-being or social interests of the local community or have done so in the recent past.

4.15 The local land charges search is made by way of a standard requisition Form LLC1 through the post or transmitted electronically, and a prescribed fee will be payable to the local authority. The fee now varies almost annually. Unless the property is clearly identifiable by its postal description, a scale plan of the property should accompany the search request. In effect this means that long-established urban properties with a well-established postal address will not require a plan but new ones and rural properties almost certainly will. The search result may take up to several weeks to come back, although councils with electronic records can provide results in days, or even hours. Presumably the Land Registry will seek to provide a swift electronic service when they eventually assume responsibility. Accordingly, a practitioner should consider dispatching the search request at the earliest opportunity to ensure that delay to the conveyancing transaction is not occasioned. The National Land Information Service (NLIS) has been developed to provide search results over a computer network. (See 4.55 for further information on NLIS.) This Internet-based system does ensure the speedy return of search results.

Personal searches

It is possible to make a personal search of the register, although not all authorities make **4.16** this easy to do. There are commercial providers of personal search results. The difficulty is not so much access but that there is no guarantee of the accuracy of the result as of course it has not been officially issued by the local authority. Because of this, compensation under s 10 of the Local Land Charges Act 1975 is unlikely to be available. Personal searches should be made only as a last resort when there is extreme pressure of time, or when contracts are to be exchanged subject to searches with the possibility of a full and proper search result being available after exchange and before completion. A back-up form of insurance should also be considered in these circumstances, and the client should of course be informed in writing of the risks attaching to the reliance upon a personal search. If a practitioner is also instructed by a lending institution as well as the buyer then, unless that lending institution specifically authorizes the practitioner to proceed on the basis of a personal search result, the transaction should not proceed without there being an official search result to hand.

On 29 September 2006, a Search Code was introduced to try to set quality standards **4.17** across the private property search industry. The Search Code seeks to provide protection for homebuyers, sellers, conveyancers, and mortgage lenders, who rely on the information included in property search reports undertaken on residential property within the UK. The Search Code falls within the control of the Property Codes Compliance Board (PCCB), the details of which can be found at **http://www.propertycodes.org.uk**. The role of the PCCB is to ensure that private organizations providing property search reports comply with the Search Code. The Search Code is sponsored by the Council of Property Search Organisations and is responsible for setting the standards included in the Code, which will be reviewed at regular intervals with key industry bodies to ensure best practice.

Enquiries of the local authority

Accompanying the request for a search in the LLC register, practitioners also submit a set **4.18** of questions directed to the local authority. The questions are about topics that can be of critical consequence to a property owner and the answers to them are therefore just as important to receive as the result of the search of the LLC register. With effect from 4 July 2016 there is a set of pre-printed standard enquiries on Form CON29. These are made up of 'standard enquiries of local authority (2016 edition)'—CON29 Part I—and 'optional enquiries of local authority (2016 edition)'—CON29O Part II. Paper-based search requests must be submitted in duplicate. The Law Society consulted on proposed amendments to the CON29 and CON29O enquiry forms from 26 June to 1 August 2013. The aim of the consultation was to inform the production of updated CON29 and CON29O enquiries. Some of the proposed changes resulted from new issues, such as assets of community value and the community infrastructure levy. Other proposed amendments aimed to take account of recent legislative changes such as the Growth and Infrastructure Act 2013. The Law Society launched the new forms in July 2016.

4.19 There are now just three question sections in Part I, but each has several subsections. The three sections are concerned with:

1. Planning and building regulations;
2. Roads and public rights of way;
3. Other matters, which include nearby road schemes, traffic schemes, and contaminated land concerns.

Part II optional enquiries cover 22 different and very varied topics, including questions about noise abatement, food safety notices, hedgerow notices, and common land town and village greens.

4.20 Local authorities used to answer questions about drainage arrangements for properties. These are now controlled by local water and sewerage companies in almost every local authority area, and a separate standard form of drainage and water search (called CON29DW) has been agreed with Water UK, the body that represents water companies in England and Wales. However, questions on agreements for combined drainage and on agreements and consents for building over sewers have been retained, since those old agreements and consents may still be recorded in local authority records. We recommend that practitioners submit a separate drainage and water search to the local sewerage company, in addition to submitting the standard enquiries to the local authority. See 4.50 for further details of water searches.

4.21 Form CON29 should always accompany the local land charge search request. The questions in themselves are straightforward. However, in the main all that is represented is a rather confusing list of 'Yes' and 'No' answers adjacent to the number of the question concerned. This therefore means that practitioners must either memorize the questions or, more practically, have a reminder list to hand when looking at the usually dislocated answers. In time a 'feel', through familiarity, will be developed for the more important sections and alarm bells will ring if the answer is problematic. However, caution should be exercised, as familiarity with the form may induce a cursory look at the answers that might result in an important answer being overlooked.

The contents of CON29

4.22 To assist the busy practitioner in an understanding of the varying importance of the questions in Part I of CON29, they are now considered individually. Thereafter, we will look at some of the questions in Part II and guide practitioners in how to make selections from these optional enquiries. Please note that the following guidance notes look at the version of the forms in force at the time of publication.

Part I Standard enquiries, applicable in every transaction
1. Planning and building decisions and pending applications

There are two subsections to the first question, which are considered below:

1.1 **Planning and building regulation decisions and pending applications** This question asks the local authority to provide a list of approvals, refusals, certificates, and pending applications relating to the property in respect of the matters set out in the question. It is in this section that practitioners will be able to discover if the subject property is affected by any important planning concerns such as planning applications, permissions, listed building applications or permissions, and any applications or permissions in respect of conservation area consents. It now also covers planning agreements. These will all be of material consequence, including conservation orders, because they place very stringent restrictions on external alterations to properties affected by them. This question now extends to listed building consent orders and certificates of lawfulness of proposed works for listed buildings. Item (l) in this section takes account of building regulations which require approvals for replacement windows, rooflights, or roof windows, or for a replacement door with over 50 per cent of the door being glazed. (Approvals are not required if the work was completed by an installer registered under the Fenestration Self-Assessment Scheme (FENSA).) This topic is covered by a change in the Property Information Form Prop 1, shown on the Online Resource Centre that accompanies this book.

1.2 **Planning designations and proposals**   This question refers to the local development plan. This covers designation of land use (e.g. town centre/shopping) affecting either just the subject property, or the area it is in. It also covers any specific proposal for the subject property itself, arising out of the plan.

2. *Roads, and public rights of way*

This is an important section for the client in that it will indicate whether or not the local authority has adopted the road (i.e. will now maintain it at their expense) on which the subject property abuts. Alternatively, the answer will indicate whether there is or is likely to be a road-making agreement and bond. A road-making agreement will usually be between a developer and the local authority, setting out the terms upon which the roads in a new development are to be handled. Again, this is of importance when the client is buying a property on a new estate (please see Chapter 11 in relation to the particular concerns of which you need to be aware when you are involved in a conveyance within a newly built estate). The practitioner will want to reassure the client that the road is maintained at the public expense, or that it will be under the terms of a road-making agreement supported by an appropriate bond (Highways Act 1980, s 38). The bond, a financial guarantee, is pertinent to ensure that no liability will fall on the buyer to pay. If the property is not new but abuts an unadopted road, buyers should be made aware that if the local authority does decide to adopt it, the frontagers to the road could be liable for substantial road-making charges pursuant to s 219 of the Highways Act 1980. (There can also be problems of access over such roads, and rights of access must be carefully considered.) The question also covers footways and footpaths named in the application for the search.

This question now extends to details relating to public rights of way. Questions are raised about any public right of way that abuts or crosses the subject property to ascertain if any exist, are in the course of being applied for, being stopped up, diverted, or altered. If so, the final question (2.5) asks for a plan showing the approximate route.

3. *Other matters*

There are 15 subsections to the third question. They are preceded by the question: 'Do any of the following matters apply to the property?' This approach therefore covers those questions to which generally the satisfactory answer, from the buyer's viewpoint, is in the negative. If there is a positive answer the form goes on to enquire how copies of relevant documents can be obtained.

3.1 **Land required for public purposes**   This covers inclusion of the subject property in a category of land required for public purposes within Schedule 13, paras 5 and 6 to the Town and Country Planning Act 1990.

3.2 **Land to be acquired for road works**   A positive answer here will be concerned with land to be acquired for highway construction or improvement. Any disclosure should be reported to your client and, if applicable, the lender.

3.3 **Drainage**   The first part of this question is concerned with Sustainable urban Drainage Systems (SuDS). A SuDS is an alternative to conventional ways of managing surface water. In built environments they aim to mimic the way rainfall drains in natural systems, avoiding many of the problems typically caused by surface water runoff from developments. The questions seek to ascertain if the property is served by such a system or within the boundary of the property and whether the owner is responsible for maintenance. Alternatively, if a payment for a SuDS affects the property, who bills for the surface water drainage charge?

3.4 **Nearby road schemes**   This is a critical enquiry, and one to which great attention should be paid. Answers will highlight road schemes within 200 metres of the property, including alterations and improvements to existing roads as well as flyovers, underpasses, and roundabouts, or the widening by construction of one or more traffic lanes. The question will also reveal proposals at the early stage of issue for public consultation. Clearly, if there is a positive answer to any part of this enquiry, further details should be sought from the department concerned. Details of the department within the authority will be given in the answer. Exchange should be delayed until the buyer and any potential mortgagee have seen and accepted the road schemes in relation to the subject property. Wherever possible, plans of the road scheme should be obtained and shown to the buyer.

3.5 **Nearby railway schemes**   This question asks about the possible construction of a railway, monorail, light railway, or tramway within 200 metres of the property. It now also asks if there are any proposals for a railway, tramway, light railway, or monorail within the local authority's boundary. The council are required to give details of schemes notified to them as well as their own schemes. The reply must include details of light railways, tramways, and monorails, as well as ordinary railway proposals. Plainly, if a reply indicates that a railway is proposed, then a prudent purchaser should seek a detailed plan of the proposed route to see how the line of the railway might affect the property. All schemes should be listed where the centre line of the railway is within 200 metres of the subject property. If your client intends to purchase a property close to a line within the London Underground system, then you can request details from the Operational Estate Manager, London Regional Transport, Townsend House, Greycoat Place, London SW1P 1BL and a plan showing the location of the subject property will be required. An alternative address for London Underground is Customer Service Centre, London Underground, 55 Broadway, London SW1H 0BD.

3.6 **Traffic schemes**   This question is concerned with road closure and traffic schemes within 200 metres of the subject property. The question has been extended to include traffic calming (e.g. road humps), residents' parking, minor widening/improvement, pedestrian crossings, cycle tracks, and bridge construction. Clients will consider that this is a critical enquiry and one to which great attention should be paid. Wherever possible, plans of the relevant traffic scheme should be obtained and shown to the buyer, especially where the road affected is the one serving the subject property.

3.7 **Outstanding notices**   This enquiry is another example of a critically important question, particularly for buyers of commercial property. Answers here will disclose formal notices issued by the council under the Public Health Acts, Housing Acts, or Highways Acts. So, for example, if your client is buying a restaurant, this is where you should look to see if the seller has got into difficulty with hygiene regulations. Practitioners should note that notices under the Health and Safety at Work legislation are now included, as are notices regarding flood and coastal erosion risk management; and that the old reference to 'informal' notices has been dropped in view of uncertainty as to what comprised an informal notice. The effect of this is that answers will cover formal statutory notices only.

3.8 **Contravention of building regulations**   This will reveal whether the council has authorized any proceedings in respect of any contravention of any provision in building regulations. This is an important area to check when the client is buying a new or newly converted property. A buyer would not incur liability with the council as a consequence of a breach of these regulations. However, proceedings of this nature would of course indicate that there were structural matters of concern to the council and therefore to the buyer. (See also 4.109 for enquiries of the seller regarding building regulations.)

3.9 **Notices, orders, directions, and proceedings under Planning Acts**   The question contains a list of 13 different matters covered by the question. This includes enforcement notices and stop notices. The local authority will list all such notices, and an answer to 3.9 will show whether any that have been issued have been complied with to their satisfaction. Furthermore, an answer should bring to light any other contravention of planning control. Where entries are disclosed, full details should be obtained from the planning authority to see how extensively the property might be affected.

This answer will also reveal if the council has resolved to make a direction pursuant to Art 4 of the Town and Country Planning (General Permitted Development) Order 1995 (as amended), which in effect deprives the owner of land of the right to permitted development in relation to the use classes defined within the Order. (For a further explanation of the nature and effect of the Town and Country (General Permitted Development) Order, see 4.94.) Of course if an actual order has been made, it will be shown as an entry in the search result. If the council has decided to disallow permitted development rights of any particular class in the neighbourhood of the subject property then the buyer should be informed. The buyer can then consider if the restriction adversely affects the intended use of the subject property. Furthermore, an answer to 3.9 will disclose if the council has resolved to make orders revoking or modifying any planning consents, or discontinuing an existing planning use. Of particular importance to residential buyers is the fact that answers will also disclose if the subject property is going to be affected by a tree preservation order, or a listed building enforcement notice. If there is such a tree preservation order, it would be prudent to advise the client to check with a surveyor to ensure that the tree does not and will not in the future adversely affect the property, either structurally or by blocking light. Enquiries should also be made of the council to ascertain the subject matter of the listed building enforcement notice.

3.10 **Community Infrastructure Levy (CIL)**   The Community Infrastructure Levy is a planning charge, introduced by the Planning Act 2008 as a tool for local authorities in England and Wales to help deliver infrastructure to support the development of their area. It came into force on 6 April 2010 through the Community Infrastructure Levy Regulations 2010 (see 4.107). The first question asks if there is a CIL charging schedule. This is then followed by detailed questions seeking to ascertain if various notices have been served, such as a demand notice. Question (d) should be carefully considered, as this asks if the local authority has received full or part payment of any CIL liability. Similarly, the answer to question (h) should be considered carefully, as this asks if any enforcement measures have been taken.

3.11 **Conservation area**   This will confirm if a conservation area not disclosed in the official certificate of search affects the subject property. This will cover all such areas that were designated before 31 August 1974. The reason for this is that after that date conservation areas became land charges and are disclosed in searches of the LLC registry. However, the question will also ascertain if the property is in a recently declared, but as yet unregistered, conservation area. A buyer will want to know if the property is in such an area as there will, as a result, be limitations on development. Even minor alterations can be disallowed in a conservation area, and so this information may be crucial for a buyer intending to alter, demolish, or improve the property. In the past, grants have been available to homeowners in conservation areas to enable them to support the conservation of the property or to put it back into the condition it may have been in originally (e.g. the removal of modern window shapes and their replacement with the original style of windows).

3.12 **Compulsory purchase**   In addition to those orders disclosed on the official certificate of search, this answer will show if the subject property is likely to be affected by a compulsory purchase order issued by the local authority. (It should be noted that this answer would not cover other authorities entitled to obtain such orders, e.g. the utility companies such as a water company. Where there might be another authority involved, a direct enquiry should be made of that authority.) Both proposed and actual orders should be disclosed. Either way, an adverse answer will normally deter a buyer from proceeding.

3.13 **Contaminated land**   Under s 78 of the Environmental Protection Act 1990, local authorities are now required to answer questions about contaminated land. From 1 April 2000, local authorities must inspect land for contamination and ensure its remediation. (There are questions in Part II of the enquiry form directed to the local authority that cover other areas of concern relating to pollution; see later in this section for details.) The council must keep a register of land identified as contaminated and will show details about remediation. Answers to the question should give such details. Other parts of question 3.13 cover land that is at risk from nearby contaminated land.

3.14 **Radon gas**   A positive answer here will reveal if records show that the property is located in an area known for radon gas pollution. The property may be in an area where precautions against radon are required in new buildings. Buyers in parts of Devon, Cornwall, Derbyshire, Northamptonshire, and Somerset are advised particularly to note an answer to this question, as these are all areas that could be affected by natural radon gas emissions. Radon gas might cause lung damage, and possibly lung cancer. This question is therefore an important one in these particular locations. There is further guidance available from the Government at **https://www.gov.uk/government/collections/radon**, where there is also a link to the UK Radon site at **http://www.ukradon.org/**. This site contains further guidance regarding this potential health hazard and has a map of radon-affected localities in England and Wales. Radon information for homeowners can be found at **http://www.ukradon.org/sectors/householders**. Small radon detectors can be sent directly to householders by post, and returned at the end of a three-month period. Radon causes invisible damage to the plastic inside the detector. This damage can be measured and used to calculate the radon level. The householder is sent the result by letter. Concerned homeowners can order a radon detector pack from the Public Health England website **http://www.UKradon.org**. The estimated radon potential for an individual home can also be obtained through the same website. To arrange a Radon survey, interested parties should contact the Centre for Radiation, Chemical and Environmental Hazards, Chilton, Didcot, Oxon, OX11 0RQ, telephone 01235 822622.

3.15 **Assets of community value**   The questions here seek information about any nominations affecting all or part of the subject property that might be an asset of community value. (As to these assets see 4.14 (g) for further details of the scheme). If the scheme applies, then subsequent questions seek to find out the prevailing circumstances, for example (b) (iii) seeks to find out if any community interest group has asked to be treated as a bidder for the property. Clearly these questions should be carefully considered when dealing with susceptible properties such as local public houses or community halls.

Part II Optional enquiries

Part II of CON29 contains a further 22 optional enquiries (4–22) that may be asked of the local authority. These optional enquiries are set out in form CON29O. However, they must be specifically selected and additional fees will be payable. The best guidance for practitioners is that they should consider the necessity for any of these additional enquiries in the context of the particular circumstances of each purchase. For example, if a rented property were being purchased, it would be sensible to select question 9 dealing with houses in multiple occupation. Similarly, if the property is in the countryside, it would be sensible to select question 7, which covers parks and countryside issues such as whether or not the subject property is within a National Park. (This is important as it then imposes an additional layer of planning control exerted by the National Park Authority.) In relation to potentially contaminated land and the effects of pollution, question 10 is about noise abatement; question 17 covers hazardous substances consents; and question 18 covers environmental and pollution notices. Question 20 is a question that was introduced in 2002. This is to highlight the power local authorities have to serve notices under the Hedgerows Regulations 1997. (The Hedgerows Regulations 1997 were made under s 97 of the Environment Act 1995 and came into force on 1 June 1997. They introduced new arrangements for local planning authorities in England and Wales to protect important hedgerows in the countryside, by controlling their removal through a system of notification.) Question 22 (Common Land and Town or Village Green) is dealt with at 4.23.

Again, it should be noted that there is no priority attaching to the answers given by the council. However, it would be liable in negligence for answers prepared wrongly or recklessly. The extent of the council's liability will be judged in each case on the facts.

Some local authorities will answer these enquiries for personal applicants but they will not guarantee the accuracy of their replies! Perhaps of greater importance is that in many personal search applications the council will not answer all the questions in Part I. As such, a personal result is really of very limited use and should be used only as a last resort, with the client being made fully aware of the limitations of such a search result. It is unlikely that any prudent mortgagee would accept a personal search result in these circumstances.

Commons registration search—Part II Optional Enquiry 22 on Form CON29O

The case of *G & K Ladenbau (UK) Ltd v Crawley and de Reya* [1978] 1 WLR 266 brought **4.23** home to conveyancers the need always to consider the necessity for a commons registration search. In that case it was held that a solicitor should make this search if the property had never been built on or was the subject of very recent development, and that the solicitor would be liable in negligence if he or she did not carry out the search. Accordingly, if the subject property is unbuilt or newly built, then this search must be made. The search should also be made if the subject property is located next to a village green or common. The search is in the form of three questions of the local authority at question 22 on Form CON29O under the heading 'Common Land and Town or Village Green'. First, is the property or any land adjoining it registered common land under the Commons Registration Act 1965 or the Commons Act 2006? Second, is there any prescribed information about maps or statements and registered pursuant to the terms of the relevant statutes? If there are entries, question three asks how copy details can be obtained. An answer from the council will disclose if the land in question is a village green or a common. If a registration is disclosed by the search result, the buyer should be informed, as there could be the very real possibility of an adverse entry giving rise to such extreme possibilities as grazing cattle on the front lawn of a property. If the land is subject to a registration under this particular provision, it will almost certainly mean that no development or fencing off will be possible. The fact that planning consent may have been granted is irrelevant. It is for this reason, if for no other, that a commons search can be vital. A fee for the extra question is payable. A plan may be required. There is no priority or protection available for the search result. It may be possible to make this search via the NLIS; see 4.55.

Coal mining search

4.24   The purpose of this search is to reveal if the subject property is within an area of past or present coal mining, or indeed possibly future mining. This is of major importance as coal mining causes subsidence and subsidence damages buildings. Furthermore, coal mining is and has been an activity in areas that one now does not normally associate with coal, such as Kent. In each case a prudent practitioner should consult the Law Society's *Coal Mining Directory* to see if the property is located within an area where a coal mining search is required. You can also check by using the postcode search facility available at **https://www.groundstability.com**, the website for the Coal Authority (see 4.25). The Law Society's *Guidance Notes* of 1994 contain a list of towns and parishes that may be affected by mining either in the past, at present, or in the future. However, in this regard the guiding principle should be if in doubt, always make a search. Further information can be obtained by telephoning the Coal Authority customer services information line on 0845 762 6848. This search now covers brine extraction; see 4.32(c) for further details. However, the Cheshire Brine Subsidence Compensation Board is intending to take the provision of the brine searches back in-house from 1 April 2018 and is in the process of inviting tenders for that work from appropriate suppliers.

4.25   The Coal Authority was established by Parliament in 1994 to undertake specific statutory responsibilities associated with licensing coal mining operations in Britain alongside handling subsidence damage claims. These searches are now sent to the Coal Authority on Form CON29M. The fee is payable to the Authority for issuing the result, and a plan of the property can be required. On payment of an additional fee an expedited search result can be obtained. The result will highlight past workings, any subsidence arising, and any proposed workings. There is no priority or protection available for the search result. Residential coal searches now include insurance cover. This cover will be available to owners of property to mitigate against any loss of value up to a maximum of £20,000; and which is attributable to any material change of the mining information in a subsequent residential mining report from that contained in the report from which the insurance derives. The intention is to address the concern of practitioners about how long a mining report remains valid. This insurance will not cover commercial properties. Non-residential searches are possible for an increased fee. A practitioner should carefully note all answers to the standard enquiries in a coal mining search result as they can sometimes appear complex. Even when simply stated, the buyer should be advised of all answers, especially where future mining proposals have been disclosed. The buyer should be asked in these circumstances whether there is still an intention to proceed with the purchase notwithstanding the likelihood of future mining in the immediate locality. The Coal Authority now offers an interpretive report service. For an additional fee, this type of report will provide more detailed analysis and advice about mine entries. It will include a risk assessment as to whether the subject property is within a zone of ground movement. The search may be submitted electronically through the NLIS (see 4.55). For access to the online coal mining reports service and information about these searches, see **https://www.groundstability.com**, where online searches can be requested.

Index map search

This search should be made in all transactions where the subject property remains unregis- **4.26** tered. The Land Registration Act 2002 (the Act) affects the nature and content of this search. It is now made on HM Land Registry Form SIM and a fee can be payable. (Where no or not more than five registered titles are disclosed the fee is £4.) A plan to scale should be supplied. The search is sent to the appropriate Land Registry local office. The search is required because it will reveal on Form SIMR if all or part of the property is already registered at Land Registry. It will also reveal any pending applications for first registration, or a caution against first registration. It will give details of all titles affecting the property, both freehold and leasehold. (Commonhold will also be involved to the extent that if an applicant has received an official copy of a common parts title, and is applying for the title number of a commonhold unit, then the common part title number must be quoted on the form.)

In 2014, the Land Registry launched a free MapSearch service, a searchable online version of the index map. It allows business customers to locate any registered property in England and Wales without having to apply to the Registry for the information. With MapSearch a business customer can establish whether land and property in England or Wales is registered, view the location of registered land and property, obtain title numbers, details of freehold or leasehold tenure, and other registered interests, and save a PDF of any MapSearch made by them. In effect this is a free self-serve search of the index map. It is not covered by the Land Registry indemnity scheme. Therefore if this is required a SIM search is necessary. As at March 2016, Land Registry says that since the introduction of MapSearch there has been a reduction by over 50 per cent of SIM searches.

Plainly, if the property is registered or registered in part, the seller must be asked to remedy **4.27** what would seem to be a problem with the title before the buyer can proceed. A practitioner should also make sure that there have not been any dispositions that could give rise to first registration since 1 December 1990, when the whole of England and Wales became an area of compulsory registration. For example, if there has been a conveyance for value since that time and registration has not thereafter taken place, the seller has no title to sell until registration has taken place (see *Pinekerry Ltd v Kenneth Needs (Contractors) Ltd* (1992) 64 P & CR 245; see also s 7 of the Land Registration Act 2002, which makes unregistered transfers void for want of registration). Subscribers to the Land Registry Portal may use the facility to apply for a search of the index map electronically.

The Act continues the obligation of Land Registry to keep an index that shows what **4.28** registered titles and cautions against first registration affect any particular piece of land (s 68, and Land Registration Rules, r 10). It is possible for anyone to search the index map to find out if a particular piece of land is registered and, if so, under what title number. The Land Registry Rules 2003 specify the forms to be used (Form SIM) to make a search of the Index, the way in which the searches can be delivered to the Registry, and how the results of the searches will be delivered, on Form SIMR. There is also an index under the Land Registration Rules 2003, being an Index of Franchises and Manors, as well as an index of proprietors' names under r 11. To search for a name, an applicant can use Form PN1 (application for a search in the index of proprietors' names). A franchises and manors search may be useful when purchasing a substantial farm property. It would reveal the existence of any manorial rights, such as sporting or mineral rights, or franchises such as the right to hold a market or take a toll in a particular area.

Land charges search

This is a search of the Central Land Charges Register set up under the provisions of the **4.29** Land Charges Act 1925 as amended. The entries in this register in the main relate to unregistered land, and searches of the register are usually carried out after exchange of contracts. However, if the seller deduces title before exchange, a search will be possible and is to be recommended before rather than after exchange. This is because if a problem is disclosed by the search the buyer can always easily withdraw before there is a binding contract. A detailed examination of this search will be made in Chapter 8 dealing with pre-completion procedures.

4.30   Even where title has not been deduced, a land charges search against the seller can be made and will disclose important matters, including whether or not there are bankruptcy or other financial charges registered. Furthermore, the search will also disclose in unregistered land if the spouse of the seller (if not a co-owner) has registered a Class F land charge to protect rights of occupation in the property to be sold. Plainly, if there is such a registration, then it must be better to know about this as early as possible to allow time for negotiations to take place for the removal of the registration. (Under the Family Law Act 1996, a non-owning spouse has by virtue of his or her marriage to the owning spouse a right of entry and occupation of the matrimonial home. This right subsists with the marriage and in the case of registered land will be registrable as a notice in the charges register. Civil partnership unions are now covered by similar legislation and with comparable rights of occupation.) The search is made at the Government land charges department in Plymouth against the names of the estate owners, not the land, and for their periods of ownership stated as full years. Subscribers to Land Registry Portal service have the facility to lodge applications for searches at the Land Charges Department electronically. Search requests can also be made through the NLIS (see 4.55). You can fax a search request, but you must hold a variable direct debit account to use this service. You must use the prescribed form K15, K16, or K19 and fax it to: 0300 006 6699. The result will be posted to you. Land charge searches are not available to Land Registry account holders by telephone as the telephone search service has been abolished. Land charges enquiries can made on their Customer Support line on 0300 006 0411.

Company search

4.31   The Companies Register at Companies House contains the details of every private or public company registered in England and Wales. Where a buyer is purchasing a property from a company, a search at Companies House is necessary, especially where the property being purchased is unregistered. The search result will confirm if the selling company has the power to sell property under the constitution of the company (in the memorandum and articles of association). The search result will also highlight whether the company is being wound up, which could prevent the company from contracting to sell property. Whenever a company is selling land, be it registered or unregistered land, a company search must be carried out after exchange, i.e. before completion. Further details are set out in Chapter 8 concerned with pre-completion procedures and searches. Online searches are available from the Companies House website at **https://www.gov.uk/government/organisations/companies-house**.

Other searches dependent upon the location of the property

4.32   England and Wales can be viewed as a patchwork of exclusive localities—exclusive in the sense that each locality can have a speciality all to itself. Consequently, searches can be specialized or localized depending on the location of the subject property. Examples are:

(a) **Limestone-mining searches** If the property is located in Dudley, Sandwell, Walsall, or Wolverhampton, a search should be sent to the local council asking about limestone mining. The result will reveal the presence, or absence, of disused underground workings that could cause subsidence.

(b) **Clay-mining searches** If the property is located in Devon or Cornwall, a search should be sent to the Kaolin and Ball Clay Association asking about clay mining. The result will reveal the presence or absence of any operations which could cause subsidence. There is a postcode search possible where you enter your postcode to check whether or not you are in a Kaolin (china clay) or Ball Clay area. The web address for this is **http://www.kabca.org/postcode-search.php**.

(c) **Brine-extraction searches** Brine extraction is a method of mining for underground salt. If the property is located in Cheshire or Greater Manchester, a search should be sent to the Coal Authority asking about brine-extraction works in the locality. The result will reveal the presence or absence of old workings that could cause subsidence. (See 4.25 for details of the Coal Authority.) The authority responsible for the issue of these reports may well change. The Cheshire Brine Subsidence Compensation Board is intending to take the provision of the brine searches back in-house from 1 April 2018 and is in the process of inviting tenders for that work from appropriate suppliers. The Coal Authority, along with the Cheshire Brine Subsidence Compensation Board, is working with the Law Society regarding this change in process and will issue an update when more information is available.

(d) **Tin-mining searches** If the property is located in Devon or Cornwall, a search should be sent to Cornwall Consultants Limited (**http://www.cornwallconsultants.com/mining-searches/**) asking about tin mining. The search result will reveal the presence or absence of disused mines that could cause subsidence. In fact this company assists with the following mining searches:
  • Metalliferous Mining—for properties in Cornwall, Devon, and Somerset where tin, copper, lead, silver, and iron mining was widespread for over 3000 years;
  • Bath stone & Fullers Earth—for properties in areas of Bath, northeast Somerset, and west Wiltshire, where localized extraction of these deposits has been carried out since Roman times and remains active today.

(e) **The New Forest** If the property is located in Hampshire (and possibly parts of Dorset too), and is in or near to the New Forest, then a search could be considered with the Verderers of the New Forest. This is because by s 11 of the Commons Registration Act 1965 the New Forest was excluded from the provisions of that Act. This search may confirm if the land is common land or is affected by common rights (details can be found at **http://www.verderers.org.uk**). On the website there is a statement to the effect that '[t]here is no definitive register showing what lands within the Forest are subject to common rights. The Clerk to the Verderers may in many cases be able to give an informed opinion as to the likelihood of particular pieces of land being subject to rights, but this will be no more than general guidance. Persons investigating the title of land within the Forest will, in the final resort, have to rely on their own researches.'

Apart from the kind of localized searches listed above, there are other less common but **4.33** countrywide searches that practitioners should know about. They can be of particular importance where the property is near to a river or canal:

(a) **Rivers** The Environment Agency (and previously the National Rivers Authority) maintains details of all rivers, streams, and brooks. If the subject property is next to a watercourse, then a search will be necessary. It will provide details of liability for repairs to, and maintenance of, river banks as well as for floods from the river, etc. Flooding is also considered at 4.44. See also **https://www.gov.uk/government/organisations/environment-agency**.

(b) **Canals** The Canal and River Trust (formerly British Waterways Board) maintains details of all canals in the country. If the subject property is next to a canal, then, for the same reasons as set out in (a), a search by way of a letter should be sent to the Trust. The search can also enquire about rights of way, etc. affecting the towpath. See also **http://canalrivertrust.org.uk/**.

(c) **Railways**   Following privatization, Railtrack and now Network Rail have indicated that they would not assist with searches. It might be possible to elicit some information from the local authority under question 3.5 of CON29 Part 1; see 4.22. In London you can make enquiries of Transport for London (TfL); see its website at **http://www.tfl. gov.uk**.

(d) **Rent registration**   If a buyer is purchasing a rented or partly rented property, then a search should be made to check on registered rents under the Rent Act 1977. These should be directed to the local rent officer or First-tier Tribunal Residential Property Division. It is an offence for a lessor to charge more than the registered rent.

(e) **Chancel repairs**   This is a historical anomaly. A chancel is the part of a church containing the altar, sanctuary, and choir, usually separated from the nave and transepts by a screen. If the subject property is in a parish with a vicar of a medieval church, then there can be a liability to contribute to the cost of repairs to the chancel of that church. The client should speak to the local vicar and a letter should go to the Public Record Office. There was a report in *The Guardian* (11 March 2000, p 24) where it was stated that two homeowners were shocked to receive a bill for nearly £100,000 for work done to the chancel of the local parish church. As a result of ownership of a local property and the effects of the Chancel Repairs Act 1932, they were liable to pay. It appears that the Human Rights Act 1998 will not protect owners of such properties in future, and so practitioners should advise clients of the potential dangers of chancel repairs liability. See *PCC of Aston Cantlow v Wallbank* [2003] UKHL 37 in [2003] 7 PLC 47. There was a follow-up report in *The Guardian* (29 September 2009) that the Wallbanks—one of the parties in the above decision—'are being forced to sell because of an old law that makes them liable for major repairs at the church . . . . They hope to raise around £500,000 to cancel the liability, pay for the repairs and meet their legal bills—around £250,000.' However, the Land Registration Act 2002 took away from chancel repairs the status of an overriding interest (by abolishing s 70(1)(c) of the 1925 Act). As a transitional provision, the Land Registration Act 2002 (Transitional Provisions) (No 2) Order 2003 (SI 2003/2431) extended the overriding status of this interest for a transitional period of ten years. After 13 October 2013 chancel repairs have to be protected by an entry in the register. Until 13 October 2013 chancel repairs liability existed as an overriding interest, but thereafter the transitional arrangement ended. From that date the liability will not affect buyers where there is no registration (notice), but the liability will continue to affect owners whether or not there is a notice. So until 13 October 2013, in registered land, chancel repair liability was an overriding interest not requiring registration while, in unregistered land, the liability bound owners of the land. After 13 October 2013, in registered land, the liability is not an overriding interest and so the church must register protective entries to bind purchasers. Meanwhile owners will still be bound until a sale occurs. The church can still register, provided there has been no prior sale. In unregistered land, the church needs to register a caution against first registration but cannot do so if there has been a change in ownership. If there is no such caution registered the buyer takes free of the liability. A commercial search provider currently offers a screening report that establishes if a property is located within the boundary of a 'risk parish' which could charge for chancel repairs. 'Chancelcheck' is available online at **https://www.clsl.co.uk/find-out-more/chancelcheck/#intro**. Where potential risk is identified, the same company offers indemnity insurance.

(f) **Agricultural credits**   Where agricultural land is being purchased, an agricultural credits search should be made where a working farmer occupies farm buildings either as an owner or as a tenant farmer. The Agricultural Credits Act 1928 allows farmers to arrange bank floating charges. If there is a registration by the bank at the Land Charges Registry, a buyer will take subject to it; hence the need for this search. The search should be sent to the Agricultural Credits Department of the Land Charges section of Land Registry in Plymouth.

Physical search or inspection of the property

A buyer should always be advised to inspect the subject property prior to exchange. The reasons for the inspection are fivefold, each of which is considered in the following paragraphs.   **4.34**

To check the state and condition of the property

No buyer should purchase a property without fully inspecting the condition of all buildings being purchased. This is true for both residential and commercial transactions. In general a seller is under no obligation to reveal defects in the property. There is no warranty given about the state of the property and consequently all buyers should obtain their own survey report before contracting to purchase it. Practitioners should always bear in mind that the common law principle of *caveat emptor* ('Let the buyer beware') still applies to conveyancing transactions. Indeed, in the Standard Conditions (SCs), SC 3.2.1 states that the buyer accepts the property in the physical state it is in at exchange of contracts. (There is the same condition in the Standard Commercial Property Conditions (SCPCs).) A prudent buyer will therefore use the services of a professional adviser such as a chartered surveyor to inspect the condition of all buildings. Accordingly, it should also be carefully noted that in *Low v RJ Haddock Ltd* [1985] 2 EGLR 247 it was held that a buyer suing over damage caused by tree roots might be contributorily negligent if that buyer did not arrange a survey at the time of purchase. It therefore follows that every buyer should obtain a full survey report. However, if buyers do not, what other forms of redress will be available to them?   **4.35**

If there is a fault in the structure can the buyer sue the seller?

In general a seller is under no obligation to reveal defects in the property. There is no warranty given about the state of the property and it is of course for this reason that all buyers should obtain their own survey report before exchanging contracts. Remember that SC 3.2.1 provides that the buyer accepts the property in the physical state it is in at the date of the contract (unless the seller is building or converting it). However, if the seller has taken steps actually to cover up a physical defect, then this might be deemed to be a fraudulent misrepresentation. The misrepresentation would be that the property is free of that defect and as a consequence the seller could be liable. See the case of *Gordon v Selico Co. Ltd* [1989] 1 EGLR 71.   **4.36**

If the buyer purchased with the assistance of a mortgage, is there the possibility of a claim against the lender's surveyor? Certainly a surveyor who is neglectful and slack in his preparation of a survey report privately commissioned by the buyer is liable in negligence. (This is reinforced by s 13 of the Supply of Goods and Services Act 1982, whereby a term is implied that the report will be carried out with reasonable skill and care.) The damages will be the difference between the contractual purchase price and the true market value (see *Perry v Sidney Phillips and Son* [1982] 1 WLR 1297).   **4.37**

The surveyor will be under a duty of care of course to the lender (see *London and South of England Building Society v Stone* [1983] 1 WLR 1242). The question that must therefore be asked is whether the buyer is entitled to a similar duty. The case of *Yianni v Edwin Evans and Sons* [1982] QB 438 clearly shows that a surveyor will also owe a duty of care to the proposed borrower as well as to the lender. In this case it was held that if a report   **4.38** for a mortgagee was negligently prepared and as a result the buyer suffered loss, the buyer could sue the surveyor in negligence. In *Yianni* the buyer did not see the report, but the court was of the view that the surveyor had missed obvious structural defects and owed a duty of care to the buyer. This was further confirmed by the House of Lords in the case of *Smith v Eric S Bush* [1990] 1 AC 831. It was held that where a surveyor was instructed by the lender to survey a 'modest' house, the lender's surveyor did indeed have a duty of care owed to the borrower. It also had to be understood that the borrower would not be arranging his own survey and would rely on the lender's report.

4.39 The *Smith* case also highlighted the court's willingness to strike down exclusion clauses that are unfair and unreasonable and which contravene ss 2 and 3 of the Unfair Contract Terms Act 1977. Thus the report cannot exclude liability by the incorporation of an exclusion clause where a 'modest' house is concerned. This was again confirmed by *Merrett v John RH Babb* [2001] EWCA Civ 214, where a surveyor was held to owe a personal duty of care for a negligent valuation report.

To check who is in actual occupation of the property

4.40 This is critically important as the seller may not be the only person in actual occupation of the property and others could be entitled to occupy the property, notwithstanding that they are not co-selling. It is of real importance to check that there are no undisclosed occupants within the property who could claim rights of occupation and thereby delay, or indeed defeat, completion. For example, a spouse may have registered a protective entry giving rights of occupation even though he or she is not a legal owner. (Indeed, the Family Law Act 1996 greatly extended those who are entitled to enjoy and claim rights of occupation. Furthermore, parties to a civil partnership union are entitled to the same rights of occupation.) Adult children may be in occupation and may have rights. Beneficiaries under a trust may be in occupation and yet the seller may be the trustee who is not in occupation. Whether the land is registered or unregistered will not affect the position in that in both cases a buyer will be concerned to ascertain details of third-party occupiers. Schedule 3, para 2 to the Land Registration Act 2002 covers registered land. Unregistered land is governed by *Hunt v Luck* [1902] 1 Ch 428 and s 199(1)(ii)(a) of the Law of Property Act 1925. As well as physically inspecting the property, a buyer will also raise written enquiries about who is in occupation. This is dealt with at 4.70.

To check the boundaries

4.41 A buyer will want to be sure that the contract correctly describes the property and that the boundaries on the ground are the same as those shown on the title (in registered land as shown on the Land Registry title plan or in unregistered land within the title deeds) and in the contract.

To check on rights and easements affecting or benefiting the property

4.42 Patent defects in title (i.e. those apparent on inspection) do not need to be disclosed by a seller. Such a defect could be a right of way affecting the property. It is therefore important to inspect the property for evidence of rights of way such as signs, a stile, used pathways, or gates. If the buyer finds any evidence of easements adversely affecting the property then of course these should be referred to the seller without delay.

To check that the fixtures and fittings contracted to be sold are in the subject property just prior to exchange

4.43 The contract for sale may include a list of items included in the sale, or there could be items listed in replies to enquiries. In either case the buyer will want to be sure that the listed items actually exist and are within the subject property.

Environmental searches (including flooding)

In every transaction, both residential and commercial, a conveyancer must consider whether **4.44** contamination is a relevant issue. Searches and enquiries should be made about environmental concerns. The *UK Finance Mortgage Lenders' Handbook* says that a buyer's practitioner should 'carry out any other searches which may be appropriate to the particular property, taking into account its locality and other features'. Furthermore, practitioners should not merely rely on any contaminated land information obtained from the local authority in the reply to question 3.12 of the enquiries in the local authority search. This is because the detail supplied is likely to be insufficient, being limited to land identified by the local authority as contaminated or potentially affected by nearby contaminated land. An environmental search result should also reveal if the subject property is affected by contamination, whether directly (e.g. contaminants on the land) or indirectly (e.g. contaminants on nearby land). Failure to discover contamination could lead to liability under the Environmental Protection Act 1990. Liability for remediation rests with the 'appropriate person' (s 78). In the first instance this will be the original polluter. However, if that person cannot be traced, liability will then rest with the current owner. It is for this reason that this search result is now so important.

It is possible to make a search with the Environment Agency, but the results can take time **4.45** to be issued and the information likely to be available may not be widespread enough to be of real benefit. However, environmental searches can be obtained from the Landmark Information Group (**http://www.landmark.co.uk**), and they can assist with both residential and commercial properties. For residential properties, a 'RiskView Residential' report can be requested (tel. 0844 844 9966), which will cover current contaminating and polluting processes, coal mining areas, and radon-affected areas, as well as risk of subsidence and flooding. Commercial search results 'RiskView Commercial' are also available from the same company. At a more basic level, environmental risk can be checked without cost on the Internet at **https://reportfinder.landmark.co.uk/?source=homecheck**. The same company offers practitioners online searches at **http://www.homecheckpro.co.uk**. It will also provide a certificate, where possible, confirming that the subject property is not likely to be described as 'contaminated land' as defined by s 78 of the Environmental Protection Act 1990.

Flooding

The Environment Agency estimates that one in six homes (5.2 million) in England are **4.46** at risk from flooding. Of these, 2.4 million are at risk from flooding from river or the sea alone, with 3 million at risk from surface water alone and 1 million at risk from both. An estimated 200 homes are at risk of complete loss to coastal erosion over the next 20 years or so and 2,000 could potentially become at risk during this period. The Environment Agency has made maps available on the Internet that show areas potentially liable to flooding. This is a free service and can be accessed using a property postcode at **http://watermaps.environment-agency.gov.uk/**. The maps do not indicate the level of risk. An additional pre-contract enquiry of the seller asking whether the subject property had ever been affected by flooding would also seem prudent. Whether or not a property might be affected by flooding is now very important as some insurers will not cover a property for water damage if the insurer considers the property to be at risk of flooding.

The Government has been working with insurers to come up with a solution so that the **4.47** many properties lying in high flood-risk areas might be insured at affordable premiums without placing costs on other policy holders or the taxpayer. The funding of the scheme is to be borne from a levy on the insurers calculated in accordance with their market share as well as through premiums. 'Flood Re' is a flood re-insurance scheme and is a not-for-profit company managed by the insurance industry which commenced in April 2016. The scheme is to offer assistance to those at high risk of flooding, with calculation of the assistance available based on the level of Council Tax banding of the property in question. When the insurer identifies the property as high risk it will cede that part of the policy to Flood Re. In the event of a flood claim the insurers pay the customer and recoup the cost from Flood Re. Accordingly, homeowners insured but at risk will not notice any difference, as they will continue to be insured by their home insurer. Homes built after 1 January 2009 will not be covered: this is to avoid incentivizing unwise building in known high flood-risk areas. Commercial properties, including commercial leasehold properties, will not be included. Leasehold blocks with three residential units or fewer will be eligible for Flood Re providing the freeholder responsible for purchasing the buildings insurance lives in the block and the building meets the other required eligibility criteria. Further details can be found at **https://www.floodre.co.uk**.

4.48   The Law Society has produced a practice note to help solicitors protect clients from flood risk, especially those looking to buy property in flood-risk areas. The practice note provides solicitors with guidance to help their clients appreciate any flood risk, as well as to identify searches, reports, and investigations that may be needed to address the risks of property transactions in flood risk areas. This guidance can be seen at **http://www.lawsociety.org. uk/advice/practice-notes/flood-risk/**.

Indemnity insurance and contaminated land

4.49   There is an alternative approach. Countrywide Legal Indemnities offer an insurance solution. The insurance policy on offer is intended to cover homeowners against the potential liability for remediation costs of any contaminants found on their land. Full details can be found at **http://www.countrywidelegal.co.uk**, or by telephone on 01603 617617. The cover includes any shortfall in the market value of the property as a result of the remediation work having been carried out. Either way, conveyancing practitioners need to issue either a search request or arrange insurance to cover this potential area of concern.

Water and drainage searches

4.50   Local authorities used to answer questions about water supply and drainage arrangements for properties. Local sewage companies in most of England and Wales now have responsibility for this. There is a drainage and water supply search and all the water companies use it in a common format. It has been available since 1 April 2002. The search (CON29DW) now covers details on water supply, metering, and the proximity of a public sewer. Details of the search are available at **http://www.con29dw.co.uk**.

4.51   The water companies have agreed to provide extracts of sewage (and water supply) maps and base their search replies on model answers, which will explain the different circumstances that might affect a property. The search result could draw attention to the fact that a property owner may have to meet or contribute to the cost of repairs to a private drain and sewers as well as private supply pipes.

4.52   The full drainage and water enquiry search result will cover the following points:

- the name and address of the local water supply company if different from the company operating the sewerage system;
- whether there is a public sewer within the boundaries of the property;
- whether there is a public sewer within 100 feet of the property;
- whether the property is connected to the public water supply;
- whether there is a water main within the boundaries of the property;
- whether the property has foul drainage and surface water drainage to the public sewer;

- the basis on which foul drainage charges are paid, i.e. by water rates or water meter;
- whether there is a separate charge for surface water drainage and, if so, how it is calculated;
- whether a currently private sewer is subject to an adoption agreement (usually for a new property), and the current position in the adoption procedure;
- whether there is a current agreement or consent to construct a property or an extension to a property over or in the vicinity of a sewer.

Details of the English Water Service Companies can be obtained from Water UK at Queen **4.53** Anne's Gate, London SW1H 9BT (tel 020 7344 1844; **http://www.water.org.uk**). Water UK represents the water companies.

There will be a fee payable for the search. The water companies try to limit their liabil- **4.54** ity in respect of search results, especially when dealing with commercial properties where there was a liability cap at £5,000. Water companies have now agreed to increase profes- sional indemnity cover to £2 million for commercial property searches, and these should be marked 'commercial property' on the front of Form CON29DW. The fees will be greater than for residential searches; details may be seen at **http://www.con29drainagewater.co.uk/**.

THE NATIONAL LAND INFORMATION SERVICE (NLIS)

As a conveyancing reform, the NLIS is one of the most exciting initiatives currently being **4.55** developed to provide national information on land and property. The possibilities of the service are extensive and could involve many different public and private data sources. It should involve a wide user base capable of accessing diverse applications where most will be of particular interest to conveyancers. This is because it brings together in one point of enquiry almost all the different agencies involved in a conveyance, such as the local authority, Land Registry, the local water companies, Companies House, the Environmental Agency, and the Coal Authority.

The idea behind the NLIS is to create an environment which will allow speedy and simple **4.56** access to a wide range of land and property information, held on the databases of many different public- and private-sector groups. The objective is that this wide range of data will be available from a single point of enquiry. (See **http://www.nlis.org.uk** for further information.)

The conveyancing process discussed in this book requires access to many different data **4.57** sources. It is often the time it takes in making searches that causes the worst delays in the house-buying process. The NLIS was piloted to see if it could speed up that process. A pilot application was concluded successfully in the Bristol area, and it achieved this improve- ment in access to data sources. The main data providers of interest to conveyancers are now available to practitioners via NLIS as listed below:

- local authority search (LLC1, CON29R, CON29O);
- Land Registry (a wide range of searches are available);
- water utilities (drainage and water CON29DW);
- Coal Authority (mining and brine extraction);
- Environment Agency (flooding);
- Forestry Commission;
- Highways Agency (road building and maintenance);
- electricity (national grid);
- gas (pipelines);
- telecommunications (cabling);

- London Transport (London Underground and Docklands Light Railway);
- Civil Aviation Authority (airports);
- The Canal and River Trust (canals);
- Ordnance Survey (maps and plans);
- specialty searches (radon, clay, tin mining, limestone, gypsum, Cheshire Brine, Cornish Tin, Chancel Repairs); and
- company searches.

4.58 The NLIS operates (having gone live in February 2001) in England and Wales through NLIS-licensed channels. Practitioners can set up facilities to carry out searches via these companies. The details of the search providers can be found on the NLIS website. See **http://www.nlis.org.uk** for further information. NLIS announced in 2017 that it had delivered over 24 million official electronic conveyancing searches since 2001. At the time of publication there were five search providers, known as 'BigPropertyData', 'IndexPI', 'Legalinx', 'SearchFlow', and 'Thames Water Property Searches' for NLIS channels. Their web addresses can be found at **https://www.nlis.org.uk/what-is-nlis**.

4.59 Eventually the NLIS will use Britain's first comprehensive gazetteer of addressable properties: the National Land and Property Gazetteer (NLPG). All addresses will be given a unique identifier, called a 'Unique Property Reference Number' (UPRN), which will be used to cross-reference data for conveyancing searches. Indeed, there is already a section in the new CON29 for practitioners to insert the NLPG UPRN to assist in identifying the subject property.

4.60 The NLIS is a very welcome development for all conveyancing practitioners. Local authorities are increasingly computerizing their records to enable search results to be issued electronically. NLIS users can access information from 410 local authorities, national parks, Land Registry, the Coal Authority, the Environment Agency, and water companies. NLIS has processed over 24 million searches and around 290,000 searches are being completed monthly through NLIS. It covers an estimated 30 per cent of all property searches for residential house sales. Every local authority (there are 410) processes NLIS search requests; 98 per cent of them receive and return searches electronically.

THE EFFECT OF THE PROTOCOL

4.61 It is interesting to note that when the Law Society Conveyancing Protocol was first issued in the early 1990s there was a requirement for the seller to obtain the local authority search. The 2011 edition of the Protocol continues the reversal of the previous specifications contained within the first two editions of the Protocol that the seller should obtain a local authority search on the subject property. Since 1 May 1994, the Protocol has reverted to the traditional position of requiring the buyer to obtain the local authority search at the buyer's sole expense. What the 2011 Protocol says is that the obtaining of search results by the seller is optional. Accordingly, the 2011 edition of the Protocol now really has little or no effect on traditional conveyancing practices with regard to searches. It is still the case that a buyer must obtain or carry out at his or her own expense all necessary searches. Indeed, it always was the case that the Protocol did not pass this responsibility to the seller for any other search beyond the local authority search. (Having said this, it should be noted that the Protocol does stipulate that if the title is unregistered, the seller's solicitor must make a land charges search against the seller and any other appropriate names, and also make an index map search. In practice, it would seem that this is rarely done.) The full text of the Protocol is set out in Appendix 3.

KEY POINTS SUMMARY

PRE-CONTRACT SEARCHES

Unless otherwise agreed, the practitioner acting for the buyer should always make a local **4.62** authority search.

- Reflect on the location of the subject property to enable you to decide which other searches are relevant to this particular property, for example is it in an urban environment or is it located in a rural setting? Location is also crucial when considering the necessity for a coal mining search and other unusual searches.

- On receipt of the local authority search, always make a double-check of the result. First, carefully scan the land charges disclosed in the result and then carefully check all answers provided by the local authority, taking care to have in mind any specific instructions from the client, for example concerning planning requirements, etc.

- In unregistered land always carry out an index map search. Is the property in an area of recent compulsory registration and only partly registered? If it is, consider the necessity for an index map search.

- Always advise clients of any onerous or unusual replies or results to any of the searches and request their written instructions in response.

- If the Protocol is being used and the land is unregistered, the seller's solicitor should carry out both an index map search and a land charges search.

- Consider the need for an environmental search, or arrange insurance cover in the alternative.

- Always check to see if the subject property might be affected by flooding, and if it is, report the findings to the client and check the position regarding the availability of insurance cover for water damage.

B PRELIMINARY ENQUIRIES

WHY RAISE ENQUIRIES?

As has been said at the start of this chapter (and because it is so important it is worth **4.63** repeating), *caveat emptor* ('Let the buyer beware') remains a cornerstone of conveyancing in England and Wales. As such, a buyer will need to find out as much as possible about the subject property before contracts are exchanged. This is true for both residential and commercial conveyancing transactions. The simple yet compelling reason for this is that the buyer must take the property in whatever condition it is, at the point when there is a binding contract for the purchase. The law imposes a clear obligation on the buyer to find out as much as possible about the property because the common law recognizes that the seller has only a limited duty of disclosure. The buyer must carry out all appropriate enquiries before entering into a binding contract to purchase the subject property. If a buyer does make all necessary enquiries of the seller, and gets sensible answers, an informed decision can then be taken about the nature and suitability of the property. This will be based on all the information obtained prior to exchange. However, this does mean that conveyancing practitioners acting for the buyer will raise vast numbers of enquiries on the basis that if they do not they might be seen as acting negligently. It is not unusual to see such enquiries stretching over 20 or more pages and comprising dozens of multi-sectioned questions. Of course a seller can refuse to give answers, but if this happens then a buyer may immediately back out of the proposed transaction on the basis that the seller must have something to hide.

4.64 The seller's practitioner must also be aware of the problems associated with giving vague or qualified replies, such as 'not to our knowledge but no warranty or representation is given' or 'not so far as the seller is aware'. The court will construe such answers as implied representations that the seller has no actual knowledge of a matter and that the seller has made all investigations that a careful conveyancer should have made (see *William Sindall plc v Cambridgeshire County Council* [1994] 1 WLR 1016).

4.65 Preliminary enquiries have been greatly affected by procedural changes brought in by the Law Society's Conveyancing Protocol (see 4.76). Practitioners should acquaint themselves with the contents of the old-style printed traditional forms of enquiries before contract as well as with the new Property Information Forms. By doing this you will come to appreciate the ways in which the forms differ and how the conveyancing process has been, to a limited extent, streamlined with the adoption of the Protocol approach.

4.66 Many conveyancing practitioners have adopted the Protocol 'enquiry' forms even when they are not actually using the full Protocol process. However, some remain tradition-ally minded and use pre-printed forms, or their own in-house preliminary enquiry forms. These questions, sometimes called preliminary enquiries and sometimes called enquiries before contract, are listed in duplicate and submitted to the seller. (Two copies are issued as a convenient and helpful practice, enabling the seller's practitioner to retain a copy of the questions with replies as a file copy.) Whatever form is used, the intention remains the same: to seek out answers from the seller about any matters that affect or could affect the subject property.

4.67 It should be noted that in the 2011 Protocol it says that a solicitor acting for a buyer should 'raise only those specific additional enquiries required to clarify issues arising out of the documents submitted (by the seller) or which are relevant to the particular nature or location of the property or which the buyer has expressly requested'. It goes on to state that the buyer's solicitor should 'resist raising any additional enquiry including those about the state and condition of the building'. The desire here is to avoid extra ques-tions that are better dealt with elsewhere, say in the survey. Finally, the Protocol states that 'indiscriminate use of standard additional enquiries may constitute a breach of this Protocol'.

4.68 There is some overlap between enquiries and planning in that there should always be plan-ning enquiries appropriate to most, if not all, transactions. This overlapping area is dealt with in 4.90 and 4.95.

WHAT ENQUIRIES SHOULD YOU RAISE, AND WHEN?

4.69 A cynic might say that a prudent conveyancing practitioner should practise defensive law-yering and issue as many enquiries as possible. Adopting the blunderbuss approach is not uncommon among practitioners. Those who adopt this format are driven by the view that if they ask as many questions as possible, they can say that they have done all in their power to protect the interests of their client. This is a possible argument but one that does nothing to speed up the conveyancing process or to enhance the reputation of conveyan-cing practitioners. With a little care and prior preparation, enquiries can be made specific to each property being purchased. Indeed, as was noted by the Law Society when it started to prepare the Protocol, many questions asked of the seller can be answered elsewhere and in many cases are better directed elsewhere (see 4.70).

A set of core enquiries

One sensible way of selecting appropriate enquiries is to adopt a set of enquiries that will **4.70** be issued for all properties—i.e. core enquiries—with a second, more selective set tailored to the subject property. If this style is adopted, the following core enquiries are suggested as being appropriate to all properties:

(a) **Boundaries and fences**   The buyer will want to know about the ownership of all the boundary walls and fences, as well as repairing responsibility if this differs from owner-ship. This should include boundaries comprised in hedges and ditches and the internal boundaries of flats, maisonettes, or offices.

(b) **Disputes**   Clearly a buyer will want to know all about past and present disputes of all kinds affecting the property. Indeed, it is now clear that the seller would be liable in damages for misrepresentation for not informing the buyer that there has been a dis-pute with the neighbours giving rise to complaints about noise. In *McMeekin v Long* [2003] 29 EG 120, sellers were held liable in damages amounting to £67,000 for having given incorrect replies to enquiries about disputes with neighbours. The moral is clear: sellers must be completely honest in replies to enquiries about disputes with neighbour-ing land owners or occupants.

However, it was reported in *The Independent* that 'a couple who were forced to sell their house at a loss after learning it might contain body parts of a girl murdered by her father' could not claim damages for the sellers' non-disclosure of the history of the property. It seems the sellers answered 'No' when asked if there was any other information the buyers had a right to know. The court held that this was not dishonest (*The Independent*, 28 February 2004), and see *Sykes v Taylor-Rose* [2004] EWCA Civ 299.

(c) **Notices**   Similarly, a buyer will also want to know about and see copies of all notices affecting the subject property; and clearly, if the seller has received any, he or she must be under a duty to disclose. All correspondence with the local or other competent authority should be copied to the buyer.

(d) **Services**   The buyer will want to know about the gas and water supply, and whether or not mains drainage and mains water are available. If mains drainage is not connected, questions must be asked about any private drainage facility, for example a septic tank. Conveyancers in large towns and cities can all too quickly forget that many proper-ties in rural environments will not be on mains drainage, and enquires will therefore be important to check on the necessity of easements if this is the case. Furthermore, a recent development is the growing installation of water meters. Again, a buyer will want to know about this possibility, especially if the client is likely to be a high-volume consumer of water (e.g. a family with several small children) and thereby incur greater expense as a result of the presence of the meter.

(e) **Guarantees**   If the property is new or recently built (i.e. within the last ten years), the buyer will want to be reassured that there is in existence a 'Buildmark' guarantee issued by the National House Building Council (NHBC) (for further details on the NHBC, see Chapter 11). Without such a guarantee, many lending institutions simply will not lend. A buyer will also be concerned to find out about the existence of specialist wood treat-ment and damp-proofing guarantees, and any other guarantees such as those given for double glazing. This kind of guarantee is not available for commercial property.

(f) **Exclusive facilities**   The subject property may enjoy an exclusive facility, such as a right of way to and from it, and the buyer will most certainly want full details. While the copy deeds will confirm the existence of the right, they may not provide details of any payments made for it, or indeed the possibility of increase or arrears. This is the kind of information to be sought in this enquiry.

(g) **Shared facilities**   Following on from the previous enquiry, a buyer will need to know about facilities used in common with owners or occupiers of adjoining or adjacent land. The same kind of detail will be required as for exclusive facilities.

(h) **Occupiers**   This is a critical enquiry. A question should be raised that refers to any possible rights accruing to a non-owning occupant. The immediate example is of course the non-owning spouse or cohabitee, who could very well have rights of occupation which have not been highlighted in the copy deeds supplied. Rights of occupation are guaranteed to parties to a civil partnership union in the same way as for married couples. Clearly a prudent purchaser will want a list of all adults in occupation of the property, and possibly all those near adulthood, together with an indication of what rights they might have or be claiming (see 4.40).

(i) **User**   A buyer will want to be reassured that the permitted use for planning purposes is the use to which the buyer intends to put the property after completion, and that the actual use is the permitted use. See 4.100 and 4.101 for further details. An enquiry should be made to see if the subject property has been or may be affected by being considered an asset of community value (see 4.14).

(j) **Fixtures and fittings**   This is an area fraught with difficulty. When is a fixture a fitting, or merely contents in the property? Clearly a buyer will want to know what the seller is going to take and what is to be included in the sale. However, what this entails is not entirely clear. Cases that have gone all the way up to the Court of Appeal have used a two-question test. First, how securely has the item been attached to the land; and second, why was it attached? So in *TSB Bank plc v Botham* [1996] EGCS 149, the bath and taps were fixtures and the kitchen cabinets were held to have become fixtures. However, fitted carpets and curtains were mere fittings, as were the light fittings. Perhaps the simplest guidance that can be provided to the client is to indicate that, unless otherwise agreed with the seller or buyer, fixtures are deemed to be included in the sale of the property whereas fittings are not.

(k) **Flooding**   It would seem prudent to enquire of the seller whether the subject property has ever been flooded. This is not always apparent from the survey result, even though it is a topic a prudent surveyor should cover. Linked to this could be another question asking if insurance cover has ever been refused and, if so, why.

(l) **The Green Deal**   This is a government initiative seeking to save energy and reduce carbon emissions. It covers works required to homes to make them 'green', including the following:
   - cavity wall insulation;
   - solar panels;
   - boilers;
   - hot water systems;
   - replacement double glazing;
   - insulation and lighting systems;
   - micro wind generation;
   - ground source pumps and;
   - biomass boilers.

Further details about the Green Deal can be found at **https://www.gov.uk/green-deal-energy-saving-measures**.

If a property is to be sold and is subject to a Green Deal, information must be disclosed—Green Deal (Disclosure) Regulations 2012. But what is the position if the buyer has no notice of the Green Deal? If the buyer gets their first energy bill that shows a Green Deal of which they were unaware, they may challenge the obligation to repay the Green Deal loan and disclaim liability. This must be done within 90 days from receipt of the bill. The debt then remains with the outgoing seller, who will be liable for full repayment! Enquiries need to be made of the seller, as you will need to know the terms of the Green Deal and be able to advise the client. So when acting for the seller make sure the Energy Performance Certificate (EPC) includes all the details of the Green Deal. If you are acting for the buyer, ensure all consents were available for the works and be ready to advise on the financial implications.

(m) **Easements, the 2002 Act, and pre-contract enquiries** A purchaser of registered land may find it very difficult to discover easements and profits that are not otherwise noted on the register. This is compounded by the fact that the non-user of an easement or profit, even for many years, will fail to raise any presumption of abandonment (see *Benn v Hardinge* (1992) 66 P & CR 246). The 2002 Act effectively provides that no easements or profits expressly granted or reserved out of registered land after the Act comes into force can take effect as overriding interests. This is because such rights will not take effect at law until they are registered, i.e. they are registrable dispositions (s 27(1)). In addition, no equitable easements or profits, however created, are capable of overriding a registered disposition (reversing the decision in *Celsteel Ltd v Alton House Holdings Ltd* [1985] 1 WLR 204). It follows that only a legal easement or profit can be overriding in relation to a registered disposition (Schedule 3, para 3(1)).

Moreover, certain categories of legal easement and profit are excluded from overriding status altogether. These cannot be overriding interests unless they either have been registered under the Commons Registration Act 1965, or have been exercised within one year prior to the registered disposition in question. They are:

(i)   those that are not within the actual knowledge of the person to whom the disposition was made; and

(ii)   those that would not have been obvious on a reasonably careful inspection of the land over which the easement or profit is exercisable.

Importantly, it therefore follows that a buyer of registered land for valuable consideration will be bound by an easement or profit that is an overriding interest only if:

(i)   it is registered under the Commons Registration Act 1965; or

(ii)   the buyer actually knows about it; or

(iii) it is patent, i.e. obvious, from a reasonable inspection of the land over which the easement or profit is exercisable, so that no seller would be obliged to disclose it; or

(iv)   it has been exercised within one year before the date of purchase.

As a result of this, buyers' pre-contract enquiries should request sellers to disclose:

(i)   any unregistered easements and profits affecting the land of which they are aware; and

(ii)   any easements or profits that have been exercised in the previous 12 months.

This makes good practical sense for all conveyancers. There will be those with the benefit of unregistered easements and profits that have not been exercised for more than a year. These persons should immediately protect their rights either by lodging a caution against first registration if the servient land is unregistered, or by registering them if the servient land is registered. These are important practical steps of which conveyancers should be aware.

The Act contains a transitional provision to allow existing easements or profits which are overriding interests at the time the Act comes into force but which would not qualify under the new provisions to retain their overriding status (Schedule 12, para 9). This is something of which buyers should be made aware, and appropriate enquiry made of the seller at the pre-contract stage. A further transitional provision states that for three years after the Act comes into force any legal easement or profit that is not registered will be an overriding interest (Schedule 12, para 10). This period expired on 13 October 2006.

(n) **Assets of community value** The Localism Act 2011 provides for a scheme affecting property called 'assets of community value'. It requires a local authority to maintain a list of 'community assets' that will comprise land and or buildings. Nominations for community assets can be made by parish councils or by groups with a connection with the community. Individuals cannot nominate community assets. If the nomination is accepted, the group will be given time to come up with a bid for the asset when it is sold. It would therefore seem prudent to make enquiries about whether this might apply to your subject property.

Leasehold enquiries

4.71 Where the subject property is leasehold and, in particular, a flat or maisonette, prudent practitioners will also utilize a set of standard preliminary enquiries about the maintenance and service charges, including the insurance arrangements for the property. The following enquiries are suggested as being most of the core leasehold enquiries we consider appropriate to such properties, and most of these enquiries could also apply to the acquisition of some leasehold business premises:

(a) **Relevant names, etc.**   It is a great help to the buyer and the buyer's conveyancer if the seller can accurately confirm the names and addresses of the lessor, any superior lessor, the lessor's managing agent if any, and the lessor's solicitors.

(b) **Ground rent**   The buyer will want to see a clear last receipt for ground rent to make sure that there are no outstanding disputes or claims and to ensure that the rent is paid up to date.

(c) **Service charges**   This is a critical area for buyers, who will want to be sure that they are not taking over any service charge arrears. Similarly, buyers will want to know if there are any large bills looming on the horizon which they will have to pay. It is not unknown for a seller to decide to sell just before the landlord embarks on a large painting scheme of the block containing the subject property!

(d) **Insurance arrangements**   This is another important area as lending institutions will always want to be sure that the property is insured for the full reinstatement value, and for a comprehensive set of perils. Normally leases stipulate that a lessor must insure, and not the lender, who would otherwise insure. This being so a full copy of the current policy should be requested.

(e) **Covenants**   The buyer will want the seller's written confirmation of the absence of breaches of covenant known to the lessor and, indeed, any that exist but have not come to the attention of the lessor. For example, if the property has been altered or if there have been any additions to it, then those works may have required the lessor's consent. In the absence of such consent there will be a breach of covenant.

4.72 The Law Society has issued a new conveyancing form called LPE1. It is used for collecting information about a subject property where that information is held by landlords, management companies, and managing agents. The kind of information that the form intends to gather will normally be about ground rent, insurance, and service charges. The sections within the form cover contact details, transfer and registration details, ground rent service charge, and insurance information, and list required documents such as service charge accounts for the last three years. This form should be used when a lessor or management company must be contacted to obtain information about a leasehold property that is in the process of being sold. Form LPE1 went into a second edition on 1 October 2015. It now includes new questions aimed to reduce the need for additional enquiries, for example with regard to any transfer fees payable on sale. A buyer's leasehold information summary form, (LPE2), has also been introduced. This seeks to give the buyer details of the buyer's key financial responsibilities such as ground rent, service charges, insurance premiums, and possible future costs arising out of these.

Standard pre-contract enquiries should always be edited to make them suitable for a par- **4.73**
ticular property. For example, where a buyer is proposing to purchase agricultural land,
together with a farm as a going concern, extra enquiries are always required. In particular,
a buyer will need to know about specific farming matters such as milk quotas, agricultural
tenancies, grazing rights, and environmental protection matters, as well as more common
concerns such as easements and services. All these elements should be expanded upon by
extra enquiries.

Some printed forms of preliminary enquiries try to limit liability by including a disclaimer **4.74**
of responsibility for inaccuracies. Practitioners will immediately appreciate that if such a
disclaimer is allowed it would greatly enhance the chances of limiting liability when dealing with replies to enquiries. It would seem that s 11(3) of the Unfair Contract Terms Act
1977 puts the burden of proof on practitioners in these circumstances, which militates
against the effectiveness of such a clause. In *First National Commercial Bank plc v Loxleys*
(1996) 93 (43) *Gazette* 20, it was held that the solicitors were required by the Act to show
that it was fair and reasonable for the firm to rely on the standard disclaimer to release
them from all liability having regard to all the circumstances of the case. The decision in the
case was that there was a reasonable cause of action and that the disclaimer did not prevent
the case from going to trial. In effect, it is clear that the courts will not view disclaimers
with any great sympathy, and will use the Act to strike them down wherever possible. The
moral for the busy practitioner is to ensure the accuracy of all answers given rather than
to rely on a disclaimer. Some practitioners use this decision as a reason for them not to
complete Part II of the Property Information Forms (see 4.78).

Lastly, as a comment on the whole subject of preliminary enquiries we would like to refer **4.75**
you to a letter in the *Law Society Gazette* of 7 September 1994 in which it was suggested
that all enquiries before contract could be reduced to just one, namely: 'If we asked the
usual silly questions would you give the usual worthless answers?' (LSG 91/32, 7 September 1994, p 14).

THE EFFECT OF THE PROTOCOL

A modernized system of residential conveyancing was introduced by the Law Society in **4.76**
1990 in the form of the National Conveyancing Protocol. The intention of the Protocol
was to streamline, and thereby expedite, the system of conveyancing. The hope was that
by introducing the Protocol the time between the buyer making the offer and contracts
being exchanged would be greatly reduced. To ensure that the Law Society's intention was
fulfilled the Protocol envisaged the adoption of standardized documentation. In the case
of pre-contract enquiries this meant the introduction of new enquiry forms that were to
be used in all Protocol conveyancing cases. These were called by the Law Society 'Property
Information Forms'. The critical change, and indeed the novel element, brought in by the
Protocol was that these were issued and completed by the seller's practitioner with, of
course, the assistance of the seller.

The Protocol forms

The old-style preliminary enquiry forms have been replaced by client questionnaires **4.77**
that form an integral part of the Protocol. The fifth edition of the Protocol brought with
it a revision of these questionnaires. The revised forms are listed below with their form
reference number. The Law Society recently updated its Protocol forms and these are the
forms as listed below; other forms have been discontinued. The following list highlights
the current forms that continue within this portfolio of Law Society-approved forms:

Forms used in residential conveyancing:

- TA6 Property information form (2013 edition);
- TA7 Leasehold information form (2013 edition);
- TA8 New home information form;
- TA9 Commonhold information form;
- TA10 Fittings and contents form (2013 edition);
- TA13 Completion information and undertakings (2nd edition).

4.78 The 2013 edition Protocol Property Information Forms can, for ease of reference, be accessed via the Online Resource Centre for this book, together with the Fixtures and Fittings Form. TA6 is a single set of questions required in almost all transactions, and, while TA7 will be used with TA6, TA7 is meant to elicit leasehold information required in the conveyancing process. (Form TA6 now includes the statement: 'Japanese Knotweed is an invasive plant that can cause damage to property. It can take several years to eradicate.' The form then requires the seller to give a warranty as follows: 'Is the Property affected by Japanese Knotweed? Yes/No or not known.' Conveyancing practitioners should be aware of the Property Codes Compliance Board Invasives Code that exists to guide members of the Invasive Non-Native Specialists Association working to control and eradicate invasive non-native species such as Japanese Knotweed, Giant Hogweed, Himalayan Balsam, or any other invasive non-native species. Details of the Association can be found at **www.innsa.org**.)

4.79 The standard Fixtures Fittings and Contents Form (TA10) has proved in practice to be a useful and straightforward form. It must be completed directly by the seller. It lists various items that might be in or around a property to be sold, and then in three columns allows the seller to indicate if the item is included in the sale, excluded, or not at the property.

4.80 Practitioners should note that the Standard Conditions Contract (fifth edition) includes a specific special condition numbered 3, which states that the contents set out on any attached list are included in the sale (or in the alternative the attached list of fixtures are specifically excluded from the sale). It is therefore intended that the enquiry form is actually attached to the contract and is to form part of the written agreement. (By attaching and referring to the list there can be no question of the condition falling foul of the provisions of s 2 of the Law of Property (Miscellaneous Provisions) Act 1989 in that the written contract will thereby incorporate all the agreed terms.)

4.81 The Property Information Forms will, therefore, continue in this revised edition. They are certainly easier to understand than most traditional forms of preliminary enquiries, and in this respect are real improvements on the conventional forms of pre-contract enquiries. However, one main criticism of preliminary enquiries is their length. Several stretch over far too many sides of densely printed paper and raise questions which would be better directed elsewhere.

4.82 There remains the difficulty of reconciling the professional obligation on the buyer's conveyancing practitioner to make all proper and reasonable enquiries on behalf of their client with the aim of the Protocol, that of streamlining the enquiry process. The difference between this element in the Protocol procedures and the buyer's conveyancing practitioner's overriding duty to the client now appears to be very slender. It seems inevitable that either the printed Protocol forms will continue to expand, or they will be accompanied by copious extra enquiries raised by anxious or perhaps prudent solicitors. It is only natural for careful conveyancing practitioners to incline towards more, rather than fewer, questions. This is, of course, in the perhaps vain hope that, notwithstanding the Property Information Forms, by asking as many questions as possible, practitioners might be able to avoid negligence claims by dissatisfied clients. However, it should be remembered that the 2011 Protocol states that 'indiscriminate use of standard additional enquiries may constitute a breach of this Protocol'. Furthermore, the Protocol guidance makes it clear that if such enquiries are submitted the seller's solicitor is under no obligation to deal with them.

COMMERCIAL PROPERTY ENQUIRIES

The Commercial Property Standard Enquiries (CPSEs) are a set of documents which have **4.83** been drafted by members of the London Property Support Lawyers Group under the sponsorship of the British Property Federation (BPF). Contributions were also made by a number of other firms and individuals. The CPSEs are endorsed by the BPF and it is anticipated that they might become industry standard pre-contract enquiries for commercial property conveyancing. The following explanation and details are taken from the guidance notes to the CPSEs issued with the enquiries themselves.

The CPSEs comprise the following documents and the latest edition of them is version 3, **4.84** to take account of the changes required by the Land Registration Act 2002 and other subsequent changes in the law and practice:

1. GN/CPSE—Guidance notes on the Commercial Property Standard Enquiries;
2. CPSE.1—General pre-contract enquiries for all commercial property transactions;
3. CPSE.2—Supplemental pre-contract enquiries for commercial property subject to tenancies;
4. CPSE.3—Supplemental pre-contract enquiries for commercial property on the grant of a new lease;
5. CPSE.4—Supplemental pre-contract enquiries for commercial leasehold property on the assignment of the lease;
6. CPSE.5—Enquiries before surrender of a rack rent commercial lease;
7. CPSE.6 and CRC enquiries—These new enquiries are necessary to deal with issues arising under the Carbon Reduction Commitment Energy Efficiency Scheme 2010 (CRC). The CRC is a mandatory carbon emissions reporting and pricing scheme to cover all organizations using more than 6,000 MWh per year of electricity (equivalent to an annual electricity bill in 2008 of about £500,000). This may affect many commercial property companies. The CRC came into force in April 2010 and aims to significantly reduce UK carbon emissions not covered by other pieces of legislation. The primary focus is to reduce emissions in non-energy-intensive sectors in the UK. CPSE.6 may be utilized when a commercial property is subject to a residential tenancy or tenancies. The enquiries themselves are lengthy and occasionally quite complicated. To address this issue CPSE.7 (version 1.0) general short-form pre-contract enquiries for all property transactions were issued in July 2015 and are a reduced set of enquiries that can be selected in place of the longer set comprising CPSE.1.

Details of the CPSEs can be seen at **https://uk.practicallaw.thomsonreuters.com/6-502-** **4.85** **2923?transitionType=Default&contextData=(sc.Default)&firstPage=true&bhcp=1**. Any reproduction of the enquiries must bear the logo of the BPF. Any user of the forms must not change the text of the documents. If a user wishes to raise any additional enquiries in the documents comprising the CPSEs, the user must do so in a separate document that identifies clearly those additional enquiries as being separate from, and additional to, the CPSEs. The enquiries in the CPSEs are intended as a standard minimum for use in any commercial property transaction. It is expected that additional specific enquiries may be raised for any subject property and also in relation to transactions involving newly constructed or extensively altered buildings.

4.86 CPSE.1 is designed to cover all commercial property transactions and will (together with any additional enquiries relevant to the particular transaction) be sufficient if the transaction deals only with a freehold sold with vacant possession. (CPSE.1 was updated on 28 February 2014 to include enquiries relating to concealment of planning breaches, assets of community value, and Community Infrastructure Levy.) The following supplemental enquiries are intended to be used in conjunction with CPSE.1. Which particular additional form or forms will be required will depend on the individual circumstances of each transaction. The following supplemental forms are available: CPSE.2, where the property is sold subject to existing tenancies; CPSE.3, where a lease of a property is being granted; and CPSE.4, where the property being sold is leasehold.

The contents of CPSE.1 (version 3.5)

4.87 The enquiries in CPSE.1 cover the following topics:

1. Boundaries and extent;
2. Party walls;
3. Rights benefiting the Property;
4. Adverse rights affecting the Property;
5. Title policies;
6. Access to neighbouring land;
7. Access to and from the Property;
8. Physical condition;
9. Contents;
10. Utilities and services;
11. Fire safety and means of escape;
12. Planning and building regulations;
13. Statutory agreements and infrastructure;
14. Statutory and other requirements;
15. Environmental;
16. Occupiers and employees;
17. Insurance;
18. Rates and other outgoings;
19. Notices;
20. Disputes;
21. Community Infrastructure Levy (CIL);
22. Commonhold;
23. Stamp Duty Land Tax (SDLT) on assignment of a lease;
24. Deferred payment of SDLT;
25. Value Added Tax (VAT) Registration information;
26. Transfer of a business as a going concern (TOGC);
27. Other VAT treatment;
28. Standard-rated supplies;
29. Exempt supplies;
30. Zero-rated supplies;
31. Transactions outside the scope of VAT (other than TOGCs);
32. Capital allowances.

4.88 All of these general enquiries relating to commercial property will be considered in more detail within Chapter 12.

4.89 A perusal of these standard questions will highlight a complete absence of enquiries asking for details of overriding interests that need to be disclosed to Land Registry on form DI under rr 28 and 57 of the Land Registration Rules 2003. This is because standard enquiry 4.5 asks the seller about all interests under Schedules 1 and 3 to the Land Registration Act 2002 that have not been revealed by means of the copy documents provided. It is, therefore, up to the buyer to determine which of those interests need to be disclosed to Land Registry. However, there is now a Disclosable Overriding Interests Questionnaire within this Commercial Enquiries scheme. The questionnaire asks the client to disclose any rights which affect the property of which he or she is aware. It is for the practitioner instructed to decide which (if any) of them are disclosable overriding interests which need to be submitted to Land Registry at the same time as the application for registration. It is envisaged that the questionnaire will be given to the buyer or tenant before exchange of contracts. It can be used either on the purchase of a commercial freehold or a commercial leasehold property, or on the grant of a new commercial lease. Currently, there is no sanction for failing to disclose such an interest.

KEY POINTS SUMMARY

PRELIMINARY ENQUIRIES

Which forms are you using or should you use—Protocol or not, pre-printed or not, core and/ **4.90** or additional?

- What extra questions need to be asked that are specific to the subject property?
- What specific enquiries should you raise consequent upon any particular instructions you may have received from the client?
- Always advise your client of any onerous or unusual replies or results to any of the preliminary enquiries and request written instructions in response.
- In commercial transactions can you utilize the CPSEs?

C TOWN AND COUNTRY PLANNING

PLANNING AND CONVEYANCING

The current extensive town planning legislation seeks to control the development of land **4.91** and buildings (Town and Country Planning Act 1990, s 57(1)). In particular, this section stipulates that 'planning permission is required for the carrying out of any development of land'. Development is defined by s 55 as being of two kinds:

(1) 'the carrying out of building, engineering, mining or other operations in, on, over or under land'; and
(2) 'the making of any material change in the use of any buildings or other land'.

By this definition legislation has been put in place to control almost all aspects of the use, **4.92** enjoyment, and redevelopment of land throughout the country. As a consequence it is important that practitioners know the basics of planning law in sufficient detail to enable them to advise their clients about any effect the legislation might have on the subject property.

If a client intends to carry out development in the manner defined by the Act, then planning **4.93** permission will be required. This can be obtained in one of two ways: either by a permission deemed to have been given as a consequence of the effects of the Town and Country Planning (General Permitted Development) Order 1995, and the Town and Country Planning (General Permitted Development) (Amendment) (No 2) England Order 2008 (SI 2008/2362); or by a formal application for planning permission submitted to the local planning authority. If the 1995 Order does not apply, then an express application will need to be made.

Permission under the Town and Country Planning (General Permitted Development) Order 1995 (as amended)

4.94 This Order grants blanket permission for certain kinds of specific development, for example the erection of fences is a development that will not (subject to height restrictions) require express planning consent. Similarly, the exterior painting of a property is covered by the Order, subject to the painting not amounting to advertising. Perhaps the most important blanket approval is that for small extensions to an existing dwelling house. These small extensions, such as a rear kitchen extension, are subject to restrictions on size and position but otherwise can be made without the necessity for express planning permission. The Order contemplates various classes of permitted development such as Class D within Part I of the Order, which permits the erection or construction of a porch outside any external door of a dwelling house. However, the Order includes detailed limitations to the dimensions of several of the classes of permitted development. These limitations affect size and height as well as external appearance. The Town and Country Planning (General Permitted Development) (Amendment) (No 2) England Order 2008 (SI 2008/2362) sets out the extensive detail of these limitations.

4.95 Planning authorities can exclude the effect of all or part of the Order if they deem it expedient to do so. Action under this provision is termed an 'Article 4 Direction'. This is so because Article 4 of the Order provides authority for such exclusions. The purpose of this restrictive provision is to allow a planning authority to control all aspects of development in great detail. This permits the authority to control even minor development activities such as the installation of double glazing or a plastic front door where it is appropriate to do so, say in a conservation area. The Secretary of State will normally be required to consent to the creation of an Article 4 Direction, but not in relation to listed buildings. (See 4.18 and, in particular, Question 9 of the enquiries of the local authority.)

4.96 The Town and Country Planning (General Permitted Development) (Amendment) (England) Order 2013 (SI 2013/1101) has amended the position regarding changes of use. This permits certain changes of use between classes A, B, C, and D including, for a time-limited period, the change from B1 (offices) to C3 (dwelling houses). As for the time limit, the Order provides that development is not permitted where the building was not used for a use falling within Class B1(a) (offices) immediately before 30 May 2013 and the use of the building falling within Class C3 (dwelling houses) was begun after 30 May 2016.

Planning permission given by the local planning authority

4.97 An applicant has the choice of making an application either for outline planning permission or for full planning permission. An outline application will elicit a response from the planning authority without the expense of having to prepare a full and comprehensive application involving detailed plans. The planning authority can impose conditions attaching to the outline consent. If an outline consent is granted it can be expressed to be subject to 'reserved matters' thereafter being resolved to the satisfaction of the planning authority. Reserved matters will relate to the detail of the application, such as the external appearance of the property, or perhaps means of access to it.

4.98 If there are reserved matters, it will mean that a full application will be necessary to obtain approval for the applicant's proposals in relation to the reserved matters, which must be made within three years of the outline consent. Moreover, the work itself must start within five years from the outline consent (Town and Country Planning Act 1990, s 92).

The alternative to an application for outline approval is a full planning application. The **4.99** planning authority can impose conditions attaching to the full planning consent. For planning consents granted before 24 August 2005, the work itself must start within five years from the date of the full planning permission. For consents issued after that date, the period has been reduced to three years; see the Planning and Compulsory Purchase Act 2004. Practitioners should advise applicants who intend to delay that the planning authority has further powers under s 94 of the Town and Country Planning Act 1990. If the work has started but not progressed very far, and/or the authority is of the view that the development will not be completed within a reasonable period, the authority can serve a completion notice on the owner or developer. This notice stipulates that the planning permission will cease to have effect after the expiry of a stated period, which must not be less than 12 months. If work is carried out after the end of the notice period it will, in effect, be unlawful as the consent will no longer be valid.

CHANGES OF USE

A buyer may be unaware of a change of use at the subject property even though that cur- **4.100** rent user is unlawful, i.e. has come about without permission for the new use from the local planning authority. A property—for example, a new flat above a shop—can appear on inspection to be quite in order. However, the prior use may have been retail or offices; and in the absence of any consent for a residential flat, there may have been a material change of use for which planning consent should have been obtained. It is, therefore, crucial that a conveyancer is satisfied that the existing use is the permitted use authorized by the local planning authority. An even more difficult example is the conversion of a house into flats. Although the whole property use remains residential there is, in fact, a material change of use requiring planning permission as the property is now in multiple occupation (Town and Country Planning Act 1990, s 55(3)(a)).

Use classes

Types of use are defined in the Town and Country Planning (Use Classes) Order 1987, which **4.101** originally listed 16 separate classes. (Other use classes have been introduced since 1987.) The following are of the greatest importance to a conveyancing practitioner. Changes of use *within* a class do not require planning consent, while changes *between* classes may do:

(a) **Class A1 shops**   This class includes post offices, travel agencies, Internet cafés, hairdressers, dry-cleaning agencies, and the retail sale of goods other than hot food. Thus no planning permission is required for a former greengrocery to be used by a travel agent because they are in the same class. This class will also include a retail warehouse used as a point of sale of goods to the public even though the size is such that it is not exactly a shop! This will still be the case even if a part of the building is used for storage. (If, however, the main element is storage, then A1 cannot apply and the class will be B8 covering storage and distribution centres.)

(b) **Class A2 financial and professional services**   This allows property to be used for the provision of financial services or professional services (not being health or medical services), or any other service appropriate to a shopping area where such services are intended for visiting members of the public. This class has been declared in an effort to support the growing advice and financial services industry. Accordingly, insurance brokers, solicitors, accountants, surveyors, architects, and mortgage brokers will all be covered by the same class. Furthermore, the class will also include law centres, as well as banks and building societies. However, the critical element is the availability of the service to visiting members of the public. This class does not include betting offices or payday loan shops.

(c) **Class A3 food and drink**   This class has been amended since 21 April 2005, and is now restricted to restaurants and cafés. The class will therefore not cover pubs, takeaways, and bars. Please see 4.102.

(d) **Class B1 business**   This class covers offices other than those covered by A2, for research and development of products or processes, or for any other industrial process. At first inspection this would seem a very wide class. However, there is a very restrictive condition in that the use is permitted only if it can be carried out when in a residential area without detriment to the amenity of the area. This detriment could be noise, vibration, smell, fumes, smoke, soot, ash, dust, or grit. Accordingly, this form of business use is clearly going to be a problem if it is intended for an area that is primarily residential and the use could be noisy, etc.

(e) **Class B2 general industrial**   This is the class that permits any use for the carrying on of an industrial process not covered by B1, or by other provisions in the Order covering special industrial processes (e.g. alkaline works and other types of heavy industry that tend to emit noxious fumes or effluent).

(f) **Class C1 hotels and hostels**   This class clearly covers the use of buildings as hotels or hostels, and will include boarding houses and guest houses. However, none of these will fall within this class if the use includes a serious element of care for persons in residence. In these circumstances class C2 will apply. There is a definition of 'care' within Article 2 of the Order.

(g) **Class C2 residential institutions**   This class covers buildings used for the provision of personal care or treatment, and residential educational facilities.

(h) **Class C3 dwelling houses**   This class will allow the use of property for the accommodation of a family, as well as the coming together of up to six individuals as a single household. This would, therefore, allow the accommodation of five persons suffering from a disability with a warden or other person caring for them. The limit is fixed at six, and the property must be used as a single household. This ensures that other forms of multiple occupation cannot fall within this class. As mentioned, the use of a single dwelling house as two or more separate dwellings (i.e. the conversion of a house into several flats) is stated by the Act to be a material change of use for which planning consent will be required (Town and Country Planning Act 1990, s 55(3)(a)).

(i) **Class C4 Houses in multiple occupation**   This class covers small, shared dwelling houses occupied by between three and six unrelated individuals, as their only or main residence, who share basic amenities such as a kitchen or bathroom.

Changes to the 1987 Use Classes Order

4.102   From 21 April 2005, there were changes to the use classes that were created by the 1987 Order. That order was amended by the Town and Country Planning (Use Classes) (Amendment) (England) Order 2005, which substituted for the former A3 (food and drink) three new use classes:

1. restaurants and cafés (A3);
2. drinking establishments (pubs and bars) (A4); and
3. hot-food takeaways (A5).

Table 4.1 General permissions for change across classes authorized by the Town and Country Planning (General Permitted Development) Order 1995 and the Planning (General Permitted Development) (Amendment) (England) Order 2005

From	To
A2, financial and professional services (in this case the subject premises must have a display window at street or ground-floor level)	A1 shop
A3, restaurants and cafés	A1 shop, or A2 financial and professional services
A4, drinking establishments (pubs and bars)	A1 shop, or A2 financial and professional services
A5, hot-food takeaways	A1 shop, or A2 financial and professional services

Accordingly, A3 is restricted to restaurants and cafés, and excludes pubs, bars, and take- **4.103** aways. Pubs and bars have their own use class, A4, and takeaways are given a new use class, A5. (Planning consent will not be needed for a change of use from A4 or A5 to A3, but any other change of use will require planning permission.)

Internet cafés are now within use class A1 (shops), and motorcar showrooms are excluded **4.104** from A1, meaning that planning permission will be needed for such a change of use.

The General Development Order also allows as permitted development specific changes **4.105** between different-use classes, and the information set out in Table 4.1 should be noted as being particularly relevant.

There are other approved changes involving B1 (business), B2 (general industrial), and B8 **4.106** (storage and distribution), and changes of use within those classes.

As a consequence of The Town and Country Planning (General Permitted Development) (England) Order 2015 (SI 2015/596) a number of new permitted development rights have been allowed: the conversion of retail premises to restaurants/cafes (Class C); the existing permitted development to convert a shop to a deposit-taker is replaced by a wider right to convert a shop to a premises providing financial and professional services (Classes D and F); the conversion of retail premises to assembly and leisure (Class J); the conversion of casinos or amusement arcades to dwellinghouses (Class N); and the conversion of premises used from storage or distribution centre uses to dwellinghouses (Class P).

Certain uses do not fall within any use class and are considered in a class of their own, i.e. 'sui generis'. Such uses include, but are not limited to, betting shops, payday loan shops, theatres, and scrap yards.

Community Infrastructure Levy

The Community Infrastructure Levy is a planning charge, introduced by the Planning Act **4.107** 2008 as a tool for local authorities in England and Wales to help deliver infrastructure to support the development of their area. It came into force on 6 April 2010 through the Community Infrastructure Levy Regulations 2010. Development may be liable for a charge under the Community Infrastructure Levy (CIL) if a local planning authority has chosen to set a charge in its area. Once planning permission is granted, collecting authorities will issue applicants with a levy liability notice. Applicants should then assume liability to pay the levy charge prior to commencement of development. The levy charge becomes due when development commences.

PLANNING ENQUIRIES

4.108 A buyer will want to be sure that the intended use for the subject property will be permitted under the planning laws. Similarly, the buyer will want to consider if an application for planning permission will be necessary in the light of the buyer's intentions for the subject property so far as demolition, rebuilding, alterations, and additions are concerned. Indeed, a buyer will want to be sure that there are no onerous conditions attaching to a consent affecting the subject property. (This can be particularly important as planning authorities have been known to grant consents personal to the applicant, and only mention this in the conditions.) Accordingly, enquiries will be required to cover all these concerns, although much of the relevant information will be disclosed in a local authority search result. Indeed, if the local authority has taken enforcement action by way of an enforcement notice or stop notice, this will be disclosed in the local authority search result and, in particular, within the replies to the enquiries directed to the local authority. Ultimately, the reason behind planning enquiries is that substantial penalties may be incurred for breaches of the planning law.

Core planning enquiries

4.109 The following is a list of enquiries that should be made of the seller and represents a core of appropriate questions to which specific enquiries should be added:

(a) **Alterations and additions**   A prudent buyer will want to know if there have been any alterations and/or additions and, if so, when they were made. In this way the buyer can decide if a planning consent authorizing those building works needs to be seen. It is still the case that small-scale alterations or additions can fall within the Town and Country (General Permitted Development) Order 1995 where this form of blanket consent is available for small changes such as a simple shed or garage. (However, in conservation areas, specific planning consents will still be required notwithstanding the Order.)

(b) **User**   The seller should be asked to confirm two points: first, the nature of the current use (and when this commenced); and, second, that this is the permitted use for planning purposes. This will be in addition to any information disclosed in the local authority search and will, therefore, disclose any discrepancies between the information from these two sources. If any such discrepancies come to light they must be investigated with the local planning authority and the seller. An enquiry should be made to see if the subject property has been or may be affected by being considered an asset of community value; see 4.14.

(c) **Advertising**   Because s 55(5) of the Town and Country Planning Act 1990 stipulates that the use of an external part of a property for advertising will require planning consent, if there is any advertising on the subject property, questions should be asked about planning consents for the advertising hoarding. This enquiry will apply to both residential and commercial property, for example end-of-terrace properties with a hoarding attached to the flank wall, and flats located above shops.

(d) **Building regulations**   Whenever building works are carried out they must comply with various building regulations such as the Building Regulations 1991, which came into force on 1 June 1992. These regulations are in place to ensure adequate standards of building work that are minimum standards covering various topics, including health and safety and energy conservation. (From 31 December 2004 electrical building works require building regulations consent and the work must be completed by a qualified electrician.) Practitioners need to appreciate that the requirement for building regulation approval is an entirely separate requirement from planning matters, and must be dealt with where there are any building works. There is a requirement for plans to be filed with the local authority which will, on satisfactory completion of the works, issue a final certificate called a certificate of compliance.

However, the decision in the case of *Cottingham v Attey Bower & Jones (A Firm)* [2000] EGCS 48 sent a ripple of concern through the conveyancing profession. Rimmer J held the solicitors for the claimants to have acted negligently by failing to take all reasonable steps to obtain copies of building regulation consents. The judge mentioned in his judgment that injunction proceedings under s 36(6) of the Building Act 1984 enable a local authority to take enforcement proceedings at any time after the works have been carried out. This provision in effect creates an unlimited obligation on conveyancers to seek copy building regulation approvals. There is a need for a common-sense approach to the problem that could be addressed by the adoption of the following procedures:

(i) Raise a specific enquiry of the sellers for copies of all building regulation consents for the last ten years. This period is suggested as it reflects the period for planning matters (see 4.111). (Building regulations first appeared in 1845, but it is unlikely that you will be able to obtain copies of all consents since then.)

(ii) If the response is incomplete and copies are not available, or none appears to have been obtained, both the buyer and any lender need to be advised of the problem. They should both be advised to refer the problem to the surveyor for advice as to how best to proceed, if at all.

(iii) Ask the client to confirm that you can ask the local authority for copies, with the warning that if there is no building regulation consent the council will be on notice of unauthorized building works where they can take enforcement proceedings.

(iv) If the local authority indicates that there is no consent, then ask the client to confirm that you can apply to the council for a Regularisation Certificate pursuant to the Building Regulations 2000. The client must appreciate that this will incur extra cost and will delay the exchange of contracts.

(v) Alternatively, Countrywide Legal Indemnities (tel: 01603 617617) has available a 'Lack of Building Regulation Consent' insurance. The policy offers cover up to a tiered number of limits of indemnity at least in respect of any works carried out at the subject property provided they were fully completed 12 months prior to the date cover is taken out.

(e) **Assets of community value** The Localism Act 2011 provides for a scheme affecting land and premises called 'assets of community value'. It requires a local council to maintain a list of 'community assets'. Nominations for community assets can be made by parish councils or by groups with a connection with the community. Individuals cannot nominate community assets that can include land and property. If the nomination is accepted, the group will be given time to come up with a bid for the asset when it is sold. It would therefore seem prudent to make enquiries about whether this might apply to your subject property.

Replacement windows and FENSA certificates

New building regulations applied from 1 April 2002 to the installation of replacement **4.110** windows and doors under the Building (Amendment) Regulations 2002 (SI 2002/440). As a result, the conveyancer for a buyer must raise enquiries with the seller covering replacement windows. The latest edition of the Property Information Form now includes question 10.2(c) to cover this topic (see the Online Resource Centre which accompanies this book). In essence, all replacement windows, rooflights, roof windows, and glazed doors have to comply with the building regulations. Confirmatory certificates will be available either from the local authority, or from FENSA (Fenestration Self-Assessment through the Glass and Glazing Federation Self-Assessment Scheme).

ENFORCEMENT NOTICES AND STOP NOTICES

4.111 If the local authority becomes aware of a breach of planning control, it has the power to issue and serve an enforcement notice. Failure to comply with an enforcement notice can amount to a criminal offence for which magistrates can impose a fine of up to £20,000. Accordingly, where development has been carried out without permission or a condition has not been complied with, the authority can serve such a notice on the owner or occupier, or on anyone else interested in the subject property. Where enforcement action is contemplated, it must be taken within four years of any operational development (i.e. such as the erection of a new building). The four-year period runs from when the operations were substantially completed. Similarly, a four-year period for enforcement operates for changes of use of any building to use as a single dwelling house, running from when the fresh use commenced. In the case of any other breach of planning law, the enforcement action period is ten years from the date of any breach. Any other breach will include changes of use other than operational development, or a change of use to a single dwelling house. The four-year rule therefore applies to the change of use of a building to a single dwelling house. The four-year rule also applies to building works such as a flat conversion. If a notice is validly served, then the recipient can appeal to the Secretary of State on one or more of the grounds for appeal set out in s 174 of the Town and Country Planning Act 1990. These grounds include indicating that planning permission ought to be granted and that the proposals, if they occur, do not constitute a breach of planning control.

4.112 While an enforcement notice is under appeal it has no effect. The consequence of this is that the alleged improper use can continue. If the authority wishes to terminate the use forthwith on service of an enforcement notice, then it must also issue and serve a stop notice. The planning authority can rely on s 183 of the Town and Country Planning Act 1990, which empowers it to issue stop notices which effectively prohibit any use or activity contained or mentioned in the allied enforcement notice. A stop notice will not prohibit the use of any building as a dwelling house (Town and Country Planning Act 1990, s 183(4)). Accordingly, a stop notice will arise only in the context of an enforcement notice.

BUILDING REGULATIONS

4.113 Whenever any meaningful building works are carried out to a property they must comply with a range of building regulations. These regulations are in place to ensure adequate standards of building work, and impose minimum standards covering a variety of areas, including energy conservation and health. Building works must comply with all relevant regulations. Practitioners should advise their clients of the need to obtain building regulations approval as an entirely separate requirement from planning. It is, in effect, an additional requirement. Before the works start, the developer should advise the local authority, and deposit with it plans of the proposed works. Once the works have been completed, the developer should seek from the local authority a final certificate. This is a certificate of compliance confirming that the works have been carried out to the satisfaction of the local authority, and in accordance with the Regulations. If the local authority intends to take action as a consequence of any suspected breach of the Regulations, it must do so within 12 months of the alleged breach (Building Act 1984, s 36(1); Public Health Act 1936, s 65).

However, the 12-month time limit is capable of extreme enlargement. In that context the **4.114** case of *Cottingham v Attey Bower & Jones (A Firm)* [2000] EGCS 48 is of great concern to practitioners, and its implications are discussed at 4.109.

KEY POINTS SUMMARY

TOWN AND COUNTRY PLANNING

- Does the client want to make any changes to the subject property? If so, will the building **4.115** works or change of use require planning permission?

- If a change of use is proposed, will it require formal consent, or will it come within a use class, or will it be allowed by the blanket approval available under the General Development Order?

- Does the client want to minimize cost by testing the waters with an outline planning application, or is a full application more appropriate?

- If the property is newly built, always ask to see building regulations approval, the certificate of compliance, and a copy planning permission for the whole development.

- When checking planning consent ensure that all the conditions attaching to the consent are seen and be sure that they have all been complied with.

- Always advise clients of any onerous or unusual replies or results to any of the searches and enquiries in so far as they relate to planning matters, and request the client's written instructions in response.

- Obtain copy building regulations consent for the last ten years. If the record is incomplete, consider indemnity insurance.

PRACTICAL CHECKLISTS

SEARCHES

Acting for a buyer

- Is the property rural or urban, and is a plan required? **4.116**

- If not sure, or newly built, do a commons registration search.

- If rural, or on the edge of a town or village, do a commons registration search.

- Check to see if the property is in an area of current or previous coal mining and do a coal mining search if necessary.

- Is the seller a company? If so, do a company search, possibly online at **http://www.companieshouse.gov.uk**.

- Is the property unregistered? If so, do an index map search.

- Is the property unregistered? If so, do a land charges search.

- Has the property been physically inspected and, if so, with what result?

- Are any minor searches required, for example for a property in Cornwall, a clay-mining search?

- Consider the need for an environmental search (particularly to cover flooding risks).

- Is the Protocol being adopted; and if it is, will the seller provide any searches?

- If the Protocol is not being used, do all searches. If the Protocol is to be used, do all necessary searches, having ascertained a response to the previous checklist item.
- When issuing a local authority search request, decide on which extra pre-printed questions should be asked in Part II of the Form.
- In relation to the local authority search result, including replies to enquiries of the council:
  - check all local land charges disclosed and always advise clients of any onerous or unusual replies or results, and request the clients' written instructions in response;
  - check all replies to enquiries and always advise clients of any onerous or unusual replies or results, and request the clients' written instructions in response;
  - always make a file note of the date of dispatch of the searches made on a specific property file and do not exchange contracts until all search results are in and approved, and the client has seen and approved full details.

ENQUIRIES

Acting for a buyer

4.117
- Is the Protocol being adopted, and if it is, has the seller provided a full set of completed Protocol-style enquiry forms?
- If the Protocol is being adopted and if the seller has provided a set of completed Protocol-style enquiry forms, are there any specific additional enquiries you need to raise?
- If the Protocol is not being utilized, which forms are you using; or should you use Protocol or not, pre-printed or not, core and/or additional?
- If the Protocol is not being utilized, what extra questions need to be asked that are specific to the subject property?
- What specific enquiries should you raise consequent on any particular instructions you may have received from the client?
- Consider the need for a specific enquiry about flooding.
- Always advise your client of any onerous or unusual replies or results to any of the preliminary enquiries, and request written instructions in response.
- Always make a file note of the date of dispatch of the enquiries made on a specific property file, *and do not* exchange contracts until all enquiries have been answered satisfactorily and the client has seen and approved full details.
- If the transaction involves commercial property, consider using the CPSEs.

PLANNING

Acting for a buyer

4.118
- Have all appropriate enquiries been sent to the seller and to the local planning authority?
- Does the client want to make any changes to the subject property that will amount to 'development' as defined by the Town and Country Planning Act 1990?
- If so, will the building works or change of use require express planning permission?
- If a change of use is proposed, will it require formal consent, or will it come within a use class, or will it be allowed by the blanket approval available under the General Development Order?
- Does an Article 4 Direction exclude the blanket approval so as to affect the subject property?

- If the property is newly built, obtain a copy of the building regulations approval as well as a copy of the planning permission and place these with the deeds on completion. Consider indemnity insurance if the detail is incomplete.

- Ensure that all the conditions attaching to a planning consent are seen and check that they have all been complied with.

- If the subject property has had recent replacement windows or doors or there are recent electrical works has there been buildings regulations compliance?

- Always advise your client of any onerous or unusual replies or results to any of the searches and enquiries in so far as they relate to planning matters, and request the client's written instructions in response. *Do not* exchange contracts until all enquiries have been answered satisfactorily, consents seen and approved, and the client has been supplied with full details of all planning matters and approves the position as reported.

5

DEDUCTION AND INVESTIGATION OF TITLE

INTRODUCTION

5.01 Deducing title is the process by which the seller demonstrates to the buyer that the seller owns the land and can convey it. Conversely, the process of investigating title is the means by which the buyer ensures that the seller does own the land, and can convey it. This is done by examining the title that the seller has deduced. Alternatively, the seller is entitled to show that the land is owned by another person whom the seller can compel to convey, for example in the case of a sub-sale (see 3.165).

5.02 We shall discuss briefly when these procedures are carried out and then consider in more detail the methods for deducing and investigating title in both registered and unregistered land. Special considerations arise when investigating title which is, or was, vested in someone whose powers as an estate owner are limited in some way, such as a trustee or personal representative. These will be examined from 5.65. As a practical illustration we have designed an abstract of an unregistered title which is set out from 5.165. This is followed by some suggested requisitions which might be raised by a practitioner, together with explanations of the requisitions.

TIME FOR DEDUCTION AND INVESTIGATION OF TITLE

Traditional approach

5.03 In unregistered title the process of deducing and investigating title can be lengthy and complex, and for this reason they were traditionally carried out after contracts had been exchanged. In this way the parties were able to defer any escalation in legal costs until they were sure that the other party was legally obliged to proceed. As we shall see, the expansion in registered titles has made the whole process generally much simpler. This has been a significant factor in the shift towards deduction and investigation of title *before* exchange. Another reason for this has been the increase in dependent sale and purchase transactions. For a buyer, in particular, it is generally advantageous to investigate title before exchange. Although a buyer can lawfully withdraw from a contract if a seller is unable to make good title, this is small comfort to a buyer who has already exchanged on a related sale.

Modern approach

Accordingly, the accepted practice today is to deduce and investigate title before exchange **5.04** of contracts. Moreover, it is a requirement of the Protocol (assuming the parties are using it) that the seller deduces title at the same time as the draft contract and other pre-contract documents are sent to the buyer. Importantly, Standard Condition (SC) 4.2.1(a) bars the buyer from raising any requisitions on the title shown by the seller before the contract is in force. However, the buyer may raise requisitions on matters coming to his attention for the first time after the contract is in force (SC 4.2.2).

Time limits

SC 4.3.1 lays down time limits for deducing title and raising requisitions. These are only **5.05** of academic interest where deduction and investigation of title occur before exchange. However, the time limits could in theory result in the buyer being out of time for raising objections when an unregistered title is verified, normally on completion. (See 5.50 for a discussion of verification of title.)

DEDUCTION OF TITLE TO UNREGISTERED LAND

The evidence of title to unregistered land is contained in the title deeds. The seller will **5.06** therefore deduce title by supplying the buyer with particulars of the deeds, tracing a chain of ownership through to the current seller (or someone whom the seller can compel to convey). The buyer should insist that the seller deduces title from at least 15 years before the date of the contract (this applies both at common law and under the SCs), and the chain of title must commence with a good root (i.e. the starting point for the period of ownership) duly stipulated in the sale contract. The constituent elements of a good root are now explained.

A good root of title

Although there is no statutory definition of a good root, the description given in Williams, **5.07** *A Treatise on the Law of Vendor and Purchaser* (4th edn, 1936), is well established. Essentially a good root is a document which:

(a) deals with or shows ownership of the whole legal and equitable interest in the property (the buyer will normally be concerned only with the legal estate; if the proper conveyancing procedures are adopted, any equitable interests should be overreached and thus will not bind the buyer: see *City of London Building Society v Flegg* [1988] AC 54);

(b) contains an adequate, identifiable description of the property. A mortgage will fail this test if it lacks a full description of the property (mortgages often refer to a fuller description in the conveyance to the mortgagor) and, similarly, an assent will fail if it simply vests the property, 'for all the estate or interest of the deceased'; or does nothing to cast doubt on the title (a document will cast doubt if it depends for its effect on an earlier instrument, such as a power of attorney (see *Re Copelin's Contract* [1937] 4 All ER 447)), but such 'doubt' can be overcome if the seller can prove that the earlier document still subsisted at the time of its execution (see 5.100 for a discussion of the problems associated with documents executed under a power of attorney);

(c) is at the date of the contract at least 15 years old (Law of Property Act 1925, s 44, as amended by the Law of Property Act 1969, s 23 (before 1970 the period was 30 years)).

5.08 Provided that the above criteria are fulfilled, the practitioner should appreciate that the best document to use as a root is a conveyance on sale or, failing that, a legal mortgage. These deeds are preferable to gifts of title, such as a voluntary conveyance or an assent, where it is unlikely that any prior title investigation was made before completion of the gift. As a general rule, if there is included within a title a conveyance on sale which satisfies the above criteria, the buyer should insist on the conveyance as the root.

5.09 The following documents should never be accepted as roots of a title: a will (it only operates in equity); a lease (it does not deal with the freehold estate); a pre-1926 conveyance subject to a mortgage (the legal estate is not vested in the mortgagor); and an equitable mortgage (it only operates in equity). If the property being sold is leasehold, a copy of the lease itself should be deduced.

Risks for buyer in accepting short title

5.10 There are dangers for the buyer in accepting a root which is less than 15 years old at the date of the contract. These can be summarized as follows:

(a) The buyer will be bound by incumbrances which would have been discovered had the buyer investigated for the full 15 years. In accepting a short title the buyer has constructive notice of them.

(b) The buyer will lose any rights to compensation from the State under s 25 of the Law of Property Act 1969. This compensation is for loss arising from undiscovered land charges registered against an estate owner who owned the land before the date of the document that *should have been used* as the root. The compensation is available only if such incumbrances would not have been discovered by a prudent buyer who investigated a proper 15-year title.

(c) An important practical point: Land Registry will probably not grant absolute title on the buyer's application for first registration after completion. It may also place a 'protective' entry in the charges register to cover the possibility of undisclosed easements or restrictive covenants, i.e. 'subject to such easements or restrictive covenants as may have been imposed thereon and are still subsisting'.

(d) As a result of the above the title to the property will become less marketable and less attractive to potential buyers and lenders.

Methods of deducing an unregistered title

5.11 There are two methods of deducing unregistered title; one is by a traditional abstract of title and the other, used almost universally these days, by an epitome of title.

Abstract of title

5.12 The conveyancer will rarely prepare an abstract of title today as this was a practice which evolved before the arrival of photocopying machines. Not wishing to part with possession of the original deeds, the seller's practitioner would draft a summary or précis of the contents of the deeds (often resembling a conveyancer's secret code). This avoided the need to write out the entire document, word for word. From time to time you will still encounter abstracts, as practitioners will sometimes use an old abstract from a previous conveyance, and then supplement it with their own epitome of the more recent title.

Epitome of title

This is the preferred modern method of deducing unregistered title. It involves the preparation of a list or schedule, in chronological order, of all the material title deeds and events which form the chain of title, for example a conveyance, a mortgage, or a death. The practitioner then attaches to the schedule photocopies of the relevant documents. All photocopies should be fully legible with copy plans correctly coloured.   **5.13**

An example of the front page of an epitome is set out in Appendix 6. Note how each document is numbered and described, and indications are given of whether a photocopy or abstract is supplied, and whether the original will be handed over on completion (in some transactions the seller will, on completion, retain the originals and just give examined copies to the buyer, e.g. on a sale of part).   **5.14**

Documents to include in the abstract or epitome

The seller's practitioner must be able to demonstrate an unbroken chain of ownership, beginning with the root of title and ending with the document vesting title in the current seller. Thus all documents dealing with the legal and equitable estate during this period should be deduced, for example conveyances, evidence of change of name, evidence of devolution on death, memoranda endorsed on title deeds, discharged legal mortgages, and a power of attorney under which a document has been executed (even if the power was executed before the root of title).   **5.15**

In addition to powers of attorney, it may be necessary to deduce other documents dated prior to the root of title. For example, an earlier conveyance may contain a fuller description of the land than that found in the root document (e.g. by reference to a plan). Furthermore, any document creating binding equitable interests, such as restrictive covenants, must be produced in order to discharge the seller's contractual duty of disclosure (see 3.27).   **5.16**

Documents that need not be included in the abstract or epitome

These can be summarized briefly as follows: **5.17**

(a) Previous land charges search certificates technically do not need to be included. However, it is customary and helpful for buyers if the seller does include them. (Note that they *must* be included if the Protocol is being used.)
(b) Leases that have expired by effluxion of time do not need to be included. (However, leases *surrendered* post-root should be included.)
(c) Documents relating to equitable interests which are discharged or will on completion be overreached, for example an equitable mortgage, need not be included.
(d) Pre-root documents save for those mentioned above, i.e. powers of attorney, or an earlier disposition containing a fuller property description or creating enforceable covenants. These should be included.

DEDUCTION OF TITLE TO REGISTERED LAND

Official copies of title

The Land Registration Act 2002 imposes no restrictions on the rights of the parties to the contract to make their own arrangements as to what evidence of title the seller must deduce. However, the SCs, the Standard Commercial Property Conditions (SCPCs), and the   **5.18**

Protocol require the seller at his own expense to provide the buyer with official copies of the registered title. SC 4.1.2 and SCPC 7.1.2 provide that for registered title the seller will supply official copies of the items referred to in rules 134(1)(a) and (b) and 135(1)(a) of the Land Registration Rules 2003, so far as they are not to be discharged or overridden at or before completion. These items are:

- the individual register;
- any title plan referred to in the register; and
- any document referred to in the register and kept by the Registrar (e.g. a conveyance containing covenants).

5.19 Every buyer's practitioner should insist on receiving up-to-date official copies of the registered title. The 2011 Protocol states that the official copies should be no more than six months old at the date of submission.

Making the application

5.20 The seller's practitioner's application to Land Registry for official copies of the title on Form OC1 will incur a fee. Applications can also be made online and official copies printed off on water-marked paper. When the official copies are sent to the buyer it is good practice to state in the covering letter that they should be held to order pending exchange of contracts. In this way, if the buyer decides not to proceed, the official copies will have to be returned and the seller can pass them on to another prospective buyer without incurring the cost of applying for another set.

5.21 For deduction of title in a situation where the seller is not yet registered as proprietor of the land, and for sub-sales, you are referred to 3.158 and 3.165, respectively. Deducing title to leasehold property is dealt with separately in Chapter 10.

INVESTIGATION OF TITLE

5.22 The seller's practitioner should investigate his own client's title before drafting the contract. The reasons for this were explained at 3.12.

5.23 The buyer's practitioner will investigate the evidence of title produced by the seller's practitioner and will raise queries (requisitions) on any matters which are unsatisfactory or unclear. In residential conveyancing the buyer's practitioner will normally also act for the buyer's lender. The lender will be concerned to ensure that there are no defects in title which would adversely affect the lender's ability to sell the property and recover the loan. In commercial conveyancing any lender is usually represented by a separate firm of solicitors who will carry out their own investigation of title.

Good and marketable title

5.24 The buyer's practitioner must ensure that the title is good and marketable and free from incumbrances which may adversely affect the use and enjoyment of the property. If you are acting for the buyer's mortgagee as well, it is important to appreciate your duty to your mortgagee client. You should check that the title is acceptable in conformity with the mortgagee's instructions, in particular, regarding any special conditions in the mortgage offer. Also check the mortgagee's requirements in the *UK Finance Mortgage Lenders' Handbook* (see Appendix 12). The typical lender is seeking an assurance from you that no title deficiencies exist which may reduce the property's value or adversely affect the lender's ability to dispose of its security on the open market.

One area of concern is where there appears to be a breach of covenant on the title. The **5.25** various options open to practitioners are now considered. These are applicable to both registered and unregistered land.

Breach of covenant

If an enforceable covenant appears to have been breached, the seller should be asked to **5.26** remedy the breach immediately. If this is not possible the seller should be asked to consider the following possibilities to resolve the problem:

(a) indemnity insurance;
(b) obtaining the retrospective consent of the person with the benefit of the covenant; or
(c) applying to the Upper Tribunal (Lands Chamber) for the covenant to be removed from the title.

As far as indemnity insurance is concerned, it should be noted that a common requirement **5.27** of insurance companies is that no one (e.g. the person with the benefit of the covenant) should have been contacted in connection with the breach. Accordingly, it is generally wiser to try the indemnity route first.

(a) Indemnity insurance

This involves arranging at the seller's cost an indemnity insurance policy from a reputable insurance company, in which the buyer, successors in title, and any mortgagee are insured against loss which may arise as a result of the breach. The insurer will normally require a copy of the conveyance or Land Registry entry imposing the restriction, a statutory declaration from the owner of the property confirming that no enforcement action has been taken, and counsel's opinion (if taken). Insurance is unlikely to be offered if the covenant was created recently (i.e. within the last 10–15 years). This is because of the increased risk of enforcement. (Title insurance is also available in respect of unknown covenants affecting property, e.g. where a registered title refers to a conveyance containing restrictive covenants but no copy has been filed at Land Registry).

(b) Consent or release by person who now owns the land with the benefit

You may consider contacting the person who has the benefit of the covenant to obtain retrospective consent to the breach. Alternatively, you may seek agreement to a release or variation of the covenant. Should payment be required for the release or variation, this should be borne by the seller. Land Registry will remove a restrictive covenant from the register only if clear evidence is shown that the person purporting to release the covenant has the right so to do. The Registry will thus need to inspect the title to the benefiting land to establish who currently has the benefit of the covenant. Obviously this may not be easy in respect of covenants created many years ago. Indeed, it is often the case that the evidence produced of ownership is insufficient. If so, the Registry will add an entry to the register indicating that a deed is only 'expressed' to release the land from the covenant. Such an entry is not conclusive and should be approached with caution by intending buyers and lenders.

(c) Application to the Upper Tribunal (Lands Chamber)

An application can be made to the Upper Tribunal (Lands Chamber) for an order that the covenant be removed from the title. This is unlikely to be successful unless the covenant is old and redundant. It is seen rather as an act of last resort, and can be prohibitively expensive (do ensure that the application is made at the seller's cost—on the basis that it is the seller's problem).

If a breach-of-covenant problem cannot be resolved, the buyer (and any lender) should **5.28** be advised very carefully about the various options available to remedy the situation and, if a proper solution cannot be found, withdrawal from the transaction may be the only alternative.

Registered land—investigating title

5.29 The buyer's practitioner must examine carefully the up-to-date official copies and other documents referred to on the register which have been received from the seller's practitioner. They must be compared against the information given in the draft contract. You should consider in particular the following:

- Confirm whether the estate is freehold or leasehold.
- Does the title number correspond with the one given in the draft contract?
- Consider the class of title: is it absolute, possessory, good leasehold, or qualified? (Anything less than absolute title will generally be considered to be unsatisfactory.)
- Does the land described in the contract correspond with the title description?
- Consider the title plan. Check that the land being bought is included within the title.
- Are there any colourings or hatchings on the title plan that indicate rights of way or that land has been removed from the title?
- Is the seller in the contract the same as the registered proprietor? If not, who has the ability to transfer the land?
- Are there any incumbrances in the register, and how will these affect the buyer? Which of these will be discharged or removed on completion? (Always ensure that mortgages will be discharged on completion.)
- Has the buyer in the draft contract agreed to buy the land subject to the incumbrances that will remain on the title after completion?

Adverse entries

5.30 If there are discrepancies, or if other adverse entries are present which protect third-party interests (e.g. a notice), you should raise these as requisitions with the seller's practitioner. Other examples might be the presence of a restriction, a caution against dealings (registered pre-13 October 2003), a Home Rights notice, an apparent breach of covenant (see 5.26), or possibly covenants referred to on the title but details of which were not given to Land Registry on first registration. Your requisition should identify the defect or problem and require the seller to remedy it (if necessary, at the seller's cost).

5.31 **Restrictions**   A restriction (entered in the proprietorship register) makes it apparent either that the powers of the proprietor are limited, or that a prior condition must be met before a disposition can be registered. The presence of a restriction does not necessarily mean there is a title defect, because the seller may be in a position to satisfy the terms of the restriction. It is a matter of examining the precise terms of the restriction, as the wording will indicate what procedure must be followed to conduct a valid disposition of the land. The buyer must either follow that procedure or require the seller to remove the restriction on or before completion. For example, if there is a co-ownership restriction indicating a tenancy in common (see 2.25), it may be the case that the purchase money will actually be paid to two trustees (or that a second trustee is being appointed), in which case the buyer can safely accept the position. However, if one of two trustees has died, then a second trustee must be appointed to satisfy the restriction.

5.32 A restriction may cause problems where it has become inoperable. An example of this is where a restriction on a leasehold title requires the certificate of a management company (or its solicitor) before a transfer is registered but the management company has been struck off for failing to submit annual returns and so cannot give the certificate. In these circumstances an application should be made to Land Registry for the restriction to be disapplied on the basis that there is no reason why the transfer should not proceed (see Land Registry Practice Guide 19). The restriction therefore remains on the register in case the company is restored to the Companies' Register at a later date.

An owner who is not living at their registered property (and who does not intend to do so) **5.33** can request the entry of a Form RQ restriction. This is a counter-fraud measure which is designed to help prevent forgery. The restriction requires a conveyancer to certify that they are satisfied that the person transferring or mortgaging the property is the same person as the owner. Clients who are absent abroad or who own second homes should consider registering this type of restriction.

Notices   A notice is an entry in the register in respect of the burden of an interest affecting **5.34** the registered estate, for example a restrictive covenant. Apart from a bankruptcy notice (which is noted in the proprietorship register), notices will be entered in the charges register. The entry of a notice does not guarantee that the interest that it protects is valid, or even exists. A notice will simply ensure that the priority of the interest protected will not be automatically postponed on the registration of a subsequent registrable disposition for value. A notice may either be an agreed notice or a unilateral notice.

The buyer should treat unilateral notices in the same way as cautions against dealings **5.35** (see 5.36), i.e. insist on their removal on or before completion. An application to cancel a unilateral notice must be made on Form UN4. When the Registrar receives an application to cancel he will serve notice on the beneficiary of the notice, who then has 15 business days in which to object to the application, failing which the notice is cancelled. Any dispute about whether the notice should be cancelled that cannot be resolved by agreement will be referred to the Land Registry Adjudicator.

Cautions against dealing   The presence of a caution against dealings (only registrable before **5.36** 13 October 2003) is linked to a third party claiming an interest in the property. No dealing with the property can be registered until the cautioner has been given an opportunity to substantiate the claim (known as the 'warning-off' procedure). Accordingly, the buyer's practitioner should insist either that the caution is removed immediately, i.e. before exchange, or that an undertaking is received from the seller's practitioner to remove the caution on or before completion.

The same approach should be taken by a buyer if a Home Rights notice has been registered **5.37** by the seller's spouse or civil partner, who should also be asked to release all rights and vacate the property on completion (see 3.21 regarding home rights).

Although cautions against dealings were abolished by the Land Registration Act 2002, **5.38** transitional provisions allow cautions registered before the Act came into force to operate as before, i.e. the warning-off procedure is still used. The general equivalent of the caution under the new regime is the unilateral notice (see 5.35).

Inhibitions   Another pre-Land Registration Act 2002 entry known as an inhibition may **5.39** be found on the proprietorship register. This is likely to relate to the bankruptcy of the proprietor before 13 October 2003, and will prevent any disposition of the land until it is removed. As with cautions against dealings, inhibitions have been abolished since 13 October 2003, leaving restrictions and notices as the only means of protecting third-party interests over registered land.

Searches and overriding interests

In addition to the above, the buyer's practitioner must carry out a Land Registry search **5.40** before completion to update the information in the official copies (see 8.18 on pre-completion searches).

5.41 The buyer's practitioner must also check at the pre-contract stage for any overriding interests which are not entered on the register but which will bind the buyer irrespective of notice (e.g. rights of persons in actual occupation, local land charges, legal easements, and leases for seven years or less). Overriding interests can be discovered through the buyer's inspection of the property, a local land charges search, and pre-contract enquiries of the seller (in which the seller is asked to disclose details of occupier's rights and adverse interests).

Unregistered land—investigating title

5.42 Following completion of the purchase of unregistered land you will need to apply for first registration, and your aim will be to obtain an absolute title for the client. Land Registry lawyers will check your title investigation, and unless you have done your job properly you may not receive an absolute title on first registration. How, then, should you go about this most vital and often complex part of the conveyancing process? The following important matters should always be considered. Any defects or queries should be raised with the seller's practitioner as requisitions on title requiring the seller to remedy them, if necessary at the seller's cost. A working example of raising requisitions on an unregistered title appears at 5.165.

Good root of title

5.43 First, check that the root of title offered by the seller is a good one and is at least 15 years old at the date of the contract (see 5.07 for what constitutes a good root). You must then trace chronologically, from the root document, a chain of ownership all the way down to the current seller; a chain which is complete and without missing links. For example, if Jones and Clark bought the land previously, make sure it is they who later sell, not Jones and Smith or even Jones and Clarke (spelling discrepancies should always be raised).

Evidence of change of name

5.44 Ensure that you see evidence of any change of name. For example, if a previous owner purchased the property as an unmarried woman using her maiden name, and then after her marriage sold using her married name, you would want to see a certified copy of the marriage certificate.

Evidence of death

5.45 Ensure that you see evidence of the death of any estate owner since the root of title. For example, if a beneficial joint tenant has died and the survivor has subsequently sold, you would want to see a certified copy of the death certificate (there may be other considerations regarding co-ownership—see 2.22).

Examine each document in the chain for possible defects

5.46 Having traced the chain of ownership you should now examine carefully each document in the abstract or epitome, checking for any deficiencies or omissions. Examples of defects might be a mortgage taken out by a previous estate owner which has not been discharged, or an improperly executed document. Check that all appropriate documents have been correctly stamped (see 5.51).

Description of property

5.47 Ensure that the description of the property in the most recent conveyance or other document accords with that which the client is buying in the contract. This is a fundamental point that will always be checked by Land Registry on first registration. There should be consistency throughout the epitome, and care will be needed where the deeds show a previous sale of part has taken place (see 5.49). Insist on seeing copies of all plans in documents correctly marked and coloured.

Incumbrances and rights

Ensure that there are no incumbrances disclosed by the deeds, other than those disclosed **5.48**
in the draft contract. Copies of all covenants, easements, and other adverse interests should
be supplied even if they pre-date the root of title. Where the property is affected by incumbrances, consider whether they will impede your client's proposed use and enjoyment of the
property. Remember that an incumbrance, if capable of being protected by registration as a
land charge, will not bind your client purchaser unless it has been protected as such at the
Land Charges Department (e.g. a restrictive covenant D(ii) land charge). Ensure also that
the property benefits from all necessary easements, such as rights of access and drainage.

Sales of part

In the history of an unregistered title there may have been a sale(s) of part of land (other- **5.49**
wise known as a 'sale-off'). When investigating title you should be able to identify a sale
of part where the description of land in one conveyance is of a smaller area than that
described in an earlier conveyance. Comparing conveyance plans can be useful in this
respect. If a sale of part has previously taken place, the buyer should check the following:

(a) The seller of the part would have kept the original deeds relating to the whole in order
to prove title to the retained land at a later date. But you should ensure that there was
included in the sale-of-part conveyance an acknowledgement for production and undertaking for safe custody of the original deeds which were retained by the seller (see 7.70
for further details and clause 7 in the precedent for conveyance in Appendix 7). If such
a clause was omitted from the sale of part conveyance, a separate acknowledgement
should be requested.
(b) Ensure that a sale-off memorandum was endorsed on the previous conveyance, i.e. the conveyance to the seller when he purchased the whole. This memorandum gives notice of the
sale-off, and affords protection against any negligent or fraudulent later reconveyance of
the part conveyed (see 8.99 for further details and s 200 of the Law of Property Act 1925).
(c) Ensure that in respect of those deeds and documents the originals of which you will not
be receiving on completion, you have confirmation from the seller's solicitors that properly examined copies or an examined abstract will be provided on completion. Note that
these copies or the abstract must be properly marked as examined against the originals;
mere photocopies will not suffice (see 8.98; Law of Property Act 1925, s 47(9)).

Searches, inspection, and verification

The buyer's practitioner must before completion carry out a search of the Central Land **5.50**
Charges Registry, and advise the client to inspect the property. The practitioner must also
verify the title, i.e. check the abstract or epitome against the original deeds. This is normally
done at completion by comparing the photocopy documents in the epitome against the original deeds. However, practitioners should note that they may be precluded from raising objections at completion if they are out of time for raising requisitions under SC 4.3.1 or SCPC
7.3.1 (this is normally six working days after the date of the contract). Accordingly, if the
title is complex or if you have any suspicions about the validity of the title, we recommend
that you verify it before the time limit expires (i.e. probably before the date of completion).

Stamping of documents

Unstamped or incorrectly stamped documents are not good roots of title; neither are they **5.51**
valid links in a chain of title. Accordingly, they will not be accepted by Land Registry on
an application for first registration. Moreover, they cannot be produced as evidence in civil
proceedings in order to prove title (see Stamp Act 1891, s 14(4); *McGuane v Welch* [2008]
EWCA Civ 785).

5.52 The buyer's practitioner should verify correct stamping by referring to stamp duty tables (which practitioners' firms should have) showing the different rates and thresholds which have applied over the years. Check both for *ad valorem* duty and the particulars delivered (PD) stamp. A document which does not require *ad valorem* duty should contain a certificate of value, an example of which is contained in clause 8 of the conveyance in Appendix 7. Late stamping should be carried out by the seller at the seller's cost. Stamping is considered again in 9.21. Stamp duty was replaced by stamp duty land tax (SDLT) on 1 December 2003.

Checking valid execution of documents

5.53 When investigating an unregistered title a practitioner must always check that each document in the chain of title has been properly executed. If this is not the case, the title may not have passed to the present seller. The current methods of execution for different documents are considered in Chapter 7. The requirements for valid execution changed on 31 July 1990 when the Law of Property (Miscellaneous Provisions) Act 1989 came into force. Before that date, a deed executed by an individual was 'signed, sealed, and delivered'. Since then a deed no longer has to be sealed, but it must say on the face of it that it is intended to be a deed (s 1(2)). This rule applies to every deed, whoever executes it. Accordingly, an attestation by an individual after July 1990 will read, 'signed as a deed'. The signatures of the parties must be properly witnessed.

5.54 The rules governing execution of deeds by companies also changed on 31 July 1990, with the insertion of a new s 36A of the Companies Act 1985. Companies no longer need to affix their common seal; execution can be achieved simply by the signatures of a director and secretary, or two directors, provided the document is expressed to be executed by the company. The signatures do not have to be witnessed. A company seal is nevertheless still effective.

5.55 Should the land have already been registered? Finally, check whether the unregistered land your client is acquiring should already have been registered. Was it in a compulsory area on the date of a previous conveyance? If it was, require the seller to apply for first registration immediately at the seller's expense.

Discharge of mortgages

5.56 When a buyer raises requisitions on a title, either in respect of registered or unregistered land, it is good practice to ask for confirmation that any existing mortgage of the seller will be discharged on or before completion (see Chapter 9 for a discussion of the procedures involved).

Registered land

5.57 In registered land, discharge of the seller's existing mortgage will be effected by filing a completed Form DS1 at Land Registry or through an e-DS1 (see 9.08). As far as mortgages taken out by a previous owner are concerned (i.e. before the seller owned the property), a buyer of registered land is not concerned about these as long as they have been removed from the charges register. The buyer simply needs to be satisfied that the seller's mortgage(s) will be discharged on or before completion.

Unregistered land

5.58 In unregistered land the buyer should always inspect the title to ensure that any prior mortgages have been effectively discharged. If not, they are still incumbrances on the title, and the buyer may take subject to them. The following matters should therefore be considered.

Non-building-society mortgages—unregistered land

A mortgage given to a person other than a building society (e.g. a bank) is discharged by a **5.59**
receipt endorsed on the mortgage deed, signed by the lender, and naming the person making payment (Law of Property Act 1925, s 115). If payment is made by someone other than
the person entitled to the equity of redemption, the receipt may operate not to discharge
the mortgage but to transfer it to the person making payment (Law of Property Act 1925,
s 115(2), and see *Cumberland Court (Brighton) Ltd v Taylor* [1964] Ch 29). Difficulties
could arise if payment is made by a trustee or personal representative on behalf of a borrower, so in these cases the receipt should expressly state that it is not intended to operate
as a transfer of the mortgage.

A transfer of mortgage could also technically occur if, in error, the discharge is dated after **5.60**
the date of the next conveyance by the borrower. The reasoning behind this is that payment is made by the borrower who, at the date of receipt, is someone other than the person
entitled to the equity of redemption (this is now the new owner who technically bought the
property subject to the mortgage). The practitioner ought to check that there is no subsisting C(i) land charge protecting any *puisne* mortgage, and that the seller (or seller's lender)
holds the deeds (not someone else possibly claiming them as security for a mortgage). This
being the case, the practitioner may safely accept the position, despite the date error.

Building society mortgages—unregistered land

Building society mortgages may be receipted as described in 5.59 or, alternatively, by using **5.61**
a receipt prescribed by s 13(7) and Schedule 4 to the Building Societies Act 1986. This is a
simpler form of receipt, which does not need to name the person making payment. It must
be sealed by the society and countersigned by someone acting under the authority of the
society's board of directors.

Mortgage on sale of part—unregistered land

On a sale of part, the whole of the mortgage is not normally discharged on completion, and **5.62**
a receipt is thus inappropriate. Instead the mortgagee will issue a release from the mortgage
of the part being sold. The mortgagee either joins as a party to the purchase deed to release
it, or executes a separate deed of release.

Mortgagee selling

When a mortgagee is selling under its power of sale, the buyer takes free from the seller's **5.63**
mortgage, which therefore does not need to be discharged (Law of Property Act 1925,
s 88(1)(b) for freeholds, and s 89(1)(b) for leaseholds). Contrast this with sales by receivers
considered at 5.73.

KEY POINTS SUMMARY

DISCHARGE OF MORTGAGES

- The buyer should raise a requisition of the seller seeking confirmation that the seller's exist- **5.64**
ing mortgage (if any) will be discharged on or before completion.

- In registered land the buyer is only concerned with mortgages presently noted on the register
of title.

- In unregistered land, the buyer must examine the abstract or epitome to ensure that all previous mortgages have been validly discharged. (On an earlier sale of part, a deed of release
of part is more likely.)

- In unregistered land, the receipt on the mortgage should not be dated later than the date of the next transaction in the chain, otherwise the mortgage will be transferred, not discharged.

- In unregistered land, for non-building-society mortgages, the person making payment must be named and must be the person entitled to the equity of redemption; otherwise the mortgage is not discharged, but transferred.

- In unregistered land, if an inadvertent transfer has occurred, check that it was only a technical slip by conducting a land charges search against the person who bought from the borrower, and asking the seller to confirm the whereabouts of the deeds.

PERSONS DISPOSING OF LAND IN DIFFERENT CAPACITIES

5.65 There are special title considerations where the person disposing of the property is not the sole legal and beneficial owner. In unregistered land, these considerations will also be of relevance so far as previous estate owners are concerned. We begin with an explanation of sales by mortgagees.

Mortgagees

5.66 A mortgagee may exercise its power of sale and convey the mortgaged property in its own name provided a power of sale exists, has arisen, and has become exercisable. These requirements and the explanations which follow apply equally to registered and unregistered land:

(a) **Power of sale exists** A power of sale is implied in every mortgage made by deed unless, unusually, the power is expressly excluded in the deed itself (Law of Property Act 1925, s 101(1)(i)). A legal mortgage must be made by deed (Law of Property Act 1925, s 85), and so it follows that a legal mortgagee will always have a power of sale unless the power has been expressly excluded.

(b) **Power of sale has arisen** The power of sale arises on the legal date for redemption of the mortgage, which is when the mortgage money, in theory, becomes due. This date is normally specified in the deed to be a date within the first six months of the mortgage.

(c) **Power of sale has become exercisable** *Prima facie* the power of sale becomes exercisable if one of the events in s 103 of the Law of Property Act 1925 occurs, namely a formal demand for payment has not been complied with for three months, interest is unpaid for two months, or the borrower is in breach of some other condition of the mortgage. In practice, however, the modern mortgage deed will generally exclude s 103 and then expressly strengthen the mortgagee's position by enlarging the statutory grounds.

Acting for a buyer

5.67 For conveyancing purposes, when acting for a buyer from a mortgagee, or when investigating an unregistered title which includes an earlier sale by a mortgagee, the buyer's practitioner will only need to be concerned with points (a) and (b) at 5.66. There is no need for the buyer to check whether the mortgagor was or is in default because even if the power is not exercisable, the buyer will still receive a good title (Law of Property Act 1925, s 104(2)). The question of whether the power can be properly exercised is a matter between mortgagor and mortgagee.

5.68 Thus the buyer's practitioner, in determining whether a sale by a mortgagee was (or will be) valid, should simply inspect the mortgage deed to verify (a) that the power of sale is not excluded (bear in mind that an exclusion would be exceptional); and (b) that the legal date for redemption has passed. If either of these has not occurred, the mortgagee cannot convey or transfer the legal estate.

Effect of sale by mortgagee

The mortgagee conveys the legal estate free from subsequent mortgages, but subject to any **5.69** mortgages having priority to the selling mortgagee. The buyer's practitioner should therefore ensure that the selling mortgagee discharges any subsisting prior mortgages from the proceeds of sale in the same way as a mortgagor who is selling would discharge a subsisting mortgage. On completion of the sale, the mortgage under which the power of sale is exercised is not discharged (allowing the mortgagee to pursue the borrower for any arrears), but the buyer takes free from it.

Acting for selling mortgagee

The seller's practitioner must ensure that the power of sale has become exercisable (see **5.70** 5.66), otherwise the mortgagee may be liable in damages to the borrower. In addition, the seller's practitioner should ensure that the mortgagee is able to give vacant possession on completion—it may be necessary to obtain a court order for possession if the property is not already vacant.

The mortgagee should be made aware of its duty to obtain the best price for the property **5.71** reasonably obtainable on the open market (see *Cuckmere Brick Co. Ltd v Mutual Finance Ltd* [1971] Ch 949, CA; Building Societies Act 1986, Schedule 4). However, this is not a matter of concern to the buyer. Once the mortgage debt is discharged, if there are any surplus monies, these must be passed by the selling mortgagee to any subsequent mortgagee and failing that, to the borrower personally. Again, this is of no concern to the buyer.

The Unfair Terms in Consumer Contracts Regulations 1999 (SI 1999/2083) may possibly **5.72** apply in a sale by a commercial mortgagee to a private individual. The Regulations are explained in Chapter 11.

Sale by receiver

In some situations, usually involving commercial property, the mortgagee will appoint a **5.73** receiver under its charge to collect rents and then perhaps to sell the property. A receiver selling mortgaged property is deemed to be the agent of the *borrower* (Law of Property Act 1925, s 109(2)), and thus a buyer from a receiver will not by right take free from any subsequent mortgage. It follows that a buyer in these circumstances must treat the receiver as he would a borrower selling, and insist that all outstanding mortgages are discharged on completion.

KEY POINTS SUMMARY

SALE BY MORTGAGEES

- Acting for the seller, ensure that power of sale exists, has arisen, and is exercisable. Is a court **5.74** order required to secure vacant possession? Mortgagee should sell for best price reasonably obtainable.

- Acting for the buyer, examine the mortgage deed and check that the legal date for redemption has passed (i.e. that the power of sale has arisen). Ensure that any prior mortgages are cleared off on completion.

- If buying from a receiver, all mortgages must be cleared off on completion because the receiver acts as agent for the borrower.

Personal representatives

5.75 Personal representatives (PRs) become involved in the conveyancing process because the legal estate in the deceased's land vests in the PRs. (But on the death of a beneficial joint tenant the deceased's beneficial share will *not* form part of the deceased's estate but will instead pass to the surviving joint tenant under the right of survivorship.)

5.76 If the deceased left a will, the PRs (known as executors) apply for a grant of probate. If the deceased did not leave a will, the PRs (known as administrators) apply for a grant of letters of administration. The generic term for both types of grant is a grant of representation and it is the grant that confers authority on the PRs to dispose of the legal estate. Accordingly, a buyer from a PR should not complete the purchase until the grant has been issued. (This may cause problems if a seller dies between exchange and completion; see 6.91.)

The assent

5.77 If land is left to a beneficiary under a will, the PRs will vest the land in the beneficiary through a document known as an assent.

5.78 **Registered land**   In registered land the assent must be in the form prescribed by the Land Registration Rules 2003 (Form AS1 for transfer of whole, and Form AS3 for transfer of part, of a registered title). Unlike in unregistered land (see 5.79), there is no risk of the same piece of land being mistakenly disposed of twice. Land Registry is required to assume that the assent has been made to the right person (Land Registration Rules 2003, r 162).

5.79 **Unregistered land**   If the legal estate is to pass, the assent must be in writing (it need not be by deed unless the beneficiary is entering into a new covenant, e.g. an indemnity covenant). The assent must be signed by all proving PRs, and it must name the person in whose favour it is made (Administration of Estates Act 1925, s 36(4)). Even if the PR and the beneficiary are one and the same, an assent by the PR (in favour of himself) is still required in order to change the capacity in which the property is held from PR to beneficial owner (*Re King's Will Trusts* [1964] Ch 542). An assent is in itself sufficient evidence that the person in whose favour it is made is the person entitled to the legal estate. This rule applies provided there is no memorandum endorsed on the grant of any *previous* assent or conveyance (Administration of Estates Act 1925, s 36(7), and see 5.85–5.86). Accordingly, it is not necessary to check the will for confirmation that the assent was made to the right person (as we have seen, the will is not deduced in any event).

PRs selling

5.80 If the deceased died intestate, or if the deceased's will directs that the land shall be sold (the proceeds being distributed to those entitled), then all proving PRs should execute a purchase deed of the land in the normal way. A PR in whom power is reserved is not a 'proving PR' as such and does not have to be a party to the deed. (Since July 1995, all proving PRs must also be parties to the sale contract—see the Law of Property (Miscellaneous Provisions) Act 1994, s 16.) A single appointed PR is able to give a valid receipt for purchase money and can thus overreach the beneficial interests under the will or intestacy (Law of Property Act 1925, s 2(2)). This should be contrasted with the position of a trustee selling, where payment to at least two trustees (or a trust corporation) is required for overreaching to occur.

Acting for a buyer from PRs

5.81 **Registered land**   The buyer will obtain a good title provided the transfer deed is executed by all proving PRs and the buyer receives a certified or office copy of the grant of representation. There is no need for PRs to become registered proprietors unless they intend to retain the land for any length of time, for example until a beneficiary reaches full age. If the PRs decide to register themselves this can be achieved by a simple application to Land Registry accompanied by the grant. If the PRs are selling as registered proprietors, a buyer will not require sight of the grant. Registered titles are not subject to ss 36(6) and (7) of the Administration of Estates Act 1925, referred to at 5.83.

Unregistered land   In unregistered land the situation is more complex because a prudent **5.82** buyer might reasonably ask: 'How can I be sure that the PRs have not already disposed of the property to someone else, perhaps by mistake?' This is of concern to a buyer not only where the current seller is a PR, but also where the buyer is investigating an unregistered title which includes an earlier disposition by a PR.

Section 36(6) statement   Help is available in the form of s 36(6) of the Administration of **5.83** Estates Act 1925. This section provides that where a conveyance by PRs contains a statement that there has been no previous assent or conveyance by the PRs, the buyer is entitled to rely on this statement as sufficient evidence of its truth, *even if it is wrong*. The moral for the buyer therefore is always to ensure that a s 36(6) statement is or was included in any conveyance by PRs (the statement is normally contained in the recitals to the conveyance). The term 'buyer' in this context includes a lessee and mortgagee but not an assentee, so it is unnecessary to include a s 36(6) statement in an assent.

There are three caveats to the s 36(6) protection rule that the buyer's practitioner should heed: **5.84**

(a) A s 36(6) statement is *sufficient* evidence of its truth, not conclusive evidence. Accordingly, other factors may affect the situation; for instance, where a buyer has knowledge of a previous disposition by PRs or is aware of suspicious circumstances, a court may not permit the buyer to rely on the statement. An example of this occurred in *Re Duce and Boots Cash Chemists (Southern) Ltd's Contract* [1937] Ch 642, where the recitals in an assent referred to the terms of the will, which showed that the assent had clearly been made to the wrong person. The buyer was deemed to have constructive knowledge of it.
(b) A s 36(6) statement will not protect a buyer if the PRs (or later, a beneficiary) have already sold the land to another buyer for valuable consideration.
(c) The buyer is not protected if the grant of representation is endorsed with a memorandum (i.e. a note) of a previous disposition by the PRs—such a memorandum constitutes notice of the disposition. A discussion of this now follows.

Memorandum on the grant   On completion of an earlier assent or sale of unregistered **5.85** land by PRs, the beneficiary or buyer (as the case may be) should have insisted that a brief memorandum of the transaction was endorsed on the grant of representation. Under s 35 of the Administration of Estates Act 1925, this can be demanded, at the cost of the estate. The reason for the memorandum is to alert anyone dealing with the PRs in the future that a disposition of the land has been made and to prevent that person from possibly taking the benefit of a s 36(6) statement in the conveyance from the PRs (see 5.83). (Technically a previous *buyer's* title cannot be usurped (see caveat (b) in 5.84) but to avoid doubt it was still best practice to endorse a memo on completion of purchases as well as assents.)

Today, an endorsement of a memorandum on a grant is strictly unnecessary because the **5.86** disposition will be one which induces first registration, for example a conveyance/transfer or assent. The registration of the disposition will prevent any land being disposed of twice, and a future buyer will of course be investigating a registered title.

Acknowledgement for grant   Subsequent buyers of the land may need to inspect the origin- **5.87** al grant of representation. A disposition of unregistered land by PRs (e.g. an assent or conveyance) should therefore contain an acknowledgement of the right to production of their grant (see also 7.77).

KEY POINTS SUMMARY

PERSONAL REPRESENTATIVES

5.88   • Do not complete a purchase from PRs until the grant has been issued. Ensure that all proving PRs execute the purchase deed.

     • Unless the land is registered or the transaction induces first registration (e.g. assent or conveyance), ensure on completion that a memorandum of the transaction is endorsed on the grant.

     • When investigating an unregistered title which contains an earlier disposition by PRs, ensure that a memorandum recording that disposition was endorsed on the grant. Also ensure there are no other endorsements on the grant recording *previous* dispositions.

     • When investigating an unregistered title containing a disposition by a beneficiary as beneficial owner, ensure that the land was properly vested in the beneficiary by an assent. This applies even if the PR and the beneficiary are the same person (see *Re King's Will Trusts* [1964] Ch 542).

     • When examining an earlier conveyance of unregistered land by PRs, check that it contains a s 36(6) statement confirming that no previous disposition of the land was made by the PRs, together with an acknowledgement for future production of the original grant.

     • When PRs are selling land registered in the name of the deceased, all proving PRs must execute the purchase deed and a certified copy of the grant must be handed to the buyer.

Co-owners

5.89   It is a fundamental principle of English land law that where land is held jointly, a trust is created. The law regulating trusts and co-ownership changed on 1 January 1997, when the Trusts of Land and Appointment of Trustees Act 1996 came into force. The 1996 Act replaced the old concept of 'trust for sale' with a new 'trust of land'. The Act applies retrospectively so that even trusts for sale created before 1997 are now known as trusts of land.

Trusts of Land and Appointment of Trustees Act 1996

5.90   Under the 1996 Act, trustees no longer have an overriding duty to sell as they once had under a trust for sale. Beneficiaries under a trust of land have a statutory interest in possession giving them a right to occupy the land as long as occupation remains a purpose of the trust (s 15). This stems from the modern recognition that beneficiaries have an interest in land rather than an interest in the proceeds of sale or equity of redemption (i.e. money). In this respect the doctrine of conversion is abolished as the land is no longer regarded as personal property (s 3).

Overreaching

5.91   Although the rights of beneficiaries have been improved under the 1996 Act, practitioners should appreciate that the doctrine of overreaching has not been abolished. This was confirmed by the Court of Appeal (*Birmingham Midshires Mortgage Services Ltd v Sabherwal* (2000) 80 P & CR 256). It remains the case that a buyer (including a mortgagee) is not concerned with the beneficial interests under a trust of land provided the buyer pays the purchase money to at least two trustees or a trust corporation (see Law of Property Act 1925, ss 2 and 27; *City of London Building Society v Flegg* [1988] AC 54). However, if payment is made to a sole trustee, the buyer takes subject to any beneficial interests under the trust. Despite the overreaching principle, a prudent purchaser should always insist that any adult occupiers of the subject property release any rights they may have, and agree to vacate on completion.

Disposition by sole surviving co-owner

Tenants in common One potential area of risk for buyers is where one of two equitable **5.92**
tenants in common has died. Suppose A and B hold the legal estate on trust for themselves
as tenants in common. If A dies, B will hold the legal estate on trust for himself and those
entitled under A's estate. If B now sells, a prudent buyer must insist that B appoints a second trustee to sell with B so that overreaching can occur; otherwise the buyer takes subject
to the interests of those entitled under A's estate. The appointment of the second trustee
should be made by deed.

As an alternative, if A left his equitable share to B under his will, A's PRs would vest A's share **5.93**
in B by an assent. In this case the buyer could accept a sale by B alone if devolution of A's equitable share to B could be proved, i.e. by production of the grant of probate and the assent to B.

Joint tenants Alternatively, co-owners may hold their equitable interests as joint tenants. **5.94**
In this case, the equitable interest of a deceased joint tenant will pass automatically to the
survivor, who is freely able to sell the whole legal and equitable interest. Accordingly, there
is no need to appoint a second trustee. There is, however, a need for the buyer to see proof
of death, either by the death certificate or the grant of representation.

Is it a tenancy in common or joint tenancy? How does the buyer from a sole surviving **5.95**
co-owner know whether the co-owners held as joint tenants or tenants in common? The
answer to this question rests on whether the land is registered or unregistered:

(a) **Registered land**

If the co-owners are tenants in common, a restriction will have been entered on the proprietorship register. Under the terms of the restriction, a sole survivor cannot dispose
of the property except under an order of the court. A second trustee must therefore be
appointed. (Of course, there is no need to appoint another trustee if the legal title is
already owned by at least two registered proprietors.)

The wording of the restriction is:

No disposition by a sole proprietor of the registered estate (except a trust corporation) under
which capital money arises is to be registered unless authorized by an order of the court.

A previous form of wording (pre-13 October 2003) may also be encountered:

No disposition by a sole proprietor of the land (not being a trust corporation) under
which capital money arises is to be registered except under an order of the Registrar or
of the court.

If there is no restriction in the proprietorship register you may assume that the co-owners **5.96**
are joint tenants in equity. A buyer may then safely deal with the survivor of them on proof
of the death of the deceased co-owner. Accordingly, a sale by a sole surviving equitable joint
tenant of registered land presents no conveyancing problems. Land Registry will simply
accept a transfer by the survivor, accompanied by the death certificate of the deceased. The
register is definitive and, in the absence of the above restriction, the buyer will know that
the seller is a surviving joint tenant.

(b) **Unregistered land**

Here the conveyance under which the co-owners purchased the land should be examined.
This will usually state whether they are joint tenants or tenants in common. If nothing
is said there will be a presumption of a joint tenancy (in accordance with the equitable
maxim, 'Equity follows the law'), unless the conveyance contains words of severance (e.g.
'to A and B equally') or there are other circumstances indicating a tenancy in common,
for example unequal contributions to the purchase price. If in doubt, you should treat the
seller as a surviving tenant in common and insist on the appointment of a second trustee.

5.97 **Sale by sole surviving joint tenant** In unregistered land a prudent buyer might reasonably ask: 'How can I be sure that the joint tenancy has not been severed, thereby converting it into a tenancy in common? Can I be sure that the appointment of a second trustee is not necessary?' The buyer is afforded protection by the Law of Property (Joint Tenants) Act 1964. This Act applies to sales of unregistered land since 1925, and is therefore retrospective in its effect. It enables a buyer in good faith from a sole surviving joint tenant of unregistered land to assume that there has been no severance of the joint tenancy provided the following conditions are fulfilled:

(a) No bankruptcy petition or order has been registered as a land charge against any of the joint tenants. Thus you should conduct an appropriate land charges search against their full names or, if already made against previous estate owners, check the earlier search.

(b) No memorandum of severance of the joint tenancy has been endorsed on the conveyance to the joint tenants. Thus you should inspect the abstract or epitome and/or raise a requisition for confirmation of this.

(c) The conveyance by the survivor states that the survivor is solely and beneficially entitled to the land (this is normally found in the recitals of the conveyance). For conveyances dated before the Law of Property (Miscellaneous Provisions) Act 1994 came into force (1 July 1995) the survivor could alternatively have conveyed simply as beneficial owner.

5.98 If there is any doubt about whether all three conditions have been met, or if the buyer actually knows there has been a severance (note the requirement of good faith), the survivor should be treated as a tenant in common, and a second trustee appointed.

KEY POINTS SUMMARY

DISPOSITIONS BY CO-OWNERS

5.99 • A buyer should not be concerned about beneficial interests behind a trust provided payment is made to at least two trustees (or a trust corporation).

• It is nevertheless advisable to obtain a release of any rights or interests that may be apparent in respect of the subject property, for example rights of an occupier who has a beneficial interest behind a trust.

• All surviving trustees should be a party to the transfer or conveyance. If it is necessary to appoint a new trustee, this is done by deed of appointment and all surviving trustees should be a party to that deed.

Registered land

• On a sale by a sole surviving co-owner, is there a restriction entered in the proprietorship register, protecting beneficial interests?

• If a restriction is present, the co-owners were tenants in common. To effect overreaching, insist on the appointment of a second trustee to join in selling the legal estate (unless devolution of the deceased's equitable share to the survivor can be proved).

• If there is no restriction, the co-owners were joint tenants. A transfer from the survivor alone can be safely accepted, accompanied by the death certificate.

Unregistered land

• On a sale by a sole surviving co-owner, were the co-owners joint tenants or tenants in common? Read the conveyance to the co-owners when they purchased to find out.

- If dealing with a surviving tenant in common, insist on the appointment of a second trustee to join in selling the legal estate (unless devolution of the deceased's equitable share to the survivor can be proved).

- If dealing with a surviving joint tenant, then, provided the three conditions in the Law of Property (Joint Tenants) Act 1964 are met, you can assume severance has not occurred and safely accept a conveyance/transfer from the survivor alone, together with the death certificate. If the conditions are not met, insist on the appointment of a second trustee to join in selling the legal estate.

Attorneys

A person may authorize another to act on that person's behalf in dealing with his property. **5.100** This authorized person is known as an attorney. An appointment of an attorney may be necessary where someone is infirm, or unavailable to sign an important document. In addition, a person who is selling property and about to go overseas on business may wish to appoint his practitioner to be his attorney. (In this case the practitioner should ensure that no conflict of interest arises.) The authority is formally conferred by a document known as a power of attorney, which must be made by deed (Powers of Attorney Act 1971, s 1(1)). Powers of attorney made before October 1971 are governed by ss 126–128 of the Law of Property Act 1925. The person conferring the authority is known as the principal. The different types of power are now considered together with the impact of the Trustee Delegation Act 1999, which came into force on 1 March 2000.

Different types of power of attorney and the impact of the Trustee Delegation Act 1999

There are various categories of power, the most common of which is the general power. **5.101** This grants the attorney authority under s 10 of the Powers of Attorney Act 1971 to deal with all the principal's assets. It can be granted quite simply as follows:

> I appoint AB to be my attorney in accordance with s 10 of the Powers of Attorney Act 1971. Signed as a deed, etc.

The donor of the power may decide to limit the attorney's powers so that the attorney **5.102** can handle only specified assets, for example a designated property, or deal only with a particular transaction.

For co-owners (i.e. trustees of land), a general power may only be used by a joint proprietor **5.103** if the donor of the power has a beneficial interest in the property (or in its income or sale proceeds). This is laid down by s 1 of the Trustee Delegation Act 1999. If a trustee uses a general power under s 1, then the attorney must record that the trustee has a beneficial interest in the property. This statement must be made either at the time the power is exercised (e.g. by a clause in the transfer deed or other document being signed by the attorney) or within three months of the power being exercised. A buyer may rely on such a statement as conclusive evidence of its truth. The following provisions would be acceptable in the transfer deed or other disposition:

Additional provision as follows:

> [Name of attorney] confirms that [donor of the power] has a beneficial interest in the Property at the date of this [transfer, charge, etc.].

Or

Adapt attestation clause as follows:

> Signed as a deed by [name of donor of power], who has a beneficial interest in the Property at the date of this [transfer, charge, etc.], acting by [his/her] attorney [name of attorney] in the presence of . . .

Or

Expand words of signature as follows:

> Thomas Churnside by his attorney Roger Woolley who confirms that the donor has a beneficial interest in the Property at the date hereof.

5.104 A separate written statement can be made provided it is dated within three months of the date of the disposition executed by the attorney.

5.105 Alternatively, a joint proprietor may use a trustee power under s 25 of the Trustee Act 1925 as amended by s 5 of the Trustee Delegation Act 1999. The trustee power can be used whether or not the trustee has a beneficial interest in the land but trustee powers cannot last longer than 12 months from the date of the power. Trustees who hold no beneficial interest in the trust land may only delegate by means of a trustee power, not a general power.

5.106 A further type of power is a security power, which is rarely used. This enables a mortgagee to exercise a power of sale under an equitable mortgage.

5.107 All of the categories of power mentioned above (save for the security power) are revoked automatically upon the donor's death, mental incapacity, or bankruptcy. Express revocation is of course also possible.

Enduring powers of attorney

5.108 Unlike the general, special, and trustee powers, an enduring power is not revoked by the donor's subsequent mental incapacity. However, if incapacity occurs, the power must be registered with the Court of Protection (or, after 1 October 2007, with the new Public Guardian), after which it is incapable of revocation (unless mental capacity is revived). The power must be executed in the form prescribed by the regulations under the Enduring Powers of Attorney Act 1985 (currently the Enduring Powers of Attorney (Prescribed Forms) Regulations 1990 (SI 1990/1376)). There are special rules governing enduring powers once the power has been registered at the court. These are very similar to those found in s 5 of the Powers of Attorney Act 1971, which afford protection to buyers with no knowledge of revocation (see 5.113 and generally s 9 of the 1985 Act). It is no longer possible to create new enduring powers of attorney (see 5.109).

5.109 Before the Trustee Delegation Act 1999 came into force, an enduring power had an important practical benefit for conveyancers in that it could be used to appoint a sole co-trustee (e.g. husband and wife) as attorney (1985 Act, s 3(3)). This was not permitted under either a general or a trustee power. However, one effect of the Trustee Delegation Act 1999 is to repeal s 3(3) of the 1985 Act. The position now is that a sole co-trustee cannot for all practical purposes be appointed as attorney (e.g. wife for husband). This is because s 7 of the Trustee Delegation Act 1999 provides that a receipt for capital money will only overreach beneficial interests if an attorney acts with at least one other person. Thus a transfer signed only by one person both as proprietor and as attorney for the other proprietor (e.g. in a husband-and-wife situation) would not be acceptable. This reinforces the 'two-trustee' overreaching principle, and closes the loophole that previously existed under the Enduring Powers of Attorney Act 1985.

Lasting power of attorney

5.110 Since 1 October 2007, it is no longer possible to create an enduring power of attorney. This is because ss 9–14 of the Mental Capacity Act 2005 replaced it by two types of new lasting powers of attorney (LPAs). One LPA covers property and financial affairs, while the other covers the donor's welfare. Unlike an enduring power, an LPA cannot be validly used by the donee until it is registered with the Public Guardian. A person dealing with a donee of an LPA will receive protection if he has conducted a search with the Public Guardian which has revealed that the LPA has been registered, and he is unaware that the LPA was invalid or has been revoked. A search can be done by e-mailing Form OPG100 to the Public Guardian. The form is downloadable from **https://www.gov.uk/government/publications/search-public-guardian-registers/**. For more detail on LPAs see the Lasting Powers of Attorney, Enduring Powers of Attorney and Public Guardian (Amendment) Regulations 2009 (SI 2009/1884). An enduring power of attorney made before 1 October 2007 remains valid.

Acting for a buyer

There are essentially two concerns for the buyer's practitioner: is the attorney properly authorized to act, and has the power been revoked? **5.111**

Is the attorney properly authorized? The buyer's practitioner should examine a certified copy of the power and check that the attorney is (or was) duly authorized to act in the particular transaction. Often this is simply a case of checking there is no limitation in the power. This applies both when acting for a buyer from an attorney and, in unregistered land, where the epitome reveals an earlier disposition by an attorney. You are entitled to see a certified copy of the power even if it pre-dates the root of title (Law of Property Act 1925, s 45(1)). You must also check that the power was properly executed as a deed. **5.112**

Has the power been revoked? Once you are satisfied that the attorney has (or had) power to make the disposition, you must check that the power was not in fact revoked before the disposition was made. Buyers are afforded protection in this regard by s 5 of the Powers of Attorney Act 1971. This provides, *inter alia*, that even if the power was revoked, the transaction by the attorney is still valid provided the person dealing with the attorney (i.e. the buyer) did not actually know of the revocation. **5.113**

There is a presumption that the buyer did not know of the revocation if the disposition occurred within 12 months of the date of the power. However, if the disposition occurred later than 12 months from the power, the buyer must make a statutory declaration, declaring that he or she was unaware of any revocation at the time. This declaration must be made before or within three months after completion of the *subsequent disposition* by the person making the declaration. So, if your client buys from an attorney whose power is more than 12 months old, arrange for your client to make a statutory declaration following completion (assuming it is true). Because of these complications, the best practice on the part of the donor is to renew the power of attorney on an annual basis if the attorney has ongoing functions. **5.114**

Enduring powers Once an enduring power has been registered with the Court of Protection (or since 1 October 2007 the new Public Guardian) the power is incapable of revocation and the attorney's full authority to act is restored. **5.115**

Registered land

When you apply to register a disposition made in exercise of a power of attorney, Land Registry will require the original or a certified copy of the power (certified on each page) to be lodged with the application (Land Registration Rules 2003, r 61). If the power is an enduring or lasting power and has been registered at the Court of Protection (or new Public Guardian), the Registry will require an office copy of it (if it has been registered it will have the Court of Protection or Public Guardian stamp on it). When buying from an attorney holding an enduring or lasting power it is, therefore, sensible to make a search of the new Public Guardian to see if an application to register has been made. **5.116**

If the disposition by the attorney occurred more than 12 months after the power was granted, the Registry may require an appropriate statutory declaration of non-revocation referred to at 5.114. Note that the Registry will accept a certificate of non-revocation in a letter from the solicitors who acted for the person who dealt with the attorney (often a more practical alternative). A form of declaration/certificate acceptable to Land Registry is set out on the Online Resource Centre. **5.117**

5.118 Rule 61 of the Land Registration Rules 2003 offers another option for practitioners. Land Registry will accept a conveyancer's certificate which states that the power of attorney is in existence. The certificate must also state:

(a) the statutory provision under which the power is made (if any);

(b) the date of the power;

(c) that the conveyancer is satisfied the power is validly executed as a deed, and authorizes the attorney to execute the document on behalf of the donor of the power; and

(d) that the conveyancer is holding either the original power, or a copy by which its contents may be proved, or a document evidencing the power's existence under the relevant statutory provisions.

5.119 The aim of the conveyancer's certificate is to ease the transition to electronic conveyancing. The intention in future is that the certificate will be submitted electronically without the need to produce paper documents. For more information on powers of attorney and registered land, see Land Registry Practice Guide 9.

KEY POINTS SUMMARY

DISPOSITIONS BY AN ATTORNEY

5.120
- A joint proprietor may only use a general power if the donor of the power has a beneficial interest in the property.

- If a trustee uses a general power the attorney must make a statement that the trustee has a beneficial interest in the property.

- This statement must be made either at the time the power is exercised or within three months of the power being exercised. A buyer may rely on the statement as conclusive evidence of its truth.

- A joint proprietor may use a trustee power whether or not the trustee has a beneficial interest in the land, but trustee powers cannot last longer than 12 months.

- Trustees who hold no beneficial interest in the trust land may only delegate by means of a trustee power, not a general power.

- A person buying from an attorney (and subsequent buyers in unregistered land) must inspect the power to check that the attorney is (or was) duly authorized.

- If the power was granted more than 12 months before the date of the disposition by the attorney, the person dealing with the attorney (e.g. the buyer) should make a statutory declaration of non-revocation.

- Best practice for donors is to review a general power on a 12-monthly basis if the attorney has ongoing functions.

- When applying to Land Registry to register a disposition by an attorney, lodge a fully certified copy of the power (or office copy if the enduring power or lasting power is registered with the Court of Protection or Public Guardian). Alternatively, a conveyancer's certificate under LRR 61 may be used.

- When buying from an attorney holding an enduring power or lasting power, it is sensible to make a search of the Public Guardian to see if an application to register has been made.

Charities

Registered land

5.121 If you are dealing with registered land owned by a charity, you should check the proprietorship register for any restriction on the power of the charity to dispose of the land. The restriction may require the Charity Commissioners' or the court's consent before the sale can proceed and, if so, this must be obtained if the buyer is to get good title (see generally Land Registry Practice Guide 14 *Charities*).

Many charities will have the old 'Form 12' or 'Form E' restriction requiring the consent of **5.122** the Charity Commissioners. Since the enactment of the Charities Act 2011, in many cases it will be possible to avoid an order from the Charity Commissioners by following the procedures laid down in ss 117–121 of that Act. These are discussed at 5.124.

Unregistered land

If you are dealing with unregistered land, the disposition may also require the consent of **5.123** the Charity Commissioners or the court (see 5.124). Larger charities are usually exempt from the relevant provisions of the Charities Act 2011, but smaller charities are usually not exempt. A buyer from an exempt charity should obtain evidence of the exemption from the seller and the charity can then be dealt with as if it were a normal seller.

If the charity is not exempt, the consent of the court or the Charity Commissioners must be **5.124** obtained unless all the conditions under ss 117–121 of the Charities Act 2011 are satisfied. These are: the charity must obtain a qualified surveyor's written report on the proposed disposition; it must advertise the disposition under the surveyor's guidance; it must procure the best terms reasonably obtainable; and it must not sell to a 'connected person' (e.g. a trustee or employee of the charity). Where the court's or Commissioners' consent is required, it should be obtained before contracts are exchanged (or the contract should at least be made conditional upon consent being given), otherwise the transaction will be illegal and void.

The deed effecting the disposition (e.g. transfer or conveyance) must certify that the land is **5.125** held by or on trust for the charity and state whether the charity is exempt. If not exempt, the deed must also certify that ss 117–121 of the Charities Act 2011 have been complied with. For dispositions by charities made before the 2011 Act came into force (14 March 2012), you will need to consider the earlier Charities Acts.

KEY POINTS SUMMARY

DISPOSITIONS BY CHARITIES

- If the land is registered, comply with the terms of any restriction in the proprietorship register. **5.126**
- If the charity is exempt from the Charities Act 2011, ask for evidence of exemption and proceed as normal.
- If the charity is not exempt, check whether the conditions of ss 117–121 of the Charities Act 2011 have been satisfied. If not, the consent of the court or the charity commissioners will be required before, or as a condition of, exchange of contracts.
- Ensure that the purchase deed contains the appropriate certificate by the charity.

Companies

Traditionally the investigating practitioner was required to inspect the objects clause in the **5.127** company's memorandum to ensure that the company had the requisite power to buy or sell the land (i.e. that it was not acting beyond its powers, *ultra vires*). The current law is governed by ss 35A and 35B of the Companies Act 1985, inserted by the Companies Act 1989, s 108. The *ultra vires* rule is now restricted in that a person dealing in good faith with a company is not required to check that the disposition is permitted by the company's memorandum. Neither is such a person required to check if there are limitations on the directors' powers to bind the company; indeed, actual knowledge that the transaction is outside the directors' powers will not of itself constitute bad faith (1985 Act, s 35A(2)(b)). Section 35(1) of the Companies Act 1985 is of equal or greater significance in this context because it provides that the capacity of a company to enter into a transaction cannot be called into question by reason of anything in its memorandum, regardless of the good faith of the person dealing with the company.

Registered land

5.128 When a company applies to be registered as proprietor, Land Registry will require details of the company's powers to hold and dispose of land. The certificate given on Form FR1 is the usual way of establishing this. If the company's powers are limited in any way, the Registry will enter a restriction on the proprietorship register. In the absence of a restriction, the buyer of registered land from a company may assume that the company's powers are not limited.

Foreign companies

5.129 The practitioner should always check the powers of a foreign company, if necessary, in conjunction with a lawyer from the jurisdiction in which the foreign company was incorporated. Foreign companies include those which are registered in the Isle of Man and the Channel Islands. It is also important to check Land Registry requirements regarding execution, etc. (see: the Land Registration (Execution of Deeds) Rules 1994 (SI 1994/1130); Foreign Companies (Execution of Documents) Regulations 1994 (SI 1994/950)). See 7.18 for the form of execution by a foreign company. Note that it may be necessary to furnish proof that the foreign company's execution of a document complies with the law of the foreign country. Moreover, if the company's documents are not in English or Welsh, Land Registry will require a certified translation.

Minors

5.130 A person under 18 years of age is entitled to hold an equitable interest in land, but cannot hold a legal estate. A purported disposition of a legal estate to a minor made before 1 January 1997 takes effect as an agreement to create a strict settlement (strict settlements are explained in 5.154). Section 2 of the Trusts of Land and Appointment of Trustees Act 1996 prohibits the creation of new strict settlements, so a disposition of this kind made on or after 1 January 1997 takes effect as a trust of land. In either case, the legal estate is retained by the seller on trust for the minor until the minor reaches majority (Law of Property Act 1925, s 19(1)). A conveyance made to an adult and a minor jointly operates to transfer the legal estate to the adult, who holds it on trust for both of them (Law of Property Act 1925, s 19(2)).

5.131 The proper method of granting a minor an interest in land is to create a trust of land, vesting the legal estate in the trustees. A contract for sale to a minor is binding unless the minor repudiates it before attaining the age of 18, or within a reasonable time thereafter. If the contract is repudiated, the court may require restitution of property or money which passed under the contract (Minors' Contracts Act 1987, s 3).

5.132 When buying registered land, the buyer can assume that the registered proprietor has full capacity unless an appropriate restriction appears on the proprietorship register. If a minor is inadvertently registered as proprietor, the register can be altered and any person suffering loss may be indemnified from State funds (Land Registration Act 2002, Schedules 4 and 8—see 1.102 generally regarding alteration and indemnity).

5.133 A minor cannot convey a legal estate, but there is a presumption that the parties to a conveyance (including a lease or mortgage) are of full age (Law of Property Act 1925, s 15).

This is rebuttable, however, and if you suspect that the seller might be under 18, it would be sensible to ask for a certified copy of the seller's birth certificate.

Persons suffering from mental disorder

A person suffering from mental disorder (i.e. for the purposes of conveyancing, someone **5.134** who does not understand the nature of the transaction) can validly enter into a contract for the sale or purchase of land, or convey land for valuable consideration, but cannot make a gift (see *Elliot v Ince* (1857) 7 De GM & G 475). However, if at the time of the transaction the buyer knew of the other person's incapacity, the transaction is voidable at the instance of the mentally disordered person, his or her receiver, or PRs (see *Broughton v Snook* [1938] Ch 505).

Appointment of receiver

If a receiver is appointed (under the Mental Health Act 1993, s 99), the receiver is the **5.135** person with control of the patient's property (under supervision of the court), and any subsequent disposition by the mentally disordered person will be void. If the receiver wishes to deal with land registered in the patient's name, Land Registry will require evidence of the receiver's authority to act, namely, a copy of the order of appointment. The receiver may apply to become the registered proprietor. If so, Land Registry will enter a restriction on the proprietorship register stating that no disposition by the proprietor (i.e. the receiver) will be registered unless made pursuant to a court order.

VOLUNTARY DISPOSITIONS

A voluntary disposition is one made by gift or at an undervalue (i.e. a significantly low **5.136** price). A transfer between spouses on marriage breakdown may qualify as a voluntary disposition, depending on the circumstances. A voluntary disposition can be effected either during the lifetime of the donor or after the donor's death, by an assent. As we have seen, it is preferable not to use a voluntary disposition as a root of title because title investigation is not normally carried out at the time of the voluntary transaction.

Risk of losing property if donor becomes bankrupt

Another difficulty with voluntary dispositions is that if the donor or undervalue seller later **5.137** becomes bankrupt, in certain circumstances a court can set aside the voluntary disposition upon application by the donor's trustee in bankruptcy (this means that the trustee can reclaim the property from the current owner). Thus, where you are acting for a buyer investigating an unregistered title which includes a voluntary disposition, you will need to determine whether the voluntary disposition is capable of being set aside. The relevant law is contained in ss 339–342 of the Insolvency Act 1986 as amended by the Insolvency (No 2) Act 1994. (Section 2 of the 1994 Act inserted a new s 342(2A) into the 1986 Act.)

The first point to appreciate is that once five years have elapsed, the voluntary disposition **5.138** cannot be set aside. So, if the voluntary transaction took place more than five years ago, you simply need to carry out a land charges search against the donor's name from the date when the donor acquired the property until five years after the donor disposed of it. If no bankruptcy entries are revealed, you can proceed safely. If there are bankruptcy entries, you will need to contact the trustee in bankruptcy to find out whether an application to set aside has been or will be made.

5.139 If the voluntary disposition occurred less than five years ago, the position is more complicated. The buyer from the donee will receive good title as long as the property is bought
for value and the buyer acts in good faith. However, in two situations there is a rebuttable
presumption of bad faith, and in either of these situations you should appreciate that the
voluntary disposition may be set aside. The presumptions of bad faith are:

(a) where the buyer has 'dual notice' both of the insolvency proceedings against the donor
and of the voluntary disposition itself; or

(b) where the buyer is an 'associate' of the donor or donee (e.g. spouse, ex-spouse, employer,
employee, partner, or partner's relative: see definition in s 435 of the Insolvency Act 1986).

5.140 The dual notice position under (a) above has been the subject of much debate. It has been
argued that a prudent buyer from a donee should still refuse to buy the property until
five years have elapsed from the voluntary disposition. This is because the donor's subsequent bankruptcy within the five-year period could make the property unmarketable.
For example, suppose a donor makes a gift to a donee, who then sells at full value to P1
within five years of the gift. At the time of P1's purchase, P1 receives a clear bankruptcy
search against the donor. Subsequently, however, and before the five years have passed,
two events occur: the donor becomes bankrupt, and P1 decides to sell to P2. It is arguable
that the donor's trustee in bankruptcy could reclaim the property from P2 because P2 has
dual notice both of the donor's bankruptcy (constructive notice through registration of
the bankruptcy) and of the voluntary disposition (this will be apparent from an inspection of the deeds, assuming the title is unregistered). A properly advised P2 will thus not
proceed because of the risk of the donor's bankruptcy. Accordingly, a properly advised P1
would not buy from the donee in the first place because P1 cannot sell it on.

5.141 The Law Society has taken leading counsel's opinion on the issue, and the opinion is reproduced in (1995) 92 (35) *Gazette* 31. Counsel advises that it would be hard to imagine a
situation in which a court would penalize a genuine purchaser acting in good faith. Moreover he puts forward strong arguments to resist any application by a trustee to set aside in
these circumstances.

First registration

5.142 Prior to 15 November 1999, on first registration of freehold or leasehold land, Land Registry entered a note in the proprietorship register where it believed that there had been an
undervalue transaction (either to the applicant or a predecessor in title) that could become
the subject of proceedings by the donor's trustee in bankruptcy (or liquidator or administrator if the donor is a company) for the recovery of the property.

5.143 The Insolvency Act note took the following form:

> The land having been the subject of a transaction at an apparent undervalue dated . . . made by
> [*full name of donor*], the registered title may be subject to the provisions of [s 339/238] of the
> Insolvency Act 1986. [*NB*: s 339 will be referred to in the case of an individual donor; s 238
> will be referred to in the case of a company donor.]

5.144 Practitioners should appreciate that as voluntary dispositions have been compulsorily
registrable since 1 April 1998, a purchaser today of an unregistered title, when examining
an epitome of title, should not come across a deed of gift within the last five years.

5.145 Land Registry's current practice is to dispense with all Insolvency Act entries. Given the
increased triggers for first registration introduced by the Land Registration Acts 1997 and
2002, the Registry has taken the view that there is no longer any justification for treating a
donee of unregistered land differently from a donee of registered land. Land Registry will

therefore make no new Insolvency Act entries and existing entries will be cancelled without application.

Voluntary dispositions of registered land

The position regarding voluntary dispositions of registered land is that unless notice of a **5.146** voluntary disposition is given by an entry in the register, a buyer should be unaware of any previous voluntary disposition (unless aware from another source), and so a buyer in these circumstances will not have the 'dual notice' referred to in 5.139. Accordingly, unless the buyer of registered land is an 'associate' (or has knowledge from another source), there is a clear presumption of good faith on the buyer's part. You should be aware, though, that since 1 April 2000 the register includes details of the price paid by the proprietor. If this appears to be well below the market value of the property at the time, then the provisions of the Insolvency Act 1986 should be borne in mind.

It is current Land Registry practice to cancel all existing Insolvency Act entries on regis- **5.147** tered titles without application.

Voluntary dispositions: a safe and practical approach for practitioners

The *UK Finance Mortgage Lenders' Handbook* provides that if the instructing practitioner **5.148** is aware that the title to the property is subject to a deed of gift or a transaction at an apparent undervalue completed within five years of the proposed mortgage, then the practitioner must be satisfied that:

(a) the lender will acquire its interest in good faith; and
(b) the lender will be protected under the Insolvency (No 2) Act 1994 against its security being set aside.

If the practitioner is unable to give an unqualified certificate of title, the practitioner **5.149** must arrange indemnity insurance. In these circumstances the following safeguards are recommended:

(a) obtain (at the seller's expense) a statutory declaration from the donor (or undervalue seller), that at the time of the voluntary disposition the donor (or undervalue seller) was solvent and did not become insolvent as a result of the disposition and that the donee was not an associate of the donor (or undervalue seller);
(b) obtain (at the seller's expense) an insurance policy from a reputable insurer indemnifying your client (and any mortgagee) against loss arising from the insolvency of the donor (or undervalue seller);
(c) conduct a bankruptcy search against the donor (or undervalue seller) to assist in rebutting any presumption against good faith on your client's part.

Voluntary dispositions by companies

If a company becomes insolvent, voluntary dispositions made up to two years prior to **5.150** the insolvency to persons 'connected' to the company can be set aside by the court on the application of the company's liquidator. Connected persons include a director, an associate and, importantly, a company within the same group (see Insolvency Act 1986, ss 249 and 435). A proposed buyer from a connected person in these circumstances should therefore wait until the two years have elapsed. In particular, you should beware of property transfers between group companies within the last two years.

5.151 If a company's voluntary disposition was made within the last two years to someone not 'connected' to the company, the liquidator or administrator can ask the court to set aside the transaction if the current buyer has 'dual notice', as referred to in 5.139. It follows that a buyer should conduct a company search against a donor or undervalue seller company to ensure that no insolvency proceedings were begun within the two years after the voluntary disposition.

5.152 In addition to a clear companies search, Land Registry will require the following evidence to show that the property cannot be recovered from the buyer:

(a) confirmation in writing by the buyer's solicitor that there was no pending petition for an administration order or a winding-up order against the donor company at the date of the transfer to the buyer; and

(b) a certificate by the buyer confirming that the buyer is not the donee and is not (and was not at the time of the undervalue transaction) an associate of, or connected with, the donor or donee.

KEY POINTS SUMMARY

VOLUNTARY DISPOSITIONS

5.153 • In registered land, unless notice is given on the register of a previous voluntary disposition within the last five years, a buyer for value acting in good faith can proceed safely. If there is an insolvency note on the register, a buyer should insist on a declaration of solvency by the donor or undervalue seller, together with indemnity insurance arranged at the seller's expense. Conduct a bankruptcy search against the donor or undervalue seller to rebut any presumption of bad faith.

• In unregistered land, if a voluntary disposition took place more than five years ago, conduct a land charges search against the donor or undervalue seller's name from the date when that person acquired the property until five years after he or she disposed of it.

• Conduct a company search against a donor or undervalue seller company to ensure that no insolvency proceedings were commenced within two years of the voluntary disposition. If still within the two-year period, insist on a declaration of solvency and indemnity insurance, as above.

• If a company has made a voluntary disposition to a 'connected person' (e.g. between companies in the same group) within the last two years, do not buy the property until the two years have elapsed.

SETTLED LAND

Abolition of the strict settlement

5.154 Under s 2(1) of the Trusts of Land and Appointment of Trustees Act 1996, subject to two exceptions, new settlements under the Settled Land Act 1925 can no longer be created. (The two exceptions relate to the saving of existing settlements: see s 2(2).) The 1996 Act came into force on 1 January 1997, and any purported new settlement made on or after that date will become a trust of land. Settlements created before 1 January 1997 remain unaffected by the new legislation save for charitable, ecclesiastical, and public trusts formerly governed by the Settled Land Act 1925, which are now converted into trusts of land.

5.155 Today's conveyancing practitioner will rarely encounter settled land, but it is obviously important to know how to deal with it if the time arrives. Before the 1996 Act came into force a home-made will could have inadvertently created a settlement, for example through a gift to a minor (see 5.130 regarding minors generally), or a gift to a spouse for life. Constraints of space prohibit any lengthy explanation of settled land conveyancing, but we set out below some useful practical tips when dealing with settled land. We begin with a brief background to the subject.

Before 1997, a strict settlement usually arose where successive equitable interests were created by a trust instrument setting out the terms of a settlement. This might have been a will appointing trustees and leaving land say to X for life, remainder to Y for life, remainder to Z. A vesting instrument would be used to vest the legal estate in the first tenant for life (X). Then, upon X's death the trustees would become X's special PRs by obtaining a special grant of representation limited to the settled land. **5.156**

The PRs would execute an assent (the vesting instrument) vesting the land in Y. On Y's death the land would cease to be settled land because under the terms of the settlement Z would become absolutely entitled. Z would receive the legal estate from Y's PRs by an ordinary assent. **5.157**

If there is no tenant for life (e.g. if the tenant for life is a minor), the legal estate is vested in the statutory owners (normally the trustees). The statutory owners have the same powers as the tenant for life. A disposition by the tenant for life (or statutory owners) must be authorized either by the vesting instrument or by the Settled Land Act 1925 (note, the Act does authorize a sale). If not authorized, the disposition is void. **5.158**

Acting for a buyer from a tenant for life (or statutory owners)

Subject to minor exceptions, a buyer is not concerned with the terms of the settlement set out in the trust instrument. Under s 110(2) of the Settled Land Act 1925, the buyer may assume that the vesting instrument was made to the correct person provided the vesting instrument contains the 'statutory particulars' laid down in s 5(1) of the Act. These particulars are: **5.159**

(a) the names of the trustees;
(b) the name of any person entitled to appoint new trustees;
(c) a description of the land;
(d) a statement that the land is vested in the tenant for life; and
(e) a statement of any extension of the powers of the tenant for life.

Unless extended by the trust instrument, the Act imposes certain restrictions on the power of the tenant for life to deal with land (e.g. regarding mortgaging and leasing). However, the tenant for life (or statutory owner) has an unfettered power of *sale* which cannot be restricted by the trust instrument. In this regard the tenant for life must obtain the best price reasonably obtainable for the property (Settled Land Act 1925, s 39(1)), although s 110(1) of the Act provides that a buyer in good faith shall be taken to have given the best price (see *Weston v Henshaw* [1950] Ch 510 and *Re Morgan's Lease* [1972] Ch 1). **5.160**

By s 18 of the Act, the buyer must pay the purchase price to at least two trustees of the settlement (or a trust corporation). Accordingly, the trustees must also be made parties to the purchase deed in addition to the tenant for life (or statutory owners). Provided payment is made to at least two trustees, the interests under the settlement are overreached and attach to the proceeds of sale, the buyer taking free of them. **5.161**

Reverting to our example above and to summarize, if you were acting for a buyer from Y (as tenant for life), you would ensure that the last vesting instrument (the vesting assent to Y) names Y as the tenant for life. You would then take a conveyance from Y, ensuring at the same time that you pay the purchase money to all the trustees of the settlement (being at least two in number), who would also be parties to the conveyance. The interest of Z in remainder would then be overreached. **5.162**

Registered land

5.163 The position in registered land is much simpler. The tenant for life (or statutory owner) is registered as the proprietor and appropriate restrictions are entered in the proprietorship register (Land Registration Rules 2003, r 186 and Schedule 7). The buyer in these circumstances must of course ensure that the terms of the restriction are satisfied. When the tenant for life dies, if there is a new tenant for life under the terms of the settlement, the special PRs of the deceased will execute a vesting assent in favour of the new tenant for life, who in turn will apply to Land Registry to be registered as proprietor of the land.

KEY POINTS SUMMARY

SETTLED LAND

5.164 • When acting on the sale of unregistered land, ensure that the seller is the tenant for life (or statutory owner) in whose favour there is a vesting instrument. In registered land, the tenant for life (or statutory owner) should be the registered proprietor.

• When acting for the buyer of registered land, simply comply with the terms of any restriction in the proprietorship register.

• When acting for the buyer of unregistered land note the following:

    • The buyer is not concerned with the terms of the settlement but the buyer must pay the purchase money to at least two trustees or a trust corporation.

    • A disposition by the tenant for life (or statutory owner) must be authorized either by the vesting instrument or by the Settled Land Act 1925 (the Act does authorize a sale).

    • The buyer should check the statutory particulars in the vesting instrument (e.g. an assent) and can assume that they are correct.

A PRACTICAL EXAMPLE OF INVESTIGATING AN UNREGISTERED TITLE AND RAISING REQUISITIONS

5.165 Your client is purchasing The Corner House, Chiltern Road, Pitton. The property has an unregistered title and title has been deduced using the following abstract. In the draft contract, the root of title is expressed to be a conveyance of 20 October 1990 and the seller is stated as Flora Nicholson. The property came within an area of compulsory registration on 1 December 1990.

5.166 At the end of the abstract (see Table 5.1) there are some suggested requisitions on the title with a brief explanation of each requisition.

Table 5.1 Investigating an unregistered title

	ABSTRACT OF THE TITLE of Flora Nicholson to freehold property known as 'The Corner House' Chiltern Road Pitton in the County of Cornshire
7 January 1980	OFFICIAL CERTIFICATE of search in HM Land Charges Register No 217432 against Charles Lane revealing no subsisting entries
13 January 1980 Stamp £1,000 PD Stamp	BY CONVEYANCE of this date made between CHARLES LANE of The Corner House Chiltern Road Pitton in the County of Cornshire (thereinafter called 'the vendor') of the one part and BENJAMIN EDWARDS of 24 Rothesay Avenue Pitton in the County of Cornshire (thereinafter called 'the purchaser') of the other part

RECITING seisin of the vendor and agreement for sale IT WAS WITNESSED as follows:

1. IN pursuance of the said agreement and in consideration of the sum of £50,000 paid to the vendor by the purchaser (receipt acknowledged) the vendor as beneficial owner thereby conveyed unto the purchaser

ALL THAT premises fronting Chiltern Road Pitton aforesaid comprising 1.9 acres or thereabouts and delineated and described on a plan annexed to a Conveyance dated 18 January 1975 made between (1) Colin Todd and (2) Hugh Bell (hereinafter called 'the said Conveyance') AND ALSO ALL THAT messuage or dwelling house erected thereon and known as 'The Corner House' Chiltern Road Pitton aforesaid TOGETHER with the full benefit and advantage of the right of way granted by the said Conveyance over and along the road shown coloured brown on the said plan TO HOLD unto the purchaser in fee simple SUBJECT to the covenants and the conditions contained in the said Conveyance

2. COVENANT by the purchaser with the vendor to observe and perform the said covenants and conditions and to indemnify

EXECUTED by both parties and ATTESTED

24 August 1990	OFFICIAL CERTIFICATE of search in HM Land Charges Register No 328557 against Benjamin Edwards revealing no subsisting entries
20 October 1990	BY CONVEYANCE of this date made between the said BENJAMIN EDWARDS of 'The Corner House' Chiltern Road Pitton in the County of Cornshire (thereinafter called 'the vendor') of the one part and SHARON MUNRO of 49 Nobbs Hill Pitton in the County of Cornshire (thereinafter called 'the purchaser') of the other part

RECITING seisin of the vendor and agreement for sale IT WAS WITNESSED as follows:

1. IN pursuance of the said agreement and in consideration of the sum of £65,000 paid to the vendor by the purchaser (receipt acknowledged) the vendor as beneficial owner thereby conveyed unto the purchaser ALL THAT the before abstracted premises together with the said dwelling house built thereon TOGETHER with the full benefit and advantage of the before abstracted right of way

TO HOLD unto the purchaser in fee simple SUBJECT to the covenants and the conditions contained in the said Conveyance

2. COVENANT by the purchaser with the vendor to observe and perform the said covenants and conditions and to indemnify

EXECUTED by both parties and ATTESTED

20 October 1990	BY MORTGAGE of this date made between the said SHARON MUNRO (thereinafter called 'the mortgagor') of the one part and BLAKEY BANK LTD of 10 High Street Blakey (thereinafter called 'the mortgagee') of the other part. After reciting seisin of Mortgagor in fee simple IT WAS WITNESSED that in consideration of the sum of £40,000 paid by the mortgagee to the mortgagor (receipt acknowledged) the mortgagor as beneficial owner thereby charged unto the mortgagee

ALL THAT before abstracted property

PROVISO for cesser and other usual clauses

EXECUTED by mortgagor and ATTESTED

17 November 1990	WILL made on this date by said SHARON MUNRO appointing DUNCAN MUNRO and SHEILA MUNRO, her parents, to be her executors
12 December 1990	Death of the said SHARON MUNRO

19 January 1991	Grant of Probate to the said will issued out of Blakey District Probate Registry on this date to the said DUNCAN MUNRO and SHEILA MUNRO
29 July 1991	BY ASSENT of this date the said DUNCAN MUNRO and SHEILA MUNRO assented to the vesting of the before abstracted property in ELIZABETH CAMPBELL
14 January 2009	BY CONVEYANCE of this date made between the said ELIZABETH CAMPBELL of The Corner House Chiltern Road Pitton in the County of Cornshire (thereinafter called 'the vendor') of the one part and ALASTAIR NICHOLSON and FLORA NICHOLSON of 2 Mill Road Pitton in the County of Cornshire (thereinafter called 'the purchasers') of the other part
	RECITING seisin of the vendor and agreement for sale IT WAS WITNESSED as follows:
	1. IN pursuance of the said agreement and in consideration of the sum of £90,000 paid to the vendor by the purchaser (receipt acknowledged) the vendor as beneficial owner thereby conveyed unto the purchasers
	ALL THAT the before abstracted premises together with the said dwelling-house built thereon TOGETHER with the full benefit and advantage of the before abstracted right of way TO HOLD unto the purchasers in fee simple as tenants in common in equity SUBJECT to the covenants and the conditions contained in the said Conveyance
	2. COVENANT by the purchasers with the vendor to observe and perform the said covenants and conditions and to indemnify
	EXECUTED by both parties and ATTESTED
14 January 2009	BY MORTGAGE of this date made between the said ALASTAIR NICHOLSON and FLORA NICHOLSON (thereinafter called 'the mortgagors') of the one part and CORNSHIRE BUILDING SOCIETY of 14 Broad Street Blakey (thereinafter called 'the mortgagee') of the other part
	After reciting seisin of mortgagors in fee simple IT WAS WITNESSED that in consideration of the sum of £65,000 paid by the mortgagee to the mortgagors (receipt acknowledged) the mortgagors as beneficial owners thereby charged unto the mortgagee
	ALL THAT before abstracted property
	PROVISO for cesser and other usual clauses
	EXECUTED by mortgagors and ATTESTED

Suggested requisitions on the above title with a brief explanation of each

5.167 (a) **Please supply a copy of the conveyance dated 18 January 1975.** The abstract of title as deduced does not contain an adequate description of the property. Although a pre-root 1980 conveyance has been abstracted, it does not adequately describe the property. It is clear from the contents of the 1980 conveyance that the property is fully described in the 1975 conveyance. This conveyance also creates a right of way and imposes covenants and conditions, which, provided they are registered as D(ii) land charges, will bind a purchaser for value. Accordingly, we are entitled to examine the 1975 conveyance, notwithstanding that it is dated prior to the root of title.

(b) **The 1990 land charges search certificate is out of date. Please supply copies of all land charges search certificates in your possession.** The October 1990 conveyance was not completed within 15 working days of the August 1990 search certificate and so the latter cannot be relied on as evidence that there are no subsisting entries against Benjamin Edwards. The seller's solicitors will be asked to see whether the search was renewed, and also to check for other search certificates which, if they exist and are valid, will obviate the need for the buyer's solicitor to carry them out now.

(c) **The conveyance of 20 October 1990 does not appear to have been stamped. Please clarify and, if necessary, confirm that it will be stamped before completion at the seller's expense.** The 1990 Conveyance is the only conveyance abstracted which does not indicate a stamp beneath the date in the margin. The conveyance does not contain a certificate for value so it seems likely that the *ad valorem* stamp and particulars delivered (PD) stamp were overlooked. The importance of this requisition is that an improperly stamped document is not admissible in evidence (Stamp Act 1891, s 14). A buyer is entitled to have every deed forming a link in the chain of title properly stamped (see *Whiting v Loomes* (1881) 17 ChD 10, CA).

(d) **The mortgage dated 20 October 1990 does not appear to have been discharged. Please confirm that a receipt for all money due under the mortgage, naming Sharon Munro and properly executed by Blakey Bank Ltd, is endorsed on the mortgage deed.** The buyer's solicitor must ensure that all mortgages revealed by the abstract have been properly discharged. The receipt referred to above is that prescribed by s 115 of the Law of Property Act 1925 for unregistered land. The section also provides that the receipt should name the person making the payment. Here, we should check that the person named in the receipt as making the payment was the then owner of the property (Sharon Munro), otherwise the receipt may not discharge the mortgage but instead operate to transfer ownership of it from the original mortgagee (Blakey Bank Ltd) to the person named as making the payment. (See also *Cumberland Court (Brighton) Ltd v Taylor* [1964] Ch 29.)

(e) **Please supply a copy of the grant of probate dated 19 January 1991 and confirm that the original or an examined copy will be handed over on completion.** It is likely that the original grant has been retained by the personal representatives. However, the grant is still a document of title and, as such, a subsequent buyer is entitled to receive at least an examined copy of it.

We will need to see a copy of the grant to be sure that all proving PRs named therein duly joined in the subsequent assent in favour of Elizabeth Campbell. This is a requirement imposed by s 68 of the Administration of Estates Act 1925.

We must also check the grant for any memoranda endorsed thereon. There should be one endorsement only, namely that of the assent to Elizabeth Campbell. The absence of such an endorsement would constitute a defect in title as the assent may theoretically have been defeated by a later sale of the land by the personal representatives to a buyer who took from them a written statement that they had made no previous assent or conveyance of the land (i.e. a statement under Administration of Estates Act 1925, s 36(6)).

(f) **Please confirm that the assent dated 29 July 1991 contains an acknowledgement for production of the grant of probate dated 19 January 1991.** Whenever an original document of title is retained on completion (in this case, the grant of probate) the buyer (or in this case the assentee) and successors in title are entitled to an acknowledgement of the right to production of the original (see *Cooper v Emery* (1844) 1 Ph 388). This is because a subsequent owner of the land may need to inspect the original at a later date. The benefit of the acknowledgement runs with the land.

(g) **Please explain why the title was not registered following completion of the conveyance dated 14 January 2009 and confirm that the sellers will register the title with title absolute at their own expense before completion.** The facts tell us that the land became compulsorily registrable on 1 December 1990. Accordingly, the 2009 conveyance would have induced compulsory registration and the seller must therefore regularize the position immediately. It is noted that in 1991 an assent did not induce first registration. (Our other requisitions will be rendered superfluous if the seller can achieve registration with title absolute, but this seems unlikely at present given the apparent defects in title.)

(h) **Why is Alastair Nicholson not selling the property in conjunction with Flora Nicholson? Please deduce devolution of title from them jointly to Flora alone.** Unless Alastair also joins in the contract there will be a break in the chain of ownership and a consequent defect in title. It is apparent from the conveyance of 14 January 2009 that Alastair and Flora purchased the property as tenants in common. Accordingly, if Alastair has died, a second trustee will need to be appointed to overreach the equitable interests under his will or intestacy. Alternatively, he may have conveyed his interest to Flora (perhaps pursuant to a divorce settlement), in which case a copy of the conveyance to Flora will be required.

(i) **Please confirm that the mortgage dated 14 January 2009 will be discharged on or before completion.** It is essential that all subsisting mortgages are discharged on or before completion. Normally, the seller's solicitors give the buyer's solicitors on completion an undertaking in Law Society Form to discharge the mortgage from the proceeds of sale. It is therefore prudent to raise this point at the requisitions stage.

LOST OR DESTROYED TITLE DEEDS

5.168 If land or charge certificates were lost or destroyed, it used to be the case, before the Land Registration Act 2002 came into force, that an application could be made to Land Registry for replacement certificates to be issued. As land and charge certificates have ceased to be issued since 13 October 2003, any application for replacement certificates is no longer necessary.

5.169 If unregistered title deeds are lost or destroyed, an application for first registration can be made on Form FR1. This will be accompanied by a statutory declaration as to the circumstances of the loss or destruction, the past history of the title, and evidence of the applicant's possession of the land. An absolute or good leasehold title will be granted only if the loss or destruction can be adequately explained. Otherwise, at best only a possessory title will be granted. Where the deeds have been lost the application should include an undertaking from the applicant's solicitor or licensed conveyancer to produce them to Land Registry if they are subsequently found. See rule 27 of the Land Registration Rules 2003 and Land Registry Practice Guide 2, available at **https://www.gov.uk/government/publications/first-registration-of-title-where-deeds-have-been-lost-or-destroyed/**.

PRACTICAL CHECKLISTS

ACTING FOR THE SELLER

5.170 • Initially investigate your own client's title, as you will have to disclose any incumbrances and defects in title in the draft contract. Anticipate any requisitions the buyer is likely to raise.

• Modern practice is to deduce title before exchange. This is obligatory if the Protocol is being used.

• For unregistered land, choose a good root at least 15 years old and show an unbroken chain of ownership down to the current seller. An epitome is easier to prepare than an abstract. Make sure all photocopies are accurate and plans properly coloured.

- For unregistered land you may be retaining original documents on completion (e.g. on a sale of part). If the Protocol is being used, you should assist the buyer's practitioner by marking the epitome as examined against the originals. The buyer thus receives the epitome already marked up.

- For registered land, deduce title by supplying up-to-date official copies of title (including title plan and other relevant documents).

- If, unusually, deduction and investigation of title are carried out after exchange, comply with the time limits in the general conditions of the contract (including those for answering requisitions). See SC 4.3.1.

ACTING FOR THE BUYER

- Your primary duty is to check that the title is good and marketable, free from adverse incumbrances. Bear in mind your duty to the buyer's mortgagee as well (assuming you are acting). **5.171**

- If the land is unregistered, ask yourself whether your client will obtain absolute title on first registration. Consider referring a difficult title problem to land registry for guidance.

- For unregistered title, check first that there is a good root, and then ensure there is an unbroken chain of ownership through to the seller. Finally, check each document in the title for defects, for example improper stamping or execution.

- Raise requisitions regarding any problems. If, unusually, title is investigated after exchange, comply with any contractual time limits regarding raising requisitions. Otherwise obtain satisfactory replies to requisitions *before* exchange. Consider indemnity insurance if necessary.

- If in your title investigation you come across a disposition by someone acting in a special capacity, for example mortgagee, PR, charity, etc., then have regard to the issues we have discussed in this chapter.

- When investigating unregistered land, if there has been a previous sale of part, consider the matters at 5.49.

6

PREPARING FOR AND IMPLEMENTING EXCHANGE OF CONTRACTS

A BEFORE EXCHANGE

ACTING FOR THE BUYER—MATTERS TO ATTEND TO BEFORE EXCHANGE

Financial arrangements

6.01 When you are taking instructions at the beginning of a transaction we have seen that you would check that the buyer's proposed financial arrangements are in order (see 2.32). In particular, you would have ensured that sufficient funds would be available both to complete the purchase and to pay for the costs and disbursements, including Land Registry fees and stamp duty land tax (SDLT). The funding would be achieved either directly from the client's own resources or, more usually, through a combination of the client's own resources, a mortgage loan, and the proceeds of any related sale (unless of course the client is a first-time buyer).

Mortgage offer

6.02 The typical buyer of a residential property will almost invariably require a mortgage, and it is for the practitioner to ensure before exchanging contracts that an acceptable written offer of mortgage is made and, if necessary, duly accepted. In this regard you should make sure that you receive the written offer yourself: do not rely merely on the client's word that it has been issued. Moreover, read the mortgage conditions carefully (both general and specific) and, after discussing the terms with your client, establish in your own mind that the mortgage offer is acceptable both to the client and to you as the professional. (For a discussion of the common types of mortgage, see Chapter 2.)

Advising client on mortgage terms

You must always advise the client about the precise terms of the mortgage offer. Be clear in **6.03** your own mind that the client understands the terms and can comply with them. General conditions (found in the small print or separate booklets) will apply across the board to all mortgages by a particular lender. Common examples are: not to make alterations to the property and not to let the property without first obtaining the lender's consent. Many people taking out a mortgage for the first time do not always appreciate that these restrictions exist, so it is important to draw them to their attention. There may also be special conditions relating to the particular mortgage, for example a requirement to carry out certain repairs, or a requirement for the client to take out an endowment policy with a named assurance company. Remember that advising on endowment policies raises the possibility of investment business under the Financial Services and Markets Act 2000. The Act and its ramifications for conveyancers are discussed in 2.55.

Special conditions in mortgage offer

You should ensure that any special conditions in the mortgage offer can be met by the **6.04** client. The following special conditions occur frequently (refer also to Chapter 7).

(a) **Retention for repairs** The lender's survey report may recommend that essential repairs are made, for example to the roof. As a result, the lender may impose a mortgage condition that a specified sum is held back from the mortgage advance until the repairs have been carried out. If so, the client will of course have to fund the shortfall in order to complete; moreover, the client will also have to pay for the cost of the repairs after completion. One tactic worth considering where a mortgage retention is made for repairs is to seek an agreement from the seller to reduce the purchase price by the amount of the retention. If you are fortunate enough to agree a price reduction and you act for both borrower/buyer and lender then, subject to your duty of confidentiality to your borrower client, you have a duty to inform the lender of the price reduction. As an alternative to a price reduction it may be possible to agree in the contract a 'repairs allowance'. The effect of this is to leave the contract price the same but on completion the seller receives from the buyer the balance due less an agreed amount for the repairs. Thus the cost of the works is effectively funded by the seller. If a repairs allowance is agreed the buyer's practitioner should still, with the buyer's consent, advise the buyer's lender. This is because of the obligation to inform your client lender of any price alteration or other information which could be relevant to the lending decision (see *Alliance and Leicester Building Society v Edgestop Ltd* [1994] 2 EGLR 229).

(b) **Retention for making up roads and drains** This may be made in respect of a new property, to cover the risks associated with the developer defaulting in making up the roads and drains. (This potential problem is considered further in 11.45.) The borrower/buyer may in the circumstances of such a retention seek to persuade the developer/seller to agree a similar retention from the balance due on completion until the mortgage retention is eventually released. Developers are, however, notoriously reluctant to agree to this.

(c) **Mortgage indemnity guarantee** If the loan exceeds a certain percentage of the lender's valuation of the property (normally between 70 per cent and 80 per cent, depending on the lender) the lender may require some additional security. This is to cover a situation in which the borrower defaults and the lender is subsequently forced to sell the property at a loss (i.e. for less than the outstanding debt). The additional security takes the form of a separate indemnity guarantee policy protecting the lender against this risk. The insurance company offering the guarantee charges a single premium (normally several hundred pounds), which the lender pays initially and then either deducts from the mortgage advance or adds to the loan account. Either way the borrower ends up paying the premium and must be made aware of the position.

6.05 Do ensure that the mortgage advance will be available by the proposed completion date. If it does not arrive in time, your client will be unable to complete on the due date unless monies are found from another source. Accordingly, your client's deposit paid on exchange may be forfeited and, in addition, your client may be forced to pay damages to the seller (see Chapter 9; also 7.108, concerning your report on title to the lender).

Solicitor's mortgage instructions

6.06 In most conveyancing transactions, the buyer's solicitor will also be acting for the lender. The lender's instructions will usually be issued at the same time as the mortgage offer. A typical set of mortgage instructions to a solicitor can be seen in Figure 6.1.

Deposit

6.07 This subject is discussed fully in 3.76–3.91. The deposit paid on exchange is normally 10 per cent of the purchase price, but it would be open for you to reduce the amount actually paid on exchange by the amount of any preliminary deposit which your client may have paid to the estate agent.

Figure 6.1 Typical set of mortgage instructions to a solicitor

CORNSHIRE BUILDING SOCIETY

Dear Sirs

Please act for the Society in the mortgage in accordance with the latest version of the *UK Finance Mortgage Lenders' Handbook for England and Wales*. We enclose a copy of the Offer of Advance, the Mortgage Deed for execution by the borrower and a report on title for you to complete and return to us. We certify that these instructions comply with the SRA Code of Conduct 2011.

Yours faithfully

Cornshire Building Society

OFFER OF ADVANCE

Date: 3 July 2018

Lender: Cornshire Building Society 5 High Street Blakey Cornshire CL1 3EH

Borrower's full name and address: Dennis Carter, 18 Falkland Road Blakey Cornshire CL2 4TY

Solicitors: Richards Abbey & Co., East Chamber Blakey Cornshire CL1 2EG

Account number: 1234567

Property to be mortgaged: 4 Longstaff Street Blakey Cornshire

Tenure: Freehold

Purchase Price: £1,200,000

Amount of Loan: £600,000

Repayment Term: 25 years

Interest Rate (variable): 3.95%

Buildings Insurance Cove: £800,000

General Conditions:

1. The General Conditions of the Lender apply, which are detailed in the enclosed booklet 'Information about your mortgage'.

2. This Offer of Advance may be varied or withdrawn if the mortgage is not completed within six months or if something occurs which in our view makes it undesirable for the loan or any part of it to be made. You must tell us of any changes in personal circumstances (e.g. loss or change of employment/pay) which occur before the mortgage is completed.

Special Conditions:

1. Lender's solicitors to obtain and place with the title deeds an undertaking signed by the Borrower to carry out the following repair work to the Property within six months of completion:
   - Replace cracked titles on roof
   - Repair chimney flashings

2. Lender's solicitors to confirm existence of legal right of way to the Property.

3. The Borrower's existing mortgage with the Halifax secured on 18 Falkland Road Blakey to be redeemed on or before completion.

4. Homeguard Insurance will be arranged as requested, details of which are as follows: Cornshire Homeguard—Buildings Option A reinstatement value £800,000.

YOUR HOME IS AT RISK IF YOU DO NOT KEEP UP REPAYMENTS ON A MORTGAGE OR OTHER LOAN SECURED ON IT.

Cleared funds   You must ensure that you have cleared funds for the deposit before exchange **6.08** occurs. This means that not only must you receive the client's cheque for the deposit, but you must also allow time for it to clear through your firm's account. The reason for this is that SC 2.2.4 requires the deposit to be paid either by electronic means from an account held in the name of a conveyancer at a clearing bank to an account in the name of a conveyancer, or by cheque drawn on a solicitor's or licensed conveyancer's client account. Increasingly firms are requiring clients to send them funds via the credit transfer system rather than by cheque.

Funding the deposit   If your client has a related sale it may be possible to fund the deposit **6.09** in other ways. Your client may be able to utilize the deposit receivable on a related sale; your client might consider offering a deposit guarantee instead of a money deposit; a bridging loan might also be a possibility. All of these methods (including the risks of bridging finance) were examined in some detail in Chapter 3 but a further word should be mentioned here about undertakings.

Bridging finance and undertakings

If a bank has offered the client bridging finance, the bank will invariably require your firm's **6.10** undertaking to repay the bridging loan from the proceeds of the client's related sale (note that a bridging loan will normally only be available where the client has a related sale). Indeed, the *whole* of the net proceeds are normally requested, so that the balance received, after the bridging loan has been repaid, is credited to the client's bank account.

6.11 Before giving the undertaking you will need to consider its terms very carefully to ensure that you can comply with them. The bank is likely to have a standard form of undertaking but you should always consider whether this is satisfactory both to you and your client. Remember when undertaking to pay money that such payment should be conditional upon your firm actually receiving the funds in the first place. Furthermore, you should obtain from your client prior irrevocable written authority to give the undertaking. Such authority may take the following form:

> To [name of your firm]
> I [insert client's name and address] hereby irrevocably authorize you to give an undertaking in the Form set out attached and accordingly to pay the net proceeds of sale of [insert address of sale property] after deduction of your costs and disbursements to [insert name of bank].

6.12 The undertaking should not be given until just before exchange, once you are satisfied that there are no outstanding matters.

Approving searches and enquiries

6.13 A buyer's practitioner must be satisfied with the results of all relevant pre-contract searches and enquiries, including the enquiries made of the seller's practitioner (see generally Chapter 4). Any outstanding matters must be resolved to the satisfaction of the client and the practitioner before contracts are exchanged. Increasingly, traditional pre-completion searches are also being carried out by practitioners before exchange, for example bankruptcy search against the buyer (see Chapter 8).

Approving survey

6.14 As we have seen, *caveat emptor* ('Let the buyer beware') applies to the purchase of land, and the buyer (and any lender) must be satisfied with the outcome of the survey before proceeding to exchange of contracts. Surveys are examined in more detail in 2.68–2.81.

Approving title

6.15 As we saw in Chapter 5, the preferred modern approach is to investigate title before exchange, and indeed many contracts expressly prohibit the raising of requisitions on title after exchange. Accordingly, acting for the buyer and lender you will have to be satisfied that the title (whether it is registered or unregistered) is good and marketable and free from incumbrances which might adversely affect the value of the property or its use and enjoyment. All outstanding requisitions on title should be resolved to your satisfaction before contracts are exchanged.

Reporting to the buyer

6.16 You have a duty to use reasonable care and skill in giving such advice as the particular transaction demands, having regard to the level of knowledge and expertise of your client (see *Sykes v Midland Bank Executor and Trustee Co. Ltd* [1971] 1 QB 113). So you would generally give fuller advice to a first-time buyer than you would to, say, an experienced property developer (see *Aslan v Clintons* (1984) 134 NLJ 584). Failure to give adequate advice may constitute breach of your duty, entitling the client to damages. Your advice to the client may be given orally or in writing, or by using both methods. For the avoidance of doubt it is best practice, at the very least, to report in writing.

Oral report

Ideally, you should try to report to your client in person, as well as in writing. A sensible **6.17** approach would be to start by sending your client copies of the relevant documentation, such as replies to pre-contract enquiries, local search, draft contract and, for registered land, official copy entries. In your covering letter you could invite the client to read the documents and to arrange an appointment with you to discuss the points arising from them. When, subsequently, you meet the client you can go through the papers, explaining their significance and highlighting any adverse matters which may be revealed. Some examples: the replies to enquiries may disclose a neighbour dispute; the title may contain covenants prohibiting business use or imposing fencing obligations; the local search may show that a flyover is being built within 200 metres of the property. Your meeting will also give you an opportunity to discuss the terms of your client's mortgage offer (if any), and the result of the survey.

A full attendance note of your advice should be kept on file and your oral advice confirmed **6.18** in a letter to the client. The letter is helpful for the client for future reference, and the written record of your advice will also protect you against the forgetful client who later complains that certain matters were not brought to his or her attention. Dictate the attendance note and letter immediately after the interview when matters are still fresh in your mind.

Written report

Of course, it may not be practicable to report to the client face to face, in which case you **6.19** will make a full written report. Write the report in language which the individual client can understand. It should refer to all matters which may adversely affect the client's use and enjoyment of the property. In particular:

(a) Advise that the property is being bought in its actual state and condition and that the client must be satisfied with the survey.

(b) Explain the significance of the searches you have carried out (e.g. coal mining, commons, local land charges). In respect of the local search: advise whether the road fronting the property is publicly maintained; advise whether there are any plans for new roads in the immediate vicinity of the property; report that the search relates only to the subject property, not neighbouring properties. In respect of the water search: advise whether foul and surface water drainage is connected to the public sewers and whether the water supply is connected to the public water system.

(c) In respect of the purchase contract: confirm the property description (if appropriate by reference to a plan); confirm the price and deposit arrangements; advise who will bear the risk of insurance between exchange and completion (see 6.64); explain any special conditions.

(d) In respect of the seller's replies to enquiries (or Seller's Property Information Form): highlight any adverse matters; draw the client's attention to the Fixtures, Fittings and Contents Form so that the client knows which items the seller is taking and which are being left; advise which boundaries the seller has maintained.

(e) Give the client information about outgoings: advise the client which band the property is in for council tax purposes; advise on the current annual charge for water rates; if the property is leasehold, advise on the likely level of any service charge the client will have to pay.

(f) In respect of the title: if registered, confirm the class of title (e.g. absolute); advise about any covenants which bind the property and any rights to which the property is subject; advise whether the property has the benefit of any rights or easements (e.g. a right of way along a private accessway).

(g) If the client is obtaining a mortgage, explain the main terms of the mortgage offer and draw the client's attention to the general mortgage conditions and any special conditions.

Advise that the property is at risk if repayments are not maintained or if the mortgage conditions are breached. Unless it is a fixed-rate or capped mortgage, advise that the lender is entitled to raise the interest rate. Advise of any retentions by the mortgagee.

(h) If the property is leasehold, explain the main terms of the lease, in particular, the tenant's covenants and the landlord's right to forfeit if the covenants are breached (see generally Chapter 10 on leases).

(i) Finally, invite the client to telephone you if any matters in the report are unclear, or if the client has any questions or queries.

Approving the draft contract

6.20   The buyer's practitioner should consider the terms of the draft contract scrupulously in the light of the buyer's instructions, the replies to pre-contract enquiries, the results of searches, and the title investigation. If amendments to the contract are necessary, these should be written in red ink and the contract then returned to the seller's practitioner for consideration. You should retain a copy of the amended contract on your purchase file.

6.21   When negotiations on the terms of the draft contract have been concluded, the seller's practitioner will prepare two fair copies of the contract; one for signature by the seller and one for signature by the buyer. Both copies of the contract must be identical. The two parts should incorporate all the agreed amendments because otherwise, even if a purported exchange occurs, no contract will come into existence (see Law of Property (Miscellaneous Provisions) Act 1989, s 2; *Harrison v Battye* [1975] 1 WLR 58, in which only one part of the contract was amended to reflect an agreed reduced deposit). The date of the contract and the date of completion should not be inserted in the contract until the moment of exchange.

Signing the contract

6.22   The client buyer will of course need to sign the contract before exchange, although the signature need not be witnessed. It is standard conveyancing practice to have two identical contracts, one signed by the seller and the other signed by the buyer, which are then exchanged so that the buyer receives the seller's signed contract, and the seller receives the buyer's signed contract. If this practice of exchange is to satisfy s 2 of the Law of Property (Miscellaneous Provisions) Act 1989, the buyer and seller must each sign one of two identical copies.

6.23   If you are reporting to the buyer in person, then this is a good time for the buyer to sign the contract in your presence (assuming the terms are agreed). You can then hold the signed but undated contract on file in readiness for exchange. If it is not practicable for you to see the client, then the contract can be sent for signature with your written report. Ask the client to return the signed contract as soon as possible together with, if required, a cheque for the deposit (or the balance thereof). Emphasize that the contract should *not* be dated when signed.

Signing contract on behalf of others

6.24   One trustee or co-owner (including a co-purchaser) may sign on behalf of the other trustees or co-owners but the practitioner should ensure that they have all given their authority, not only to sign the contract but also to proceed with the transaction. Similarly, one partner may sign on behalf of the other partners provided the transaction has been authorized by the partnership. A company officer (e.g. director) can sign on behalf of the company provided the company has authorized the transaction. As far as personal representatives (PRs) are concerned, s 16 of the Law of Property (Miscellaneous Provisions) Act 1994 provides that *all* proving PRs must be parties to the contract (and purchase deed). However, one can sign the contract on behalf of all, provided authorization for signature has been given.

Practitioner signing contract on client's behalf

It is possible for the conveyancing practitioner personally to sign the contract on behalf of **6.25** the client, and in practice this is often done to save time. Strictly speaking, however, you should sign only if you have been formally appointed as the client's attorney (as attorney you can sign in your own name or the client's), or if the client has given you express authority to sign, preferably in writing. In *Suleman v Shahsavari* [1988] 1 WLR 1181, a solicitor acting without authority was held liable in damages for breach of warranty of authority. On a sale by auction, an auctioneer has implied authority to sign for both parties.

Buildings insurance

This is covered in 6.64. If the buyer (or buyer's mortgagee) is to insure the property after **6.26** exchange, arrangements should be put in place before exchange, so that all that is needed after exchange is, at most, a simple telephone call to put the policy on risk. The seller's insurance policy should always be maintained until completion in case the buyer does not complete.

Synchronization

If the buyer is relying on money from a related sale in order to assist the finance of the **6.27** purchase (i.e. the purchase is dependent on the sale), then the practitioner must synchronize exchange of contracts on both sale and purchase transactions. The ways of achieving synchronization by telephonic exchange are discussed from 6.40. The dangers of not synchronizing become apparent in the following scenario:

(a) You exchange on the purchase before the sale.
(b) Your client's purchaser withdraws before you can exchange on the sale.
(c) Your client is legally bound to complete the purchase but is unable financially to do so. Your client is thus in breach of the purchase contract.
(d) Even if your client can secure alternative funds to complete (e.g. bridging loan), your client will end up with two properties.

If you fail to synchronize exchange of contracts on a related sale and purchase, and the client **6.28** suffers loss, you will be negligent (see *Buckley v Lane Herdman and Co.* [1977] CLY 3143).

ACTING FOR THE SELLER—MATTERS TO ATTEND TO BEFORE EXCHANGE

The contract

As we have seen, when acting for the buyer, the draft contract must be approved, the client **6.29** must understand its contents, and a fair copy of the contract must be signed. These considerations apply equally when acting for the seller and you should refer to 6.20 and 6.22. In addition, any non-owning occupiers will be expected to sign the contract to release any rights and agree to vacate on or before completion (see 3.19).

Seller's mortgage

Sale of whole

If the subject property being sold has an existing mortgage secured on it, the buyer will of **6.30** course require the mortgage to be repaid and discharged on or before completion (repayment is normally made from the sale proceeds on completion). The contract will confirm this indirectly as the mortgage will not be mentioned as an incumbrance subject to which the property is being sold.

6.31 Accordingly, the seller's practitioner must always ensure before exchange that there will be sufficient funds available from the proceeds of sale (and/or other sources) to discharge the mortgage. Failure to do so will amount to negligence on your part if the client suffers loss. You should request a redemption statement from the lender for confirmation of the outstanding mortgage debt.

Sale of part

6.32 If only part of the seller's property is being sold, it will not be necessary to discharge fully any mortgage on the property (although the seller may choose to do so if sufficient monies are available). The buyer will merely be concerned to ensure that the part of land being bought is released from the mortgage. The seller's practitioner must therefore enquire of the existing mortgagee how much is required for the release of the part being sold, and ensure that at least this sum will be available on completion to forward to the mortgagee.

Synchronization

6.33 If the seller is expecting to purchase another property at the same time as he or she is selling a property, then you must synchronize exchange of contracts on both sale and purchase transactions. The ways of achieving synchronization by telephonic exchange are discussed from 6.40. The dangers of not synchronizing become apparent in the following scenario:

(a) You exchange on the sale before the purchase.
(b) Your client's seller withdraws before you can exchange on the purchase.
(c) Your client is legally bound to complete the sale and does so.
(d) Your client has no property to move into and will have to find temporary accommodation and arrange furniture storage.

6.34 It is worth repeating that if you fail to synchronize exchange of contracts on a related sale and purchase, and the client suffers loss, you will be negligent (see *Buckley v Lane Herdman and Co.* [1977] CLY 3143).

B IMPLEMENTING EXCHANGE OF CONTRACTS

METHODS OF EXCHANGE

6.35 As we have seen, the contract becomes legally binding not when the two parts are signed but when they are exchanged. There are three main methods by which exchange of contracts can be effected: in person; by post (or document exchange); and, most commonly, by telephone.

Exchange in person

6.36 In this method the parties' practitioners meet, normally at one of their offices. They physically exchange their respective clients' signed contracts and the buyer's practitioner hands over the client account deposit cheque. The completion date is written in and the contracts are then dated. A personal exchange is recognized as being the safest method because it is an instant exchange and the practitioners can personally check that the contracts are identical. However, exchange in person is rarely used today unless the two offices are closely situated. Pressures of time and the need for synchronization in chain transactions make personal exchanges largely incompatible with the requirements of modern conveyancing.

Exchange by post (or document exchange)

In this method the buyer's practitioner posts the buyer's signed contract and the cheque **6.37** for the deposit to the seller's practitioner. Upon receipt, the seller's practitioner posts the seller's signed contract to the buyer's practitioner. It may also happen the other way round by the seller sending his contract first. If the SCs are being used, SC 2.1.1 confirms the common law postal rule on acceptance laid down in *Adams v Lindsell* (1818) 1 B & Ald 681, namely that the contract comes into existence not when the second copy is received but when the second copy is *posted* (or deposited at the document exchange). Thus, even if the contract is lost in the post, a binding contract still exists.

We do not recommend postal exchange where either party has a linked transaction, i.e. a **6.38** dependent sale or purchase. The reason for this is the time lag between the first contract being posted and the second contract being posted, and during this time either party is of course free to change his mind and withdraw.

Exchange by telephone

This is the most common method of exchange used by practitioners today. The moment **6.39** of exchange occurs at the point in the telephone conversation when the practitioners agree that contracts are actually exchanged. The decision in *Domb v Isoz* [1980] Ch 548 formally endorsed the practice of telephonic exchange and, following a recommendation by Templeman LJ, the Law Society subsequently produced formulae for use by practitioners (see 6.40–6.53). As the formulae involve the use of professional undertakings they should be used only between firms of solicitors and licensed conveyancers, i.e. not where unqualified persons are involved. Any variations of the formulae should be recorded on the practitioners' files and confirmed in writing, in case of any later disputes.

TELEPHONE FORMULAE

Operation of formulae

Formula A

This formula should be used when one party's practitioner (usually the seller's) holds *both* **6.40** signed parts of the contract, together with the deposit cheque. (The buyer's practitioner will have forwarded the buyer's contract and deposit cheque to the seller's practitioner to be held to order in readiness for exchange.)

On the assumption that it is the seller's solicitor who holds both parts of the contract, for- **6.41** mula A works as follows (S = seller's practitioner; B = buyer's practitioner):

(a) S confirms holding the seller's signed contract and the buyer's signed contract and deposit cheque.
(b) S and B agree that S will insert the agreed completion date in each contract.
(c) Exchange is formally agreed by B releasing the buyer's contract and S agreeing to hold the seller's contract to B's order.
(d) S undertakes to forward the seller's contract to B that day, either by first-class post, personal delivery, or document exchange.

Following exchange, the practitioners must write file memos recording: their own names, **6.42** the date and time of exchange, the formula used (and any variations to it), the completion date, and the amount of the deposit being paid.

Formula B

6.43 This formula should be used when both practitioners hold their own clients' signed contracts (and the buyer's practitioner has cleared funds for the deposit). The practitioners confirm that they hold the signed contracts, they insert the agreed completion date, each agrees to hold his or her client's contract to the other's order, and they undertake to send the contracts out that day (plus, for the buyer, the deposit cheque). File memos should be made after exchange recording the details of the conversation (see formula A at 6.40).

Formula C

6.44 **Use in a chain** This formula should be used where there is a chain of transactions and the deposit monies are to be sent directly to another firm further up the chain. The practitioner at one end of the chain (X) telephones the practitioner next in line (Y). Both practitioners confirm that they hold their clients' signed contracts. X undertakes that X will definitely exchange with Y if Y rings back X before a specified time later that day requesting X to exchange. The same undertakings are then given to the other practitioners in the chain until the penultimate one in the chain is reached. Now at the end of the chain, a formula B exchange can occur between the penultimate practitioner and the practitioner at the end (assuming they are both ready). Thereafter the other contracts can be exchanged, one by one, back down the chain as the return calls are made. Thus the first call (e.g. by X to Y) activates formula C part 1; the return call (e.g. by Y to X)—when the exchange occurs—activates formula C part 2.

6.45 **File memos** File memos should be made in respect of the conversations in parts 1 and 2, respectively. The part 1 memo will record the date and time of the conversation, the names of the practitioners speaking, any agreed variations to formula C, the final time later in the day for exchange, the completion date, and the name of the practitioner to whom the deposit is to be paid (formula C assumes a 10 per cent deposit). The part 2 memo will record the request to exchange, the time of exchange, and the identities of the speakers.

6.46 **Points to remember** The following points should also be noted regarding formula C:

(a) Each caller activating part 1 (e.g. X—see 6.44) must give the name of another person in the office who could take the part 2 return call if X is unavailable. X is undertaking that X or that other person will be available up to the final time for exchange.

(b) Formula C cannot be held over to the next day. If exchange does not take place during the day, the whole process must be restarted and part 1 will be reactivated on another day.

(c) The contract must allow the deposit to be passed on up the chain and it must ultimately be held by a practitioner as stakeholder (this is permitted by the Standard Conditions (SCs)). Consequently, you may well find yourself undertaking that another practitioner will be sending deposit monies. Be aware that this is an undertaking to do something which is outside your direct control.

(d) You should obtain the client's express irrevocable authority (preferably in writing) to exchange using formula C. Unless the client's authority is irrevocable, there is the risk that the client will instruct you to withdraw from the transaction after you have given (in part 1) the undertaking that you will definitely exchange if requested to do so. This would leave you in 'no man's land' because if you now accept your client's instructions and refuse to exchange, you will be in breach of your undertaking. However, if you go ahead and exchange, you will be in breach of your duty to your client by acting contrary to your client's instructions.

A practical example of exchange of contracts by telephone (using formulae B and C)

6.47 We act for Emily Logsdail selling 19 Minster Yard for £1 million and buying 9 Castle Hill for £900,000. The Standard Conditions of Sale, fifth edn, are adopted in both contracts.

We have received from the buyer's practitioner on 19 Minster Yard the buyer's signed part of the contract and cheque for the 10 per cent deposit. We hold on file both Emily's sale and purchase contracts duly signed by her. We are instructed to exchange contracts today.

We will telephone the practitioner acting on the sale of 9 Castle Hill and also the practitioner acting for Emily's buyer of 19 Minster Yard to verify that they are both ready to exchange today. A convenient completion date for all parties will have to be agreed in principle. **6.48**

We must check that the practitioner acting on the sale of 9 Castle Hill holds a signed contract which is identical to the part signed by our client. We will advise them that we have a signed contract and 10 per cent deposit is available. The SCs permit our client to use the sale deposit for the deposit on her related purchase, provided it is held ultimately by a solicitor as stakeholder (SC 2.2.6). Accordingly, we must check that there is no special condition in the 9 Castle Hill contract providing for the deposit to be held as agent for the seller. **6.49**

Once we are satisfied on this point, we will ask the buyer's practitioner on 19 Minster Yard to 'release' the buyer's part of the contract to us until a time later in the day. The release of the contract is important to aid synchronization where there is a dependent sale and purchase. The effect of releasing the contract is that the buyer's practitioner on 19 Minster Yard undertakes to exchange if, by an agreed time later in the day, we ring back to request an exchange. This gives us the security to exchange on Emily's related purchase of 9 Castle Hill and then to ring back the buyer's practitioner on 19 Minster Yard to exchange. **6.50**

Following the release of the 19 Minster Yard contract, we will telephone the practitioner acting on the sale of 9 Castle Hill to effect a telephonic exchange under Law Society formula B. This is the appropriate formula where each practitioner holds their own client's signed part of the contract. We will advise the seller's practitioner that our client's signed contract is identical to the seller's part. We will then formally agree the exchange and, as a result, undertake to send to the other side today (by first-class post or document exchange) our client's signed part of the contract. In addition, we will send the other side our firm's client account cheque for the deposit of £90,000. The remaining £10,000, being the balance of the 19 Minster Yard deposit, will be retained by us as stakeholder in accordance with the Standard Conditions. **6.51**

We will then immediately ring back the buyer's practitioner on 19 Minster Yard to effect a formula A exchange. This is the appropriate formula where one practitioner (ourselves) holds both the seller's and buyer's signed parts of the contract. We will undertake to send our client's signed contract to the buyer's practitioner today. **6.52**

We will prepare appropriate memos for our files recording the details of our conversations and, in our covering letters to the other practitioners, confirm the details of the telephonic exchanges. **6.53**

Fax and e-mail

An exchange of faxes or e-mails is not a valid method of exchanging contracts. For a case involving a fax, see *Milton Keynes Development Corporation v Cooper (Great Britain) Ltd* [1993] EGCS 142. The common law rule is reinforced by SC 1.3.3, which provides, in effect, that where the delivery of a document is essential (e.g. exchange of contracts), transmission by fax or e-mail is not a valid means of delivery. Faxes or e-mails may be used, however, to activate the Law Society's formulae for telephonic exchange. **6.54**

C AFTER EXCHANGE

ACTION TO BE TAKEN IMMEDIATELY AFTER EXCHANGE

The following points should be noted:

6.55 If the exchange has taken place by telephone, then appropriate memos and letters to the other side must be written in compliance with undertakings that have been given, if necessary accompanied by the signed contracts and deposit cheques. Remember to date the contract with the date of exchange and insert the agreed completion date. Also, enter the completion date in your diary so that it is not overlooked.

6.56 Telephone the clients to inform them that you have exchanged and to confirm the completion date. Confirm your telephone conversation in writing.

6.57 The seller's practitioner should also write to the seller's mortgagee, if any, requesting a redemption statement calculated to the date of completion with a daily rate of interest thereafter in case completion is delayed.

6.58 If the buyer is to insure the property from exchange of contracts (see 6.64), the buyer's practitioner must ensure that the insurance policy is activated immediately after exchange. In practice the buyer's mortgagee will normally arrange the insurance and this will often occur automatically, without any need for you to contact the mortgagee. However, the matter must be checked in each case. (Indeed, it is worth checking the position *before* you exchange as the last thing you want is to find yourself exchanging at 5 p.m. on a Friday only to find that the insurers cannot be contacted until Monday morning.)

6.59 If deemed appropriate, the buyer's practitioner should protect the contract by registration (see 6.74).

6.60 Lastly, it is courteous for the seller's practitioner to contact the estate agents, if any, who acted on the sale to advise them of the exchange and completion date. The agents will no doubt send you their commission account for you to discharge out of the proceeds of sale on completion.

THE EFFECT OF A BINDING CONTRACT

6.61 As soon as there is a valid contract, the beneficial ownership in the property passes to the buyer (see *Lysaght v Edwards* (1876) 2 ChD 499). Consequently, the buyer at common law bears the risk of any loss or damage to the property, subject to the seller's duty to look after the property (see 6.62). In *Hillingdon Estates Co. v Stonefield Estate Ltd* [1952] Ch 627, the buyer was forced to complete even though between exchange and completion the property was made subject to a compulsory purchase order by the local authority. The buyer is, however, entitled to any increase in value of the property between exchange and completion. The seller has a lien over the property for the balance of the purchase money.

SELLER'S DUTY AS TRUSTEE

6.62 The seller retains ownership of the legal estate as a qualified trustee for the buyer until the estate is transferred by the purchase deed. The trusteeship confers on the seller a duty to exercise reasonable care to keep the property in the same condition as it was at the date of the contract (see *Clarke v Ramuz* [1891] 2 QB 456, CA). Accordingly, in winter, the seller should keep the heating on to ensure that the water in the pipes does not freeze (see *Lucie-Smith v Gorman* [1981] CLY 2866). The seller should also replace any slates or windows which may become broken between exchange and completion, and should probably also tend any garden of the property (see *Foster v Deacon* (1818) 3 Madd 394). The seller's duty continues even if the seller vacates before completion (see *Lucie-Smith v Gorman*), but the seller's duty will end if the buyer is allowed into occupation before completion (see 6.77).

During the seller's trusteeship the seller is entitled to remain in possession and to receive **6.63** any rents and profits, but must also discharge the outgoings of the property such as council tax and water rates.

RISK AND RESPONSIBILITY FOR BUILDINGS INSURANCE

A practitioner will be negligent if proper advice is not given concerning risk and insurance **6.64** and the client suffers loss as a result. It will be necessary for the practitioner to consider these matters at the draft contract stage because the question of who bears the risk of insurance of the property will depend upon the terms of the contract.

Standard Condition 5.1 If the standard conditions are being used, SC 5.1.1 reflects **6.65** the open contract position by stating that the property is at the risk of the buyer from the date of the contract. It is therefore important for the buyer (or if the buyer requires mortgage finance, the buyer's mortgagee) to arrange adequate insurance of the property from the moment of exchange. This is because if the property is damaged (e.g. by fire), the buyer will still be contractually bound to complete the purchase.

SC 5.1.2 states that the seller is under no obligation to insure the property unless: **6.66**

(a) the contract provides that a policy effected by or for the seller and insuring the property or any part of it against liability for loss or damage is to continue in force; or
(b) the property or any part of it is let on terms under which the seller (whether as landlord or as tenant) is obliged to insure against loss or damage.

SC 5.1.3 goes on to provide that if the seller is obliged to insure under SC 5.1.2, then the seller is to do everything necessary to maintain the policy and permit the buyer to inspect the policy or evidence of its terms. Moreover, if before completion the property suffers loss or damage, the seller must pay to the buyer on completion the amount of the policy monies which the seller has received, so far as not applied in repairing or reinstating the property. If no final payment has been received, the seller must assign to the buyer at the buyer's expense, all rights to claim under the policy in such form as the buyer reasonably requires. Pending execution of the assignment, the seller must hold any policy monies received in trust for the buyer. Lastly, if the seller is obliged to insure under SC 5.1.2 he must cancel the policy on completion of the sale of the property.

Commercial property

SCPCs were introduced in 1999 for commercial transactions and these are discussed more **6.67** fully at 12.92. Under the SCPCs the buyer also assumes the risk from exchange of contracts.

The problem of double insurance

There are potential difficulties arising out of a situation where two or more insurance com- **6.68** panies insure the same property, i.e. double insurance. If the parties agree to use SC 5.1.1, we have seen that the buyer must insure the property from exchange. However, the seller will also be advised to keep his existing policy ongoing until completion in case the buyer defaults and the transaction does not complete. Indeed, the terms of the seller's mortgage are likely to require this. In this event, whose insurance company will meet the claim? Each company may say that the other should meet it and, in any event, they will not pay out twice for the same damage. This could result in the unhappy situation of the buyer and seller receiving only part of the whole claim. For a case on double insurance, see *National Farmers Union Mutual Insurance Society Ltd v HSBC Insurance (UK) Ltd* [2010] EWHC 773.

Agreeing abatement in price

6.69 This dilemma is addressed by SC 5.1.5, which provides that if payment under a policy effected by or for the buyer is reduced because the property is covered against loss or damage by an insurance policy effected by or on behalf of the seller then, unless the seller is obliged to insure the property under SC 5.1.2, the purchase price is to be abated by the amount of that reduction. A clause to similar effect is contained in the SCPCs (SCPC 8.2.4(b)).

Insurance and leases

6.70 SC 5.1.4 provides that where the property is leasehold and the property, or any building containing it, is insured by a reversioner or other third party, the seller must use reasonable efforts to ensure that the insurance is maintained until completion. If before completion the property or building suffers loss or damage the seller must assign to the buyer on completion (at the buyer's expense) such rights as the seller may have in the policy monies, in such form as the buyer reasonably requires.

6.71 **LPA 1925, s 47** If the SCs are not being used the practitioner should be aware of the effect of s 47 of the Law of Property Act 1925 (SC 5.1.6 specifically excludes s 47). This section enables a buyer to claim loss from the seller's insurance policy, if one exists. It provides that insurance money payable to the seller after the date of the contract in respect of loss or damage to the property shall be paid to the buyer on completion (or upon receipt, if later) as long as: (a) the contract does not exclude s 47; (b) the buyer pays a proportionate part of the insurance premium; and (c) the insurance company gives its consent.

6.72 **Fires Prevention (Metropolis) Act 1774** In addition, the practitioner should be aware of s 83 of the Fires Prevention (Metropolis) Act 1774. Under this statute, if there is damage to a property by fire, a 'person interested' in the property can compel the insurance company to apply the insurance proceeds towards the reinstatement of the property. There is some doubt about whether a buyer under a contract for sale would constitute an interested person for the purposes of the Act, but in *Rayner v Preston* (1881) 18 ChD 1 there is an *obiter dictum* indicating that a buyer of land would be included within the definition. The operation of the Act is not confined solely to the metropolis of London (*ex parte Gorely* (1864) 4 De G J & S 477).

KEY POINTS SUMMARY

RISK AND INSURANCE

6.73 • After exchange the seller is a qualified trustee of the legal estate and owes a duty to the buyer to exercise reasonable care to keep the property in the same condition as it was at the date of the contract.

• Under an open contract, the SCs, and the SCPCs the risk passes to the buyer on exchange of contracts. In this case the buyer (or buyer's mortgagee) should insure from the moment of exchange. However, look carefully at SCs 5.1.2 and 5.1.3 (or SCPC 8.2), which contain detailed provisions (the seller may already be obliged to insure, e.g. under a lease or pursuant to the contract).

- Under an open contract, if the buyer does not insure and the property suffers damage from fire, etc., the buyer may be assisted by the seller's lack of care, s 47 of the Law of Property Act 1925 or the Fires Prevention (Metropolis) Act 1774.
- Whoever assumes the risk, the seller should always maintain his existing insurance until completion just in case damage occurs, the buyer defaults, and completion does not occur.
- Unless the seller is obliged to insure, SC 5.1.5 allows the buyer an abatement in the purchase price if any insurance proceeds are reduced because of the existence of the seller's insurance policy (i.e. the problem of double insurance). SCPC 7.1.4 also provides for this.

PROTECTING THE CONTRACT BY REGISTRATION

A contract to purchase land is an estate contract and unless the buyer's practitioner pro- **6.74** tects the contract by registration, it will not bind a purchaser of the legal estate. If the property has an unregistered title, the appropriate protective registration is a C(iv) land charge against the name of the estate owner at the Central Land Charges Department in Plymouth. (In the case of a sub-sale, the estate owner will not be the seller in the contract but the person from whom the seller has contracted to buy—see 3.165 generally regarding sub-sales.) If the property has a registered title, the appropriate protective registration is a notice in the charges register of the title.

Standard practice is not to register

If a practitioner fails to register a contract which subsequently becomes void resulting in **6.75** loss to the buyer, the practitioner will be liable in professional negligence (see *Midland Bank Trust Co. Ltd v Hett, Stubbs and Kemp* [1979] Ch 384; *Wroth v Tyler* [1974] Ch 30). Despite this, it has become standard practice not to register the contract except in the following situations:

(a) where a dispute arises between the parties; or
(b) the buyer becomes suspicious of the seller possibly seeking to dispose of the property to someone else; or
(c) more commonly, where there is a long period of time between exchange and completion (e.g. in excess of six weeks).

Notwithstanding current practice, you should always bear in mind your professional duty **6.76** to your client and, if in any doubt, you should register the contract. Note that an option to purchase or a right of pre-emption should always be protected by registration.

OCCUPATION BY THE BUYER BEFORE COMPLETION

Background

Once contracts are exchanged the seller will sometimes receive a request from the buyer **6.77** for access to the property before completion, perhaps to take measurements for carpets or curtains, or to take a final look around before moving in. A request of this nature should not cause any problems for the seller provided the keys are not handed over and the buyer's visit is supervised, usually by the estate agent who negotiated the sale.

Dangers for seller

Occasionally, however, the buyer will want to begin decorating or to carry out alterations, **6.78** or even move in before completion. The seller should treat such requests with caution for the simple reason that the property does not properly belong to the buyer until the balance of the purchase price has been paid and the title to the legal estate has been transferred. Once in possession, a buyer might easily lose his motivation to complete. Moreover, a residential occupier cannot be compelled to vacate without an eviction order from the court (Protection from Eviction Act 1977, s 2). An even worse scenario for the seller would be inadvertently to create a tenancy in which the buyer acquires security of tenure. In this case the seller may be hard-pressed to recover possession at all.

Alternatives

6.79 In the light of these dangers, if a buyer in a straightforward transaction requests anything more than a simple inspection, a prudent seller should refuse; after all, the buyer should not have long to wait until completion. Another possibility could be for the parties to agree an earlier completion, if this is convenient, but you will need to consider the effect of this on any related sale or purchase, because it may be that other parties in the chain do not wish to complete earlier (see also 6.90 on varying the terms of the contract).

Conditions of entry

6.80 Despite this advice, there will be times when the seller will consider permitting the buyer into occupation before completion. For instance, there may be a very long period between exchange and completion, or the property may be in need of urgent repairs which the buyer has undertaken to carry out. If this is the case the seller will have to think carefully about the conditions under which the buyer will be allowed to occupy.

Common law and SC 5.2

6.81 The position at common law if the buyer goes into possession before completion is that the seller's liability to maintain the property ceases, and the buyer is required to pay interest on the balance of the purchase monies. This alone is insufficient to protect the seller from the risks mentioned at 6.78 but, if the SCs are used, help is at hand in SC 5.2. The principal protection afforded to the seller under SC 5.2 is that the buyer occupies as licensee, not as tenant. The effect of this is that the buyer is conferred no security of tenure (see generally the comments of Templeman LJ in *Street v Mountford* [1985] AC 809 at 827).

Terms of buyer's licence

6.82 The terms of the buyer's licence set out in SC 5.2.2 are summarized below, but the parties should not hesitate to formulate their own additional conditions or amendments if the circumstances warrant it. For example, the condition not to alter the premises will require amendment if works are being permitted—the precise nature of the works must be specified (see also SC 5.2.3 discussed at 6.85). The following is a summary of the licence conditions in SC 5.2:

(a) the buyer to keep the property in as good a state of repair as it was when the buyer went into occupation (fair wear and tear excepted) and not to alter the property;

(b) the buyer to pay the seller a licence fee at the 'contract rate' (see 3.74 for an explanation of this term) on the balance of the purchase price for the period of the licence;

(c) the buyer cannot transfer the licence and only the buyer and members of the buyer's household are allowed to occupy;

(d) the buyer is responsible for outgoings and other expenses relating to the property, but is entitled to any rents and profits from any part of the property which he does not occupy;

(e) if the property is leasehold the buyer must not do anything which puts the seller in breach of his obligations in the lease; and

(f) the buyer must quit the property when the licence ends (SC 5.2.4 provides for termination of the licence on the earliest of: completion date, rescission of the contract, or upon five working days' notice given by one party to the other).

The buyer is obliged to pay the licence fee only while the licence subsists. The licence will **6.83** normally cease on the contractual completion date so if the buyer delays completion, the seller cannot, on the face of it, recover the licence fee for the extra period of occupation until completion actually takes place. However SC 5.2.5 assists the seller in this regard by entitling him to recover compensation (at the same rate as the licence fee) for the period of the buyer's continued occupation. (The seller will also be able to claim compensation for delayed completion at the contract rate—see SC 7.2; and Chapter 9.)

Specific performance

If a buyer in occupation refuses to complete at all, the seller can sue for specific perform- **6.84** ance. Practitioners should note that the court may give the buyer the option of paying the balance of the purchase price plus interest into court, rather than ordering the buyer to give up possession (see *Greenwood v Turner* [1891] 2 Ch 144).

SC 5.2.3

It should be noted that under SC 5.2.3 the buyer is not in occupation for the purposes of **6.85** SC 5.2 'if he merely exercises rights of access given solely to do work agreed by the seller'. This might cover the case where the seller grants a licence for access for cleaning or perhaps for minor decoration, in which case no licence fee is payable unless otherwise agreed. Note that for SC 5.2.3 to apply, the works must be agreed by the seller and so the buyer must do no more than the agreed works.

SC 5.2.6

SC 5.2.6 provides that the buyer's right to raise requisitions is unaffected by the buyer's **6.86** occupation. This changes the common law rule that, by taking possession, the buyer is accepting the seller's title. (The point is largely academic because today's prudent buyer should already have raised requisitions while investigating title before exchange.)

Advising the client

Lastly, on a practical note, if occupation is agreed before completion, the practitioners for **6.87** seller and buyer must each explain the conditions of the occupation agreement to their respective clients, and obtain their confirmatory instructions. The consent of any mortgagee should also be obtained if this is a requirement of the mortgage.

Commercial property—occupation by buyer before completion

The SCPCs are silent on the matter of the buyer's occupation before completion. **6.88**

KEY POINTS SUMMARY

OCCUPATION BY THE BUYER BEFORE COMPLETION

- The safest course for the seller is not to allow occupation before completion—simply make **6.89** the buyer wait or, if possible, complete early.

- If occupation is agreed, the seller should grant a licence only and impose stringent conditions (e.g. those contained in SC 5.2). On no account must a tenancy be created.

- Under the SCs, if the buyer exercises rights of access given solely to do work agreed by the seller, the buyer is not in occupation for the purposes of SC 5.2. Accordingly, no licence fee is payable unless otherwise agreed.

- Under SC 5.2.5, a buyer in occupation who delays completion can be charged a licence fee for the continued occupation, as well as interest for delayed completion.

- Both seller and buyer should be advised of the proposed conditions of occupation and their instructions confirmed.

- Any mortgagee's consent will normally have to be obtained—check the mortgage conditions.

VARIATION OF THE CONTRACT BETWEEN EXCHANGE AND COMPLETION

6.90 It is perhaps appropriate at this stage to be reminded of the rules concerning variation of a contract for the sale or other disposition of land. A typical variation might occur where the parties decide after exchange to agree a different date for completion. This occurred in *McCausland v Duncan Lawrie Ltd* [1997] 1 WLR 38, where the solicitors exchanged for completion on 26 March but subsequently realized that this was a Sunday, so they exchanged letters agreeing 24 March instead. The Court of Appeal held that the purported variation was unenforceable because any variation of the contract must comply strictly with the provisions of s 2 of the Law of Property (Miscellaneous Provisions) Act 1989. This means that there has to be a further exchange of documents, signed by the parties, referring to the original contract and the subsequent variation. On a purely practical level, in most cases of this kind no problems will occur because the parties will not fall out, but practitioners should note the inherent dangers in merely agreeing variations in correspondence.

D DEATH OR INSOLVENCY OF CONTRACTING PARTIES BETWEEN EXCHANGE AND COMPLETION

DEATH

6.91 The death of one of the parties to the contract between exchange and completion does not affect the validity of the contract, or the obligations contained in it. The deceased's PRs are, therefore, bound to complete the transaction in accordance with the terms of the contract just as if they were themselves the contracting party. This obligation applies equally to any surviving co-seller or co-buyer of the deceased.

Service of notice on deceased owner

6.92 Sections 10–14 of the Law of Property (Miscellaneous Provisions) Act 1994 provide that if, at the time of service, the person serving the notice knows of the estate owner's death, notice must be served on (i.e. addressed to) the deceased and the deceased's PRs at the deceased's last-known address. A copy of the notice must also be served on the Public Trustee. This may be relevant where it is necessary to serve a notice to complete (notices to complete are discussed in 9.93). Conversely, if the person serving notice is, at the time of service, unaware of the estate owner's death, then service on the deceased alone at his or her last-known address will constitute valid service.

Death of seller

Single seller

As we saw in Chapter 5, a PR cannot give good title until the Probate Registry has **6.93** issued the grant of representation. Accordingly, the buyer from a PR can lawfully refuse to complete until the grant is issued. This may cause completion to be delayed beyond the contractual completion date and any resultant liability for compensation and damages would fall naturally on the deceased's estate (see 9.81 regarding liability for late completion).

Expedited grant　Despite this, if the Probate Registry is made aware of the real possibility **6.94** that damages could be awarded against the estate, the Registry will normally grant leave for the issue of an expedited grant (i.e. one which is processed more quickly than normal). The practitioner acting for the deceased's estate should, therefore, acting on instructions, apply for an expedited grant and at the same time notify the buyer's practitioner of the situation. It may be the case that once the other side (and possibly others in the chain) know of the seller's death they may be willing to postpone completion in the knowledge that an expedited grant is forthcoming.

Limited grant　It is also possible to apply for a limited grant of representation, i.e. a grant **6.95** that is limited to dealings with the subject property. This could be quicker than waiting for a full grant and it is worth enquiring with the local Probate Registry as to the likely timescale involved.

Allowing buyer into possession　Another viable solution to the problem of delay is for the **6.96** PRs to allow the buyer into possession of the property on the contractual completion date under licence, while postponing actual completion until the expedited grant is received. Although the estate may still be liable for compensation in respect of delayed completion, at least the PRs can claim a licence fee from the buyer who is in occupation (see 6.77 on occupation before completion).

Death of one of three or more co-sellers

In this situation the sale can proceed as normal because there are still at least two trustees **6.97** of the legal estate, the minimum number required to satisfy the overreaching provisions of s 27 of the Law of Property Act 1925 (see 5.91 concerning overreaching). The death certificate (or a certified copy) should be produced as evidence of death.

Death of one of two co-sellers

Are they joint tenants or tenants in common?

If one of two co-sellers (e.g. husband and wife) dies, the situation is more complex and you **6.98** should refer to 5.91 which deals fully with dispositions by a sole surviving co-owner. In short, if the two co-sellers held as joint tenants, then the right of survivorship will apply and the deceased's share will accrue automatically to the survivor who, as the sole beneficial owner, can complete the sale. The death certificate (or a certified copy) should be produced as evidence of death.

The practitioner can verify whether the co-sellers were joint tenants by checking whether there **6.99** is any restriction on the proprietorship register (assuming the title is registered). If the title is unregistered, you will need to read the conveyance to the co-owners for an indication of whether they held as joint tenants or tenants in common, and consider also the requirements of the Law of Property (Joint Tenants) Act 1964 (see 5.97 for a discussion of this statute).

6.100 **Appointing second trustee** Conversely, if at the time of the deceased's death the two co-sellers were tenants in common, the buyer's practitioner should insist that the seller appoints a second trustee so as to overreach the equitable interests under the deceased's estate. The appointment can be included in the purchase deed or, more commonly, by a separate deed of appointment. The second trustee is very often one of the PRs of the deceased or a beneficiary under the deceased's estate, but there is no obstacle to appointing the seller's practitioner, provided no conflict of interest arises.

Death of buyer

Options for PRs

6.101 The PRs of the deceased buyer may feel, quite understandably, that they do not wish to complete the purchase, especially if the property was being bought for the deceased's own occupation. However, as we have seen, the PRs are bound to complete in accordance with the contract. The obvious difficulty for them is that any mortgage offer may now be withdrawn, and in these circumstances the PRs will have to find the purchase monies from elsewhere. Unless the seller can be persuaded to end the contract, which is unlikely, the property will simply have to be bought and then sold again as soon as possible. The PRs should not complete until the grant of representation has been obtained, so it may be necessary to apply for an expedited grant. The seller will have a claim against the deceased buyer's estate for any loss caused by delay.

Death of co-buyer

6.102 If one of two or more co-buyers dies between exchange and completion, the surviving co-buyer(s) will of course still have to complete the purchase. The death of a co-buyer may also affect the terms of any mortgage offer (possibly leading to its withdrawal if the deceased was the main breadwinner) and this should be checked with the lender, who must in any event be advised of the death.

KEY POINTS SUMMARY

DEATH OF A CONTRACTING PARTY BETWEEN EXCHANGE AND COMPLETION

6.103
- The contractual obligations are unaffected and the deceased's PRs are bound to complete.
- Advise the other side. It may be necessary to seek either a termination of the contract (unlikely) or a postponement of the completion date.
- If the other side does not agree to the above and completion is likely to be delayed, apply for an expedited or limited grant of representation, advising the Probate Registry that the estate risks incurring liability for breach of contract.
- If one of three or more co-sellers dies, the sale can proceed as normal.
- If one of two co-sellers dies, check whether they held as joint tenants or tenants in common. If the latter, it will be necessary to appoint a second trustee.
- Unless the deceased's share passed by survivorship enabling a surviving co-seller(s) to sell the whole beneficial estate, do not complete until the grant of representation has been issued.
- On the death of a sole buyer, any mortgage offer is likely to be withdrawn, so the PRs will have to find alternative funding.
- If you need to serve notice on a deceased estate owner, address it to the deceased and the deceased's PRs at the deceased's last-known address; also send a copy to the Public Trustee.

INSOLVENCY

Background

Bankruptcy proceedings are normally begun by a creditor presenting a petition in bankruptcy **6.104** against a debtor (although it is possible to petition for one's own bankruptcy). If it is shown that the potential bankrupt is unable to pay his or her debts as they become due, the court will make a bankruptcy order. Control of the bankrupt's assets passes to the official receiver. A trustee in bankruptcy is then appointed and the bankrupt's assets vest automatically in the trustee by virtue of s 306 of the Insolvency Act 1986. Company insolvency is examined briefly in 6.119.

Registration by the court

Petition in bankruptcy

A petition in bankruptcy is registered by the bankruptcy court against the name of the **6.105** potential bankrupt in the register of pending actions at the Central Land Charges Department in Plymouth. This will be revealed by any land charges search against the potential bankrupt's name. If in addition the potential bankrupt owns registered land, the court will register a notice in the proprietorship register of the registered title. The effect of this is that any subsequent disposition of the registered title will be subject to the claims of the creditors (unless the subsequent disposition has been afforded priority protection by an official search—see 8.22 regarding official searches).

Bankruptcy order

When a bankruptcy order is made the bankruptcy court will register it in the register of **6.106** writs and orders, again at the Central Land Charges Department in Plymouth. This will also be revealed by any land charges search against the bankrupt's name. If, in addition, the bankrupt owns registered land, the court will register a restriction in the proprietorship register of the title. (Before the Land Registration Act 2002 came into force on 13 October 2003, Land Registry entry was known as a bankruptcy inhibition.) This prevents any subsequent disposition of the title except by the trustee in bankruptcy (unless, as mentioned at 6.105, the disposition has been afforded priority protection by an official search) (see generally s 86 of the Land Registration Act 2002).

The registration of the bankruptcy order lasts for one year (Enterprise Act 2002, s 256). **6.107**

Seller's bankruptcy

Disposition is void

As soon as a bankruptcy order is made, any disposition by the bankrupt (e.g. a transfer **6.108** or conveyance of land) between the time of the presentation of the petition and the time when the bankrupt's property vests in the trustee in bankruptcy is void unless made with the court's consent (Insolvency Act 1986, s 284). However, because registration constitutes notice, a purchaser (which includes a lessee or mortgagee) of a legal estate in good faith for money or money's worth will not be bound by a petition or bankruptcy order which, in error, has *not* been registered by the court (for unregistered land, see Land Charges Act 1972, ss 5(8) and 6(5); for registered land, see Land Registration Act 2002, s 86). Note, however, the words 'in good faith': a purchaser with *actual* knowledge of the bankruptcy proceedings will not be acting in good faith and will thus be bound.

Acting for the buyer

If you are acting for a buyer of a registered title, you should appreciate that the registra- **6.109** tions at the Land Charges Department (either in the register of pending actions, or in the register of writs and orders) do not constitute notice to the purchaser. Accordingly, it is not necessary for you to conduct a land charges search against the seller of a registered title. Indeed, s 86(7) of the Land Registration Act 2002 expressly provides that the purchaser of a registered title is under no duty to make a land charges search. Thus, for registered title the only registrations which constitute notice are those entered on the registered title itself (i.e. for bankruptcy purposes, a notice following a bankruptcy petition, or a restriction following a bankruptcy order).

6.110 If your relevant searches reveal any bankruptcy entries, the buyer should not accept a transfer or conveyance from the seller, but should wait instead for the appointment of the trustee in bankruptcy and take a transfer or conveyance from the trustee. The bankrupt cannot be a party to the purchase deed, and 'the seller' in the deed should be the trustee personally. The attestation clause in the purchase deed should read as follows:

> signed as a deed by [insert full name of trustee in bankruptcy], (the trustee of the estate of [insert full name of bankrupt]) in the presence of:

6.111 The buyer's practitioner should ask to see a copy of the bankruptcy order together with documentary proof of the trustee's appointment. This in turn will be required by Land Registry on the subsequent registration of the purchase (or first registration).

Disclaiming contract

6.112 Under s 315 of the Insolvency Act 1986 it is possible for the trustee to disclaim the sale contract if it is unprofitable or onerous. Such a disclaimer has the effect of releasing the trustee from any obligation to fulfil the contract. In practice the trustee will rarely disclaim a sale contract unless it was made at an undervalue, or as a preference (note that the trustee cannot disclaim simply to secure a higher price from another buyer: see *Re Bastable, Re, ex parte Trustee* [1901] 2 KB 518, CA).

6.113 If the trustee disclaims the contract and the buyer suffers loss as a result of the seller's bankruptcy, the buyer must prove in the bankruptcy as an unsecured creditor. For example, if the buyer rescinds the contract and the deposit was not paid to the seller's practitioner as stakeholder (i.e. it was held as agent), the buyer will no doubt have difficulty in recovering the deposit because it was probably released to the seller after exchange. This demonstrates an inherent danger of the buyer agreeing to allow the deposit to be held as agent rather than stakeholder (see 3.82 regarding deposits). The seller's trustee may in certain circumstances be sued for specific performance of the contract (see *Freevale Ltd v Metrostore (Holdings) Ltd* [1984] Ch 199).

Co-ownership

6.114 A bankruptcy order will sever an equitable joint tenancy. If the property is held by two or more persons, it is classified as trust property (i.e. a trust of land). If one of the co-owners becomes bankrupt, the trust property (i.e. the legal estate) will not vest in the trustee in bankruptcy, but the beneficial interest of the bankrupt co-owner will do so. The sale of the legal estate can proceed as normal, simply by the trustee in bankruptcy joining in the purchase deed with the other co-owner to consent to the sale of the bankrupt's beneficial interest.

Buyer's bankruptcy

Position of trustee

6.115 The trustee in bankruptcy of the buyer takes over the benefit of the contract and may choose either to complete the purchase or to disclaim the contract if it is considered to be onerous. The seller can serve notice on the trustee requiring him or her to complete or disclaim the contract within 28 days. If the buyer has a mortgage offer, doubtless it will be revoked by the bankruptcy and so the trustee will probably have difficulty in funding the balance of the purchase price. This may tempt the trustee to disclaim but the problem with not completing the contract is that the deposit paid on exchange will probably be forfeited and the seller may sue the bankrupt's estate to recover further loss and/or claim specific performance (Insolvency Act 1986, s 315(5) and *Re Parnell, Re, ex parte Barrell* (1875) LR 10 Ch App 512).

Insolvency Act 1986 s 284

Section 284 of the Insolvency Act 1986 (see 6.108) also applies to the seller on the bank- **6.116** ruptcy of the buyer. This means that if the seller, with notice of bankruptcy proceedings against the buyer, accepts purchase money (which would include a deposit on exchange) from the buyer, the buyer's trustee in bankruptcy can reclaim the purchase monies. Of course it is unlikely that a bankrupt, or potential bankrupt, would be able to complete. If the purchase is funded by a mortgage, the mortgagee will carry out a bankruptcy search against the buyer just before completion, and if a bankruptcy entry is revealed, then the mortgage offer will be withdrawn. A bankrupt who is not buying with a mortgage should have no other funds! The problem for the seller is perhaps more acute on exchange with the possibility that the deposit could be reclaimed. As there is no duty on the seller to make a land charges search against the buyer, it is submitted that 'notice' of bankruptcy proceedings means actual notice.

If a seller after exchange becomes aware of bankruptcy proceedings against the buyer **6.117** he should wait to complete with the trustee or, alternatively, serve notice to complete to make time of the essence, thus enabling him ultimately to rescind the contract for delay (see *Sargeant v National Westminster Bank plc* (1990) 61 P & CR 518, CA; and 9.93).

Bankruptcy of a co-buyer

If one of two or more co-buyers goes bankrupt, his or her beneficial share in the property **6.118** vests in the trustee in bankruptcy. In these circumstances any mortgage offer made to the co-buyers may be withdrawn, which would probably make completion very difficult. If, however, the non-bankrupt co-buyer is still able to complete, the bankrupt's equitable interest would be held on trust by the co-buyer for the trustee who, understandably, might subsequently seek an order for sale in order to pay off creditors.

Company insolvency

If a company becomes insolvent between exchange and completion, the position is very **6.119** similar to that of individuals. The liquidator may choose either to complete the contract or, if onerous, to disclaim it, with the same rights applying *vis-à-vis* buyer and seller as discussed at 6.115. If the liquidation is voluntary, the directors' powers cease on the appointment of the liquidator. In a compulsory winding up (but not a voluntary winding up) the liquidator requires the approval of the court or the liquidation committee before taking proceedings to compel a buyer to complete.

Disposal by company

Any disposal of a company's property after a winding-up petition has been presented is **6.120** void unless sanctioned by the court. A buyer from a company in this situation will therefore usually wait until the liquidator has been appointed and accept a transfer from him. Unless the court vests the legal estate in the liquidator (which is rare), technically the company will complete the sale, with the liquidator attesting the purchase deed on the company's behalf (see 7.20 concerning the form of execution).

6.121 **Formalities** A buyer from a liquidator must ensure that the formalities of the liquidator's appointment have been satisfied. In this respect the practitioner should consult rr 4.100–4.105 of the Insolvency Rules 1986 (if necessary, guidance can be sought from the Insolvency Practitioners' Control Unit, Ladywood House, 45–46 Stephenson Street, Birmingham B2 4UP; tel 0121 698 4000).

Administrative receiver

Floating charge

6.122 If an administrative receiver is appointed, the floating charge under which the receiver was appointed should be read to establish the extent of the receiver's powers (the receiver will also have the powers set out in Schedule 1 to the Insolvency Act 1986). The appointment of the administrative receiver will crystallize the floating charge so that the charge becomes fixed, and on completion of the sale the buyer must insist that the property is released from the fixed charge in the normal way. The buyer from a receiver will require a certified copy of the document appointing the receiver. To avoid personal liability the receiver will execute the purchase deed on behalf of the company, which is still technically the seller (or buyer) of the property.

Effect of Enterprise Act 2002

6.123 If the company's floating charge was entered into on or after 15 September 2003 when the relevant provisions of the Enterprise Act 2002 came into force, the chargee will be unable to appoint an administrative receiver. It must instead appoint an administrator using an out-of-court administration procedure. The administrator owes a duty to all creditors, not just the chargee. As with an administrative receiver, a buyer from an administrator should check the validity of the appointment and insist on a certified copy of the appointment. Both administrators and administrative receivers must be qualified insolvency practitioners.

KEY POINTS SUMMARY

INSOLVENCY

6.124
- On a registered title a notice will alert the buyer that a petition in bankruptcy has been presented against the registered proprietor; a bankruptcy restriction (or, prior to 13 October 2003, an inhibition) will alert the buyer that a bankruptcy order has been made.

- The bankruptcy proceedings will also be registered at the Land Charges Department. These registrations are relevant for buyers of unregistered land only—it is not necessary to conduct a land charges search against the seller when buying registered land.

- A buyer who has relevant notice of bankruptcy proceedings should wait to take a transfer from the trustee in bankruptcy, not the seller.

- The buyer's practitioner should ask to see a copy of the bankruptcy order together with documentary proof of the trustee's appointment. Similarly, a buyer from a liquidator or administrative receiver of a company requires written evidence of the appointment.

- Any disposition by a bankrupt (including payment of purchase money) after the presentation of the petition is void. The same rule applies on company insolvency.

- A bankruptcy order will sever an equitable joint tenancy. The bankrupt co-owner's beneficial interest vests in the trustee, who must execute the purchase deed with the surviving co-owner(s).
- Anyone buying from, or selling to, a company being wound up should deal with the liquidator of the company. A person dealing with a liquidator must ensure that the formalities of the liquidator's appointment have been observed.
- The appointment of an administrative receiver will normally crystallize a floating charge so that it becomes a fixed charge on the company's property. A buyer must ensure that the property is released from the fixed charge.

PRACTICAL CHECKLISTS

BEFORE EXCHANGE

Acting for buyer

- Has a satisfactory mortgage offer been received and are the mortgage conditions acceptable to you and your client? Ensure that all conditions can be met. **6.125**
- Taking into account the net mortgage advance, the proceeds of any related sale and all costs and disbursements, does your client have sufficient funds to proceed with the purchase?
- How much deposit is being paid and to whom? Obtain cleared funds before exchange. If bridging finance is required, you will need to give an undertaking to the lender.
- Is the result of the client's survey satisfactory? Ensure that the survey carried out was more than a mere valuation.
- Are the results of all searches and replies to pre-contract enquiries satisfactory? Check that all queries have been resolved.
- Is the title in order? Check that all requisitions have been dealt with satisfactorily.
- Have the terms of the contract been agreed? Check that all agreed amendments are included in the final form of contract.
- Report in writing to the client fully on all aspects of the transaction and obtain the client's signature to the contract.
- Has a completion date been agreed in principle?
- It will be usual for the buyer to insure the property from exchange, so if appropriate make all necessary arrangements so that the policy can be brought into force on exchange.
- If there is a related sale, ensure that you achieve synchronization of the purchase and sale. Are all transactions in the chain ready to proceed?
- Decide on which method of exchange to use.

Acting for seller

- If the seller has a mortgage, ensure that there will be sufficient sale proceeds to discharge it. On a sale of part the lender must agree to release the part being sold from the mortgage.
- How much deposit is being received and from whom?
- Have the terms of the contract been agreed? Check that all agreed amendments are included in the final form of contract.
- Report to the client on the contract, and obtain the client's signature to the contract.

- Has a completion date been agreed in principle?
- If there is a related purchase, ensure that you achieve synchronization of the sale and purchase. Are all transactions in the chain ready to proceed?
- Decide on which method of exchange to use.

ACTION TO BE TAKEN IMMEDIATELY AFTER EXCHANGE

6.126
- Advise the client.
- Make a diary entry of the completion date.
- If exchange was by telephone, prepare necessary memoranda for the file(s).
- Comply with any undertakings given on exchange, for example to dispatch contract and deposit cheque.
- If appropriate, the buyer's practitioner should arrange insurance of the property.
- The seller's practitioner should request a redemption statement from any mortgagee(s).
- The seller's practitioner should advise the estate agent (if any).
- If appropriate, the buyer's practitioner should protect the contract by registration.
- If the completion date is near, the buyer's practitioner should apply for pre-completion searches (see Chapter 8).

7

THE PURCHASE DEED AND MORTGAGE

A THE PURCHASE DEED

INTRODUCTION

The principal purpose of the purchase deed is to transfer the legal estate in the property **7.01** from the seller to the buyer. The transfer of a legal estate is void unless it is made by deed (Law of Property Act 1925, s 52(1)). There are statutory exceptions to this rule contained in s 52(2), the most relevant for practitioners being: assents by personal representatives (PRs) (see 7.77), the grant of a short-term lease not exceeding three years (which includes periodic tenancies), and vesting orders made by the court.

The purchase deed is traditionally drafted by the buyer's practitioner once exchange of **7.02** contracts has occurred. Its contents are governed by the terms of the contract; whereas the contract sets out what the parties have agreed, the purchase deed actually puts those terms into effect. In some cases the seller may wish to draft the purchase deed, for example when selling new properties on an estate where uniformity of documentation is important (see Chapter 11 on new properties). Section 48(1) of the Law of Property Act 1925 permits the seller to draft the deed in the form the seller requires by an appropriate clause in the contract (and to charge a reasonable fee for supplying the engrossment). The 2011 Protocol suggests that the seller's solicitor may wish to draft the purchase deed at the same time as the contract is drafted much earlier in the transaction, i.e. pre-exchange. Although some practitioners are doing this, the practice as yet is not widespread.

GENERAL MATTERS

Procedure

7.03 The standard procedure is for the buyer's practitioner to submit two copies of the draft purchase deed to the seller's practitioner for approval, and to keep an extra copy on file for reference (in case minor points are raised over the telephone or by e-mail). If the draft is approved as drawn, the top copy can be used as the engrossment (see 7.08) provided it is printed on durable A4 size paper (this is a requirement of r 210 of the Land Registration Rules 2003). If the seller requires extensive amendments, these should be written clearly in red ink on one copy of the draft, which should be returned to the buyer's practitioner, while a copy of the amended draft is kept on the file for reference. A seller's amendment typically arises where the buyer has overlooked the inclusion of a clause required by the contract, for example an indemnity covenant.

Time limits

7.04 Where the Law Society Standard Form of Contract is being used practitioners should submit, approve, and engross the draft purchase deed within the time limits laid down in SC 4.3.2. A breach of the time limits may be of importance if one of the contracting parties later claims compensation for delay in completion. Under SC 7.2.1, if there is default by the parties in performing their obligations under the contract (e.g. the buyer submits the draft purchase deed out of time) then the party whose total period of default is the greater must pay compensation to the other (see 9.85 where this is discussed further).

7.05 In essence, the time limits are as follows. The draft deed must be submitted at least 12 working days before the completion date; the seller's practitioner has four working days to approve it; the buyer's practitioner must then send out the engrossment at least five working days before completion. SC 4.3.4 provides that if the period between the date of the contract and the completion date is less than 15 working days, the time limits are reduced *pro rata*. Fractions of a working day are rounded down (but cannot be less than one working day). By way of an example, if the completion date is ten working days after exchange, the time limits are reduced by two-thirds (i.e. ten divided by 15) so that the draft deed must be submitted at least eight working days before the completion date.

7.06 The Standard Commercial Property Conditions (SCPCs) contain identical time limits (SCPC 6.3).

Parties to the deed

7.07 In most cases the parties to the deed will simply be the seller and the buyer. However, it may be necessary for others to be made parties in the following situations:

(a) Where a second trustee of the legal estate has been appointed to effect overreaching of a beneficial interest, the second trustee and the seller will give a receipt for the purchase price and transfer the property jointly.
(b) In a sub-sale the seller, buyer, and sub-buyer are all made parties to the deed, the property being transferred by the seller to the sub-buyer at the direction of the 'first' buyer (3.165 deals with sub-sales).
(c) Where a seller company is in liquidation or receivership the liquidator or receiver is made a party to the deed to give a receipt for the purchase price (the company will, however, still transfer the property).

(d) Conversely, where an individual seller is made bankrupt, the seller's trustee in bankruptcy will transfer the property. The bankrupt seller is not a party to the deed in this case (see 6.104 on bankruptcy). If a joint proprietor is made bankrupt the other joint proprietor(s) will also be party to the deed.

(e) On a sale of part of mortgaged property the seller's mortgagee may join in the deed to release the part being sold from the mortgage. However, it is more common for the mortgagee to give a separate deed of release (in unregistered land), or execute Form DS3 (in registered land).

The engrossment

The engrossment is the final form of deed which is formally executed. As mentioned at 7.03, it is a Land Registry requirement that durable A4 size paper is used. The buyer's practitioner will prepare the engrossment, incorporating all the agreed amendments. However, as we have seen, if the seller approves the draft as drawn, the top copy of the draft can be used as the engrossment. **7.08**

If the buyer is to execute the deed (see 7.10 regarding valid execution), it is good practice for the buyer to do so first, before sending it across for the seller to execute. This saves time, but the prudent seller will also be disinclined to part with an executed deed before the money is actually received on completion. In these circumstances, the buyer's practitioner should make it clear that the buyer has executed the deed 'in escrow', which means that the deed has no legal effect until the deed has also been executed by the seller, i.e. this is a condition of the buyer's execution. You are reminded of the time limits for delivery of the engrossment laid down in SC 4.3.2 and SCPC 7.3.2 (see 7.04). **7.09**

VALID EXECUTION

Generally

In order to transfer the legal estate the seller must always execute the purchase deed (Law of Property Act 1925, s 52). However, the deed need only be executed by the buyer if the buyer is either making a declaration (e.g. as to co-ownership), or entering into new obligations (e.g. giving the seller an indemnity covenant, or agreeing new covenants on a sale of part). For a detailed description of the rules relating to the proper execution of transfers of registered land reference should be made to Schedule 9 and r 206(3) of the Land Registration Rules 2003). There is also useful Land Registry practice material that summarizes the requirements. **7.10**

Although often done, in practice we do not recommend that buyers' practitioners undertake that their clients will execute the purchase deed after completion. This would be an undertaking to do something which is outside the practitioner's control because the practitioner cannot force the client to sign anything. (Sometimes a buyer's practitioner will offer a qualified undertaking to use best or reasonable endeavours to obtain his client's execution after completion. This should also be resisted as there would still be no guarantee that the buyer will actually do so.) **7.11**

Formalities

The transfer of the legal estate must be by deed and, to be a valid deed, the document must state clearly on its face that it is a deed (Law of Property (Miscellaneous Provisions) Act 1989, s 1). It is no longer necessary for a deed to be sealed (although a company may still **7.12** use its seal), but it must be signed by the necessary parties in the presence of a witness, and delivered. Although the deed takes effect on delivery, the word 'delivered' is not necessary in the attestation clause. A typical attestation clause for execution by an individual would read as follows:

> Signed as a deed by [full name of seller]
> in the presence of
> [signature, name, and address of witness]

Witness

7.13 To avoid any inference of coercion or undue influence, the adult witness should be independent from the person signing the deed (e.g. not the signatory's spouse, relative, or another party to the deed). The witness should sign, and then write his or her address and occupation below. If the witness's signature is illegible the full name should also be written in block capitals. It is quite in order for a practitioner to witness the client's signature. Indeed, this is often done as the practitioner must ensure that the client understands the purpose and contents of the deed before the client signs it.

7.14 If the practitioner sends the purchase deed to the client for signature and return, the practitioner's covering letter should explain the purpose and contents of the document and contain clear instructions as to its execution. Ideally the letter should also specify a date by which the signed document should be returned to the practitioner and request that the client leaves the document undated (it is dated on actual completion). Many practitioners write in pencil at the top, 'Do not date'.

Execution by a company

7.15 A company is no longer required to have a common seal and thus a deed can be properly executed by the signatures of a director and secretary, or two of the company's directors. The attestation clause for execution by a company would typically read as follows:

> Executed as a deed by ABC Ltd acting by
> WX Director . . . and
> YZ [Director] [Secretary] . . .

7.16 Alternatively, the company's common seal can still be used, in which case the form of attestation would read as follows:

> Executed as a deed by affixing the common seal of ABC Ltd
> in the presence of:
> Signature of director
> Signature of [director] [secretary]

7.17 As with an individual's attestation, the word 'delivered' is not necessary. Section 36A(5) of the Companies Act 1985 provides that delivery is presumed at the date of execution unless proved to the contrary. In addition, s 44(2) of the Companies Act 2006 provides that a document is validly executed by a company if it is signed on behalf of the company by either two authorized signatories (the company's directors and the company secretary) or by a director of the company in the presence of a witness who attests the signature.

7.18 If any of these methods of execution is adopted, the buyer from a company incorporated in England and Wales is entitled to assume that proper execution has occurred. For a discussion of foreign companies, see 5.129. Where the deed is to be executed on behalf of a foreign company having a common seal, the form of execution appropriate to a company registered under the Companies Acts may be used with such adaptations as may be necessary in place of execution by a person or persons acting under the authority of the company. Where the deed is to be executed on behalf of a foreign company without using a common seal, the form of attestation would read as follows:

> Signed as a deed and on behalf of (name of company), a company incorporated in (territory), by (full name of person(s) signing), being [a] person(s) who, in accordance with the laws of that territory, is (or are) acting under the authority of the company.

Execution by an attorney

A person signing as an attorney may sign either in the attorney's name or in the name of the person on behalf of whom the attorney is acting (see 5.100 regarding powers of attorney). For example, where XY is the principal and AB is the attorney, use either 'Signed as a deed by AB as attorney on behalf of XY' or 'Signed as a deed by XY by his attorney AB'. **7.19**

Execution by a receiver or liquidator

Law of Property Act 1925 receiver ('LPA receiver')

A mortgagee may appoint a receiver under s 101(1)(iii) of the Law of Property Act 1925. This is often done to assist in the collection of rents and to manage the property. If the lender subsequently wishes to sell the property, an LPA receiver's powers are more limited than those of an administrative receiver due to the constraints of statute (see Law of Property Act 1925, s 109). In particular, an LPA receiver has no statutory power to execute a deed on behalf of a company (although a well-drawn legal charge will confer an express power). Under s 109(2) an LPA receiver is deemed to be the agent of the mortgagor, and this enables an LPA receiver to execute a transfer or conveyance as the mortgagor's attorney, for example: **7.20**

> Signed as a deed by [name of mortgagor] acting by his/her attorney [name of LPA receiver] in the presence of: [signature, name and address of witness]

The LPA receiver should sign the mortgagor's name beside the attestation clause and add the words, 'by his/her attorney'. The LPA receiver should then sign his or her own name underneath. **7.21**

An LPA receiver should not execute a transfer or conveyance in his or her own name because of the risk of personal liability (see *Plant Engineers (Sales) Ltd v Davis* (1969) 113 SJ 484). **7.22**

An alternative way of handling the sale of mortgaged property following the appointment of an LPA receiver is for the mortgagee itself to exercise its power of sale and execute the purchase deed as the seller (see 5.66 regarding sales by mortgagee). **7.23**

Administrative receiver

Administrative receivership is applicable only to corporate mortgagors and the statutory definition of an administrative receiver is to be found in s 29 of the Insolvency Act 1986 (buyers should check that the criteria in this section are satisfied). In general terms, an administrative receiver has power to sell and execute documents on behalf of and in the name of the company (Insolvency Act 1986, s 42 and Schedule 1). A suitable form of attestation acceptable to Land Registry would read as follows: **7.24**

> Signed as a deed by [company name] Ltd by its administrative receiver [name of receiver] appointed under a [debenture] dated [date] in favour of [debenture holder] in the presence of: [Signature, name and address of witness]

7.25 The administrative receiver should sign the company's name beside the attestation clause and add the words, 'by its receiver'. The receiver should then sign his or her own name underneath.

Liquidator

7.26 The purpose of liquidation is to realize the assets of a company and distribute the proceeds to creditors (and possibly shareholders if there is a surplus). Except in very rare cases (see Insolvency Act 1986, s 145), the liquidator will act as agent of the company and can dispose of the company's property as agent. The attestation for execution by a liquidator is achieved simply as follows:

> The common seal of [company name] Ltd (in liquidation) was affixed to this deed in the presence of: [Signature of liquidator] [company seal]

7.27 For further information regarding the land registration aspects of transactions effected by receivers (and administrators), see the appropriate practice material issued by Land Registry.

Virtual signing or execution

7.28 In a situation where not all the parties are physically present at a meeting, clients may pre-sign the document and their solicitor will then send the signature page to the other side by e-mail or fax. In *R (on the application of Mercury Tax Group Ltd) v Revenue and Customs Commissioners & Ors* [2008] EWHC 2721 the court made it clear that, as far as deeds are concerned, the signature and attestation must form part of the same physical document. The court went on to say that as far as contracts (not deeds) are concerned, the requirement is that the document to be signed must exist as a discrete physical entity at the moment of signing. To avoid uncertainty, the City of London Law Society has recommended that the following procedures be adopted:

(i) Once the documents have been agreed, the final execution copies should be e-mailed (in PDF or Word format) to the parties and their solicitors. For convenience, a separate PDF or Word document containing the signature page may also be sent (although this is not essential).

(ii) Each signatory prints and signs the signature page only. There is no need to print off the full document.

(iii) The client sends back to the solicitor: (a) a scanned (PDF) copy of the signature page; and (b) a copy of the full version of the document (PDF or Word). The parties can then use these copies to exchange or complete.

Although it is recommended that these procedures be followed, some firms may prefer simply to arrange for each party to print off the contract or deed in full, then execute the signature page and e-mail back a scanned PDF of the executed signature page. For more information on the execution of deeds generally, see Land Registry Practice Guide 8 *Execution of Deeds*, **https://www.gov.uk/government/publications/execution-of-deeds/practice-guide-8-execution-of-deeds**.

TYPES OF PURCHASE DEED

7.29 The type of purchase deed used will depend on whether the land being transferred is registered or unregistered. For registered land the deed must be in the form prescribed by the Land Registration (Amendment) Rules 2008. For unregistered land there is no prescribed form, and the practitioner may use either the traditional form (a conveyance for freeholds; an assignment for leaseholds), or alternatively, where the title is subject to first registration, a Land Registry transfer. The various forms of purchase deed are now considered and we begin with the most commonly used, the transfer. Note that Land Registry transfer forms can be downloaded free of charge from **http://www.landregistry.gov.uk**.

Transfer

A transfer deed is used for the transfer of registered land and should be used for all registered titles, freehold or leasehold. It may also be used for the transfer of unregistered freehold or leasehold land where the title is required to be registered for the first time after completion. The form of transfer is prescribed by the Land Registration (Amendment) Rules 2008. The two main forms are: **7.30**

- TR1: Transfer of *whole* of registered land, or *whole* of unregistered land where the title is subject to first registration; and
- TP1: Transfer of *part* of registered land, or part of unregistered land where the title is subject to first registration.

These forms can be accessed via the Online Resource Centre accompanying this book. **7.31**

Completing the forms

Completing the forms is very easy and self-explanatory, but the points in the following paragraphs should be noted. **7.32**

Property description   If the property is already registered the title number is inserted in box 2. The property description then follows. On a transfer of part, a full description of the part being sold, including a plan showing the property edged red, will have been agreed in the contract. The description and a duplicate plan can now be incorporated in the transfer. The land being retained by the transferor should also be defined and marked on the plan edged blue. The plan should be to a stated scale and must not be merely for identification purposes. The description need not mention appurtenant rights and benefits shown on the register as these will pass as part of the title. Any other rights or benefits not shown on the register will also pass by virtue of s 62 of the Law of Property Act 1925. **7.33**

Date   The date of the transfer is left blank until completion. **7.34**

Consideration and receipt   The statement of consideration is sufficient to satisfy the provisions of s 5 of the Stamp Act 1891, which states that the consideration must be stated on the face of the deed. It is customary for the consideration to be written in words and figures. In commercial conveyancing where VAT is payable in addition to the purchase price, the amount stated should include the VAT. Any additional monies paid for chattels should not be included in the consideration on the transfer; a separate receipt should be given for chattels. **7.35**

In the consideration box, the transferor is stated as receiving the consideration. This statement of receipt of the purchase money is important to the buyer for three reasons: **7.36**

1. It acts as authority to the buyer to pay the purchase money to the seller's practitioner (Law of Property Act 1925, s 69), so if the seller's practitioner absconds with the money it is the seller's loss not the buyer's.
2. The receipt acts as sufficient discharge to the buyer (Law of Property Act 1925, s 67).
3. The receipt is evidence that the seller's lien over the property for the unpaid purchase price is at an end.

For transfers since April 2000, Land Registry will note the price paid on the register. If the buyer wishes the price to remain confidential and avoid the 'price paid' entry, the transfer should simply state 'the purchase price stated in the contract'. Land Registry should not ordinarily call for sight of the contract in order to ascertain the price. **7.37**

7.38 **Title guarantee**   The seller's title guarantee implies covenants for title under the Law of Property (Miscellaneous Provisions) Act 1994. The form of title guarantee will have been agreed at the contract stage and, as we saw in the contract chapter (see 3.97), the parties often agree to modify the effect of the 1994 Act by agreeing the following clause in the purchase deed:

> In the covenant implied by s 2(1)(b) of the Law of Property (Miscellaneous Provisions) Act 1994 the words 'at the Buyer's cost' shall be substituted for the words 'at his own cost'. This can be inserted in the additional provisions box.

7.39 **Declaration of trust**   Where the buyer is more than one person the declaration of trust box should be completed stating whether the buyers are joint tenants or tenants in common (and their respective shares if unequal). Land Registry Form JO may be used instead. This form is useful if there is a short time between exchange and completion, when it might not be possible to obtain the signatures of the buyers on the purchase deed. Conveyancers may also use Form JO where they do not wish the purchase deed signed by the seller to leave their possession.

7.40 **Additional provisions**   The additional provisions box will be used for such matters as definitions of terms not previously defined (e.g. 'the retained land'), new rights granted or reserved, new covenants, agreements, declarations, and other provisions agreed between the parties in the contract. You should check the special conditions in the contract for any agreed additional clauses. If the contract provides for such matters as new easements, covenants, or declarations, then they must be inserted expressly in the transfer, for it is the transfer that creates them (the contract is merely the agreement to create them). The precise form of wording will already have been agreed in the contract and can be taken directly from it. If more space is required, Form CS can be used as a continuation sheet, which should be securely fastened to the main form.

7.41 To counter any suggestion that the covenants on the part of the transferee may be unenforceable by the transferor's successors in title, the benefit of the covenants should be expressed to be annexed to each and every part of the transferor's retained land. The following wording could be used:

> For the benefit and protection of the Retained Land or any part or parts thereof and so as to bind so far as may be the Property into whosesoever hands the same may come the Transferee hereby covenants with the Transferor that the Transferee and the persons deriving title under him will at all times hereafter observe and perform the restrictions and stipulations set out in the schedule hereto.

7.42 Technically, the burden of the covenants need not be expressly annexed to the land being transferred as this is implied by s 79 of the Law of Property Act 1925 (see *Federated Homes Ltd v Mill Lodge Properties Ltd* [1980] 1 WLR 594). However, it is best practice to do so.

Negation of implied easements

7.43 On a sale of part, the seller should have included a special condition in the contract agreeing to negate any implied grants of easement in favour of the buyer over the seller's retained land. A declaration to this effect should now therefore be made in the transfer. A suitable form of wording which would follow the wording of any special condition might read as follows:

> It is hereby agreed and declared that the Transferee shall not by implication or otherwise become entitled to any rights of light or air which would restrict or interfere with the free use of the Retained Land for building or other purposes.

Indemnity covenant

7.44 Under SC 4.6.4 and SCPC 6.6.4 an indemnity covenant will be required where the sale is subject to any obligation on which the seller will remain liable after completion. If this is the case the indemnity covenant should be inserted in the additional provisions box. A typical indemnity covenant would read:

> The Transferees jointly and severally covenant to observe and perform the covenants referred to in [Entry No 1] of the charges register and to indemnify the Transferor against any future liability for their breach or non-observance.

Acknowledgement for production An acknowledgement for production is generally not required in a transfer of part of registered land. No further production of the seller's title is required. In transfers or conveyances of part of unregistered land however, it is still good practice to require an acknowledgement for production (see 7.69). **7.45**

There are two exceptions to the general rule that an acknowledgement for production is not required in registered land; both are unusual and rarely encountered. The first concerns a sale of part of a registered leasehold title. Here, the seller retains the lease on completion and so the buyer will require an acknowledgement in respect of the lease. The other exception is on a sale of part of registered land which has less than absolute title (i.e. possessory, qualified, or good leasehold). Here, the buyer will require an acknowledgement for any deeds retained by the seller which relate to the part of the title not covered by registration (i.e. normally pre-registration deeds). **7.46**

PRs selling registered land do not need to acknowledge the future production of the grant. This is because Land Registry will accept a certified copy of the grant as evidence of the title of the PRs. **7.47**

When the transfer form is submitted to Land Registry for registration of a dealing with registered land it should be accompanied by Form AP1. If the land is unregistered, the form should be accompanied by Form FR1 (see generally Chapter 9). **7.48**

Transferring unregistered land

Practitioners may, if they prefer, use a conveyance instead of a transfer. Indeed a conveyance is sometimes still used for complex sales of part where many additional clauses may be required. If a transfer form is being used to transfer unregistered land, it should be completed in the same way as for registered land, but the following should be noted: **7.49**

(a) leave the title number box blank;
(b) include a full description of the property in the property box. If the transfer is of the whole of the transferor's title, refer to the last unregistered title deed that contained such a description. The description might read, for example: '10 Broad Street Reading RG1 3EH as is more particularly described in conveyance dated 2 May 1978 made between . . .'; and
(c) if the transferor is giving a title guarantee, refer in the additional provisions box to any incumbrances subject to which the property is being transferred (e.g. easements, covenants).

Other less common forms of transfer

These are: **7.50**

- TR2: Transfer of whole of registered land under a power of sale conferred by a registered charge;
- TP2: Transfer of part of registered land under a power of sale conferred by a registered charge;
- TR3: Transfer of a registered charge;
- TP3: Transfer of a portfolio of titles (including part);
- TR4: Transfer of a portfolio of registered charges; and
- TR5: Transfer of a portfolio of titles (whole only).

7.51   All transfer forms are available in printed form from law stationers, or may be reproduced by individual firms electronically from commercial forms packages (see Chapter 1, Section D). Alternatively, firms can get their own word-processed versions approved by the Forms Unit at Land Registry.

Modifying implied leasehold covenants for title

7.52   SC 3.2.2 and SCPC 7.6.4 limit a leasehold seller's implied covenants for title under s 4(1)(b) of the Law of Property (Miscellaneous Provisions) Act 1994. The effect of these conditions is that it is not implied that the lessee's repairing covenants in the lease have been performed (the reason for this is that *caveat emptor* should apply). Moreover, SC 4.6.3 states that if the property is leasehold, the transfer should contain a statement that the covenants set out in s 4 of the 1994 Act will not extend to any breach of the tenant's covenants in the lease relating to the physical state of the property. Accordingly, if the contract incorporates either the SCs or SCPCs, the transfer should include a declaration to this effect, for example:

> The covenant by the seller under s 4(1)(b) of the Law of Property (Miscellaneous Provisions) Act 1994 is modified so that the seller is not liable for any subsisting breach of a condition or lessee's obligation relating to the physical state of the property which renders the lease liable to forfeiture.

Leasehold indemnity covenants

7.53   **'Old' leases**   In respect of leases granted before 1 January 1996, under s 24 of the Land Registration Act 1925, the buyer impliedly covenanted with the seller to pay the rent, to observe and perform the covenants in the lease, and to indemnify the seller against future breach of the covenants. This section applied whether or not the transfer was for value (compare the position in unregistered land—see 7.75). The Land Registration Act 2002 (which repealed the Land Registration Act 1925) replicates the effect of s 24 of the 1925 Act (2002 Act, Schedule 12, para 20). Some sellers' practitioners still prefer to have an express covenant by the buyer in the transfer to this effect, but practitioners drafting the deed (i.e. for the buyer) should take note that the statute renders an express covenant unnecessary for leases granted before 1 January 1996.

7.54   **'New' leases**   However, the implied statutory indemnity is abolished for 'new' leases, i.e. those created on or after 1 January 1996. This is because an outgoing lessee does not require an indemnity, as the lessee's liability to the lessor ceases once the lessee disposes of the leasehold interest (see generally Landlord and Tenant (Covenants) Act 1995, and in particular s 14). If the outgoing lessee enters into an authorised guarantee agreement (AGA), the matter of indemnity is governed by the law relating to guarantees (s 16(8)). This will generally allow a guarantor to be indemnified by the person whose liability has been guaranteed.

Conveyance

7.55   The conveyance is the traditional form of purchase deed for unregistered land. As mentioned at 7.49, the practitioner will sometimes use a conveyance (instead of a transfer) for a more complex sale of part, where additional clauses are required. A precedent for a conveyance of part of an unregistered title is set out in Appendix 7 and there now follows a brief explanation of its constituent parts.

Commencement

7.56   The conveyance begins with the commencement ('This Conveyance . . . '), date (not to be inserted until completion), and the description of the parties (who are defined for ease of reference).

Recitals

The recitals are introduced by the word, 'WHEREAS'. They describe the purpose of the **7.57** deed, i.e. what it is intended to do, and may also give background information about the title. Although recitals are strictly unnecessary (*Earl of Bath and Earl of Montague's Case* (1693) 3 Ch Cas 55), they can be a useful drafting aid, allowing the reader to identify the deed's purpose without the need to read the main body of the document.

Examples When we considered the deduction and investigation of unregistered title in **7.58** Chapter 5, we noted that PRs selling property should include a statement in the recitals that no previous assent or conveyance of the subject property has been made (Administration of Estates Act 1925, s 36(6)). We saw also that a sole surviving joint tenant will include a recital confirming his or her sole beneficial entitlement (Law of Property (Joints Tenants) Act 1964, s 1).

Other points to note concerning recitals are as follows: **7.59**

(a) A recital of fact in a deed at least 20 years old is deemed to be correct unless proved to the contrary (Law of Property Act 1925, s 46(6)).
(b) A person may be estopped from later denying the accuracy of a statement in a recital (see *Cumberland Court (Brighton) Ltd v Taylor* [1964] Ch 29).
(c) If the main (i.e. operative) part of the deed is ambiguous, the recitals may be consulted for clarification (see *Jenner v Jenner* (1866) LR 1 Eq 361).

Operative part

The operative part of the deed is introduced by the words, 'NOW THIS DEED WITNES- **7.60** SETH'; this is known as the testatum. There then follows a statement of the consideration and a receipt clause (discussed at 7.35 in the context of a transfer of whole), followed by the operative words 'hereby conveys' and a statement of the title guarantee (agreed at the contract stage).

Parcels clause

Next is the parcels clause, which describes the extent of the property being conveyed, intro- **7.61** duced by the words, 'ALL THAT'. This again will have been agreed at the contract stage and the same description can be used. You are reminded that the accuracy of the property description is particularly important on a sale of part, where a plan is essential to identify both the subject property and the seller's retained land. See 3.110 for a full discussion of plans.

A statement of the rights or easements which benefit the land comes after the property **7.62** description (introduced by the words, 'TOGETHER WITH'), and then reference is made to any rights reserved in favour of the seller (introduced by the words, 'EXCEPTING AND RESERVING'). Once again the precise terms of the newly created rights and reservations will have been agreed at the contract stage and are now replicated in the purchase deed in separate schedules (as is the case in our precedent). Remember that the contract is the agreement to create these rights; the purchase deed actually creates them.

Habendum and existing covenants

Next come the words, 'TO HOLD the same unto the Buyers in fee simple SUBJECT TO . . .'. **7.63** This describes the estate being conveyed and refers to the existing covenants subject to which the property is being sold (i.e. the 'Incumbrances' in the contract). Despite express reference to the 1957 covenants in our precedent, they will only bind the buyers if they are registered as D(ii) land charges.

Negation of implied grant

7.64   Clause 2 in the precedent is a declaration negating any implied grant of easement in favour of the buyer.

Indemnity covenant

7.65   Clause 3 is an indemnity covenant given by the buyers in respect of the 1957 covenants. It is appropriate here presumably because the seller, when he bought, gave an indemnity covenant to his seller. If he had not done so then the chain of indemnity covenants would have been broken and there would be no need for an indemnity covenant in this conveyance (see 3.99, and SC 4.6.4 and SCPC 6.6.4 regarding indemnity covenants).

New covenants

7.66   Clause 4 imposes new obligations or covenants on the buyers, which are itemized in the fifth Schedule. Again the terms of these will have been agreed at the contract stage and can be reproduced word for word.

Declaration of trust

7.67   Clause 5 is a declaration by the buyers that they hold the beneficial estate as joint tenants (as opposed to tenants in common).

Powers of trustees

7.68   Clause 6 enlarges the powers of the buyers as trustees. As noted in the precedent, since 1 January 1997 this clause is no longer necessary as s 6(1) of the Trusts of Land and Appointment of Trustees Act 1996 gives trustees of land all the powers of an absolute owner (unless the powers have in the instant case been expressly restricted). We have included the clause for the sake of completeness as it will of course be found in pre-1997 conveyances.

Acknowledgement and undertaking

7.69   Clause 7 is the acknowledgement and undertaking clause, which is appropriate when a seller of unregistered land retains original documents of title on completion. In sales of whole the seller will of course hand over all the deeds to the buyer but in a sale of part the seller is entitled to keep the deeds because they constitute evidence of title to the retained land (Law of Property Act 1925, s 45(9)). In this situation the buyer will on completion instead receive examined copies of the originals (which for conveyancing purposes are as good as the originals). However, in the future the buyer might need to produce the originals (e.g. to prove in court the exact position of a boundary), and accordingly the seller should acknowledge that if required by the buyer they will be produced. The effect of the seller's acknowledgement for production is that the buyer has the right to the production of the relevant documents at the buyer's expense (Law of Property Act 1925, s 64(4)).

7.70   The buyer will also want to know that the retained original deeds will be properly looked after. Unless the originals are held by a mortgagee or the seller is selling in a fiduciary capacity the seller should therefore also undertake for their safe custody. The effect of this undertaking is that the buyer can claim damages if the documents are destroyed, or lost, other than by fire, or other accident.

7.71   The benefit of the clause runs with the land and thus benefits the buyer's successors in title without needing to be repeated in a later conveyance. The burden also runs with the deeds so that the person with custody of the deeds remains bound. In our precedent, the seller's retained deeds, duly acknowledged in clause 7, are listed in the sixth Schedule.

In addition to sales of part, another situation in which an acknowledgement clause will be **7.72** necessary is on a sale of unregistered land by PRs in which the PRs keep the original grant of representation. In this situation the acknowledgement will be given in respect of the grant.

Certificate of value

Since the introduction of Stamp Duty Land Tax (SDLT) on 1 December 2003, a certificate **7.73** of value is no longer required in a purchase deed. However, for illustrative purposes clause 8 is an example of a certificate of value (prior to 1 December 2003) where the purchase price did not exceed the old stamp duty threshold of £60,000.

Testimonium

The formal and rather old-fashioned introduction to the parties' execution of the docu- **7.74** ment ('In Witness . . . ') is known as the testimonium. It is not used in a transfer deed.

Assignment of unregistered leasehold land

An assignment may be used instead of a transfer where the practitioner is dealing with the **7.75** transfer of unregistered leasehold land. As with a conveyance, the use of an assignment may be recommended in more complex transactions where additional clauses are required and it is helpful to consult a precedent. An assignment will be in a similar form to a convey-ance, but the following matters should be noted:

(a) The recitals will give brief details of the lease (date, parties, term, etc.), explain how the seller became the current leaseholder, and confirm that the lessor has consented to the assignment (if consent is required).
(b) The operative words will be, 'the seller assigns'.
(c) The habendum will read, 'to hold unto the buyer for all the residue now unexpired of the term created by the lease'.
(d) If the SCs have been used in the contract, you should include a clause in the assignment modifying the seller's implied covenants for title as referred to at 7.52 in the context of a transfer of a registered leasehold title.
(e) For leases granted prior to 1 January 1996, if the assignment is for value, under s 77 of the Law of Property Act 1925 the buyer impliedly covenants with the seller to pay the rent, observe, and perform the covenants in the lease, and indemnify the seller against any future breach. If the assignment is not for value, s 77 does not apply and the seller should insist on an express indemnity from the buyer in the assignment (this reflects the contractual position under SC 4.6.4 and SCPC 7.6.5).

The implied statutory indemnity under s 77 is abolished for 'new' leases, i.e. those created **7.76** on or after 1 January 1996 (see 7.54).

Assent

An assent is the document used by PRs to transfer land to a beneficiary under a will or intes- **7.77** tacy. All proving PRs must be parties to the assent. The form of assent in registered land cases is prescribed by the Land Registration Rules 2003 (Form AS1 for whole and Form AS3 for part) and must always be used. There is no prescribed form for unregistered land but it will usually follow a similar format to that of the traditional conveyance (containing recitals, operative part, etc.). As explained in 5.85, on completion of an assent of unregis-tered land a memorandum should be endorsed on the grant of representation noting that an assent of the land in question has been made. As the land will be subject to first registra-tion following the assent, it may be more convenient to use Form AS1 or AS3 in preference to an unregistered form of assent.

Formalities

7.78   The assent must be in writing and must name the assentee, i.e. the person in whose favour it is given. Although an assent transfers a legal estate, it does not have to be made by deed unless it contains a covenant by the assentee (e.g. an indemnity covenant to the personal representatives in respect of covenants affecting the title).

7.79   An assent should not be used by PRs who are selling land to a third party. The correct purchase deed in this case is a transfer, conveyance, or assignment in the normal way.

KEY POINTS SUMMARY

WHICH FORM OF PURCHASE DEED TO USE

7.80
- If the land being purchased is the whole of a registered title (freehold or leasehold), use Land Registry Form TR1.
- If the land being purchased is part of a registered title (freehold or leasehold), use Land Registry Form TP1.
- If the land being purchased is unregistered, use TR1 (whole) or TP1 (part) (freehold or leasehold).
- If the land being purchased is unregistered and the transaction is complex (e.g. sale of part), it may be easier to use a precedent conveyance (for freehold) (see Appendix 7) or assignment (for leasehold).
- If PRs are transferring land to a beneficiary under a will or intestacy, use an assent (there is a prescribed Form AS1 for registered land (AS3 for part)).
- If PRs are selling land to a third party, use a transfer, conveyance, or assignment as appropriate.

DRAFTING CONSIDERATIONS

Refer to contract

7.81   Once the form of deed has been established (i.e. transfer, conveyance, etc.), the actual drafting of it is not difficult provided you remember that the contents of the deed are governed by the contents of the contract. For example, on a sale of part, if new easements or covenants are to be created, the actual wording of these will have been agreed in the contract and it will simply be a matter of reproducing the same clauses in the purchase deed. Likewise the description of the property, including reference to any plan, will have been settled at the contract stage and can be copied from the contract.

Use of precedents

7.82   There may be some clauses that will not be reproduced word for word in the contract. Reference to them may instead have been made in the SCs. For example, SC 4.6.5 provides for the seller to give an acknowledgement and undertaking in respect of documents which the buyer will not receive on completion. Accordingly, the buyer's practitioner will have to draft this clause and best practice would be to consult a precedent (see clause 7 in the precedent conveyance in Appendix 7). Precedents are always worth having by your side for reference, but do not copy the precedent slavishly; adapt it to suit your needs and make sure it is up to date.

7.83   Punctuation is generally not used in the drafting of a deed. The reason for this is to help prevent any fraudulent alteration of the deed (e.g. by inserting a comma) which could change its meaning.

Plans

You will recall from the contract chapter that plans are generally necessary only where part **7.84** of the seller's property is being sold. On a sale of part of registered land, r 213 of the Land Registration Rules 2003 provides that a plan is generally required. The only exception is where the part being dealt with is clearly identified on the title plan of the registered title. This would rarely be the case, and as a matter of good practice a plan should always be used on a transfer of part. The plan must be accurate with all colourings and markings correctly made, and it must be tightly bound into the engrossed deed. Metric measurements must be used on the plan (Unit of Measurement Regulations 1995 (SI 1995/1804)). The verbal description of the property in the main body of the document should naturally refer to any plan. The plan should be to a stated scale and must not be merely for identification purposes.

If any discrepancy arises between the plan and the verbal description in the deed, it is a **7.85** matter of construction as to which should prevail. If the plan is described as being 'for identification purposes only', then the verbal description prevails. If the property is 'more particularly delineated or described' on the plan, then the plan will prevail (see *Neilson v Poole* (1969) 20 P & CR 909).

Signing plans

Unregistered land

In unregistered land, if the deed incorporates a plan (e.g. on a sale of part), best practice **7.86** will dictate that the plan should also be signed by the signatories to the deed (although this is not obligatory). By signing the plan the signatories are confirming that the plan is an indispensable part of the deed.

Registered land

On a transfer of registered land, the Land Registration Rules 2003 prescribe that all par- **7.87** ties who execute the deed must also sign the plan. This acknowledges that the plan is an integral part of the document. See generally 3.110 regarding the importance of good plans.

B THE MORTGAGE

INTRODUCTION

The concerns that the buyer has about the subject property largely coincide with those of **7.88** the lender. Before drawing down the loan advance the lender must be sure that the subject property is adequate security for the loan. If the borrower defaults in paying the mortgage instalments, the lender may wish to exercise its power of sale and, if the title is defective, the lender's concern will be that the sale monies could be insufficient to discharge the debt. Accordingly, the lender will insist on a good and marketable title to the subject property, free from incumbrances or restrictions likely to affect the property's value or marketability, or the enforcement of its legal charge.

In Chapter 2 we reviewed the common types of mortgage, general mortgage advice for **7.89** borrowers, and some professional conduct issues. Now we will deal with other practical matters which will be of concern to those acting for the lender, either alone or in conjunction with the borrower. In particular we will consider the lender's instructions to the practitioner, the potential danger of conflicts of interest, non-owning occupiers, the certificate of title, advising on the provisions in the mortgage deed, execution and completion of the mortgage deed, and post-completion formalities. We will also consider further advances, subsequent mortgages, and mortgage fraud. For a full explanation of the discharge of mortgages (e.g. on completion of a sale) see 9.08–9.11.

JOINT REPRESENTATION OF BORROWER AND LENDER

7.90 As the lender's interests are closely linked to those of the buyer, the lender will usually instruct the buyer's practitioner to act in perfecting the new mortgage on the property. This dual representation is permitted by Indicative Behaviour 3.7 of the Code of Conduct provided:

- the mortgage is a 'standard mortgage' (see below) of property to be used as the borrower's private residence;
- the practitioner is satisfied that it is reasonable and in the client's best interests for the practitioner to act; and
- the certificate of title required by the lender is in the form approved by the Law Society and the Council of Mortgage Lenders (CML) (see 7.108).

A 'standard mortgage' is defined in Indicative Behaviour 3.7 of the Code of Conduct as a mortgage provided in the normal course of the lender's activities, where a significant part of the lender's activities consists of lending and the mortgage is on standard terms. In other words, the material terms of the mortgage documentation are not negotiated between the lender and borrower, as they are standard.

It follows that a practitioner will normally be able to act for both lender and borrower in a straightforward mortgage of residential property where the lender is an institutional bank or building society lending on standard terms. However, if the mortgage is not on standard terms (e.g. in a commercial transaction, or a private mortgage), or the property is being used by the borrower other than as his residence (e.g. buy-to-let mortgage) the lender and borrower must be separately represented. A large majority of solicitors' firms in England and Wales are on the principal institutional lenders' 'panel' of solicitors for this purpose, although it is significant that sole practitioners are rarely so instructed. Sadly, this is because the incidence of dishonesty in the profession has been highest among sole practitioners, who are thus regarded by lenders as a high-risk category.

Practitioner's instructions

7.91 Instructions will normally be received at the same time as the client's written mortgage offer, and the instructions and mortgage offer must be read carefully to ensure that all general conditions and any special conditions can be met (see 6.01–6.06). Some offers require formal written acceptance from the borrower and this will also need to be checked. Practitioners should be aware that standardized mortgage conditions could possibly be caught by the Unfair Terms in Consumer Contracts Regulations 1999; see 11.15–11.16 for an explanation of these Regulations.

Identity check

7.92 Both lender and practitioner must ensure that the Money Laundering Regulations 2007 are complied with and, to this end, procedures must be in place for obtaining satisfactory evidence of the borrower's identity. As a result, an important development in recent years has been the common instruction to practitioners to verify and obtain evidence of the identity of the borrower. The most reliable evidence of identification is a passport and safe practice is to inspect the borrower's full passport to confirm the person's identity before the mortgage is signed. Also keep a copy of the passport on file for future reference if necessary.

It should be noted that some mortgagees stipulate in their instructions to practitioners **7.93** that the mortgagee must be advised of any blood, family, or business relationship between the borrower and/or any seller or prospective lessor. The instructions should therefore be read carefully and, if necessary, appropriate enquiries made of the borrower to establish whether such a relationship exists.

Special conditions

The following special conditions are commonly encountered: **7.94**

(a) **Buildings insurance**   For freehold properties it is normally a requirement that buildings insurance is arranged through the institutional lender's block policy. You should advise the borrower of the cost of the annual insurance premium. In the case of leases the lender will normally wish to inspect and approve a copy of the lessor's policy covering the building.

(b) **Life assurance**   For an endowment mortgage the lender will usually require a life policy to be formally assigned to it or simply deposited with the deeds. Some lenders are content for the policy to be held by the borrower. If the policy is a new one, make sure it is in force before completion. Check also that the age of the insured has been admitted on the policy and that the first premium has been paid. If it is an existing policy, you should check with the insurance company that it has not received any earlier notice of assignment in favour of another lender. If it has, the policy cannot be assigned to the current lender. Advise the client of the effect of an assignment, namely, that upon death the policy proceeds will be paid to the lender.

(c) **Mortgage indemnity guarantee**   If the amount of the loan is above a certain percentage of the property's market value (e.g. 75–80 per cent), the institutional lender will often arrange a mortgage indemnity guarantee policy. The policy is designed to compensate the lender for loss suffered as a result of the property subsequently being sold by the lender (under its power of sale) for less than the sum then owing on the mortgage account. A single premium of several hundred pounds is payable, which the lender will either deduct from the mortgage advance or add to the mortgage account. The practitioner will need to advise the borrower who, in turn, will have to provide any shortfall in the monies required to complete.

(d) **Retentions**   If the property is in need of repair, the lender's surveyor will often recommend that a retention from the advance be made pending completion of the works. A retention may also be made when the property is on a new estate and the road and sewer agreements are not yet in place (see 11.45–11.49). Again the borrower must be advised and be able to supply the shortfall to enable completion to occur. In the case of a repairs retention, the borrower must also be warned that the cost of carrying out the repairs may exceed the amount of the retention.

UK Finance Mortgage Lenders' Handbook

The *UK Finance Mortgage Lenders' Handbook* has been adopted by most institutional **7.95** lenders and sets out standardized instructions to conveyancing practitioners. Conveyancers are encouraged to access the handbook via the website of the Council of Mortgage Lenders at **https://www.cml.org.uk/lenders-handbook/** or the lenders' own websites (see also Appendix 12). As a result of the mortgage market review in 2014, the lender's conveyancer is now required to inform the lender straightaway if the seller has not owned the property for at least six months. Any sub-sale must also be reported.

7.96 The handbook is divided into three parts. Part 1 sets out the main instructions and guidance, which must be disclosed by the conveyancers. Part 2 details each lender's specific requirements which arise from those instructions. Part 3 applies where the conveyancer is representing only the lender in a residential conveyancing transaction, i.e. there is separate representation of the borrower and the lender. Practitioners must ensure that they carry out their lender client's instructions as set out in the handbook.

Building Societies Association Standard Mortgage Instructions

7.97 On 1 January 2010 the Building Societies Association (BSA) introduced a new set of standardized mortgage instructions, which are being used in some residential transactions involving BSA members. This is partly because some building societies want to remain independent of the CML while others are reluctant to pay the higher fees charged by the CML. Accordingly, if a building society lender instructs you, check your instructions to see whether the BSA instructions or the *UK Finance Mortgage Lenders' Handbook* is applicable. The BSA instructions are very similar to those of the *UK Finance Mortgage Lenders' Handbook*. For further information see **https://www.bsa.org.uk/information/mortgage-instructions/**.

Mortgages of leases

Mutual enforceability of covenants

7.98 Instructions from a lender where the security involves a long lease invariably provide that the lease must include a covenant on the part of the lessor to enforce other lessees' covenants in the block. If this covenant is not present, the lease will, to all intents and purposes, be unmortgageable. This aspect of leases is discussed more fully in 10.51–10.54, but merits a mention here. Remember that if you complete a mortgage secured on a lease that does not contain a mutual enforceability covenant, the likelihood is that you are negligent. If the covenant is absent (perhaps because the lease was granted many years ago), you should insist that it is incorporated now, at the seller's expense, through a deed of variation of the lease. If the seller or lessor will not agree to this, the purchase and mortgage should not proceed.

7.99 **Other defects in leases** Other defects in long leases to which lenders rightfully object are forfeiture on lessee's bankruptcy, inadequate rights of way and services, and inadequate lessor's repairing obligations. These and other defects are discussed more fully in Chapter 10. Also check the tenant's covenants in the lease to establish whether it is necessary to obtain the lessor's consent before mortgaging the leasehold title.

Conflicts of interest and confidentiality

7.100 Acting for lender and borrower inevitably raises the spectre of conflict of interest and you should be on your guard. One difficulty is that the nature of any relevant information (e.g. a bankruptcy entry) will be confidential to the borrower client. As a matter of conduct, therefore, you will need to obtain the borrower's consent before passing on any confidential information to the lender. This is unless the lender can show to your satisfaction that there is a *prima facie* case of fraud. If the borrower refuses consent to disclose, you should send, if requested, only those parts of your file that relate to work done for the lender or documents relating to the borrower's retainer, but in which a lender has a common interest. Examples of such documents would be a copy of the executed mortgage deed, pre-contract enquiries, search results and related correspondence, title information, contract for sale, requisitions, and draft purchase deed. Note that some lenders ensure that borrowers sign a waiver of confidentiality at the time of the mortgage application. In this case you may need to disclose your whole file to the lender, but do check the client's waiver for details of what can be disclosed and check also that the waiver has not lapsed. The Law Society has published a useful practice note on how to respond to a request from a lender for all or part of the solicitor's residential conveyancing file (see **http://www.lawsociety.org.uk/ support-services/advice/practice-notes/lender-requests-for-files/**).

A conflict of interest will also arise if you discover that the borrower intends to breach a **7.101** condition of the mortgage offer (e.g. to use the property for business purposes when such use is prohibited). In this situation you must explain to the borrower that a conflict has arisen and you can no longer act for the lender, and you must consider carefully whether to continue acting for the borrower. As you can no longer act for the lender, the lender's papers should be returned. However, due to your duty of confidentiality to the borrower (which continues even after termination of the borrower's retainer) you cannot disclose the reason why you can no longer act. You must simply inform the lender that a conflict of interest has arisen and leave it at that.

Non-owning occupiers

A principal concern for the lender is that a person occupying the property with the bor- **7.102** rower (e.g. a non-owning spouse or civil partner) may acquire an interest which would be binding on the lender. The lender would then be unable to sell the property free from the occupier's interest. However, following the decision in *Abbey National Building Society v Cann* [1991] 1 AC 56 this appears to be extremely unlikely. In this case the House of Lords held that a non-owning occupier's equitable interest could not come into existence until after completion of the purchase (and contemporaneous mortgage), and so the occupier's interest could not bind the lender. Moreover, their Lordships also expressed the view that an occupier's knowledge that the borrower is taking out a mortgage will probably be sufficient to postpone the occupier's rights behind those of the lender (subsequently confirmed in *Equity and Law Home Loans Ltd v Prestidge* [1992] 1 WLR 137).

Occupier postponing rights

Notwithstanding the decision in *Abbey National Building Society v Cann*, lenders are natur- **7.103** ally cautious about occupiers and will usually want to know whether any adult will be in occupation of the property after completion in addition to the buyer/borrower. The vigilant lender will require an occupier to sign a declaration postponing any interest behind that of the lender. It is important that the practitioner for the lender/borrower ensures that the occupier obtains independent advice before signing this declaration. This is because of the conflict between the interest of the occupier and that of the lender/borrower and also the possibility of the borrower exerting undue influence on the occupier to sign the declaration.

To avoid a conflict of interest and to counter any suggestion of undue influence the lender **7.104** must take reasonable steps to ensure that the signatory has an adequate understanding of the nature and effect of the transaction. Effectively this means the practitioner must ensure that the signatory is separately advised (see *Barclays Bank plc v O'Brien* [1994] 1 AC 180). Your recommendation for separate advice and/or representation should be recorded in writing for future reference if necessary.

Non-acquisition mortgages

Lastly, it should be noted that lenders are potentially more at risk from occupiers' interests **7.105** where the mortgage is being secured on property which is already owned by the borrower (rather than assisting in a contemporaneous purchase). The reason for this is that the occupier is already present in the property. Consequently lenders should take special care to protect against occupiers' interests when taking second or subsequent charges (see 7.135).

Advising a spouse—impact of the *Etridge* case

7.106 In *Royal Bank of Scotland v Etridge (No 2)* [2001] 4 All ER 449, the House of Lords laid down guidelines for solicitors advising a spouse being asked to agree to a husband's (or wife's) business debts being secured on the matrimonial home. These guidelines also apply to cases where anyone in a non-commercial relationship has offered to guarantee the debts of another, for example a parent and child. Although a solicitor should exercise his own skill and judgement in advising on the merits of each transaction, the 'core minimum' guidelines when advising a spouse are as follows:

- Be satisfied that you have the necessary expertise and time to interpret or advise on what may be very detailed financial information.
- Be satisfied that you can properly act for the wife as well as the husband, i.e. that there is no conflict of interest.
- Obtain full financial information concerning the husband's account. This will normally include information on the purpose for the new facility, the indebtedness, the amount and terms of the borrowing, and a copy of any application form.
- Meet the wife face to face in the absence of the husband (telephone calls and letters are not sufficient).
- Confirm the wife's understanding of the transaction, and correct any misapprehension she may have.
- Explain in non-technical language the nature of the documents and their practical consequences, for example if the husband's business fails, the risk of losing her home and being made bankrupt.
- Emphasize the seriousness of the risks involved.
- Explain the length of time the security will last.
- Explain that the wife has a choice and that the decision to proceed is hers and hers alone.
- If the wife wishes to proceed there should be clear confirmation from her that this is the case, and she should authorize you to provide written confirmation of this to the lender.

7.107 You should also consider the following matters of good professional practice:

- Who will pay your fee for advising the wife? If the wife decides not to guarantee the proposed loan, will your fees get paid at all?
- Open a separate file and send the wife a retainer letter which clearly defines your relationship with her.
- Keep a clear record of your advice, especially if the transaction appears to be to the wife's disadvantage. Consider asking the wife to countersign a copy of that advice.
- The wife's authority for you to provide a 'certificate' to the lender should be given in writing.

Certificate of title and request for mortgage advance

7.108 In conjunction with the *UK Finance Mortgage Lenders' Handbook* a compulsory standard-form certificate of title has been agreed between the Law Society and the Council of Mortgage Lenders. This should be used by conveyancers when reporting to their lender clients and requesting the mortgage advance. The certificate of title can be downloaded from the Law Society website (**http://www.lawsociety.org.uk/advice/articles/sra-handbook-and-approved-certificate-of-title/**). There is also a short-form version of the certificate (also available on the website) which states that the conveyancer gives the Certificate of Title referred to in IB (see 3.8) of the Solicitors Regulation Authority (SRA) Code of Conduct 2011, published by the Law Society, as if the same were set out in full, subject to the limitations contained in it.

If, as a result of your investigation of title, searches, and enquiries, you consider that the **7.109** title is not acceptable, you must draw this specifically to the lender's attention.

A practitioner who is in any doubt about whether a particular adverse matter will result **7.110** in the mortgage offer being withdrawn should of course have referred the matter to the mortgagee before contracts were exchanged. Indeed, to avoid delay, all queries should be referred to the lender as soon as they arise, which will normally be at the investigation of title stage, i.e. before exchange.

Request for mortgage advance

The certificate of title will include a request to the lender for the mortgage advance. As some **7.111** lenders require several days' notice of draw-down of funds, the form should be submitted to the lender in good time for completion. It is a breach of the SRA to draw against a lender's cheque before it has cleared, and at least three days should be allowed for clearance.

In most cases the lender will agree to send the advance monies by telegraphic transfer, **7.112** deducting the transfer fee from the advance. The advance monies are regarded as clients' money and as such must be paid into client account.

Release of funds

Pending completion the practitioner holds the mortgage advance on trust for the lender **7.113** and must comply with the lender's instructions. Non-compliance will constitute a breach of trust; see *Target Holdings Ltd v Redferns* [1996] AC 421. In particular do not release funds and complete until the borrower has properly executed and you have received the mortgage deed (and any other security documentation). If there is any delay in completion, the lender's instructions may require the advance to be returned, with interest.

Bankruptcy search

In all cases before the advance is drawn down the lender will require confirmation that the **7.114** borrower is not bankrupt and that there are no insolvency proceedings. The practitioner for the lender should therefore conduct a bankruptcy search against each individual borrower's full name at the Land Charges Department (Form K16 is used for a 'bankruptcy only' search). If the borrower is a company, a company search should also be conducted to ensure that the company is not in liquidation and that there are no winding-up proceedings.

The *UK Finance Mortgage Lenders' Handbook* (see Appendix 12) details stringent require- **7.115** ments for solicitors and licensed conveyancers setting out what lenders expect conveyancers to do when acting for them. A checklist is given at 7.163.

COMMERCIAL MORTGAGES

In relation to a mortgage of commercial property, the lender will normally instruct an **7.116** independent firm. In these circumstances the buyer's practitioner must ensure, before committing the buyer to exchange of contracts, that the lender's practitioner is satisfied with the title, the results of searches, and all other matters.

Requesting information

The borrower's practitioner will be asked to supply copies of all relevant documentation **7.117** relating to the transaction. Invariably, this will include a full abstract or epitome of title or official copies of the registered title, all necessary searches, replies to pre-contract enquiries, planning permissions, details of all occupiers (the same considerations apply as in 7.102–7.104) and, if the borrower is also buying, the dated and signed contract, replies to requisitions, pre-completion searches, and the approved draft purchase deed.

Investigation of title, etc.

7.118 The lender's practitioner is essentially double-checking the work of the borrower's practitioner. Inevitably this results in duplication of work, but is unavoidable unless the lender is prepared to accept a certificate of title from the borrower's practitioner. If the lender's practitioner has any queries, these should be raised with the borrower's practitioner as formal requisitions. These in turn will be raised by the buyer's practitioner with the seller's practitioner. Although the lender's practitioner will attend to the post-completion work, the borrower's practitioner will normally be expected to supply a completed Land Registry application form (see Chapter 9 for post-completion procedures).

Undertaking for costs

7.119 The lender's practitioner will also insist on an undertaking from the borrower's practitioner to be responsible for the lender's costs whether or not the matter proceeds to completion. This is primarily to cover abortive fees. Such an undertaking should be given up to a maximum specified sum, and only with the borrower's express authority. The borrower's practitioner should always consider the merit of obtaining monies in advance from the client before giving such an undertaking.

Procedure

7.120 The lender's practitioner will prepare the security documentation (e.g. mortgage deed) and stipulate that its contents must be properly explained to the borrower. It is normally a requirement that the documentation is executed in the presence of the borrower's practitioner, who will sign as witness. Unless completion occurs at a meeting attended by the lender's practitioner, the latter will normally appoint the borrower's practitioner to act as agent on completion. This is on the basis that the borrower's practitioner holds the mortgage advance to order pending completion and undertakes to supply immediately thereafter the following: all documents of title, the executed security documentation, a Land Registry application form and, if the borrower is buying as well, the executed purchase deed and Form DS1 (or in unregistered land, the seller's vacated charge). If the matter proceeds to completion, the lender's practitioner's costs and other payments, such as SDLT, and Land Registry fees, will be deducted from the mortgage advance.

Further reading

7.121 An analysis of the specialist field of secured lending in relation to commercial development projects is contained in Chapter 8 of our companion volume, R. Abbey and M. Richards, *A Practical Approach to Commercial Conveyancing and Property* (5th edn, OUP, 2016).

THE MORTGAGE DEED

7.122 A legal mortgage must be made by deed (Law of Property Act 1925, s 85). Apart from this requirement, it need take no other prescribed form, although in registered land r 103 of the Land Registration Rules 2003 provides that a legal charge may be in Form CH1. Although not compulsory at present, Form CH1 is seen as something of a 'stepping-stone' towards a standard compulsory form of charge when e-conveyancing is introduced.

7.123 Typically the institutional lender will supply its own printed mortgage form, which is sent to the practitioner along with the 'instructions pack'. The practitioner will then simply complete the blanks (name of borrower, property address, etc.) in readiness for execution by the borrower before completion. (For an endowment mortgage where the benefit of a life policy is to be assigned to the lender, the borrower will also execute an assignment of life policy deed.)

Explanation of terms

Before execution of the mortgage deed it is vitally important that you explain to the bor- **7.124** rower the nature and effect of the deed and its contents. The following matters should always be explained to the client:

(a) Point out the initial rate of interest and amount of the first monthly repayment; explain that the lender may vary them at any time (unless the mortgage is fixed rate).
(b) Explain the borrower's covenants, such as the covenant to keep the property in good repair, not to make alterations without the lender's consent, and any prohibition against letting or sharing possession without the lender's consent (lodgers often help to pay the mortgage).
(c) The borrower must understand that if there is any default on mortgage repayments or breach of covenant, the lender has the right to call in the loan and sell the property.
(d) Any penalty charges for early repayment should be explained (this is often the case in initially attractive-looking fixed-rate packages).
(e) If the mortgage secures 'all monies' owed to the lender, a breach of this mortgage would entitle the lender to call in other loans (if any) made to the borrower. Most mortgages are all monies charges. Where there are joint borrowers, this would include sums advanced to them individually on sole mortgages on other properties (see *AIB Group UK plc v Martin* [2002] 1 WLR 94, HL).
(f) The lender's right to insure the property and recover the premiums from the borrower should be explained; the mortgage deed normally contains an express power for the lender to insure, extending the statutory power under s 101(1)(ii) of the LPA 1925.

Guarantors

Any guarantor signing the deed should be told to take independent legal advice before sign- **7.125** ing. This is because the guarantor may become liable instead of, or as well as, the borrower for all the money owing under the deed.

Execution and completion

If the mortgage monies are being used to finance a contemporaneous purchase, the mort- **7.126** gage deed must be properly executed by the relevant parties before completion of the purchase. A good time for signing is when you see the client to explain the mortgage terms, and you can then act as the client's witness as well. There is no need for the lender to execute the deed unless, unusually, the lender is entering into new covenants.

You will date the mortgage deed the same date as the purchase deed, although technically **7.127** the mortgage is completed fractionally later (on the basis that the client cannot mortgage the property until he actually acquires it). You should check the lender's instructions at this stage as some lenders require to be advised as soon as completion takes place.

A typical form of mortgage deed used by institutional lenders is set out in Appendix 13. **7.128**

POST-COMPLETION STEPS

You are referred to Chapter 9 for a full explanation of the post-completion steps following **7.129** a purchase, but it is worth mentioning here the special duties owed to a lender.

Registration by company borrower

7.130 If the borrower is a company incorporated in, or with an established place of business in, England and Wales, the mortgage must be registered at the Companies Registry within 21 days of completion (Companies Act 2006, s 860). If it is not registered, the charge will be void against the company's creditors or a liquidator or administrator. It is important not to delay in registering the charge as an extension of time cannot be given without a court order and such orders are rarely made. You should also note that Land Registry's practice is not to raise a requisition requiring a charge to be so registered. The Registry will instead simply enter a note in the charges register referring to the relevant section of the Companies Act.

Registration at Land Registry

7.131 To perfect the mortgage, the mortgage deed need not be stamped but, critically, the mortgage must be entered as a registered charge on the charges register of the title. When the land acquired is an existing registered title, remember to lodge your application to Land Registry before the expiry of the priority protection period of your official search. If the land acquired is unregistered, you must apply for first registration (and registration of the mortgage) within two months of completion. In addition to the original mortgage, Land Registry will require a copy of it, certified by you as being a true copy.

Notice of assignment of life policy

7.132 If the borrower has assigned a life policy to the lender, you will need to give notice of this to the life company so that the company is aware that the lender is entitled to the proceeds of the policy. Standard-form notices of assignment are usually sent as part of the lender's instructions pack so it will simply be a case of completing the form. Send off the notice in duplicate, asking for one copy to be returned receipted for placing with the deeds.

Leases

7.133 If the mortgaged property is leasehold, check the notice requirements in the lease. It will usually be necessary to give notice to the lessor of any mortgage of the leasehold estate within a set time, and to pay a fee. The notice should be given in duplicate with a request that one copy be returned receipted.

After registration

7.134 When the title information document is returned by Land Registry, remember to check that the lender's mortgage duly appears in the charges register and that the registered title is otherwise in order. Lastly, if required by the lender, remember to send the title information document and other deeds and documents to the lender for safe keeping (some lenders specifically request that pre-registration deeds should not be sent). Schedule the documents in triplicate and send two to the lender, keeping the other for your file. Ask the lender to return one copy of the schedule, signed as an acknowledgement of safe receipt. Bear in mind that some lenders may not want any papers at all, so check your instructions.

FURTHER ADVANCES

7.135 A further advance is an additional loan from a borrower's current lender, which is usually secured by the lender's existing charge on the property. An example of when a further advance might be requested is when a property owner is seeking to finance works to the property, for example to build an extension. In these circumstances the lender will want to approve the building proposals and ensure that there will be sufficient value (or 'equity') in the property to cover the increased indebtedness.

For an endowment mortgage the lender may require the premiums on the life policy to **7.136** be increased in order to enhance the maturity value of the policy. If the existing mortgage secures not only the initial advance but also further advances (which is usually the case), there will be no need for the borrower to execute a further mortgage deed.

SUBSEQUENT MORTGAGES

Introduction

A subsequent mortgage is a separate charge taken by a second or subsequent lender as **7.137** security for a new loan. Further advances and subsequent mortgages both operate typically in circumstances where the borrower is not seeking financial assistance for the acquisition of a property; the mortgaged property is already owned by the borrower.

As with further advances, a lender intending to take a subsequent mortgage must ensure **7.138** that there is sufficient equity in the property, taking into account the monies owed to prior mortgagees. The subsequent lender should also check that any further advances that in future may be made under the prior mortgages will not rank in priority ahead of its own intended security (see 7.146 on tacking).

As when acting for a first mortgagee, you must investigate title and carry out all necessary **7.139** searches to ensure that the property can be safely accepted as security. In addition you must check that the prior mortgage deeds contain no covenant on the borrower's part prohibiting the creation of further charges. Breach of this restriction could lead to enforcement proceedings against the borrower by the prior mortgagee (although it will not make the subsequent charge invalid). It is typically the case that the lender's consent is required before any subsequent charge is created. In the case of registered land you should check the register for any restrictions confirming this position.

Right of consolidation

A subsequent lender should also check whether any prior lender has a right to consolidate **7.140** mortgages on different properties. In practice, this right is invariably reserved by a clause in the mortgage deed excluding s 93 of the Law of Property Act 1925, which imposes a statutory restriction on consolidation.

The effect of consolidation is to permit the lender to refuse to discharge the mortgage on **7.141** the subject property until the loans secured on the borrower's other properties have also been repaid. Naturally this might adversely affect a subsequent lender's position. Accordingly, a lender who is considering a subsequent charge should enquire whether the prior lender has a charge secured on other properties of the borrower and, if so, whether the borrower has ever been in default.

A subsequent mortgagee has no control over the exercise by the first mortgagee of its **7.142** power of sale. If the first mortgagee chooses to exercise its power of sale and discharge its debt, there is the obvious danger that insufficient proceeds will be available to pay off the subsequent lender's debt. This of course is the inherent danger of taking a subsequent mortgage—there is no guaranteed security.

Priority of mortgages

Subject to the comments at 7.145 in relation to unregistered land, legal mortgages will **7.143** rank in priority according to their order of registration, not their order of creation. Thus, following completion of a mortgage, it is essential that the appropriate registration of the charge is made within the priority period of your pre-completion search. Section 48(1) of the Land Registration Act 2002 confirms that registered charges are 'to be taken to rank as between themselves in the order shown in the register'.

Registered land

7.144   In registered land, a legal charge should be protected by substantive registration as a registered charge (Land Registration Act 2002, Schedule 2, para 8). An equitable charge is an equitable interest, and as such is protected by a notice. Equitable charges of registered land can no longer be protected by notice of deposit (Land Registration Rules 1995 (SI 1995/140)). It is no longer possible to create a legal mortgage of registered land by demise or sub-demise (Land Registration Act 2002, s 23(1)).

Unregistered land

7.145   In unregistered land, subsequent legal mortgages are protected by the registration of a C(i) land charge, and equitable mortgages by a C(iii) land charge. Such registration constitutes actual notice to a third party pursuant to s 198 of the Law of Property Act 1925. (Remember that first legal charges of unregistered land are protected simply by the deposit of the deeds with the lender; there is no registration of a first legal mortgage in unregistered land.)

Tacking

7.146   Further advances may be 'tacked' onto the original loan, giving them priority for repayment over other monies lent and secured by another lender's charge created between the time of the original loan and the time of the further advance. The 'tacked' further advance is treated as having been made at the same time as the original loan. An example of tacking is as follows:

(a) X buys Blackacre with the aid of a loan from M secured by a first mortgage on Blackacre.
(b) X then gives a second mortgage of Blackacre to M2 to secure a separate loan from M2.
(c) M then makes a further advance to X under its first mortgage. If tacking applies, the further advance will take priority over M2's charge.

When does tacking apply?

7.147   The rules governing tacking differ somewhat according to whether the land is registered or unregistered.

7.148   **Unregistered land**   In unregistered land s 94(1) of the Law of Property Act 1925 prescribes the following circumstances in which tacking of further advances will apply:

(a) The subsequent lender consents to the further advance having priority (e.g. in a deed of priorities).
(b) The original lender has no notice of the subsequent lender's mortgage at the time of the further advance.
(c) Irrespective of notice, the original lender is under an obligation in the mortgage deed to make further advances.

7.149   It is worth mentioning two matters concerning notice in relation to circumstance (b) above. First, to prevent tacking of a further advance, the subsequent lender should serve written notice of the subsequent charge on the original lender. This is necessary where the original mortgage expressly secures 'a current account or other further advances'. In other words, mere registration of a land charge (C(i) or C(iii)) is insufficient notice for this purpose (s 94(2)). (It follows that a land charges search is superfluous when making a further advance on unregistered land.)

Second, once notice has been served the prior lender is obliged to forward the deeds to **7.150** the subsequent lender as soon as the prior charge has been discharged. It is therefore good practice to serve notice on a prior lender in all cases (irrespective of whether the land is registered or unregistered).

Registered land   In registered land the general rule is that registered charges rank in prior- **7.151** ity according to their order of registration (Land Registration Act 2002, s 48(1)). How- ever, s 49 of the Land Registration Act 2002 governs the priority of further advances (i.e. whether they can be tacked).

A registered chargee may make a further advance in priority to any subsequent registered **7.152** charge if the first chargee making the further advance has not received from the subse- quent chargee notice of that later charge (s 49(1)). Thus the first lender can make a further advance on the security of an existing charge if that first lender has not received notice from another lender that a subsequent charge has been created. Rule 107 of the Land Registration Rules 2003 governs how the receipt of the notice is effected.

Section 49 of the 2002 Act also allows further benefit to first lenders who make further **7.153** advances in two additional ways. First, the lender may make a further advance that ranks in priority if the advance is made as a result of an obligation to do so in the original mortgage deed and that obligation was noted in the register (s 49(3)). Section 49(4) allows a lender to make a further advance ranking in priority if the parties to the original charge agree a maximum amount for the security for the loan, and where that agreement of the maximum is noted on the register. The application to note the agreement on the register should be made on Form CH3 (Land Registration Rules 2003, r 109). As long as the sums due to the first lender do not exceed the maximum loan amount specified, the subsequent loan or loans up to the agreed maximum will take the same priority over any subsequent charge.

Deed of priorities

Many institutional lenders will prefer all parties to enter into a deed of priorities. This **7.154** deed will serve to regulate the extent of the lenders' priorities and will also incorporate any necessary consent to the creation of the subsequent charge. A well-drawn deed will leave no room for doubt or argument. The deed of priorities can be the subject of a note on the title register and this should be done as a matter of good practice.

Digital mortgages

Land Registry is planning to launch a new digital mortgage service in 2018. This will **7.155** be designed to enable borrowers to sign mortgage deeds digitally, speed up the re-mortgage process, and improve the customer experience. A new liability risk arises with this service because HM Land Registry (HMLR) will certify the identity of a borrower when that person provides a digital signature in advance of registration. This liability sits outside of the scope of HMLR's existing statutory compensation scheme (Schedule 8, Land Registra- tion Act 2002). The risk of the new liability occurring is considered low. The new process, where the borrower's identity has to be verified through GOV.UK Verify combined with HMLR's independent security processes, should in theory reduce the overall risk of fraud.

KEY POINTS SUMMARY

FURTHER ADVANCES AND SUBSEQUENT MORTGAGES

- On a further advance, check the lender's requirements, for example if it is an endowment **7.156** mortgage, do the premiums on the life policy need to be increased?

- If the original mortgage secures further advances, it will not be necessary for the borrower to execute a separate mortgage.

- If a prior lender has reserved the right of consolidation, a prospective subsequent lender should enquire whether the prior lender has mortgages secured on other land owned by the borrower.

- When acting for a prospective subsequent lender always check that the prior charge allows subsequent mortgages to be created and obtain consent from the prior mortgagee if necessary.

- When acting for a prospective subsequent lender, investigate title and carry out all necessary searches and enquiries in the normal way. Pay special attention to non-owning occupiers who must postpone any rights.

- A prospective subsequent lender should check whether any further advances by the prior lender will be 'tacked' onto the original loan and thus take priority over the subsequent lender's charge (see 7.146 for when tacking applies).

- When considering tacking, check in particular whether the prior lender is under an obligation to make further advances, or whether there is an agreed maximum amount under the prior charge (in registered land, to be effective, these must be noted on the register).

- Subsequent lenders should serve written notice of their charge on any prior lender.

- Registered charges rank in priority according to their dates of registration, not their dates of creation. Ensure that your application to register the charge is made within the priority period of your official search.

- In the interests of clarity, the borrower and all lenders will find it wise to enter into a deed of priorities and, if the land is registered, have it noted at Land Registry.

MORTGAGE FRAUD

7.157 The increased incidence of mortgage fraud arose in the climate of the 1980s property boom when dishonest professionals and others quickly understood that illegal profit could be made from sharply rising property prices. It was partly as a result of the subsequent recession and fall in prices that many of these crimes involving fictitious borrowers and false valuations came to light.

7.158 As a conveyancing practitioner, you must be ever-watchful for the possibility of mortgage fraud. If you become aware that your client is engaging in fraudulent activities of any kind, you are obliged as a matter of professional conduct to discontinue acting for the client. Bear in mind that if you continue to act in these circumstances you risk one or more of the following:

(a) disciplinary proceedings from your professional body for breach of the professional conduct rules;

(b) civil proceedings for negligence or breach of contract, for example by a lender who has suffered loss;

(c) criminal prosecution for aiding and abetting a fraud or conspiracy to defraud. A guilty verdict invariably means a custodial sentence and being struck off the roll.

7.159 You should appreciate that simply by playing a part in the transaction in which a fraud is being perpetrated, you risk being implicated in the criminal activity itself. Be aware that other professionals (e.g. valuers, estate agents) may be involved in a mortgage fraud 'ring'. It is no defence to say that you were simply carrying out the conveyancing work. A court may conclude that you are implicated in the criminal activity because, as a professional, you carried on when a reasonably competent practitioner would have reported the situation. It is therefore of vital importance to know when a mortgage fraud might occur. We have outlined at 7.160 some typical fraudulent situations; be aware of them and be on your guard. If you ignore suspicious circumstances you do so at your peril. The Law Society has issued a useful practice note on mortgage fraud (**http://www.lawsociety.org.uk/advice/ practice-notes/mortgage-fraud/**).

Suspicious circumstances

(a) **Adjustments to the purchase price**   Ensure that the true price is written on all rele-   **7.160** vant documentation (e.g. contract, purchase deed), that it corresponds with the figure quoted in the mortgage offer, and that the sum quoted on the lender's report on title is the same figure.

You may receive instructions that the seller will accept less than the original price, perhaps because of a repairs allowance or because the buyer owes the seller money. You are obliged to inform your client lender of any price alteration or other information relevant to the lending decision (see *Alliance and Leicester Building Society v Edgestop Ltd* [1994] 2 EGLR 229). This is because it may affect the lender's decision to lend as much as the original advance, or even whether to continue lending at all.

If your borrower client refuses to consent to this disclosure, there is a conflict between your duty to act in the lender's best interest and your duty of confidentiality towards the borrower. Accordingly, you should cease acting for the lender and best practice would be to cease acting for the borrower as well.

(b) **False identity cases**   Your client could be trying to conceal an existing mortgage, or attempting to forge his spouse's signature on a document to assist in obtaining a business loan. Always take instructions from both husband and wife in person. If necessary, inspect the client's passport to verify identity, and also verify the identity of the firm acting for the other side if your firm has not encountered them before. For a case involving mortgage fraud and an imposter client, see *LSC Finance Ltd v Abensons* [2015] EWHC 1163 (Ch).

(c) **Unusual instructions**   The seller could instruct you to send the proceeds of sale to another person. Discuss it with the client and find out why this is required. Perhaps the client wants you to witness a deed which is already signed. It is important not to witness a signature unless the document is actually signed in your presence. If it is already signed, the signatory must sign it again in your presence.

(d) **Unusual transactions**   Perhaps a client instructs you to buy several properties from one person; or you become instructed in a sub-sale at a massive profit; or your client intends to use an alias. Be on your guard—these types of dealings are unusual and suspicious.

(e) **False mortgage applications**   If you believe that your client has made an inflated declaration of income and the client will not correct it, you must refuse to continue to act.

(f) **False property valuations**   You must refuse to continue to act if you believe that the lender's valuation is significantly higher than the true market value of the property. Naturally you are not an expert in these matters, but if the property is situated locally or your firm acted on a recent conveyance of it, you may be expected to have an opinion of its worth. (Some mortgage instructions require practitioners to advise the lender of the sale price shown in any document where the property has been conveyed or transferred within the last year.)

(g) **Money not paid through your firm's account**   A client buyer could tell you that he or she has already paid the deposit or balance of the purchase price (less the mortgage advance) direct to the seller. This should arouse your suspicion. Best practice is to insist that all monies are paid through and acknowledged by the practitioners acting for the parties.

KEY POINTS SUMMARY

MORTGAGE FRAUD

7.161
- When acting for more than one client (e.g. joint borrowers), take instructions from each client in person; to avoid forgery best practice is for all borrowers to sign the mortgage deed in your presence.

- Be aware of your duties to your lender client, the possibility of conflicts of interest, and your duty of confidentiality towards your borrower client.

- Inform your lender client of any price alteration or other information that may be relevant to the lending decision. However, you also have a duty of confidentiality to your borrower client, so the borrower must consent to any disclosure you make to the lender.

- If your instructions are unusual or the transaction is unusual, ask your client for a full explanation. If your client is attempting to commit a fraud or if you are in any doubt about your client's motives, discontinue acting.

- Ensure that all monies are paid through practitioners' accounts, not between the parties direct.

- Be on your guard against false mortgage applications and inflated property valuations. If in doubt, make further investigations; do not accept the situation and just proceed with the transaction.

- If you become suspicious about any transaction you must take appropriate steps and, if necessary, stop acting for the client.

- For further guidance, see the Practice Note on mortgage fraud available on the Law Society's website.

PRACTICAL CHECKLISTS

THE PURCHASE DEED

7.162
- Ensure that the form of purchase deed is correct.
  - The most common deed in operation is the TR1 transfer of whole for registered and unregistered land. TP1 is used for the transfer of part of registered and part of unregistered land.
  - Comply with any time limits in the contract regarding submission of the draft, approval, and engrossment (e.g. SC 4.3).
  - The contents of the purchase deed are governed by the contents of the contract; ensure that all agreed clauses are included in the draft but no more.
  - The approved draft deed should be engrossed on durable A4 paper.
  - Explain the contents of the deed to the client and arrange for valid execution prior to completion; advise the client to leave the deed undated until completion has occurred.

ACTING FOR THE LENDER

7.163
- Check the lender's instructions and ensure that all general and special conditions have been or will be fulfilled.
  - Investigate title to the property and conduct all necessary searches and enquiries. The property must have a good and marketable title; it should be free from incumbrances or restrictions likely to affect its value or marketability, or the enforcement of the lender's legal charge.

- All non-owning occupiers who will be in occupation after completion must sign a consent form and release all rights in favour of the lender; ensure that such occupiers are independently advised.

- Conduct a bankruptcy search and/or company search against the borrower; ensure that the results are clear.

- Ensure that vacant possession of the property will be given if this is a condition of the mortgage offer; if necessary arrange a final inspection.

- Ensure that all security documentation is properly executed by the borrower before completion of the mortgage; the terms of the mortgage deed and other documentation must be fully explained to the borrower.

- Report on title to the lender and request the advance monies in good time before completion.

- Check that the price in the contract, purchase deed, mortgage deed, and any other documentation is the same as that quoted in the mortgage offer and instructions; the lender must be advised of any price alteration.

- If required, advise the lender of completion.

- If required, after completion give notice of assignment of life policy to the insurance company.

- A charge created by a company borrower must be registered at the Companies Registry within 21 days of completion.

- After completion of a second or subsequent mortgage serve notice of your client's mortgage on the prior lender(s).

- Apply to register the mortgage (and any transfer) at Land Registry before your pre-completion search protection period expires; first registration applications should be made within two months of completion.

- On completion of the registration by Land Registry, check that the registration is correct; if requested by the lender, send all relevant documents to the lender for safe keeping, requesting one copy of your schedule to be returned receipted.

THE *UK FINANCE MORTGAGE LENDERS' HANDBOOK*

- Check that the lender's instructions contain a certificate that they comply with the SRA Code **7.164** of Conduct.

- Check that all mortgage conditions have been complied with.

- Read the lender's valuation and check your file to ensure that any assumptions made by the lender's valuer as to tenure, easements, boundaries, and restrictions are correct.

- Check your borrower client's identity—ask to see a passport if necessary.

- Check that there is no possibility of mortgage fraud or money laundering.

- Check the identity of the seller's practitioners—verify in a professional directory if necessary.

- Advise the lender if the agreed purchase price is different from that in the lender's instructions.

- Advise the lender of any reduction in the purchase price.

- Advise the lender (with the borrower's consent) of any intention by the borrower to take out a second mortgage soon after completion.

- Advise the lender of any incentives given to the buyer (e.g. 'cash backs' or price discounts).

- Advise the lender if any part of the purchase price has not passed through your firm's client account (save for any holding deposit of up to £500), for example direct payments from buyer to seller.

- Advise the lender if the seller has not owned the property for the last six months, and give details.

- Advise the lender if the fee-earner in your firm conducting the transaction is also the borrower or is related to the borrower.
- Ensure that you have clear searches, including a bankruptcy search against your borrower client.
- Repeat your local search if it will be more than six months old at completion.
- Check the lender's instructions for details of mortgages which need to be discharged on completion, for example on the borrower's related sale.
- Check that the title is good and marketable and free from anything that may materially adversely affect the value of the property or its future marketability.
- Obtain defective title indemnity insurance if necessary, for example for flying freehold, possessory or good leasehold title, breach of covenant, inadequate repairing obligations or easements, missing deeds, etc.
- Check for no undervalue transaction within the last five years. If so, take appropriate action (see 5.136).
- Check that the buildings insurance policy accords with the lender's instructions where someone other than the lender insures (e.g. a lessor).
- If required by the lender, ensure that the lender's interest is noted on the insurance policy.
- If required by the lender, the insurer must confirm that it will notify the lender if the policy is not renewed.
- Your bill should itemize separately your fees for acting for the lender.
- Before completion you should be in funds for Land Registry fees and any SDLT.
- Check that there is no conflict of interest between borrower and lender (e.g. where borrower intends to break a mortgage condition) or any other conflict of interest.
- Ensure that any third party (e.g. a prospective non-owning occupier) receives independent advice.
- For leaseholds generally (see Chapter 10):

  (a) Ensure you have a clear receipt for the last ground rent.

  (b) Ensure there is no provision for forfeiture on bankruptcy of the tenant or any superior tenant.

  (c) Ensure there is a mutual enforceability covenant allowing the tenant to enforce other tenants' covenants in the block.

  (d) Check that the lessor's covenants for repair and maintenance of the structure and common parts are adequate.

  (e) Check that you have the current name and address of the lessor and any management company and that, if limited companies, neither have been struck off the register.

  (f) Are you satisfied with the last three years' accounts of any management company? If not, send them to the lender for clearance.

  (g) If the management company is controlled by the tenants you must keep with the deeds an up-to-date copy of the company's memorandum and articles of association, the borrower's share certificate, and a blank transfer signed by the borrower.

  (h) Check that any management company has an interest in land and that the lessees are all members of it. If this is not the case, the lessor should be obliged to carry out the management company's obligations should it fail to do so.

  (i) If required, check that the lessor's consent to the proposed assignment has been obtained.

Note: for full information, consult the *UK Finance Mortgage Lenders' Handbook* at **https://www.cml.org.uk/lenders-handbook/**.

8

PRE-COMPLETION PROCEDURES AND COMPLETION

In this chapter we will consider the procedures that precede completion and then what takes place at the time of completion.

A PRE-COMPLETION PROCEDURES

WHAT ARE PRE-COMPLETION PROCEDURES?

Although conveyancing is about land, land law, and its practical application, it is also **8.01** about money being paid for the transfer of valuable assets, both large and small. This is nowhere more clearly demonstrated than at completion. It is at this critical point in the conveyancing process that large amounts of money will change hands. Indeed, it is also at this point that extremely costly errors can occur. Pre-completion procedures exist to minimize the likelihood of errors occurring, and more particularly to ensure that both parties to an agreement are in a position at completion to honour their contractual obligations. Accordingly, and to ensure that completion takes place without delay or difficulty, preparatory steps prior to completion will need to be taken by both the seller and buyer.

In the past it has been the traditional practice to investigate title after exchange and therefore to raise requisitions on title after exchange. This practice has declined almost to the point of extinction. Accordingly, some traditional post-exchange and pre-completion procedures are considered elsewhere in this book (see also 8.03). Relevant procedures which are considered elsewhere in the book are:

(a) requisitions on title (see Chapter 5);
(b) the traditional deducing and investigation of title (see Chapter 5);
(c) the purchase deed, preparation, etc. (see Chapter 7);
(d) mortgages and bridging finance (see Chapter 7);
(e) procedure at death of the seller after exchange of contracts (see Chapter 6);
(f) procedure at death of the buyer after exchange of contracts (see Chapter 6);
(g) procedure at insolvency of the seller after exchange of contracts (see Chapter 6);
(h) procedure at insolvency of the buyer after exchange of contracts (see Chapter 6).

Recent changes to pre-completion procedures

8.02 Recently, and in an effort to speed up the process, solicitors acting for sellers have taken to issuing the draft transfer at the same time that they send out the draft contract along with pre-answered standard pre-completion requisitions. (The Protocol requisitions form is now called a 'Completion Information and Undertakings (second edition) form', Form TA13.) This change is also promoted in the latest edition of the Law Society's Conveyancing Protocol. As this change in timing is not universally adopted we will continue to explain the conveyancing process by way of the more traditional approach, but practitioners need to be alive to the possibility of the new approach being more commonly adopted as time progresses.

Standard-form pre-completion requisitions

8.03 A requisition, in the context of conveyancing, is a formal written question that requires a formal written answer. There may be some confusion in your mind about the place of requisitions in the conveyancing process. In the past, requisitions on title were raised after exchange because in conveyancing transactions following very traditional pathways, title was not deduced until after exchange. Only incumbrances were disclosed with the draft contract, not the full title. However, modern conveyancing practice has forced the early disclosure of the full title and certainly this has been the case with registered land for some time. As a consequence the nature of requisitions has changed, and those that are raised after exchange are now standard-form pre-completion requisitions. This format has been adopted in the Law Society Conveyancing Protocol with the use of a form called the 'Completion Information and Undertakings' form. The title of the form itself no longer refers to 'requisitions' as the questions asked are really not about the title but are concerned with arrangements for completion.

8.04 Most practitioners have adopted a pre-printed form for requisitions, using either forms pre-printed by themselves, or those issued by law stationers. Alternatively, the Protocol Form is used. Whichever form is used, the purpose of it is to sort out completion arrangements rather than raise detailed questions about the title. We examine at 8.05 the form used in the Protocol as an introduction to standard-form pre-completion requisitions. Thereafter we look at a non-protocol form of Requisitions on Title (see 8.08).

The Protocol Completion Information and Undertakings Form

8.05 The form was introduced with the third edition of the Protocol in 1994. It has been revised several times and is now in a 2011 edition termed a second edition. It is a core element of the Law Society's Conveyancing Protocol. The revised version (2011 second edition) is available via a web link listed in Appendix 8. Apart from producing a standard pre-completion requisitions form, the document was also drawn up to ensure that practitioners 'are aware of the danger of giving thoughtless undertakings to discharge mortgages hence the many warnings on the form' (*A Guide to the National Protocol; Transaction 2001* (Law Society, 2001)). Indeed, the heading includes a clear warning that replies to two questions (3.2 and 5.2) on the form are treated as a solicitor's undertaking. Under the new 2011 Protocol it is suggested that the seller supplies replies to this form, post exchange, without the buyer needing to send the seller a blank form.

The Protocol questions/requisitions

8.06 The requisitions/questions are explained in the following paragraphs.

Question 1 This is concerned with the giving of vacant possession and is in two parts. The first part assumes vacant possession will be available on completion and asks where the keys will be and at what time the seller will vacate. The second part requests the usual authority to the tenant from the seller to pay future rent after completion, to the buyer.

Question 2 This is in two parts and is concerned with the title deeds and documents. The questions are not about the nature of the title, but are merely procedural. The first is limited to unregistered properties and asks about the whereabouts of the deeds. (It is limited in this way following the abolition of land or charge certificates, which used to represent title deeds for registered land prior to their elimination on 13 October 2003 by the Land Registration Act 2002.) The second question asks for a list of what is to be handed over at completion.

Question 3 This is about completion and is in two parts. The first asks where completion is to take place, and the second part requests confirmation that, if completion is by post, the Law Society's Code for Completion will apply. This is the first section where undertakings will apply, and certainly this is the case for the Code for Completion (see Appendix 10). The current version splits the second part into two requests for confirmation. The first covers the Code for Completion. However, the second part asks for confirmation of the mortgages covered by a later question (see Question 5 below).

Question 4 This is in two sections and is about money. The first asks for a statement of how much is expected to be paid on completion. The question goes on to say that if the exact amount payable on completion is not just the balance of the purchase money, receipts or demands are also requested in support of any apportionments. The second asks for bank details for a bank transfer of monies at completion. There is no mention of payment by banker's draft because the fifth edition of the Standard Conditions requires payment by bank transfer only.

Question 5 This is called 'Mortgages and charges' and contains a blunt warning: 'A reply to requisition 5.2 is treated as an undertaking. Great care must be taken when answering this requisition.' The reason for this is clear. Sloppily worded answers can mean a practitioner having to redeem previously unknown mortgages, probably from his own resources. There are three sections but all are concerned with the discharge of mortgages or charges. The first asks for a list of all mortgages (or charges) secured against the subject property that you as the seller's practitioner will pay off on completion. You should immediately note that by listing the mortgages you are in effect confirming that they will be discharged on completion. If you are in any doubt on this point, do not list anything until you know there are sufficient monies to pay off all the mortgages. The question specifically includes any repayment of any discount under the Housing Acts right-to-buy legislation where a former council tenant is selling soon after buying the property. In these circumstances a refund of a right-to-buy discount will be payable to the original seller. The second section asks if you undertake to discharge the borrowings listed in the first section. It goes on to require Forms DS1, DS3, the receipted mortgages, or confirmation that notice of release or discharge in electronic form has been given to Land Registry as soon as the seller's conveyancer receives them. It will be clear from these questions that no answer must be given unless and until it is clear that there will be sufficient monies available on completion to pay off the lenders. The third section seeks confirmation that where the Code for Completion is to be adopted, the seller is the authorized agent of every lender listed in the answer to Question 5.2 as being a proprietor of every mortgage to be redeemed at completion. This takes account of the decision in *Patel v Daybells* [2000] EGCS 98; [2001] PNLR 43: see 8.104; and 8.107 for further guidance on the point at issue.

Lastly, the form contains one further warning that the replies should only be signed by **8.07** someone with authority to give undertakings on behalf of the firm or practitioner replying. (A secretary or unqualified assistant should never be called upon to sign in this way.) This is followed by a separate section for signatures and dates. There is no space for additional requisitions as it is contemplated that all such questions will have been asked and dealt with prior to this stage in the transaction.

A non-Protocol form of requisitions on title

8.08   Apart from the Protocol form, probably the most popular other form that is used by practitioners is the standard 'Oyez' Requisitions on Title issued by the Solicitors' Law Stationery Society Ltd. You can find a link to a copy of this form on the Online Resource Centre accompanying this book.

Non-Protocol requisitions

8.09   The questions within the Oyez form are now considered in detail.

Question 1   This question seeks to ensure that the information already supplied to the buyer is complete and up to date. The question seeks details of variation. This is in contrast to the first question in the Protocol form discussed at 8.06. A typical answer may read 'None known save as may have been made in any subsequent correspondence or the contract.' It is then for the buyer's practitioner to try to work out what this might refer to, thereby highlighting how unhelpful such a response can prove to be.

Question 2   There are four subsections. The first is a statement made to the seller requiring receipts to be produced in support of apportioned outgoings that relate to the subject property. The second subsection relates to leasehold properties. It covers two questions. The first requires the seller to produce the last ground rent receipt or demand, together with the same documentation for the last fire insurance premium. The second raises the all-important query, i.e. does the last receipt make any mention of a subsisting breach of any of the lease covenants? This is of importance as a clear ground rent receipt can be taken to signify that at the time of the issue of the receipt there were no breaches of covenant to which the lessor may refer. The third section deals with apportionments when the subject property is commonhold. Included is a requisition about any reference in the receipts to a breach of any of the provisions of the commonhold community statement (see 10.113 for details relating to commonhold). The fourth subsection simply asks for a completion statement, i.e. a statement showing the monies to be paid on completion, including any apportionments of outgoings relating to the subject property. (See 8.79 for information on completion statements generally.)

Question 3   This covers queries about the title deeds, and subdivides into two sections: one for unregistered land; and the second for registered titles. There are three parts to the unregistered section, and the first asks for confirmation purposes for an exact list of the original documents that will be handed over at completion. This takes into account that, with a sale of part, not all of the abstracted documents will be handed over. Because of this the second question asks for the identity of the person or company that will give an acknowledgement for production for any deeds not handed over at completion. Following on from these two points, the third question asks the seller to explain why some deeds are to be retained, for example because there is a sale of part.

The second section of this question is for registered land. The question asks for search purposes if there is a Land Registry-approved estate plan, and on what date the plan was approved. This is information that may be required to enable a Land Registry search of part Form OS2 to be completed. (See 8.31 for further information about the completion of Land Registry searches of part.)

Question 4 This is the most important question in the form, as it deals with mortgages and their redemption. It has two parts. The first part simply asks the seller to list the mortgages to be redeemed on or before completion. The second part has three subsections that need to be completed for each mortgage listed in the first answer. The first of these asks for confirmation of what form of mortgage release is offered, and seeks confirmation that it will be handed over at completion. The second subsection requests a solicitor's undertaking if the release is not going to be available at completion. Following on from that, the third subsection then asks for an indication of the suggested terms of the undertaking proposed. Great care is needed when replying to this requisition. Please see the guidance set out in reply to Question 5 of the Protocol form set out at 8.06.

Question 5 This question covers matters arising from possession of the subject property. A conveyancing contract will either provide for vacant or part possession, or will be subject to tenancies. Accordingly, this question is in two parts covering contracts for sale with vacant possession, or subject to a tenant or tenancies. The vacant possession subsections are straightforward and procedural. The second part requests that written authorities for future rental payments by the tenant in the subject property to the buyer be handed over at completion. This is required to ensure that the buyer receives the rents once completion has occurred.

Question 6 This is a short yet important question about notices. It asks for the name and address of a party to whom notice should be given of the dealing with the subject property. The most common occurrence of this would be in leasehold assignments or transfers, where the lease contains a covenant requiring notice of the change of ownership to be given to the lessor on completion. The problem with the question is that it is rarely answered properly. This is because most practitioners refer the buyer to answers to preliminary enquiries where virtually the same question is asked prior to exchange of contracts.

Question 7 The final question uses tick boxes and is procedural, covering completion arrangements. The boxes cover the venue for completion, bank details for electronic money transfers, and (in the alternative) banker's draft details. The final tick box asks for confirmation that the seller will comply with the Law Society's Code for Completion by Post. (The reference to banker's draft details is redundant when using the Standard Conditions (SCs) as these only allow payment by bank transfer.)

8.10 The form has a last section in which the right to raise further requisitions is reserved. Best practice dictates that at this point the answer should be 'subject to contract'. This is because of time limits that are likely to be included in the contractual terms for the raising of requisitions. There is such a provision in the general conditions, hence the need to show that this right to raise further requisitions must be subject to the overall terms of the contract. There is also space to raise additional subject property-specific requisitions.

PRE-COMPLETION WHEN ACTING FOR THE SELLER

8.11 In many ways, this is an easier period for the practitioner acting for the seller, in comparison to the heavier burden experienced prior to exchange. When acting for the seller, it is invariably harder to push to an exchange than it is to move to completion once exchange has taken place. Perhaps this then is the proof, if any were needed, of the effect of paying a deposit on exchange. An exchange of contracts supported by a deposit will concentrate the mind of the buyer on completion, as failure to complete will endanger the deposit.

8.12 When the seller has a mortgage on the title, then there is one particularly important pre-completion step, i.e. the necessity to obtain redemption figures for all outstanding mortgages on the title so as to ensure that the property can be sold free of mortgage. (It is also sensible at the same time to ask for a daily rate of interest charged by the lender so that if there is any delay in redeeming the mortgage, fresh figures will not be required for a short delay as the additional interest due can be calculated by reference to the daily rate.)

8.13   When requesting the redemption figures, you should ensure that all accounts (all borrowings) with the lender are covered by their redemption quotation. The problem for practitioners is that some lenders have more than one reference for a borrower, for example where there has been a further loan or additional charge. You need to make sure that the amount advised by the lender covers all monies due to them at completion. A questionnaire completed by the client asking them to provide details of all accounts and loans due to lenders should assist. Always check the charges register to make sure that all mortgages listed in it have been covered by up-to-date redemption statements.

Dealing with estate agent accounts

8.14   If the seller is selling through an estate agency, once contracts have been exchanged there is the question of who is to deal with the estate agents' commission account. It is appropriate to inform the estate agents once contracts have been exchanged and to confirm a binding contract, and particularly the completion date. However, in many cases the agents will be fully informed and will submit their commission account to you on exchange. It is inappropriate actually to ask for the estate agents' account. When you receive it, it is best simply to advise the agents that you will take your client's instructions on the account. In this way the agents will not be in a position to assert that anything you have written should be interpreted as an undertaking to pay their account. The point here is that it has been known for disappointed agents to try to seek payment from the seller's practitioner when the seller has not or will not pay the commission account. If the above procedure is adopted, then there can be no doubt that the liability to pay the estate agents rests solely with the seller.

8.15   The seller's practitioner must ensure that the purchase deed, which is usually prepared by the buyer, is acceptable and complies with the terms of the contract. He or she must also ensure that it is signed by the seller (and witnessed), in readiness for completion. It is also prudent to prepare Form DS1 (charge release form) in readiness for completion. (See 8.101 for details of the need for Form DS1.) See 8.119 for a detailed checklist of pre-completion steps for the seller's conveyancing practitioner.

PRE-COMPLETION WHEN ACTING FOR THE BUYER

8.16   This is a busy time for the conveyancing practitioner acting for the buyer. Once exchange has taken place an immediate check is required to see if the contractual terms pass an insurance obligation on to the buyer at the time of the formation of a binding agreement. If they do, then insurance arrangements must be made without delay. Requisitions (usually of just a procedural nature rather than in relation to the title) must be issued to the sellers, along with a draft transfer. If the buyer is utilizing mortgage finance, the mortgage deed must be prepared and executed, in readiness for completion. The balance of the purchase price after taking into account the deposit must be calculated and collected from the client in good time for completion. If the buyer is relying on mortgage finance, then a clear report on title will be required by the lending institution before it will release the mortgage advance. Lastly, all relevant pre-completion searches must be made and checked to ensure that the buyer is ready to complete by the contractual completion date.

As can be seen, this is a considerable list to be worked through within whatever period **8.17** is fixed by the contract. Indeed, with the pressure on practitioners to compress the time between exchange and completion, it is no surprise that modern practice is to deal with the investigation of title before rather than after exchange of contracts. In many cases a decision is made at an early stage to reduce the time between exchange and completion to a very short period. To enable this to happen, practitioners will carry out post-exchange work before exchange. Thus, to enable completion to take place very soon after exchange the preparation of requisitions, transfer deed, and searches is dealt with before an exchange has taken place. This depends on cooperation between seller and buyer and, in particular, requires the full title to be disclosed at the same time as the draft contract is issued. Modern conveyancing practice now means that this is done in almost all conveyancing transactions. See 8.119 for a detailed checklist of pre-completion steps for the buyer's conveyancing practitioner.

PRE-COMPLETION SEARCHES

Pre-completion searches are a critical part of the overall conveyancing process. However, **8.18** the results of these searches can be riddled with all sorts of pitfalls for the unwary practitioner. In the first place there is the obvious point that with two current land law systems, registered and unregistered, there will always be confusion for the ill-prepared about which searches to make. Second, there is also the potential for confusion arising from the dual role of acting simultaneously for the buyer and the lender. Lastly, there is the assortment of different but relevant searches that can confuse. The buyer's practitioner will be the person to carry out pre-completion searches. This is because the buyer (and the buyer's lender) will want to ensure that the title is in order and is free from undisclosed incumbrances and is therefore freely mortgageable. (Of course if the lender is separately represented, then the lender's practitioner will carry out all searches on behalf of the lender. Sometimes a lender's practitioner will pass on this obligation to the borrower's practitioner.)

Pre-completion searches are made to ensure that the information with regard to the title **8.19** supplied prior to exchange remains the same up to completion. So in the case of registered land the search will refer to the date of the copy registers supplied by the seller, namely, the issue date of the official copies from the Registry, and will disclose any changes since that time. As to unregistered land, the search may disclose many different types of entry, such as any mortgages not detailed in the abstract of title and which have been created as a second or subsequent charge since the seller purchased the property.

There is another purpose to these searches and that is to obtain a protective period during **8.20** which completion and registration can take place and during which the buyer will have priority over anyone else seeking to register an entry against the subject property.

Registered land

A buyer will be supplied with official copies of the registers of the title of the subject prop- **8.21** erty prior to exchange. A binding agreement will have been put in place for the sale and purchase of the property on the basis of the title disclosed in those official copies. These are dated and timed by Land Registry, and the title is therefore accurate only as at the date and time of the official copy entries. It is imperative that a search is carried out from the date of those official copy title details to see if there have been any entries made after the date of the official copies. Because protective entries can be made, for example a unilateral notice or a restriction on the bankruptcy of the registered proprietor, there may be entries made since the date of the official copy entries that even the seller may not know about. Thus an official search with priority is used to protect a transaction for value that affects the registered subject property, for example a purchase, lease, or charge. The search prevents registration of an adverse interest for 30 business days (the priority period) to allow the purchaser, lessee, or lender to lodge the protected application.

Registered land search requirements

8.22 In all cases a practitioner acting for a buyer should insist on receiving, prior to exchange, official copy entries that are less than 12 months old. The reason for this lies with best practice. It is appropriate that practitioners work from reasonably up-to-date official copy details rather than relying on old, out-of-date official copies that could very well not show all subsisting entries. Mere photocopies of the title are not acceptable, as they cannot include an issue date and time and might be very out of date. Official copies will be admissible in evidence to the same extent as the original plan and registers of which they are copies (Land Registration Act 2002, ss 67 and 120). Moreover, the accuracy of the official copies is guaranteed by statute (Land Registration Act 2002, s 67).

8.23 An application for an official search must be directed to the Land Registry office that is responsible for the area in which the subject property is located. A fee will be payable for the search request, and can be paid by cheque. Credit accounts are no longer available for payment of land registry fees; the only other payment method is by variable direct debit. The registry variable direct debit scheme is one where the value being debited varies, as does the frequency of the debit, to accord with the nature of the applications involved. All services delivered through the Portal must be paid for using this scheme. Where required, the payment method should be indicated on the application form by ticking the appropriate tick box. Land Registry will issue a direct debit notification every time a collection of fees is due. The notification will contain details of the key account, the collection it is in respect of, the total amount to be collected, and the date of collection. Searches can be submitted to the Registry by post or online via the National Land Information Service (NLIS) or the Land Registry Portal. Details can be seen at the website of Land Registry at **https://www.gov.uk/government/organisations/land-registry**. The Land Registry Portal enables users to lodge searches of the whole of titles (Form OS1) via their own computers. The applicant enjoys instant priority from the time the search is made (see 8.29). Other appropriate applicants can also electronically deliver a homes rights search (HR3). Searches cannot now be made over the telephone as this service was terminated by Land Registry at the end of 2012, nor can they be faxed. (According to Land Registry demand for this service had reduced by 96 per cent since 2003, with almost 92 per cent of applications now ordered online, compared with 6.8 per cent by post and 1.5 per cent by telephone.)

The effect of a registered land search

8.24 A Land Registry pre-completion search is important not only for the purpose of revealing the state of the title at the time of the search, but also because it will confirm the state of the title at the point of registration. This will be done as a consequence of priority having been given to the search applicant. The effect of this is that any entry due to be made in the registers of the subject property during the priority period will be postponed in favour of the application to register on behalf of the person making the search. The priority period is 30 working days from the search certificate date. The effect of the priority period is, in effect, to freeze the title and the entries in the registers to those disclosed in the official copies as varied, if at all, in the search result, but only until the expiry of the priority period (Land Registration Act, s 72).

8.25 Should completion be delayed, it may be possible to make another search prior to the completion of the transaction. However, it is of vital importance to realize that the second search does not extend the first priority period. In these circumstances it would be possible for a third party to make a search between the two searches and, as a result, obtain priority.

The person named on the search application is the person entitled to priority. The position **8.26** is complicated because most buyers proceed on the basis of a mortgage so that the mortgagee will also require priority protection. To avoid the necessity of making two searches—one for the buyer and the other for the lender—a search is made in the name of the lender, and the buyer takes advantage of the lender's priority period. Accordingly, where a practitioner acts for the buyer and lender, the Land Registry search should always be in the name of the lender (Land Registration Rules 2003 (SI 2003/1417), r 151).

Errors in search results

A practitioner who relies on a Land Registry search result that contains an error is not answer- **8.27** able for any loss that may arise as a result. Indeed, unlike s 10(4) of the Land Charges Act 1972 which relates solely to unregistered land, the search result is not conclusive (see *Parkash v Irani Finance Ltd* [1970] Ch 10, where a buyer of registered land had to take the property subject to a caution that was not disclosed on the pre-completion official certificate of search result). As a consequence, a buyer has merely a remedy in a claim for compensation by reason of the indemnity available under s 103 of, and Schedule 8, para 1(1)(c) to, the Land Registration Act 2002. This is compensation from the public purse and payments are made fairly regularly. (In Land Registry's *Annual Report and Accounts 2012–13*, indemnity claims were listed by amounts paid for each type of claim. There were ten claims arising out of official searches where the total substantive loss including costs was £8,057. This is in the context of 1,019 claims for that year with total gross losses, including costs, of £11,895,796.)

There are several types of Land Registry search forms, including: **8.28**

- Form OS1, search of the whole of a title (see 8.29);
- Form OS2, search of part of a title (see 8.32);
- Form OS3, non-priority searches (see 8.33);
- Form HR3, mortgagee search (see 8.39).

Form OS1, search of the whole of the title

This search is the standard pre-completion search affording the searcher priority when the **8.29** whole of the registered title is being purchased, mortgaged, or leased. A small fee is payable and the search should be submitted to the Land Registry office serving the area in which the subject property is located. The fees vary from time to time. Current fee levels can be checked on the Land Registry website at **https://www.gov.uk/government/organisations/land-registry**. If an OS1 search is sent to the Registry, it will issue the search result on a standard form. In the past the problem with the standard form result was that it did not mention the address or description of the subject property, and from a practical point of view it is sometimes difficult to be sure to which file the search result belongs. Use should be made, therefore, of the facility offered on Form OS1 for giving a reference that will be quoted on the result form.

Form OS1 requires the searcher to insert the title number, a description of the property **8.30** (usually the postal address), and the names of the registered proprietors. (If the searcher is a buyer in a sub-sale contract, then the original seller must be quoted as the registered proprietor, and not the contractual seller. This is because the original seller will still be the proprietor on the title register and not the contractual seller who, by reason of the transaction being a sub-sale, will not have yet completed.) The applicant's identity must then be given along with the reason for the search, for example the applicant intends to purchase, mortgage, or lease the subject property comprising the whole of the registered title or possibly convert to commonhold. Where a mortgage is involved, you should bear in mind the point examined at 8.26 regarding searching in the name of a lender, rather than a buyer, to avoid the wasteful necessity of two searches. A 'search from date' must be stated, being of course the date of the official copies supplied by the seller. There is now also the option to insert 'FR' instead of a date, and this option will arise for a pending first registration search (see 8.35 for details).

8.31   **The effect of using the wrong search form**   It is not uncommon for a buyer of part of a registered title to submit a Form OS1 prior to completion. This is incorrect, as the right search is OS2 discussed at 8.32. If by mistake OS1 is used, this will cause problems on other potential transactions of part affecting different elements of the title. This is because if there are searches of part submitted for other sections of the title, then the search of whole will be disclosed, no doubt to the considerable concern of the practitioner on the receiving end of this worrying result. There is a further problem highlighted in the July/ August 1999 issue of *The Practical Lawyer* at p 6, regarding a case where a property was being purchased at auction. The buyer's conveyancers carried out a search of the whole by telephone, even though only part of a registered title was being purchased. A clear search was issued with priority. Completion and an application followed this for registration within the priority period. When the conveyancers did make the application, the Registry then told them that a prior application was already being actioned for the same part of the title. Even though the applicant had made a search, had priority, and had applied for registration in the priority period, Land Registry indicated that the first applicant would be registered in priority. This is because a search of the whole, in the view of Land Registry, will not give priority in a purchase of part of a registered title. Therefore neither application had a claim to protection from a priority period, and it was therefore 'first come, first served'; see also (1999) 21 LSG 44. Accordingly, practitioners should make sure that Form OS1 searches are used only when buying the complete title (Land Registration Rules 2003, r 147(3)).

Form OS2, search of part of the title

8.32   This search is used when the subject property forms part of a larger title from which it is being sold. In many respects it is the same as an OS1 search save that it does not relate to the whole of the title. Because of this difference, practitioners must remember not only to describe the subject property carefully in the search, but also to describe it in one of two alternative ways. The search of part must describe the subject property either by reference to a plan attached to the search request, or by a plot number shown on an estate plan which has been given prior approval by Land Registry. (An approved estate plan will normally be used on the sale of new properties within a large estate: see Chapter 11.) If the search is to be accompanied by a plan it must be submitted in duplicate, and best practice dictates that the plan should be to scale, ideally show a north point, and should clearly mark the subject property and should make clear on what floor level the property is located when it is a flat in a block. The search plan should not be marked 'for identification purposes only'. In view of the difficulties mentioned in 8.31 about a transfer of part, it is now even more important that search plans are entirely accurate. Both alternatives are referred to in the search form and one only must be selected. If the search refers to an approved estate plan, the date of the approval must be mentioned on the search request along with the plot number. The other information required in the search of the whole also applies to a search of part, and priority details are also the same. The applicant must state a 'search from date', being of course the date of the official copies supplied. There is now also the option to insert 'FR' instead of a date, and this option will arise for a pending first registration search (see 8.35 for details).

Form OS3, non-priority searches

8.33   Forms OS1 and OS2 exist for the benefit of a person or company that (for valuable consideration and at arm's length) is buying, leasing, mortgaging, or converting to commonhold all or some of a registered title. The forms cannot be used in other circumstances. Accordingly, an OS3 search should be used in cases other than these. For example, a lender, pursuant to its power of sale, which is selling the mortgaged property, should make an OS3 Land Registry search to ascertain the existence or not of any subsequent mortgages on the title. The purpose of this is that if, after the sale, the first mortgagee has a surplus over the redemption sum required, the balance should be paid to any subsequent mortgagee in full or part satisfaction of the second charge, and so on down the list of lenders involved in the title. Similarly, a buyer of an equitable interest in the subject property will also wish to make a final search and, because of the nature of the interest being purchased, Form OS3 must be used, as the other searches relate to legal estates (Land Registration Rules 2003, r 155).

In cases where this search is used, the search result will disclose entries subsequent to the **8.34** official copies in the possession of the searcher, but it will not give any priority to that searcher. However, the likely circumstances in which such a search will arise are such that priority will be of little or no consequence.

Form OS1 and pending first registration of whole

Inevitably, applications to Land Registry for first registration of a title will take longer to **8.35** process than simple dealings of existing registered titles. This can lead to problems when the applicant for first registration then wishes to sell before the first registration application has been completed. The problem for the prudent practitioner is that although a registered title has yet to be issued, an application for a search in the land charges registry would not be appropriate as the buyer will ultimately receive a registered title, and there is a pending first registration application at the Registry. As a consequence, the appropriate search is the OS1 search form, which allows a search-from date to indicate that there is a pending first registration lodged at the Registry. A fee is payable.

The search result will disclose if Land Registry has received any applications affecting the **8.36** subject property that will give rise to an adverse entry on the title when issued. This search result will afford priority, and the result will be in relation to the period from the date of the pending first registration application to the search date. Provided the searcher makes the dealing application within the priority period, he will take free of any other application that might otherwise intervene.

Accordingly, practitioners should use Form OS1 (or OS2) wherever there is a pending first **8.37** registration application lodged at the Registry at the time when they must search the as yet unregistered title.

Form OS2 and pending first registration of part

This search is the same as discussed in 8.35 but relates solely to dealings affecting part **8.38** of the pending application title. In both cases, part and whole of title, there is no need to quote to Land Registry, in the search application, the date of the pending first registration application. Form OS2 should be used on a purchase of part of a title subject to a pending application for first registration. A fee is payable, and an accurate plan in duplicate showing the part of the title forming the part to be sold should also accompany the OS2.

Form HR3, mortgagee search

Where, as a consequence of the default of the borrower, a lender wishes to enforce its rights **8.39** as a mortgagee of a home, it must first serve notice of the action on any non-owning spouse or a party to a civil partnership union who has registered a protective entry on the title in respect of rights of occupation. The search discloses whether any notice or caution is registered to protect a spouse's or civil partner's right of occupation under the Family Law Act 1996, the Matrimonial Homes Acts 1967 or 1983, or the Civil Partnership Act 2004.

It is possible for entries to have been made of which the lender is unaware (e.g. a notice), and in these circumstances the mortgagee can make a search to update the title utilizing Form HR3, which will disclose homes rights registrations. (A caution would exist to protect entries made before 13 October 2003 under legislation prior to the Land Registration Act 2002.) The Land Registry Portal system allows the online delivery of homes rights searches.

Search results

8.40   The search result that all buyers expect is one that confirms that there have been no adverse entries made on the title of the subject property since the date of the official copies supplied by the seller to the buyer. Clearly, if there are adverse entries these must be carefully noted and referred back to the seller for an explanation. Beyond an explanation, the seller must be required to remove or deal with the entries to the entire satisfaction of the buyer, so that the buyer at completion can acquire a clear and unencumbered title. Indeed, the seller may well be under a contractual obligation to give good title, and will therefore be required to deal with the adverse entries disclosed on the search result.

8.41   Practitioners need to be aware that after 13 October 2003 they need to be able to interpret results that can relate to both pre- and post-Land Registration Act 2002 entries. So it is possible that a search result will give details of entries made under the old and the new law, such as a new-style unilateral notice as well as an old-style caution. It remains the case that registrations made before 13 October 2003 remain valid even though the form of registration such as a caution cannot now be made.

Real-time priority

8.42   The priority for searches until fairly recently referred to just a date. Now it refers to a date and time, i.e. real time. Real-time priority (RTP) arises where an application is given priority from the moment, i.e. the actual time, it is entered on a day list maintained at and by Land Registry. From 29 May 2001, Land Registry extended RTP so that all substantive applications and priority searches are given priority from the time they are entered on the day list, i.e. the actual time of receipt. Applications will be given a priority date and time: for example, 1 June 2014, 12:34:56. Land Registry takes the view that RTP will help to facilitate e-conveyancing in the longer term (see Chapter 1 regarding e-conveyancing).

8.43   Official copies of registers and title plans will show a time as well as a date. This information will be completed automatically by computer in most cases. Copies of deeds are not affected. The time will be important because it will be possible for different versions of the register to exist on the same day. Forms for new properties will also carry a date and time.

8.44   RTP will be extended to all priority searches, however lodged. This means that applicants will be able to lodge OS1 searches as soon as telephone and direct access services are opened, rather than waiting until 11.00 a.m. Priority under searches will expire at midnight (rather than 9.30 a.m.) on the thirtieth working day following the priority date of a search. There is no significant change to the procedures for lodging applications protected by priority searches—they must still be received during the priority period, but by 12 noon rather than 9.30 a.m. on the last day of the period. This will allow Land Registry to add protected applications to the day list before priority expires at midnight. Search results will be based on changes made since the start of the search from date; no search from time will be requested. RTP is covered by the Land Registration Rules 2003.

8.45   **Outline applications**   From 29 May 2001 applicants, by way of an outline application (OLA), may reserve priority for certain applications that cannot be protected by an official search; for example, registering a charging order, a deed of gift, a restriction, or a notice. The application is made by telephone and can only be made in respect of a whole title, not part. For an OLA to be effective, a duly completed application form, together with the supporting papers, must be lodged by 12 noon on the fourth working day, including the day the OLA was entered on the day list. (This is similar to the requirements for an official search.) The paper application quoting the correct reference number of the OLA must be lodged at the correct Land Registry office with the appropriate form (e.g. AP1, as required, which must refer to the previously delivered OLA). A fee is payable for an OLA.

Land Registry Practice Guide 12—official searches and outline applications can be found at https://www.gov.uk/government/publications/official-searches-and-outline-applications/ practice-guide-12-official-searches-and-outline-applications#types-of-official-search.

Unregistered land

When dealing with unregistered land, the most critical pre-completion search is made in **8.46** the Central Land Charges Register (CLCR). Full searches in this register are only necessary when dealing with unregistered land and are completely irrelevant so far as registered land is concerned. The correct search form is Form K15 (not to be confused with a mere bankruptcy search, also sent to this registry, which is K16). An application for an official search must be directed to the CLCR, which is located in Plymouth and covers all of England and Wales. A small fee will be payable for the search request and can be paid by cheque or by the Registry variable direct debit scheme. The Registry variable direct debit scheme is one where the value being debited varies, as does the frequency of the debit, to accord with the nature of the application involved. All services delivered through the Portal must be paid for using this scheme. Where required, the payment method should be indicated on the application form by ticking the appropriate tick box. The Registry will issue a direct debit notification every time a collection of fees is due. The notification will contain details of the key account, the collection it is in respect of, the total amount to be collected, and the date of collection. Searches can be submitted to the Registry either by post, online via the Land Registry Portal or the NLIS, or by fax, but they cannot be requested over the telephone as Land Registry terminated this service at the end of 2012. The search result confers a priority period of 15 working days on the searcher/applicant. Accordingly, if completion takes place during this period, the searcher/applicant will take free of any entries placed on the register between the date of the search and the completion date, on the proviso that completion did indeed take place within the priority period. (You should note that it is not necessary to apply for first registration of title within the search priority period; the time limit is simply two months from the completion date: see s 6(4) of the Land Registration Act 2002.) Applicants can now ask for search results to be issued electronically. No paper certificate is issued. A result in PDF format (electronic form) is issued instead. In 2016/17 the Registry issued 1,683,809 full and bankruptcy searches out of the Land Charges Register (see the Land Registry's *Annual Report and Accounts 2016–17*). Of that total just 172,098 were full searches, with the remainder being bankruptcy or insolvency searches. (This total of full searches was down 2.23 per cent on the previous year, while bankruptcy searches were up 9.96 per cent.) This is a clear indication of the continued decline in the number of unregistered conveyancing transactions.

Central Land Charges Register

The register is a computer database of the names of estate owners and any charges registered **8.47** against particular estate owners' names. Practitioners will therefore appreciate the difference between unregistered land when searches are made against owners and former owners using their names, rather than the registered land practice of searching against the land title. Practitioners must therefore list the names of estate owners disclosed in the abstract or epitome of title for land charge search purposes. If the abstract or epitome includes search results against listed names, then a fresh search will not normally be required. See further details regarding names to be included in a K15 search request in 8.55.

8.48 **The registers** There are five registers in the Land Charges Register; entries made are classified as follows, and will be referred to below in the same way on search results. The five registers are:

- a register of land charges;
- a register of pending land actions;
- a register of writs and orders affecting land;
- a register of deeds of arrangement affecting land;
- a register of annuities.

8.49 **Land charges** Land charges are classified into six categories, each of which is labelled by a letter. Some of these categories have sub-categories, as set out in the following paragraphs.

Class A (Land Charges Act 1972, s 2(2)) This is a rarely encountered financial charge arising from little-used statutory provisions, and occurring only after a court application. Examples include the right of a landlord to compensation under s 86 of the Agricultural Holdings Act 1986; a charge registered pursuant to s 12 of the Landlord and Tenant Act 1927 where a business lessor registers in respect of compensation paid to a lessee for improvements to the subject premises. A full list of Class A land charges appears in Schedule 2 to the Land Charges Act 1972.

Class B (Land Charges Act 1972, s 2(3)) This is another financial charge arising from statute (and not a court application), and is also uncommon in practice. An example is the statutory charge over property that the Legal Services Commission can claim pursuant to s 16(6) of the Legal Aid Act 1988, and s 10(7) of the Access to Justice Act 1999. These land charges are imposed automatically as a result of the effects of statute, which is why they are different from the first category.

Class C comprises four sub-divisions and contains many of the most important land charges encountered in practice:

Class C(i) (Land Charges Act 1972, s 2(4)(i)) This is the first of the more commonly encountered entries and relates to the registration of a *puisne* mortgage. This is a legal charge that does not have protection by the deposit of the title deeds. This situation will arise in unregistered land where this mortgage is a second legal charge. The first lender will have the title deeds, and consequently a registration of this kind will afford protection to the second lender, who of course will be unable to claim the protection of actual possession of the deeds. Without this form of registration, a buyer of the mortgaged estate would be unaware of second and subsequent charges, and it is for this reason that registration is required.

Class C(ii) (Land Charges Act 1972, s 2(4)(ii)) This is called a limited owner's charge. As this involves an equitable charge by a tenant for life (or by a statutory owner) in relation to settled land, and relates to tax payable on death, it will be appreciated that it is not often encountered in practice. It is an equitable charge in relation to inheritance tax paid by the tenant for life.

Class C(iii) (Land Charges Act 1972, s 2(4)(iii)) This is a general equitable charge. It is a pot-pourri of various miscellaneous items (not registrable under C(i)) and can cover different matters, for example a seller's lien for unpaid purchase monies. The potential items covered by this class are defined in a negative way, i.e. not covered elsewhere (see *Uziell-Hamilton v Keen* (1971) 22 P & CR 655). Annuities can also be protected by this charge.

Class C(iv) (Land Charges Act 1972, s 2(4)(iv)) This is an estate contract. It is commonly encountered in practice as it affords protection in relation to contracts made by estate owners (sellers), or others entitled to take a conveyance (buyers), where the contract relates to the conveying or creation of a legal estate. Accordingly, if a binding contract is made either party can register this protective entry, although in practice it is usually the buyer who will seek protection. This will be the case particularly if completion is delayed or is contractually a long time off, or if the buyer does not trust the seller. Equally, if the seller has cause to mistrust the buyer a protective registration is possible. A conditional contract is registrable even though the condition remains outstanding and unfulfilled at the date of registration of the estate contract (see *Haslemere Estates Ltd v Baker* [1982] 1 WLR 1109).

Other than ordinary conveyancing contracts, this entry also protects options to purchase, options to renew leases, and rights of pre-emption. Therefore, it should be noted that if a lease contains a right for the lessee to claim a lease renewal on expiry of the original term, this right must be protected by registration for it to be binding on a buyer of the lessor's estate (see *Phillips v Mobil Oil Ltd* [1989] 1 WLR 888).

Class D comprises three sub-divisions: 8.50

Class D(i) (Land Charges Act 1972, s 2(5)(i))   Another rarity, this is a charge obtained by the Inland Revenue for unpaid tax payable on death. If there is unpaid inheritance tax, the Inland Revenue can register this form of protective entry.

Class D(ii) (Land Charges Act 1972, s 2(5)(ii))   This registration covers restrictive covenants created after 1925, other than restrictive covenants in a lease or pre-1926 restrictive covenants. Lease covenants are not registrable because their enforceability will depend on the law relating to covenants in landlord and tenant terms. See Chapter 10 for further details. Additionally, freehold, pre-1926 restrictive covenants cannot be protected by this registration, as the traditional doctrine of notice will apply.

Class D(iii) (Land Charges Act 1972, s 2(5)(iii))   This is a post-1925 equitable easement. Easements that are not legal must be protected by registration in this class. Furthermore, a contract to create an easement will also be registrable (see *ER Ives Investment Ltd v High* [1967] 2 QB 379).

Class E (Land Charges Act 1972, s 2(6))   This class is virtually outmoded as it originally protected pre-1926 annuities. This form of annuity is a charge against a legal estate in land to secure an annual or other form of instalment income. Such charges are very rarely seen in practice.

Class F (Land Charges Act 1972, s 2(7))   This class originally arose from the provisions of the Family Law Act 1996 (and prior to that the Matrimonial Homes Act 1967) relating to a spouse's right of occupation, i.e. matrimonial home rights. Civil partnership unions are now covered by similar legislation with comparable rights of occupation. Where there is a non-owning spouse or partner in occupation, that spouse or partner can register a Class F charge to protect a right of occupation, to protect his or her homes rights. Failure to register will mean that the occupying spouse or partner loses all protection against a buyer for value of the home in question.

Register of pending land actions (Land Charges Act 1972, s 5)   A pending action is any pro-   8.51
ceeding or action in court relating to land or an interest in land, including a charge over land. Perhaps the most important example of the kind of pending action disclosed in this way is a petition in bankruptcy. If the seller is shown to be subject to a pending bankruptcy action, completion must not occur unless steps are taken to deal with the entry and ensure that the buyer receives good title. Other examples of pending actions include claims for a property transfer by a spouse in divorce proceedings, and boundary disputes. By s 8 of the Land Charges Act 1972, registrations of pending actions last for five years; if they are not renewed they will cease to be valid. Renewal is permitted by s 8 of the Land Charges Act 1972.

Register of writs and orders (Land Charges Act 1972, s 6)   The purpose of this register   8.52
is to afford assistance in the enforcement of judgments and court orders. Writs and orders

concerned with land and bankruptcy orders made by a court will benefit from registration in this register. As with the register of pending actions, the period of validity is five years, and renewal pursuant to s 8 of the Land Charges Act 1972 is also available. A charging order is registrable, as is an order made pursuant to the provisions in the Access to Neighbouring Land Act 1992. Non-registration means that a buyer will take free from the writ or order.

8.53   **Register of deeds of arrangement (Land Charges Act 1972, s 7)**   Under s 1 of the Deeds of Arrangement Act 1914, a deed of arrangement is a document entered into by a debtor with creditors whereby control over the debtor's property is relinquished, with a view to avoiding bankruptcy proceedings. Registration is by a creditor or trustee. Registration is valid for five years but renewal is possible. The effect of non-registration is that the arrangement is void against a buyer of the land involved in the arrangement.

8.54   **Register of annuities (Land Charges Act 1972, s 1(4))**   This register deals with pre-1926 annuities and is more or less obsolete. An annuity is a fixed sum payable at specified intervals, usually annually, over a period such as the recipient's life or in perpetuity in return for either a single premium, or premiums paid in instalments. Post-1925 annuities may be registered as Class C(iii) land charges or, possibly, as Class E charges.

Names and searches

8.55   A land charges search should be made against the seller and all estate owners disclosed in the abstract or epitome of title, and diligent practice dictates that the search is made against all estate owners since 1925. The search will also need to mention the period of years of ownership for each estate owner, together with an indication of the county in which the property is located. County names required by the search should be correctly entered, and former county details should be stated: for example if a property was formerly in the county of Middlesex, this should be mentioned as well as the 'new' county location. This applies to several 'new' counties such as Cumbria. With regard to London, parts of Greater London were previously in outlying counties, i.e. not actually part of an administrative area of London such as the London County Council, and became part of the (now defunct) Greater London Council in 1965. These former details, such as the former county being Middlesex, should always be mentioned in the search request.

8.56   It is possible that there may be an entry on the register against a previous owner not known to the buyer as the period of ownership was before the root of title. If the root of title in the contract is a conveyance to the seller 16 years ago, the buyer will see just one deed, i.e. that conveyance, and can only search against one name, that of the seller.

8.57   The unsatisfactory point here is that the buyer will be bound by prior entries against previous owners but will be unable to call for pre-root title details (under s 198 of the Law of Property Act 1925 the buyer is deemed to have notice of all such registrations even though they are undiscoverable). It is possible that compensation may be available for an undiscoverable and adverse land charge under s 25 of the Law of Property Act 1969. If the buyer had no knowledge of the charge, the charge was registered against an owner not disclosed in the abstract or epitome of title (and the root of title was at least 15 years old), the buyer may seek compensation from public funds. (The buyer may be able to take action against the seller if the seller knew about the incumbrances but did not disclose them; see the seller's duty of disclosure in 3.28.)

8.58   To avoid this problem a practitioner should requisition:

1. title from 1925; or
2. names of title owners from 1925; or
3. all previous land charge search results that are with the deeds.

Searches carried out on behalf of previous buyers may be relied on, and it may be possible **8.59** to construct the preceding chain of ownership for reassurance in this way.

The effect of errors in search applications   Because a registration is made against the name **8.60** of an estate owner, it is crucial that the name is correctly and exactly quoted in the search application. (See *Oak Co-operative Building Society v Blackburn* [1968] Ch 730, where a buyer registered a C(iv) estate contract in the name Frank David Blackburn, but the correct name was Francis David Blackburn. It was held that a search against the wrong name was invalid. This was so even though the registration itself was against a wrong name.)

Best practice is to quote the name (or names if more than one version) that appears in the **8.61** title deed by which the estate owner took the title (see *Standard Property Investment plc v British Plastics Federation* (1985) 53 P & CR 25, and *Diligent Finance Co. Ltd v Alleyne* (1972) 23 P & CR 346). Accordingly, great care must be taken as to the accuracy of names, and practitioners should ensure that all former names, if known, are searched against. This will apply to companies and to individuals.

Land charge searches and deceased owners   In the case of a deceased owner, a land char- **8.62** ges search should be made against the full name of the deceased for the period between death and the present day where the deceased was the proprietor of the property at the date of death. Otherwise, a search against the deceased estate owner should be made up to the next conveyance for value. This is because land charges are capable of being registered against deceased estate owners.

Effect of registration or non-registration

Section 198(1) of the Law of Property Act 1925 provides that registration of an entry in **8.63** any of the five registers constitutes actual notice of whatever is registered. This will be the case against all persons and companies and for all purposes to do with the land affected by the registration. As a consequence of this provision, searches are carried out to ensure that a buyer is aware of all registrations of which, by statute, a purchaser is deemed to have notice. Accordingly, the effect of an official search certificate is that it is conclusive in favour of a searcher. (It will give the searcher priority, and will also protect the practitioner for the searcher against any errors in the search; see s 12 of the Land Charges Act 1972, which confirms that anyone obtaining an official search result is not answerable for any loss arising from an error within the search result.)

The effect of non-registration   The effect of non-registration varies with the different **8.64** registers, as set out in Table 8.1.

Table 8.1 The effect of non-registration

A, B, C(i), C(ii), C(iii), and F	Void as against a purchaser/lessee/mortgagee for valuable consideration of the subject property or an interest in it unless registered (Land Charges Act 1925, s 4).
C(iv) and D	Void as against a purchaser *of a legal estate* in the land for money or money's worth unless registered (Land Charges Act 1925, s 4).
Pending action	Void as against a buyer for valuable consideration if not registered (Land Charges Act 1925, s 5).
Writ or order	Void as against a buyer for valuable consideration if not registered (Land Charges Act 1925, s 6).
Arrangement deed	Void as against a buyer for valuable consideration if not registered (Land Charges Act 1925, s 7).

8.65 The case of *Midland Bank Trust Co. Ltd v Green* [1981] AC 513, HL, confirms that if a buyer has actual knowledge of a registrable interest but there has been no registration of the interest, that knowledge is immaterial and irrelevant.

Search results and old searches

8.66 The search result, the official search certificate, will show either subsisting entries or that there are none. It will also confer priority, so that if the buyer completes within the 15-working-day priority period starting from the date of the certificate, then he will take free of any entries made after the certificate date (Land Charges Act 1972, s 11(5)). Another period of priority will be conferred by new searches sent to Plymouth. The requirement is to complete within this time limit and not to make a first registration application. The Land Registration Act 2002, s 6(4) allows a two-month period from completion to apply for first registration.

8.67 As has been mentioned earlier (see 8.55), old search certificates should be requested in requisitions in the expectation that they will be supplied and contribute to a search covering all the estate owners since 1925. Another reason for seeking such results is to check that they have been completed correctly (names are accurate, etc.), then there will be no need for a fresh search against the names disclosed in the old searches and the buyer will not incur the expense of additional search fees.

8.68 If entries are revealed, the items disclosed should be scrutinized to sift out those that might be expected from others that were previously unknown. If the property is subject to restrictive covenants, a buyer can expect to see an entry in the D(ii) category. If completion was delayed, a buyer could well encounter a C(iv) entry made to protect the relevant delayed contract for the purchase of the subject property. However, if an unexpected entry is disclosed, two steps should be taken. First, a requisition should be issued to the seller requesting an explanation and the removal of the land charge. Second, the buyer should apply to the Land Charges Registry for an office copy (an official copy), of the entry. If the copy is of a significant registration, and it was not an incumbrance to which the property was expressed in the contract to be subject, then the seller will be liable to remove the charge. If it cannot be removed the seller will plainly be in breach of contract, because he is now selling something different from that which he contracted to sell. Sometimes the entry is irrelevant, and in these circumstances the seller's solicitor should be required to certify in writing that the entry disclosed does not relate to the subject property. When requested to provide such a certification a practitioner acting for a seller must take great care, as a certificate in these terms can constitute a professional undertaking in respect of which liability could fall on the practitioner.

Acting for a lender

8.69 The present practice, in the vast majority of residential conveyancing cases, is for the buyer's practitioner to act for the buyer's lender at the same time. While this has come about, no doubt, as a result of economic pressures (so that the buyer need only pay one conveyancing practitioner rather than two), it does mean that additional searches will be necessary. This is because the practitioner must ensure that there is a good and marketable title to the subject property not only for the buyer but also for the buyer's lender. However, the lender must also be satisfied that a loan can be granted in favour of the proposed borrower. This means that there must be checks made for the lender in relation to both the subject property and the borrower. In the majority of commercial loans the lender is usually separately represented.

8.70 Title searches for mortgagees are the same as those for a buyer: OS1 and OS2 searches for registered land, and K15 searches for unregistered land, and company searches if appropriate.

Lenders will also require a bankruptcy-only search against all proposed borrowers. These are made on Form K16 and are also sent to Plymouth to the CLCR as a search in the registers of pending actions and writs and orders. In this way all registered bankruptcy petitions and orders will be disclosed. Clearly, if an entry is disclosed, the lender must be informed without delay, and the mortgage will almost certainly not proceed. It is critical that the full names of the borrowers be stated precisely, and all former names and aliases must also be given. Results can be awkward in that sometimes entries will be disclosed against a surname only. If this happens consideration must be given to supporting information, such as the address and, if necessary, an office copy (an official copy) should be sought on Form K19. It is appropriate, when you are completely satisfied that the entry does not apply to certify for the lender on the search result that the entry does not relate to the borrower.

Buying from a company

If the seller is a limited company there will be an additional search that will apply to both registered and unregistered land. Where a company is selling, a search of the companies register at Companies House should be carried out. This can be done either in person, or through search agents. Some basic company information is also available online at **https://www.gov.uk/government/organisations/companies-house**. There is no formal or prescribed method or form for this search. There is no priority period of protection available for a company search. Because of this lack of protection for a buyer, the search should be made just before completion to ensure that the information to be relied on is up to date at completion. In large-scale commercial conveyancing transactions, two company searches will be made; one immediately after exchange and the second on the morning of completion. If you as the buyer's representative have any cause to doubt the standing of the selling company, then we recommend, wherever possible, that you carry out a company search on the day of completion. **8.71**

The Land Registration Act 2002 is quite clear in that it states that the grant of a legal charge is a registrable disposition (s 27(2)(f)). It also states that the effect of non-registration at the Registry of a mortgage means that it is void and takes effect as a mere contract made for valuable consideration to create the mortgage (s 7(2)(b)). It is therefore clear that no company charge whatever, be it fixed or floating, will affect a buyer unless it is protected by some form of registration at Land Registry, such as registration in the charges register or even possibly a notice or restriction. **8.72**

Why search?

A company search will still be necessary because a buyer may wish to be sure that the company still subsists and has not been struck off the register, for example for failing to file returns. If it has been struck off the companies register, then the company ceases to exist in law and cannot therefore enter into a deed, transfer, or conveyance. If the company is subject to winding-up proceedings, these will be shown by a company search. This is information that a buyer needs to be aware of in the context of imminent completion. (Section 127 of the Insolvency Act 1986 renders any disposition of property owned by a company void if made after the commencement of winding-up proceedings.) There is no need to carry out a company search to check on financial charges made by the company as they will bind a buyer only if they are registered at Land Registry. **8.73**

In the case of unregistered land the company search is very important. The search will reveal subsisting floating charges, specific (or fixed) charges created before 1 January 1970, and the commencement of any winding-up proceedings. All three are of material importance to a buyer and, if disclosed in the search result, would clearly be adverse. No purchaser should proceed until the seller has in the appropriate way shown how and when the **8.74** adverse entry is to be dealt with. Bearing in mind that any disposition by a company subject to winding-up proceedings is void (Insolvency Act 1986, s 127), it will be appreciated just how important a company search can be.

8.75   Company searches are usually carried out by search agents who will inspect the records available at Companies House. Some limited free information is available online at **https://www.gov.uk/government/organisations/companies-house**, for example a list of disqualified directors and the companies' name and address index with basic company information. This information includes the company registration number, date of incorporation, company type, nature of business, and registered office.

Physical inspection of the subject property

8.76   Lastly, the subject property should be inspected prior to completion. The reason for this is primarily to check on exactly who is in occupation. The existence of a third-party occupant might amount to an overriding interest to which the purchase would be subject (as was the case in *Williams and Glyn's Bank Ltd v Boland* [1981] AC 487). The reasons for and purpose of a physical inspection were explored in detail in 4.34. The contract for sale may include a list of items included in the sale, or there could be items listed in replies to enquiries. In either case the buyer will want to be sure that the listed items actually exist and are within the subject property.

8.77   Another reason for a physical inspection is when it is a new property which must be examined to list any problems that need to be dealt with by the developer. A 'snagging list' should be compiled by the buyer as soon as the developer asserts that the property is ready for completion. This will be done by revisiting the property with or without a surveyor, and listing all the outstanding defects that need to be remedied by the seller.

Other searches

8.78   Other searches can also prove necessary in particular circumstances applicable to a subject property. These include:

(a) **Enduring powers of attorney search**   If the purchase deed is to be executed by a person authorized by an enduring power of attorney the buyer's practitioner should carry out a search (on payment of a small fee and utilizing Form EP4) of the records maintained by the Court of Protection. (Remember that Enduring Powers of Attorney have, since 1 October 2007, been replaced by Lasting Powers of Attorney (LPA): see 5.110 for further details.) An LPA can only be used once it is registered with the Office of the Public Guardian. You can search if this has been done by submitting Form OPG100 to the Office of the Public Guardian. The form is on the **https://www.gov.uk** website. If those records show no registration having been made or pending, then completion can take place. If registration is disclosed the transaction may still complete provided the donor is still alive.

(b) **Probate search**   There can be occasions when a seller includes reference to a grant of representation in an abstract or epitome of title but without actually supplying the original or a copy of that grant. It might also be the case that on completion the original or a marked copy of the grant will not be available to the buyer. In these circumstances a buyer should carry out a search at the Principal Probate Registry with a view to ensuring that the grant has not been revoked or, if a limited grant, that it has not expired. A search can be requested by post and a fee will be payable. The deceased's full name, date of death, and last address should be quoted. On the assumption that a proper grant was issued, an office copy of the grant can then be sought if still required.

COMPLETION AND FINANCIAL STATEMENTS

Many and varied completion statements are commonly encountered in conveyancing trans- **8.79** actions. Statements sent to the client are usually called financial statements; those sent to the buyer are called completion statements. There are three main forms of completion statement:

(a) **A financial statement prepared by the seller's practitioner for the seller**   The purpose of this statement is to show the seller how much will be left over on completion by way of the net proceeds of sale, either to be applied towards an allied purchase or as the simple net proceeds of sale.

(b) **A completion statement prepared by the seller's practitioner for the buyer's practitioner** The purpose of this statement is to show the buyer how much is expected to be paid over at completion. Clearly if this is only the balance of the purchase price after taking into account the deposit, then a full-blown statement is unnecessary. These statements can be quite complex and lengthy when the subject property is leasehold. In these circumstances the statement will have to include apportionments of monies paid in advance, or still outstanding and due to be paid. This might include ground rent, insurance, rent, and service charges.

(c) **A financial statement prepared by the buyer's practitioner for the buyer**   The purpose of this statement is to show the buyer how much will be needed to complete the purchase of the subject property. This will normally be prepared and issued shortly after exchange so that the buyer can put his practitioner in funds in good time for completion. If the figures are to be fully comprehensive, a bill of costs should accompany this statement. Failure to complete using cleared funds is a breach of the Solicitors' Accounts Rules.

Completion statements are sometimes referred to as financial statements by practitioners. **8.80** However, as a guide to their usual format, examples of all three of the above are provided in Appendix 9.

PRE-COMPLETION PROCEDURES

Acting for the buyer

- When acting for buyer and lender together and if purchasing registered land, apply for a Land **8.81** Registry search in the name of the lender only; in this way the buyer will also obtain the benefit of the search priority protection.

- When buying from a company, consider the necessity of a company search to check on the continuing ability of the vendor company to sell.

- Do not get confused about what search is required.

- For registered land:
  (a) OS1 (buying the whole title), OS2 (buying part of the title);
  (b) K16 land charges bankruptcy search against the buyer, if you are also acting for a lender;
  (c) company search if buying from a company.

- For unregistered land:
  (a) K15 full land charges search against past and present estate owners, post-1925;
  (b) K16 land charges bankruptcy search against the buyer if you are also acting for a lender;
  (c) company search if buying from a company.

- If buying unregistered land, try to get pre-root title details for your land charges search or all old land charge search results.

Acting for the seller

- Where the title is subject to a mortgage, obtain redemption figures immediately after exchange.

- If the title is registered, ensure Form DS1 is prepared (but left undated) before completion, or take a copy of the charges register, to ensure the necessary details of the registered charge can be entered on the form to be sealed by the lender after completion.

- If the title is leasehold, make sure you get all up-to-date receipts and demands relating to ground rent and service charge payments (including buildings insurance premiums) for apportionment, and check that the last receipt for ground rent is clear, i.e. that there are no alleged outstanding breaches of covenant.

- Double-check that you hold all the deeds and documents of title due to be handed over at completion. Consider passing to the buyer all obsolete land or charge certificates.

B COMPLETION

8.82 Completion is the time when the balance of the purchase price is paid by the buyer to the seller in exchange for the deeds, executed purchase deed, keys and, if the contract so provides, vacant possession. In unregistered land the transfer or assignment constitutes the passing of title of a legal estate and this is effectively completion of the transaction: see *Killner v France* [1946] 2 All ER 83 (subject to the requirement to submit the title to Land Registry for first registration). This is not the case in registered land, where the passing of title of a legal estate is only completed with the registration of the buyer as the registered proprietor at Land Registry. On a practical basis, as the buyer is obliged to register, completion is at the time the money is handed over in exchange for the transfer. However, practitioners must always remember to proceed with registration, and to do so within their search priority period, without which no legal title will vest in the buyer.

8.83 No old and now redundant land or charge certificates (pre-13 October 2003 registered land deeds) need to be lodged at Land Registry when applying for a dealing, or be placed on deposit when concerned with the registration of a transfer of part. If they are sent to Land Registry they will be destroyed.

DATE, TIME, AND PLACE FOR COMPLETION

8.84 When contracts are exchanged it is usual to insert the completion date in the agreement, there having been prior negotiations between the parties to reach the agreed completion date. The most common choice for a completion period used to be either one month, or 28 days, from exchange. A move away from this timescale to a much shorter period has taken place in recent years. It is not unusual to see a completion period of just 14 days or less. The period can be of any length, reasonable or not but, if the SCs are used and no period is stipulated in the contract, or if the date is overlooked at the time of exchange, SC 6.1.1 provides that completion is due on the twentieth working day after exchange. This condition goes on to provide that time is not of the essence for the completion date. (See Chapter 9 regarding post-completion procedures, and delays and remedies in relation to the concept of time being of the essence.)

8.85 This condition means that if completion is subject to delay, this will give rise to a claim for damages by the party who has not caused the delay. Moreover, SC 7.2 will apply (compensation for late completion, i.e. interest on the unpaid balance of the purchase price as stipulated in the contract). If time is not of the essence, the innocent party cannot withdraw from the obligations within the agreement (where time is of the essence immediate withdrawal from the contract is possible if completion is not on the completion date). Because making time of the essence imposes a tremendous burden on the contractual parties to complete on the due date, it is unusual to see it applied to ordinary conveyancing contracts. Bearing in mind that there are other factors involved that may not be under your control (e.g. mortgagees, the postal system, local authorities, the banking system, etc.), making time of the essence is not to be recommended.

Time for completion

As the pace and demand on the conveyancing system have increased, it is not only the date for completion that must be considered. The latest time for completion on the completion date must also be negotiated and will figure in almost all conveyancing agreements. Certainly SC 6.1.2 now, in effect, sets a final time of 2 p.m. on the day of completion. It does so by providing that if completion does not take place by that time completion is deemed to be overdue and interest will be payable. This does not mean that completion cannot take place that day. However, if completion cannot take place before 2 p.m. it simply means that interest will be payable (if demanded) for late completion. In many cases completion will be after this time, but practitioners often take the view that the pragmatic approach is not to call for interest but simply to complete, as the amount of interest involved would be quickly swallowed up by the cost of seeking payment. (See Chapter 3 concerning the negotiation of a time earlier than 2 p.m. for completion.)

8.86

Normally completion will take place at the offices of the practitioner acting for the seller. SC 6.2 provides that completion is to be effected somewhere in England and Wales, being either the offices of the seller's solicitor or at some other place which the seller reasonably specifies. SC 6.2.1 states that both parties to the contract are to cooperate in agreeing arrangements for completing the contract. Rarely will the deeds remain with solicitors acting solely for a lender. This will happen if the lender is separately represented, or possibly if the lender has commenced repossession proceedings. In these circumstances completion may have to take place at the lender's solicitors' offices, although efforts should be made to persuade such solicitors to allow the seller's solicitors to deal with completion and redemption together. They cannot be compelled, however, to agree this arrangement. It is worth repeating that a final check of all searches should be made just before completion and the buyer should make one last inspection of the property.

8.87

WHEN YOUR CLIENT IS SELLING AS WELL AS BUYING: SYNCHRONIZATION

It is fundamental to a client who is selling and buying, in the absence of any express instructions to the contrary, that the completion of the two transactions be on the same day. In effect the sale must be synchronized with the purchase to enable the net sale proceeds to be applied towards the purchase price. If there is a whole chain of transactions, of which the client's sale and purchase form part, then for much the same reason, all of the transactions in the chain must fall for completion on the same date; with purchase following sale right along the chain. Occasionally, such chains will be very long and delay can be expected if your transaction is at the wrong end. Without the ability to transfer money swiftly via computer payments very few such chains would be possible. We also suggest that if you are at the very end of a long chain, you investigate the possibility of monies 'bypassing' some of the parties so that some payments can be made further along the chain. Where this is proposed written authorities to

8.88

complete in this way should be sought from all the parties involved, including those being 'bypassed'. It is vital to ensure that everyone involved is ready and able to complete and will hand over deeds, etc. on the assumption that completion will proceed in this fashion.

MECHANICS OF COMPLETION

8.89 Completion can be dealt with in various ways: in person, by appointing an agent to complete on your behalf, or through the post. Until the early 1980s most completions were in person. With increasing economic pressures, practitioners have been forced to look to other, cheaper methods of completion. Postal completions will normally prevail in domestic conveyancing cases. In all forms of completion the practitioner for the buyer should pay close attention to the acquisition deed, be it a transfer, or assignment. It should be checked to make sure that it has been properly executed and can be dated with the date of completion. An individual who is selling should have an independent witness to his or her signature. The witness must also sign and put in his name and address. If a company is executing then care should be taken to ensure that one of the two ways of executing a deed by a company is properly effected. (A company can either seal a deed with the company seal, or the deed can be signed by two directors, a director and the secretary, without the seal—see s 36A of the Companies Act 1985 introduced by the Companies Act 1989. The Companies Act 2006 restates the provisions in the Companies Act 1985 as regards a company seal. This means the company can execute documents, as currently, either by using its company seal or by the document being signed by two authorized signatories, for example two directors or a director and a secretary who will sign by wording showing the form was 'Executed as a deed by' the signing parties in their capacities as officers of the company.) If an attorney has signed, a check should be made to ensure that the deed has been executed in one of the two permissible ways for an attorney (i.e. A.B. by his attorney C.D. or C.D. as attorney for A.B.).

Deeds and unregistered land

8.90 Where there is a sale of part of a title the seller will, if the property is unregistered, retain the deeds. The buyer will want to examine his or her copy deeds against the originals and mark them up at completion as so examined. (The wording is 'examined at the offices of' [insert the name and address of the seller's solicitors], and this is then followed by a signature of the examining practitioner for the buyer, together with a note of his or her firm's name and address, and the date.) In this way the buyer will acquire an examined abstract or epitome of title that will, with the purchase deed, constitute the title deeds for the part sold off.

8.91 If completion is to take place in person, the buyer will be able to examine the abstract. If there is an agency completion, the agent can examine the abstract. (This will be so in Protocol cases, as the seller agrees to act as the buyer's agent in these circumstances.)

Personal completions and agency completions

8.92 Completion in person will normally be at the offices of the seller's practitioner. As has been noted, SC 6.2 provides that completion is to be effected somewhere in England and Wales, being either at the offices of the seller's solicitor or at some other place which the seller reasonably specifies. We recommend personal completion in all cases where the transaction is either particularly complicated or where the price is very substantial. This is because a personal completion will enable the buyer's practitioner to inspect and approve the signed purchase deed and all other deeds and documents prior to paying over the completion monies. This ensures certainty. There can be no doubt whether or not all the buyer's requirements have been fulfilled as they will have been checked through at the completion meeting. Reliance need not be placed on an agent or the seller's practitioner. Personal completions take longer and cost more, but the risk of errors or omissions is minimized. In the majority of ordinary house or flat purchases, completion will be by post.

SC 6.7 of the fifth edition now states that 'the buyer is to pay the money due on completion **8.93** by a direct transfer of cleared funds from an account held in the name of a conveyancer at a clearing bank and, if appropriate, an unconditional release of a deposit held by a stakeholder'. This means that the only method of payment at completion and authorized by the SCs is by direct electronic bank transfer. As a result, unless SC 6.7 is amended no other method of payment, for example by a banker's draft, can be made. (It should be noted that if a solicitor acting for a seller were to accept a cheque payment at completion without having the client's prior confirmatory instructions so to do then this acceptance would be an act of negligence (see *Pape v Westacott* [1894] 1 QB 272).) Accordingly, if the conveyancers acting for the parties to the contract agree, completion can be by banker's draft but SC 6.7 must be amended to allow for this method of payment. Direct payments are to be preferred as banker's drafts as they are drawn directly on the issuing bank (or building society, if it is a building society cheque) rather than on the account of a customer, and signed by a bank or building society official. A banker's draft is not a cheque but, like a cheque, is subject to the Bills of Exchange Act 1882 and is cleared in the same way as a cheque over several business days.

Following the Bank of England's takeover of the Clearing House Automated Payment System (CHAPS), and its impact on the definition of 'clearing bank' in the Standard Conditions of Sale and Standard Commercial Property Conditions, revisions to these conditions have been settled. The new wording is: '"clearing bank" means a bank admitted by the Bank of England as a direct participant in its CHAPS system'. **8.94**

Since this is the only change being made to the current editions, the forms will now be known as:

- the Standard Conditions of Sale (5th edn, 2018 revision);
- Standard Commercial Property Conditions (3rd edn, 2018 revision).

Leasehold completion requirements

Lastly, when buying a leasehold property, remember to inspect the last receipt for ground **8.95** rent to make sure it is an unqualified clear receipt. If there is a clear ground rent receipt, you can assume that in the absence of any other information to the contrary, of which you have had notice, there are no subsisting breaches of covenant affecting the subject property, to which the lessor may refer.

Agency completions

An agency completion occurs where the practitioner acting for the buyer cannot or does **8.96** not wish to attend at a personal completion. As a consequence, and perhaps to avoid a postal completion, the buyer's practitioner will appoint another practitioner to attend at completion as an agent. The agent will attend at completion and do all things necessary in the same manner as would have been the case had the buyer's practitioner attended. The usual reason for an agency completion is that the seller's practitioner has an office located well away from the buyer's practitioner and, because a personal completion is preferred, a local agent must be appointed. The agent will require full and detailed instructions, and should be supplied with these, supported by copy documents, well before completion. Appropriate arrangements concerning the purchase funds need to be put in place. This will normally necessitate a telegraphic transfer of the completion monies to the agent either the day before or early on the morning of the day for completion. In these circumstances the agent will be entitled to charge for the service provided and it is recommended that the fee be agreed in writing when the agency arrangement is first considered.

Inspecting the title, especially in unregistered land

8.97 The SCs set down time limits for the approval and verification of the title to be sold (SC 4 title and transfer). All that you are doing is checking to see that you receive all the deeds and documents that constitute the title. In registered land this should be straightforward. Accordingly, you will at a completion of registered freehold land receive just a transfer or a transfer with an e-DS1 or DS1 undertaking (see 8.101). If the registered property is leasehold you should also receive the registered lease itself.

8.98 With unregistered land the need for inspection of title is even greater. Approval or rejection of the title comes with requisitions (not after, and certainly not at, completion). Even so, even after approving the title, it could well be complex, with many different deeds contained within it. Each document should be inspected to ensure it is the original, that all the pages remain together, and that any plans referred to are bound up within the deed. If within the title there has been a sale of part, then some original deeds may not be available. (Section 47(9) of the Law of Property Act 1925 authorizes a seller to retain deeds and documents of title when that seller retains any part of the land comprised in that title.) A careful check must be made to ensure that at completion examined copies (and not photocopies) or an examined abstract are handed over. A prudent approach would be to check the documents received against the abstract or epitome produced with the contract so that each item can be ticked off as the deeds are inspected. If you are acting for the seller, you will want a receipted schedule signed by the buyer's practitioner to confirm what was handed over at completion, and to ensure that at a later date there can be no doubt about precisely what was made available at completion.

Memoranda endorsements in unregistered land

8.99 With unregistered land gradually disappearing, albeit at an increasing pace, practitioners run the risk of overlooking some of the more forgettable yet important aspects of unregistered conveyancing. One such aspect relates to the endorsement of a memorandum of sale. Where a deed or document of title is not to be handed over at completion, a memorandum of the sale should be endorsed on the most recent retained deed. Thus, where there is a sale of part out of a larger unregistered title, a memorandum of sale should be endorsed on the last deed in the title retained by the seller (Law of Property Act 1925, s 200). If the sale is by a PR, s 36(5) of the Administration of Estates Act 1925 affords the buyer the right to insist on such an endorsement on the grant of representation. (The Law of Property Act 1925, s 200, also gives a buyer the right to call for a memorandum of sale to be endorsed on the most recent deed on the seller's retained title where the deed to the buyer imposes new restrictive covenants or easements.)

8.100 The purpose of such an endorsement is to afford the buyer protection against a later reconveyance of the same land by either a negligent or fraudulent seller. A suitable form of memorandum would read:

> By a transfer/conveyance dated the day of 20 A.B. [the seller] of [address] transferred/conveyed to C.D. [the buyer] of [address] the freehold title in the property situate at and known as [insert here a description of the property; more than just the postal address is required properly to identify the land in question; a repeat of the description in the purchase deed would be sensible] (being part of the property comprised in the within-written conveyance) and the right of C.D. to the production of the within-written conveyance was acknowledged.

Dealing with the discharge of the seller's mortgage

Conveyancers for both parties to the contract will normally agree the arrangement to apply **8.101** at completion for the discharge of the seller's mortgage and will do so after exchange, when dealing with post-exchange standard-form requisitions. Indeed, most pre-printed forms of requisitions include a standard question on the mortgage discharge arrangements. Whatever is agreed, these arrangements should cover all the subsisting mortgages on the title and not just the first and most obvious mortgage. Inevitably, where there is a first mortgage and the seller has received instructions to deal with redemption for the lender, sale proceeds will be applied immediately after completion for the purposes of redemption. This being so, the vacating receipt for unregistered mortgages or Form DS1 for a registered charge will not be available on completion. In these circumstances, practitioners must rely on professional (and enforceable) undertakings. Such undertakings must only be taken from solicitors or licensed conveyancers, and not from an unqualified person whose 'undertaking' will of course be unenforceable. A professional body, such as the Law Society, will ensure that the undertaking is complied with. The Law Society has issued a recommended form of undertaking and we endorse its use by practitioners wherever possible (see (1986) 83 LSG 3127). The wording is:

> In consideration of you today completing the purchase of [insert subject property postal address or description] we hereby undertake to pay over to [insert identity of the lender] the money required to discharge the mortgage/legal charge dated [insert date of mortgage/legal charge] and to forward the receipted mortgage/legal charge/Form DS1 to you as soon as it is received by us from [insert identity of lender].

Remember that a receipted mortgage or legal charge is appropriate for unregistered land, **8.102** and Form DS1 (or e-DS1) is appropriate for registered land. Thus, you would not refer in your undertaking to Form DS1 on completion of an unregistered land transaction. Similarly, you would not refer to a receipted mortgage or legal charge in a registered land transaction.

A problem arises when the lender is not a member of the Council of Mortgage Lenders (CML). **8.103** (The same problem arises for some members of the CML who explicitly reject the proposition that they must accept responsibility for incorrect redemption statements.) Members will stand by redemption statements issued by them before completion and relied on at completion and which may ultimately prove to be incorrect. In effect this means that a deed of discharge, forming the subject matter of an undertaking, will be issued even if the lender has issued incorrect figures (and therefore has received incorrect redemption monies). This is not the case for non-members, who can disagree over the amount required to redeem even though completion may have already taken place and undertakings been issued. In these circumstances actual redemption may need to take place along with completion, probably at the offices of the lender or the offices of the lender's solicitor. A redemption statement should be read carefully to check assumptions made by the lender about payments to be made by the borrower. It might assume that the next instalment due before completion but after the date of the statement will be made. If it does, the seller must make that payment or a shortfall will arise.

Another problem arises out of the decision in *Patel v Daybells* [2000] EGCS 98 (QBD, **8.104** 19 July 2000). Gray J held that a solicitor could be held to be negligent in relying on a solicitor's undertaking. The judge posed three questions. First, does the acceptance of the undertaking involve foreseeable risk? Second, could that risk have been avoided? Third, if so, was there an act of negligence in failing to avoid that risk? The judge considered that there was a risk in the industry standard practice of undertakings and that a different form of completion (probably based on attendance) can avoid the risk. Frankly, the decision may be accurate but it is definitely not practical.

8.105 The decision would seem to require practitioners to call for the availability of Form DS1 at completion. However, lenders will not provide the form at that time, as they have not yet been paid.

8.106 One way to address the difficulty is to ensure that the seller's practitioner is also the agent of the seller's lender. If then the agent fails to redeem by paying over an incorrect amount, the dispute will be between the agent (the seller's practitioner) and principal (the seller's lender), because with this procedure the lender will be bound to redeem. Express appointment as agent by the lender is required, and the buyer's practitioner should ask for a copy of the letter of appointment as confirmation. In practice this is unlikely to be forthcoming and the risks attendant on industry standard completion undertakings will remain. See a general discussion about this awkward case in the *Solicitors Journal* (20 October 2000, p 947). See also 8.114(c) for further practical assistance.

8.107 Lastly, a buyer's practitioner needs to exercise special care where the seller has a high-value mortgage. In the *Patel* case it was stated that there could be 'exceptional circumstances' where accepting an undertaking at completion was negligent. This could be where the value of the seller's mortgage exceeds the minimum level required for indemnity insurance for solicitors. This is currently £1 million, so if a buyer's practitioner is aware of this situation prevailing, either the cover must be increased, or the seller's solicitors must warrant that the insurance cover exceeds the amount required to redeem (or Form DS1 must be available at completion).

e-DS1

8.108 An e-DS1 is an electronic form of discharge submitted by lenders through the Land Registry Portal. The e-DS1 acts as both the evidence of discharge and the application to remove the charge from the register. An e-DS1 can only be lodged for a discharge of whole of the land charged and replaces the END.

8.109 When acting for a buyer and you understand that an e-DS1 is to be used, then you should proceed with the transaction in the same way as you would with a traditional form of purchase, except that you will need to allow for the different method of discharge by agreeing on a revised form of undertaking.

8.110 The revised form of undertaking could take the following form:

> In consideration of your today completing the purchase of (subject property) we hereby undertake forthwith to pay over to (the lender) the money required to discharge the mortgage/legal charge dated (insert date) and to forward to you a copy of the lender's letter confirming successful redemption of their charge and lodgement of an e-DS1 at HM Land Registry as soon as we receive it from the Lender.

8.111 The Land Registry website used to include a list of e-DS1 users that included the Nationwide Building Society, Lloyds TSB Bank plc, as well as many other banks and building societies throughout England and Wales. The use of the e-DS1 has become so widespread in conveyancing that such a list is now unnecessary.

Postal completions

8.112 Practitioners have, in recent years, realized that they can no longer afford the luxury of traditional completions that were dealt with in person. Moreover, with greater emphasis on registered land and with the whole country being compulsorily registrable from the start of the 1990s, personal completions have become less important, and certainly less popular, among practitioners, almost to the point of extinction. However, how their replacement—i.e. the postal completion—is governed is open to doubt, perhaps as a direct consequence of its somewhat haphazard development. The lack of any express regulation prompted the Law Society to issue in 1984 a suggested method of control and this is examined at 8.113. However, the Law Society Code is not the only method for postal completions. Informal ad hoc arrangements can be made between the parties. Plainly the terms of the agreed procedure need to be clearly expressed and understood so that there can be no doubt about the arrangement. In many cases the seller's practitioner will be prepared to act as the buyer's agent, without fee, on completion and will send all the required deeds and documents to the buyer as soon as the completion monies have been received. Similarly, where the transaction is quite straightforward the buyer might be prepared, particularly if the seller does not have a mortgage to discharge, to send the completion monies to the seller's practitioner on the strength of an undertaking to send all the necessary deeds and documents once the completion monies have been paid over. However, the warnings mentioned at 8.104 arising from *Patel v Daybells* [2000] EGCS 98 (QBD, 19 July 2000) should be considered before agreeing to complete on the strength of undertakings.

Completion and the Protocol

Since 1990 the Law Society has tried to urge practitioners, and in particular solicitors, to adopt all the elements of the Law Society's Conveyancing Protocol. One such element is the inclusion of the Law Society's Code for Completion. This inclusion underpins the use of postal completions in residential conveyancing transactions. (See 8.114 for a detailed examination of the code for completion by post.) **8.113**

The Law Society's Code for Completion by Post

A new version of the Code was issued in April 2011 and supersedes the previous version from 1998. An area of potential confusion has arisen from the dissemination of the Law Society's Conveyancing Protocol and the fact that some conveyancing transactions will proceed within it and some will not. Those that do will, in the absence of agreement to the contrary, complete in accordance with the Law Society's Code for Completion 2011 (the Code). Those that do not will only complete within the terms of the Code if both practitioners acting for the parties to the contract specifically agree to adopt the Code. (Some pre-printed forms of preliminary enquiries, and requisitions on title, actually ask the seller whether or not the Code can be adopted for completion.) Thus, if the Code is to be used in non-Protocol conveyances, it must be expressly adopted by both sides (preferably in writing), but for Protocol cases the Code will apply unless otherwise agreed. In all cases, if a practitioner considers that to adopt the Code would create a conflict between the interests of the client and the requirements of the Code, then the Code must not be adopted. **8.114**

The Code provisions

The main provisions of the Code are: **8.115**

(a) The crucial element of the Code is that the buyer's solicitor appoints the seller's solicitor as his or her unpaid agent for completion. The buyer's solicitor is now required to use reasonable endeavours to ensure that sufficient funds are collected from the buyer and any mortgage lender in good time to transmit to the seller's solicitor on or before completion. The seller's solicitor is to provide to the buyer's solicitor replies to completion information and undertakings in the Law Society's standard form at least five working days before completion.

(b) The buyer's solicitor should provide full instructions for the 'agent' relating to the buyer's requirements. These instructions must clearly set out for the seller's solicitor what the buyer's solicitor requires him to do and what is to be sent on from the seller to the buyer after completion has been effected.

(c) The seller's solicitor must confirm that he has been appointed the authorized agent of any mortgagee authorizing the receipt of monies required to redeem. This section was introduced to the Code as a consequence of the decision in *Edward Wong Finance Co. Ltd v Johnson, Stokes and Master* [1984] AC 296, PC. This was a Hong Kong case where monies were handed over against an undertaking regarding the forwarding of the deeds and the discharge of the existing charge. Sadly, this was a case where the seller's solicitor unlawfully absconded with the completion monies without having paid anything to the lenders. Even though the buyer's solicitors had acted in accordance with the general practice of the legal community within the colony, it was held that they were negligent in the way they arranged completion. To get around the problem the seller must be appointed the mortgagee's agent. In this way, if the same circumstances arose, the mortgagee could not refuse to complete because of the default of its agent. If there is any doubt, then we suggest you ascertain the amount required to redeem and on the day of completion send the redemption amount direct to the mortgagee and the balance to the seller's solicitor.

(d) The buyer's solicitor will send the completion monies by bank telegraphic transfer (a CHAPS payment) and on receipt the completion takes place. Until completion has taken place, the seller's solicitor will hold the purchase monies to the order of the buyer's solicitor. At the point of completion the deeds and documents are held by the seller's solicitor as agent for the buyer's solicitor and no lien can be claimed.

(e) That day (i.e. the day of completion), the deeds and documents must be sent to the buyer's solicitor, and once posted properly they are at the buyer's risk.

(f) Adopting the Code involves the giving of a professional undertaking that will be enforced through the Law Society.

(g) The Code can be used only if there is no obvious conflict, but if such conflict exists, the appointment of an agent would be inappropriate.

(h) Bearing in mind the decisions in *Angel Solicitors (A Firm) v Jenkins O'Dowd & Barth* [2009] EWHC 46 and *Clark v Lucas LLP* [2009] EWHC 1952 (Ch) (cases on undertakings), the undertaking to redeem charges within the Code includes confirmation that a satisfactory redemption statement has been obtained from the lender(s). In essence this means that the amount for redemption is known and ascertained and as a consequence that the undertaking can and will be fulfilled.

(i) Lastly, it should be noted that nothing in the Code shall override any rights and obligations of either the seller or the buyer under the terms of the sale contract or otherwise.

The outcome of completion

8.116 The necessary outcome of completion for the seller is to receive the full purchase monies, including (especially if leasehold) all apportionments.

8.117 Two further points are worth noting. First, in theory, where a deposit is being held by a practitioner as a stakeholder, the buyer's practitioner should give the stakeholder a written release authorizing payment of the deposit to the seller. Bearing in mind that in many cases the seller's solicitor or licensed conveyancer will be the stakeholder as well, it is rare for there to be such a written release, as it is simply implied. If, unusually, the deposit is with the selling agents a written release would be necessary. Second, if the buyer offers to pay in legal tender (here meaning banknotes), you should immediately be concerned about the dangers of money laundering. Where you act for that buyer you need to be sure that the client is not committing a money laundering offence. A practitioner is in danger of committing an offence by not reporting such circumstances. Efforts should therefore be made to investigate the source of these cash funds and the identity of the client.

The buyer wants to receive the complete set of deeds and documents of title to enable him **8.118** to rely on them to show good title to the subject property. With registered land, title to the property will only pass to the buyer on completion of the registration process at Land Registry. Accordingly, steps must be taken in the search priority period not only to pay stamp duty land tax (if necessary) but also to submit the registration application to Land Registry. These aspects are dealt with in 9.21.

KEY POINTS SUMMARY

COMPLETION

Acting for the seller

- Check you have all the necessary deeds, that you have prepared Form DS1 or, if appropri- **8.119** ate, e-DS1, or a vacating receipt for a mortgage of unregistered land, and that you have the executed purchase deed.

- To minimize personal risk and liability, wherever possible only give undertakings about redemption in the form approved by the Law Society.

- If you are asked to act as an agent on completion, consider whether there is likely to be a conflict. If there is, you must decline.

- Be aware that in Protocol cases (and in non-Protocol cases but where the Code is being adopted) the Code for Completion incorporates professional undertakings.

Acting for the buyer

- Check all searches to ensure they exist and remain in force and ensure the buyer carries out a final inspection immediately before completion.

- Can you accept an undertaking from the seller regarding the mortgage? Preferably not if the lender is not a member of the Council of Mortgage Lenders.

- Seek written confirmation that the seller's practitioner is the agent of the lender at completion.

- Is it cost-effective to complete in person? Do you trust the seller's practitioner? If not, complete in person or appoint an agent.

- In a long chain can you make 'bypass' arrangements to ensure the monies will be with the seller's practitioner before the last time for completion?

PRACTICAL CHECKLISTS

PRE-COMPLETION

Acting for the seller

- Immediately after exchange obtain redemption figures for all subsisting mortgages. **8.120**

- Immediately after exchange check on the insurance position and leave insurance in place until completion.

- On receipt of the estate agents' commission account simply write back advising you are taking your client's instructions or make no reply at all.

- Reply to any standard-form pre-completion requisitions raised on behalf of the buyer.

- Approve the purchase deed.

- Arrange for the seller to execute the engrossed purchase deed.
- If the property is leasehold, obtain from your client receipted accounts or recent demands to enable apportionment as at the completion date.
- If the property is leasehold, obtain all necessary consents to the sale from lessors, management company, etc.
- Draft your bill of costs and ensure it includes all disbursements.
- Prepare a completion statement and seek instructions on the estate agents' commission account, and where the net proceeds of sale should be sent.
- Finalize completion arrangements and prepare Form DS1, e-DS1, or the mortgage vacating receipt, with any undertaking in respect thereof drawn up in accordance with Law Society recommendations.
- If the property being sold is tenanted, prepare an authority to the tenant to pay all future rent from the completion date to the purchaser.
- Check you are in possession of all the deeds if any are required by the buyer at completion.
- Check where the keys will be and how they are to be handed over on the day of completion. They are normally released by the estate agents.
- If there is an old land or charge certificate in existence, agree with the client that it will be given to the buyer at completion, even though it no longer serves as proof of title.

Acting for the buyer

- Forthwith on exchange check on the insurance and ensure that it is in place if the burden passed from the seller to the buyer on exchange of contracts.
- Raise standard-form pre-completion requisitions and approve answers.
- Draft the purchase deed.
- Engross the approved purchase deed and if required arrange for the buyer to execute it and send it to the sellers for signature to be held in escrow pending completion.
- Engross the mortgage deed and arrange for the buyer to execute it.
- Ensure that all first premiums for new endowment life policies for any endowment mortgage are paid, and therefore the policies will be issued in time for completion.
- Prepare and dispatch all necessary final searches and approve or action search results.
- Obtain and approve the seller's completion statement with all supporting receipts or recent demands.
- If the subject property is leasehold, ensure the last receipt for ground rent is clear and available for inspection at or before completion.
- Prepare and dispatch to the lenders their report on title and request the mortgage advance.
- Draft your bill of costs and ensure it includes all disbursements.
- Calculate and request the balance required to complete (including all costs and disbursements) from the buyer.
- Finalize completion arrangements, and if completing by post ensure that the seller's practitioner will act as your agent without charge on completion.
- Ask the seller's practitioner to confirm that he acts as agent for the seller's lender in relation to redemption at the time of completion.
- Ensure that there is a final pre-completion inspection of the property to check on vacant possession, fixtures and fittings to be left, etc.

- On a sale of part, examine copy documents against originals and mark them as so examined (done by the seller in all Protocol cases).

- If an old land or charge certificate exists, agree with the seller's practitioner that it should be handed over at completion with any pre-registration deeds.

COMPLETION

Acting for the seller

- Prepare a schedule of deeds and documents to be handed over at completion and obtain the **8.121** buyer's practitioner's signature thereon to confirm the transmission of these documents.

- Agree the time and place for completion and the style of completion—postal, agency, or in person.

- Make sure the seller is moving out and (if the contract so provides) ascertain the time that full vacant possession will be available, i.e. when the property will be empty.

- If there is an old land or charge certificate (where the charge is to be fully repaid), take instructions about the redundant certificate. Will the seller wish to keep it, or agree to pass it over? It is no longer proof of title, but best practice means the buyer should have custody of it with any pre-registration deeds.

- When seeking payment of the sale price along with apportionments ensure that the buyer's practitioner has a completion statement and copy receipts or current demands.

- Post off the deeds and purchase deed immediately on receipt of the purchase monies by bank transfer.

- Ensure the keys are released and the selling agents duly informed of completion.

- If the land is unregistered, remember to attach all necessary endorsements on the most recent title deed (normally only on a sale of part) and a memorandum on any relevant grant of representation.

Acting for the buyer

- When completion is by post make sure all the proper safeguards (undertakings, etc.), are in place and evidenced in writing.

- If completing in person, on receipt of the deeds and documents of title always check that all the expected documents have indeed been passed over to you. Tick off each one using a checklist.

- In registered land, ask for the old land or charge certificate (if still in existence) and executed transfer (and original lease if the title is an existing registered leasehold).

- If the seller has a mortgage, ensure that you obtain the seller's practitioner's undertaking to redeem in the form suggested by the Law Society together with his confirmation of appointment as agent on completion for the seller's lender.

- Check the execution of the purchase deed and inspect any relevant powers of attorney in support and obtain certified copies of the powers.

- If relevant, inspect original grants of representation and compare with your previously supplied office copy grants.

- Inspect and approve all original receipts or current demands relevant to the details in the completion statement.

- If the subject property is subject to a tenancy, obtain a rental authority issued by the seller or the seller's practitioner authorizing the tenant to pay all future rent to the buyer or as the buyer directs.

9

POST-COMPLETION PROCEDURES: DELAYS AND REMEDIES

9.01 This chapter deals with two areas that present conveyancing practitioners with some of the more challenging parts of the conveyancing process: first, post-completion procedures; and, second, dealing with delays and seeking appropriate remedies. As a consequence you will be concerned with time limits, with 'what if' scenarios, and with the mechanics of Stamp Duty Land Tax (SDLT) and title registration. In particular, delays affecting conveyancing contracts, and the consequential remedies available, are a fertile source for conflict between conveyancing practitioners. However, one element to be considered at the commencement of this chapter is what is the effect of completion?

9.02 At common law, the contract is considered to be at an end as it is deemed to have merged with the purchase deed. This is called the doctrine of merger. The result of this is that the buyer can only sue the seller under covenants for title through title guarantee, contained or referred to in the purchase deed; there is no right to sue under the contractual terms. (Merger takes effect only where the contract and purchase deed cover the same subject matter. If the contract contains ancillary matters, then these will not be affected by merger.) However, SC 7.3 provides that 'completion does not cancel liability to perform any outstanding obligation under this contract'. This has the effect of negating the doctrine of merger. Accordingly, if you want merger to apply, then an express special condition must be incorporated excluding from the agreement the effect of SC 7.3. In the absence of such an exclusion the buyer will still be able to sue the seller for breach of contract once completion has occurred. In practice SC 7.3 is rarely excluded.

A POST-COMPLETION PROCEDURES

9.03 Just when the practitioner thinks a sigh of relief is in order because completion has taken place, it is suddenly realized that there is still more to do. The fact that completion has successfully taken place does not mean that the practitioner for either party to the contract can simply down tools and turn to something else. Post-completion tasks are few and comparatively simple for the seller's practitioner. The reverse can be true for the buyer; stamping, title registration, and allied topics beckon.

9.04 Whether you are acting for the seller or the buyer, your client will expect, first, a telephone confirmation and, second, a written confirmation of the completion of the transaction. In some cases a lender will require confirmation of the completion of its loan, but if this is the case that confirmation should be in writing. (Some lenders require written confirmation on their own pre-printed form.)

If you are acting for a lender alone, you will need to obtain the deeds (if any), purchase **9.05** deed and mortgage and, if necessary, arrange stamping and registration in much the same way as is the case for the buyer. Your obligation is to perfect the mortgage, and to achieve this all post-completion procedures must be strictly adhered to.

In the case of a new mortgage by a company borrower, a certified copy of the mortgage must **9.06** be lodged and accepted for registration by the Registrar of Companies within 21 days of completion. (This must be accompanied by Form MR01, particulars of mortgage or charge, as required by Part 25 of the Companies Act 2006. (The certified copy will be retained at Companies House and made available for the public register. You should not submit the original written mortgage or charge.) Form MR01 should only be used to register charges created on or after 6 April 2013 by companies registered in England and Wales.) If you fail to comply with this very strict time limit, you cannot register the mortgage without an order of the court, and such orders are given only in exceptional circumstances. Failure to register is an unanswerable case of professional negligence that would have to be referred to your indemnity insurers. There is a fee payable for the registration of a charge at Companies House. The papers and fee should be sent to Companies House, PO Box 716, Crown Way, Maindy, Cardiff CF14 3UZ (DX 33050). The Companies Act 2006 sets out this requirement in Part 25 of that Act (ss 860–877) and came into force on 1 October 2009. Since 6 April 2013 applications to register charges can also be submitted electronically. You can file online using the 'WebFiling' facility at Companies House. Details can be seen at **https://www.gov. uk/government/organisations/companies-house/about/about-our-services#webfiling**.

ACTING FOR THE SELLER

After completion the seller's practitioner may have one major duty to perform. If the seller **9.07** has a mortgage, then this must be redeemed and paid in full (unless there was a sale of just part of the mortgaged property). However, there can be other functions, and all are considered in the following paragraphs.

Paying off lenders

At completion the buyer's practitioner will have insisted on an undertaking to discharge **9.08** all mortgages and no doubt the Law Society recommended form of undertaking will have been provided. (See 8.101 for the wording of this undertaking.) There are now two types of undertaking: first, the traditional style involving Form DS1 and, second, a different Form to cover Electronic Discharges (the e-DS1), see 8.102 and 8.108 for details. Both procedures for paying off lenders are set out at 9.11. To ensure that the terms of the undertaking are fully complied with, steps must now be taken to deal with the redemption of the mortgages affecting the subject property.

Redemption arrangements

You will have obtained, prior to completion, redemption statements for the mortgages **9.09** affecting the property to be sold. Once completion has taken place, and preferably on the day of completion, the redemption monies must be sent to the lenders in full settlement of the debt due to them. The method of transmission of these monies is dictated by the calculation of the redemption statement. Some lenders issue a statement calculated to a month end. In these circumstances, and on the assumption that completion has not taken place at the end of the month, a payment by a client account cheque sent by post will be acceptable. If, however, the statement is calculated to the day and has a daily rate, the redemption monies can be sent by post, but extra days of interest must be added until the cheque is received and cleared. This would normally add an extra seven days to the total interest. It will probably be more economic for the client if the monies were sent by bank transfer and with the client paying the fee for this, usually in the region of £25. This can normally be accomplished on the day of completion.

9.10   In addition to submitting the redemption monies, proof of payment is required. In registered land this is by way of Form DS1 (see (a) at 9.11). Land Registry is seeking to move from DS1s to e-DS1s (see 8.108 and (c) at 9.11). In unregistered land a mortgage vacating receipt endorsed on the mortgage deed itself is appropriate (see (b) at 9.11 for details).

9.11   The methods for paying off lenders are:

(a) **Form DS1—registered land**   This is a very simple form that repeats the title details (county, location, title number, and description of property), and in which you must insert the name and address of the registered lender and the dates of the mortgage. The deed must be executed by the lender and dated with the date of completion. (However, see 5.60 for potential problems where the discharge is after completion.) You will need to refer to official copies of the registers to complete Form DS1, as you will need to insert the date of the mortgage. (Evidence of identity form ID1 or form ID2 will be required if the lender is not a UK bank or building society and it is not represented by a conveyancer, and the person lodging the application is unable to confirm identity.)

(b) **Mortgage vacating receipt—unregistered land**   The position is a little more complicated for unregistered land. Mortgages will be released by way of a receipt usually endorsed on the back of the original deed. The receipt, also known as a vacating receipt, must be executed by the lender and dated with the date of completion.

In both cases an undertaking will have been given at completion, and the sealed document should therefore be sent to the buyer's practitioner as soon as it is received back from the lender. When sending it on to the buyer a request should be made for the undertaking to be returned, fully discharged, i.e. released.

(c) **Electronic Discharge (e-DS1)—registered land**   When an e-DS1 is to be used, the lender will inform Land Registry of the discharge of their mortgage over whole titles to land by an electronic submission of the form, sent through the Land Registry's Portal. It is intended that e-DS1 will replace Form DS1. Receiving an electronic submission direct from the lender should reduce delays and help identify cases where a difficulty exists. Although the charge will not be cancelled immediately, in many cases the application will be processed automatically by the Land Registry computer system so the charges register will be updated quickly, possibly in a matter of seconds. Land Registry will issue an electronic acknowledgement to the user.

The form of undertaking required when an e-DS1 is being used could be as follows:

> In consideration of your today completing the purchase of (subject property) we hereby undertake forthwith to pay over to (the lender) the money required to discharge the mortgage/legal charge dated (insert date) and to forward to you a copy of the lender's letter confirming successful redemption of their charge and lodgement of an electronic discharge at HM Land Registry as soon as we receive it from the Lender.

(d) **Release of part—registered land**   In registered land, Form DS3 is required when releasing part of a title from a registered charge. If the mortgage was granted prior to 13 October 2003, the lender will still require the redundant charge certificate because even though it is not proof of title it will contain the original charge over the retained land. Form DS3 should show the extent of the released land by reference to a scale plan.

(e) **Electronic discharges—registered land**   Land Registry has also introduced a different system with selected lenders regarding the electronic discharge of registered mortgages. An Electronic Discharge (ED) is a discharge of a registered charge sent electronically by a lender direct to Land Registry. Land Registry's computer system makes a number of checks and if everything is in order, it cancels the charge entries. In most cases, the charge entries will be cancelled immediately and automatically on receipt of the discharge. An ED cancels the charge entries automatically and, in most cases, immediately. It does not require a separate formal paper application to discharge the charge. It is a computer-to-computer system-driven process. As a result of this modification, an alternative undertaking should be requested and provided at completion. The following recommended form of undertaking was drafted specifically in connection with the discharge of Nationwide Building Society mortgages during the original ED Pilot scheme:

In consideration of your today completing the purchase of (subject property) we hereby undertake forthwith to pay over to Nationwide Building Society the money required to discharge the mortgage/legal charge dated (insert date) and either to forward to you a copy of the lender's letter confirming successful redemption of their charge and lodgement of an electronic discharge at HM Land Registry as soon as we receive it from the Lender.

An electronic discharge can only be sent for a discharge of whole. Further details of EDs can be found in the Land Registry Practice Guide 31 (**https://www.gov.uk/government/publications/discharge-of-charges**). EDs have now been supplemented by e-DS1s.

Other issues

Apart from the discharge of mortgages the seller's practitioner must deal with other interconnected items and issues. For example, there may be land charges to register (e.g. new restrictive covenants as D(ii)), or registrations to remove at the land charges registry. Other concerns are listed in the following paragraphs. **9.12**

Life policies

If an endowment mortgage is discharged on completion but one or more life policies were not utilized to contribute to the redemption of the loan and are not linked to a new endowment mortgage, steps should be taken to advise the life offices of the removal of the charge on the policies. Notice can be given in the following format and should be sent to the head office or assignments section of the life company concerned: **9.13**

TAKE NOTICE that by a deed of reassignment dated the [insert the day the mortgage of life policy was discharged] the policy or policies of assurance described in the schedule hereto were reassigned by [insert the name and address of the former lender] back to [insert the name and address of the client/policyholder] absolutely. Dated the [insert the date].
[In the schedule give, for each policy the policy number, the life company and the full names of the policy holders.]

There will of course need to be a deed of reassignment, either endorsed on the mortgage of life policy or separate from it. This is a very simple deed in the form of a release of the charge over the policy by the lender. Without this step being taken problems will arise should a claim be required on the policy. This will be because the records at the life office will show that there is still a charge registered with them in favour of the old mortgagee. **9.14**

If your client is considering surrendering the policy, you should advise that there are alternatives, for example selling the policy to a trader in endowment policies or auctioning it, which might realize more than the surrender value offered by the life company. **9.15**

Estate agents' fees

9.16 If you are instructed to pay the selling agents' fees or charges, then you must do so within a reasonable time of completion, and obtain a written form of receipt for the payment. The receipt may be required by the seller if the cost may be a permitted deduction for capital gains tax purposes (as is the case for legal fees in connection with the disposal).

Deeds retained

9.17 Where there is a sale of part, in unregistered land deeds will be retained in relation to the property remaining in the ownership of the seller. If they are not required to be returned to a subsisting lender, you should ask for the seller's instructions on where the deeds should be kept. Many practitioners offer to retain the deeds for no charge. If the deeds are kept in this way, they must be placed in a fire-proof location such as a safe or strong room. If this is not done, then the practitioner would be failing in his duty to the client in relation to the safe storage of the deeds. Where there is a sale of part of registered land there are no deeds, so the land or charge certificate if you possess one, should not be lodged at Land Registry to meet the dealing to be lodged in relation to the part sold of the seller's property. (This is because from 13 October 2003, no new certificates will be issued and old certificates do not prove title.)

Costs

9.18 On the assumption that a bill has been delivered to the account, remember to transfer your costs with all paid disbursements from the client account to your office account.

Satisfaction survey

9.19 You may wish to consider issuing to the client, at the final point of contact a satisfaction survey through which you and your firm can seek some feedback on the handling of the transaction. Such a survey should highlight areas that you control and which can therefore be improved. It should also demonstrate to the client that there is an intention on your part to improve the service offered to clients, something that might persuade the client to return in the future with new work.

ACTING FOR THE BUYER

9.20 The buyer's practitioner has a far busier time after completion and is also burdened with time limits, the breaching of which can lead to major financial consequences for the practitioner, rather than the client. It is, therefore, critical to ensure that the post-completion procedures and time limits are fully understood and strictly adhered to, particularly with regard to the payment of stamp duty.

Stamp Duty Land Tax (SDLT)

Introduction

9.21 SDLT is a tax created by the 2003 Budget (called Land Tax or SDLT), based on taxation of transactions rather than deeds or documents, which was the case under the old stamp duty regime. It is assessed directly against the buyer rather than the property being purchased. It would seem that SDLT was introduced for three reasons: first, to further the Government's desire to modernize; second, to anticipate the needs of e-conveyancing; and third, to try to limit tax avoidance.

SDLT practice and procedure

The SDLT regime came into force on 1 December 2003. Section 43 of the Finance Act 2003 **9.22**
defines land transactions as being the focus for Land Tax and is an extremely wide definition covering dealings in estates and interests including those that are equitable. The starting threshold in England for the payment of Land Tax is £125,000 for residential property,
but £150,000 for non-residential or commercial property.

First-time buyers' relief

There are different rules if your client is buying their first home. A first-time buyer gets a **9.23**
discount (relief) that means your client pays less or no tax if:

- Your client completes their purchase on or after 22 November 2017;
- the purchase price is £500,000 or less;
- and of course the client and anyone else your client is buying with, are first-time buyers.

Thus first-time buyers will pay no SDLT on the first £300,000 of the purchase price with
the remainder being charged at 5 per cent. No relief can be claimed where the total price
exceeds £500,000. A first-time buyer is defined as someone who has never owned a freehold
or leasehold interest in a dwelling before and who is purchasing their own or main residence.
If there are joint purchasers all of them must be first-time buyers to be eligible for the relief.

The SDLT for land transactions with an effective date on or after 4 December 2014, for **9.24**
transfers of land and buildings (consideration paid), is set out at 9.25.

Conveyancers should note that there is guidance on the Revenue and Customs website **9.25**
at **https://www.gov.uk/stamp-duty-land-tax-rates**. A selection of simple questions should
lead to the Revenue's view of the status of a subject property. In essence if a property is used
as a residence, the Revenue will consider the subject property on sale to be residential. If an
office or shop is sold, then it will be considered non-residential. Practitioners also need to
be aware that transactions under either threshold (£125,000 or £150,000), will be taxed at
0 per cent but may still require a land transaction return to be completed for these transactions. The following transactions do not require a return to be lodged:

- freehold transactions of £40,000 or less; or
- leasehold purchases of leases of seven years or more where the value is £40,000 or less
  and the annual rent is £1,000 or less; or
- leasehold purchases of leases of less than seven years where the total value of the transaction is not more than the residential or non-residential SDLT threshold. Furthermore, if
  your client uses alternative property financial arrangements, for example to comply with
  Sharia law, then you don't have to pay SDLT or file a return.

Details of the land transaction returns are set out at 9.26. The Revenue will be
implementing a regime of random checks to verify that the correct Land Tax has been paid.

The Revenue will require the completion and submission of a land transaction return to **9.26**
their data capture centre in Merseyside within 30 days of completion of the transaction.
(Payment is required either on completion or when there is substantial performance of
the contract. This will be if the buyer goes into possession or pays a substantial amount,
probably 90 per cent of the price.) HM Revenue & Customs (HMRC) having consulting on whether the 30-day period should be reduced to 14 days have now proposed a
14-day deadline introduction by the tax year 2019–2020. The centre address is HMRC
BT Stamp Duty Land Tax HM Revenue & Customs BX9 1LT. Alternatively, you can send
the return using the DX system to: Rapid Data Capture Centre DX725593 Bootle 9. SDLT
returns can also be filed online. Whether you decide to use HMRC's software or that of a

commercial provider, you need to register before you can start filing SDLT returns online. If you are an individual filing a return without a solicitor or licensed conveyancer you will need to complete a paper return. If a return is filed late the buyer will be liable to a fixed penalty of £100, or if more than three months late, £200. The buyer may also be liable to a tax-related penalty, not to exceed the tax payable. To claim first-time buyer relief, code 32 should be entered at box 1.9 of the SDLT return.

SDLT is charged at increasing rates for each portion of the price.

Residential properties

9.27 Assuming you are not a first-time buyer, you'll pay:

- nothing on the first £125,000 of the property price;
- 2% on the next £125,000;
- 5% on the next £675,000;
- 10% on the next £575,000;
- 12% on the rest (above £1.5 million).

A worked example of a residential property SDLT calculation:

If you are not a first-time buyer and you buy a property for £275,000, you'll pay £3,750 of SDLT. This is made up of:

- nothing on the first £125,000;
- £2,500 on the next £125,000;
- £1,250 on the remaining £25,000.

Corporate bodies

SDLT is charged at 15 per cent on residential properties costing more than £500,000 bought by bodies such as:

- companies;
- collective investment schemes.

Non-residential and mixed-use properties

For non-residential and mixed-use properties the purchaser pays the following rates of SDLT:

- property price, premium or value up to £150,000 (annual rent no greater than £1,000) = 0%;
- properties between £150,001 and £250,000 = 2%;
- properties over £250,000 = 5%.

HMRC have proved the following example of how this commercial SDLT tax is calculated.

If you buy a freehold commercial property for £275,000, the SDLT you owe is calculated as follows:

- 0% on the first £150,000 = £0;
- 2% on the next £100,000 = £2,000;
- 5% on the final £25,000 = £1,250;
- total SDLT = £3,250.

9.28 When should a land transaction return be completed? The SDLT return should be submitted to notify:

1. any transfer of a freehold or assignment of a lease for consideration, whether or not giving rise to a charge;
2. any transaction for which relief is being claimed;

3. the grant of a lease for a contractual term of seven years or more or which gives rise to a charge;
4. any other transaction giving rise to a charge.

However, the following transactions do not require a return to be lodged:

- freehold transactions of £40,000 or less; or
- leasehold purchases of leases of seven years or more where the value is £40,000 or less and the annual rent is £1,000 or less; or
- leasehold purchases of leases of less than seven years where the total value of the transaction is not more than the residential or non-residential SDLT threshold.

The following transactions are not notifiable and as such no Land Tax return is required: **9.29**

- the acquisition of a freehold or leasehold interest in land for no chargeable consideration (note that there will normally be chargeable consideration where there is a gift of property subject to an existing debt such as a mortgage);
- transactions made in connection with the ending of a marriage.
- transactions varying the dispositions made, whether effected by will or laws of intestacy, within two years after the person's death not involving any consideration in money or money's worth;
- a transaction which effects something other than a major interest in land chargeable with tax at 0 per cent. An example of such a transaction would be an interest, which is not a major interest in land, such as the grant of an easement where the consideration does not exceed £125,000. This would attract Land Tax at 0 per cent, provided it is not linked to any other transaction that would bring the total consideration to more than £125,000. Notification would not be required.

Higher rates of Stamp Duty Land Tax (SDLT) on purchases of additional residential properties

Higher rates of SDLT are now charged on purchases of additional residential properties, such as buy-to-let properties and second homes, with effect from 1 April 2016 (Table 9.1). The higher rate is 3 per cent above the current SDLT rates. HMRC has issued a guide (Figure 9.1) to check if a party is liable to pay this additional charge.

Buyers will be charged on the portion of the value of the property that falls into each band.

Table 9.1 Rates of Stamp Duty Land Tax (SDLT) for additional residential properties

Band	Existing residential SDLT rates	New additional property SDLT rates
£0*–£125,000	0%	3%
£125,000–£250,000	2%	5%
£250,000–£925,000	5%	8%
£925,000–£1.5 million	10%	13%
Above £1.5 million	12%	15%

HMRC have provided two examples of how this extra SDLT will be calculated—

Example 1:

An additional residential property is purchased for £200.000. SDLT is calculated as follows:

- 3% on the first £125,000 = £3,750;
- 5% on the remaining £75,000 (the portion between £125,000 and £200,000) = £3,750;
- total SDLT due is therefore: £3,750 + £3,750 = £7,500.

Figure 9.1 HMRC guide to payment of SDLT charges on purchases of additional residential properties

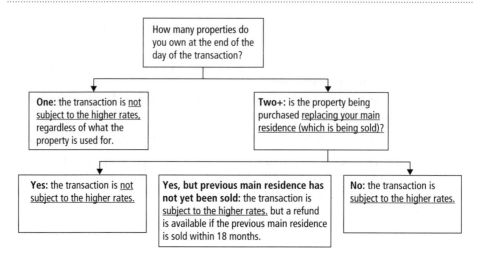

Example 2:

An additional residential property is purchased for £100,000. SDLT is calculated as follows:

- 3% on £100,000 = £3,000.

9.30 The land transaction return, Form SDLT1 (supplemented by SDLT2, 3, and 4) replaces the former 'Stamps L(A)451' (the Particulars Delivered or PD form). Furthermore, the Land Tax system means that certificates of value in conveyancing documentation are now redundant and should be excluded from all purchase deeds.

9.31 For most transactions, submission of the land transaction return and correct payment will be all that is required. Payment may be made by cheque enclosed with the return, by electronic payment (BACS, CHAPS, etc.), or at a bank or a building society. If you have a debit or credit card from a UK card issuer, you can pay your SDLT online, see **https://www.gov. uk/guidance/pay-stamp-duty-land-tax#by-debit-or-credit-card-online**.

9.32 The supplementary forms deal with the following circumstances:

1. SDLT2—where there are more than two sellers and/or two buyers;
2. SDLT3—where land is involved and further space is required in addition to the space provided on SDLT1;
3. SDLT4—for complex commercial transactions and leases.

Welsh Land Transaction Tax

9.33 Since April 2018, Land Transaction Tax (LTT) has replaced UK Stamp Duty Land Tax (SDLT) in Wales. Like SDLT, LTT will be payable when a party buys or leases a building or land over a certain price. The legislation will broadly be consistent with SDLT, preserving the underlying structure and mirroring key elements. Higher rates of SDLT on purchases of additional residential properties (including second homes) came into effect on 1 April 2016, and the higher rates also apply in Wales as part of the LTT legislation.

Tables 9.2 and 9.3 show the main Welsh non-residential (commercial) and residential tax rates and bands.

Table 9.2 Land transaction tax (LTT) main non-residential rates

Price threshold	LTT rate
£0–£150,000	0%
£150,000–£250,000	1%
£250,000–£1 million	5%
Above £1 million	6%

Table 9.3 Land transaction tax (LTT) main residential rates

Price threshold	LTT rate
£0–£180,000	0%
£180k–£250,000	3.5%
£250k–£400,000	5%
£400k–£750,000	7.5%
£750,000k–£1.5m	10%
Above £1.5m	12%

Completion of the SDLT forms, written and online

The land transaction return must be completed in black ink and must be signed by the **9.34** buyer(s). The buyer's solicitor or conveyancer must not sign the return. This is because it is the buyer's responsibility to ensure that the information contained in the land transaction return is correct and complete. However, the buyer may request that their solicitor or conveyancer be authorized to handle correspondence on their behalf, by completing box 59 of the land transaction return. It is also vital for practitioners to remember to complete box 58. This will enable them to receive the certificate of payment from the Revenue (rather than the buyer), and which will be required to enable the application for registration to Land Registry to be completed. Of particular importance to practitioners is the provision that each land transaction return has a unique reference number, so photocopies cannot be used. Furthermore, the form requires each national insurance number for every buyer. This being so it would seem prudent for practitioners to ask for this information when taking instructions from the client at the start of the transaction.

Practitioners can also make SDLT applications online. SDLT returns can be completed **9.35** online at **https://www.gov.uk/stamp-taxes-online-how-to-use-the-service**. Before using this online facility, practitioners must register for the service. Details are available from the website. If filing online, it is appropriate to pay online. One major benefit of making an online application is the ability to submit returns by the agent for the client (the buyer's practitioner), without the taxpayer having to sign. Clearly the practitioner must have the express written authority of the client to do this and the client should always see and approve the completed return before it is filed online. The simplest approach to achieve this arrangement would be for the authority to be obtained from the client in the signed client case letter obtained at the start of the transaction, with a copy of the return being e-mailed to the client on completion. There is also a commercial provider for the electronic submission of SDLT forms. They can be found at **http://www.sdlt.co.uk**. They say that their service provides online submissions direct to the Revenue and that it eliminates SDLT Form rejections, and that SDLT5 Certificates (see 9.37) can be printed instantly by your own printer. There is a small charge for each successful transaction; no client signature is required on the SDLT return.

SDLT and leases

9.36 When you buy a leasehold property, the amount of SDLT you pay depends on whether it's an existing lease or a new one. If it is an existing lease, you only have to pay SDLT on the consideration. This is the same as if you had bought a freehold property. The same rates, thresholds, and conditions for deciding whether to complete an SDLT return apply. However, the changes to stamp duty also usher in a changed regime for the rental element of commercial leases. The new charge will be at a rate of 1 per cent on the net present value (NPV) of the total rent payable over the term of the lease. Future rents will be discounted at 3.5 per cent per annum in order to arrive at the NPV. Leases where the NPV of the rent over the term of the lease does not exceed £125,000 on residential property and £150,000 for commercial property will be exempt. The Revenue has suggested that change in the regime could mean that some 60 per cent of all commercial leases could avoid any SDLT on the rental element. For example, if the net present value of the rent for a non-residential lease is £200,000, the amount of the net present value over the threshold is £50,000. Therefore you have to pay SDLT on £50,000 at the rate of 1%: that is, £500. There is an online calculator for SDLT payable in leasehold transactions at **https://www.tax.service.gov.uk/calculate-stamp-duty-land-tax/#/intro**. Returns are not required involving leasehold purchases of leases of seven years or more where the value is £40,000 or less and the annual rent is £1,000 or less, and, leasehold purchases of leases of less than seven years where the total value of the transaction is not more than the residential or non-residential SDLT threshold. Remember, from 4 December 2014, SDLT is charged at increasing rates for each portion of the price for a leasehold property over £125,000 for residential leasehold property and £150,000 for commercial leasehold property.

The SDLT5 or certificate of payment

9.37 Once the Revenue has received and processed a proper Land Tax return and payment it will issue a certificate of payment. This is called a Land Transaction Return Certificate or SDLT5. The certificate is issued under s 79 of the Finance Act 2003 and evidences that Land Tax has been accounted on the particular transaction notified to the Revenue. This must be sent to Land Registry to enable an application to register to proceed. If you make a successful online SDLT application you can get an instant SDLT5 downloaded to your computer. Finally, the rule that deeds were inadmissible in court if they were not stamped no longer applies. Unstamped deeds and documents (dated on or after 1 December 2003) can therefore be relied on in court should reference to them be required.

9.38 An attempt to evade SDLT can amount to a criminal offence. An obvious example is to try to apportion inappropriately the consideration in the contract between the property being purchased and fixtures and fittings within it. If the value ascribed to the fixtures and fittings is not accurate, for example it is inflated well beyond the true value, this could be seen to be a fraud on the Revenue (see *Saunders v Edwards* [1987] 1 WLR 1116). If there is such an apportionment, the values must be accurate as between the property and the fixtures and fittings. Where there is such an apportionment, it is recommended that the contract contains a list of the fixtures and fittings, showing the true value for each item in the list as well as the total.

KEY POINTS SUMMARY

STAMP DUTY LAND TAX

- It is assessed directly against the buyer rather than the property being purchased.   **9.39**
- The Revenue will require the completion and submission of a land transaction return to their data capture centre in Merseyside within 30 days of the completion of a transaction.
- If a return is filed late the buyer will be liable as a minimum to a fixed penalty of £100, or if more than three months late, £200.
- Section 43 of the Finance Act 2003 defines land transactions as being the focus of Land Tax and is an extremely wide definition covering dealings in estates and interests (including easements and equitable interests).
- The starting threshold for the payment of Land Tax is £125,001 for residential property, but £150,001 for commercial property.
- There are different starting thresholds and bands in Wales.
- Transactions under either threshold (£125,001 or £150,001), will be taxed at 0 per cent but will still require a land transaction return to be completed where the consideration exceeds £40,000.
- The Land Tax return contains a box that is completed to show that relief is being claimed. Nothing else is required to make the claim for relief and no certificate is needed in any deed.
- Bear in mind the availability of the first-time buyer relief, but this must apply to all the buyers, not one or two, or several.
- Since 1 April 2016 there has been a 3 per cent SDLT surcharge when an additional residential property is bought by someone who already owns a home, i.e. second homes and 'buy-to-let' properties.
- The Land Tax system means that certificates of value are also now redundant and can be excluded from all purchase deeds.
- The land transaction return must be completed in black ink and must be signed by the buyer(s). The buyer's solicitor or conveyancer is not permitted to sign the return but an online application can be made with the client's authority.
- The buyer may request that their conveyancer be authorized to handle correspondence on their behalf, by completing box 59 of the land transaction return. It is also vital for practitioners to remember to complete box 58. This will enable them to receive the certificate of payment from the Revenue (rather than the buyer), and which will be required to enable the application for registration to Land Registry to be completed.
- Each land transaction return has a unique reference number, so photocopies of the tax forms cannot be used.
- The form requires a national insurance number for every buyer. This being so it would seem prudent for practitioners to ask for this information when taking instructions from the client at the start of the transaction.
- The following transactions are not notifiable and as such no Land Tax return is required:
    1. the acquisition of a freehold or leasehold interest in land for no chargeable consideration;
    2. transactions made in connection with the ending of a marriage;
    3. transactions varying the dispositions made, whether effected by will or laws of intestacy, within two years after the person's death not involving any consideration in money or money's worth;
    4. a transaction which effects something other than a major interest in land chargeable with tax at 0 per cent. An example of such a transaction would be an interest, which is not a

major interest in land, such as the grant of an easement where the consideration does not exceed £125,000. This would attract Land Tax at 0 per cent, provided it is not linked to any other transaction that would bring the total consideration to more than £125,000.

- Consider making SDLT applications online. It is quicker and easier and self-validating; mistakes in the completion of the form will be automatically highlighted and will require correction before acceptance.

Registration of title

9.40   Registered land was considered in depth in Chapter 1; please refer to that chapter for details of the system of registered land conveyancing. In this section we will be looking at the mechanics of formal applications for registration. This will be concerned with first registration of a previously unregistered title and registration of dealings with registered land, both of the whole of the title and part of the title. However, to start there is an examination of what are the correct documents that should be sent to Land Registry on a dealing or on first registration. Registration applications generally are vital to the interests of buyers. Without them being made or being made correctly, the legal title may not pass to the buyer, who may lose priority to a third-party application affecting the title to the subject property. There are several explanatory and practice leaflets online that can assist practitioners with their registration applications at **https://www.gov.uk/government/organisations/land-registry/**. You may need to inform the client that the price paid for the subject property is now noted on the register (see Land Registration (No 3) Rules 1999). If your client wishes to avoid having this information entered on the registers open to the public, this must be considered before the transfer is approved. Land Registry will not make an entry where it is impracticable to do so. If the consideration is dependent on terms in a document it does not see within a registration application then no entry will be made. As from 3 March 2008 Land Registry requires evidence of identity for applicants who are not legally represented. This covers applications to register a transfer, lease, mortgage, or discharge of a mortgage in paper form. This is to try to lessen fraudulent registration applications. Practice guide 67 on the Land Registry website explains when evidence of identity is required and how it should be given. It is aimed at conveyancers.

The documents that should be sent to Land Registry

9.41   It used to be the case that all original deeds and documents were sent to Land Registry to ensure that registration of each transaction is properly completed. Now if you are applying for First Registration, you must send to the Land Registry original supporting documents. For all other applications, they recommend sending certified copies, as they destroy original documents once they have made a scanned copy. For applications submitted through e-DRS, the Land Registry only accept certified copies. In first registration cases these original deeds and documents are lodged together with a Land Registry application form, the details of which are set out in 9.51 and 9.55. Certified copies can also now accompany the Land Registry application forms. However, Land Registry introduced a new method of lodging some applications from 18 February 2002. Practitioners who use the Land Registry Portal can now lodge applications to change the register electronically. Initially, this covers only simple applications, but Land Registry plans to develop the process to allow more complicated applications. The service is called 'e-lodgement' to differentiate it from 'e-conveyancing', which it is not. There is also e-DRS, considered at 9.43.

9.42   **E-lodgement**   You can lodge the following types of application using e-lodgement:

- application to be registered as a person to be notified of an application for adverse possession;
- application to cancel a caution against dealings;
- change of property description;

- change of address;
- change of name by marriage or deed poll;
- death of a joint proprietor;
- application for registration of a notice of home rights;
- application for renewal of registration in respect of home rights;
- application for cancellation of a home rights notice;
- application to enter a standard form of restriction;
- application for an order that a restriction be disapplied or modified;
- application to withdraw a restriction;
- application to enter a unilateral notice;
- application to remove a unilateral notice;
- application for the cancellation of a unilateral notice;
- application for upgrading of a title;
- application to withdraw a caution.

e-DRS (Electronic Document Registration Service)   With e-DRS, you can send and receive **9.43** applications to change the register electronically, for example AP1s. You submit applications to change the register electronically and attach scanned copies of supporting documents. There are no additional fees for using e-DRS. The fees payable for submitting applications via e-DRS are based on the current Land Registration Fee Order. (The current Order gives a 50 per cent reduction for electronic applications.)

The following application types may be submitted by e-DRS:

- dealings of whole of registered land for up to 50 registered titles;
- most types of dealing transaction that are currently received by post;
- transfers of part; and
- first registrations of leases as well as lease extensions.

All applications will be received and responded to electronically, creating an audit trail **9.44** that will help to prevent fraud. Firms can have an electronic record of every document that they send to Land Registry. There is no risk of losing hard copy documents as they never leave your offices. If a form or document does not need a 'wet' signature it can be uploaded in electronic format (pdf, tiff, gif, or jpg). So an AP1 application form can be signed with a typed signature and does not need to be printed and scanned. Common examples of documents that need a wet signature include TR1 and mortgage documents. They must be scanned so Land Registry can examine the execution and ensure it is compliant with current legislation. Since 14 March 2016, Land Registry portal users are able to view information about their applications using a new search facility called 'Application Enquiry'. The new application allows customers to search using the title number or the Land Registry reference number to find more details about their application, including:

- progress status, such as: received, priority protected, in progress, or delayed;
- reason why an application has been delayed, where applicable; and
- full priority period for official searches.

The land registry has also introduced e-Despatch for users of its online portal. If you send your registration applications in the post, you will receive the application results online in your PDF download area in the portal. The only exception to the new system is for first registrations, which will continue to be returned by post. Firms that are currently not signed up to the online portal will continue to receive their results in the post.

Land Registry will send you confirmation if your application has been successfully submitted. **9.45** When received, the application is processed in the same way as a paper application. Land

Registry send you the completed documents electronically and you can retrieve them from your portal 'PDF Downloads' area. You can sign up to the Land Registry e-notification service to receive alerts when documents have arrived in your 'downloads' area. If you submit an application and Land Registry raises a requisition it will be sent to you electronically. Simply select the 'Reply to requisition service' in the portal and resubmit any amended attachments.

9.46 Generally, in all applications where there is a sale by a personal representative (PR), an office copy of the grant of representation to the estate of the deceased registered proprietor will need to be included. Similarly, if a document has been executed by an attorney, a certified copy of the power of attorney must also be included in the application. Finally, where SDLT is payable Land Registry will always require a certificate of payment (SDLT5) with the registration application. This is also required even if the transaction is taxed at 0 per cent, i.e. under the thresholds (£125,000 or £150,000).

9.47 On 10 November 2008 Land Registry changed its prescribed forms including all forms involved in the registration of transfers. These changes were to the prescribed mandatory Land Registry forms and also to provide for the inclusion of confirmation of identity panels to application forms AP1, FR1, and DS2 and the introduction of the requirement, in some circumstances, to provide confirmation relating to the identity of unrepresented parties. Practitioners must use the changed forms or their applications will be rejected.

9.48 **Evidence of identity on making a registration application**   Land Registry, in an attempt to reduce fraudulent registration applications, has added identity panels to application forms AP1, FR1, and DS2. Evidence of identity will always be required for transfers, leases, charges, and applications for first registration. (Evidence is not required where the value of the land is worth less than £5,000.) Conveyancers making a registration application must list all parties to the transaction and where a party is not represented by a conveyancer a separate section on the form (section 2) must also be completed.

9.49 **Existing registered titles; dealings with whole or part**   These applications must be lodged at Land Registry within the priority period given on the pre-completion Land Registry search result. Where the land is registered and the dealing is with the whole of the title, any existing old land or charge certificate should not be sent to Land Registry with the dealing application cover AP1 (application to change the register). Form AP1 can be seen in the Online Resource Centre accompanying this book. The application should be accompanied by the transfer deed and all new mortgages. Land Registry will require a certified copy of each mortgage sent for registration with a clear indication of priority. The certification can be in the following form:

> I/We hereby certify this to be a true copy of the original [signed, here signed in the firm name or by the practitioner applying].

Land Registry Early Completion Policy

9.50 In cases where e-DS1 is not being used, all discharges of previous mortgages on Form DS1 must be lodged with the application. In this regard, early completion is a policy governing applications to discharge mortgages that Land Registry has applied since 3 August 2009. The policy will apply to all situations where an application for a discharge of whole has been made with another application but proof of satisfaction (evidence of the discharge of the charge) has not been provided. In essence, if there is no DS1 or other satisfactory proof of the mortgage discharge, Land Registry will reject the application for discharge but complete any other accompanying applications where it is possible to do so, such as a transfer of title. The entries relating to the existing charge will be left in the register until proof of redemption is received by Land Registry. If the discharge of a charge is the sole application, regardless of the method of discharge Land Registry will reject it if proof of redemption has not been supplied. Accordingly, if a property has been sold and the buyer submits the registration application without adequate proof of redemption Land Registry will vest the property in the new owner but will leave the old owner's mortgage in the charges register. To avoid this, proper evidence of redemption, for example a DS1 or evidence of the electronic equivalent, should always be included with the registration application.

On a dealing making a transfer of part the appropriate application cover is also the AP1, **9.51** which now covers both whole-of-title and part-of-title dealings. (Form AP1 can be seen on the Online Resource Centre accompanying this book.) The buyer will not need a land or charge certificate. Otherwise the documents will be the same as for a dealing with the whole of the title. However, it is possible that a mortgage discharge will be of part with the charge remaining on the residue of the seller's title. In this case Form DS3 will be required, but it should have with it a scale plan showing the area to be released from the charge. This will be required from the seller's lender and must accompany the AP1 application form. Where SDLT has been paid SDLT5 must be lodged with the application for registration. (SDLT5 will be required even if no tax was payable for transactions worth more than £40,000. Transactions above that figure and taxed at 0 per cent will still require an SDLT1 to be submitted.)

After 13 October 2003, no land or charge certificates (old redundant registered land title **9.52** deeds) need be lodged at the Registry when applying for a dealing, or placed on deposit when concerned with the registration of a transfer of part.

The appropriate Land Registry fee must accompany the application. Fees are set out in the **9.53** Land Registration Fees Order 2013 (SI 2013/3174) and are listed in scales according to the consideration paid for the property. In this fee order there is a new provision that makes a 50 per cent reduction for customers who submit transfers of whole, charges of whole, transfers of charges, and other dealings of whole applications electronically. Fees can only be paid by cheque or direct debit.

First registration   At present, s 6(4) of the Land Registration Act 2002 requires applica- **9.54** tions for first registration to be made within two months of completion. Transactions that induce first registration are dealt with in 1.14. The application cover required is normally Form FR1 for both freehold and leasehold properties. Form FR1 can be seen on the Online Resource Centre accompanying this book. In both cases the Registry requires a list in triplicate of all documents lodged within the cover form, and Form DL is required for this purpose. The registrar will want to see all the documents of title to enable a decision to be taken as to the class of title to be granted. In first registration cases, original documents must be produced. Consequently, practitioners should include and list:

(a) all the documents of title as abstracted, including all old land charges search results;
(b) all searches and pre-contract enquiries with replies;
(c) the original contract;
(d) requisitions on title with replies;
(e) the original executed conveyance, or transfer, or deed of assignment with certified copy;
(f) the buyer's mortgage deed, if any, with a certified copy;
(g) all receipted discharged mortgages, including any paid off by the seller; and
(h) if the property is leasehold, the lease (and a certified copy where a new lease is being granted).

Land Registry fees   The appropriate Land Registry fee must accompany the application. **9.55** Fees are set out in the Land Registration Fees Order 2013 (SI 2013/3174) and are listed in scales according to the consideration paid for the property. In this fee order there is a new provision that makes a 50 per cent reduction for customers who submit transfers of whole, charges of whole, transfers of charges, and other dealings of whole applications electronically. Fees can only be paid by cheque or direct debit. Where SDLT has been paid, SDLT5 must be lodged with the application for registration. (SDLT5 will be required even if no tax was payable for transactions worth more than £40,000. Transactions taxed at 0 per cent will still require an SDLT1 to be submitted where the consideration exceeds £40,000.) Land Registry offers a reduction of 25 per cent in the fee for voluntary first registration of title to land. This reduction is intended to encourage voluntary first registration of title to land. The fee for a voluntary application for first registration will continue to be payable in accordance with Land Registry's principal fees scale (Scale 1), but the amount payable will be reduced. The full Scale 1 fee will continue to be payable for compulsory applications for first registration. Land Registry provide details of their fees on their website at **https:// www.gov.uk/government/organisations/land-registry/**. The contact details for the 15 Land Registry local offices can also be found at the same website. There is an online fee calculator available at **http://landregistry.data.gov.uk/fees-calculator.html,** where the calculator covers the main provisions of the Land Registration Fee Order for applications received at Land Registry offices. The Fee Calculator consists of three stages. First, you select the type of application; second, you enter the property value and/or the rent payable (if applicable); and third, you click a button to calculate the fee automatically.

9.56 Land Registry has issued a Guide (March 2014), at **https://www.gov.uk/government/ publications/registration-services-fees**, giving general guidance about their fees. It also offers Practice Guide 49, which details why they reject applications for registration. It gives advice on how to avoid the rejection of an application. Practice Guide 50 gives guidance on requisitions Land Registry may raise on applications and what practitioners can do to avoid these questions from the Registry.

Existing registered titles; registration of dealings

9.57 In all cases, dealings must be registered within the priority period of the pre-completion Land Registry search. In many cases the practitioner acting for the buyer will be ready to apply for registration save for the provision of Form DS1, duly sealed by the seller's lender. Where this is so, you need to wait for Form DS1. Pursuant to its policy of early completion (see 9.50), Land Registry rejects an application to register if the DS1 is not lodged, despite any undertaking or any copy DS1 lodged. The danger is that if you wait for Form DS1 you might overlook lodging the application within the priority period. To avoid this, diarize dates to call for the DS1 or to renew your search. Where e-DS1 is being used this concern regarding the absence of Form DS1 is irrelevant so the registration application can proceed without delay. If you are only lodging a DS1, i.e. you are simply discharging a mortgage and not registering any other dealing, rather than also using an AP1 you can use a DS2 application that can be printed on the back of the DS1. Form AP1 can be seen on the Online Resource Centre accompanying this book.

First registrations

9.58 Applications must be made within two months of completion (Land Registration Act 2002, s 6(4)), failing which the legal title will not vest in the buyer until an application has been completed by the Registry. Failure to register will result in the transfer becoming void. In this situation, the transferor will hold the legal estate on a bare trust for the transferee (s 7(2)(a)). Any grant of a lease or mortgage will become void for want of registration and take effect as a contract to grant or create the lease or mortgage (s 7(2)(b)). Either way, the buyer's practitioner should not allow this to occur (see *Brown and Root Technology Ltd v Sun Alliance and London Assurance Co. Ltd* [1997] 1 EGLR 39 for an example of what can occur in this 'registration gap' and the problems that can arise as a direct consequence). Although leasehold applications will, as mentioned at 9.54, be on Form FR1, it is possible that you will be required to register a pre-existing leasehold title rather than the grant of a new lease. In these circumstances this too is within Form FR1. This form can be seen on the Online Resource Centre accompanying this book. The form always requires the applicant to state the class of title applied for. This is particularly important for leases, bearing in mind the implications of a good leasehold title (see 1.49).

Transfers of whole

These will form the majority of all applications to Land Registry and the usual documents required in such applications are listed in 9.41. SDLT5 will be required for transactions over £40,000.

9.59

Transfers of part

Where a transfer of part also contains new restrictive covenants, a full certified copy of the transfer is required by Land Registry. SDLT5 will be required.

9.60

Where to send your application

Members of the public should send applications and correspondence to:

9.61

Land Registry Citizen Centre PO Box 74 Gloucester GL14 9BB.

Business customers should send applications and correspondence by Royal Mail or DX to:

Post-Land Registry, (insert a customer team's office name, for example 'Telford office'. If you do not have a customer team, insert the name of your closest office from the list below), PO Box 75 Gloucester GL14 9BD DX—Land Registry (insert a customer team's office name, for example 'Telford office'. If you do not have a customer team, insert the name of your closest office from the list below), DX 321601 Gloucester 33.

Offices

- Birkenhead
- Coventry
- Croydon
- Durham
- Gloucester
- Hull
- Fylde
- Leicester
- Nottingham
- Peterborough
- Plymouth
- Telford
- Wales
- Weymouth

You should remember that you can submit applications online by signing up to business e-services and by using the e-DRS facility. Benefits include a 50 per cent fee reduction for some application types, no postage costs, an electronic audit trail, and reduced processing times.

Dematerialization of charge certificates

Prior to the Land Registration Act 2002, it was possible for lenders to request Land Registry to retain their charge certificates pursuant to s 63 of the Land Registration Act 1925. Where the charge certificate was retained, the charges register will show the registered charge in the usual way, but there will be an additional entry. This will state: 'The charge

9.62

certificate relating to the charge dated [date of the particular charge] in favour of [proprietor of the particular charge] is retained in HM Land Registry ([Land Registration Act 1925, s 63]).' Remember, however, that there can be other charges registered against the same title for which charge certificates may have been issued. Notwithstanding the effects of the Land Registration Act 2002, practitioners may still see this entry. It is now irrelevant as land and charge certificates have been abolished and therefore have no legal effect.

9.63   There is one complication for practitioners when dealing with s 63 procedures, and that is in relation to other deeds for the subject property. When you come to sell, you will need to locate these other deeds. For example, regarding a lease, you will need a copy of the lease to prepare the contract, as well as for the buyer's practitioner.

Welsh language on the register

9.64   From 1 October 2001, registered properties in Wales have register templates issued by Land Registry in a bilingual format. In this way, headings and standard information will appear in Welsh and English. Furthermore, individual entries will appear in the language of the source document. This will allow a 'dual-language register', reflecting the language choice of the current proprietor.

Title Information Document

9.65   This is issued by the Registry following a change to the register, for example on first registration or registration of a dealing. It is a copy of the register showing the up-to-date position at the time of its issue. This document does not represent the deeds to the property and merely serves as title information. It should not be sent to the Registry with subsequent applications. If no changes have occurred to the title plan, then no copy will be issued as part of the Title Information Document. As such in most cases only copy entries will be seen. Practitioners should appreciate that only official copies serve as proof of title. Official copies may be issued as the Title Information Document.

Land Registry requisitions

9.66   If you complete an AP1 or FR1 and in doing so include your e-mail address, then Land Registry will issue any requisitions on the application by e-mail. If you want these to be sent by post omit your e-mail address.

Other issues

9.67   The buyer's practitioner has many different issues and concerns to cope with after completion that are not related to stamping or registration. The main ones are listed in the following paragraphs.

Deeds retained

9.68   Where there is a transaction and the client will retain the deeds (as the title is unregistered and there is no mortgage), the client's instructions should be obtained on where the deeds should be kept. Many practitioners offer to retain the deeds for no charge. If the deeds are kept in this way, they must be placed in a fireproof location such as a safe or strong room. If this were not done, then the practitioner would be failing in his duty to the client in relation to the safe storage of the deeds.

Registration with the lessor

9.69   Almost all leases include a covenant on the lessee's part requiring the lessee to give notice to the lessor of all transfers, assignments, mortgages, or other dealings affecting the legal title. The purpose of the clause is to ensure that the lessor is aware of who is the lessee and therefore responsible for the performance of all the covenants in the lease and, in particular, the payment of rent. The covenant normally stipulates a time limit for giving notice, usually 28 days from the date of the deed or completion, and calls for copies of the relevant documents (the transfer, mortgage, etc.) to be lodged with the lessor's solicitor. A fee may be required by the terms of the covenant, payable to the lessor's solicitor. (If the fee is stated, then that is all that must be paid as the VAT is deemed to be included in that figure. However, many covenants state the fee and go on to provide that VAT will also be payable on the fee by the lessee.) Notice should be given in duplicate so that a receipted copy can be placed with the deeds. Law stationers issue notice of assignment forms but it is quite permissible to give notice by letter.

Notice of assignment   The following could serve as the basis for a notice of assignment: **9.70**

> To [lessor] of [address] [insert the date] With regard to the Lease made the [here insert the date of the lease] between (1) [insert the name of the original lessor] and (2) [insert the name of the original lessee] relating to [here insert the postal address or description of premises] ('the Lease') TAKE NOTICE that by a transfer or an assignment dated the [insert the date of the assignment or transfer] the Lease was transferred or assigned by [insert the name and address of the outgoing lessee] to [insert the purchaser, transferee or assignee] of [the incoming lessee's address] ('the Purchaser') for the residue of the term granted by the Lease.

Some modern leases do not state a fee but refer to a 'reasonable fee'. In these circumstances   **9.71**
you will need to agree what is reasonable before the lessor's solicitor will receipt the notice.

Share transfer registration

Particularly when dealing with leasehold properties, it may be that each owner in the block   **9.72**
or development is entitled to own a share or shares in a management company. If there is such an arrangement, the share certificate should be obtained on completion along with a stock transfer form completed and signed by the seller. These two documents should then be submitted to the secretary of the company with a request that a new share certificate be issued in the name of the buyer. The new certificate should be kept with the deeds. In many cases these companies are limited by guarantee and therefore do not have or issue share certificates. Where this is the case the change of ownership (and hence guarantee) should be confirmed in writing to the company secretary. A membership certificate may be issued.

Life policies

Many mortgages are endowment mortgages where the loan is secured not just on the sub-   **9.73**
ject property, but also on one or more life insurance policies. Where this is so, the buyer's practitioner must ensure that as well as the charge on the property a mortgage of the life policy or policies is in place. This will normally be by way of an assignment of the benefit of the life policy from the borrower in favour of the lender; the purpose being that the proceeds of the policy are meant to be sufficient in due course to repay the loan. Furthermore, notice of the mortgage, by way of an assignment of the policy or policies, must be given to the life office. If notice is not given, the life company will not know of the interest of the lender (see the Policies of Assurance Act 1867). Accordingly, notice should be given and the following form can be used and should be sent to the life company head office or assignments section:

> To: [insert the life company name and address] TAKE NOTICE: RE: POLICY NO. [insert the policy number]: That by a DEED OF ASSIGNMENT/MORTGAGE OF LIFE POLICY dated the [insert the date of the deed] (certified copy enclosed) [it is best practice to send the life company a copy of the deed] and made between the Assignor [here insert the name of

the borrower] of [insert the borrower's address] of the one part and the Assignee [insert the lender's name] of [insert the lender's address] of the other part, the Assignor assigned to the Assignee absolutely a Policy of Assurance on the life of [insert the name of the life assured] granted by the [insert the life company name] and being the Policy numbered above with all bonuses and money assured by or to become payable under the said Policy and the full benefit thereof TO HOLD unto the Assignee as in the assignment mentioned above.

That you are requested to pay all money which may become payable under the said policy to the Assignee or as the Assignee may direct.

[Insert the date of the giving of the notice.]
Please receipt and return the enclosed copy of this notice.

9.74 When sending the deeds to the lender you should also send the original life policy document, all previous assignments and reassignments, all receipted notices of assignments, and the receipted notice sent to you by the life office regarding the latest mortgage assignment.

Costs

9.75 On the assumption that a bill of costs has been delivered to the client, remember to transfer your costs with all paid disbursements from the client account to your office account.

Other final issues

9.76 There are various final checking procedures that, if carried through properly, will bring the transaction to a satisfactory conclusion. When the Registry returns the Title Information Document to you, always check to see that no mistakes or omissions have been made by you or the Registry. Thereafter the remaining deeds should be sent to the mortgagee for retention while the loan remains in existence. (This is if the lender requires them. Check your instructions. Otherwise pass them on to your client.) Remember that even if there is no charge or land certificate, other deeds may have to go to the lender, such as an original lease relating to a leasehold title. The deeds and documents should be fully listed in a schedule in duplicate for receipting by the lender. All search results should be sent with the deeds, including the latest local authority search result. The documents should be sent by recorded or registered delivery and not by ordinary post. Some mortgagees do not want, or prefer not to receive, a large bundle of pre-registration deeds and documents. As can be appreciated, if they did in each case, this would only increase their storage costs. However, the unwanted pre-registration deeds should not be destroyed. It is always possible that they could be used to resolve a problem at a later date. Either the client or the practitioner should retain these pre-registration deeds, just in case they are needed. Before sending the deeds to the lender, take a copy of the contents of the Title Information Document and send the copy set to the client. This will reassure the client of the contents of the registered title and will assist if reference has to be made to the title in the future, for example should a dispute arise about boundaries, etc. Lastly, you should make one last check of the file to make sure that there are no outstanding items to be dealt with before the file is put away for storage.

Satisfaction survey

9.77 You may wish to consider issuing to the client, at the final point of contact, a satisfaction survey through which you and your firm can seek some feedback on the handling of the transaction. Such a survey should highlight areas that you control and which can therefore be improved. It should also demonstrate to the client that there is an intention on your part to improve the service offered to clients, something that might persuade the client to return in the future with new work.

Annual Residential Property Tax, now called Annual Tax on Enveloped Dwellings

The Annual Tax on Enveloped Dwellings (ATED) (formerly called the Residential Property **9.78** Tax) is a tax payable by companies that own high-value residential property (a 'dwelling'). It took effect on 1 April 2013. The tax is due on high-value residential property and is payable each year. An ATED return is required if the subject property is a dwelling and it is in the UK and it was valued at £2 million or more on 1 April 2012, or at later acquisition and it is owned partly or completely by a company (or collective investment vehicle, for example unit trust).

The tax is in the following bands as set out in Table 9.4:

Table 9.4 Chargeable amounts for 1 April 2018 to 31 March 2019

Property value	Annual charge
More than £500,000 but not more than £1 million	£3,600
More than £1 million but not more than £2 million	£7,250
More than £2 million but not more than £5 million	£24,250
More than £5 million but not more than £10 million	£56,550
More than £10 million but not more than £20 million	£113,400
More than £20 million	£226,950

From 1 April 2016 a first band came into effect for properties with a value greater than £500,000 but not more than £1 million, with an annual charge of £3,500.

ATED applies to residential property (a 'dwelling'). A dwelling may be all or part of a residential or mixed-use property. Sometimes a dwelling is part of a larger, mixed-use property that has parts not used for residential purposes. Only the residential part would have ATED payable on it. If a property consists of a number of self-contained flats, each flat will usually be valued separately.

In March 2013 HMRC renamed this tax the Annual Tax on Enveloped Dwellings. This is because the dwelling is said to be 'enveloped' as the ownership sits within a corporate 'wrapper' or 'envelope'.

In the Budget of 2014, the Chancellor of the Exchequer announced a reduction in the threshold from £2 million to £500,000, to be introduced over two years. Since 1 April 2015 a new band has come into effect for properties with a value greater than £1 million but not more than £2 million, with an annual charge of £7,000. For future years these charges will be indexed in line with the previous September Consumer Prices Index.

KEY POINTS SUMMARY

POST-COMPLETION PROCEDURES

- Where you are dealing with a new mortgage granted by a company, you must ensure the **9.79** mortgage is registered at Companies House within 21 days of completion. (Address all correspondence to 'The Mortgage Section' to hasten delivery.)

- Where SDLT is payable, collect the tax from the client before completion to make sure the tax is paid to the Revenue within the time limit to avoid any penalty fee being charged. Make sure the client has completed and signed the SDLT return and that boxes 58 and 59 on the form have been completed appropriately.

- As a faster alternative, consider making the SDLT application online.

- Always ensure you submit your registration application for a dealing within the priority period fixed by your Land Registry search result or, if a first registration, within two months of completion.

- Be prepared to deal with Land Registry identity verification requirements.

- Always check the contents of the Title Information Document on its issue from Land Registry and, where there is a mortgage, send to the lender a deeds schedule in duplicate for receipting. (Retain the deeds where the lender's instructions state they are not required.)

- Make sure you send all relevant deeds to the lender, such as leases or deeds of covenant.

- Send a photocopy of the title to the client for information and retention.

- Never overlook transferring your profit costs out of the client account into your office account.

- Make a final check of your file to make sure there are no forgotten points or items still to be dealt with.

B DELAYS AND REMEDIES

DELAYS

9.80 In an open contract where there is no agreed completion date, completion must take place within a 'reasonable time' (see *Johnson v Humphrey* [1946] 1 All ER 460). In a contract regulated by the SCs the completion date will either be specified on the front page within the particulars or, more rarely, by SC 6.1, 20 working days after the date of the contract. This arrangement for completion is straightforward, but what is the position if completion is delayed?

Late completion

9.81 The problem for practitioners is what can be done if one of the parties delays completion. It is plain that such a delay will be a breach of contract, and it was held in the House of Lords in *Raineri v Miles* [1981] AC 1050 that failure to complete was a breach entitling the innocent party to a claim for damages arising from the delay. Can an injured party, immediately on the happening of the breach, terminate the contract? It would seem not, because this remedy is only available to the innocent party if time was of the essence in relation to the completion date. When time is of the essence, there is no leeway for delay; completion must be on the date specified, failing which all remedies will be available to the aggrieved party. Section 41 of the Law of Property Act 1925 tried to regulate time clauses in property contracts but only achieved further confusion: see *Stickney v Keeble* [1915] AC 386 (on a similar provision of previous legislation) and *United Scientific Holdings Ltd v Burnley Borough Council* [1978] AC 904, illustrating how differently the courts have interpreted this statutory provision.

9.82 It now seems to be that if a contract states a completion date without qualification, that date is not a strict and binding date that would allow the innocent party to withdraw from the contract on the occasion of the breach. On the other hand, if it is expressly stated that time is of the essence, then a strict interpretation arises and if there is a failure to complete on the stipulated date there will be a breach of contract of such magnitude that the innocent party will be free to pursue all remedies, which can include immediate termination or rescission of the contract.

Time of the essence

Time will be of the essence for a conveyancing contract: **9.83**

(a) if the parties agree to it being written into the contract; or
(b) where a notice to complete has been correctly served; or
(c) where time is of the essence by necessary implication from the surrounding circumstances of the case.

In a contract regulated by the SCs, SC 6.1 specifically states that time is not of the essence   **9.84**
unless a notice to complete is served (see 9.93–9.99). The parties to the contract can vary
this term to make time of the essence but this cannot be achieved unilaterally. To make time
of the essence the SCs should be varied to delete the word 'not' from SC 6.1, and the words
'unless a notice to complete has been served' should be replaced with 'without the necessity
for the service of a notice to complete'. In addition the words 'time shall be of the essence
of the contract' should be inserted next to the stated completion date. Although this second
element is not essential it will remind all parties of this critical element of the agreement.

In the absence of an SC 6.1 provision declaring that time is not of the essence, it may   **9.85**
become of the essence where the time of completion is clearly expressed to be an essential,
almost paramount, term. Examples are *Harold Wood Brick Co. Ltd v Ferris* [1935] 1 KB
613, where completion was required 'not later than . . . ', and *Barclay v Messenger* (1874)
43 LJ Ch 449, where if the purchase monies were not paid by a certain date the contract
would be null and void. Time of the essence will also arise on the giving of a notice to
complete (see 9.93).

Time of the essence may arise by necessary implication (see *Parkin v Thorold* (1852) 16   **9.86**
Beav 59) and particularly from the surrounding circumstances of the transaction. For
example, time of the essence will be implied in a contract concerned with the sale of a business as a going concern where delay would have a material and probably adverse effect
(see *Smith v Hamilton* [1951] Ch 174 regarding the sale of a shop as a going concern).
The same would be the case for a sale of a wasting asset such as a short leasehold interest
(see *Pips (Leisure Productions) Ltd v Walton* (1980) 43 P & CR 415, which was concerned
with the sale of a 21-year lease with 15 years unexpired). However, in all these cases if the
express contract terms are to the contrary, i.e. they include a provision such as SC 6.1,
then the express term in the agreement will supersede any implication of time being of the
essence (see *Ellis v Lawrence* (1969) 210 EG 215, where the contract included express
terms for the service of a notice to complete and, even though the sale was of a business as
a going concern, the express terms negatived any implication of time being of the essence).

What, then, are the implications where time is not of the essence and yet one party has   **9.87**
delayed completion? One element of this predicament is clear; the injured party cannot
refuse to complete the contract. If the injured party seeks to establish grounds for terminating the agreement, then the appropriate course of action is to make time of the essence, and
a notice to complete should be served on the delaying party without further ado (see 9.96).

Consequences of delay: compensation

Where there is delay in completing a transaction that delay, however short, will amount   **9.88**
to a breach of contract. If there is delay, even of a matter of hours (or even minutes), the
innocent party is entitled to seek damages for any loss occasioned as a result of the delay.

In the circumstances of a brief delay of a few hours any loss sustained is unlikely to be such as to justify making a claim in the courts for breach of contract. As a result it has become the norm to include compensation provisions within the express contract terms. These compensatory terms do not preclude a claim in the courts, but where such steps are taken any compensation paid under the contractual terms must be taken into account when computing damages.

9.89 The common law has made provision for compensation, but if certainty is required, compensation terms should always be included in a conveyancing contract. The common law position is that where completion is delayed in an open contract, the buyer will be entitled to any income from the property but must bear all outgoings. Furthermore, if the seller remains in the subject property he or she will be required to pay a fee for occupation unless the delay has arisen as a consequence of any default by the buyer. The seller will be entitled to interest on the unpaid purchase monies. The level of interest is likely to be at the level allowed on the court short-term investment account under the Administration of Justice Act 1925 (see *Bartlett v Barclays Bank Trust Co. Ltd* [1980] Ch 515). If the seller causes the delay then he must pay the outgoings. Accordingly, the position at common law seems to be that the intention is to deal with the parties as if completion had actually taken place even though in reality no such step has been taken. Notwithstanding that the innocent party will be entitled to seek damages, it is clear that to allow open contract provisions to prevail in these circumstances would be unwise.

Compensation and the Standard Conditions

9.90 The Standard Conditions (SCs) contain clear and precise provisions for compensation for a breach of contract that arises from delayed completion. SC 7.2 states that if a party to the contract defaults and delays completion, the defaulting party must pay compensation to the innocent party. Compensation is quantified as interest at the rate specified in the agreement as the 'contract rate' to the intent that the interest is on the unpaid purchase price. If a deposit has been paid and the buyer is in default, interest is calculated on the unpaid balance of the purchase price, or the total purchase price if the seller is in default. Interest is payable for each day that there is delay. SC 7.2.4 states that if the subject property is tenanted then the seller can elect to take the rent rather than interest. Accordingly, if the rent is likely to exceed the value of the interest, notice should be served on the defaulting buyer to confirm that the rent is to be taken by the seller rather than interest. Of course SC 7.2.4 can be varied in the special conditions to allow the seller to take the interest and the rent should the buyer default and delay completion. SC 7.2 also contemplates the possibility of both parties being in default. In these circumstances the party at greater fault must pay compensation.

9.91 The interest rate defined by the SCs as being the 'contract rate' is 'The Law Society's interest rate from time to time in force'. This is declared each week in the Law Society's *Gazette*. It can also be found at **http://www.lawsociety.org.uk/advice/articles/law-society-interest-rate/**. There is space on the front of the contract for an alternative rate to be declared and this could be, for example, 'four per cent above the base rate of Lloyds Bank plc or such other lending rate as the bank shall declare in place thereof'.

9.92 Where interest is allowed by the contract it will be payable on completion being delayed even if this is only by a matter of minutes. The SCs stipulate a time and day for completion, see SC 6.1.1 and SC 6.1.2. If the time limit is breached but completion takes place on the contractual date, completion is deemed to take place the next working day and interest will accrue. The worst time for this to occur is on a Friday when three days' interest will arise for the period over the weekend to the next working day, being the following Monday. All this will be allowed by the contract even though completion actually took place late on the previous Friday.

Notices to complete

As we have seen, in a conveyancing contract time is not of the essence if regulated by the **9.93** SCs unless the special conditions provide otherwise. As a result an innocent party suffering from a delayed completion cannot consider the agreement as repudiated following the defaulting party's delay. This is an unsatisfactory position because the defaulting party may have no intention whatsoever of completing and yet the contract would in theory subsist. To bring the matter to a head and to terminate the agreement, the innocent party must take steps to precipitate a change, and this will be by way of a notice to complete. The notice will in all cases give a final date for completion, failing which there will be no further time for the defaulting party. Time is now of the essence of the contract. The notice can inform the defaulting party that unless completion takes place by the date stated in the notice, the party serving the notice will be entitled to all remedies, including a repudiation of the agreement. Because notices to complete deal with timing, practitioners need to reflect on two elements. First, when can the notice be served? And, second, how long must the notice be before it expires?

When can a notice to complete be served?

Where there is an open contract this is open to doubt. The reason is that a notice to com- **9.94** plete can be served only if sufficient time has elapsed so that any further delay would be unreasonable and unfair as far as the innocent party is concerned. The party serving the notice must be ready, willing, and able to complete, failing which the notice will be invalid.

Where the SCs apply the position is perfectly clear. SC 6.8.1 states that at any time on or **9.95** after the date fixed for completion, either party who is ready, able, and willing to complete may give the other a notice to complete. SC 1.1.3 goes on to define when a party is ready, able, and willing, i.e. he would have been in a position and ready to complete but for the default of the other party, and in the case of the seller, even though the property remains subject to a mortgage, if the amount to be paid at completion will be enough to pay off the mortgage.

How long should the notice-to-complete period be?

In an open contract the period for completion should be that within which it would be **9.96** reasonable to allow completion to be effected when all the outstanding steps are taken into consideration. Again this is open to doubt and so, where the SCs are being used, SC 6.8.2 states that the parties are to complete the agreement within ten working days of giving the notice to complete. The ten-day period excludes the day on which the notice is given. The condition goes on to state the essential wording, namely, 'for this purpose, time is of the essence of the contract'. Lastly, and for what it is worth, SC 6.8.3 states that a buyer who delays completion and has paid less than a 10 per cent deposit at exchange must pay the remaining monies required to make up a full 10 per cent deposit, and must pay these monies immediately on receipt of the notice. In practice this is unlikely to happen if the reason for not completing is a lack of finance. However, the seller can claim the full 10 per cent deposit.

Failure to comply with a notice to complete

If there is still no completion after the service and expiry of a notice to complete, the SCs **9.97** which set out what is to be done are SC 7.4, where the buyer is in default, and SC 7.5, where the seller defaults. If SC 7.4 comes into operation, the seller may rescind; and if there is rescission, the seller may forfeit the deposit, resell the property, and claim damages. These provisions are not exclusive and the seller therefore retains all other rights and remedies that may also be available. If SC 7.5 is operative, the buyer may rescind; and if there is rescission, the buyer can demand repayment of the deposit with any interest thereon. Again, these provisions are not exclusive and the buyer therefore retains all other rights and remedies that may otherwise be available (see also s 49 of the Law of Property Act 1925 discussed in 9.113). In both cases the conveyancing papers must be returned and any protective registrations cancelled. The notice is binding on both parties and not just the party originally in default (see *Quadrangle Development and Construction Co. Ltd v Jenner* [1974] 1 WLR 68, CA). Thus time is of the essence for both the seller and the buyer (see *Oakdown Ltd v Bernstein and Co.* (1984) 49 P & CR 282).

The form of notice to complete

9.98 If you need to serve a notice to complete in connection with a contract incorporating the SCs, the following is a suitable precedent. It will be addressed to the defaulting party:

> On behalf of [insert your client seller/buyer and address] we hereby give you NOTICE that with reference to the contract dated [insert the date of the agreement] and made between [insert the seller's full names and the buyer's full names] for the sale and purchase of [insert the property address or description in the contract] we place on record the fact that the sale/purchase of the property has not been completed on the date fixed in the contract for completion. We further give you NOTICE that the seller/buyer [delete the party not ready] is ready able and willing to complete. We therefore give you NOTICE pursuant to condition 6.8 of the Standard Conditions of Sale (5th edition) and require you to complete the contract in compliance with that condition.

9.99 This can be given by letter or a separate form, but either way it should be sent to the defaulting party in such a way that you will be able to prove delivery, i.e. service of the notice. (We suggest the Royal Mail's recorded delivery service with advice of receipt.) If you use a letter, you can also draw the recipient's attention to the period of notice (ten working days excluding the day of service) and what the contract provides in SC 7.4 (buyer's failure) or 7.5 (seller's failure), should completion not take place within the time limit set by the notice. If you are selling on behalf of a mortgagee, amend SC 6.8.2 to include your lender client as a party being 'ready, able and willing' to complete. The point is that a mortgagee selling under a power of sale will not be a registered proprietor and the defaulting party might assert that as a result your lender's client was not ready and able to complete.

REMEDIES

9.100 In the large majority of conveyancing transactions completion occurs without difficulty and title passes unhindered from seller to buyer. However, there will always be cases where completion does not occur or, though it does occur, a dispute over the subject property arises after completion. The following sections cover first, what remedies are available if completion has not taken place and, second, what remedies are available if a dispute and potential consequential claim arise after completion. In all cases where a claim is necessary, specialist litigation assistance should be suggested to the client as the best way of advancing it.

9.101 It is always open to a party to a conveyancing contract to try to limit any liability by the inclusion of a clause excluding liability for a breach of contract. To be valid the exclusion clause must be contained in the written agreement and must deal with the kind of breach that has arisen (see *Curtis v Chemical Cleaning and Dyeing Co.* [1951] 1 KB 805).

Exclusion clauses must be very carefully worded as the courts will construe any ambiguity within the clause against the party seeking to rely on it. Conveyancing contracts do not fall within the ambit of the Unfair Contract Terms Act 1977, save for claims arising out of misrepresentation and, as such, there is no test of reasonableness that can apply to an exclusion clause in a conveyancing contract (other than for misrepresentation). (See, however, the Unfair Terms in Consumer Contracts Regulations 1999 discussed in 11.15.)

Conveyancing practitioners need to consider whether court proceedings are probable. If they are, then the case should be passed as soon as possible to a litigation solicitor. **9.102**

Where the contract has not been completed

Where a contract has not been completed, and where a cause of action has arisen, an innocent party to that contract can consider four available and different remedies. These remedies are: **9.103**

(a) specific performance;
(b) a claim for compensation by way of damages;
(c) rescission; and
(d) a vendor and purchaser summons.

Specific performance

Specific performance is an equitable remedy by way of a discretionary order of the court that is intended to compel the defaulting party to perform and complete the contract for the sale and purchase of land. The remedy is available to both buyer and seller where the other party has committed a breach of contract and where an award of damages would be insufficient compensation for the party suffering loss. (This would be the case in most conveyancing matters bearing in mind the unique nature of the subject matter of most conveyancing contracts.) The remedy can be sought together with a claim for damages or rescission, or indeed on its own, depending on the nature of the contractual dispute and the claims arising therefrom. However, in due course, and certainly by the time of the hearing, the claimant must elect to select one remedy. If a judgment for that one remedy is granted, it will thereby preclude recourse to the other remedies. SCs 7.4 and 7.5 make it clear that an innocent party's right to apply for an order for specific performance is not precluded by the fact that a notice to complete has been served and not complied with. **9.104**

The completion date need not have passed before bringing a claim for specific performance. In *Hasham v Zenab* [1960] AC 316, the seller after signing the contract then tore it up, plainly with the intention of trying to avoid the contractual liability. Immediately after this incident and before the completion date the buyer applied for specific performance. The reverse position, that of delay, must also be considered in this context. In *Lazard Bros and Co. Ltd v Fairfield Properties Co. (Mayfair) Ltd* (1977) 121 SJ 793, the court held that simple delay without possession of the property is not in itself a bar to the remedy of specific performance. In this case a delay of two years was held not to be a bar because the defendant had not been prejudiced by the delay. It is therefore apparent that delay ('laches') will not necessarily defeat a claim for specific performance unless the defendant is going to be prejudiced as a consequence. Indeed, a buyer who actually takes occupation can rely on an equitable title and not claim specific performance for as long as ten years without losing the right to the award (see *Williams v Greatrex* [1957] 1 WLR 31, CA). **9.105**

Specific performance is an equitable remedy, and the principles of equity will prohibit an award where it would breach equitable principles. So, for example, where there is an element of fraud or illegality, or the award would cause one party exceptional hardship, the court will refrain from granting an order for specific performance. If damages would **9.106** properly compensate the innocent party for the loss sustained then the court will order damages and not specific performance. Even where an order for specific performance is obtained, damages can still subsequently be ordered if the innocent party cannot enforce the order (see *Johnson v Agnew* [1980] AC 367). An award for damages can be made pursuant to s 50 of the Supreme Court Act 1981. However, it should be remembered that specific performance can be awarded before the contractual date for completion of the transaction, i.e. where a serious breach is likely to occur steps can be taken to seek an order for specific performance even though a breach of contract has yet to arise. See *Manchester Diocesan Council for Education v Commercial and General Investments Ltd* [1970] 1 WLR 241 and *Oakacre Ltd v Clare Cleaners (Holdings) Ltd* [1982] Ch 197 for examples of how the courts will make such decisions.

Damages, including forfeiting or returning the deposit

9.107 There is a general consideration of damages in 9.127. However, it is appropriate to consider at this point the question of damages and the forfeiting of any deposit. In essence, where a claim for damages is to be advanced, credit must be given for any deposit forfeited by the seller. (This is also true for any compensation payments made pursuant to SC 7.2.) Section 49(2) of the Law of Property Act 1925 empowers the court, if it thinks it appropriate, to order the repayment of any deposit where it has refused to make an order for specific performance. It has been held that the court has an unfettered discretion to order the return of the deposit if this is the fairest way of dealing with the dispute (see *Universal Corporation v Five Ways Properties Ltd* [1979] 1 All ER 522, CA). This particular section of the enactment does not seem to allow a partial return of the deposit (see guidance on deposit returns in *Tennero Ltd v Majorarch* Ltd [2003] EGCS 154). It has more recently been decided that parties to an agreement cannot contract out of the effect of s 49(2): see *Aribisala v St James* [2007] EWHC 1694 (Ch).

Rescission

9.108 Rescission has over time gathered two meanings. First, it can mean an order of the court whereby the parties are put back into such a state as would have prevailed had the contract never existed. In effect the court will order the 'undoing' of the conveyancing contract. This may be ordered where there has been a claim arising out of some vitiating factor such as fraud, mistake, or misrepresentation. This form of rescission is dealt with in 9.117. Second, rescission can mean the result of the innocent party accepting the repudiation of the agreement as a consequence of the defaulting party's breach of a major term in the agreement. Rescission can arise by a term in the conveyancing contract, or by agreement, or by an order of the court.

9.109 **Rescission and the SCs**   The SCs refer to rescission in two different circumstances:

(a) **SC 7.1**   This condition allows rescission for misrepresentation. SC 7 allows rescission where any statement or plan in the contract or the negotiations leading to it is or was misleading or inaccurate as a consequence of an error or omission. However, SC 7.1.1(b) limits this provision by allowing rescission only where there is an element of fraud or recklessness, or where, if the innocent party took the property, it would, prejudicially, be substantially different from that which the innocent party expected as a result of the error or omission. This is the one area of conveyancing contracts where an exclusion clause is subject to the reasonableness test within s 11 of the Unfair Contract Terms Act 1977.

(b) **SC 8.3**   Where the subject property is leasehold, and where the lease terms require the landlord's consent or licence to a change of tenant, if that licence to assign is not forthcoming, either party can seek rescission.

It is always open to the parties to a contract to agree to rescind the contract. This is rescission **9.110** by agreement, i.e. the parties mutually agree to put aside the agreement and to undo its effect.

In the past the courts have been reluctant to allow a claimant to seek rescission and, in **9.111** the alternative, damages. However, it would seem that the modern position is to allow this alternate claim (see *Johnson v Agnew* [1980] AC 367). It seems that where the contract is rescinded as a result of the other side's breach, rescission and damages will be allowed. If rescission is sought as a consequence of a vitiating element there can be no claim for damages. (This is not so for misrepresentation, when s 2(1) of the Misrepresentation Act 1967 permits the innocent party to claim damages and rescission.)

To summarize, if there is misrepresentation or mistake, rescission can arise on the funda- **9.112** mental basis of the undoing of the contract. If there is a defective title, failure to complete or misdescription, rescission can arise for the breach of contract. Lastly, rescission can also arise under the terms of the contract. If this is the case, then the contract terms govern when it is exercisable, and the ramifications thereof.

Vendor and purchaser summons

Section 49(1) of the Law of Property Act 1925 provides that '[a] vendor or purchaser of **9.113** any interest in land . . . may apply in a summary way to the court, in respect of any requisitions or objections, or any claim for compensation, or any other question arising out of or connected with the contract', and if such an application is made, the court can 'make such order upon the application as to the court may appear just'. This procedure allows either party to a conveyancing contract to apply to court for its deliberation on a point of dispute without having to apply for specific performance. An example of what could give rise to a summons of this kind is a reference to the court to ascertain if the seller has shown good title and thus complied with the terms in the contract to that effect. If the court did decide that good title had not been shown, the court could order the return of the deposit with interest and costs. Other examples of the kind of dispute that can be referred to the court are whether or not a requisition is valid and whether or not there has been a valid notice to complete. However, the procedure cannot be used to test the validity, or existence, of a contract.

After completion

Completion of a conveyancing contract narrows down the available remedies. In the main **9.114** it is the buyer who will commence proceedings as the seller will have the sale proceeds. If, unusually, the doctrine of merger effectively puts paid to the terms of the contract (see the discussion of merger at the beginning of this chapter), the aggrieved buyer can only sue for damages on the covenants for title through title guarantee, implied in the purchase deed (see 9.115). Other post-completion remedies are considered subsequently.

Covenants for title—title guarantee

The doctrine of merger stipulates that, subject to any contractual terms to the contrary, on **9.115** completion the contract terms merge with the purchase deed and are thereby extinguished. (However, SC 7.3 states that completion does not cancel liability to perform any outstanding obligation under the contract.) As a consequence, after completion the primary remedy is a claim for breach of title guarantee. Title guarantee is governed by the Law of Property (Miscellaneous Provisions) Act 1994.

The title guarantee regime contemplates three possibilities: full title guarantee, limited title **9.116** guarantee, or no guarantee at all. In the last situation the contract will offer no form of guarantee whatsoever, to the intent that there will be no post-completion remedy arising out of the guarantee available to an innocent party in the event of a dispute arising after completion. The other two possibilities are full and limited guarantee, and are in effect statutory guarantees that will be implied in a purchase deed by the use of the phrases 'with full guarantee' or 'with limited guarantee'. SC 4.6.2 stipulates that the seller is to transfer the property with full title guarantee, but subject to SC 4.6.3 (this refers to SC 3.1.2 and the matters affecting the property, i.e. incumbrances).

9.117   With title guarantee the contract need not refer to the capacity of the seller but only to the level of guarantee on offer. There is nothing in the Act that prohibits the extent or the level of guarantee being modified further by the terms of the contract.

9.118   **Covenants and title guarantee**   If the seller sells with full title guarantee, the seller covenants that:

(a) the seller has the right to sell the property;

(b) the seller will at the seller's cost do all things that can be reasonably done to give to the buyer the title the seller purports to give;

(c) if the nature of the title to the subject property is not clear, it is freehold;

(d) if the property is registered, the buyer will receive at least the class of title that prevailed before the transfer;

(e) the seller will provide reasonable assistance to enable the recipient to be registered as proprietor of the registered land;

(f) if the interest is registered, the disposition is of the whole interest;

(g) where the interest passing is leasehold, the disposition is of the whole of the unexpired portion of the term of years created by the lease, the lease still subsists and there is no subsisting breach that could give rise to forfeiture; and

(h) the person making the disposition disposes of it free from all charges and incumbrances and from all other rights exercisable by third parties other than those that the person does not and could not reasonably be expected to know about. (Remember that the contract will include specific reference to incumbrances to which the sale is expressly subject.)

9.119   If the seller sells with limited title guarantee, the seller covenants that all the covenants set out above will be complied with save the last covenant, which is replaced by the following:

> the person making the disposition has not since the last disposition for value subjected the property to charges or incumbrances which still exist, or granted third-party rights which still exist.

9.120   Title guarantees are covenants that run with the land and can therefore be enforced by successors in title. As a remedy, a breach of these implied covenants is equivalent to a claim for a breach of contract with all the attaching rights. Because completion has taken place it is probable that the only likely result would be an order for damages. A practitioner will normally advise the client to offer a full title guarantee. However, a limited title guarantee should be suggested for a sale by a PR or trustee. No doubt sellers of commercial property will seek to sell with limited title guarantee, but there is really no reason why the buyer should accept this, on the assumption that there is no difficulty with the subject title.

Other post-completion remedies

9.121   These remedies cover, *inter alia*, fraud, innocent misrepresentation, and mistake, as well as rectification. They cover situations where one or more of these factors apply and the transaction could as a consequence be set aside. (This has become known as rescission, in respect of which there will be a complete undoing of the conveyancing agreement, provided there is an entitlement to rescind.)

Misrepresentation   A misrepresentation is an untrue factual statement made by one **9.122** party and relied on by the other, which induces the other party to enter into the contract and, as a consequence, suffer loss. A misrepresentation can be deliberately dishonest and is then termed a fraudulent misrepresentation. Of a lesser degree, the misrepresentation can be simply careless and is then termed a negligent misrepresentation. Alternatively, and of a lesser degree again, the misrepresentation may be made innocently and be a genuine mistake, whereupon it will be termed an innocent misrepresentation. If there is a suggested fraud (see *Derry v Peek* (1889) 14 App Cas 337 for a test of what will amount to fraud), the aggrieved party may sue for damages (by way of the tort of deceit) and rescind the contract. The problem here is that the party alleging fraud must prove it. This is likely to be difficult and costly. Consequently, claims are more usual at the lesser degree of negligent misrepresentation. In this case, the innocent party may take action pursuant to s 2 of the Misrepresentation Act 1967 for either damages or rescission of the contract. If the misrepresentation was innocent the only remedy available is rescission.

Misdescription   A misdescription is an error in the property particulars of the contract. A **9.123** patent example would be to state incorrectly the tenure as freehold when it is in fact leasehold, or *vice versa*. If the misdescription is sufficiently significant it will entitle the innocent party to seek rescission and damages. A significant misdescription is one that would lead to the innocent party being deprived of what he thought he was going to receive under the terms of the contract (see *Watson v Burton* [1957] 1 WLR 19). Most such cases give rise to a claim under the Misrepresentation Act 1967.

Non-disclosure   Non-disclosure can also arise where the seller has not complied with an **9.124** obligation to disclose matters in the contract or in documents referred to in the contract. Again, if the non-disclosure is sufficiently significant to lead to the innocent party being deprived of what he thought he was going to receive under the terms of the contract then that party may seek to rescind the contract.

Rectification   Rectification can arise in different ways. Both the contract and purchase **9.125** deed can be the subject of rectification. If the contract is involved, then an application to the court can be made. If rectification is ordered to correct either an omission or an incorrectly recorded contract term, then the court has the discretion to set the date on which the contract is effective. If the purchase deed is involved, again an application to the court can be made to ensure that all the terms in the contract, and which should be in the purchase deed, are incorporated in it. Section 65 and Schedule 4 to the Land Registration Act 2002 set out the grounds on which an application to correct an entry within a registered title can be made. Rather than rectification, the 2002 Act refers to 'alteration' of the registers. Under the Act, rectification is just one kind of alteration. (It is an alteration involving the correction of a mistake which prejudicially affects the title of a registered owner (Schedule 4, para 1).) A right of indemnity will flow from rectification. The order for rectification is discretionary, and the court will not make an order if it would be unjust to the registered proprietor to do so. Section 103 and Schedule 8 permit an indemnity to be claimed from the Chief Land Registrar, *inter alia*, by a person who has suffered loss as a result of any rectification of the register. This indemnity is not available to a claimant who is deemed to have caused or contributed to the loss by fraud or a lack of proper care. Since changes to the Land Registry indemnity rules made with effect from 27 April 1997, indemnity payments will be made whether or not there has been actual rectification.

9.126 The First-tier Tribunal (Property Chamber; Land Registration), formerly the Adjudicator to HM Land Registry, has the power (on direct application to the Tribunal) to rectify or set aside a conveyancing document (Land Registration Act 2002, s 108(2)). This is an important function as previously the Registrar could only refer such matters to the High Court, which inevitably resulted in delay and further costs. This power applies only in relation to a document which does any one of the following:

(i) effects a qualifying disposition of a registered estate or charge where that disposition is either a registrable disposition or one which creates an interest which may be protected by a notice, for example a transfer, grant of a lease, or a deed creating a restrictive covenant; or

(ii) is a contract to do the above; or

(iii) effects a transfer of an interest which is the subject of a notice in the register, for example a conveyance of a *profit à prendre* that was noted on the register but not registered with its own title, and there was an error in that conveyance.

Damages

9.127 A claimant involved in a claim arising from an uncompleted or completed conveyancing contract may be entitled to damages. The general common law rules on damages will apply to a conveyancing contract claim in just the same way as for all other contracts (see *Hadley v Baxendale* (1854) 9 Ex 341 for remoteness of damages). The party entitled to claim will be able to seek to recover losses arising naturally from the breach, or losses that can reasonably be supposed to have been contemplated by both parties to the agreement, as the probable result of the breach of contract.

9.128 Substantial damages can be claimed, especially where the contract has not been completed. In *Beard v Porter* [1948] 1 KB 321, the transaction was not completed because the seller could not comply with the contract and give vacant possession to the buyer. As a consequence substantial damages were awarded to the purchaser based on the difference between the purchase price and the value of the property still subject to the tenancy, as well as other consequential costs. Similarly, in *Cottrill v Steyning and Littlehampton Building Society* [1966] 1 WLR 753 a seller knew that the buyer was intending to develop the subject property. The seller failed to complete. The substantial damages awarded were based on the potential profit the buyer would have made had the transaction been completed properly. Wasted expenses can also be claimed, including wasted legal fees and proper surveying fees. Other expenses claims are likely to fail, for example the cost of carpets and curtains purchased before the property purchase has actually taken place. The courts take the view that these are expenses a prudent buyer should not incur until completion has taken place.

9.129 The SCs limit any potential claim for damages in cases of misrepresentation. SC 7.1.1 states that when there is a material difference between the description or value of the subject property as represented and as it is, the injured party is entitled to damages. This effectively limits any claim for damages for misrepresentation to this difference.

9.130 Damages will be assessed as at the date of the breach (see *Johnson v Agnew* [1980] AC 367), but if that principle is likely to cause injustice, the court will assess damages at another date (see *Forster v Silvermere Golf and Equestrian Centre Ltd* (1981) 42 P & CR 255). However, damages are not a mechanism by which the claimant can be put into a better position than that which would have prevailed had the transaction been completed. In all cases there is a duty to mitigate the loss, i.e. the claimant must take all reasonable steps to reduce or even avoid the loss (*Raineri v Miles* [1981] AC 1050 at 1064). This duty applies to either a buyer or a seller seeking damages. For example, if a buyer is forced to store furniture as a result of a breach of contract by the seller, the storage charges should be at a reasonable level, i.e. not the most expensive, as the buyer will be under a duty to keep these costs down.

Liens

A seller will be entitled to claim a lien (i.e. a right to retain possession of another's property pending discharge of a debt) over the subject property in relation to any unpaid element of the purchase price. The lien is in effect an equitable charge enforceable by the court by way of an order for the sale of the property or for the setting aside of the contract. The lien should always be protected by a caution or notice on the title in registered land and as a C(iii) registration for unregistered land. **9.131**

A buyer is entitled to claim a lien if the deposit is returnable and was paid over originally to the seller's practitioner as agent for the seller. The lien claimed will be in respect of the deposit monies. The lien should be protected by registration. SC 6.5.1 prohibits any entitlement on the seller's part to a lien over the title deeds after completion and after the buyer has tendered all the money due to be paid over at completion. If the seller wants to have this entitlement available the contract terms must be varied to that effect to enable enforcement of other payments or the performance of other contractual obligations. **9.132**

KEY POINTS SUMMARY

DELAYS AND REMEDIES

- If the other party is late for completion, remember that under the SCs either party is entitled to claim compensation for delay at the contract rate of interest on a daily basis, until completion takes place. **9.133**

- If you decide to serve a notice to complete, always do so in a way that enables you to prove service (personal delivery, recorded delivery with advice of receipt, etc.), and remember the period of notice *excludes* the day on which the notice is given.

- Remember that once issued a notice to complete cannot be withdrawn, although the time period set out in the notice can, by mutual agreement, be extended provided both parties acknowledge that time remains of the essence.

- Specific performance can be claimed along with damages and rescission, but the claimant must at the eventual hearing select one remedy in respect of which judgment is to be sought.

- Does the contract include any form of exclusion clause that might limit liability? If it does, is it in any way ambiguous? If it is, remember ambiguity is construed against the person seeking to rely on the exclusion clause.

PRACTICAL CHECKLISTS

POST-COMPLETION

Acting for the seller

- If completion is by post, inform all parties by phone of completion, i.e. the seller, the practitioner acting for the buyer and, if any, the selling agents, so that the keys for the subject property can be released. **9.134**

- Commit to the post on the day of completion the deeds and documents of title with the executed and dated purchase deed, and keep a dated file copy of the purchase deed.

- If the subject property is subject to a mortgage, send, on the day of completion, sufficient redemption monies to the lender along with Form DS1 for registered land and the mortgage deed for receipting in unregistered land.

- If the mortgage is an endowment one, send to the lender all the mortgages of life policies for release, and also give notice of reassignment to the life companies.

- When the receipted documents are returned to you from the lenders, remember to check the details; and if all is well send Form DS1 or vacated mortgage to the buyer's practitioner with a request that you be released from your undertaking given at completion.

- On receipt of the released mortgage of life policy and receipted notice or reassignment from the life office, send to the client the original policy and all released mortgages of life policies and notices as these will be required by the client should a policy claim arise.

- Pay to the client the net proceeds of sale and supply full accounts, including a note of your own charges, if you have not already done so; or alternatively apply the net proceeds towards an allied purchase if these are your instructions.

- Make sure you have transferred monies to your office account for all costs and prepaid disbursements.

- If you have instructions to do so, pay the estate agents their commission charges and request a receipted account from them.

- Remind the client to cancel all standing orders to the lender, any buildings insurance, and payments to the local authority in the nature of council tax.

- If there is a sale of part and the deeds are in your possession, ensure that you have instructions about their custody and, if they are to remain with you, place them all within a fireproof safe.

Acting for the buyer

- Advise the buyer, and the buyer's lender, that you have effected completion in accordance with the contract terms.

- Ensure that the seller's practitioner has sent, or will have sent later on the day of completion, all the deeds and documents to you in the post.

- On receipt of the purchase deed deal with the stamping requirements, being SDLT for purchases currently exceeding £125,000 (or £150,000, depending on where the property is). Ensure the SDLT is paid within 30 days of completion to avoid any penalty fee for late payment.

- From 6 April 2011 a 5 per cent rate of SDLT applies on the purchase of residential property for more than £1 million. From 22 March 2012 a 7 per cent rate of SDLT applies on the purchase of residential property for more than £2 million. The Government introduced a 15 per cent rate of SDLT to be applied to residential properties over £2 million purchased by non-natural persons, such as companies. This new rate took effect on 21 March 2012.

- Since 1 April 2016 there has been a 3 per cent SDLT surcharge when an additional residential property is bought by someone who already owns a home, i.e. second homes and 'buy-to-let' properties.

- Consider if your client is entitled to claim the SDLT first-time buyer relief. If the price of the subject property exceeds £500,000 then no relief is available.

- If the title is unregistered, submit the deeds for first registration within two months of completion; and if the title is registered, submit the dealing for registration within your search priority period.

- Make sure you use the correct form for your Land Registry application and include certified copy mortgages. Also include a certified copy transfer where it is a transfer of part imposing new restrictive covenants and remember to include the appropriate Land Registry fee. Include SDLT5.

- Be prepared to comply with Land Registry identity verification requirements.

- Consider using the e-DRS online application service.

- If there is a mortgage created by a limited company, make sure the mortgage is registered at Companies House within 21 days of the completion date, and remember this is an unequivocal deadline incapable of extension without recourse to the court.

- Give notice of assignment to life offices of any life policies forming part of the security for the lender.

- If the subject property is leasehold and if the lease terms require it, give notice of assignment or transfer to the lessor's practitioner, pay any requisite fee, and request a receipted copy of the notice to be placed with the deeds.

- If the subject property is subject to a tenancy, give notice to the tenant of the change of ownership and indicate to whom all future rent should be paid.

- When the Title Information Document is received back from the Registry, check the new entries carefully and refer it to the Registry if there are any errors in need of correction.

- Send all relevant deeds and documents (e.g. a registered lease) to the lender, if the lender requires them.

- Make sure you have transferred monies to your office account for all costs and prepaid disbursements.

- If the deeds are in your possession (i.e. there is no mortgage on the title), ensure you have instructions about their custody and, if they are to remain with you, place them all in a fire-proof safe.

DELAYS AND REMEDIES

- Has the time for completion set out in the contract elapsed?   **9.135**

- If it has, does the client want you to serve a notice to complete, i.e. have you taken instructions approving this step?

- If you have instructions, have you served a notice using the appropriate wording and in such a way as to enable you to prove service of the notice?

- Has the period set out in the notice expired; and if so does the client want to rescind the agreement, sell the property elsewhere, and sue for damages?

- Is there some other form of breach of contract? If so, have you obtained a full history of the conveyancing transaction with all supporting papers; and what remedy does the innocent party want?

- Are you able to quantify the client's loss arising from the breach? If so, how much is that loss?

- Is it economic sense to commence proceedings bearing in mind the costs that will be incurred?

- Apart from the other party to the contract might there be a claim elsewhere, for example against a conveyancing practitioner or surveyor in negligence?

10

LEASEHOLDS AND COMMONHOLD

In this chapter we will consider leases and their contents and how statute regulates their existence. We also consider briefly commonhold developments.

A AN INTRODUCTION TO LEASEHOLDS

GENERAL INTRODUCTION

10.01 A lease is an agreement, usually by way of a deed, by which an estate in land or property is created, but only for a finite term. This seems simple enough, but if there is one area in conveyancing that really demonstrates the client's need for a competent practitioner then this must be it. The reason for this is simply that leasehold conveyancing is full of pitfalls and problems for the unwary or ill-informed buyer. The explanation for this apparent complexity is contained in the nature and format of the lease document itself. Over time leases have become increasingly longer, with scores of covenants, conditions, provisos, and rights included to try to cover every possible eventuality. Moreover, different types of leases with diverse contents are required to deal with different types of property. No one lease is exactly the same as another. It is this uniqueness that demands that, if you act for a potential buyer or lessee, each lease must be closely scrutinized and, if necessary, amended. If you act for the seller/potential lessor, then each lease must be carefully drafted. There is some crossover between the contents of this chapter and Chapter 12 because much of commercial conveyancing focuses upon leases. When this occurs you will see reference made to where the relevant information can be found elsewhere. Leases are a very important part of a conveyancer's work. Flats now make up one-quarter of all housing in the UK. Research by the Royal Mail has shown that London alone has 1.8 million flats (see *The i* newspaper, 13 January 2017).

One current problem relates to the normally small ground rent paid on long residential **10.02** leases. Some recently granted leases have included rent increase provisions that meant in some cases rents doubled every ten years. (So, e.g., a commencing rent would be at £250 per annum but after just 50 years could be £4,000.) This kind of high rent and the resultant high cost of buying in the freehold (enfranchisement, see 10.107) has led the Government to announce in December 2017 its intention to stop houses being newly sold on long leases. They intend to introduce legislation before the end of the current parliament. There is also the possibility of reducing onerous ground rents to zero. The details of the proposals are not currently known.

Residential and commercial leases

In this chapter we will, in the main, be concerned with residential leases. We deal with com- **10.03** mercial leases and their specific requirements in Chapter 12. Students commonly get confused about the differences in the way residential and commercial leases are dealt with by conveyancing law and practice. The main reason for these differences is that the duration of a residential lease when granted will be much longer than for a commercial lease. As a result the lease contents will differ dramatically because clauses in a long lease will diverge from those in a short lease. Furthermore, lenders will require clauses in residential leases that would be unlikely to appear in commercial leases and *vice versa*. The best example is a provision permitting the lessor to forfeit the lease on bankruptcy. This is always required by a lessor of commercial property but would never appear in a residential lease (see 10.46). These differences will be highlighted in both this chapter dealing with residential concerns and in Chapter 12, when the commercial perspective will be highlighted. Many clauses will appear in both types of lease and some details are common to both.

Draft lease approval

When a new lease is proposed, the lessor's practitioner will draft a lease and send the draft for **10.04** approval to the practitioner acting for the lessee. The draft will then be amended in red (ink) on behalf of the lessee, re-amended in green (ink) on behalf of the lessor and so on, with the draft lease passing between the two sides. The 'travelling draft' will then pass back and forth until it reaches a form that is agreed between the parties. Traditionally this was achieved using a printed 'travelling draft'. The contemporary methodology uses an electronic file version incorporating changes highlighted in colours using a 'track changes' facility in common word-processing packages. This is then sent between the parties as an attachment to e-mails.

WHAT YOU MIGHT EXPECT IN A LEASE

Land Registry prescribed clauses leases

Land Registry has issued rules requiring certain lease contents to be in a particular position **10.05** in registrable leases (new leases with a term of more than seven years). As a result they are called prescribed clauses leases. These provisions were contained in the Land Registration (Amendment) (No 2) Rules 2005 (SI 2005/1982). The compulsory requirements have been limited to a set number of 'prescribed clauses' with a requirement that these particular clauses must appear at the start of the lease. New Rule 58A states that '. . . a prescribed clauses lease must begin with the required wording or that wording must appear immediately after any front sheet'. A prescribed clauses lease will cover any lease the term of which triggers compulsory registration and which is granted on or after 19 June 2006. The information that must appear at the lease commencement includes:

- the lessor's title number;
- the parties to the lease;
- a full description of the property being leased;
- prescribed statements (those required by statute, e.g. involving a charity or pursuant to the Leasehold Reform and Housing and Urban Development Act 1993);
- the term for which the property is leased;
- any premium;
- prohibitions or restrictions on disposing of the lease;
- rights of acquisition such as a contractual right for the tenant to renew the lease (an option to renew); and
- easements.

10.06   This information would appear to be straightforward and should not prove a major concern to practitioners involved in the drafting of commercial leases. It would seem sensible to structure all leases, even those that will not be subject to compulsory registration, so as to place this information at the front. Please see Appendix 14 for a guide to completing prescribed clauses. This is from Land Registry Guidance (see LR Practice Guide 64— **https://www.gov.uk/government/publications/prescribed-clauses-leases**).

10.07   A residential lease will have its unique features. The date, parties, consideration, and parcels (the property description) will all apply specifically to the subject property. Similarly, the habendum (the term of the lease and the start date of that term), as well as the reddendum (the amount of the rent and the frequency of payment with the payment dates), will also specifically relate to the property. However, there will be some elements that should appear in most (if not all) such leases. These are further considered below from two perspectives.

Acting for a lessor

10.08   A lessor will require the lease to include clauses and/or covenants that adequately protect the reversionary interest. To that end the lessor will include a long list of obligations, of covenants requiring the lessee to do and not to do various things. Above all else, the lease must contain the most important protection for the lessor, which is a right of re-entry. (The lessor's right to end a lease is one of the legal interests stipulated by s 1 of the Law of Property Act 1925, i.e. 'Rights of entry exercisable over or in respect of a legal term of years absolute . . .'.) If the lessee should fail to pay the rent, the lease must contain a right for the lessor to re-enter the subject property to forfeit the lease. This right should be extended beyond the failure to pay rent to a breach of any of the lease covenants. Practitioners should note that without an express right of re-entry a lessor can merely sue for a breach of covenant. The right of re-entry can also be extended to enable the provision to be operative should the lessee become bankrupt or make an arrangement with creditors. This is a problem for lenders; see 10.46.

Acting for a lessee

10.09   A lessee will also require essential clauses or covenants, but these are in many cases entirely opposite to those favoured by the lessor. A lessee will seek to limit the number and extent of the lease covenants. A prudent lessee will also seek covenants from the lessor to perform the obligations resting with the lessor, for example to keep the main structure of the property of which the subject property forms part insured and in good repair. These competing interests between the two parties to the lease require careful representation by practitioners.

Covenant enforcement by lessor

A lessee will also want to see an arrangement in a lease whereby the lessor will, on explicit **10.10** prerequisite terms, enforce covenants in another lessee's lease in the same building. This requirement arises from the limitations of privity of contract and estate. For example, one lessee living next door to another may play loud music late at night despite a covenant in the lease prohibiting such behaviour. The lease agreement is between the lessor and lessee. The next-door lessee has no contractual relationship with the other lessee. The only person who can enforce any of the lease covenants is the lessor. It is this relationship, or the lack of it, that gives rise to the enforcement requirement. For leases granted on or after 11 May 2000, the position can be changed by the effects of the Contracts (Rights of Third Parties) Act 1999. The Act enables direct enforcement of lease covenants between lessees. However, the Act is capable of express exclusion and in many business leases is excluded. A typical lessor's enforcement covenant of the kind indicated would read:

> If so requested by the lessee, to enforce the covenants on the part of the lessee entered into by any of the other lessees of any other part of the building of which the demised premises forms part PROVIDED ALWAYS that the lessee making this request shall do so in writing, and shall at the same time indemnify the Lessor against all costs claims and expenses in respect of such enforcement, and the lessee will further provide such security for these costs claims and expenses as the Lessor may reasonably require.

You will no doubt appreciate that the lessee may wish to avoid the part of the covenant **10.11** requiring an indemnity, while the lessor will insist on it. Another such clause is a covenant by the lessor to observe and perform the lessee's covenants in respect of any vacant flats in the block in which the subject property is located. The lessee will want this clause to ensure that the lessee's covenants apply to all flats in the block, whether they are occupied or not. The lessor will resist the obligation as being one that could potentially put the lessor to some expense.

These are typical examples of the conflicting interests that drive the drafting and selling **10.12** of leases. In all cases the following covenants, *inter alia*, will normally represent the battleground between lessor and lessee.

Typical lease covenants and other provisions

As you might expect, most of the onerous covenants in a lease are for the lessee to perform, **10.13** such as to pay the rent, keep the property in good and substantial repair or condition, and pay for the insurance of the property and any maintenance charges. There are both positive and negative covenants in a lease. An example of a positive requirement already mentioned is to pay all rents. Examples of negative covenants include not to alter the property in any way, not to apply for a planning consent that directly affects the property, and not to use the property other than as described in the lease. The following are typical covenants found in most residential leases and which will form the subject of negotiations between both parties to the intended lease.

To pay rent and other outgoings, including service charges

A covenant to pay rent is fundamental and should appear in all leases that include a rental **10.14** obligation. The lessee will want to introduce another clause that suspends the payment of rent if the property is destroyed or damaged by an insured risk. The lessor should agree this provided the lessor can control the insurance of the whole property and thus include loss of rent as an insurable risk. This leads on to the consideration of the payment of other outgoings such as insurance (see 10.15). This can be by way of an additional rent and the lease can be drafted to give effect to this. Similarly, any service charge payable can be made a rent in the same way. (This benefits the lessor because if there are arrears these can be recovered as a rent, rather than as a result of a breach of covenant. As a consequence, a notice pursuant to s 146 of the Law of Property Act 1925 can be avoided. However, statute may limit this power, depending on the nature of the property.) The lease should stipulate that the rents are payable in advance, failing which they will be payable in arrears. If the lease includes a rent review provision allowing the rent to be increased (and/or decreased) at regular intervals, there should also be a specific covenant requiring the lessee to enter into review procedures and to pay the rent at the reviewed level. Rent reviews are rare in residential leases, which tend to include fixed increases at regular intervals. The lease will also require the lessee to pay all outgoings applicable to the subject property such as council tax and water rates.

Insurance covenants

10.15 Insurance can be dealt with in one of two ways. First, the lessee can be made to covenant to insure or, second, the lessor can agree to insure. Where the lease is of a whole house or of one of two maisonettes, then it would be sensible to expect the lessee to insure. However, where there is a building in multiple occupation, the converse should apply so as to ensure that there is an appropriate level of cover rather than the patchwork of different policies that would occur if all the lessees insured separately. In this situation the lessor should arrange insurance so that the whole of the building can be covered by one policy, with all the lessees obliged by way of a lease covenant to pay, perhaps as a rent, a proportion of the annual premium. Where the lessor insures, a prudent lessee will want to see the lease include a covenant requiring the lessor to expend any monies claimed and received from the insurance company on reinstating the damaged or destroyed property. This is particularly so where reinstatement will be necessary to all parts of the building to give support to the subject property itself. Some lessees might at this point require the lessor to make up any deficiency in the insurance proceeds from the lessor's own resources. Clearly the lessor will resist such an onerous obligation. The point will have to be negotiated. If the lessor does accept the point, it is an incentive to over-insure the premises, rather than under-insure. A typical lease insurance provision would read:

> to insure and keep insured the building of which the demised premises forms part against loss or damage by the Insured Risks [with the Insured Risks defined elsewhere in the lease, i.e. fire, storm, tempest, flood etc.] and such other risks as the lessor's surveyor for the time being considers necessary in the full cost of reinstatement together with architects' surveyors' and other fees payable together with the costs of site clearance and the securing of the damaged property and making good any shortfall out of the lessor's own monies.

10.16 The lessee will also want a covenant requiring the lessor to supply a copy of the policy on request, as well as details of the existing cover by way of a copy of the current policy cover schedule and the current premium receipt.

10.17 An insurance provision should require either the lessor or the lessee, depending on who is covenanting to insure, to arrange insurance cover in the full reinstatement value. The cover should also include all architects' and surveyors' fees incurred in connection with the rebuilding or reinstatement of the property. This will ensure that the property is not under-insured. Damage caused by the action of terrorists is no longer covered in normal buildings policies and separate cover for damage occasioned in this way must be arranged, in particular for property located near potential targets, for example in the main cities near major stations, etc. This needs to be covered in the insurance covenant.

To keep the property in good repair

10.18 This is an area considered in detail at 12.44–12.52. For residential properties, as was the case for insurance, where the lease is of a whole house or of one of two maisonettes, it would be sensible to expect the lessee to keep the house or maisonette fully repaired. However, where there is a building in multiple occupation, the converse should apply. This is to ensure that there is an appropriate level of consistent repair instead of a patchwork of different levels of repair that would occur if all the lessees dealt with repairs separately.

Who repairs what part of a property as between the lessor and the lessee is considered at **10.19** 12.46.

The standard of repair   The standard of repair required is considered in depth at 12.48.   **10.20**

To ensure compliance with repairing obligations modern leases will always include a cov- **10.21** enant allowing the lessor to enter the demised premises, on prior written notice, to view the state of repair. If the repairing covenant is in breach, the lessor will then be able to serve a notice on the lessee calling for work to be carried out to ensure the proper repair of the subject property. Moreover, the lessor, in the case of default by the lessee, will have the benefit of a further covenant enabling the lessor to enter the subject property to carry out the necessary repairs and to charge the lessee for the cost of the work required (see *Jervis v Harris* [1996] 1 All ER 303, CA).

User

It is possible for the lease to include a covenant imposing an absolute restriction on the les- **10.22** see against changing the use from any user precisely stated in the lease. In the case of a residential lease it is desirable that the user clause be such that there can be only one permitted use that cannot be changed. The reason for this is that this form of extremely restrictive covenant will guarantee conformity of use amongst all the lessees and ensure that there is no breach of planning law. Such a clause could read:

> not to use the demised property other than a residential house/flat/maisonette and for no other purpose whatsoever.

Because the covenant is absolute the lessor cannot be compelled to allow a change of use. **10.23** If a change is agreed in negotiations, it can be effected by a deed of variation to the terms of the original lease.

Qualified covenants   The covenant can be qualified requiring the lessor's consent before **10.24** the use can be changed, and this is more commonly seen in commercial leases; for details see 12.54. There is no statutory provision that implies that the lessor's consent cannot be unreasonably withheld, as is the case with alienation covenants (see 10.26). Section 19(3) of the Landlord and Tenant Act 1927 provides that if a consent for a change of use is required, then the lessor is not allowed to demand a premium or extra rent for giving that consent. The lessor can require costs to be paid by the applicant, including all legal fees. A premium or extra rent can be demanded if alterations to the structure of the property are also proposed.

Some residential lease user clauses stipulate that the property should be in the occupa- **10.25** tion of one family only. This should be resisted by the lessee as unnecessarily limiting and very much out of touch with modern lifestyles. A better alternative would be to include a covenant on the lessee not to permit the use of the property so as to overcrowd the subject premises, i.e. not to allow the property to be occupied beyond a stated maximum number.

Alienation

In this context, the term 'alienation' covers covenants against assignments, underlettings, **10.26** mortgages, and other material dealings with the legal estate. There is no such restriction against alienation unless there is express provision to that effect in the lease. Many leases include a covenant whereby the lessee cannot assign the lease without the prior written consent of the lessor, such consent not to be unreasonably withheld. Some leases extend this provision to include sub-lettings as well as assignments. If the lease states that the lessor's consent is required but does not refer to reasonableness, then statute adds this qualification (Landlord and Tenant Act 1927, s 19(1)(a)). The Landlord and Tenant Act 1988 requires the lessor to deal with applications for consent to an assignment within a reasonable time of the making of the application. Should the lessor fail to do so the lessee can, if the lessee has suffered loss as a consequence of the lessor's delay, sue the lessor for damages for breach of statutory duty.

10.27 The alienation covenant is of great concern for business leases and will therefore be considered in greater detail in Chapter 12. It is now considered inappropriate to fetter a lessee's right to deal freely with a long leasehold legal estate. The lessee of such an estate should be able to deal with it unchecked, just as any absolute owner would in relation to a fee simple. Therefore the question for a practitioner should be: is there any restriction against alienation; and if so, should there be such a provision in the lease of the subject property? Frankly the answer is in the negative where the lease is a long lease of residential property. However, there can be exceptions. For example, the lease may require an incoming lessee, before being registered with the lessor as the new leaseholder, to enter into a direct covenant with the lessor to observe all the terms and especially the covenants in the lease. (The lessor will require this because there is no privity of estate after the assignee sells on.) The same arrangement could be predicated upon the incoming lessee applying for licence to assign. The licence would then incorporate an observance covenant in the same format. A typical clause of this kind would read:

> . . . not to assign transfer underlet or part with or share possession of the demised premises or any part thereof without the written consent of the Lessor PROVIDED ALWAYS that it shall be lawful for the Lessor to withhold such consent unless before the assignment transfer or under-lease is completed the lessee procures the execution of and delivers to the lessor a deed to be prepared by the Lessor's legal practitioner at the full cost of the lessee and which contains a covenant by the proposed assignee transferee or sub-lessee to perform and observe during the term assigned transferred or granted the covenants by the lessee and the conditions contained in this lease in the same manner as if such covenants and conditions were repeated in full in that deed.

10.28 Modern leases will include a covenant requiring the lessee to give notice to the lessor or the lessor's solicitor of all assignments, sub-lettings, or other material dealings with the legal estate. This is perfectly reasonable in that it will enable the lessor to be aware of exactly who is entitled to the leasehold estate and who should be in occupation of the subject property. A fee will usually be payable for registering the notice with the lessor's solicitor.

Alterations, additions, and/or improvements

10.29 Clearly the reversioner will want to ensure that unauthorized alterations do not take place. Furthermore, the reversioner will want to be sure that the alterations that do take place are such that the integrity of the structure will not be adversely affected. This will also be the case for additions and improvements. Lessees of long residential leases will argue that they should be free to do what they like with their property. Certainly this would seem to be a tenable argument where the lease is of a house. However, it is less tenable where the lease is of a flat or maisonette. Clearly in these circumstances, alterations, additions, and improvements could very well affect adjacent or adjoining property, and the lessor may therefore feel that there should be controls over what may be done by the lessee in the way of alterations.

10.30 A covenant dealing with alterations can include an absolute bar such as 'not to make or allow to be made any alterations additions or improvements to the demised premises'. If this is the prevailing covenant, the lessee cannot carry out any work whatsoever. This could be seen to be unfair to a long leaseholder, and consequently such clauses are sometimes qualified to allow the lessee to carry out non-structural alterations within the demised premises that do not cut or maim any load-bearing walls or timbers.

An absolute bar on alterations or additions must be considered unacceptable in a long **10.31** lease. If one appears in a draft, the lease should be amended to allow alterations with the lessor's written consent. To the extent that proposed alterations amount to improvements, s 19(2) of the Landlord and Tenant Act 1927 will then apply so that consent cannot be unreasonably withheld, and the lessor cannot demand any payment beyond his reasonable legal and other expenses incurred in granting consent (see *Woolworth & Co. Ltd v Lambert* [1937] Ch 37). However, to avoid any argument about whether an alteration is or is not an improvement, the clause should be amended to allow alterations or additions with the lessor's consent, such consent not to be unreasonably withheld. (This is known as a fully qualified covenant.) In this way the lessor will be required to justify any refusal of permission, ultimately in court, and would therefore not be an avenue the landlord would explore without real justification. The statute does not stop the lessor from seeking a reasonable sum should the proposed amendments diminish the value of the premises, or any adjacent premises in the ownership of the same lessor. Similarly, if the alteration or addition does not add to the letting value of the premises the statute does not prevent the lessor from obtaining from the tenant a covenant to reinstate the premises to their former condition at the end (or sooner determination) of the lease.

The nature and scope of covenants of this kind will be considered again in Chapter 12 **10.32** dealing with commercial property.

Quiet enjoyment

A covenant for quiet enjoyment is common to all leases and is discussed at 12.65. **10.33**

The purpose of the covenant is considered further at 12.66. **10.34**

Service charge provisions

Where the lessor is under an obligation to keep in good repair a building of which the **10.35** subject property forms part, the cost of those repairs will usually be recoverable from the lessee. That cost, along with other expenses incurred by the lessor in providing services (e.g. lighting and heating of common parts) on behalf of all the lessees, will form a service charge. If in the lease it is described as a rent, then that enables the lessor to distrain for arrears of a service charge rental. As can be imagined this is an area of friction between lessors and lessees. Lessees think that they have to pay too much for poorly provided services, while lessors complain that they comply with their obligations and yet the lessee fails to reimburse the lessor.

Contents of service charge clauses   There is no single right way for a lease to be prepared **10.36** in relation to service charges. However, we think that the following should apply to a lease of part of a residential block, i.e. a flat in a conglomeration of flats all paying a service charge to the one lessor:

(a) The lease may provide for a service charge payable as a rent with payments on account made quarterly at a rate to be decided by the lessor's surveyor (whose decision shall be final, save for manifest error) at the start of each year but having regard to expenditure in the previous year. At the end of the year accounts should be prepared without undue delay to reconcile payments made and received. Excess monies held should go to a sinking fund (see below), while any underpayment should be paid by the lessees within 21 days of the supply of the year-end accounts.

(b) There should also be a sinking fund created for the express purposes of ensuring that there are sufficient monies available to cover major expenses such as lift replacements or external redecoration schemes.

(c) The lessor should be obliged by a covenant to carry out clearly identified obligations listed in a schedule to the lease, including repairs and renovations to the main structure and common parts, and lighting and heating the common parts.

(d) The lessor should be obliged to provide at least two estimates where expenditure is required other than those of a moderate nature.

(e) Different lessees in the block may pay different charges. Consideration should be given to a fair distribution of the burden of payment, for example should occupants on the ground floor be required to pay towards the cost of the repair of a lift?

10.37	Many of these items are now required by statute (Landlord and Tenant Act 1985, s 18–30). Section 19 of this Act imposes a requirement of reasonableness as to service charges. Section 20 requires, where the cost of work exceeds £1,000, two estimates to be obtained, with notice being given to lessees. (Provisions within the Commonhold and Leasehold Reform Act 2002 have extended these rights to cover improvements as well as service charges: see 10.113 for more on this Act.) The best method of avoiding the potential problems in this area is to draft the lease so that the maintenance of the property is carried out by a management or maintenance company, with each lessee owning a share in that company. If this arrangement is created, then the maintenance of the whole block will be in the control of the lessees, who can control the expenditure in whatever way they wish. It is not uncommon for the lessor to transfer the freehold to such a company, on the occasion of the grant of the last lease in the block.

Service Charges and the Housing Act 1996, and Commonhold and Leasehold Reform Act 2002

10.38	Section 81 of the Housing Act 1996 imposes a more rigid structure of control on lessors seeking to exercise a right of re-entry or forfeiture as a result of failure by a lessee to pay service charges. In fact no exercise of a right of re-entry can be effected until 14 days after a court order. This does not limit a s 146 notice under the terms of the Law of Property Act 1925. However, the s 146 notice must include a statement confirming that s 81 of the Housing Act 1996 applies, and setting out its effect. If the amount of the service charge is expressly agreed by the lessee, then a court order is unnecessary. The Commonhold and Leasehold Reform Act 2002 introduced a further requirement that ground rent will not be payable unless it has been formally demanded. The demand is to be made by giving the tenant a prescribed notice. The reforms in the Act prevent the application of any provisions of a lease relating to late or non-payment (e.g. additional charges such as interest) if the rent is paid within 30 days of the demand being issued. It also introduces additional restrictions on the commencement of forfeiture proceedings for breaches of covenants or conditions of a lease. It modifies s 81 of the Housing Act 1996 to prohibit the commencement of forfeiture proceedings, including the issue of a notice under s 146 of the Law of Property Act 1925, in respect of non-payment of service charges or administration charges. This is not the case if the charge has been agreed or admitted by the tenant, or a court or the First-tier Tribunal (Property Chamber; Residential Property), formerly the Leasehold Valuation Tribunal, has determined that it is reasonable and due. It also prohibits the commencement of forfeiture proceedings for other breaches unless a court or the First-tier Tribunal (Property Chamber; Residential Property) has determined that a breach has occurred.

Mutual rights

10.39	In residential blocks in multiple occupation and where maisonettes are concerned easements, both granted and reserved, will almost certainly have to be detailed in the lease. There will need to be mutual rights by way of easements and exceptions for matters such as the paths of conducting media (i.e. gas pipes, electricity cables, sewers, etc.) serving the property that have to pass across other parts of the block. Similarly, rights of access to and from the subject property will need to be detailed showing the common areas to which the lessee may have access. The reverse will also be true. There will be other lessees who may require rights over the subject property by way of express reservations detailed in the lease. The best example would be the mutual right of lessees in a multi-occupied block to access to other parts for the purposes of emergency repairs or general upkeep. Another common element required will be a mutual proviso for support and protection between flats in a block, or maisonettes. This sounds obvious but protects the core of any multi-occupation arrangement.

Leases and Stamp Duty Land Tax

Stamp Duty Land Tax (Land Tax or SDLT) is a property tax based on taxation of trans- **10.40** actions rather than deeds or documents, which was the case for the previous stamp duty regime. It is assessed directly against the buyer rather than the property being purchased. (In Wales since April 2018, a Welsh Land Transaction Tax has replaced Stamp Duty Land Tax.)

The regime came into force on 1 December 2003. Leasehold transactions are caught by **10.41** SDLT as to the consideration paid and the rent in the lease. The starting threshold for the payment of SDLT is £125,000 for residential property, but £150,000 for commercial property. Practitioners should note that there is guidance on the Revenue & Customs website at **https://www.gov.uk/stamp-duty-land-tax-rates**. Practitioners also need to be aware that transactions under either threshold (£125,000 or £150,000) will be taxed at 0 per cent but will still require a land transaction return to be completed for these transactions. (This is different for first-time buyers of residential leasehold property; see Chapter 9 for further details of this new SDLT relief.)

For residential properties, a buyer who is not a first-time buyer will have to pay nothing on the first £125,000 of the property price, 2 per cent on the next £125,000, 5 per cent on the next £675,000, 10 per cent on the next £575,000 and 12 per cent on the rest (above £1.5 million). The starting threshold for commercial properties is £150,000. There is a 3 per cent SDLT surcharge on second homes.

Practitioners need to be aware that form SDLT4 should be used for complex commercial **10.42** transactions and leases. The changes to stamp duty brought in a changed regime for the rental element of leases and in particular commercial leases. With this system you must look separately at the rent and any consideration other than rent, for example a premium. The charge in relation to the rental element will be at a rate of 1 per cent on the net present value (NPV) of the total rent payable over the term of the lease. The Revenue charge SDLT on the NPV of the total rent payable over the term of the lease. You must work out the NPV of the rent due for each year of the lease, and then add them all together. Future rents will be discounted at 3.5 per cent per annum in order to arrive at the NPV. Leases where the NPV of the rent over the term of the lease does not exceed £150,000 for commercial property and £125,000 for residential will be exempt. The Revenue has suggested that change in the regime could mean that some 60 per cent of all commercial leases could avoid any SDLT on the rental element. Guidance on the NPV can be found on the government's website at **https://www.gov.uk/stamp-duty-land-tax-leasehold-purchases**.

Once the Revenue has received and processed a proper SDLT return and, if required, pay- **10.43** ment, it will issue a certificate of payment SDLT5. The certificate is issued under s 79 of the Finance Act 2003 and evidences that SDLT has been accounted on the particular transaction notified to the Revenue. This must be sent to Land Registry to enable an application to register to proceed. Further details on SDLT can be found at 9.21. SDLT5 must be sent to the Registry even where the consideration for the lease is below the SDLT thresholds. However, in the 2008 budget changes were made regarding the notification threshold. No notification is required where there is a grant of a lease for seven years or more where the premium is less than £40,000 or the annual rent is less than £1,000. Similarly, no notification is required on a lease assignment where the lease was granted for a term of seven years or more and the assignment consideration is less than £40,000.

DEALING WITH LEASES WHEN ACTING FOR A LESSEE OR LENDER

Introduction

10.44 Careful consideration of the lease terms of flats and maisonettes could keep a lot of conveyancing practitioners very busy. This is because lease terms will be unique to each subject property. Furthermore, the nature of that property will inevitably dictate many specific terms. Older leases failing to meet modern standards for lease contents, particularly those dictated by lenders, further compound this problem. Why should lenders be so concerned when they are not buying the leasehold legal estate itself? The basis for their involvement is an eye to the possible future for their loan. Should the borrower default, then the lender will want to realize the security by selling it on the open market, in an effort to recover all its mortgage monies. While the full value may, in the eyes of a surveyor, be seen to be secured by the subject property, this could prove to be immaterial if the lease itself is unsaleable because the contents are in some way defective. This could occur if the lease terms are insufficient or inappropriate. If you are acting for a buyer it will be your professional duty to ensure that the lease contents are sufficient for your client and for any lender for whom you are also acting in the same transaction.

UK Finance Mortgage Lenders' Handbook (formerly the CML Handbook) and leases

10.45 The Council of Mortgage Lenders (CML) (now integrated into UK Finance) issued The *CML Lenders' Handbook for Solicitors and Licensed Conveyancers England and Wales* in 1999 and it has been regularly updated since then. It is now known as the *UK Finance Mortgage Lenders' Handbook* (see Appendix 12).

10.46 A lender will not, in any circumstances, accept as security for a loan a lease that contains forfeiture on bankruptcy of the lessee. In other words, if the lease allows a right of re-entry on the bankruptcy of the lessee, the lease will not be mortgageable. The reasoning is that if the lessee did become bankrupt and the lessor forfeited, the lender's security would evaporate. Additionally, where there is a property that contains several units, all on separate leases, a lender (and indeed a lessee) would not want each lessee to be responsible for the repair of his or her own section of the structure. Clearly this would lead to an inconsistent and patchy approach to repair that can be avoided if this responsibility rests with the lessor. The same argument will apply to insurance arrangements for multi-occupied property. Moreover, any absolute prohibition against an assignment or mortgage of the whole of the subject property would be unacceptable in a long residential lease. Lastly, although strictly speaking nothing to do with leases, it is worth emphasizing that flying freeholds (i.e. freehold flats or maisonettes not attached to the ground) are unlikely to be acceptable to a lender or a buyer. In particular a flying freehold will involve positive covenants that cannot be enforced. The pivotal problem arises from the current inability to enforce positive repairing covenants against a freehold covenantor's successors in title. It is this deficiency that makes a freehold flat a poor choice in the property marketplace. (There is no reason why a leaseholder should not also own a share of the freehold with other leaseholders in the same block.) In future, the position may be changed by the Contracts (Rights of Third Parties) Act 1999. It is possible that the Act will provide a method of enforceability, but this has yet to be properly tested in the courts. Many lessors expressly exclude this Act from their leases. Commonhold will also assist. Further details can be found from 10.113.

Common lease defects

Inevitably, a lender will require a lease to contain the terms any prudent purchaser would **10.47** require. Furthermore, a lender will expect any new lease to be capable of registration with absolute title. Alternatively, if the lease is in existence, the registered title should be absolute. The following sums up what both buyer and lender require and without which the lease would be considered defective or unacceptable:

(a) The property description must be accurate as to the extent of the property, including any stairs or halls serving just one property. Where is the front door? Is the back and/ or front garden included?
(b) Are all rights of access to and from the property clearly stated? Is there an easement for support and protection? Is there a right of access to other parts around the subject property allowing the lessee to carry out repairs required for the benefit of the subject property?
(c) Has the term at least 60 years to run; how much is the passing rent and is it subject to review? Some mortgagees are reluctant to lend on a lease with less than 60 years left unexpired of the lease term.
(d) Is the lease arrangement for repair appropriate for the type of property concerned? Is this also the case for the insurance of the fabric of the property?
(e) If a service charge is required, are the lease terms sufficient to ensure proper remedial work by the lessor or management company (through an enforceable covenant to carry out work), with a covenant to pay a service charge by the lessee?
(f) Can the lessee enforce covenants through the lessor against other lessees in the other flats surrounding the subject property?
(g) The lease must not contain a forfeiture on bankruptcy provision.
(h) The lease should permit assignments without the lessor's consent as well as mortgages and other dealings with the legal estate.
(i) Use should be limited to that appropriate to the property and in accordance with planning laws.
(j) Does the lease contain covenants from the lessor and/or the lessee to cover all these various requirements?

These are the basic terms that a practitioner must consider when acting on a leasehold **10.48** acquisition. There will be further specific requirements that each individual lender will have for leasehold securities, and you should refer to the lender's instructions when you receive them prior to exchange. Refer also to the *UK Finance Mortgage Lenders' Handbook*.

Defective leases—a summary

A residential lease will be considered defective if any of the following occurs in the lease **10.49** you are considering for your client buyer:

(a) the lease contains a forfeiture on bankruptcy provision;
(b) the lease fails to include proper repairing covenants that ensure the ongoing maintenance and renewal of the main structure, roof, foundations, and common parts. This will require the involvement of the lessor or management company; the property is in a newly constructed block of flats where the developer is not offering a National House

Building Council (NHBC) guarantee or similar guarantee scheme. Although not strictly a lease defect, many mortgagees will not lend in the absence of this protection;

(c) the lease does not include a covenant by the lessor to take action against another lessee for breach of covenant at the request of a lessee who agrees to indemnify the lessor for that action;

(d) the lease has inadequate insurance provisions, or the lessor is under no obligation to look after unlet or unsold property in a large block.

10.50 There is one particular point to note in relation to maisonette leases. Where there are two maisonettes on lease, it has been the occasional practice also to transfer the freehold of the flats to the lessees at the time of the granting of the lease. However, in doing so the transfer is in two parts. This means that each lessee is the freeholder for the other maisonette. This sounds a simple solution that, in theory, sets up a commonality of responsibility for repairs and maintenance. However, there is one major flaw: one of the two freehold titles will be a 'flying freehold'. This is poor conveyancing practice and this arrangement should not be contemplated. Instead the single freehold title could be vested in the joint names of the two lessees, or in a limited company jointly owned by the lessees.

LIABILITY ON COVENANTS IN LEASES: ENFORCEMENT

Introduction

10.51 For many years it was the case that the original lessor and lessee were liable to each other under the covenants in their lease for the full term granted by the lease. As a consequence of the effects of privity of contract this liability remained enforceable in the courts even if the lessee had subsequently assigned the residue of the term of the lease. The practical effect of this was that a lessee could be sued for arrears of rent even though that lessee had not been the tenant in occupation for many years and where there had been various subsequent lessees liable to pay rent under the terms of the original lease. (It gets worse—in *Selous Street Properties Ltd v Oronel Fabrics Ltd* [1984] 1 EGLR 50 it was held that where a later tenant carries out improvements that increase the rental value, the original tenant must pay rent at that higher level even though the works were carried out after the original tenant ceased to be involved as a result of having assigned the residue of the term of the lease.)

Reform

10.52 This outdated element of landlord and tenant law has led to some very unfair situations where an original tenant has been called on to pay rent many years after assigning its interest in the subject property. A measure of reform was made by the provisions of the Landlord and Tenant (Covenants) Act 1995 and the details of the changes are set out at 10.111. These provisions apply only to new leases created on or after 1 January 1996. In essence a lessee who assigns such a lease automatically enjoys a release through statute of any continuing liability under the lease covenants. However, a lessor can require the outgoing lessee to enter into a form of guarantee stipulated by the statute and known as an authorised guarantee agreement (AGA). The statute made a major change to the law—the benefit and burden of lease covenants pass automatically on assignment without any question of whether or not they touch and concern the land. The successor in title, the assignee, will take the benefit and burden of the lease covenants by reason of statute and the assignor, the original lessee, will be released from liability. This has made a major dent in the lessor's armoury of privity of contract.

10.53 Where a buyer is purchasing a flat in a block containing many other similar flats and where all are on long leases, the doctrine of privity of contract can cause major problems where one lessee is involved in a dispute with another about the enforcement of lease covenants. To enable enforcement to take place, and for all lessees in the block to know the extent of the lease terms for all occupants of the block, the lease should state that all the leases granted for the block will or do contain the same terms as that for the subject property. Coupled with this there should be a covenant by the lessor on request by one lessee (and with that lessee agreeing to indemnify the lessor's costs) to enforce lease covenants against another lessee. Without this provision one lessee has no legal right to enforce covenants against another lessee as the covenant is not with the other lessee but with the lessor. However, the lease can be drawn up to include a covenant between the lessor, lessee, and all the other lessees in the block. If this appears, each lessee can take action against any other lessee.

Since 11 May 2000, when the Contracts (Rights of Third Parties) Act 1999 came into force, **10.54** the direct enforcement of covenants between lessees may be possible, but only in relation to leases granted on or after that date and where the lease does not expressly exclude the Act.

LEASE VARIATIONS

Where a lease has been granted by deed, an effective variation of the lease must and can be **10.55** made only by deed. It has been the practice in the past for practitioners to issue 'side letters' to give effect to an agreed variation. If tested in court, this form of arrangement is doomed to failure. (It should fail as a result of s 2 of the Law of Property (Miscellaneous Provisions) Act 1989, as it is unlikely that such a letter will be signed by both parties or that it contains all the terms. Even a collateral personal agreement that tried to effect a lease variation was set aside by the court (see *Allied Dunbar Assurance plc v Homebase Ltd* [2002] 27 EG 144.)) Furthermore, if the lease being varied is already registered at Land Registry, the deed of variation must be submitted to the Registry so that it can note the variation on the title. The deed of variation is ineffective in law until it is properly registered, although it would probably be effective in equity. Practitioners should remember that where the variation is of a registered lease which affects the length of the original term of the lease or the extent of the demised property, Land Registry considers the deed of variation to be evidence of surrender and re-grant. In effect this means that the 'lease' will be registered and dated from the date of the variation, but will by implication refer back to the terms of the original lease. There is therefore a re-grant on the terms as varied by the deed of variation. Furthermore, the new 'lease' will be covered by the terms of the Landlord and Tenant (Covenants) Act 1995 whereby, without realizing it, a lessor may give a lessee a method of escaping liability under lease covenants that would otherwise not be available. If there is no wish on the part of the lessor to allow such a release to be available to the lessee, then a variation should, of course, be avoided.

KEY POINTS SUMMARY

AN INTRODUCTION TO LEASES

- In the light of the type of lease to be given or taken by your client, are the terms contained **10.56** within it suitable to a lease of that kind? Try to step back and take an overview to ensure the contents are suitable.

- When instructed by buyer and lender, always remember your dual obligation to ensure that the lease to be purchased suits both your clients and their individual requirements and instructions.

- In particular, are the insurance arrangements suitable to the type of subject property? In brief, if the property is a house, the lessee should insure; if a flat, the lessor should insure; if a maisonette, either will do. The same is true for repairs.

- If your client is buying a long residential lease, reject clauses restricting alienation except if the restriction is there to ensure a direct covenant between the lessor and your client the assignee.

- When acting for a proposed lessee intending to buy a leasehold residential property with a mortgage, never agree a lease that allows forfeiture on bankruptcy as this will not be acceptable to a lender.

- Always ensure the lease to be purchased contains a lessor's covenant allowing one lessee to enforce lease covenants against another lessee through the assistance of the lessor.

- If the lease is registrable, always make sure all the prescribed clauses required by Land Registry have been included.

B NEW LEASES

10.57 A new lease is granted by a lessor or landlord and is taken by a lessee or tenant. (It is best practice in any one deed to adopt one pair of titles, for example by using lessor and lessee or landlord and tenant.) The lease may be preceded by a contract to grant the lease, but if there is no contract there is no binding relationship until the lease is formally granted. The lease will almost always be in two parts, the original part executed by the lessor and the counterpart executed by the lessee. Both parts will be identical; and when exchanged and dated the lease will, at the moment of exchange, come into formal and legal existence and thereby create a brand new legal estate. The lessor will be able to receive not only any premium to be paid on the grant of the new lease but thereafter any periodically recurring rent provided for in the lease.

LEASE-SPECIFIC CHANGES IN THE CONVEYANCING PROCESS

Introduction

10.58 While in many ways the leasehold conveyancing process is much the same as that for a freehold, there are specific and necessary differences. Before the draft contract can be prepared a draft lease must be drawn up which will form the subject of the agreement. It is perfectly possible to adopt the same contract forms, incorporating the SCs, used on a freehold sale for a leasehold disposal, whether this is to be the grant of a new lease, or an assignment or transfer of an existing lease. (SC 8 deals with leasehold property; SC 8.1 covers existing leases, and SC 8.2 new leases. If the lessor's consent is required, this is covered by SC 8.3.) When the contract is drafted it should be sent to the buyer's practitioner, together with the proposed form of draft lease in duplicate. The draft contract and lease will then be approved with or without amendments. After exchange the agreed form of lease must be engrossed and executed in duplicate by the contractual parties, in readiness for completion. Where necessary the seller will have to obtain all necessary consents for the grant of the new lease from either or both the seller's mortgagee and superior title holder. At completion the buyer may be required to pay lease-specific outgoings in advance such as rent and service charges. There will possibly be SDLT on the lease rental as well as the consideration, and Land Registry forms are required for any application to the Registry for first registration of a registrable lease. (Section 6 of the Land Registration Act 2002 stipulates that first registration must take place within two months of the completion of a grant of a new lease for a term of more than seven years, or the assignment on sale of an existing lease where the term left to run exceeds seven years at completion.)

Deducing title; entitlement to inspect the superior or freehold title

On the grant of a lease, the lessee has no automatic right to investigate the lessor's free- **10.59** hold title unless the lessor agrees otherwise. (Law of Property Act 1925, s 44(2), specifically provides that the intended lessee shall not be entitled to call for the title to the freehold.) If this is the case the purchase contract should contain a provision requiring the seller to deduce the freehold title. SC 8.2.4 requires the seller to deduce a title which will enable the buyer to register the lease at HM Land Registry with an absolute title. (Indeed, s 44(4A) says that these provisions stopping an intended lessee from calling for the superior title do not apply to a contract to grant a lease if the grant will be an event within s 4(1) of the Land Registration Act 2002, i.e. events which trigger compulsory first registration.) In these circumstances the freehold title will have to be deduced to ensure the grant of an absolute title. Accordingly, the purchase contract must be checked first, to ensure it is drawn up on the basis of the fifth edition of the SCs and, second, that no attempt has been made in the special conditions of that contract to limit or exclude SC 8.2.4. If the superior title is not investigated the lessee runs the risk that the lease may not have been validly granted or may not bind a mortgagee of the freehold, for example the freehold may be in mortgage and the mortgage may specifically preclude the borrower or seller from granting any leases. There is also the risk of being bound by unknown third-party interests affecting the freehold, such as overriding interests or other interests protected by entry on the registers of the freehold title when the lease was granted. These risks are unacceptable to the lessee.

Specific matters when dealing with sub-leases

There are special and particular problems in relation to matters of title where sub- or **10.60** under-leases are concerned. These matters are examined in greater detail in the following paragraphs.

Rules regarding deduction of title

A sub-lessee can call for the superior lease out of which the sub-lease is to be granted **10.61** together with all assignments of that lease for the last 15 years. However, s 44(2) of the Law of Property Act 1925 prohibits a call for the superior leasehold and/or freehold title. This is a problem in unregistered land but is less so for registered land because the registers are now open to public inspection and the buyer can buy official copies of the freehold title (and all superior leasehold titles) direct from Land Registry. The moral is that if the land is unregistered, you should demand a copy of all superior titles before the new sub-lease is granted. Furthermore, if the term of the new lease will exceed seven years SC 8.2.4 gets around this difficulty by requiring the seller to deduce title to the buyer in such a way as to enable the buyer to register the sub-lease with title absolute. In other words the superior titles must be disclosed. This will only apply to leases to be granted for a term exceeding seven years. Shorter leases will fall into the s 44 title trap.

Another real problem arises over the use of the property. The user clause in the sub-lease **10.62** may conflict with the user provisions in an unseen superior title. If this occurs, the practitioner who drew up the sub-lease would be considered to have acted negligently in preparing the lease without regard to the user restrictions in the superior title. Furthermore, the superior title may include a requirement that any sub-lease may only be granted with the superior lessor's consent. Clearly all consents must be obtained before a sub-lease is granted. (Also see SC 8.3, which contains provisions that will apply if consent to sub-let is required from a superior title owner. At worst, if no such consent is forthcoming, rescission is possible.)

Consistency with head lease

10.63   It is important to ensure that the covenants and conditions in any sub-lease remain consistent with those in any superior lease. It is therefore imperative to see the superior lease to ensure that the terms of the sub-lease do not conflict with the superior lease terms. It would be plainly inconsistent if the head lease required the lessor to repair the subject property while the sub-lease required the sub-lessee to repair the subject property. This is all the more important when you consider that the sub-lessor will almost certainly require an indemnity in the sub-lease, from the sub-lessee, against breaches of the covenants in the superior lease. Consequently, consistency of covenants will make sure the sub-lessee will be able to ensure compliance with covenants in both leases.

Sub-lessee's right to seek relief from forfeiture

10.64   If the head lessor forfeits the head lease, then the sub-lessee does have the right to apply for relief against forfeiture of the superior lease without which the sub-lease could be lost. If a head lease is terminated by forfeiture, all sub-leases will cease, along with the superior lease. To try to prevent this, s 146(4) of the Law of Property Act 1925 allows sub-lessees to apply for relief against forfeiture of the superior lease. This relief is discretionary and if an order is made, it will take effect as a new lease between the lessor and sub-lessee on terms deemed appropriate by the court.

ACTING FOR THE LESSOR

10.65   The draft lease must reflect the precise wishes of the lessor and the particular nature of the property to be sold. If the lessor wishes to sell a flat within a block but retain control of that block, the lease terms must reflect these instructions. There will be times when the lessor will instruct you to proceed in a way that is unsatisfactory, for example the lessor may want to grant a new lease for a flat in a block, getting rid of all responsibility for the lessor, who only wants to receive the rents. This may mean you will be required to draw up a lease that is unsaleable, being unacceptable to a lender as a consequence of the absence of proper repairing arrangements for the whole block. To draft such a lease would be bad conveyancing practice. If this situation does occur, you should write to your client expressing as clearly as possible your reservations about the nature of your instructions, and invite your client to reconsider. If the instructions remain the same, our advice is to stand firm and not proceed: it could amount to professional negligence to do so.

The lessor and a management company

10.66   You could suggest to the lessor that there is an alternative to simply giving each lessee their own individual repairing and insuring responsibilities, and that is to pass these responsibilities to a management company. Each lessee would be given a share in the management company and the lessor would receive the rents without any further liability for future maintenance and insurance arrangements. Furthermore, if there are freehold covenants, the lease should include a covenant on the part of the lessee to observe and perform those covenants with an indemnity against any future breach.

Draft lease and contract

10.67   When drafting the contract you will need to insert in the particulars the estate and term to be offered to the buyer. You can do this by express reference or by attaching the draft lease to the contract as an annexure. (SC 8.2.3 states 'The lease is to be in the form of the draft attached to the contract.') With a new long lease, nothing more about deducing title needs be said as SC 8.2.4 stipulates that '[i]f the term of the new lease will exceed seven years, the seller is to deduce a title which will enable the buyer to register the lease at the Land Registry with an absolute title'. This should therefore require the seller to deduce the superior title.

Contracts (Rights of Third Parties) Act 1999

A lessor will also need to consider whether or not to allow the Contracts (Rights of Third **10.68** Parties) Act 1999 to apply to the new lease. If the lessor does not want the Act to apply, then a specific written exclusion must be included in the lease deed. Section 1 of the Act provides that a person not a party to a contract will be able to enforce a term of the contract if the term of the contract purports to confer a benefit on the third party. However, if it appears that on a proper construction of the contract no such enforceability was intended then the third party will be unable to enforce such terms. The following will exclude the Act: 'The parties to this lease agree that the Contracts (Rights of Third Parties) Act 1999 shall not apply to it.' (The Standard Conditions (fifth edition) state that unless expressly stated nothing in the contract will create rights pursuant to this Act in favour of anyone other than the parties to the contract.)

ACTING FOR THE LESSEE

Introduction

On receipt of the draft lease and contract you should check both very carefully to make **10.69** sure that they describe and demise the subject property accurately. You must also be sure that your client understands the relevance of all the lease terms. To ensure that this is so, you should write to your client with a detailed report on all the terms in the lease. In this way the buyer cannot in the future allege that you did not advise him of any particular provision that may cause future problems.

The draft lease and contract, lessee concerns

Points of concern about the draft lease and contract terms that should be carefully con- **10.70** sidered include the following:

(a) In the description of the subject property in the lease: are all the walls, floors, and ceilings included or excluded?
(b) Is there a garden at the front and/or rear and if so do either or both form part of the property to be purchased?
(c) Are there adequate rights of access to and from the subject property over the parts leading to the premises?
(d) Are there mutual rights of support, protection, and entry for repairs?
(e) Is the buyer aware of rental at the levels shown in the draft? What are the provisions for rental increases or review? Check that these are not onerous.
(f) Are the lessee's covenants reasonable and in particular is there any restriction on alienation; and if so is that restriction fair to a long leaseholder?
(g) Does the lease allow forfeiture on bankruptcy? If so, take steps immediately to remove this provision.
(h) Is there a covenant requiring the lessor to enforce covenants against other lessees in the block? This must be included.

(i) Does the contract make proper and exact reference to the estate and term to be sold to your client?

(j) Are there any lease-specific special conditions and if so are they acceptable in the context of your instructions for the buyer?

Other issues

10.71 If the buyer intends to purchase with the assistance of a mortgage, you must make sure that the lease terms accord with the lender's requirements. You must therefore check the details of the mortgage offer and the *UK Finance Mortgage Lenders' Handbook* together with any particular requirements the lender may list with the client's offer of mortgage. On exchange of contracts, re-check the insurance arrangements and if the lessor insures, make sure the interest of the buyer and the buyer's lender are noted on the lessor's policy of insurance. The purpose of this is to make sure that the insurance company is aware of the buyer's involvement in the property in the event that there is a claim on the policy. Be sure of who must engross the original of the lease and the counterpart. It makes sense to agree to a contractual term permitting a modest fee payable to the lessor's practitioner for the preparation of a counterpart lease engrossment to be executed by the lessee. It will save you time and will ensure uniformity between the two lease parts. On completion make sure you pay all SDLT including any due on the rent, and apply for first registration using the correct Land Registry application form. If the reversionary title is registered, the buyer's practitioner must carry out an official search against the reversionary title, and apply for first registration of the new lease within the priority period. The application must include the original lease together with a certified copy.

10.72 The Law Society has issued a conveyancing form called LPE1. It is used for collecting information about a subject property where that information is held by landlords, management companies, and managing agents. The kind of information that the form intends to gather will normally be about ground rent, insurance, and service charges. The sections within the form cover contact details, transfer and registration details, ground rent service charge, and insurance information, and the form lists required documents such as service charge accounts for the last three years. This form should be used when a lessor or management company must be contacted to obtain information from them about a leasehold property that is in the process of being sold. A buyer's leasehold information summary form, (LPE2), has also been introduced. This seeks to give the buyer details of the buyer's key financial responsibilities such as ground rent, service charges, insurance premiums, and possible future costs arising out of these.

Giving notice

10.73 There is one further lease-specific task to be performed after completion where the new lessee has purchased with a mortgage. Most modern leases require notice of assignment and charge (or mortgage) to be given to the seller's solicitor. Where there is the grant of a new lease clearly only notice of charge must be given along with the payment of any fee for the registration. There is a double obligation where you also act for the lender as it is important that the lessor is aware of the lender's interest in the property should the lessee, in the future, breach any of the terms of the lease.

KEY POINTS SUMMARY

NEW LEASES

10.74 • Does the new lease contain all the terms considered appropriate to the type of property to be sold or purchased?

- Does the new lease contain any terms that are unacceptable to the buyer's lender or to the buyer? (Be aware of possible onerous rental increases.)

- Has the contract been drafted properly in the context of the proposed terms of the new lease, and what lease-specific special conditions are there and are they acceptable?

- On the assumption that the lease requires it, have you remembered to give notice of the buyer's charge to the lessor and have you paid the registration fee?

C EXISTING LEASES

Introduction

Where a lease is in existence and is to be conveyed to an assignee, the process will be effected **10.75** by a transfer in the case of registered leasehold land, or an assignment when the lease is not registered. (However, the assignment may very well induce first registration and as such a transfer should be used.) It is possible to adopt the same pre-printed contract forms, incorporating the SCs, normally used on a freehold sale for an existing lease disposal. In effect there is just one specific SC: SC 8.1.2 states, 'The seller having provided the buyer with copies of the documents embodying the lease terms, the buyer is treated as entering into the contract knowing and fully accepting those terms.' This covers a sale where the lease terms are not all in the one document, i.e. where there has been a subsequent deed of variation of the original lease terms. It also states that there is a clear assumption that all the necessary copies have been supplied and the buyer therefore takes the property in full knowledge of the lease terms and is deemed to have accepted the transaction on that basis.

LEASE-SPECIFIC CHANGES IN THE CONVEYANCING PROCESS

The conveyancing process involved in the sale of a leasehold property will be very similar **10.76** to that for a freehold property. Perhaps the major variation is in relation to conditions in the lease that impose prerequisite conditions to any disposal. As we have seen, the lease can contain covenants on the part of the lessee not to assign or transfer the property without first ensuring either that the lessor's consent is obtained, or that the incoming lessee has entered into a deed of covenant with the lessor or a management company. Further details from the buyer's perspective are given in 10.85. Otherwise many of the variations in the process will be concerned with maintenance and service charges and more procedural changes. These are highlighted in the following paragraphs.

ACTING FOR THE SELLER

Deducing title

If you are acting for the seller, the main concern will be to ensure that you can and have **10.77** deduced title so that there will be no delay on exchange or completion. Where an existing lease is concerned, just as for freehold properties, there will be two possible ways that title should be deduced.

First, the Land Registration Act 2002 imposes no restrictions on the rights of the parties **10.78** to the contract to make their own arrangements as to what evidence of title the seller must deduce. Schedule 10, para 2 provides:

(1) Rules may make provision about the obligations with respect to—
  (a) proof of title; or
  (b) perfection of title; of the seller under a contract for the transfer, or other disposition, for valuable consideration of a registered estate or charge.
(2) Rules under this paragraph may be expressed to have effect notwithstanding any stipulation to the contrary.

10.79 The Land Registration Rules 2003 are silent on the matter of what exactly should be deduced as representing the title offered for sale. The parties to the contract are free to agree whatever contractual provisions they like regarding deduction of title. SC 4.1.2 and the Protocol require the seller at his or her own expense to provide the buyer with official copies of the registered title. This is best practice in any event because recent official copies show the current position of the register. Accordingly, every buyer's practitioner should insist on receiving official copies which are less than 12 months old, as this will be required for final Land Registry searches. The buyer must also receive a copy of the lease registered at Land Registry, together with any deeds varying it or affecting it and which have been registered. As Land Registry will have examined the freehold at the time the leasehold title was issued with an absolute title, there is no necessity for the buyer to examine or investigate the freehold title. Given the fact that the leasehold absolute title is in effect guaranteed by the State, there is nothing further needed to constitute the title.

Good leasehold issues

10.80 If the property being sold is registered at Land Registry with good leasehold title, the same provisions as to the deduction of title apply, and SC 4.1.2 stipulations also apply as set out at 10.79. The buyer must also receive a copy of the lease registered at Land Registry along with any deeds varying it or affecting it and which have been registered. However, the problem for the buyer of a good leasehold title is that the registration is such that there is no guarantee of the validity of the lease, i.e. that the lease has been validly granted. The Registry will issue this class of title when the superior title, the reversionary title, has not been seen and approved by the registrar. As a consequence, a buyer faced with a good leasehold title should demand that the superior title be deduced; and because the SCs are silent on the point, an extra special condition should be inserted in the contract to that effect. (In practical terms this should be unnecessary if title is to be investigated before contracts are exchanged.) The buyer cannot persist as the law does not support this insistence. If the superior title is not available, the buyer should be advised not to proceed, as a good leasehold title may not be acceptable to a lender. The seller could be asked to upgrade the title, as a good leasehold title can be upgraded to absolute so long as an applicant is able to produce to the Registrar the freehold reversionary title together with any superior leasehold titles.

Unregistered land and the effect of s 44 of the Law of Property Act 1925

10.81 In relation to unregistered land, s 44 of the Law of Property Act 1925 provides that the buyer can insist on seeing the lease of the property that is being purchased, supported by all deeds of assignment and other legal documents dealing with the legal estate representing a period of ownership for at least the last 15 years. In this respect the title is deduced in much the same way as for freehold properties. However, the crucial difference is that where an existing unregistered lease title is to be deduced, the buyer cannot insist on seeing details of any superior titles. If the buyer needs to submit the lease for first registration and has no details of the superior title, the lease will be registered with a mere good leasehold title. This could be unacceptable to a mortgagee. To avoid this difficulty and because the SCs are silent on the point, a special condition can be inserted in the contract requiring the seller to deduce title to the freehold and any intermediate superior leasehold interests. As noted, in practical terms this should be resolved before exchange by the buyer seeing all the details of the title before a binding contract is put in place.

Information required on a sale

Obtain details of any rents, service charge, and insurance payments made by the client **10.82** seller, as you will require these to prepare answers to preliminary enquiries or Property Information Forms. You will also need to see copies of the last three years' service charge accounts as the buyer will inevitably ask for these prior to exchange. (In Protocol cases the seller's practitioner is required to ask the client to produce service or maintenance charge accounts for the last three years, where appropriate, and evidence of payment.) Check the lease to see what assignment preconditions there are and take steps to comply with them, such as making provision in the contract for the buyer to enter into a deed of covenant at the time of completion directly with the lessor. If necessary apply for a licence to assign supported by references from the buyer prior to exchange of contracts. SC 8.3 applies if a consent to assign or sub-let is required to enable completion to take place. SC 8.3.2(a) states that '[t]he seller is to apply for the consent at his expense, and to use all reasonable efforts to obtain it'. In support of this application SC 8.3.2(b) requires the buyer to 'provide all information and references reasonably required'. Either party may rescind the contract if three working days before the day for completion the lessor's consent has not been issued, or if issued it has attaching to it 'a condition to which the buyer reasonably objects'. Rescission is effected by giving written notice to the other party to the agreement; and on rescission arising in this manner, neither party is 'to be treated as in breach of contract and condition 7.1.2 applies'. (This condition provides that the deposit is to be repaid with interest and the buyer is to return any documents and to cancel any registration of the contract, i.e. the parties are to return to the position they were in as if the contract had not existed.)

If there is a management company owned by the lessees, before exchange the seller must **10.83** supply copies of the memorandum and articles of association of that management company together with, where appropriate, a copy of the seller's share certificate. (Remember if the company is limited by guarantee there will be no share certificate.)

Post-exchange matters

After exchange the buyer will no doubt supply a form of purchase deed for approval. **10.84** Where this takes the form of a deed of transfer in many cases the same form is used as if it were a freehold transaction. Ensure you have up-to-date receipts or demands for lease-specific outgoings such as rent and service charges including insurance contributions, so that these can be apportioned by way of a completion statement prepared as at the day of completion. By s 45(2) of the Law of Property Act 1925, if the receipt is produced, a buyer, in the absence of evidence to the contrary, can assume that the rent has been paid and all lease covenants performed without there being a subsisting breach.

ACTING FOR THE BUYER

Introduction

If you are acting for a buyer, you should always check the amount of time left to run on **10.85** the lease, i.e. the residue of the term granted, especially if the buyer is purchasing with the assistance of a mortgage. This is particularly so for two reasons. First, if the residue of the term is fairly limited it will be unacceptable to many lenders. Some lenders will decline to lend if the lease term has less than 60 years left to run. Second, the lender may have based the loan on a term of years stated to it by the buyer. If that figure turns out to be inaccurate, the lender must be told the correct details by you and you need to obtain its written approval to the amended details prior to an exchange of contracts. The same is true for any rental details.

Lease-specific enquiries and the contract

10.86 Where a leasehold is being purchased, lease-specific enquiries should be made covering insurance and maintenance details and should include a request for the last three years' service charge accounts along with a copy of the current insurance policy and up-to-date schedule of cover. This can be done by way of the Protocol forms, the seller's leasehold information form Part I and II. See Chapter 4 for further details.

10.87 The Law Society has issued a new conveyancing form called LPE1. It is intended to be used for collecting information about a subject property where that information is held by landlords, management companies, and managing agents. The kind of information that the form intends to gather will normally be about ground rent, insurance, and service charges. The sections within the form cover contact details, transfer and registration details, ground rent service charge, and insurance information, and the form lists required documents such as service charge accounts for the last three years. This form should be used when a lessor or management company must be contacted to obtain information from them about a leasehold property that is in the process of being sold.

10.88 Carefully check the contract to make sure it properly describes all the leasehold title to be purchased. Reference should be made in the contract to the property description in the lease. Look through the lease terms to make sure it contains all the necessary terms (see Chapter 3), and that it does not include any that should be avoided. Check to see if the lease plan remains accurate. Check the lease to see what obligations there are, if any, on any incoming lessee before the transfer can take place. If the lessor's consent is required for the transfer of the residue of the lease to your client, consider the need for references. Add together the amount of the current annual rent and service charges and obtain references for that amount. The references should be provided by the buyer's bankers, accountants, if any, and perhaps with one further reference as to the buyer's character. If the client is not known to you as an established client, you should decline to supply a reference for someone you do not know. If there is a management company, call for a copy of the memorandum and articles of association and a copy of the seller's share certificate. If the company is limited by guarantee, there will be no share certificate. Provide the buyer with a full and detailed written report of the terms of the lease and ask the client to confirm in writing that the terms of the lease are understood and accepted.

10.89 Does the lease contain all the terms considered appropriate to the type of property to be purchased? If not you may need to approach the seller with a request that a deed of variation be obtained from the lessor to correct the position. The deed of variation can include a necessary lease term or exclude an undesirable one. The terms that should be included or excluded are set out in detail in 10.05. Leases that are more than 15–20 years old tend not to include a lessor's covenant to enforce covenants by other lessees. A variation is one way in which this kind of lease can be modernized so as to include such a clause.

Issues at exchange

10.90 At the time of exchange double-check the insurance arrangements to make sure that if the lessor insures, the insurance remains current. After exchange take steps to put in place all consents to the transfer, particularly where the lessor is involved, so that the licence to assign or deed of covenant is available on completion. Remember you should use a Form TR1 transfer for leaseholds, including those that will be subject to first registration where an existing lease is being transferred.

Issues at completion

Insist on seeing the last receipt for ground rent for two important reasons. First, to make **10.91** sure the receipt is a clear one, i.e. that it does not contain any reference to any subsisting breaches of covenant. If it does, the buyer will be on notice and will take subject to that alleged breach of the terms of the lease. Second, the receipt will confirm whether or not the rental payments are up to date and whether or not there are any rent arrears. Call for a detailed completion statement showing all lease-specific payments such as rent and service charges and apportioning them at the date of sale depending on whether they are paid in arrears or in advance. Finally, in registered land make sure the seller has the original lease ready to be passed over to you at completion. Because there are no deeds in registered land the seller may only send through the signed transfer, whereas in leasehold sales the original lease must also be handed over as well.

KEY POINTS SUMMARY

EXISTING LEASES

- If the seller is seeking to sell a good leasehold title, always insist that either the title be con- **10.92** verted to absolute, or the superior title be deduced and amend the draft contract to include a special condition to that effect.

- If the seller is seeking to deduce an unregistered lease, because of s 44 of the Law of Property Act 1925, always insist before exchange and, if necessary, by way of a contract special condition that the superior title(s) be deduced so that an absolute title can be granted at the time of the application for first registration.

- If you are acting for a seller of an existing lease, make sure you have details of all lease-specific outgoings as well as copies of the last three years' service charge accounts.

- If you are acting for a buyer, make sure the lease terms are acceptable to your client and the client's lender and supply references if needed in support of an application for licence to assign if required by the terms of the lease. The financial references should be for the total of the annual rent and the current annual service charge payments.

D STATUTES AND LEASES

Perhaps because of the complex nature of leases or the more interventionist nature of **10.93** recent governments, over the last 30 years statutes dealing with leases have increased in number and effect. Several are particularly important to conveyancing practitioners. The following is a selection of some of the key statutes.

LEASEHOLD REFORM ACT 1967

This statute applies to long leases of houses, i.e. those for a term exceeding 21 years (Lease- **10.94** hold Reform Act 1967, s 3 as amended). Previously, a qualifying lease had to be at a low rent. However, ss 137–149 of the Commonhold and Leasehold Reform Act 2002 ('the

2002 Act') have abolished the low rent rule. It was the case that a 'house' could include a house where part is used for business purposes (see *Tandon v Trustees of Spurgeons Homes* [1982] AC 755), or where it has been converted into flats where the conversion is vertical (see *Sharpe v Duke Street Securities NV* (1987) 55 P & CR 331). However, what constituted a house came under further judicial scrutiny in *Day v Hosebay Ltd, Howard de Walden Estates Ltd v Lexgorge Ltd* [2012] UKSC 41. In this case the Supreme Court looked again at how the definition of a house was dealt with for enfranchisement purposes. The decision was a short one based almost entirely on the current use of the premises in question. The court decided that the buildings in *Hosebay* were not houses 'reasonably so called'. The fact that they might look like houses and might be referred to as houses for some purposes was not sufficient to displace the fact that their use was entirely commercial.

10.95   The statute does not apply to a flat or maisonette. In effect, provided there is attachment to the land and occupation of the whole of the 'house', the Act could apply. Previously, a potential claimant had to have resided at the house for at least three years. Sections 137–149 of the 2002 Act have abolished this residence requirement. It is replaced with a requirement that the lessee/claimant must have held the lease for at least two years.

10.96   On paying the lease value calculated in accordance with formulae stipulated by the 1967 Act as subsequently amended by the 2002 Act, the lessee may thereby enfranchise. If the lease is in its early stages the value will be low and on acquisition the lessee can merge the lease into the freehold. The Act sets out what terms are to be stipulated in the freehold transfer. The statute contemplates the inclusion of such terms as are required to put the parties in the same position as they were in under the lease. As an alternative to buying the freehold the lessee can call for an extended lease of a further 50 years. Where this form of extension is required the rent will be fixed at a modern ground rent and will be open to review after 25 years.

10.97   A notice in a prescribed form should be served on the lessor. Once served, a contract is created by statute that must be protected by registration. This should be by way of a C(iv) land charge for unregistered land, or a notice for registered land. If the parties to the statutory contract cannot agree on the price, the valuation can be referred to the Lands Chamber. This is part of the Upper Tribunal and has power to determine a range of disputes and appeals concerning land in England and Wales. It replaced its predecessor, the Lands Tribunal, in 2009. On completion the lessee must pay the lessor's costs, both surveying and legal.

10.98   Qualifying rights will now also pass to PRs of deceased tenants. Leaseholders who have already extended their leases under the 1967 Act will nevertheless be able to buy their freehold after the extended lease has commenced. If their extended lease expires, they will be entitled to security of tenure by becoming a tenant of an assured tenancy under Part I of the Housing Act 1988. Lastly, if the freeholder cannot be traced, lessees will be able to apply to the county court for a vesting order, and the First-tier Tribunal (Property Chamber: Residential Property), formerly the Leasehold Valuation Tribunal, will determine the price payable.

RIGHT TO BUY—HOUSING ACTS 1985 AND 2004

10.99   These statutes give council tenants and lessees of other public bodies and institutions the right to buy the freehold or a long lease of their property. A lessee who is in occupation of a flat or maisonette can demand and buy from the lessor a long leasehold interest. To be entitled to call for a long lease (or indeed, where entitled, the freehold), the lessee must have been in occupation of the subject property as a secure tenant for five complete years (amended from two to five years by the Housing Act 2004).

If so entitled the claimant is enabled to receive a long lease for a term of not less than **10.100** 125 years and at a low rent not exceeding £10 per annum with specific limits on lease service charges. The Act applies to any local authority, the Commission for the New Towns, any county council and private housing associations, but not those of a charitable nature.

What will it cost?

As to the consideration to be paid by the claimant, this is the amount that the subject **10.101** property would realize if sold in the open market at arm's length between a willing seller and buyer (s 127 of the Act). However, there is a discount element to be taken into account which is defined in detail by the statute. The longer a claimant has been a qualifying tenant the greater the discount they can claim. However, the Housing Act 2004 imposed new maximum discount levels that varied depending on where the claimant lives. If the claim was in the South East the maximum was £38,000, while in Wales it was £16,000, and the same was the case for London. Since 21 July 2014 the maximum discount has been £77,000 across England, except in London boroughs, where it is £102,700. It will increase each year in April in line with the consumer price index.

Title registration

As to title, on completion the buyer must arrange for registration at Land Registry. To **10.102** assist in the case of unregistered titles, s 154(6) states that the lessor need only supply to the buyer a certificate stating that the seller is entitled to the reversionary estate (the freehold), and grant the new lease subject to such incumbrances, interests, or rights as may be stated in the certificate or detailed in the lease to be granted to the applicant. The format of this certificate is as approved by the Chief Land Registrar, who is required to accept it as all the evidence required of title. The new lease will include details of the discount and the clawback period (see 10.103). It will also include all rights and easements affecting the subject property. Indeed, Part III of Schedule 6 sets out items or provisions that should be included in leases granted as a result of a right-to-buy claim. The effect of this Part is to ensure that there are covenants from the lessor to keep the block in which the subject property is located in good repair, both as to the structure and the exterior elements, and to deliver a reasonable level of services in the capacity of lessor.

Clawback arrangements

After purchasing the property through the right-to-buy procedure, if the buyer then wishes **10.103** to sell, the Housing Act 2004 authorizes a five-year clawback period. If the flat (or house) is sold within five years of the original disposal, a part of the discount must be repaid to the original seller. The Housing Act 2004 provides that the amount to be repaid is lowered by the amount that represents one-fifth of the discount for each full year that passes after the original sale. In addition the amount of discount to be repaid if you sell in the five-year period will be a percentage of the resale value of the property, disregarding the value of any improvements. To ensure that this is enforced, Land Registry will place a note on the registers that there is a discount clawback entitlement for the five-year period. This should prove sufficient notice to a proposed purchaser, who must request payment on or before completion. Accordingly, if you are acting for a buyer of a property that was subject to a right-to-buy transaction always get an undertaking from the seller's practitioners before exchange to pay all monies required on completion to deal properly with the entry on the register.

LANDLORD AND TENANT ACT 1987

10.104 The Act gives tenants in a 'block', i.e. a property in multiple occupation, a right of pre-emption where the lessor intends to dispose of the freehold. This means that if the lessor intends to sell, the lessees must first be offered the chance of buying the reversionary title before there is a sale on the open market. The statute applies to property containing two or more flats. Where the premises are mixed in use, i.e. residential and commercial, the Act may still apply, depending on the percentages of occupation. If the non-residential use does not exceed 50 per cent of the whole, then the statute will apply. This is of particular concern to the owner of a shop and upper part where the upper area is subject to two or more long residential leases, where that owner wants to sell the reversion with the benefit of a commercial letting on the ground floor.

10.105 The lessor must give notice of the proposed disposal to the lessees (s 5 of the Act) and the notice will give them the right to buy the lessor's interest. At least 50 per cent of the flats must be held by qualifying tenants (in effect long leaseholders) and the block must contain two or more flats. The acquisition by the lessees can be through a nominee such as a company owned by the lessees. An auction is clearly a disposal contemplated by the Act (s 4 of the Act); and if the freeholder wishes to sell by auction, the freeholder will be obliged to offer the reversion to the lessees before the auction. If at least half of the qualifying lessees take up the offer, the lessor will be obliged to sell on the same terms as those that gave rise to the notice. It is presumed that the price will therefore be not less than the auction reserve price. The Act contains clear provisions should the lessor sell without serving the necessary notices. Section 11 provides for a notice to be served by the lessees on the purchaser requiring information about the sale, and s 12 then contains a provision to force the buyer to transfer the freehold to the lessees on the same terms as were made for the disposal to that purchaser. Any dispute about the terms, including the price, can be referred to and decided by tribunal. A further practical problem is that the time constraints contemplated by the Act are lengthy. The period during which the lessees must respond to the notice is in effect two months, with further time delays possible. Accordingly, the timing of any proposed disposal by the freeholder may be greatly delayed by the effect of this Act. Lastly, it should be noted that the Act has other weaknesses. If the freehold is owned by a company as its only asset, the owner of that company can avoid the effect of the Act should there be a desire to dispose of the property. This is achieved by selling the shares in the company rather than the freehold title.

10.106 The Housing Act 1996 amended this Act, making it a criminal offence not to notify the tenants of a proposed disposal (by imposing s 10A of the 1987 Act).

LEASEHOLD REFORM, HOUSING AND URBAN DEVELOPMENT ACT 1993

10.107 From 1 November 1993, when this statute came into force, a mechanism for the collective enfranchisement of lessees of flats within a block exists. This mechanism has been amended and greatly improved by the Commonhold and Leasehold Reform Act 2002. The intention of these amendments is the simplification of the eligibility criteria for qualifying tenants. The effect of this combination of legislation is to give most long leaseholders of flats the right, in combination, to purchase the freehold of their block.

10.108 To qualify, the leaseholder must hold a lease for a term exceeding 21 years. The 2002 reforms remove the former requirements that at least two-thirds of the leaseholders in the block must participate and that at least half of the participating group must have lived in their flats for the previous 12 months (or periods totalling three years in the last ten). The

2002 Act further removes the low rent test in the limited circumstances where this still applies (leases of less than 35 years). It also increases the proportion of the building that can be occupied for non-residential purposes from 10 per cent to 25 per cent. There is, however, a requirement that those participating in the enfranchisement must occupy half of the flats in the block (2002 Act, s 119). The purchase of the freehold and subsequent management of the building are to be carried out by a 'Right to Enfranchise Company' of which the participating leaseholders are members. All relevant leaseholders will have the right to participate in the purchase by joining the company. As well as the purchase price, on enfranchisement lessees may also have to pay the lessor's reasonable costs.

Also as a consequence of the terms of this Act, a lessee can in the alternative call for a new **10.109** lease that will extend the existing term by another 90 years (s 39). The existing requirement that the leaseholder must have lived in the flat for the last three years, or periods totalling three years in the last ten, is replaced by the 2002 reforms with a requirement that the lessee must have held the lease for at least two years. The rent to be paid will be a mere peppercorn, but a premium valued under specific terms of the statute will be payable. If the lease has less than five years to run, the lessor can seek to oppose the lessee's application where the lessor can show an intention to demolish and/or reconstruct the property and needs vacant possession to carry out these plans. If granted, the lease will have immediate effect, but will not stop subsequent collective enfranchisement action.

If collective enfranchisement is to proceed, the lessees need to serve an initial notice form **10.110** upon the lessor, including in the notice the contents required by the Act (s 13). (Only the contents are set out, not the nature of the form itself.) These include the subject premises, a plan, the proposed price, all qualifying tenants with lease details, nominee details, and the interest or interests to be procured by this process.

LANDLORD AND TENANT (COVENANTS) ACT 1995

This Act applies to all leases granted on or after 1 January 1996. All other leases will not **10.111** normally be affected by the Act. It reverses the general rule that prevailed before the Act was passed that a lessee remained liable under the lease covenants throughout the full term of the lease. The Act therefore strikes a mortal blow to the principle of privity of contract where leases are concerned. Unless the lessee has entered into an agreement designated by the Act as an 'authorised guarantee agreement' (AGA) the lessee will, on assignment, be automatically released from any liability in the future on the lessee's lease covenants (s 5(2)). An outgoing lessee who has entered into an AGA acts as guarantor for the successor in title but not beyond the time of ownership of the lease by the incoming lessee. The outgoing lessee cannot escape liability for breaches of covenant that arose during the time prior to the assignment of the legal estate, and the outgoing lessee will remain liable for such breaches after as well as before assignment. Should there be a transfer of the freehold reversion, there is no such automatic release for a lessor under the terms of the statute. However, the reversioner can seek a release by applying for it from the lessee for the time being either before or within a period of four weeks from the date of the transfer of the reversionary title. The effect of this Act cannot be excluded or altered by agreement or otherwise.

What amounts to a new lease can be of material importance, especially where there is a **10.112** variation to a lease that was granted before 1 January 1996. This is because a variation can amount to a surrender and re-grant but without being called a surrender. If the variation concerns either the lease term or the extent of the leased property, it will operate as a surrender and re-grant. If this happens, then the re-grant will amount to a new lease and will be covered by the terms of this statute. Practitioners acting for a lessor should always bear this in mind when dealing with variations, especially where the rent or the extent of the demised property is involved.

E THE COMMONHOLD AND LEASEHOLD REFORM ACT 2002

Introduction

10.113 This Act makes substantial changes to leasehold property law and conveyancing. It is intended that there will be another way in which an owner may hold a freehold estate. It will be called commonhold land, even though it actually deals with freeholds. The purpose of the new form is to address the current deficiencies in relation to the enforceability of covenants and other lease provisions between lessees. (For the same reason it also addresses the related problems with freehold flats, i.e. flying freeholds.) Each separate property in a commonhold development will be termed a unit. A unit can be either residential or commercial and the owner will be the unit-holder. Accordingly, commercial conveyancers need to be aware that the Act can apply to a shop or a light industrial unit as well as to residential flats.

10.114 There will be a commonhold association that will own and manage the common parts. It will be a company limited by guarantee where all the members will be the unit-holders. Thus unit-holders will have a duality of ownership. First, they will own their units and, second, they will own a share of the commonhold association and thus indirectly the common parts.

10.115 All commonhold will be registrable at Land Registry, which will require on registration a Commonhold Community Statement (CCS). This statement will contain the rules and regulations for the commonhold. It will be possible for owners of existing non-commonhold property to seek to convert their title to a commonhold arrangement, but 100 per cent of all owners will have to agree to the conversion. The freeholder must also consent to the conversion, without which it cannot proceed.

10.116 In summary, the unit-holder will in effect own, freehold-style, the shop, light industrial unit, or flat instead of being a leaseholder. The unit-holders will share in the running of the commonhold-held common parts and be required to pay a management or service charge. The units will not be wasting assets like leaseholds, nor will they be at the whim of a freeholder and/or its management policies.

10.117 SC 9 in the fourth edition (and not the fifth edition) deals with dispositions of commonhold property. SC 9.3 states that the buyer having received copies of the memorandum and articles of association of the commonhold association and the CCS, enters into the contract fully accepting the terms of these documents. If the sale is of part of a commonhold unit, then SC 9.4 requires the seller to seek the consent of the commonhold association for this sale of part. It also allows rescission should consent not be forthcoming. Commonhold is considered in more detail in 10.118.

Commonhold

10.118 This is a new form of land ownership of registered freehold land. It can apply to both residential and commercial developments. The idea is based on cooperation between a community of freehold owners living within a defined location. It gives owners of individual units in a development the security of freehold ownership. It allows them to control and collectively manage their own common areas. It allows positive obligations to be enforceable against successors

in title of individual units. In July 2012 the old CML published another part of its *Lenders'*
Handbook for Solicitors and Licensed Conveyancers England and Wales (now known as the
UK Finance Mortgage Lenders' Handbook). This sets out standard instructions in the event
that a conveyancer is representing the lender separately from the borrower in a residential
conveyancing transaction. Commonhold has not proved popular with developers and there
may be less than 20 commonhold estates across England and Wales.

Key features of commonhold

(a) **Introduction** A commonhold is a freehold community. Within the boundaries of that **10.119**
community are separate freeholders with their own units. These people are called unit-
holders. The remainder of the commonhold comprises the common parts, which are
vested in a commonhold association. This association is a private company limited by
guarantee and its only members are the freehold registered proprietors of the units
within the community. The community is then bound together by a 'local law', which is
drafted, when the community is established. This local law is known as the Commonhold Community Statement (or CCS). Schedule 2 to the Act lists the types of registered
freehold that cannot be commonhold. These include flying freeholds (e.g. no commonhold flats above a shop not forming part of the commonhold) and agricultural land.
(b) **Unit-holder** A unit-holder is the person registered as proprietor, or entitled to be
registered as proprietor, of a freehold estate in the unit (s 12). A sole unit-holder is a
member of the commonhold association. You can also have joint unit-holders (s 13).
In the case of joint unit-holders, they decide which of them is to be the member of the
commonhold association. If they do not decide, then the unit-holder who is named first
in the proprietorship register is the member.
(c) **Commonhold association** This is a private company limited by guarantee incorporated under the Companies Act 1985. It must have a memorandum of association setting
out the objects of the company. Under s 34 of the 2002 Act, one of the objects of the
company must be to exercise the functions of a commonhold association. The commonhold land must be specified. The memorandum must fix the amount each member
guarantees to contribute if the company is wound up.
(d) **Commonhold Community Statement (CCS)** This serves two purposes:
 1. It describes the development, the units, and the common parts.
 2. It sets out the rules under which it will be managed.
(e) **Common parts** The rest of the commonhold development, i.e. not included in a unit,
forms the common parts (s 25). The CCS may define one or more pieces of land within the
common parts as 'limited use areas' where there may be restrictions on who may use such
an area and what it may be used for, for example allocated parking areas for individual
unit-holders which can only be used for parking. The CCS must contain provisions requiring the commonhold association to insure, repair, and maintain the common parts (s 26).
(f) **Rules of management** The CCS will set out:
 1. the rights and duties of the unit-holders and the commonhold association;
 2. how management decisions are to be taken. Examples of duties are contained in
 s 31—they include to pay money, to carry out works, to grant access, controlling the
 use of the unit, for example residential only, not to cause nuisance or annoyance to
 neighbours.
(g) **How commonhold is created** Land becomes commonhold land because it is registered
as such. The role of Land Registry is to ensure that commonhold land is clearly defined,
that it is transferable under the general principles of land registration subject to the variations specific to commonhold, and that all associated and necessary documents within
the commonhold development are accessible to those who wish to view them.

(h) **Conversions from leases to commonhold**   Where units are already occupied by long leaseholders application can be made to convert the freehold reversion to commonhold (s 9). However, all leaseholders and their mortgagees must consent. You cannot mix and match commonhold and long leases. Typically a conversion will occur where long leaseholders own a management company that controls the freehold and they want to convert to commonhold. All leases are extinguished and registration of the commonhold common parts and units then occurs.

(i) **Dealings by the unit-holder**   The unit-holder's powers to deal with his unit are set out in ss 15–22 of the 2002 Act. He may transfer the whole of his freehold unit. The new unit-holder then notifies the commonhold association of the transfer and becomes a member of the association. The outgoing unit-holder remains liable for any arrears of service charge or other previously incurred liabilities. Transfers of part are not permitted unless the commonhold association consents in writing. The unit-holder may charge the whole of the unit (but not part) and if he grants a lease of a residential unit the lease must comply with conditions to be prescribed by regulations, for example length of lease.

(j) **Dealings by the commonhold association**   Common parts—the commonhold association may transfer land in the common parts (i.e. adding or subtracting bits). In this event, as the extent of the common parts will be changed, an amendment to the CCS will be required. The association may also create other interests in the common parts, for example an easement in favour of an adjoining development. The association's power to create charges is restricted. Essentially it can create a legal mortgage but, before doing so, it must pass a unanimous resolution to create the charge.

Other changes

10.120   The 2002 Act also made substantial changes to other aspects of leasehold property law and practice that conveyancers may encounter when dealing with leasehold properties. The following detail has been prepared from the explanatory notes to the 2002 Act prepared by the Lord Chancellor's Department:

(a) **A right to management**   The 2002 Act introduced a right for leaseholders of flats to manage their own building. It set out qualifying conditions for exercising the right and provided that eligible leaseholders must set up a company, known as a 'Right to Manage Company', in order to exercise this new right. The 2002 Act decreed the nature and format of the constitution of the company, including its memorandum and articles of association, and entitlement to membership. It set out procedures for exercising the right to manage and for the subsequent management of the building. It includes safeguards to protect the interests of the landlord and any other occupiers of the building, such as tenants on short residential leases or commercial tenants.

(b) **Changes to the Leasehold Reform Housing and Urban Development Act 1993**   The 2002 Act amended the provisions of the Leasehold Reform Housing and Urban Development Act 1993 with regard to the right of leaseholders to buy collectively the freehold of their building. The changes are set out in 10.107.

(c) **Reforms of the Landlord and Tenant Act 1987**   The 2002 Act made two changes to the 1987 statute. First, it extended the right to apply to a tribunal for the appointment of a new manager under Part II of the 1987 Act to leaseholders where the lease provides that management is carried out by a third party rather than the landlord. This would cover a company appointed by the lessees and required to manage rather than the lessor. The 2002 Act also extended and clarified the grounds on which application may be made to vary a lease under Part IV of the 1987 Act. It also transferred jurisdiction for handling such applications from the county courts to a tribunal.

(d) **Other leasehold reforms** The 2002 Act introduced a requirement that ground rent will not be payable unless it has been demanded. The demand is to be made by giving the tenant a prescribed notice. The reform in the 2002 Act prevents the application of any provisions of a lease relating to late or non-payment (e.g. additional charges such as interest) if the rent is paid within 30 days of the demand being issued. It also introduced additional restrictions on the commencement of forfeiture proceedings for breaches of covenants or conditions of a lease. It modified s 81 of the Housing Act 1996 to prohibit the commencement of forfeiture proceedings, including the issue of a notice under s 146 of the Law of Property Act 1925, in respect of non-payment of service charges or administration charges. This is not the case if the charge has been agreed or admitted by the tenant, or a court or the First-tier Tribunal (Property Chamber; Residential Property) has determined that it is reasonable and due. It also prohibits the commencement of forfeiture proceedings for other breaches, unless a court or the Tribunal has determined that a breach has occurred.

(e) Section 131 of the Housing and Planning Act 2016 amends Schedule 11 of the Commonhold and Leasehold Reform Act 2002 to add a new para 5A which will give the First-tier Tribunal (Residential Property) power to make an order preventing a landlord from charging legal costs to a leaseholder as an administration charge. The new paragraph 5A commenced on 6 April 2017.

KEY POINTS SUMMARY

STATUTES AND LEASES AND COMMONHOLD

- If your client owns a house on a long lease, he may be entitled to claim the freehold or an extension of the lease term as a result of the Leasehold Reform Act 1967. Is it a long lease of residential accommodation where the client has held the lease for at least two years? **10.121**

- If your client owns a flat or maisonette on a long lease, he may be entitled to seek collective enfranchisement as a result of the Leasehold Reform, Housing and Urban Development Act 1993. To qualify, the leaseholder must hold a lease for a term exceeding 21 years. If at least one-half of the lessees meet these criteria, and give notice to the lessor, the purchase will then proceed at the market value as prescribed in the Act.

- The Landlord and Tenant (Covenants) Act 1995 applies to all leases granted on or after 1 January 1996. Unless the lessee has entered into an AGA the lessee will, on assignment, be automatically released from any liability in the future on lease covenants. If there is an AGA then the outgoing lessee acts as guarantor for the first successor in title only.

- If your client wants to buy a flat or maisonette lease on a right-to-buy basis, is the client a qualifying tenant of a local authority or other relevant lessor, and how long a period of occupation can be claimed? These elements will dictate the possibility of the claim and the amount of any possible discount. Discount depends on location.

- The Landlord and Tenant Act 1987 gives lessees in a 'block', i.e. a property in multiple occupation, a right of pre-emption where the lessor intends to dispose of the freehold. The lessor must give notice of the proposed disposal to the tenants, and the notice will give them the right to buy the lessor's interest. The period during which the lessees must respond to the notice is two months.

- Be aware of recent changes to leasehold legislation arising out of the provisions in the Commonhold and Leasehold Reform Act 2002.

PRACTICAL CHECKLISTS

NEW LEASES

10.122
- Does the draft lease contain an accurate description of the subject property and all rights required for the full use and enjoyment thereof?
- Do the rights include rights of way, of support and protection, and access to other parts for repairs?
- Are the ground rent arrangements acceptable, particularly regarding increase?
- Are the lessee's covenants reasonable?
- Are there any lessor covenants; and if so, are they sufficiently comprehensive in the light of the nature of the subject property?
- Do the lease terms adequately cover insurance arrangements? If a house or maisonette, the lessee could insure. If a flat in a block, the lessor or management company should insure. Is there a clause calling for reinstatement on there being damage by an insured risk?
- Do the lease terms adequately cover maintenance arrangements? If a house, the lessee could have the complete responsibility to repair and maintain the subject property. If a flat or maisonette, it is best for either the lessor or a management company owned by the lessees to repair.
- Is there any restriction on user? If so, are those restrictions reasonable and/or appropriate to the subject property?
- Is there any restriction on alienation? If so, are those restrictions reasonable and/or appropriate to the subject property?
- Has the lessor offered a covenant to enforce covenants against one lessee at the request of another?
- If the lease contains a forfeiture on bankruptcy clause, demand that the clause be removed from the draft.
- Do the contract terms appear harmonious with the draft lease terms and are there any special conditions to be considered?
- Have you reported in writing on all the lease terms to your client, and has that client acknowledged that report and confirmed that it is acceptable?
- Who is to engross the lease after contracts have been exchanged, and is there a fee to be paid for this?
- If the superior title is registered, make sure the client will end up with an absolute leasehold title. Have you made an application for first registration on a form appropriate to a new long lease?
- If buying the new lease with a mortgage and if required by the lease terms, have you given notice of charge to the lessor?
- If your client is being granted a sub-lease insist on seeing all the superior titles and make sure that the contract contains SC 8.2.4.

EXISTING LEASES

10.123
- Does the existing lease to be purchased contain an accurate description of the subject property and all rights required for the full use and enjoyment thereof?
- Do the rights include rights of way, of support and protection, and access to other parts for repairs?

- Are the ground rent arrangements clear?

- Are the lessee's covenants reasonable?

- Are there any lessor covenants; and if so, are they sufficiently comprehensive in the light of the nature of the subject property?

- Do the lease terms adequately cover insurance arrangements? If a house or maisonette, the lessee could insure. If a flat in a block, the lessor or management company should insure. Is there a clause calling for reinstatement on there being damage by an insured risk?

- Do the lease terms adequately cover maintenance arrangements? If a house, the lessee could have the complete responsibility to repair and maintain the subject property. If a flat or maisonette, it is best for one agent, either the lessor or a management company owned by the lessees, to repair. Is there any restriction on user? If so, are those restrictions reasonable and/or appropriate to the subject property?

- Is there any restriction on alienation? If so, are those restrictions reasonable and/or appropriate to the subject property?

- Has the lessor covenanted to enforce covenants against one lessee at the request of another?

- If the lease contains a forfeiture on bankruptcy clause, advise the client that the lease is not acceptable, as no lender would accept it as a security for a mortgage.

- Have you raised lease-specific enquiries and have you seen a copy of the insurance policy with an up-to-date schedule of cover? Have you seen service charge accounts for the last three years?

- Are the mortgagee's requirements satisfied within the lease terms on offer?

- Are the special conditions in the contract sufficient given the lease terms covering alienation, insurance and repairs?

- On completion have you seen a clear ground rent receipt and has, if required by the lease terms, the lessor granted permission for the transmission of title to your client?

- Have you given notice of assignment (and charge) to the lessor if so required by the lease terms?

11

NEW PROPERTIES

INTRODUCTION

11.01 This chapter will consider the special areas of concern for practitioners who are required to deal with the sale or purchase of new residential properties, either recently constructed or in the course of construction. We will look at the roles of the practitioners acting for the developer and prospective buyer, respectively. We shall also consider the arrangements for roads and sewers on a new estate and the importance of insurance against structural defects in new properties. As the sale of a new property on an estate is the sale of part of an existing title, the discussions of sale of part in Chapters 3 and 5 are also relevant. For properties being sold 'off plan', i.e. before being built, the buyer must be supplied with a Predicted Energy Assessment, followed by a full Energy Performance Certificate once the property has been physically completed.

In April 2013 the Government launched a 'Help to buy' scheme to assist buyers who have a deposit of at least 5 per cent to buy a new-build home. The scheme will run until the end of the decade and covers newly built homes up to the value of £600,000. As much as 20 per cent of the cost of the home can be funded by a shared equity loan, which is interest-free for the first five years. In this way the Government effectively takes a stake in the value of borrowers' homes. The value of the shared equity loan is linked to the property's value. So, for example if the value of the property has doubled by the time the shared equity loan is repaid, the amount the borrower has to repay will have doubled as well. In year six, borrowers will have to pay a 1.75 per cent annual fee, which will rise by 1 per cent above the Retail Prices Index (RPI) measure of inflation every year after that. The remainder of the value of the property is paid for with a standard mortgage, to cover up to 75 per cent of the loan.

ACTING FOR THE DEVELOPER

11.02 There are likely to be very many plots of land on a new estate, which it is intended shall be sold to different buyers. Accordingly, each buyer will expect to receive certain essential items such as the draft contract, replies to standard enquiries, copies of the relevant planning consents, and evidence of title. As a result, a time-saving measure for the developer's practitioner is the preparation, before the first sale, of a standardized pack of documents which each buyer's practitioner will require. This package should be ready to send out as soon as notification is received that a plot has been sold.

Special care must be taken over the drafting of the contract and purchase deed which, for uniformity, should contain all the easements and covenants which are appropriate and necessary for the development. It will often be the case that the seller will refuse to negotiate any amendments to its standard-form draft documentation on the basis that a seller of multiple plots on a building estate must have uniformity and standardization of legal documentation. The possible impact of the Unfair Terms in Consumer Contracts Regulations 1999 will, however, need to be borne in mind (see 11.15). **11.03**

DOCUMENTATION

We will now consider individually the items in the package of documents to be sent to the practitioner acting for the buyer. **11.04**

Draft contract: the seller's concerns

Generally

The sale of a plot in a new development of properties will constitute a sale of part of the developer's title. It is important therefore to bear in mind the key issues relating to sale of part contracts which were considered in Chapter 3 (see 3.106–3.131). **11.05**

Accurate description

On a sale of part the seller's practitioner drafting the contract must ensure that it contains a full and accurate description of the property being sold. This should be done by reference to a scale plan attached to the contract showing the individual plot edged red. The description can be relatively short with the added words, 'more particularly described on the plan', thereby indicating that the plan is to prevail in the case of conflict or uncertainty (see *Neilson v Poole* (1969) 20 P & CR 909). **11.06**

Easements and covenants

The developer/seller will want to negate any implied grant of easements in favour of the buyer under s 62 of the Law of Property Act 1925 and the rule in *Wheeldon v Burrows* (1879) 12 ChD 31. The contract should make appropriate provision for the grant and reservation of new easements and the imposition of new covenants. The easements will cover such matters as rights of way and the right to run services over the remainder of the estate, and the right to enter to inspect, maintain, and repair accessways and services. Typical covenants will include: restricting the use to residential only, not to make any alterations without the seller's consent, and to maintain one or more fences around the plot (some new open-plan developments include a covenant not to fence off front gardens). The easements and covenants will be created in the purchase deed, not the contract, but the contract will govern the contents of the purchase deed, so the contract will normally stipulate the exact wording of the easements and covenants. **11.07**

Completion arrangements

The developer cannot be absolutely sure when the property will be physically completed and ready for the buyer to move in. Accordingly, a fixed completion date should not be agreed on exchange of contracts. The contract should provide instead for legal completion to take place within a specified period after the seller's practitioner has notified the buyer's practitioner that the property has been completed and is fit for occupation. The period in **11.08** question must be sufficient to allow time for the buyer to carry out the pre-completion searches, to request the draw-down of any mortgage advance, and for the buyer's (and probably mortgagee's) surveyor to carry out a final inspection of the property. Ten working days should be sufficient and is normally acceptable to both developer and purchaser.

Barring requisitions

11.09 The developer/seller will want to ensure that the buyer carries out the investigation of title before exchange and that no requisitions are permitted to be raised on the title after exchange. This can be covered by a special condition in the contract. The buyer should be happy with this provided there is enough time to carry out the title investigation.

Responsibility for insurance

11.10 If the subject property is not finished by the time contracts are exchanged, the seller should be responsible for it between exchange and completion. SC 5.1.1 is not appropriate as this states that the property is at the risk of the buyer from the date of the contract. This condition should therefore be excluded or amended, and the special condition doing so must make it clear that the risk remains with the seller until legal completion.

National House Building Council

11.11 If the builder is registered with the National House Building Council (NHBC), the new property will have the benefit of the NHBC Buildmark scheme which provides a ten-year insurance for structural defects (see 11.51). The contract should specify that the builder will provide NHBC protection and that the NHBC documentation will be supplied to the buyer before completion.

Extras

11.12 If the buyer is paying an additional price for 'extras' (e.g. specially designed kitchen or bathroom fittings) then, having regard to s 2 of the Law of Property (Miscellaneous Provisions) Act 1989, the contract should specifically deal with this by itemizing the extras and clearly stating the additional sum.

Deposit

11.13 To assist cash flow the developer will usually expect to receive a full 10 per cent deposit from the buyer on exchange of contracts. Moreover, the developer will want the deposit paid to its practitioner as agent for the seller rather than as stakeholder, so that the deposit can be released to the developer as soon as contracts are exchanged. The seller's solicitor should therefore cover the point and amend the Standard Conditions (SCs) by a special condition to this effect.

11.14 While it may be the intention of the developer to build the property in accordance with the agreed plans and specifications, the developer may wish to reserve a right to vary the method of construction or the materials used in the construction. The buyer may wish to qualify such a right (see 11.22).

Unfair Terms in Consumer Contracts Regulations 1999

11.15 The Unfair Terms in Consumer Contracts Regulations 1999 (SI 1999/2083) derive from an EU directive and govern contracts made between a seller or supplier of goods acting in the course of a business and a private consumer. Similar in effect to the Unfair Contract Terms Act 1977, the Regulations render void an 'unfair' term in such a contract. An unfair term is classified as one which, contrary to the requirement of good faith, causes a significant imbalance in the parties' rights and obligations arising under the contract to the detriment of the consumer. The relative strengths of the parties' bargaining power would be an important factor in determining whether a term is unfair. The burden of proof lies with the consumer.

The 1999 Regulations apply to land contracts, including mortgages and tenancy agreements (see *Khartun v London Borough of Newham* [2003] EWHC 2326). Standard-form contracts in which developers indicate that no amendments will be considered may fall foul of the Regulations. **11.16**

Draft contract: the buyer's concerns

As we have seen, it is customary for the seller to refuse to negotiate any amendments on the standardized documentation, but for a buyer's practitioner to accept this without question would clearly be a dereliction of duty to the client. The buyer's practitioner must therefore as a matter of course always consider the draft documentation carefully and seek to make amendments which properly protect the buyer's (and any lender client's) interests. **11.17**

Easements and covenants

The buyer's practitioner must be satisfied that the contract provides for the grant of all necessary easements in favour of the buyer, including the free passage of services, uninterrupted rights of access, and a right to go on to adjoining land if necessary to carry out repairs. The proposed new covenants must not unduly restrict the buyer's intended use and enjoyment of the property. In particular, the buyer's practitioner should have regard to any covenant restricting alterations to the property without the seller's consent. We suggest that the buyer should be advised to limit this in time to, say, three years, after which period the developer should have sold all remaining plots (and thus the question of whether the buyer's alterations will adversely affect the developer's ability to sell the remaining plots will not arise). Moreover, the proposed covenants must not adversely affect the future sale or marketability of the property, and in this respect any lender's instructions should be strictly adhered to. **11.18**

Final inspection

If the buyer is buying with the aid of a mortgage, the lender will not release the mortgage advance until the property has been completed to the satisfaction of the lender's surveyor. The buyer's practitioner should therefore consider a provision in the contract whereby the buyer cannot be forced to complete until the mortgagee's surveyor is satisfied in this respect. Similarly, the lender should not release the mortgage advance until the home warranty provider (e.g. NHBC) has issued a cover note confirming that the property has received a satisfactory final inspection and that the home warranty will be in place on or before completion (see 11.58). The buyer's practitioner should therefore consider a provision in the contract whereby the buyer cannot be forced to complete until a satisfactory final inspection has been carried out by the home warranty provider and a cover note issued. **11.19**

Completion

The buyer will also require a 'longstop date' for completion, being a date, say, six or nine months hence, after which the buyer may withdraw from the contract. Without this provision, if the property is never physically completed or the seller's completion notice is not served, the contract would remain open indefinitely, a state of affairs which ultimately would be unsatisfactory for both parties. **11.20**

Developer's obligations

If the property is in the course of construction, the buyer would be wise to include a contractual obligation on the developer/seller to build the property and the rest of the estate in a good and workmanlike manner in accordance with the planning permission and the agreed plans and specifications. The buyer would also want the right (together with the **11.21** buyer's lender) to inspect the property during its construction and again when it is finished. Associated with this will be a provision requiring the seller to rectify any minor defects (known as 'snagging items') either before legal completion or within a specified time thereafter. A snagging list is normally prepared by the buyer's surveyor on final inspection. A prudent buyer would also insist on a clause in the contract whereby the seller agrees to remove all builders' rubbish before completion, to erect boundary fences, and to landscape the garden and adjoining areas. (The developer may prefer to confirm these points in its replies to pre-contract enquiries rather than amend its standard form of contract.)

11.22 As we have seen, the developer may wish to reserve a right to vary the method of construction or the materials used in the construction of the new property. The buyer will be reluctant to accept such a clause unless it is qualified to provide that such variation will not diminish the value of the property or the accommodation to be provided.

Deposit

11.23 As far as the deposit is concerned, the buyer would prefer the deposit to be held by the seller's practitioner as stakeholder, so that it remains secure in the seller's practitioner's client account until completion. The argument can be made on behalf of the buyer that it may be several months before the transaction is completed and if the deposit is released to the seller and the seller later defaults (e.g. because of insolvency), the buyer as an unsecured creditor may never recover the deposit. In addition, you can make the point that the developer will be entitled to receive interest on the deposit in any event.

KEY POINTS SUMMARY

BUYER'S CONCERNS ON DRAFT CONTRACT OF NEW PROPERTY

11.24
- Do not be afraid to amend standardized draft documentation if this is in the best interests of your client.
- Check that the buyer has all necessary easements, for example for access, services, and rights of entry on to adjoining plots.
- Ensure that the proposed covenants will not adversely affect the buyer's use and enjoyment of the property or the future sale or marketability of it; consider your mortgagee's instructions.
- Allow for the buyer's and/or mortgagee's surveyor to inspect the property both before and after physical completion.
- Insist on a longstop date for completion after which your client can rescind the contract.
- The seller should be obliged to build in a good and workmanlike manner with good and substantial materials.
- Provide for the seller to rectify any snagging items, to remove all builders' rubbish before completion, to erect boundary fences, and to landscape the garden and adjoining areas.
- If the seller reserves the right to vary the methods of construction or building materials, this should be qualified by a proviso that neither the value of the property nor the accommodation shall be materially diminished.
- If the property is still in the course of construction on exchange of contracts, the risk of insurance should remain with the seller until physical and legal completion have occurred.
- The deposit is to be held as stakeholder.
- Provide for NHBC protection; all relevant documentation to be supplied to the buyer on or before completion.

Purchase deed

On the sale of a new property the form of purchase deed is usually stipulated in the con- **11.25**
tract and this is permitted by s 48 of the Law of Property Act 1925. To comply with s 2 of
the Law of Property (Miscellaneous Provisions) Act 1989 the contract must incorporate
all the terms agreed by the parties, and for this reason the agreed form of purchase deed is
annexed to the contract. Thus the draft contract and purchase deed together will be sent
in duplicate to each buyer's practitioner. As we have seen, the purchase deed will set out
expressly all necessary grants and reservations of easements together with the new covenants being created.

If the estate is registered, a Land Registry transfer of part (TP1) will be the appropriate **11.26**
purchase deed. The developer's practitioner may apply to Land Registry for prior approval
of the form of transfer, and this should be done as a matter of good practice to avoid Land
Registry raising any requisitions at a later date. In approving the form of transfer the
Registry will also guarantee that the easements granted by the transfer will be registered.
This will avoid the necessity for the seller to prove its title to grant the easements.

As the transaction is a sale of part, the transfer will of course incorporate a plan, which **11.27**
is usually based on an extract from the estate layout plan approved by Land Registry (see
11.31). The Registry will not accept a transfer plan 'for the purpose of identification only':
the plan must contain sufficient detail to identify the plot and its dimensions in relation to
nearby recognizable features.

If the land is unregistered, either a draft conveyance will be appropriate or, if preferred, **11.28**
a Land Registry transfer (as the plots will be compulsorily registrable). It may be wise,
however, for the developer to consider voluntarily applying for first registration of the
unregistered land before any of the plots are sold (see 11.36).

New lease or commonhold

If instead of the sale of a freehold, the new property is the grant of a lease, the developer's **11.29**
practitioner will prepare an agreement for lease with standard form of lease attached. In this
case it is the lease which contains the necessary grant and reservation of easements and
the imposition of covenants. If the new development is to be commonhold, have regard to
the issues considered at 10.118.

Evidence of title

Each buyer will require evidence of the seller's title to the estate so that title can be inves- **11.30**
tigated in the normal way. A detailed discussion of deduction of title is given in Chapter 5,
but we consider in the following paragraphs matters which are of particular relevance to
new properties in both registered and unregistered land.

Registered land

Land Registry approval of estate layout plan The estate layout plan is the plan prepared **11.31**
by the developer's surveyor showing the proposed layout of the development and the
individual plots (including any flats or maisonettes). Land Registry will, free of charge,
formally approve the estate layout plan of any estate which is registered or about to be registered. Such approval will assist in avoiding boundary disputes, aid the deduction of title,
and help the buyer when carrying out the pre-completion official search at Land Registry
(see 11.34 regarding Form CI).

The procedure for approval is for the developer to send to the appropriate Land Registry **11.32**
office two copies of the estate layout plan. When the Registry has approved the plan it will

retain one copy and return the second copy to the developer marked as officially approved. The plan must be based on a recent accurate land survey with the scale and orientation clearly shown (plans marked 'for identification only' are not acceptable). The preferred scale is 1:500, although scale 1:1250 may be admissible if the plot boundaries can be clearly identified. A much larger scale may be necessary if the boundaries are within a building (e.g. for flats) and this should be verified with the Registry in each case. The external boundaries of plots should be edged in colour. Where a property comprises more than one parcel of land, for example a separate parking space for a flat, the plan should identify the main parcel with a number and the ancillary parcel with the same number and a prefix (e.g. 19 for the flat, P19 for the parking space). Access drives, pathways, and common areas should all be clearly indicated on the plan. The Registry requires metric measurements on the plan.

11.33   Any subsequent variation to the layout of the estate, deliberate or accidental, must be duly notified to the Registry. This is done by returning the original approved plan accompanied by two copies of the new plan. More detailed information on Land Registry approval of estate plans can be obtained from Land Registry's Practice Guide 41.

11.34   **Form CI**   The usual method of deducing title to registered land is to supply official copies and a title plan. However, very often the title plan of an estate is large and unwieldy, and in this case the seller's practitioner may apply to Land Registry on Form OC1 for a certificate of official inspection of the title plan. This certificate on Form CI will certify that the subject property (i.e. the individual plot) to which it relates is within the seller's title. It will also indicate the entries on the title which affect the plot in question. Form CI will assist the buyer's practitioner when carrying out the pre-completion official search; instead of having to attach a plan to Form OS2, the practitioner will simply quote the plot number specified on the Form CI.

11.35   Form CI, like official copies, shows a time of issue as well as a date, for example 1 June 2018 12:34:56. The need for a time of issue arises as a result of Land Registry searches and applications acquiring priority on a 'real time' basis. Thus it is possible for different versions of the register to exist on the same day.

Unregistered land

11.36   If the land is unregistered, the seller's practitioner should prepare an abstract of the title to the estate or, preferably, an epitome of title with copy documents attached. It may be worth considering applying for voluntary first registration of the seller's title as deducing title to registered land is, of course, simpler. You should especially consider voluntary registration if the unregistered title is complex, or if there are minor defects which the Registry may be willing to disregard (i.e. the 'curative' effect of first registration).

Replies to enquiries and requisitions

11.37   The seller's practitioner should prepare replies to enquiries which can be geared specifically to the purchase of a new property, for example a dwelling on a housing estate. This saves having to respond to each buyer's own enquiries on an individual basis (save for any additional enquiries that may be raised). The seller will be diverting from the standard forms under the National Protocol and so the buyer's practitioner should be advised that the Protocol is not being used. This can be done in the covering letter (see 11.50).

11.38   Replies to standard requisitions can also be supplied at this initial stage in the transaction so that confirmation can be given that plots will be released from mortgages, and letters of non-crystallization will be issued in respect of any floating charges. Remember that as far as existing fixed charges on the estate are concerned the buyer will require, in respect of the plot being purchased, either a formal deed of release (if the land is unregistered) or Form DS3, with plan attached showing the part of the seller's title being released from the charge (if the land is registered). On the grant of a new lease the appropriate document is a consent to dealing duly executed by the mortgagee.

Other matters that can be dealt with in replies to requisitions are the arrangements for col- **11.39** lection of keys on completion and the furnishing of the seller's practitioner's bank details for transmission of funds by the buyer's practitioner on completion.

Acting for the buyer: additional pre-contract enquiries

After perusing the documentation produced by the developer's practitioner, the buyer's **11.40** practitioner should consider whether any additional enquiries ought to be raised. The following are some typical examples:

(a) You could make a simple request for confirmation of how many houses or units will be constructed on the estate and how many of these have been sold to date (you can then check that the number of units conforms with the planning consent).
(b) You should have received a copy of the road agreement and supporting bond (discussed at 11.45 and 11.46), but you might care to raise the practical question of when the seller expects to lay the final wearing surface to the roads.
(c) You could ask the seller to confirm that it will pay for all charges for construction and connection of the drainage and sewerage systems and all other services of which the property will have the benefit, for example electricity, gas, telephone, cable television. The developer may also be able to supply a plan showing the proposed route of all services to and from the property.
(d) If not already confirmed, you should seek confirmation that any residential property will have the benefit of the NHBC Buildmark scheme providing insurance protection against structural defects for up to ten years, and that the seller will supply you with all necessary documentation.
(e) The draft contract will normally provide for legal completion to take place only after the new property has been physically completed. If the seller will not agree any material amendments to the draft contract, you should ask the seller to confirm that the buyer will not be called on to complete until not only the property but also all services are finished and reasonable access to the property has been provided.
(f) If the contract permits the seller the right to vary the construction or dimensions of the property but the seller will not agree to qualify that right in the contract, you must seek to protect your client's position by raising an enquiry along the following lines: does the seller have any plans to vary the construction or dimensions of the property; and can the seller confirm that any such variation will not materially diminish the accommodation to be provided or the value of the property?
(g) On a practical note, the plot number of the property will invariably be different from the postal address. You should therefore ask the seller to supply the postal address of the property.

Planning consents and planning obligations

Copies of the express planning permissions for the estate development and any building regu- **11.41** lation approvals should be sent to the buyer's practitioner (although the approvals will not be available until the property is finished). The buyer will want to be satisfied that the local planning authority has authorized the construction of the estate and that the builder has complied, or will comply, with all conditions of the planning permissions. The seller's practitioner should also advise the buyer's practitioner of any reserved matters requiring further consent.

11.42 As part of the planning process, the planning authority and the developer may enter into an agreement under s 106 of the Town and Country Planning Act 1990 (known as a Planning Obligation). This agreement sets out the terms for the developer to provide or fund the provision of infrastructure, services, or other impact mitigation measures on or off the development site. For example, if there is insufficient capacity in local schools for new children moving into a new housing development, the council may require the developer to enter into a Planning Obligation to make a financial contribution for educational purposes. As an alternative to a s 106 agreement, the developer may give a unilateral undertaking to the council, for example to carry out certain works. Details of any s 106 agreement or unilateral undertaking that is in place for the subject development should be made available to the buyer's practitioner.

Searches

11.43 Some developers will supply with the package of documents a copy of a local authority search for the estate. This is designed to speed up the conveyancing process because a search will not need to be undertaken later by the buyer's practitioner (at added cost). However, the difficulty with this arrangement is that local searches quickly become out of date and the *UK Finance Mortgage Lenders' Handbook* provides that the search must be not more than six months old at completion. As a result many developers simply leave buyers to conduct their own local searches. If this is so, the buyer's search will generally need to be accompanied by a plan, together with a description of the new property by reference to its plot number. You should check with the relevant local authority as to their precise requirements.

11.44 If the land is unregistered, a recent index map search at Land Registry can be sent as confirmation that the land is unregistered and that no cautions against first registration have been lodged. If the land has never been built on before, it will also be helpful to supply a copy of a recent commons registration search (see Chapter 4 for a full discussion of these searches).

Road and sewer agreements under s 38 of the Highways Act 1980 and s 104 of the Water Industry Act 1991 with supporting bonds

Road agreement

11.45 The roads and street lighting on a new estate will become adopted by the local authority (and thus maintainable at the public expense) only after the estate has been physically completed. The local authority is empowered to make up the roads and charge the house buyers for the cost of doing so. The buyers will therefore require the developer to enter into an agreement with the local authority under s 38 of the Highways Act 1980, in which the developer agrees to make up the roads and street lighting to an adoptable standard (i.e. to a standard acceptable to the authority) and the authority agrees to adopt them subsequently.

Supporting bond

11.46 The buyers will be concerned that the developer may default in making up the roads (e.g. because of insolvency), resulting in the local authority making them up and charging the cost to the buyers (this is permitted under s 219 of the Highways Act 1980). To protect the buyers against this occurring, the s 38 agreement must be supported by a bond or guarantee from the developer's bank or insurer, which provides for the buyers to be indemnified for any costs paid to the local authority should the developer default.

Drains and sewers

11.47 The developer should complete a similar agreement and supporting bond in respect of the making up and adoption of the drains and sewers on the estate. This agreement is made with the local water company under s 104 of the Water Industry Act 1991.

Mortgagee requirements

It is a standard requirement of mortgagees of properties on new large estates that road and **11.48**
sewer agreements with supporting bonds are in place before completion of the mortgage.
This is confirmed in the *UK Finance Mortgage Lenders' Handbook*. If they are not in place,
the lender will usually wish to make a retention from the advance, which will be released
to the borrower only as and when the agreements come into force.

The *UK Finance Mortgage Lenders' Handbook* requires builders and developers of newly
built, converted, or renovated properties to complete a UK Finance Disclosure form. It
informs the lender what discounts and other incentives have been offered to the borrower/
purchaser and additionally includes information on other matters such as tenure type,
method of construction, and information on ground rents. The completed form must be
supplied to the conveyancer acting on behalf of the lender providing the mortgage finance
for the property. The form must be supplied to the valuer acting on behalf of the lender upon
request. The form is designed to ensure full disclosure of the financial aspects of the transaction and key information about the property. It is not meant to be used to provide a valuation. It should be completed by reference to the UK Finance FAQ, see **https://www.ukfinance.
org.uk/wp-content/uploads/2018/02/Disclosure-Form-FAQs-February-2018-Final-1.pdf**.

Small estates

If the new estate is small, the developer may decide to retain ownership of the roads and **11.49**
sewers. In this case the developer should, in the transfer or conveyance, covenant with
the buyer to maintain the private roads and sewers. The developer can then provide for
the recovery of the cost of maintenance from the individual plot owners through an estate
rentcharge under the Rentcharges Act 1977 (note that the enforcement of a rentcharge is an
exception to the general rule that the burden of positive covenants does not bind successors
in title of the covenantor).

Covering letter

The seller's practitioner should prepare a standardized covering letter for each buyer's **11.50**
practitioner enclosing the package of documents. The letter can also provide useful general information about the new estate, covering such matters as the anticipated dates for
physical completion of the buildings and details of where plans and specifications can be
inspected. A general information pack may also be useful. The seller may wish to make it
clear at this early stage that no material amendments to the draft documentation will be
accepted. The letter can also confirm that the developer is registered with the NHBC and
that the appropriate NHBC documentation will be forwarded to the buyer's practitioners
following exchange of contracts. The letter can confirm that it is not intended to use the
National Protocol (although by supplying these items at this initial stage the spirit of the
Protocol is invoked).

STRUCTURAL DEFECTS INSURANCE

Schemes available

All new dwellings and conversions should be insured against structural defects, and it is **11.51**
a standard requirement of lending institutions that new residential properties are protected in this way. Without such insurance the property will become unmortgageable and
its future marketability adversely affected. The most popular current scheme which is
now in use almost universally is the NHBC Buildmark scheme. This is discussed in detail
in 11.55.

Architect's certificate

11.52 In some cases a buyer or lender may be willing to accept an architect's certificate of completion of the building as an alternative to an NHBC warranty. This may apply, for instance, where the architect has supervised the construction of the building under a Joint Contracts Tribunal (JCT) contract (i.e. an agreement incorporating a standard set of conditions for a building contract). The insurance cover is effectively provided by the architect's professional indemnity insurers in the event of professional negligence on the part of the architect. There are, however, potential dangers in accepting an architect's certificate. In *Hunt v Optima* [2014] EWCA Civ 714, original buyers (and subsequent buyers) who received and relied upon an architect's certificate after exchange of contracts or completion were unsuccessful in a negligence action against the architect. The Court of Appeal ruled that the architect owed a duty of care only to those buyers who received the certificate *before* exchange of contracts. So if you are acting for a buyer (or subsequent buyer) or lender who is relying on an architect's certificate you should heed the warnings of this case and ensure that the client is properly advised of the potential risks.

Consultant's certificate

11.53 The lender may be willing to accept the monitoring of the development by a professional consultant employed by the borrower alone or by the borrower and the builder jointly. If so, and the *Lenders' Handbook* is being used (see Appendix 12), the professional consultant must complete a Professional Consultant's Certificate in the required form (see para 6.7.4 of the *Lenders' Handbook*).

11.54 As the NHBC Buildmark scheme is the most widely used, we set out in the following paragraphs a detailed appraisal of how it operates. Other schemes, less commonly used, are provided by the Housing Association Property Mutual (HAPM) and the Premier Guarantee for Private Housing and Completed Housing.

NHBC Buildmark

11.55 The Buildmark scheme is used when a builder who is registered with the NHBC sells a newly constructed house or flat that the builder has built or converted. Reputable builders naturally aspire to be registered with the NHBC because the NHBC's acceptance of them is a sign that they have the necessary skill and competence as a builder. You can check whether a builder is currently registered with the NHBC by going to **http://www.nhbc. co.uk/Homeowners/check-the-register/** or tel 0344 633 1000.

Basics of the scheme

11.56 The Buildmark scheme offers protection in the form of an insurance policy against structural defects in the property, including common parts, which may arise during the first ten years. The scheme is in two parts, comprising separate agreements in the form of warranties given by the builder and the NHBC, respectively. In the first part, the builder agrees that the new dwelling will be constructed in a good and workmanlike manner and in line with the requirements of the NHBC. The builder also agrees to put right any defects in the property, notified to the builder in writing, which occur during the first two years (known as the initial guarantee period) and which occur as a result of the builder's failure to comply with the NHBC requirements. In the second part, the NHBC give separate warranties (i.e. the insurance), which will compensate the buyer against loss suffered as a result of:

(a) the builder becoming insolvent before the dwelling is finished (limited to 10 per cent of the contract sum or £10,000, whichever is the greater);

(b) the builder failing to fulfil its own warranty to correct defects arising in the initial guarantee period; and

(c) any repair works to the property the cost of which exceeds £500 which occur during the eight years following the initial guarantee period. This eight-year period is known as the structural guarantee period. Cover includes double or multiple glazing and the costs of clearing up contamination as a result of action taken by a local authority or the Environment Agency.

NHBC procedure

Once contracts are exchanged the builder's practitioner sends the buyer's practitioner the following papers supplied by NHBC: **11.57**

(a) offer of cover and acceptance form; and
(b) a Buildmark booklet which sets out the terms of the scheme.

The acceptance form is signed by the buyer (or the buyer's practitioner) and returned to the NHBC. As soon as the NHBC receives the signed acceptance form, the cover will begin in respect of the builder's warranties and for any loss which is caused as a result of the builder becoming insolvent. Once the NHBC has approved the completed dwelling on its final inspection, it will issue in duplicate a notice of protection of cover for the full ten-year period (known as the 'Insurance Certificate'). One copy is placed with the deeds of the property and the other is given to the buyer together with the offer of cover form and the Buildmark booklet. **11.58**

If the new owner subsequently sells the property during the ten-year period, the successor in title will automatically take over the benefit of the insurance protection, i.e. there is no need for an assignment of the NHBC policy. The documents that should be made available to the subsequent buyer are the original offer of cover form, the Buildmark booklet, and the ten-year Insurance Certificate (in duplicate). **11.59**

NHBC has an online system for the acceptance of Buildmark cover. Conveyancers can access a secure online account to obtain all relevant documentation and utilize the system to notify NHBC when exchange of contracts and completion has taken place. NHBC validates the completion information and makes the insurance certificate available to download. For further information, visit the NHBC website, **http://www.nhbc.co.uk**. **11.60**

Claims

If it becomes necessary to make a claim under the scheme, this will be dealt with by the NHBC regional office for the subject property, where a freephone service is provided. If there are defects which are the responsibility of the builder, having arisen during the initial guarantee period, the regional office will normally arrange a conciliation meeting with the builder at the property. Where a claim is made during the structural guarantee period, the regional office will carry out an inspection to confirm the validity of the claim and the work to be carried out by the NHBC. In the event of a dispute regarding the insurance claim the matter may be referred to the Insurance Ombudsman. **11.61**

Subsidence is not generally covered under the Buildmark Scheme, and clients should be advised accordingly with a view to ensuring that subsidence is covered under their own buildings insurance. **11.62**

A prospective buyer can obtain a priority period from the NHBC to guard against the builder's insolvency. If you write to the NHBC shortly before exchange of contracts, advising them of your client's intention to exchange, the NHBC will provide you with a six-day priority period for exchanging contracts. Then, should the builder become insolvent or be removed from the NHBC register before exchange, the buyer will still be protected. **11.63**

11.64 The *UK Finance Mortgage Lenders' Handbook* includes a section on new properties (para 6.7) and practitioners should be aware of lenders' requirements (see Appendix 12). In particular, para 6.7.2 of the *Handbook* reads:

> Where the cover under a scheme referred to in clause 6.7.1 is not yet in place before you send us the certificate of title, you must obtain a copy of a new home warranty provider's cover note from the developer. The cover note must confirm that the property has received a satisfactory final inspection and that the new home warranty will be in place on or before legal completion. This does not apply to self-build schemes. Check part 2 to see what new home warranty documentation should be sent to us after completion.

11.65 The purpose of this provision is to ensure that the buyer does not move into a new property that is not satisfactorily complete. In the past, evidence has shown that some homebuyers, after moving in, have discovered serious defects such as missing doors or windows. Indeed, it has even been known for builders to offer incentives to buyers to move in before physical completion. This can lead to months of distress as homeowners desperately negotiate with the builders to remedy the defects. The *UK Finance Mortgage Lenders' Handbook* requirement that the property has passed a final inspection from the NHBC (or other provider) before the mortgage monies are requested (i.e. before legal completion) helps to avoid such problems.

Consumer Code for Home Builders

11.66 The Consumer Code for Home Builders came into force on 1 April 2010. The Consumer Code was formed by agreement between NHBC and MD Insurance Services Ltd (trading as Premier Guarantee and LABC New Home Warranty). These organizations have agreed that builders and developers registered with them will adopt the Consumer Code. The Consumer Code applies to Home Buyers who, on or after 1 April 2010, reserve to buy a new or newly converted home built by a Home Builder under the insurance protection of one of the supporting Home Warranty Bodies. The purpose of the Code is to ensure that Home Buyers are treated fairly, know what service levels to expect, are given reliable information upon which to make their decisions, and know how to access speedy, low-cost dispute resolution arrangements if they are dissatisfied.

DIFFICULTIES OF SYNCHRONIZING COMPLETION OF A RELATED SALE TRANSACTION

11.67 The client buying a property in the course of construction may well have a dependent sale transaction, and in these circumstances the client will obviously prefer to complete both transactions on the same day. In this way, the sale proceeds will be readily available to apply towards the purchase price of the new property, and the client will be able to move out of one property and into the other on the day of completion.

11.68 As we have seen, because the new property is in the course of construction, the developer/seller will be unwilling to agree in the contract a fixed completion date. Instead, the purchase contract will contain a provision whereby completion will take place a given number of days after the seller's practitioner has notified the buyer's practitioner that physical completion of the new property has taken place.

11.69 As the property the buyer is selling is not new but an existing one, it would be customary in a contract of this nature to agree a fixed completion date. However, if that were to occur, the client would have no guarantee that the completion dates on the sale and purchase would be the same. A way round this would be not to agree a fixed completion date on the sale, but seek to agree a condition in the sale contract regarding completion similar to that in the purchase contract. That is to say, completion shall take place a specified number of days after the seller's practitioner notifies the buyer's practitioner in writing that the client is ready to complete. One would want to serve this notice once the completion notice on the client's purchase is received, and in order to give some leeway, the notice period in the sale contract should be, say, one day less than the notice period in the purchase contract. As an example: if the purchase contract specified ten working days' notice of completion then, upon receipt of the same, you would prepare the sale contract notice and the following day serve it on the buyer's practitioner, notifying that completion will take place in nine working days' time, i.e. the same completion day as the purchase.

Of course if your client's buyer insists on a fixed completion date (e.g. because there is a chain behind), you would have to advise the client that it will not be possible to synchronize the two completions. If the client still wished to proceed, you would canvass two options. The client could either seek bridging finance to complete the purchase first (the consent of the existing lender may be required) or, more usually, complete the sale first and move into temporary accommodation until completion of the new property occurs. Whichever option the client decides on, you must as a matter of great importance still ensure that the *act of exchange of contracts* is synchronized, so as to prevent the client ending up with two properties or none at all. (See Chapter 6 generally regarding synchronization of exchange on related sale and purchase transactions.) **11.70**

KEY POINTS SUMMARY

SYNCHRONIZING COMPLETION OF A RELATED SALE TRANSACTION

- Try to avoid a fixed completion date in the sale contract; provide instead for a notice provision similar to that in the new property purchase contract. **11.71**
- The notice period in the sale contract should be one day less than the notice period in the purchase contract.
- If the client's buyer insists on a fixed completion date, advise client of implications of not synchronizing completion dates.
- If sale is to be completed before purchase, the client will need to arrange temporary accommodation and possibly furniture storage.
- If purchase is to be completed before sale, bridging finance will need to be arranged in order to complete the purchase.
- In any event always synchronize *exchange* of contracts.

PRACTICAL CHECKLISTS

MATTERS FOR DEVELOPER'S PRACTITIONER TO CONSIDER

- If the developer's title is unregistered, consider applying for voluntary first registration. **11.72**
- Contact the developer's lender, if any, to make arrangements for the release of the individual plots from the lender's charge as and when they are sold.

- In conjunction with the developer client, arrange for a site inspection by a qualified surveyor and preparation of an estate layout plan for approval by Land Registry.
- Draft the standard form of purchase deed and arrange for it to be approved by Land Registry at the same time as the estate layout plan.
- Ensure that road and sewer agreements with supporting bonds are, or will be, in place.
- Check that the developer is registered with the NHBC, or an alternative provider, and that all appropriate documentation is available.
- Carry out all necessary searches, copies of which are to be made available to the buyer's practitioner.
- Prepare information pack and/or covering letter.

ITEMS TO BE SENT TO THE BUYER'S PRACTITIONER

11.73
- Draft contract with draft purchase deed and plan attached.
- Evidence of title: either official copies with form CI (registered land), or abstract or epitome of title (unregistered land).
- Replies to standard enquiries and requisitions (and possibly also copy searches).
- Copy planning consents (and building regulation approvals, when available).
- Copy agreements under s 38 of the Highways Act 1980 and s 104 of the Water Industry Act 1991 with copies of supporting bonds.
- UK Finance Disclosure Form.
- Covering letter confirming that NHBC (or alternative) cover will be available and giving explanatory information concerning the development.

12

COMMERCIAL CONVEYANCING

A AN INTRODUCTION TO COMMERCIAL CONVEYANCING

In this chapter the phrase 'commercial conveyancing' covers the granting and renewal of **12.01** business (or commercial) leases as well as the buying and selling of properties that are let to business occupants. It could also include the sale and purchase of businesses as going concerns and commercial lending transactions. However, these last items are beyond the scope of this book. For a more detailed examination of all aspects of commercial conveyancing, see R. Abbey and M. Richards, *A Practical Approach to Commercial Conveyancing and Property* (5th edn, OUP, 2016).

After a concise look at Revenue matters the chapter will continue with an examination **12.02** of the key commercial area that most conveyancers will encounter in practice, the review of the contents of a commercial lease. The final section is devoted to the particular requirements a practitioner must bear in mind when acting for a client who is selling or buying a tenanted property. We will also consider, in this final section, the Standard Commercial Property Conditions (3rd edn, 2017) (SCPC) being commercial specific standard contractual terms. (Otherwise, the process of lease renewal is considered separately in Chapter 13.)

GENERAL INTRODUCTION

Commercial conveyancing requires the practitioner to focus on business (or commercial) **12.03** leases and commercial property. However, because the conveyancing involved concerns commercial investments or acquisitions and disposals, the tax regime is different from that which prevails in residential conveyancing. It is therefore critical that practitioners are aware of the basics of revenue law implications in commercial transactions.

VAT—an introduction

12.04 Value Added Tax (VAT) is a tax that is in effect a tax on turnover. VAT payments could arise both in a commercial lease and in a commercial property purchase. HM Revenue & Customs (HMRC) deal with VAT, which is currently payable at 20 per cent on chargeable items. A chargeable item is called a 'supply'. In the context of commercial property, if a lease is granted, there can be the supply of a lease by the lessor to the lessee. If a commercial property is to be sold, then there can be a supply of the subject property by the seller to the buyer. If a lease is assigned or transferred, there can be a supply of the residue of the term granted by the lease by the assignor/transferor to the assignee/transferee.

12.05 The general rule is that property transactions such as transfers, conveyances, assignments, or the granting of leases can all be exempt supplies, i.e. they do not attract a VAT charge. However, this can be reversed by written election (see 12.06). On the face of it, conveyancing transactions are exempt. Nevertheless, some transactions can be compulsorily standard-rated (i.e. paying the full rate of tax), some are zero-rated (i.e. subject to VAT but at 0 per cent), and the taxpayer always has the option to elect to tax.

12.06 Parties can register as taxable persons who can pay and receive VAT. Revenue and Customs set a threshold at which they are obliged so to register (of the value of taxable supplies, usually the business turnover figures). In the context of commercial transactions the tax can be payable either on the price paid for a commercial property, or on the rent payable by the terms of a commercial lease. Thus if the rent is £100 the VAT is added to it in the sum of £20, making £120.00 payable by the lessee at 20 per cent.

12.07 Where a person or company is required to pay VAT on a purchase price or rent, they should receive an invoice (a VAT invoice) showing how much VAT has been charged. This amount of VAT is called 'input tax'. That person or company may also charge VAT to someone else; this is called 'output tax'. VAT is payable quarterly (being a 'prescribed accounting period' by s 25(1) of the Value Added Tax Act 1994). The taxpayer can, when accounting to Revenue and Customs for the output tax received, deduct input tax paid. The net balance is then actually paid, and if input tax exceeds output tax the full amount is recoverable (1994 Act, s 25(3)).

12.08 The rate of VAT presently at 20 per cent is called the standard rate. There is another rate, called the zero rate, where there is a taxable supply but the rate of tax is zero. Otherwise a supply can be exempt, i.e. not subject to VAT at all. So, the sale of a 'greenfield' site for development is exempt (but there is an option to tax: see 12.09). The surrender of a lease is exempt, as is the assignment of a lease (but again, in both cases there is an option to tax). However, the charges levied by a solicitor or other professional instructed in a commercial transaction will involve fees together with standard-rate VAT. Similarly, construction services for the building of a commercial development are standard-rated.

VAT and leases generally

12.09 If a commercial lease is granted, the rule is that it is generally exempt from VAT (i.e. there is an exempt supply), but it is nevertheless subject to the option to tax, i.e. to make the letting taxable. The option to tax arises when the lessor decides voluntarily to give up the exemption and to opt for VAT liability at the standard rate (see s 89 of the Value Added Tax Act 1994). Notice of the election must be given to HMRC within 30 days of its being exercised and best practice dictates the use of customs form VAT 1614. The building or premises concerned will thereafter be a taxable supply instead of an exempt supply. If it is a taxable supply, on a lease of the subject premises VAT will be chargeable to the lessee. An election must be for the whole of the subject premises; an election in respect of part is not possible. This is also true for assignments and surrenders. It is in effect an option to waive the standard exemption. The lessor must be registered for VAT; and if there is such a registration, written notice must be given to HMRC within 30 days of the election having been made. As it will be for the lessees to pay the VAT on their rent, it is vital that at the same time they are advised of the VAT election. This election is personal to the elector. This means that if there are sub-lessees, the sub-lessor must also elect for VAT to be payable on the sub-lessees' rents.

Electing to charge VAT will only suit a lessor who wishes to recover VAT. Careful consid- **12.10** eration should be given to the effect of charging VAT on the rent, as many prospective lessees will be put off taking the premises where they are not registered for VAT and cannot therefore recover the VAT themselves.

There should always be a covenant in all leases to require payment of VAT in addition to **12.11** the rent. On the assumption that there is an existing lease and it is silent as to the payment of VAT, the lessee will nevertheless have to pay VAT on the rent should the lessor decide to opt to tax. However, there is one vital point to note where you are acting for a lessor who intends to grant a new lease and also intends to opt to tax. You must advise the lessor not to make the election before the grant of the new lease. If the election precedes the grant, HMRC will deem the new rent to be *inclusive* of VAT. This pitfall can be avoided by electing immediately *after* the grant of the lease, but including in the lease a covenant requiring the lessee to pay any VAT on all the rents. Lastly, bear in mind that HMRC view any rent-free period, or periods that are granted as an inducement to a new lessee, as subject to VAT. VAT will be payable on the unpaid rent.

If VAT is payable on a rent, it will also be payable on any service charge under the terms of **12.12** the same lease by which the rent is paid. In both cases the lessor can issue mere demands (and not VAT invoices), and when the rents and service charges are actually paid receipted VAT invoices should be issued. In this way the lessor can delay accounting for VAT to HMRC until the lessor receives the actual payments. This has the benefit of delaying payment of tax, as well as ensuring that no VAT payments are made on supplies where monies have yet to reach the lessor, i.e. rent arrears.

VAT and buying/selling a commercial property

If the commercial property to be sold or purchased is not new (i.e. not less than three **12.13** years old), there is an exempt supply of the property on sale. A building is said to be VAT-able when the lessor has made an election and collects rent and VAT on the rent payable by the lessee(s) of the subject premises. The option to tax arises when the lessor decides voluntarily to give up the standard exemption and to opt for a VAT liability at the standard rate (1994 Act, s 89). Notice of the election must be given to HMRC within 30 days of its being exercised and best practice dictates the use of customs form VAT 1614. The building concerned will thereafter be a taxable supply instead of an exempt supply. If it is a taxable supply, on sale of the subject premises VAT will be chargeable to the buyer. An election must be for the whole of the subject premises as an election in respect of part is not possible.

When buying a commercial investment property, the buyer will want to know whether VAT **12.14** will be payable on top of the proposed purchase price. The Standard Commercial Property Conditions of Sale (SCPCs) provide for all sums payable under the contract to be exclusive of VAT, i.e. any VAT is added to the purchase price. So the buyer is to pay the seller on completion an additional amount equal to the VAT in exchange for a VAT invoice from the seller, see SCPC 2.2. In contrast the Standard Conditions (fifth edition) at 1.4 state that the purchase price and any contents price are inclusive of any VAT. In commercial transactions if the buyer wishes to avoid paying VAT on top of any consideration, it will require a special condition to this effect. The condition will say either that the purchase price is to be inclusive of any VAT, or that the seller warrants that it has not elected to waive any exemption to VAT and will not do so on or before completion. This is especially important for buyers who make exempt supplies in the course of their businesses, for example banks, building societies, and insurance companies, because they are unable to recover their VAT payments. In part 2 of the standard contract, condition A1 covers VAT in that it can provide that this agreement does not constitute a taxable supply when a box provided is checked or ticked.

12.15   If a new freehold building (i.e. less than three years old) is sold it is subject to the standard rate of VAT. Accordingly, if a client instructs you to sell a new commercial property, the seller will be making a supply that will be standard-rated. This being so, the consideration will attract VAT at the standard rate. However, the client will want to know whether the stated price includes or excludes the standard rate of VAT. Clearly the seller will want the VAT added to the consideration. Unless there is evidence or documentation to the contrary, there will be a presumption that the stated consideration is to *include* VAT. Practitioners acting for a seller in these circumstances should ensure that there is a clear contractual term making the consideration exclusive of VAT so that the full price is paid to the seller with VAT on top of it. To omit such a clause in these circumstances would amount to a clear act of negligence. Therefore, as a matter of course, a VAT-exclusive clause should be included in all such contracts. Both the SCs (SC 1.4) and the SCPCs (SCPC 2) provide for all sums payable under the contract to be exclusive of VAT, i.e. any VAT is *added*, save in relation to the purchase price and contents only where VAT is inclusive.

12.16   **VAT and the SCPC**   The second edition of the SCPC is divided into two parts. Part 1 contains general conditions building on those in the first edition, while Part 2 contains new clauses and in particular detailed provisions covering VAT, capital allowances, and reversionary interests in flats. In general Part 1 applies unless specifically excluded, while Part 2 will only apply if expressly incorporated. Completing tick boxes on the back page of the agreement effects explicit incorporation: see SCPC 1.1.4 (a) and (b).

12.17   The standard position in Part 1 is that the seller warrants that the sale of the property does constitute a supply that is taxable for VAT purposes. Part 2 changes this in two possible ways. First, A1 states that the sale does not constitute a supply that is taxable for VAT purposes. (SCPC 2 requires the buyer to pay VAT on top of the purchase price in exchange for a proper VAT invoice.) Second, A2 covers a transfer of a going concern. In this case the seller warrants that it is using the property for the business of letting to produce a rental income.

KEY POINTS SUMMARY

VAT AND COMMERCIAL CONVEYANCING

12.18   • If a commercial lease is granted, the rule is that it is generally exempt from VAT but is nevertheless subject to the option to tax, i.e. to make the letting VATable.

   • In a commercial lease, where VAT is to be charged on the rent the lessor must be registered for VAT; and if there is such a registration, written notice must be given to HMRC within 30 days of the election having been made.

- If the election precedes the grant of a new commercial lease, HMRC will deem the new rent to be inclusive of VAT. If acting for the lessor, to avoid this problem, make sure the lease contains a covenant by the lessee to pay VAT in addition to the rent.

- The election to tax is personal to the elector and is in respect of individual properties, i.e. on a property-by-property basis.

- On the assumption that there is an existing lease and it is silent as to the payment of VAT, the lessee will nevertheless have to pay VAT on the rent should the lessor decide to opt to tax. For certainty, always ensure that there is a covenant requiring the lessee to pay VAT on rent if required.

- If a commercial property that is not new (not less than three years old) is to be sold or purchased, there is an exempt supply of the property on sale and VAT will not be payable unless the seller opts to tax.

- If a new freehold building is to be sold it will be subject to the standard rate of VAT. Accordingly, if a client instructs you to sell a new commercial property the seller will be making a supply that will be standard-rated.

- Practitioners acting for sellers should always draft contracts so as to make all sums exclusive of VAT.

- The HMRC national VAT advice service can be contacted on 0300 200 3700, where they will deal with general VAT enquiries. You will need your VAT registration number and postcode with you when you call.

Stamp Duty Land Tax

Stamp Duty Land Tax (Land Tax or SDLT) is based on the taxation of transactions in place **12.19** of deeds or documents, which was the case for the old stamp duty regime. It is assessed directly against the buyer rather than the property being purchased. The Welsh government has decided to replace SDLT with a new LTT effective from April 2018 (see 9.33).

The SDLT regime came into force on 1 December 2003. Leasehold transactions are caught **12.20** by SDLT as to the consideration paid and the rent in the lease. The starting threshold for the payment of SDLT is £150,000 for commercial properties. Practitioners should note that there is guidance on the HMRC website at **https://www.gov.uk/business-tax/stamp-taxes** regarding SDLT.

The SDLT rates for commercial property are as set out below. HMRC defines commercial as **12.21** non-residential and mixed-use land, and property where the rates are different from residential SDLT. HMRC lists the following examples of what they call non-residential property:

- commercial property, eg shops or offices;
- agricultural land;
- forests;
- any other land or property which is not used as a residence; and
- six or more residential properties bought in a single transaction.

Commercial property SDLT rates are given in Table 12.1.

Table 12.1 Commercial property SDLT rates

Property or lease premium or transfer value	SDLT rate
Up to £150,000	Zero
The next £100,000 (the portion from £150,001 to £250,000)	2%
The remaining amount (the portion above £250,000)	5%

HMRC has provided an example of SDLT calculation:

If you buy a freehold commercial property for £275,000, the SDLT you owe is calculated as follows:

- 0% on the first £150,000 = £0;
- 2% on the next £100,000 = £2,000;
- 5% on the final £25,000 = £1,250;
- Total SDLT = £3,250.

Higher rates of SDLT are now charged on purchases of additional residential properties, such as 'buy-to-let' properties with effect from 1 April 2016. The higher rate is 3 per cent above the current SDLT rates. Further details can be found in chapter 9.

12.22　The land transaction return, form SDLT1 replaces the old 'Stamps L(A)451' (the 'Particulars Delivered' or PD form). SDLT2 and 3 and 4 supplement SDLT1. SDLT2 is used where there are more than two sellers and/or two buyers. SDLT3 is used where land is involved and further space is required in addition to the space provided on SDLT1. Perhaps of greater importance in commercial property is form SDLT4, which should be used for complex commercial transactions and leases. The effect of this new tax is to abolish the need for, and the use of, the purchase deed form. Furthermore, the SDLT system means that certificates of value previously found in purchase deeds are now redundant and can be excluded from all conveyances and transfers.

12.23　SDLT includes a regime for the rental element of commercial leases. The charge will be at a rate of 1 or 2 per cent on the net present value (NPV) of the total rent payable over the term of the lease. Future rents will be discounted at 3.5 per cent per annum in order to arrive at the NPV. Leases where the NPV of the rent over the term of the lease does not exceed £150,000 will be exempt (see Table 12.2). The Revenue has suggested that change in the regime could mean that some 60 per cent of all commercial leases could avoid any SDLT on the rental element.

The rental element is represented by the following chart:

Table 12.2 SDLT on rent for commercial properties or land—new leases

Net present value of rent	SDLT rate
£0 to £150,000	Zero
The portion from £150,001 to £5,000,000	1%
The portion above £5,000,000	2%

(N.B. The net present value (NPV) is based on the total rent over the life of the lease. You don't pay SDLT on the rent if the NPV is less than £150,000.)

On the HMRC website there is a facility to work out the SDLT liability for leasehold transactions. The HMRC SDLT calculator provides the amount of liability of SDLT on lease transactions and can be found at **http://www.hmtrc.gov.uk/tools/sdlt/land-and-property.htm**.

12.24　Once HMRC has received and processed a proper SDLT return and, where required, payment, it will issue a certificate of payment. The certificate, the SDLT5, is issued under s 79 of the Finance Act 2003 and evidences that SDLT has been accounted on the particular transaction notified to HMRC. This must be sent to Land Registry to enable an application to register to proceed. Further details on SDLT can be found at 9.21.

Other taxes

If the lessor charges and receives a premium for the granting of a commercial lease, that **12.25** premium will be potentially liable to tax as a capital gain. As premiums are uncommon in the context of commercial leases, this tax liability is unlikely to be of any real consequence. However, the lessor's profit rental income will be liable either to income tax or, if a company, corporation tax. HMRC also deem a premium paid on a lease for a term of less than 50 years to be partly taxable as income. There is no double charge to tax, as the element deemed to be income will be excluded from capital gains tax. A premium paid on assignment will, potentially, attract capital gains tax as it is of course a 'disposal' which attracts this tax liability.

The Annual Tax on Enveloped Dwellings, previously called the Annual Residential Property Tax ('ATED')

The Annual Tax on Enveloped Dwellings (ATED) is a tax payable by companies that own **12.26** high-value residential property (a 'dwelling'). It is due on high-value residential property and will be payable each year. An ATED return is required if it is a dwelling and it is in the UK and it was valued at £2 million or more on 1 April 2012, or at later acquisition and it is owned partly or completely by a company (or collective investment vehicle, e.g. unit trust).

The tax rates (as shown in Table 12.3) are:

Table 12.3 Chargeable amounts for 1 April 2018 to 31 March 2019

Property value	Annual charge
More than £500,000 but not more than £1 million	£3,650
More than £1 million but not more than £2 million	£7,250
More than £2 million but not more than £5 million	£24,250
More than £5 million but not more than £10 million	£56,550
More than £10 million but not more than £20 million	£113,400
More than £20 million	£226,950

A dwelling for the purposes of this new tax may be all or part of a residential or mixed-use property. If a property consists of a number of self-contained flats, each flat will usually be valued separately. In March 2013, HMRC renamed this tax the Annual Tax on Enveloped Dwellings. This is because the dwelling is said to be 'enveloped' because the ownership sits within a corporate 'wrapper' or 'envelope'.

B COMMERCIAL LEASES

Introduction

In the past shops and offices, as well as other types of commercial property, were let on **12.27** leases, many of which are not registered in their own right at Land Registry because their lease term was not more than 21 years in duration. However, since 13 October 2003, leases of more than seven years are compulsorily registrable (s 4 of the Land Registration Act 2002). This could lead to commercial leases being limited to seven years or less. This will avoid registration and keep the lease terms off the public register.

Land Registry has issued rules requiring certain lease contents to be in a particular pos- **12.28** ition in registrable leases (new leases with a term of more than seven years). As a result, they are called prescribed clauses leases. See the Land Registration (Amendment) (No 2) Rules 2005 (SI 2005/1982). The compulsory requirements have been limited to a set number of 'prescribed clauses' with a requirement that these particular clauses must appear at the start of the lease. The information that must appear at the lease commencement includes:

- the parties to the lease;
- a full description of the property being leased;
- the term for which the property is leased;
- any premium;
- prohibitions or restrictions on disposing of the lease;
- easements.

Further details on prescribed clauses leases and the contents required by them can be found at 10.05.

12.29 The freehold will be owned as an investment by an individual or company, and that freeholder will grant such a commercial lease to an occupying lessee. The lease terms regulate the basis on which the lessee will be allowed to occupy the premises for the purposes of carrying on a business. Inevitably this has meant that there is no one common form of commercial or business lease. Practitioners will encounter a multitude of lease formats. Consequently when acting for a prospective lessee, the terms must be read carefully to make sure that none of them is of an onerous or unusual nature that might prejudice your client. When acting for a lessor almost the reverse is true. You will want to be sure that the lease properly restricts the lessee in such a way as to ensure that the property is occupied on the terms dictated by your lessor client. It is this area of conflict that requires conveyancing practitioners to consider carefully the detailed contents of commercial leases.

Exempt information documents

12.30 Commercial lessors may be concerned that registered leases will be available to the public as a result of the register being open to review by anyone. The effect of this could be that lessees might find out the lease terms for adjacent or adjoining property and this could be material to lease renewal negotiations in a large estate or could reveal concessions granted to another lessee.

12.31 However, the Land Registration Rules 2003 allow for applications to remove from public view sensitive material. If the Registry approves an application it will be an 'exempt information document', an EID. An application will be approved if the Registry is satisfied that the document contains 'prejudicial information'. Rule 131 defines prejudicial information as:

(a) information that relates to an individual who has applied for the document to be designated an EID and if disclosed to other persons (whether to the public generally or specific persons) would, or would be likely to, cause substantial unwarranted damage or substantial unwarranted distress to the applicant or another; or

(b) information that if disclosed to other persons (whether to the public generally or specific persons) would, or would be likely to, prejudice the commercial interests of the applicant, i.e. the person who applied for the document to be designated an EID.

12.32 Applications are made on Forms EX1 and EX1A. (As EX1 is a public document, unlike EX1A, do not disclose any sensitive material on this form.) The benefit of an EID is personal to the applicant and cannot be assigned or passed on. On a change of ownership a fresh application will be necessary to 'renew' the EID arrangement.

LEASE CONTENTS

A business lease should contain specific elements, and these are listed below. However, **12.33** how and where they appear in any one lease will vary greatly. Some leases will use schedules, some will not. Also remember Land Registry's requirement for prescribed clauses in registered leases (see 12.28). Consequently, practitioners must have in mind a basic list of necessary contents for a commercial lease as follows:

(a) heading, date, and parties;
(b) a clear parcels clause setting out a full description of the property (if necessary by reference to a lease plan), with all attaching rights;
(c) exceptions and reservations, i.e. a detailed list of all the rights retained by the lessor;
(d) the length of the lease term and the commencement date for that term (not always the date of the lease), known as the habendum;
(e) the rental details (known as the reddendum) including rent review clauses, frequency of payment and payment dates, and whether the rent is paid in arrears or in advance;
(f) lessee's covenants;
(g) lessor's covenants;
(h) provisos, including a forfeiture clause and other clauses regulating the mechanics of the operation of the lease terms, such as a provision for arbitration in case of dispute between the parties or a clause setting out how covenant notices are to be served (service charge details could also appear at this point);
(i) an attestation clause.

Traditional leases will follow this format without the use of schedules. Word processing **12.34** and the use of precedents have given rise to the use of schedules to the extent that some leases have all these separate elements within different schedules. This is to be recommended when compiling documents in this manner. Some of the more important elements listed above are now considered in more detail.

Payment of rent

So far as the lessor is concerned, this is the rationale for the very existence of the lease. **12.35** The lessee is allowed the use and enjoyment of the subject premises in consideration of the rental expressed in the lease. The amount to be paid must be stated in clear and definite terms. However, a lease can be granted without including a rental element or with a period of non-payment, i.e. a rent-free period. Whether there is a rent-free period or not, the lease should state a commencement date for the payment of rent and the frequency of payment. Most modern leases provide for rent to be paid quarterly in advance. Traditional quarter days are commonly used, but the more precise modern quarter days are becoming increasingly evident, e.g. the first day of January, April, July, and October. Modern leases will also include a provision referring to other payments, such as service charges, as rent. Including these payments as rent enables the lessor to use the remedies of distress and forfeit for non-payment. The remedy of distress is not available for a breach of covenant other than non-payment of rent. Modern business leases will also include a further provision allowing the lessor to collect interest on late rent.

Rent reviews

Perhaps of greatest concern to the lessor is the nature and extent of the rent review pro- **12.36** vision. Rent review clauses allow the lessor to vary the rent stated in the lease so as to increase the income from the subject property. This has been especially important in times of inflation as the lessor of a long lease at a fixed rental has been at a severe disadvantage when inflation was running at high levels. Each passing year meant that the lessor in such an unfortunate position was losing even more in real terms as inflation ate into the value of the fixed rental. To combat this potential increasing loss lessors have included in leases a provision allowing the rent to be reviewed at fixed intervals, usually only in an upward direction. (If the review mechanism permits downward reviews, as well as upward, the rent could actually be reduced on review, something that occurred in several property slumps from the late 1980s and early 1990s right through to the slump experienced in 2008–2010.) Some leases simply link the annual rent to inflation, e.g. the Index of Retail Prices (see *Blumenthal v Gallery Five Ltd* (1971) 220 EG 31). Others state the amount to be paid in the future by way of fixed increases. However, most do not state the amount of the increase but try to define in the lease how the lease rental should be revalued on review.

12.37 It therefore follows that in a rent review the critical element is on what basis the rent should be reviewed. The intention of the lessor is to move the rent to the current market value for the subject premises. However, this gives rise to the all-important question of what that market value is and how it will be ascertained. Furthermore, the procedure for triggering and handling the review is critical. These valuation and procedural elements will be considered in the following paragraphs.

Valuation

12.38 The new lease should contain a definition of a formula by which the new reviewed rent should be ascertained. The nature of what might be included in such a definition is itself a subject for a book. Certainly it has been heavily litigated. If the lease terms say the intention is to fix a 'rack rent', then this is the full rent for the property (see *Corporation of London v Cusack-Smith* [1955] AC 337). Thus such a rental would reflect the changes in the property market as assessed by a valuer or surveyor. Alternatively, if the lease required the rent to be reviewed as a 'market rent', then this will be the same as for a new lease granted under the terms of the Landlord and Tenant Act 1954, but including the factors that the Act contemplates being ignored.

12.39 There is nothing to stop the lease incorporating detailed assumptions on which the review is to be based. If the lease stipulates assumptions to be made on a rent review, then they will be central to the valuation process for the subject property. Typical assumptions are that the rent is to be reviewed at the renewal date, assuming the property is vacant for a term equal to that either originally granted or the residue of the term and for the permitted user stated in the lease. (As to the term, it can be argued that a higher rental will arise if the term is longer than the unexpired residue at the time of review. In the absence of any express lease term to the contrary, courts will assume the lease term on review to be the period of the unexpired term: see *Lynnthorpe Enterprises Ltd v Sidney Smith (Chelsea) Ltd* [1990] 2 EGLR 148, CA.) Modern rent review clauses will also allow the valuer to ignore any diminution in the value of the rental as a result of the lessee having failed properly to repair the subject property. Some review clauses also import assumptions with regard to improvements made by the lessee. If the lease is silent on the point, the rent review will be based on the nature of the premises at the time of review, including any improvements made by the lessee even though they were made at the lessee's cost (see *Ponsford v HMS Aerosols Ltd* [1979] AC 63). Assumptions can also cover sub-lettings to take into account any profit rental the lessee may be receiving from sub-lessees. Courts will also generally accept that the hypothetical lease will include a rent review: see *British Gas v Universities Superannuation Scheme* [1986] 1 All ER 978.

Procedure

Modern rent review clauses trigger the process by requiring the lessor to serve a notice on **12.40** the lessee calling for a review of the rent at the rent review date. Some trigger notices will be required by the review procedure to state what the lessor requires as a new rental. Others may simply call for the review process to be commenced. If an amount is specified, some clauses require the lessee to agree or disagree with the stated amount within a specified period. A trap exists here for the unwary. If time is of the essence for the lessee's response then, should that time limit not be complied with, the rental stated by the lessor, no matter how exaggerated it may be, will prevail as the rent for review. (Exaggeration does not make the notice ineffective: see *Amalgamated Estates Ltd v Joystretch Manufacturing Ltd* (1981) 257 EG 489.) In *Starmark Enterprises Limited v CPL Enterprises Ltd* [2001] EWCA Civ 1252, there was no mention of time being of the essence for service of the tenant's counter-notice. Nevertheless, an out-of-time counter-notice was deemed invalid because the parties to the lease had clearly stipulated the consequences of a party's failure to serve a notice within the time agreed by them.

Lessors can also be late calling for review by not complying with a timescale stated in the **12.41** lease rent review provisions. In *United Scientific Holdings Ltd v Burnley Borough Council* [1978] AC 904, it was held that unless the clause makes it so, time is *not* of the essence for a rent review clause. If the clause makes time of the essence of part or all of the procedure, then the time limits are absolute and incapable of extension. In the absence of express provision, though, delay will not defeat a lessor's claim for a rent review. Time can be of the essence even if the rent review provision does not include that actual wording. If the words of the rent review clause are such that it is possible to show that there was an intention to make time limits absolute, then the courts will infer time to be of the essence (see *Henry Smith's Charity Trustees v AWADA Trading and Promotion Services Ltd* (1984) 47 P & CR 607). Time of the essence can also arise if other wording in the lease supports this possibility. Accordingly, if the lessee can, by notice, terminate the tenancy at the review date, it has been held that this means that time is of the essence for the review (see *Al Saloom v Shirley James Travel Services Ltd* (1981) 42 P & CR 181).

Sensible rent review clauses will also have two further provisions. First, there will be the pos- **12.42** sibility of referring the rent to an arbitrator for a final decision should the lessor and lessee be unable to agree the level of the new rent. Second, there should be a clause covering what must be done in the event of a dispute between the parties. This will again sensibly entail arbitration. In both clauses, if arbitration is contemplated, it will involve provisions in the Arbitration Act 1996. Should the appointment of the arbitrator be in dispute the lease can provide that the appointment be by the President for the time being of the Royal Institution of Chartered Surveyors.

Covenants by the lessee

If you are acting for a prospective lessee, you must consider carefully the nature and extent **12.43** of all the lessee's covenants in the light of the client's intended use of the property and any other salient instructions. However, some covenants will be of more consequence to a lessee than others. Details of some of the more critical covenants commonly found in commercial leases are set out in the following paragraphs.

Repairing obligations

This is a common area of dispute between the parties, and it is therefore critical that the **12.44** repairs clauses are as clear as they can be in defining who is responsible for repairing the subject property and to what standard.

12.45   This is a subject area of great difficulty in two principal ways. First, deciding on what part of the subject property must be repaired by the lessee does rather depend on the extent of the definition of the lessee's property in the lease. Second, when the extent of the property is known the measure of the burden of the repairing liability must be clearly defined; from simple repairs necessary to deal with ordinary wear and tear, right up to the lessee being under a strict obligation virtually to replace the whole property.

12.46   Where there is a property in multiple occupation, say, an office block containing several office suites, all let to different lessees, the usual repairing arrangement is for the lessee to be required to keep in good repair the inner skin of the demised property. This would therefore require the lessee to keep properly maintained the plaster, the ceiling and flooring materials, but not much else. All structural elements of the property, including the floor and ceiling joists, the main or load-bearing walls, the roof, and foundations, should all be repairable by the lessor, with all the lessees paying a service charge to reimburse the lessor for this expense. (The further need for clear and appropriate service charge covenants flows from this form of repairing arrangement.) The rationale for this arrangement is that there is a need for a consistent approach to the whole question of structural repairs and maintenance.

12.47   On the other hand, if the lease is of the whole building, such as a lease of a shop and upper part, or indeed one office building let to one lessee, then it is common for the sole lessee to be responsible for all the repairs to the building.

12.48   **The standard of repair**   The precise standard of repair required was set out in *Proudfoot v Hart* (1890) 25 QBD 42, where it was held that the standard of repair is to be determined according to several factors, including the subject property's age and character and the environment in which the property is located. In effect this has meant that there is a clear difference in the expected standard of repair between a Victorian property and one that was built in the 1990s. As to the meaning of 'repair', the courts have made it clear this includes renewal (see *Lurcott v Wakeley and Wheeler* [1911] 1 KB 905). It should be remembered that a covenant requiring the lessee 'to put and keep the property in good and substantial repair' is particularly onerous. This is way above mere repair and will be interpreted as requiring the lessee to carry out all repairs and renewals, substantial or not, right from the start of the lease (see *Elite Investments Ltd v TI Bainbridge Silencers Ltd* [1986] 2 EGLR 43). This kind of covenant is, however, encountered frequently in practice. In addition, a covenant to keep in repair implies a covenant to put and keep in repair. As a result each lease-repairing covenant, seen in the light of the subject property, will dictate the nature and extent of the repairs required.

12.49   Most commercial leases will also include clauses calling on the lessee to decorate internally (and externally if the lessee has the total repairing liability) at regular intervals during the term of the lease. Common repainting and redecorating intervals are every five years internally, and every three years externally. Many such covenants also call on the lessee to decorate and repaint in the final year of the term whether or not this coincides with the fixed intervals. Overall, the purpose of clauses such as these is to ensure that the nature and extent of the lessee's decorating liability is clearly defined so as to ensure the proper upkeep of the subject property.

12.50   **Other covenants affecting repair**   To ensure compliance with repairing obligations modern leases will always include a covenant allowing the lessor to enter the demised premises, on prior written notice, to view the state of repair. If the repairing covenant is in breach, the lessor will then be able to serve a notice on the lessee calling for repair to be carried out. Moreover, the lessor, in the case of default by the lessee, will have the benefit of a further provision enabling the lessor to enter the subject property to carry out the necessary repairs and to charge the lessee for the cost of the work required. The lessor can also serve a notice pursuant to the terms of s 146 of the Law of Property Act 1925 calling for the lessee to comply with the lease-repairing covenants. The notice will give the lessee a fixed amount of time to comply with those covenants, failing which the lessor can seek to forfeit the lease for breach of covenant. The lessor's rights in this regard are limited by the effect of the Leasehold Property (Repairs) Act 1938. If the original term of the lease was for seven years or more and there are at least three years of the term left unexpired, then the s 146 notice must refer to the 1938 Act and inform the lessee of his right to serve a counter-notice claiming the benefit of the Act. This counter-notice must be served on the lessor within 28 days of the service of the s 146 notice. If the lessee obtains the benefit of the Act by serving a counter-notice within the time limit, the lessor cannot forfeit the lease without leave of the court (see *Associated British Ports v CH Bailey plc* [1990] 1 All ER 929). In effect it means that the lessor can neither sue for damages nor forfeit the lease without a court order allowing the lessor so to do. When making an order the court has complete discretion to impose such conditions in the order as the court deems appropriate to the particular circumstances of the case.

Repair and service charges   Where the lessor is under an obligation to keep in good repair   **12.51** a building of which the subject property forms part, the cost of those repairs will usually be recoverable from the lessee. That cost, along with other expenses incurred by the lessor in providing services (e.g. lighting and heating of common parts) on behalf of all lessees, will form a service charge. If in the lease it is described as a rent, then in the event of its non-payment, the procedure for forfeiture for non-payment of rent can be used (see 12.71). Normally there will be a service charge payable as a rent, with payments on account made quarterly at a level to be decided by the lessor's surveyor (whose decision shall be final, save for manifest error) at the start of each year but having regard to the expenditure during the previous year. At the end of the year accounts are prepared to reconcile the payments made and received. The lessor will usually be obliged by a covenant to carry out clearly identified obligations listed in a schedule to the lease, including repairs and renovations to the main structure and common parts, and lighting and heating the common parts. This obligation is usually made conditional on the lessees paying the service charge rental. Section 81 of the Housing Act 1996 imposes a new structure of control on lessors seeking to exercise a right of re-entry or forfeiture as a result of failure by a lessee to pay service charges. In effect, no exercise of a right of re-entry can be effected until 14 days after a court order. This does not limit a s 146 notice under the terms of the Law of Property Act 1925. However, the s 146 notice must include a statement confirming that s 81 of the Housing Act 1996 applies and setting out its effect. (Section 81 has been modified by the Commonhold and Leasehold Reform Act 2002; see 12.76.)

With the advent of commonhold provisions, the arrangements regarding common main-   **12.52** tenance can also apply to commercial properties. See 10.118 for more details about commonhold land.

User obligations

It is possible for the lease to include a covenant imposing an absolute restriction on the les-   **12.53** see against changing the use from any stated user precisely defined by the lease. Because the covenant is absolute, the lessor cannot be compelled to allow a change of use. If a change is agreed in subsequent negotiations, it can be made by a deed of variation to the terms of the original lease.

The covenant can be qualified, requiring the lessor's consent before the use can be changed,   **12.54** and this is more commonly seen in commercial leases. In such business leases an absolute user covenant will mean that the rental on review could be subject to a reduction in valuation.

This is because a restriction on user makes the lease less attractive to tenants and it will therefore command less as a rental. However, this limitation on the rental income can be avoided by a fully qualified covenant, i.e. including wording such as 'such consent not to be unreasonably withheld'. This is because there is no statutory provision that the lessor's consent cannot be unreasonably withheld, as is the case with alienation covenants. However, s 19(3) of the Landlord and Tenant Act 1927 does provide that if consent for a change of use is required, then the lessor is not allowed to demand a premium or extra rent for giving that consent. The lessor can require costs to be paid by the applicant, including all legal fees. A premium or extra rent can be demanded if alterations to the structure of the property are also proposed.

12.55 **Other clauses affecting the user**   In addition to the stated user clause, a modern business lease will include other clauses concerned with the use of the property. For example, there will be a covenant requiring the lessee to comply with planning law. The provision can in the alternative prohibit the lessee from making any application for planning consent so that there can be no change to the stated use if that change of use requires planning permission. Business leases will also require the lessee to covenant not to reside at the property or to sleep there overnight, as to do so would be a breach of planning law. Most, if not all, commercial leases will include a lessee's covenant not to use the property for an illegal or immoral purpose, and to do nothing within the subject premises that is a nuisance or annoyance to other neighbouring lessees.

Alteration restrictions

12.56 This is a topic of particular concern in business leases. Clearly the reversioner will want to ensure that unauthorized alterations do not take place, especially where the lease term is short in duration. Furthermore, the reversioner will want to be sure that the alterations that do take place are such that the integrity of the structure will not be adversely affected. This will also be the case for additions and improvements to the subject property that are carried out by the lessee.

12.57 A covenant dealing with alterations can include an absolute bar such as: 'not to make or allow to be made any alterations additions or improvements to the demised premises'. If this is the lease covenant, the lessee cannot carry out any work whatsoever.

12.58 **Alterations and the Landlord and Tenant Act 1927**   The lease could allow alterations to the property with the lessor's written consent. To the extent that proposed alterations amount to improvements, s 19(2) of the Landlord and Tenant Act 1927 will then apply so that consent cannot be unreasonably withheld, and the lessor cannot demand any payment beyond reasonable legal and other expenses incurred in the granting of consent for the relevant works. The statute does not stop the lessor from seeking a reasonable sum should the proposed amendments diminish the value of the premises or indeed any adjacent premises in the ownership of the same lessor. Similarly, if the alteration or addition does not add to the letting value of the premises, the statute does not prevent the lessor from obtaining from the lessee a covenant to reinstate the premises to their former condition at the end or sooner determination of the lease.

12.59 What amounts to an improvement was considered in *Lambert v FW Woolworth and Co. Ltd* [1938] Ch 883. In that case it was decided that an improvement will be considered as such from the lessee's viewpoint and whether it made the subject premises more useful or more valuable to the lessee.

12.60 **Signs**   Although not strictly speaking an alteration, most lessees will want to erect a name sign advertising their occupation of the subject property. Many commercial leases place restrictions on this by requiring the lessee to submit plans for the sign for prior approval by the lessor. Alternatively some commercial leases include a provision requiring signs to be placed in one particular location and to a specific format. This is usually used where there is, for example, a signboard within an entrance hall on which all the businesses for that building are listed.

Alienation restrictions

Consent Alienation covers covenants against assignments, underletting, mortgages, and **12.61** other material dealings with the legal estate. This covenant is of great concern for business leases. The reason for this is that a business lessor will want to know who is in occupation of the property and in particular that the financial strength of the person or company in occupation is such that the rents required by the lease will be paid. As a consequence the lessor will seek to validate intending lessees to try to be sure that they will be able to pay the rents. Once the lessor has approved the status of the incoming lessee, the lessor will normally require the proposed assignee to enter into a deed of licence. This will incorporate direct covenants between the lessor and assignee requiring the assignee to comply with the lease terms for the residue of the term of the lease. This is now subject to the terms of the Landlord and Tenant (Covenants) Act 1995 (see 12.77 regarding enforceability of covenants).

Consent required There is no restriction against alienation unless there is express provi- **12.62** sion to that effect in the lease (see *Keeves v Dean* [1924] 1 KB 685 and *Leith Properties Ltd v Byrne* [1983] QB 433). Many commercial leases include a covenant whereby the lessee cannot assign the lease without the prior written consent of the lessor, such consent usually not to be unreasonably withheld. This is known as a fully qualified covenant. Some leases extend this provision to include sub-lettings and assignments. If the lease states that the lessor's consent is required but does not refer to reasonableness then statute adds this qualification (Landlord and Tenant Act 1927, s 19(1)(a)). (The Court of Appeal issued guidelines on what amounts to reasonableness in the context of s 19 in *International Drilling Fluids Ltd v Louisville Investments (Uxbridge) Ltd* [1986] Ch 513.) However, if the lease includes an absolute prohibition, then the lessee simply cannot assign the lease and must remain in the premises for the residue of the term. Section 19(1A) of the Landlord and Tenant Act 1927 (introduced by s 22 of the Landlord and Tenant (Covenants) Act 1995) allows the parties to a lease to agree conditions or circumstances which must be satisfied before the lessor will give consent. Section 19(1A) only relates to qualified covenants against assigning, i.e. not sub-letting or charging. If the lease requires the lessee to offer a surrender of the lease back to the lessor prior to seeking an assignment, that provision is unenforceable (see *Allnatt London Properties Ltd v Newton* [1984] 1 All ER 423) unless the provision is covered under s 38 of the Landlord and Tenant Act 1954.

Alienation of part Many modern business leases will include an absolute covenant against **12.63** dealing with part of the subject premises. There are two good reasons for including such a provision. First, good estate management practice dictates that the fewer lessees there are in a block the easier it is to manage the building as a whole. However, the second reason is far more compelling. Under the Landlord and Tenant Act 1954 business lessees in occupation at the end of a business lease are entitled by statute to renew their lease. If there have been sub-lettings of parts, the lessor is required by statute to issue new leases to all the sub-lessees in occupation and not to the original lessee who became the sub-lessor but did not remain in occupation. In this way the superior lessor could accidentally end up with several lessees where originally there was one.

Timing of applications for consent Section 1(3) of the Landlord and Tenant Act 1988 **12.64** requires the lessor to deal with applications for consent to an assignment within a reasonable time of the making of the application. Should the lessor fail to do so the lessee can, if the lessee has suffered loss as a consequence of the lessor's delay, sue the lessor for damages. The lessor can attach conditions to any consent but those conditions themselves must be reasonable (1988 Act, s 1(4)). As to reasonableness, the courts have held that a serious outstanding breach of a repairing covenant will be sufficient cause to allow a lessor to refuse to grant licence to assign (see *Goldstein v Sanders* [1915] 1 Ch 549). On the other hand, an example of where refusal to grant a licence was held to be unreasonable was in *Re Smith's Lease* [1951] 1 All ER 346, where the lessor required possession of the subject premises for the lessor's own use. This was not sufficient to allow the lessor to withhold consent. Mere delay in dealing with the application for consent will amount to unreasonableness (see *Lewis and Allenby (1909) Ltd v Pegge* [1914] 1 Ch 782). However, a lessor can withhold consent to an assignment because the lessor believes that the proposed assignee's intended use would give rise to a breach of covenant (see *Ashworth Frazer Ltd v Gloucester City Council* [2002] 05 EG 133). The burden of proof is on the lessor to show that the lessor has acted reasonably. This applies as to the reasonableness of conditions to consent or refusal of consent. The lessee must make a court application seeking a declaration that the lessor has acted unreasonably. If successful, the lessee can seek an award for costs and the lessor may also be liable for damages where the claimant has suffered loss (Landlord and Tenant Act 1988, s 4).

Covenants by the lessor, including insurance

12.65 **Quiet enjoyment** A covenant for quiet enjoyment given by the lessor should be anticipated in virtually all leases. Indeed, if an express covenant is absent, an implied covenant will apply. A typical express covenant could read:

> that the lessee paying all the rents reserved by this lease and performing and observing all the covenants contained herein shall peaceably hold and enjoy the demised premises without any interruption by the lessor or any other company or person rightfully claiming under or in trust for the lessor.

12.66 The purpose of the covenant is to confirm that the lessee can physically enjoy the complete benefit of the property without the lessor adversely disturbing that enjoyment. What amounts to that disturbance has been the subject of detailed litigation. In *Browne v Flower* [1911] 1 Ch 219, the lessor was not held to be in breach of this covenant by inserting a new staircase right by the lessee's bedroom window. This was because there was no diminution of the physical enjoyment of the property; rather, the intrusion was on the lessee's privacy and not property. The courts have also held that this covenant could apply to scaffolding outside the property: see *Owen v Gadd* [1956] 2 QB 99, although this case related to a shop where the scaffolding was outside the shop door and window and consequently affected the lessee's business. In contrast, in *Kenny v Preen* [1963] 1 QB 499 the court held that the lessor's conduct where he banged on the door, sent threatening letters, and shouted abuse at the lessee, amounted to a breach of covenant for quiet enjoyment.

12.67 **Insurance by lessor** In modern business leases it is common practice for the lessor to insure but for the lessee to covenant to reimburse the lessor for the insurance premium. This is almost always the arrangement that prevails where there are several commercial lettings in one building. This is a desirable arrangement as it will be cost-effective to have one policy covering the whole building and will avoid inconsistencies of insurance cover that might arise if there was to be a separate policy for each letting. Where the lessee reimburses the lessor it would seem that the lessor is under no obligation to consider various insurers to find the cheapest premium (see *Havenridge Ltd v Boston*

Dyers Ltd [1994] 2 EGLR 73). The insured risks should be carefully defined and should clearly include damage caused by fire, storm, flooding, subsidence, burst pipes, riot, and other usual risks covered by standard buildings insurance policies. However, terrorism needs separate specific cover, and this should be precisely stated in the lease insurance provisions.

Commercial property leases—Code of Practice

The Code for Leasing Business Premises in England and Wales 2007 is the result of col- **12.68** laboration between commercial property professionals and industry bodies representing both Lessors and Lessees. The Code consists of three parts:

- ten point requirements for landlords in order for their lease to be Code-compliant;
- a guide for occupiers, explaining terms and providing helpful tips; and
- a model Heads of Terms (which can be completed online and downloaded).

The Code is voluntary, so the Government takes a keen interest in ensuring the property industry complies with this voluntary Code. The Code is endorsed by, among others:

- the Association of British Insurers;
- the British Retail Consortium;
- the Confederation of British Industry;
- the British Property Federation;
- the Federation of Small Businesses;
- The Welsh Assembly Government;
- The Law Society of England and Wales;
- The Royal Institution of Chartered Surveyors.

The Code is meant to apply to new leases and not to existing lettings. The intention of the Government-backed Code is to try to ensure that the lease parties deal with each other on an open and honest basis throughout the whole lease term. This means that if the lessee applies for a licence from the lessor, for example for alterations or change of use or assignment, the Code requires the lessor to deal with the application promptly. There are other elements that will be of relevance to both parties, especially where a guarantor is concerned, for example if the lessee defaults the lessor will, under the Code, notify any guarantor (who may also be a former lessee) of the default. The Code covers the conduct of the parties both during the negotiations for the grant of a new business lease and during the lease term. The Code remains a voluntary arrangement. The Government is monitoring its use and may, in the future, consider making it compulsory should the need arise.

FORFEITURE

All commercial leases should include a clause enabling the lessor to re-enter the subject **12.69** property and terminate the lease term as a consequence of a breach of covenant by the lessee, or of the happening of a specified occurrence. The reason for this is that without such an express provision there is no right of forfeiture available to the lessor. The usual reasons stipulated in such a clause, giving rise to the right to forfeiture, include non-payment of rent, breach of another lease covenant, and the lessee's liquidation or bankruptcy. Each of these is considered in the following paragraphs.

If the lessor wishes to forfeit, this can be achieved in two different ways. First, the les- **12.70** sor may commence court proceedings for forfeiture and seek an order for possession of the subject premises. Second, the lessor can simply peaceably re-enter the premises and thereby physically re-take possession. This second, apparently simple alternative is not without its problems. Statute imposes restrictions on this remedy. For example, if the letting involves a residential dwelling, the lessor could fall foul of the provisions of s 2 of the Protection from Eviction Act 1977. The lessor must not use or threaten violence to regain possession, as to do so could amount to a criminal offence under s 6 of the Criminal Law Act 1977. Consequently, many lessors take the view that, unless it is apparent from inspection that the lessee has abandoned the subject premises, it is far safer to apply to the courts for an order for possession. A practitioner acting for a lessor seeking to forfeit should advise his client about the potential dangers of waiver. For example, if the lessor is seeking to forfeit and then demands and/or accepts rent, the courts will infer a waiver of the right to forfeit (in *Central Estates (Belgravia) Ltd v Woolgar (No 2)* [1972] 1 WLR 1048 it was held that even a simple clerical error, whereby a rent demand was wrongly issued by the lessor's agent, will amount to an act of waiver).

For non-payment of rent

12.71 In the absence of an express provision to the contrary the lessor must make a formal demand for the rent. Most leases will include such an express provision requiring the lessee to pay the rent usually within 14 or 21 days of the payment date (one of the quarter days), whether the rent is formally demanded or not. In the absence of payment the lessor may either commence proceedings or peaceably re-enter. The lessee may be entitled to relief from forfeiture. The lessee can apply to court for this form of relief, and if the rent arrears and costs are discharged before the court hearing for forfeiture, the lessee will be so entitled. In certain circumstances the lessee can seek relief at any time during a period of up to six months from the making of the order for forfeiture or from when the lessor peaceably re-entered. See s 210 of the Common Law Procedure Act 1852 for High Court actions and s 138 of the County Courts Act 1984 for county court proceedings and for peaceable re-entry cases (see *Thatcher v CH Pearce and Sons (Contractors) Ltd* [1968] 1 WLR 748).

For breach of another lease covenant

12.72 This area is regulated by the provisions of s 146 of the Law of Property Act 1925. Usually, no enforcement steps can be taken without a notice being prepared based on these statutory requirements and served upon the lessee. The notice must:

(a) specify the particular breach complained of;
(b) if the breach is capable of remedy, require the lessee to remedy the breach; and
(c) require the lessee to make compensation in money for the breach.

12.73 A breach of a positive covenant is usually considered capable of remedy. A breach of a negative covenant is not so clear and will vary with each covenant depending upon the remediability of any harm done to the lessor (see *Expert Clothing Service and Sales Ltd v Hillgate House Ltd* [1986] Ch 340). Thus a breach of an alienation covenant, a negative covenant, has been held to be incapable of remedy (see *Scala House and District Property Co. Ltd v Forbes* [1974] QB 575). However, a covenant to reinstate a property, a positive covenant, was capable of remedy (see the *Expert Clothing* case). Other irremediable breaches include those of user covenants including specifically not to use the property for immoral purposes, for example as a sex shop in *Dunraven Securities Ltd v Holloway* (1982) 264 EG 709.

If there is non-compliance with the notice, the lessor can peaceably re-enter or obtain **12.74** possession by way of a court order. The lessee can nevertheless still seek relief from forfeiture. If there has been peaceable re-entry, the relief is available even after re-entry (see *Billson v Residential Apartments Ltd* [1992] 1 AC 494). If there is a court order and the lessor has re-entered, the right to relief is no longer available to the lessee. Relief is granted on such terms as the court thinks fit (Law of Property Act 1925, s 146(2)). If the breach complained of involves a repairing covenant, the s 146 notice may also involve the terms of the Leasehold Property (Repairs) Act 1938. If the covenant is contained in a lease for a term of at least seven years, and at the date of the service of the notice there are at least three years of that term left to run, the 1938 Act will apply. In these circumstances the s 146 notice must include explicit reference to the lessee's additional right to serve a counter-notice in writing within 28 days of the receipt of the s 146 notice, claiming the benefit of the Act (Leasehold Property Repairs Act 1938, s 1(2)). If a valid counter-notice is served, the lessor cannot take proceedings to enforce any right of re-entry or forfeiture for the continuing breach without leave of the court. Indeed, the courts have proved to be reluctant to grant such an order except in cases of substantial breach by the lessee.

Liquidation or bankruptcy

Common sense dictates that an insolvent lessee is unlikely to be able to comply with **12.75** lease covenants and it is probable that the covenant to pay rent is going to be breached sooner rather than later. This being so, most modern commercial leases will include the right to re-enter on the lessee being declared bankrupt or, if a company, being put into liquidation. The right is usually expressed to arise on the appointment of a receiver, a liquidator, or company administrator. The right to forfeit must be expressed as none is implied, and without such a clause the fact of the lessee's bankruptcy will not automatically put an end to the lease term (see *Hyde v Warden* (1877) 3 ExD 72). The lessor must serve a s 146 notice in most cases, but not where the lessee was a publican or the lease is of agricultural land (Law of Property Act 1925, s 146(9)). The bankrupt lessee, if seeking relief, must take steps to do so within the first year following the bankruptcy, failing which the right to relief is lost.

Forfeiture and the Commonhold and Leasehold Reform Act 2002

The Commonhold and Leasehold Reform Act 2002 introduced a new requirement that **12.76** ground rent will not be payable unless it has been formally demanded. The demand is to be made by giving the tenant a prescribed notice. The reforms in the Act prevent the application of any provisions of a lease relating to late payment or non-payment (e.g. additional charges such as interest) if the rent is paid within 30 days of the demand being issued. The Act also introduces additional restrictions on the commencement of forfeiture proceedings for breaches of covenants or conditions of a lease. It modifies s 81 of the Housing Act 1996 to prohibit the commencement of forfeiture proceedings, including the issue of a notice under s 146 of the Law of Property Act 1925, in respect of non-payment of service or administration charges. This is not the case if the charge has been agreed or admitted by the tenant, or a court or the First-tier Tribunal (Property Chamber), formerly the Leasehold Valuation Tribunal, has determined that it is reasonable and due. The Act also prohibits the commencement of forfeiture proceedings for other breaches, unless a court or the First-tier Tribunal has determined that a breach has occurred.

ENFORCEABILITY OF COVENANTS

Landlord and Tenant (Covenants) Act 1995

Introduction

12.77 It was, until recently, the position that the original lessor and lessee were liable to each other under the covenants in their lease for the full term granted by the first lessor to the first lessee. As a consequence of the effects of privity of contract this liability remained enforceable in the courts even if the lessee had subsequently assigned the residue of the term of the lease. The practical effect of this used to be that a lessee could be sued for arrears of rent even though that lessee had not been the lessee in occupation for many years. (The liability can be extended even after assignment. In *Selous Street Properties Ltd v Oronel Fabrics Ltd* [1984] 1 EGLR 50, it was held that where a later lessee carries out improvements that increase the rental value, the original lessee must pay rent at that higher level even though the works were carried out after the original lessee ceased to be involved as a result of having assigned the residue of the term of the lease.) This ancient element of landlord and tenant law has led to some very unfair situations where an original lessee has been called on to pay rent many years after assigning their legal estate in the subject property.

The purpose of the 1995 statute

12.78 A measure of reform has been made by the provisions of the Landlord and Tenant (Covenants) Act 1995, and details of the changes are set out in the following paragraphs. These provisions only apply to leases created on or after 1 January 1996. In essence a lessee who assigns such a lease automatically enjoys a release through statute for any continuing liability under the lease covenants. However, a lessor can require the outgoing lessee to enter into a form of guarantee designated by the statute as an 'authorised guarantee agreement' (AGA); see 12.79. The statute has made a major change to the law: the benefit and burden of lease covenants now pass automatically on assignment without any question of whether or not they touch and concern the land. The successor in title, the assignee, will take the benefit and burden of the lease covenants by reason of statute and the assignor, the original lessee, will be released from liability.

12.79 Unless the lessee has entered into an agreement formulated by the Landlord and Tenant (Covenants) Act 1995 as an AGA the lessee will, on assignment, be automatically released from any liability in the future on the lessee's lease covenants. An outgoing lessee who has entered into an AGA acts as guarantor for the successor in title, but not beyond the time of ownership of the lease by the incoming lessee. Of course the outgoing lessee cannot escape liability for breaches of covenant that arose during the time prior to the assignment of the legal estate, and the outgoing lessee will remain liable for such breaches after as well as before assignment. Should there be a transfer of the freehold reversion, there is no such automatic release for an outgoing lessor under the terms of the statute. However, the reversioner can seek a release by applying for it from the lessee, either before or within a period of four weeks from the date of the transfer of the reversionary title. The effect of this Act cannot be excluded or altered by agreement or otherwise.

12.80 What is a new lease can be of material importance, especially where there is a variation to a lease granted before 1 January 1996. This is because a variation can amount to a surrender and re-grant of a new term, but without being called a surrender. For example, if the variation concerns either the amount of the rent or the extent of the leased property, it will operate as a surrender and re-grant. If this happens, then the re-grant will amount to a new lease and will be covered by the terms of this statute. Practitioners acting for a lessor should always bear this in mind when dealing with variations, especially where the rent or the extent of the demised property is involved.

Contracts (Rights of Third Parties) Act 1999

The Contracts (Rights of Third Parties) Act 1999 ('the Act') affects covenants made on or **12.81** after 11 May 2000 (although contracting parties were able to opt into the provisions of the Act during a period of six months preceding this date, s 8(2)–(3)). It amends the law of privity of contract by enabling a third party to sue to enforce a contractual term if:

(a) the contract expressly provides that the third party should have the right to do so; or
(b) the term of the contract purports to confer a benefit on the third party unless, on a proper construction of the contract, it appears that the parties did not intend the contract to be enforceable by the third party.

The third party need not be in existence at the date of the contract/lease. A third party may **12.82** include a company not yet incorporated, or a sub-tenant or assignee of a lease. The Act gives the third party the same remedies as would have been available to it if it had been a party to the contract. The Act has a substantial impact on the mutual enforceability of leasehold covenants. If the tenant's covenants are worded so as to benefit every other tenant in the building/industrial estate, etc., then those tenants should be able to take direct action against the offending tenant without the need for mutual enforceability by the landlord. Sub-leases will also be affected.

A covenant by a head landlord in a head lease to insure the premises or provide services **12.83** will clearly benefit a sub-tenant. Under the Act the sub-tenant will be able to enforce the covenant against the head landlord even though there is no privity of estate between the sub-tenant and head landlord. Similarly, the head landlord may be able to enforce a breach of covenant by the sub-tenant in the sub-lease.

Section 2 of the Act provides that any variation of a contract may also require the consent **12.84** of a third party. That consent will be necessary if the third party has communicated his or her assent to the contract to the promisor, or if the promisor is aware that the third party has relied on the term, or should reasonably have foreseen that he would rely on it where he has in fact done so. Thus it may be necessary to obtain the consent of any sub-tenant before any variations are made to a head lease.

How to exclude the Act

As a result of this provision, many practitioners drafting leases will want to expressly **12.85** exclude the operation of the Act to obviate the need to obtain third parties' consent in the future before agreeing a variation of the lease. Moreover, if your client does not wish third parties to take the benefit of the lease covenants, then the lease should expressly exclude third parties from taking the benefit. This will put the contracting parties in the position they would have been in before the Act came into force. A suitable clause will read:

> The parties to this lease declare that the Contracts (Rights of Third Parties) Act 1999 shall not apply to it.

KEY POINTS SUMMARY

COMMERCIAL LEASES

- If you are drafting a new lease incorporating a rent review mechanism, make sure that on review **12.86** the rent cannot be reduced below the rental level that prevailed prior to the date of review. Furthermore, avoid strict time limits that make time of the essence for the review procedure.

- If you are involved with an application for licence to assign, remember that the terms of the Landlord and Tenant Act 1988 require the application to be dealt with within a reasonable time, failing which the lessee could be entitled to a claim for damages arising from any undue delay.

- In relation to user clauses, there is no statutory provision that implies that the lessor's consent cannot be unreasonably withheld, as is the case with alienation covenants. However, if there is an absolute or simple qualified covenant against changes of user it can have a deflating effect on any rental value on review. The covenant should be fully qualified, i.e. 'Not without the lessor's consent such consent not to be unreasonably withheld'.

- Practitioners acting for a lessor seeking to forfeit should advise their client about the potential dangers of waiver. If the lessor is seeking to forfeit and then demands and/or accepts rent, the courts will infer a waiver of the right to forfeit.

- If the lessor wishes to claim an alleged breach of covenant, remember that only a breach of a positive covenant is usually considered capable of remedy. A breach of a negative covenant is not so clear, and whether or not it will be capable of remedy will vary with each covenant depending upon the remediability of any harm done to the lessor.

- Remember that if you are dealing with a lease for a term of at least seven years where there are at least three years left to run, the Leasehold Property (Repairs) Act 1938 will apply. Any s 146 notice must include reference to the lessee's right to serve a counter-notice in writing within 28 days claiming the benefit of the Act. If a valid counter-notice is served, the lessor cannot take proceedings without leave of the court.

- If you act for a lessor and the original lessee of a lease granted on or after 1 January 1996 wishes to assign, seek to ensure that the outgoing lessee enters into an AGA whereby the outgoing lessee guarantees the performance of the lease covenants by the incoming lessee.

- Should you exclude the Contracts (Rights of Third Parties) Act 1999 in new leases?

- If the lease is to be registered do you need to consider applying for an EID to protect sensitive detail?

- Did your lease used to be a prescribed clauses lease?

C SELLING AND BUYING TENANTED PROPERTIES

12.87 There is a considerable commercial market in the purchase and sale of properties that are subject to the occupation of lessees with statutory security of tenure. This is particularly so in relation to property occupied by business tenants, but many of the special factors required in transactions involving commercial property will apply as well to properties sold with residential tenants. In essence, in addition to the matters of importance to a domestic seller or buyer, the terms of the letting will be of material importance in relation to the title, contract enquiries, and requisitions. These core elements are examined in the following paragraphs. First, contracts using the SCs, and, second, contracts using the SCPCs, are discussed.

12.88 Procedural changes brought about by the use of information technology are also relevant to this area of conveyancing. It was reported in the *Law Society Gazette* that one city firm has set up an online deal room for its commercial property clients. Documents are posted on the internet site; and where part or all of a portfolio is to be sold, the lawyer is given online access to speed up the sale (LSG 97/44, 16 November 2000).

CONTRACTUAL MATTERS WHERE SCs ARE USED

The seller will want to be sure that there are specific items in the contract covering the **12.89** nature of the sale and particularly to take account of the nature of the letting. If the tenant is a mere residential tenant, the basic terms of the SCs could suffice. However, clause 4 of the special conditions in the Law Society's standard form of contract should be amended so as to delete the first alternative, leaving the contract term as 'The property is sold subject to the following leases or tenancies . . .'. Thereafter the simple details of the residential lettings should be inserted. These details should refer to the lessee by name, the type of tenancy, i.e. weekly, monthly, quarterly, etc., and the amount of the rent together with the part of the property occupied if the tenancy is not of the whole of the subject property.

If the sale is of a reversion subject to residential long leases, the sale cannot proceed with- **12.90** out careful consideration of the effects of the Landlord and Tenant Act 1987, which gives the lessees in occupation a right of pre-emption. The contract will therefore need to show that the necessary steps have been taken to comply with the Act and that the lessees are not going to exercise their rights, and that therefore the sale to the non-occupant buyer may proceed. Where the letting is of a commercial nature the same approach set out above can be adopted, but further elements are of concern. In particular:

(a) Where there is a substantial commercial rental income from the property the contract will need to cover the question of rent arrears and the apportionment of rent at completion. Arrears can be dealt with by a special condition requiring the buyer to pay to the seller a sum equivalent to any subsisting rent arrears at the date of completion so that the buyer can then sue the lessee for those arrears, the point being that *Re King* [1963] Ch 459 throws doubt on whether a lessor who has sold the reversion can still sue the lessee after the sale for rent arrears that arose prior to the sale. This case therefore makes such a clause judicious; or at the very least there should be a contractual clause making the buyer assign to the seller the right to sue the lessee for those arrears.

(b) Special contractual provisions should be included if a rent review is due at the time of the contract, or if the lease is about to terminate and proceedings under Part II of the Landlord and Tenant Act 1954 are anticipated. In both cases the seller should agree not to do anything without consulting the buyer and should agree to act as the buyer reasonably directs.

(c) There may be a rental deposit paid by the lessee to the seller. If there is, the buyer will want to take over control of those monies. However, whether this will be possible will depend upon the terms of the actual deposit deed, which will need to be considered prior to exchange with the necessary steps required to effect a transfer covered in the special conditions.

SC 3.3 covers leases affecting the property. (A lease is defined by SC 1.1.1(g) as includ- **12.91** ing a sub-lease, tenancy, and agreement for a lease or sub-lease and should cover all forms of lettings but not licences.) The seller is obliged by SC 3.3.2(a) to provide full particulars of the letting with copies of any documents relating thereto so as to ensure the buyer enters into the contract 'knowing and fully accepting those terms'. To give effect to this provision the seller should supply, with the draft contract, a copy of any relevant lease or tenancy agreement along with any deeds or documents that are supplementary to them, such as a deed of variation. SC 3.3.2(b) requires the seller to inform the buyer of any lease or tenancy termination after exchange but before completion, and to act as the buyer reasonably directs, with the buyer indemnifying the seller against any consequent loss or expense. Similarly, SC 3.3.2(c) prohibits the seller from agreeing any changes to the lease or tenancy terms and requires the seller in SC 3.3.2(d) to advise the buyer of any proposed or agreed changes. Further, the buyer is, by SC 3.2.2(e), to indemnify the seller against claims arising from the lease or tenancy for the period following completion. SC 3.2.2(f) puts the burden of enquiry on the buyer as to what rent is lawfully recoverable and what legislation affects the lease or tenancy. It is for this reason, where the SCs are adopted, that the buyer must make particular enquiries about the rent and legislation as they affect the lessee in occupation, and these matters are considered in detail in the following paragraphs.

THE STANDARD COMMERCIAL PROPERTY CONDITIONS (SCPCs)

12.92 The SCPCs were issued on 17 May 1999 for use in commercial transactions. A second edition was issued on 1 June 2004 and a third edition in May 2017. A 2018 revision has also been issued, see 12.98. From the definitions section onward, it is clear that the SCPCs have been drafted with corporate lawyers in mind. For example, although the parties to the agreement are called sellers and buyers, they are referred to as 'it' rather than 'he', as is the case in the SCs. There follows an examination of the more important conditions in the SCPCs.

Introduction

12.93 In simple residential transactions the pre-printed contractual Standard Conditions of Sale (SCs), are almost universally used by conveyancing practitioners. However, if a commercial element in a proposed agreement is more complicated and in particular if there is a lessee in occupation as a commercial tenant, then the SCPCs are likely to be more appropriate. The third edition takes into account the changes in the law and practice arising from the Land Registration Act 2002 and the Commonhold and Leasehold Reform Act 2002. It also builds on the fifth edition of the SCs and now makes for VAT the default position being that the sale of the property will constitute a taxable supply.

12.94 The SCPCs are divided into two parts. Part 1 contains general conditions building on those in the previous editions, while Part 2 contains new clauses and in particular detailed provisions covering VAT, capital allowances, and reversionary interests in flats. As such the emphasis is clearly on more complex commercial transactions. In general Part 1 applies unless expressly excluded, while Part 2 will only apply if expressly incorporated. Completing tick boxes on the back page of the agreement effects express incorporation, see SCPC 1.1.4 (a) and (b).

12.95 Both sets of conditions have a front page that allows practitioners to insert basic yet vital details for the agreement such as details of the seller, buyer, the property, title information, and specified incumbrances. (By SCPC 4.1.2(a) the seller sells subject to incumbrances specified in the contract, i.e. on the front page.) The front page on the third edition of the SCPCs does not now allow for the sale of chattels to be included in the purchase price as was the case in the previous edition. On the special conditions page there is a special condition that will provide for vacant possession or for a sale subject to listed tenancies. Another special condition provides for contents to be included in the sale or to be sold separately, and an alternative listing fixtures that are specifically excluded from the sale. Finally there is a special condition on the back page that has tick boxes enabling the specific incorporation of Part 2 conditions, e.g. conditions covering VAT, capital allowances, and reversionary interests in flats.

Part 1 Conditions

Part 1 contains general conditions building on those in the previous editions. It is of inter-   **12.96**
est that there is no mention on the front page of the SCPC of title guarantee. There is such
a provision in SCPC 7.6.2 but this is subject to any incumbrances affecting the subject
property and covered by SCPC 4.1.2. However, in the special conditions there is a tick box
to select that confirms that the property is to be sold with limited title guarantee which
replaces the reference to full title guarantee in SCPC 7.6.2. There are also conditions varying methods of payment and time for completion (6 and 7). Special condition 8 can be used
in sales of part to stipulate a form of transfer that includes express terms such as covenants
or rights and reservations.

Most, if not all, conveyancing practitioners will be familiar with the SCs as they are used in
the vast majority of domestic conveyancing transactions. The SCPCs may not be so familiar. Consequently, the following section is an examination of some of the more important
features of the SCPCs.

Condition 1 General

In this section in the second edition there was a definition for 'direct credit'. The effect of   **12.97**
this was that payments at exchange and completion could not be by banker's draft and
can only be by bank telegraphic CHAPS payment transfers. The purpose of this inclusion
was to take account of the general commercial practice of requiring completely cleared
funds at exchange or completion. In the third edition there is no such definition, but
at SCPC 9.7 it states that 'The buyer is to pay the money on completion by electronic
means in same day cleared funds from an account held in the name of a conveyancer...'.
The SCPCs define when a party is ready, able, and willing to complete, i.e. when they
might be able to serve on the other party who is not so ready a notice to complete. (Such
notice is also defined as a notice requiring completion of the contract in accordance with
SCPC 9.) A party is so ready if it would complete but for the default of the other party, see
SCPC 1.1.3.

Following the Bank of England's takeover of the Clearing House Automated Payment Sys-   **12.98**
tem (CHAPS), and its impact on the definition of 'clearing bank' in the Standard Conditions of Sale and Standard Commercial Property Conditions, revisions to these conditions
have been settled. The new wording is:

> '"clearing bank" means a bank admitted by the Bank of England as a direct participant in its
> CHAPS system.'

Since this is the only change being made to the current editions, the forms will now be
known as:

- the Standard Conditions of Sale (fifth edition, 2018 revision)
- Standard Commercial Property Conditions (third edition, 2018 revision).

SCPC 1.4.1 prohibits the transfer of the benefit of the contract. Practitioners should also   **12.99**
be aware that SCPC 1.4.2 is a total prohibition against sub-sales in whole or in part.
The buyer must be named as the transferee in the purchase deed and no other party can
be mentioned unless they are a named party in the agreement. This section is therefore
close to the terms of the SCs and is there to ensure that the named buyer and only the
named buyer completes with the seller.

SCPC 1.3 recognizes the use of e-mail to deliver and serve a notice (as well as by fax). If the   **12.100**
recipient's e-mail is stated in the contract (on the back page within the section for details of
the seller's and buyer's conveyancers), then adding the e-mail address authorizes service by

e-mail: see SCPC 1.3.3(b). An e-mail is treated as being received one hour after dispatch: see SCPC 1.3.7(e).

Condition 2 VAT Standard Rated Supply

12.101 Under this condition the seller warrants that the sale will constitute a supply chargeable to VAT at the standard rate. So if the sale is not a taxable supply then Condition A1 in Part 2 should be expressly incorporated into the agreement to confirm this VAT status.

Condition 3 Formation

12.102 As to the date of the formation of the agreement, the terms cover the moment of exchange, i.e. it will be at the time of posting or at the time of deposit in the DX or by some other procedure agreed between the parties. SCPC 3.2 regarding the deposit states that the deposit (at 10 per cent) except by auction sale the buyer is to pay the deposit by electronic means in same day cleared funds from an account held in the name of a conveyancer. In contrast to domestic conveyances, most transactions where the parties are selling and/or buying tenanted properties are unlikely to be part of a chain of transactions. Consequently, the deposit is paid to the seller's solicitor as stakeholder and is to be released to the seller on completion with accrued interest. However, where there is an auction sale the deposit is to be held by the auctioneer as agent for the seller, thus enabling the seller to get hold of the deposit prior to completion. Furthermore, if there is a deposit paid at an auction sale by cheque and all or any part of the payment is dishonoured on first presentation, then the seller has an option to terminate on dishonour. The seller does not need to represent the cheque as the provision talks of first presentation and can simply give notice to the buyer that the contract has been discharged by the buyer's breach.

Condition 3 Matters affecting the property, Condition 4 Occupational leases

12.103 SCPC 4.1.2(d) has been written to put the burden on the buyer to carry out all searches and enquiries that a prudent buyer would make before entering into a contract of this type. In essence the property is sold subject to all matters that would be disclosed, for example a local authority search save for mortgages. The SCPCs now also state that the incumbrances affecting the subject property are either specified in the contract, discoverable on inspection, or disclosable in searches or enquiries. The SCPCs also state that a leasehold property is sold subject to any subsisting breach of covenant regarding the condition of the property.

12.104 Condition 5 covers leases and applies if any part of the property is sold subject to a lease (and a lease is defined as including a sub-lease, tenancy, and agreement for a lease or sub-lease). SCPC 5.1.3 states that the seller is not to serve a notice to end the lease or accept surrender and by SCPC 5.1.4 is to inform the buyer without delay if the lease ends. These elements are included in the SCPCs to prevent the seller from taking unilateral action that might adversely affect the value of the premises by ensuring that the seller cannot after exchange and before completion force the tenant out of the subject property or take steps towards ejecting the tenant. SCPC 4.2 is a leasehold condition by seeking to cover property management for the period between exchange and completion. It sets out extensive provisions for the conduct of litigation proceedings affecting leasehold premises in court or by arbitration. (However, you should note that this does not cover rent review matters that are covered by Condition 6, see 12.105.) Furthermore, the seller is not to grant or formally withhold any licence consent or approval required by the terms of the occupational lease. This means that once contracts are exchanged the seller must always seek the buyer's permission in relation to any matters that arise from the lease terms and that need the consent or involvement of the lessor. However, SCPC 5.2.7 provides that the buyer is not to withhold consent so as to place the seller in breach of a statutory duty or of an obligation to the lessee. Therefore, if the circumstances are such that the lessor should grant a licence to assign and by refusing would be in breach of a statutory duty, the buyer cannot dictate that the seller adopt this stance. SCPC 5.2.9 requires the seller to manage the property in accordance with the principles of good estate management until completion. Quite whether parties to a contract in dispute can agree as to what might amount to good estate management is open to debate.

Condition 6 Rent reviews

This was a wholly new condition included in the second edition that remains in the third **12.105** edition and covers some of the details in the first edition with expanded and new items. The purpose of the condition is to explicitly cover rent review matters that will arise between exchange and completion. SCPC 6.15.4 imposes on both seller and buyer an obligation to cooperate promptly and effectively regarding the process of the rent review and the documentation required to facilitate the review process. Most importantly neither can approve a rent without the written approval of the other: SCPC 6.15.5. The condition also covers how the cost of the rent review should be paid as between the seller and the buyer; e.g. SCPC 6.15.6 states that the seller and the buyer are to bear their own costs of the rent review process. More detailed time-related provisions follow relating to the payment of costs: see SCPC 6.15.7 and 6.15.8.

SCPC 6.2 is a new condition that applies where the seller is the lessor of a tenancy where **12.106** it is continuing under Part II of the Landlord and Tenant Act 1954 but no agreement has been reached on an interim rent or on the termination of the tenancy or the terms of the new tenancy. In this situation the seller remains responsible for negotiations but the parties to the contract must consult and co-operate between exchange and completion.

Condition 7 Title and transfer

Conditions 7.1–7.4 are the same in both sets of conditions. (Requirements for both regis- **12.107** tered and unregistered titles are set out in 7.1.2 and 7.1.3.) However, SCPC 7.6.5 has been drafted so that where the seller will, after completion, be bound by an obligation affecting the property, then provided the obligation is disclosed to the buyer before exchange the seller is entitled to an indemnity from the buyer. There must be disclosure failing which there is no binding obligation to afford any such indemnity.

If the property is registered there may be EIDs such that they may not be disclosed on **12.108** or with the official copies of the registers. Accordingly, where there are any such EIDs, the buyer should make sure that the seller is obliged by a contractual term to provide the buyer with full copies. As a precautionary measure, it may be appropriate to include this in all contracts. (EIDs are discussed in detail at 12.30–12.32 regarding commercial leases.)

SCPC 7.6.4 is a new condition. It comes into operation when the subject property is **12.109** leasehold and requires the leasehold property transfer to state that the covenants implied by s 4 of the Law of Property (Miscellaneous Provisions) Act 1994 will not extend to a breach of the lessee's covenants in the lease that relate to the physical state of the subject property.

Condition 8 Risk and Insurance

This clause expressly states that the subject property is at the buyer's risk from the date **12.110** of the agreement. SCPC 8.2.2 describes the seller's obligations about insurance in the situation where the seller is required by SCPC 8.2.1 to keep the subject property insured between exchange and completion. SCPC8.2.5 is new and covers the situation where the leasehold property insurance is maintained by the reversioner. In this situation the seller must use reasonable efforts to ensure that the insurance is maintained from exchange to completion. If after exchange and before completion the property is damaged by an insured risk, the seller is obliged to pay to the buyer on completion the amount of the policy monies received by the seller. If no final insurance payment has been made, then the seller is to assign to the buyer all rights to monies under the insurance policy and to hold any monies received in trust for the buyer.

Condition 9 Completion

12.111 In this section, being the condition regulating all matters at completion, the buyer instead of the seller is assumed to own the property from the start of the completion date. The completion date will be the actual date of completion where the whole property is sold with vacant possession, otherwise it is the date specified in the agreement. This clearly affects apportionments (SCPC 9.3.3). These are further regulated at SCPC 9.3.4, where the detailed arrangements required for completion date apportionments are set out. Sums are to be treated as accruing from day to day throughout the period for which payment is or has to be made and at the rate applicable for that period. The SCPC also covers unquantified sums such as final year-end service charges: see SCPC 9.3.5. These are to be payable with interest on late payment but because of the larger amounts involved in commercial property we suggest that it would be safer to set up an agreed retention with the buyer's solicitor by way of the special conditions. Alternatively, the seller's solicitor could retain the monies in a designated client deposit account pending settlement with the interest accruing to the seller in any event. This provision should also be covered by way of a special condition in the agreement.

12.112 SCPC 9.3.6 applies where a lease affects the property being sold and there is a service charge. On completion the buyer is to pay to the seller any element of the service charge incurred by the seller but not yet due from the tenant. In the light of this provision it is vital that practitioners acting for a buyer in these circumstances raise detailed enquiries about any such expenditure. It is therefore important that proof of payment be produced along with proof that it was necessarily incurred and repayable under the terms and conditions of the lease. This is required to avoid subsequent problems with the lessee in obtaining reimbursement, and is covered by SCPC 9.3.6(a).

12.113 SCPC 9.3.7 and 9.3.8 both seek to cover the position where there are arrears. The terms of these clauses are complicated and should be considered in detail for each subject property and amended as necessary. SCPC 9.3.7 states that SCPC 9.3.8 applies if there are arrears, there is no contractual assignment to the seller of the right to collect those arrears, and the seller is not entitled to recover any arrears from the tenant. In these circumstances SCPC 8.3.8 requires the buyer to seek to collect all the arrears in the ordinary course of management but is not obliged to commence court proceedings for their recovery or exercise the Commercial Rent Arrears Recovery (CRAR) procedure. Any monies received are to be apportioned between the parties in the ratio of the sums owed to each. Leases granted post-1995 are covered by ss 3 and 23 of the Landlord and Tenant (Covenants) Act 1995 to the extent that unless specifically assigned to the buyer, the right to collect arrears remains with the seller. This is relevant in the context of these SCPCs and the conditions required activate SCPC 9.3.8. It also means that pre-1996 leases are such that the seller will not be able to recover arrears by commencing proceedings or instructing bailiffs after completion (Law of Property of Act 1925, s 141).

Finally, in this section SCPC 9.5 says that as soon as the buyer has performed all its obliga- **12.114**
tions on completion the seller must part with the title documents. SCPC 8.7 requires payment to be by electronic means in same day cleared funds from an account held in the name
of a conveyancer. SCPC 9.8 states that at any time on or after the completion date a party
who is ready, able, and willing to complete may give to the other a notice to complete. Ten
working days is the notice period excluding the day on which the notice is given. For this
purpose time is of the essence: see SCPC 9.8.2.

Condition 10 Remedies

Little of this particular condition is changed from the SCs to the SCPCs, although there is **12.115**
one alteration of consequence for buyers. It should be noted that SCPC 10.3.1 provides
that liability for interest arises only on the default of the buyer. If the seller defaults and
delays completion, in the absence of a special condition all that a buyer can do is sue the
defaulting seller for damages. Moreover, SCPC 10.3.4 states that if completion is delayed
the seller may give notice to the buyer that it will take the net income from the subject
property until completion takes place together with any interest due pursuant to SCPC
10.3.1.

Condition 11 Leasehold property

As one might expect for a set of conditions designed to cover commercial transac- **12.116**
tions and especially those dealing with the selling and buying of tenanted properties,
this section contains substantial provisions. There are detailed alterations from the
terms of the SCs where leases are concerned and particularly in relation to the normal
requirement to obtain the consent of the lessor in a commercial lease assignment or
transfer.

Dealing first with new leases (i.e. a contract for the grant of a new lease), SCPC 11.2 reiter- **12.117**
ates the provisions of the SCs as to definitions and under the SCPCs the lease is to be in the
form of a draft attached to the agreement itself. Accordingly, it is contemplated that new
leases will be part of the actual agreement by attachment. If the lease term exceeds seven
years the seller is to deduce title to enable the buyer to register with absolute title. This
means that a lessor will have to show the lessee its superior title. To avoid this disclosure,
lessors should only grant seven-year leases or shorter.

SCPC 11.3 deals with the landlord's consent and has been substantially retained in the **12.118**
same format as that which appeared in the previous edition of the conditions. For example, SCPC 10.3.3(b) states that the seller is to enter into an AGA. Similarly, the buyer is
to use reasonable endeavours to provide guarantees of the performance and observance
of the tenant's covenants and the conditions in the seller's lease. SCPC 10.3.1(b) defines
consent as 'consent in a form which satisfies the requirement to obtain it' (see *Aubergine
Enterprises Ltd v Lakewood International Ltd* [2002] 1 WLR 2149). Completion can now
be postponed if there is a delay in obtaining the consent of the lessor (SCPC 11.3.4 and
11.3.5).

Completion can be postponed until five working days after either the seller notifies the **12.119**
buyer that consent has been given or a court has declared that consent has been unreasonably withheld. (The previous edition set a time limit of four months from completion but
this is no longer the case in the third edition.)

In previous editions there were conditions covering commonhold. These have been totally **12.120**
removed because it is rarely if ever used.

12.121   Previously this was entitled 'chattels' but now has the modern title of contents. It should be noted that in SCPC 12.4, where it now provides that ownership of any contents covered by the agreement passes to the buyer at completion, but that the contents are at the buyer's risk from exchange. This reflects the provision in the SCPC relating to the insurance risk for the subject property, where the risk also passes at the contract date. The reverse is the case for both the subject property and the chattels in the SCs (SC 10.4 states that ownership of the chattels passes to the buyer on actual completion).

Part 2 Conditions

12.122   Part 2 contains clauses and detailed provisions covering VAT, capital allowances, and reversionary interests in flats. There is nothing in the SCs that matches them. The main details of these three provisions are:

(a) **VAT**   Under SCPC 2, the seller warrants that the sale will constitute a supply chargeable to VAT at the standard rate. So if the sale is not a taxable supply then Condition A1 in Part 2 should be expressly incorporated into the agreement to confirm this VAT status. First, Condition A1 states that the sale does not constitute a supply that is taxable for VAT purposes. (SCPC 2 requires the buyer to pay VAT on top of the purchase price in exchange for a proper VAT invoice.) Second, Condition A2 covers a transfer of a going concern. In this case the seller warrants that it is using the property for the business of letting to produce a rental income.

(b) **Capital allowances**   Condition B supports a buyer in any claims it may make pursuant to the terms of the Capital Allowances Act 2001. In doing so it requires the seller to provide copies of relevant information and cooperation and assistance as the buyer may reasonably require. A practitioner can find detailed guidance on capital allowances on the HMRC website at **http://www.hmrc.gov.uk**. The conditions have also been changed to take into account changes that came into force in April 2014 regarding claims for capital allowances for expenditure on plant and machinery that is a fixture.

(c) **Reversionary interests in flats**   C1 covers the provisions of the Landlord and Tenant Act 1987 and the tenants' rights of pre-emption on a sale. The condition requires the seller to warrant that on the facts the tenants do not have any rights arising from this statute, i.e. the relevant notice has been served but no response was forthcoming. Condition C2 covers the position where the tenants are entitled to a right of first refusal in auction sales.

Conclusion

12.123   The SCPC have been expanded and greatly improved by the additional provisions included in the third edition. They are now likely to be adopted for all appropriate sales of commercial property, especially where there is a tenant in occupation or where there are VAT and/or capital allowances to be taken into consideration. Much of the SCPC replicate the terms of the SCs but this can only be of benefit to practitioners by ensuring that most will be acquainted with the details and will therefore be prepared to use these new conditions.

Adoption of the SCPCs

12.124   Should a prudent practitioner adopt these conditions for all seller clients? In theory there is no reason why this should not be done, although in practice there could be substantial resistance to this practice from buyers when they come to approve the draft agreement. In reality, the same effect can be achieved by adopting the SCs and by making specific amendments to the draft contract to take into account those changes made by the SCPCs that are relevant to the specific transaction in hand. Indeed, some of the new conditions may not be very sensible in the context of a residential sale. We take the view that the right approach is to adopt whichever set of conditions is best for the subject property, and to amend them further to make the selected conditions thoroughly appropriate to that particular property. Best practice dictates that in general a prudent practitioner should always alter a standard contract form to suit a specific property.

TENANTED PROPERTIES: THE BUYER'S PERSPECTIVE

It is clear that the heavier burden rests with the buyer's practitioner when a tenanted property changes hands. This particular form of conveyancing transaction requires extra care when raising preliminary enquiries, when looking at the title, and when raising requisitions. These matters will be considered further in the following sections.

12.125

Additional enquiries

In addition to the standard enquiries that need to be made in all conveyancing transactions, it is critical that enquiries are made with regard to the lessees in occupation and their rents paid or in arrears. It is therefore appropriate to request details of previous rent reviews along with copies of rent review memoranda recording the previous changes in rent. Service charge accounts should be requested for the last three years, with details of sinking funds and arrears that may exist in respect of these payments. Details should be requested of any permitted changes of use as these too could materially affect the future, or indeed current, rental potential. If the property is VATable, details of the VAT position will need to be investigated along with accounts of VAT payments made by lessees or details of arrears. Insurance details need to be investigated, particularly if the lessor insures the block and the lessee repays the premium. If industrial premises are being purchased, detailed environmental and contamination enquiries must be made of the seller.

12.126

Additional enquiries—residential

In addition to the standard enquiries that are always raised, and the additional enquiries mentioned at 12.122, it is appropriate to make further enquiries in relation to residential lettings in so far as they may be affected or regulated by legislation. A buyer will want to enquire as to the status of the tenant in occupation, and in particular whether the tenant can claim any form of statutory protection providing any element of security of tenure. Since 28 February 1997, s 96 of the Housing Act 1996 makes all subsequent residential tenancies assured shorthold tenancies, and they are so without the need to comply with any particular formalities such as formal notices, etc. This is not retrospective and only applies to new tenancies granted after that date. Accordingly, the date of creation of the tenancy is a crucial item of information which needs to be disclosed to the buyer and should be elicited through a specific preliminary enquiry. This is all the more so as different forms of security of tenure will apply to tenancies depending on when they were created. If the tenancy arose prior to 28 November 1980 it will be covered by the Rent Acts and will be a protected tenancy with full security of tenure. If the tenancy commenced after this date but before 15 January 1989, it could either be a protected tenancy under the Rent Acts, or it might also be a protected shorthold where there is limited security, with the lessor

12.127

being entitled to a mandatory ground for possession. Accordingly, further enquiries will be necessary to ascertain which form of tenancy will be involved. If the tenancy arose after 15 January 1989 the Housing Act 1988 applies, and the tenancy will usually be an assured tenancy with full security or an assured tenancy with limited security. This is not a complete listing as it is an area of great complexity, and if further information is required practitioners should consult additional authorities. However, you should note that there are some tenancies that will not be covered at all, such as those at a low rent, e.g. outside London not exceeding £250, or a business tenancy, agricultural holding, student or holiday letting, or a letting by the Crown or a local authority.

12.128   Further enquiries should be made as to the statutory control of the rents payable by a residential tenant. Tenancies granted after 28 February 1997 will have minimal control as a consequence of the Housing Act 1996. Tenants in these circumstances can merely, and only during the first six months of their tenancy, refer the rent to a rent assessment committee for scrutiny. Tenancies created previously will have differing elements of statutory control of rents depending on when the tenancy was first created.

12.129   **The Green Deal**   This is a government initiative seeking to save energy and reduce carbon emissions. It covers works required to homes to make them 'green', including the following:

- cavity wall insulation;
- solar panels;
- boilers;
- hot water systems;
- replacement double glazing;
- insulation and lighting systems;
- micro wind generation;
- ground source pumps and biomass boilers.

If a property is to be sold and is subject to a Green Deal, information must be disclosed, in terms of the Green Deal (Disclosure) Regulations 2012. But what is the position if the buyer has no notice of the Green Deal? If the buyer gets their first energy bill that shows a Green Deal of which they were unaware, they may challenge the obligation to repay the Green Deal loan and disclaim liability. This must be done within 90 days. The debt then remains with the outgoing seller, who will be liable for full repayment!

You will need to know the terms of the Green Deal and be able to advise the client, so if you are acting for the seller make sure the Energy Performance Certificate includes all the details of the Green Deal. If you are acting for the buyer ensure all consents were available for the works and be ready to advise on the financial implications. Take up of the Green Deal has been poor and in July 2015 the Government announced that the Green Deal would be scrapped as it had failed to deliver its objectives. In January 2017, Greenstone Finance and Aurium Capital Markets announced the acquisition of the business and assets of the Green Deal Finance Company (which administered the Government scheme), as well as its existing loan book with a principal value in excess of £40 million.

Additional enquiries—commercial

12.130   In addition to the standard enquiries that are always raised, and the additional enquiries mentioned at 12.122, it is appropriate to make further enquiries in relation to commercial lettings in so far as they may be affected or regulated by legislation. In essence a buyer will want to know how far, if at all, the lease is influenced by Part II of the Landlord and Tenant Act 1954. A buyer will want to know if there has been a court application (as if there is no clause to that effect in the lease the contracting out will be to no effect), and if so will want to see what order the court made. If the lease has been recently renewed under the terms of the Act, a prudent buyer will want details to ascertain how the length of the term eventually granted was settled along with the other terms of the lease. Perhaps of more consequence would be to see the basis on which the rental was finally settled. Valuers' reports would be of use and copies should be requested. A buyer will also want to know if the lessor originally sought to oppose the grant of the lease and why. The ground for possession would be of material interest to the buyer, especially if it related to a breach of covenant or for arrears of rent. Detailed enquiries should be directed to the seller's practitioner, seeking as much information as possible about the circumstances of any recent statutory renewal. If the lease was granted after 1 January 1996 on assignment an AGA may be involved. Enquiries should be made of the terms of this agreement. If industrial premises are being purchased detailed environmental and contamination enquiries must be made of the seller. Specimen enquiries where a property is subject to lettings may be found at the Online Resource Centre for this book.

The Commercial Property Standard Enquiries

An attempt has been made to draft some standard enquiries for commercial properties. **12.131** The Commercial Property Standard Enquiries (CPSEs) are a set of documents that have been drafted by members of the London Property Support Lawyers Group under the sponsorship of the British Property Federation (BPF). Contributions were also made by a number of other firms and individuals. The CPSEs are endorsed by the BPF, and it is anticipated that they might become industry standard pre-contract enquiries for commercial property conveyancing. These documents can be used freely and without charge, subject to the user identifying them as being part of the suite of documents comprising the CPSEs. Details of the CPSEs can be seen at **http://www.practicallaw.com**. The enquiries in the CPSEs are intended as a standard minimum for use in any commercial property transaction.

CPSE.1 is designed to cover all commercial property transactions and will (together with **12.132** any additional enquiries relevant to the particular transaction) be sufficient if the transaction deals only with a freehold sold with vacant possession. The following supplemental enquiries are intended to be used in conjunction with CPSE.1. Which particular additional form or forms will be required will depend upon the individual circumstances of each transaction. The following supplemental forms are available:

- CPSE.2—where the property is sold subject to existing tenancies;
- CPSE.3—where a lease of a property is being granted;
- CPSE.4—where the property being sold is leasehold (i.e. the lease is being assigned or transferred);
- CPSE.5—enquiries before surrender of a rack rent commercial lease;
- CPSE.6 and CRC enquiries—these new enquiries are necessary to deal with issues arising under the Carbon Reduction Commitment Energy Efficiency Scheme 2010 (CRC). The CRC is a mandatory carbon emissions reporting and pricing scheme to cover all organizations using more than 6,000 MWh per year of electricity (equivalent to an annual electricity bill of about £500,000). This may affect many commercial property companies. The CRC came into force in April 2010 and aims to significantly reduce UK carbon emissions not covered by other pieces of legislation. The primary focus is to reduce emissions in non-energy-intensive sectors in the UK.
- CPSE.7—general short-form pre-contract enquiries for all property transactions. Because the enquiries can be lengthy they may not suit all transactions. Accordingly a short form set has been issued as CPSE 7. This shortened set of enquiries contains the following topics:

1. Boundaries and extent;
2. Rights benefiting the property;
3. Adverse rights affecting the property;
4. Physical condition;
5. Contents;
6. Utilities and services;
7. Fire safety and means of escape;
8. Planning and building regulations;
9. Statutory agreements and infrastructure;
10. Statutory and other requirements;
11. Environmental;
12. Occupiers;
13. Insurance;
14. Rates and other outgoings;
15. Notices;
16. Disputes;
17. SDLT on assignment of a lease;
18. Deferred payment of SDLT;
19. VAT;
20. Capital allowances.

This form is not suitable for the purchase of development sites, or transactions involving investment property subject to multiple tenancies, or in other complex commercial transactions. CPSE.7 omits some of the questions raised in CPSE.1 (such as those relating to employees and commonhold) and simplifies many others (i.e. CIL, SDLT, and other tax questions).

CONDITIONAL CONTRACTS

Introduction

12.133   Conditional contracts are frequently encountered in commercial conveyancing, particularly in relation to conditions relating to planning permission, the buyer's local search, and the buyer's financial arrangements. Practitioners should note in particular the following important issues when drafting a conditional contract.

Planning conditionality

12.134   Where the condition relates to obtaining satisfactory planning permission it is important to define both the proposed development and the relevant planning permission itself. It should be made clear whether the proposed planning permission is outline or detailed. The buyer should be obliged to submit an application to the planning authority within a prescribed time and to pay all necessary fees. The buyer should also be required to take all necessary steps to procure the grant of the permission as soon as possible, including perhaps submitting an amended application or appealing against a refusal. In addition, the buyer should keep the seller informed as to the progress of the planning application. The contract will normally stipulate that completion of the sale shall take place a set number of days after the grant of planning permission (e.g. 14 days).

12.135   The buyer will not want to complete if planning permission is granted subject to any 'unreasonable conditions' and so these should be defined, for example as one that materially affects the cost of construction or marketability of the development. If the parties cannot agree whether a condition is unreasonable, provision should be made for reference to an independent surveyor for determination. If the relevant planning permission is not granted by a predetermined longstop date (time being of the essence), then the contract should provide for either party to rescind, and the deposit to be returned to the buyer.

Financial conditionality

Where the condition relates to the buyer's financial arrangements the contract should provide that the buyer takes all necessary steps to procure a relevant offer of finance, including completing all documents required by the mortgagee. The clause should define a relevant offer of finance as being for not less than a stipulated sum and which is not subject to any 'unusually onerous conditions'. These should also be defined, for example an interest rate above a certain percentage or an excessive arrangement fee. Alternatively, the buyer may wish to retain control by deciding for itself whether the offer of finance is satisfactory. The contract should also provide that the purchase is subject to the buyer receiving by the contractual completion date the relevant offer of finance, failing which the contract will end and the deposit will be returned to the buyer.

12.136

Search conditionality

Where the condition relates to the buyer's local search, the contract should provide that the buyer is not obliged to complete the contract unless a satisfactory local search has been received by the contractual completion date. As such, a 'satisfactory local search' should be defined, for example as one that does not reveal entries that materially and adversely affect the market value of the property or the buyer's proposed use or development. Alternatively, the buyer may wish to retain control by deciding for itself whether the result of the local search is satisfactory (although this is unlikely to be acceptable to a seller). Consideration should also be given to a clause whereby if the parties cannot agree whether a local search is satisfactory, the matter is referred to an independent surveyor for determination. The seller should impose a longstop date for fulfilment of the condition (time being of the essence), after which the seller can withdraw from the contract and repay the deposit to the buyer.

12.137

Precedent

An example of a precedent clause for a contract dependent on a satisfactory local search is set out on the Online Resource Centre for this book. As an alternative to a conditional contract the parties may consider that an option agreement is more appropriate. Option agreements are considered at 3.146.

12.138

COMPLETION MATTERS

On completion the seller must hand over not merely the reversionary title deeds and documents, but also the lease(s) or tenancy agreement(s) as well as rental authorities. These authorities should be completed in letter format and signed by the seller and addressed to the lessees authorizing them to pay all future rents to the buyer or as the buyer directs. (Standard pre-printed requisitions normally include a request that such authorities be made available on completion.) Where the subject property constitutes a dwelling, s 3 of the Landlord and Tenant Act 1985 compels the buyer to give written notice of the change of ownership to the lessee or tenant in occupation within two months of completion. Where a dwelling has been sold, s 48 of the Landlord and Tenant Act 1987 compels the lessor buyer to provide the lessee in occupation with an address in England and Wales that can be used for the service of notices.

12.139

SELLING AND BUYING TENANTED PROPERTIES

12.140 • Consider whether the sale contract should be based upon the SCs or the SCPCs:

  • If the sale is of a reversion subject to residential long leases the sale cannot proceed without the careful consideration of the effects of the Landlord and Tenant Act 1987, which may give the lessees in occupation a right of pre-emption. If the right exists, the contract will need to show that steps have been taken to comply with the Act.

  • Where there is a substantial commercial rental income from the property the contract will need to cover the question of rent arrears and the apportionment of rent at completion. Remember that SC 3.3.2(b) requires the seller to inform the buyer of any lease or tenancy termination after exchange but before completion, and to act as the buyer reasonably directs, with the buyer indemnifying the seller against any consequent loss or expense.

  • Bear in mind that where the property constitutes a dwelling, s 3 of the Landlord and Tenant Act 1985 compels the buyer to give written notice of the change of ownership to the lessee or tenant in occupation within two months of completion; and s 48 of the Landlord and Tenant Act 1987 compels the lessor buyer to provide the lessee in occupation with an address within England and Wales that can be used for the service of notices.

  • Do you need to make environmental enquiries and searches?

  • Can you use the Commercial Property Standard Enquiries? Would the short form (CPSE7) suit your transaction?

  • Do you need to use a conditional contract?

COMMERCIAL LEASE CONTENTS

12.141 • When dealing with the approval of a new lease, have particular regard to the draft terms, and especially to the contents of the provisions on the following matters, to make sure that the details accord with your client's instructions:

  • Identify the length of the lease term and the start date.

  • Identify the rental level and payment days as well as the necessity to pay other rents, for example insurance and/or service charges.

  • Ascertain the rent review provisions, frequency, and mechanics. Avoid items that make time of the essence.

  • Is the rent review upward only?

  • Who is to insure? If it is the lessor, are the lease terms sufficient to ensure the property is fully insured?

  • Alienation provisions. Will the lease allow dealings with part of the property? What conditions will be expressly imposed if permission is forthcoming?

  • Will changes of use be allowed? If not, does the lessor appreciate how this could limit the rental income?

  • Can alterations be made at the property; if so, on what terms? Will the covenant have any effect on the rent at review?

  • Are the other terms appropriate to a letting of the nature contemplated by your client as well as the subject property itself?

- Are there any potentially onerous provisions that should be brought to the attention of the proposed lessee such as interest on unpaid rent?

TENANTED PROPERTIES

- Always raise extra enquiries before contract when acting for a buyer of tenanted property; **12.142** and ensure those enquiries are employed to ascertain as much detail about the tenant and tenancy as possible.
- Always raise questions about any statutory controls affecting the tenant or the terms of the tenancy.
- Ask specifically about security of tenure provisions that may affect the lessee, and any specific statutory controls on the passing rental.
- Make sure the contract terms specifically cover the nature of the letting, be it commercial or residential.

13

BUSINESS TENANCIES AND THE LANDLORD AND TENANT ACT 1954, PART II

INTRODUCTION

13.01   Part II of the Landlord and Tenant Act 1954 (referred to in this chapter as 'the Act') regulates the ways in which business tenancies may be terminated and gives statutory protection to business tenants. A business tenant's statutory protection essentially has two parts:

(a) The right for the tenancy to continue automatically at the end of the contractual term. Accordingly, a fixed-term lease does not end on the expiry date and a periodic tenancy is not terminated by the landlord's usual notice to quit. Section 24 of the Act continues the tenancy on the same terms (except for termination provisions) and at the same rent until it is terminated in one of the ways prescribed by the Act.

(b) The right to apply to the court for a statutory renewal of the tenancy, which can be opposed by the landlord only on grounds specified in the Act. In addition, the tenant has a right to compensation for disturbance if the application for renewal of the lease is unsuccessful.

13.02   There are strict time limits for service of the various notices under the Act and for the tenant's application to the court for a new tenancy. Failure to adhere to these time limits represents one of the most common examples of solicitors' negligence. Attention to detail and a fail-safe diary or computer entry system are therefore essential when dealing with business tenancy renewals.

The Act was reformed by the Regulatory Reform (Business Tenancies) (England and Wales)   **13.03**
Order 2003 (SI 2003/3096), which came into force on 1 June 2004. The reforms do not
alter the substance of the Act and are largely procedural in nature. They are incorporated
into the text but a summary of them can be found at the end of this chapter.

AGREEMENTS TO WHICH THE 1954 ACT APPLIES

The Act applies to 'any tenancy where the property comprised in the tenancy is or   **13.04**
includes premises which are occupied by the tenant and are so occupied for the purposes
of a business carried on by him or for those and other purposes' (s 23(1)). Thus to qualify
for protection under the Act a tenant must be occupying premises for the purposes of a
business. The wording of s 23(1) as interpreted by the courts is now considered.

REQUIREMENT FOR 'TENANCY'

Section 23(1) uses the word 'tenancy', which is defined in s 69(1) of the 1954 Act as being a: **13.05**

> tenancy created either immediately or derivatively out of the freehold, whether by a lease
> or underlease, by an agreement for a lease or underlease or by a tenancy agreement or in
> pursuance of any enactment (including this Act), but does not include a mortgage term or
> any interest arising in favour of a mortgagor by his attorning tenant to his mortgagee . . .

Dangers of granting a licence

It follows that a licence cannot be protected by the Act because it is not a tenancy. However,   **13.06**
there are dangers for landlords who seek to avoid the Act by purporting to grant a licence
to occupiers of their premises. The courts have construed many so-called licences to be mere
fabrications and have held them instead to be tenancies. If the agreement has the hallmarks
of a tenancy (exclusive possession, for a term, and at a rent), then the courts will generally
construe it as such, notwithstanding that the parties may call it a licence (see *Bruton v
London & Quadrant Housing Trust Ltd* [1999] 3 WLR 150, HL). A tenancy includes an
equitable interest under an agreement for a lease as well as a sub-lease, even if the sub-lease
has not been authorized by the superior landlord (see *D'Silva v Lister House Developments
Ltd* [1971] Ch 17).

Exclusive possession

It is well known that the key factor in determining whether an arrangement is a tenancy   **13.07**
or licence is whether the occupier has been granted exclusive possession of the property
(*Street v Mountford* [1985] 2 All ER 289, HL). Exclusive possession by the occupier will
connote a tenancy, and this has been confirmed in several cases involving commercial
property. In *Esso Petroleum Ltd v Fumegrange Ltd* [1994] 2 EGLR 90, the Court of
Appeal held that exclusive possession of a petrol station had not been granted because
the licensor had reserved extensive rights over the property. These included control over
the way in which the occupier's business was to be operated as well as the physical
layout of the site. It should be noted that a reservation of a simple right of entry or
access onto the occupier's premises will be insufficient to negate exclusive possession
(see *Addiscombe Garden Estates Ltd v Crabbe* [1957] 3 All ER 563, CA). In *National
Car Parks Ltd v Trinity Development Company (Banbury) Ltd* [2000] EGCS 128, the
court held that an agreement to occupy premises as a car park did not constitute a
tenancy and was a mere licence. Here the fact that the agreement allowed the licensor

potentially to use the premises itself to park cars, and also laid down regulations as to the conduct of the licensee's business was sufficient to deny exclusive possession.

TENANCIES EXCLUDED FROM STATUTORY PROTECTION

13.08 Certain tenancies are excluded from the protection of the Act. The principal exclusions relevant to conveyancing practice are discussed in 13.09–13.25.

Fixed-term tenancies not exceeding six months (s 43(3))

13.09 Although generally excluded, it should be noted that these short, fixed-term tenancies will be protected under the Act in two situations:

(a) if they contain provisions for renewing the term or extending it beyond six months (s 43(3)(a)); or

(b) if the tenant (including any predecessor in the same business) has already been in occupation for a period exceeding 12 months (s 43(3)(b)). For the tenant to have protection, such occupation must be under either a fixed-term or a periodic tenancy, i.e. not as licensee, tenant at will, or trespasser. Note that any predecessor in the tenant's business need not necessarily have been a tenant and may have been occupying as a mere licensee, or even as freeholder (see *Cricket Ltd v Shaftesbury plc* [1999] 3 All ER 283).

13.10 The exception under s 43(3)(b) allows a tenant starting up in business to be granted up to three successive tenancies of less than six months each. This is because by the time the third tenancy is granted, the tenant will not have been in occupation for 12 months.

Contracted-out tenancies

13.11 Under s 38A of the Act, the prospective landlord and tenant may agree to exclude from the tenancy the security-of-tenure provisions of the Act (ss 24–28). The tenancy must be for a 'term of years certain' and the definition of the 'term' of the tenancy must not include any continuation, extension, or holding over period (see *Newham v Thomas Van-Staden* [2008] EWCA Civ 1414). The agreement must satisfy three statutory requirements, failing which the agreement will be void, with the consequence that the tenancy will be protected under the Act. For landlords, it is therefore vital that these requirements are observed. They are as set out in the following paragraphs.

Landlord's health warning

13.12 Before the tenant enters into the tenancy (or, if earlier, before the tenant is contractually bound to do so) the landlord must serve on the tenant a 'health warning' notice in the form, or substantially the form, set out below. The notice should be served 14 days before the tenant commits itself to the lease.

> **IMPORTANT NOTICE**
>
> **You are being offered a lease without security of tenure. Do not commit yourself to the lease unless you have read this message carefully and have discussed it with a professional adviser.**
>
> Business tenants normally have security of tenure—the right to stay in their business premises when the lease ends.
>
> **If you commit yourself to the lease you will be giving up these important legal rights.**
>
> - You will have no right to stay in the premises when the lease ends.
> - Unless the landlord chooses to offer you another lease, you will need to leave the premises.

- You will be unable to claim compensation for the loss of your business premises unless the lease specifically gives you this right.
- If the landlord offers you another lease, you will have no right to ask the court to fix the rent.

It is, therefore, important to get professional advice—from a qualified surveyor, lawyer, or accountant—before agreeing to give up these rights.   **13.13**

If you receive this notice at least 14 days before committing yourself to the lease, you will need to sign a simple declaration that you have received this notice and have accepted its consequences, before signing the lease.   **13.14**

> But if you do not receive at least 14 days' notice, you will need to sign a 'statutory' declaration. To do so, you will need to visit an independent solicitor (or someone else empowered to administer oaths).

Unless there is a special reason for committing yourself to the lease sooner, you may want to ask the landlord to let you have at least 14 days to consider whether you wish to give up your statutory rights. If you then decided to go ahead with the agreement to exclude the protection of the Landlord and Tenant Act 1954, you would only need to make a simple declaration, and so you would not need to make a separate visit to an independent solicitor.   **13.15**

Tenant's declaration

After receiving the health warning notice the tenant (or someone authorized by the tenant, e.g. his solicitor) must take the following action before entering into the tenancy (or, if earlier, becoming contractually bound to do so). The tenant (or authorized person) must sign a declaration that the tenant has received the health warning and accepts the consequences of contracting out of the Act. Provided the tenant receives the health warning at least 14 days before committing himself to the lease, the tenant (or authorized person) merely signs a simple declaration (not requiring a witness), stating that the tenant has received the notice and accepts the consequences of contracting out of the Act.   **13.16**

However, the landlord is permitted to serve the health warning notice less than 14 days before the tenant enters into the tenancy (or, if earlier, becomes contractually bound to do so). In this case, the tenant must sign a more formal statutory declaration in front of an independent solicitor (or someone else empowered to administer oaths). Thus the parties can effectively waive the 14-day period. A statutory declaration is sufficient for both long- and short-notice contracting out procedures (see *Patel v Chiltern Railway Co. Ltd* [2008] EWCA Civ 178. It is important to appreciate that however late the health warning is served, it must always be served *before* the tenant actually enters into the tenancy (or becomes contractually bound to do so). Failure to do so will make the agreement to contract out of the Act void.   **13.17**

Reference in the lease

The third requirement is that the lease must contain references to (a) the health warning; (b) the tenant's declaration or statutory declaration; and (c) the agreement to contract out. Typically, this will all be contained in a separate clause in the lease. Alternatively, a separate endorsement to this effect can be attached to the lease.   **13.18**

Tenancies at will

Tenancies at will may occur where a person occupies property with the permission of the owner but does not pay rent (see *Wheeler v Mercer* [1957] AC 416). The owner/landlord can withdraw permission to occupy at any time ('at will'), but the tenant must also have the right to terminate the tenancy at any time. Tenancies at will cannot be granted for a   **13.19** fixed term. They can be made expressly but often arise by implication. Examples of implied tenancies at will include where the tenant takes possession before the lease is formally granted (see *Javad v Aqil* [1991] 1 WLR 1007, CA), or where the tenant holds over at the end of a fixed-term tenancy (see *Cardiothoracic Institute v Shrewdcrest Ltd* [1986] 1 WLR 368). In *Hagee (London) Ltd v AB Erikson and Larson* [1975] 3 All ER 234, the Court of Appeal confirmed that an express tenancy at will did not fall within the Act. A tenancy at will is not a legal estate, as it does not fall within the definition of a term of years absolute in the Law of Property Act 1925. Landlords should beware that if they accept rent a tenancy at will may be converted into an implied tenancy, which would *prima facie* confer statutory protection on the tenant.

Service tenancies

13.20   These are tenancies granted to persons in connection with their office or employment (e.g. school caretaker) and end when the office or employment is terminated. A service tenancy granted after 1 October 1954 (the commencement date of the Act) must be in writing and express the purpose for which it was granted. Provided this occurs, a service tenancy is not protected under the Act (s 43(2)).

Agricultural holdings

13.21   Agricultural holdings are not protected by the Act (s 43(1)(a)). They are protected under a different statute, the Agricultural Holdings Act 1986. For the purposes of the 1954 Act 'agricultural holding' has the same meaning as in s 1(1) of the 1986 Act. If the tenancy appears to qualify as both an agricultural holding and a business tenancy, it will be protected as an agricultural holding only, not as a business tenancy under the 1954 Act (*Short v Greeves* [1988] 1 EGLR 1, CA). Neither the 1954 Act nor the 1986 Act applies to new lettings to new tenants since 1 September 1995. These are known as 'farm business tenancies' and are governed by the Agricultural Tenancies Act 1995.

Mining leases

13.22   Section 43(1)(b) provides that the Act does not apply where land is let under a mining lease. Under s 46, 'mining lease' has the same meaning as in the Landlord and Tenant Act 1927, s 25(1), which provides:

> The expression 'mining lease' means a lease for any mining purpose or purposes connected therewith, and 'mining purposes' include the sinking and searching for, winning, working, getting, making merchantable, smelting or otherwise converting or working for the purposes of any manufacture, carrying away, and disposing of mines and minerals, in or under land, and the erection of buildings, and the execution of engineering and other works suitable for those purposes . . .

13.23   The Court of Appeal in *O'Callaghan v Elliott* [1965] 3 All ER 111 held that the Act did not apply to a lease granted for the extraction of sand and gravel.

Tenancies of premises licensed to sell alcohol, not including hotels, etc.

13.24   The protection of the 1954 Act does not extend to tenancies of premises licensed to sell alcohol, not including hotels, restaurants, and other premises where the sale of alcohol is not the main use of the premises, which were granted before 11 July 1989. Tenancies of premises licensed to sell alcohol granted on or after 11 July 1989 are protected by the 1954 Act (Landlord and Tenant (Licensed Premises) Act 1990, s 1(1)). Off-licences have consistently enjoyed full statutory protection.

Other exclusions

The Act will also not apply in the following situations: **13.25**

(a) **National security and public interest**   Sections 57 and 58 of the Act permit the determination of business tenancies on the grounds of national security and public interest. A public interest certificate may be issued where the premises are required for the purposes of a government body such as a local authority, or development corporation, or even the National Trust (see *R v Secretary of State for the Environment, ex parte Powis* [1981] 1 All ER 788). A tenant who is precluded from obtaining a new tenancy will in certain circumstances be entitled to compensation (s 59). Sections 60, 60A, and 60B contain similar provisions applying to premises where the landlord is the Minister of Technology, the Urban Regeneration Agency, the Welsh Development Agency, or the Development Board for Rural Wales.

(b) **Where the parties to a lease agree that the tenant will be granted a new tenancy in the future (s 28)**   The agreement must specify the date of the future tenancy, and the current tenancy will end on that date. It is for the period between the date of the agreement and the date of the new tenancy that the tenant will not be protected by the Act. The agreement must comply with s 2 of the Law of Property (Miscellaneous Provisions) Act 1989 and be binding and enforceable between the parties (see *RJ Stratton Ltd v Wallis Tomlin & Co. Ltd* [1986] 1 EGLR 104, CA). To protect the agreement against any potential assignee of the reversion the tenant should register it as an estate contract. This will be a class C(iv) land charge in unregistered land, or a notice in registered land.

(c) **Where the court revokes an order for a new tenancy following an application by the tenant under s 36(2) of the Act** (see 13.190). This section allows the tenant to apply for a revocation within 14 days of the order for a new lease. It will be used by a tenant who is not satisfied with the new terms granted by the court. Following the revocation, the Act will not apply to the current tenancy, which will continue under s 36(2) for such period as the court may specify.

REQUIREMENT FOR 'OCCUPATION'

In most cases it will be fairly clear whether the tenant is in occupation of the premises.   **13.26** The courts have held that the important factors to be taken into account are the tenant's physical occupation or presence, and the measure of control the tenant exercises over those who use the premises (see *Wandsworth LBC v Singh* (1991) 62 P & CR 219, CA, in particular the judgment of Ralph Gibson LJ at 227–30). In *Hancock and Willis v GMS Syndicate Ltd* [1983] 1 EGLR 70, CA, Eveleigh LJ said (at 72):

> The words with which we are concerned import, in my judgment, an element of control and use and they involve the notion of physical occupation. That does not mean physical occupation every minute of the day provided the right to occupy continues. But it is necessary for the judge trying the case to assess the whole situation where the element of control and use may exist in variable degrees. At the end of the day it is a question of fact for the tribunal to decide, treating the words as ordinary words in the way in which I have referred to them.

Tenant vacating premises

If the tenant is forced to leave the premises because of something over which it has no con-   **13.27** trol, for example fire damage or to allow lessor's repairs, the tenant remains in occupation for the purposes of the Act (see *Morrison Holdings Ltd v Manders Property (Wolverhampton)*

Ltd [1976] 2 All ER 205). However, the tenant must continue to exert and claim a right to occupy the premises (see *Demetriou v Poolaction* [1991] 1 EGLR 100, CA and *Fairline Properties Ltd v Hassan* [1998] EGCS 169). If the tenant leaves the premises voluntarily it will be a question of fact as to whether the 'thread of business continuity' has been broken. If the thread is broken the tenant will have ceased to occupy for the purposes of the Act (see *Aspinall Finance Ltd v Viscount Chelsea* [1989] 1 EGLR 103). The longer the period of absence, the more likely it is that the thread will have been broken. For shorter periods, Simon Brown LJ in *Bacchiocchi v Academic Agency Ltd* [1998] 2 All ER 241 said (at 249):

> . . . whenever business premises are empty for only a short period, whether mid-term or before or after trading at either end of the lease, I would be disinclined to find that the business occupancy has ceased (or not started) for that period provided always that during it there exists no rival for the role of business occupant and that the premises are not being used for some other, non-business purposes. That to my mind is how Part II of the 1954 Act should operate in logic and in justice.

13.28 If the tenant is a seasonal occupier, for example it is a summer holiday business where the tenant is absent during the winter months, the tenant normally will be regarded as in occupation for the whole year (see *Artemiou v Procopiou* [1965] 3 All ER 539, CA).

Occupation by tenant's manager

13.29 Occupation by a manager or agent of the tenant may be sufficient to constitute occupation by the tenant, provided the management or agency arrangement is genuine (see *Pegler v Craven* [1952] 1 All ER 685 and *Cafeteria (Keighley) Ltd v Harrison* (1956) 168 EG 668, CA). A limited company's business that is managed by another company may also be in occupation (see *Ross Auto Wash Ltd v Herbert* (1978) 250 EG 971); and where another company within the same group occupies the premises, the occupation is treated as occupation by the tenant (s 42). Under the 2004 reforms the protection of the Act is extended to tenancies where the tenant and the business are not the same, as long as one controls the other. For example a company which is in occupation and is controlled by the tenant will be protected by the Act (s 23(1A)).

Sub-letting

13.30 Generally, if the tenant sub-lets or parts with possession of the premises it can no longer be said to be in occupation of the part (or whole) that has been sub-let. It would therefore not qualify for statutory protection in respect of the part (or whole) of the premises occupied by the sub-tenant. In *Graysim Holdings Ltd v P&O Property Holdings Ltd* [1995] 3 WLR 854, the tenant of a market hall managed it by sub-letting to stallholders who had exclusive possession of their stalls. Unusually, the Court of Appeal held that both the tenant and sub-tenant could be 'in occupation' for the purposes of the Act. However, the House of Lords held that there could be no dual occupation and reversed the decision. Importantly, their Lordships left open the possibility that the tenant may, exceptionally, reserve sufficient rights over the sub-let part to enable it to remain the 'occupier' at law. The Court of Appeal has subsequently applied the reasoning in *Graysim* (see *Bassari Ltd v Camden LBC* [1998] EGCS 27, CA).

REQUIREMENT FOR 'THE PURPOSES OF A BUSINESS'

13.31 To qualify for protection under the Act, the tenant is required to occupy the premises for the purposes of a business. The fact that they are occupied for business purposes does not necessarily mean that the tenant must carry on the business there. What is important is that the premises must be occupied for that purpose (see *Bracey v Read* [1962] 3 All ER 472 and *Methodist Secondary Schools Trust Deed Trustees v O'Leary* [1993] 1 EGLR 105, CA). A business carried on by one member of a group of companies of which the tenant company is a member is treated as a business of the tenant (s 42(2)(a)). Similarly, where a tenancy is held on trust, the carrying on of a business by the beneficiaries under the trust is treated as being the business of the tenant (s 41(1)).

MEANING OF 'BUSINESS'

The definition of 'business' in s 23(2) includes a 'trade, profession or employment and **13.32** includes any activity carried on by a body of persons, whether corporate or unincorporate'. It can be seen that the definition is narrower for an individual ('trade, profession or employment') than it is for a body of persons ('any activity'). Thus a body of persons running a tennis club was held to be a business (see *Addiscombe Garden Estates v Crabbe* [1958] 1 QB 513, CA), as was the administration of a hospital by a board of governors (see *Hills (Patents) Ltd v University College Hospital Board of Governors* [1956] 1 QB 90, CA). Similarly, a local authority's maintenance of a park was classified as a business activity under the Act (see *Wandsworth LBC v Singh* (1991) 62 P & CR 219, CA). However, an individual running a Sunday school has been held not to be within the definition of 'trade, profession or employment'. The provision of residential accommodation by way of a business venture has been classified as a business activity (see *Lee-Verhulst (Investments) Ltd v Harwood Trust* [1973] QB 204).

Mixed use

If the premises are used partly for business and partly for residential purposes (e.g. a **13.33** flat above a shop), the test is whether the business activity is a significant purpose of the occupation, or whether it is merely incidental to the occupation as a residence. It is a question of degree in each case. For example, an office block might have sleeping accommodation for staff on the top floor. Although residential in nature, the sleeping accommodation would only be incidental to the building's principal use as business premises. Conversely, one room in a dwelling house set aside exclusively for business purposes (e.g. a doctor's private consultation room at home) would not alter the fact that the significant purpose of the occupation of the property was residential. This occurred in *Royal Life Savings Society v Page* [1978] 1 WLR 1329. In *Gurton v Parrot* [1991] 1 EGLR 98, a residential tenant's conversion of outbuildings into dog kennels was held to be merely incidental to the property's use as a dwelling house. Similarly, in *Wright v Mortimer* (1996) 28 HLR 719, CA, an art historian's use of his flat for writing was held to be merely incidental to his residential use. On the other hand, a seafood importer who received business visitors and kept files, a telephone, and a typewriter in his flat, and had no other business premises, was held to occupy the flat for business purposes (see *Cheryl Investments Ltd v Saldanha* [1979] 1 All ER 5, CA).

Prohibition against business use

If the lease prohibits business use generally (e.g. 'not to use the premises for business **13.34** purposes'), the tenant cannot obtain protection from the Act simply by carrying on a business in breach of the covenant (s 23(4)). However, the Act may apply if the landlord consented to or acquiesced in the breach (see *Bell v Alfred Franks and Bartlett Co. Ltd* [1980] 1 All ER 356 and *Methodist Secondary Schools Trust Deed Trustees v O'Leary*

[1993] 1 EGLR 105, CA). The tenancy will still come within the Act if the tenant's user is merely in breach of a covenant in the lease. This may include, for example, a covenant:

(a) prohibiting use for a specified business (e.g. 'not to use as a modelling agency'—if in breach of covenant the premises are used as a modelling agency, the Act would still apply); or

(b) prohibiting use for any business except a specified business (e.g. 'not to use except as a modelling agency'—if in breach of covenant the premises are used for a business other than a modelling agency, again the Act would still apply).

METHODS OF TERMINATION UNDER THE 1954 ACT

13.35 A business tenancy protected by the Act can be terminated only in one of the ways prescribed by the Act. Until that occurs the tenancy simply continues on the same terms as the original tenancy (except for the termination provisions). The landlord or the tenant can seek an increased rent by applying to the court for an interim rent under s 24A of the Act (see 13.103).

13.36 The most widely used methods of termination are the landlord's s 25 notice and the tenant's s 26 request. These are considered at 13.47 and 13.69, respectively. The other methods of termination are:

(a) a tenant's notice under s 27(1) or s 27(2) of the Act where the tenancy is for a fixed term (these notices are used where the tenant does not wish the lease to continue or be renewed: see 13.37);

(b) a tenant's notice to quit in a periodic tenancy (provided the tenant has been in occupation for at least one month);

(c) surrender;

(d) forfeiture;

(e) forfeiture of a superior lease;

(f) notice to quit served by a mesne landlord on the superior landlord; and

(g) an agreement between the parties for a future tenancy under s 28 of the Act (see 13.25).

Tenant's notices under s 27

13.37 If the tenant has a fixed-term tenancy and does not wish it to continue, the tenant can terminate the lease by serving on the immediate landlord a statutory notice under s 27 of the 1954 Act. There are two types of notice. A notice under s 27(1) is served before the end of the contractual term, whereas a notice under s 27(2) is served after the end of the contractual term where the tenant is holding over.

Before the end of the contractual term—tenant's notice under s 27(1)

13.38 A tenant who has been in occupation under a business tenancy for at least one month and who does not wish to renew its fixed-term tenancy can serve a notice in writing on its immediate landlord under s 27(1). This notice must be served not later than three months before the end of the fixed term. The tenancy will then come to an end on the expiry of the contractual term. Section 27(1) applies only to 'a term of years certain', i.e. a fixed term. This would exclude periodic tenancies, but would include a fixed term of less than one year (see *Re Land and Premises at Liss, Hants* [1971] 3 All ER 380). It has been held that 'a term of years certain' would not include a term of 12 months and thereafter from year to year determinable on the landlord giving 12 months' notice (see *Nicholls v Kinsey* [1994] 2 WLR 622, CA).

There is no prescribed form, but a typical notice might read as follows: **13.39**

> To [name of landlord]
> of [address of landlord]
>
> From [name of tenant]
> of [address of tenant]
>
> 1. I am the tenant of [address of property] under a lease dated [date of lease] ('the Lease') made between [original parties to lease].
> 2. The Lease expires on [contractual expiry date].
> 3. I hereby give you notice under s 27(1) of the Landlord and Tenant Act 1954 ('the Act') that I do not wish my tenancy to be continued under the provisions of Part II of the Act.
>
> Dated:
>
> Signed:
>
> [signature of tenant, or on behalf of tenant]

A tenant who has served a s 27(1) notice is not permitted to serve a s 26 request (s 26(4)). **13.40** A s 27(1) notice will not affect any sub-tenancy protected by the Act.

Tenant's prior vacation   What is the position if the tenant vacates the premises before the **13.41** contractual expiry date? Is a s 27(1) notice needed? In *Esselte AB v Pearl Assurance plc* [1997] 2 EG 124, it was held that a s 27(1) notice is strictly not necessary if the tenant has ceased to occupy the premises for business purposes on or before the contractual expiry date. This is because the tenancy is no longer one to which the 1954 Act applies (i.e. not in occupation for the purposes of a business) and so cannot be continued under s 24.

The 2004 reforms amended the Act to reflect the decision in *Esselte AB v Pearl Assurance* **13.42** *plc* [1997] 2 EG 124. Section 27(1A) provides, in effect, that a fixed-term tenancy will not continue under the Act if the tenant was not in occupation at the contractual expiry date. However, in cases of doubt as to whether the tenant has fully quit the premises, it is still best practice for the tenant to serve a s 27(1) notice.

After the end of the contractual term—tenant's notice under s 27(2)

A notice under s 27(2) differs slightly from a s 27(1) notice. It is served by a tenant who **13.43** is holding over after the contractual expiry date has passed and who does not wish to renew the tenancy. As with a s 27(1) notice, the tenant must have been in occupation for at least one month. It is served on the immediate landlord, who must be given at least three months' notice expiring on any day. This is a change from the position before 1 June 2004 where the three months' notice had to expire on a quarter day.

There is no prescribed form, but a typical notice might read as follows: **13.44**

> To [name of landlord]
> of [address of landlord]
>
> From [name of tenant]
> of [address of tenant]
>
> 1. I am the tenant of [address of property] under a lease dated [date of lease] ('the Lease') made between [original parties to lease].
> 2. The Lease expired on [contractual expiry date] and my tenancy continues under s 24 of the Landlord and Tenant Act 1954 ('the Act').
> 3. I hereby give you notice under s 27(2) of the Act that my tenancy will come to an end on [date tenancy to end] by virtue of this notice.

A tenant who has served a s 27(2) notice is not permitted to serve a s 26 request (s 26(4)). **13.45** A s 27(2) notice will not affect any sub-tenancy protected by the Act. If the tenant vacates the premises after the end of the contractual term, it cannot rely on the effect of *Esselte AB v Pearl Assurance plc* [1997] 2 EG 124 and the amended s 27(1A) (see 13.42). This is because s 27(2) provides that where a fixed term continues under s 24 the tenancy will not end merely because the tenant ceases to occupy the premises. The tenant must therefore serve a s 27(2) notice to bring the tenancy to an end.

13.46 Under a new s 27(3), provision is made for the appropriate apportionment of rent to be made in the tenant's favour as at the expiry of a s 27(2) notice. The tenant may therefore recover any overpayment of rent.

LANDLORD'S NOTICE UNDER S 25

13.47 If the tenant is protected under the Act and the landlord requires the premises back at the end of the lease, the landlord must serve a s 25 notice on the tenant specifying the grounds on which the landlord is claiming possession. This is known as a 'hostile notice'. The specified grounds for possession are contained in s 30(1) of the Act and are considered at 13.117. Even if the landlord is content for the tenant to remain in possession under a negotiated new lease, the landlord must still serve a s 25 notice to end the existing lease. This is known as a 'non-hostile notice'. The landlord cannot serve a s 25 notice if the tenant has already served a s 26 request or a s 27 notice.

13.48 The s 25 notice is effective only if it is in a prescribed form. Moreover, there are strict time limits for service in that the notice must be given not less than six months, or more than 12 months, before the *termination date specified in the notice*. As will be seen, the termination date cannot be earlier than the contractual expiry date, and may well be later. If the time limits are not observed the notice will be invalid and of no effect. If the landlord client suffers loss as a result of an invalid notice, a negligence claim against the solicitors is likely to ensue.

Prescribed form and content of s 25 notice

13.49 The current prescribed form for a s 25 notice is set out on the Online Resource Centre accompanying this book. A form 'substantially to the like effect' can be used, but this is not to be recommended. To ensure that the most current form is used, the safest practice is to use a printed form from law stationers or a computer software form. If firms use their own word-processed forms there is always a danger that errors or omissions could occur, leading to possible negligence claims. Do not use forms in use before 1 June 2004.

13.50 The s 25 notice must:

(a) specify the date at which the tenancy is to end (s 25(1)). This termination date must not be earlier than the date on which the tenancy could have been terminated at common law. Thus for a normal fixed term without a break clause, the specified termination date cannot be earlier than the last day of the contractual term. And for a fixed-term lease with a break clause (as well as a periodic tenancy), the specified termination date cannot be earlier than the date on which the landlord could have ended the tenancy by common law notice;

(b) state whether the landlord would oppose the tenant's application to the court for a new tenancy, and if so on which statutory grounds (s 25(6) and (7)). Thus the landlord must decide whether the notice is 'hostile' or 'non-hostile'. The statutory grounds of opposition are considered at 13.117. The notice cannot be amended once it has been served, so the landlord should specify all the grounds on which it wishes to rely (see *Hutchinson v Lamberth* [1984] 1 EGLR 75, CA);

(c) if the s 25 notice states that the landlord would not oppose the tenant's application for a new tenancy, it must set out the landlord's proposals as to (i) the property to be comprised in the new tenancy (either the whole or part of the property comprised in the current tenancy); (ii) the new rent; and (iii) the other terms of the new tenancy (s 25(8)). This is a new provision introduced by the 2004 reforms;

(d) be given and signed by, or on behalf of, the landlord. If there is more than one landlord, all their names must be given (see *Pearson v Alyo* [1990] 1 EGLR 114). If there are joint tenants, the notice must be served on all of them unless the joint tenancy is held by a partnership. In this case, s 41A of the Act permits the landlord to serve only those tenants who are partners involved in running the business;

(e) relate to the whole of the demised premises, not part only (see *Southport Old Links Ltd v Naylor* [1985] 1 EGLR 129). This applies even where the tenant has sub-let part of the premises. Where, after the grant of the tenancy, the reversion becomes vested in different landlords, the landlords should either serve a notice jointly, or serve separate notices which can be read together (see *M & P Enterprises (London) Ltd v Norfolk Square Hotels Ltd* [1994] 1 EGLR 129);

(f) be served on any sub-tenant where the tenant has sub-let the *whole* of the premises. This is provided the sub-tenancy satisfies s 23 (see also 13.92 regarding s 40).

Omission of prescribed information   If the prescribed information is omitted from the s 25 notice, is it still valid? The test, as laid down by Barry J in *Barclays Bank Ltd v Ascott* [1961] 1 WLR 717, is whether the notice gives 'the proper information to the tenant which will enable the tenant to deal in a proper way with the situation, whatever it may be, referred to in the statement of the notice'. The Court of Appeal approved this test in the later cases of *Tegerdine v Brooks* (1977) 36 P & CR 261, *Morrow v Nadeem* [1986] 1 WLR 1381, and *Bridgers v Stanford* [1991] 2 EGLR 265. Ultimately it will be a question of whether a reasonable recipient would have been misled by the notice (see *Sabella Ltd v Montgomery* [1998] 1 EGLR 65, CA, where a notice omitting the 'Act Quick' warning and other notes was held to be invalid). Accordingly, if the form is not materially different from the prescribed form, then it will generally be considered valid (see *Sun Alliance and London Assurance Co. Ltd v Hayman* [1975] 1 WLR 177).   **13.51**

Error or defect in s 25 notice   If the notice contains an error or is incorrectly completed, is it still valid? The test was laid down by the House of Lords in *Mannai Investment Co. Ltd v Eagle Star Life Assurance Ltd* [1997] 3 All ER 352. Essentially, the court has to decide, first, whether the error in the notice is obvious or evident and, second, whether, despite the error, the notice read in its context is sufficiently clear to leave a reasonable recipient in no reasonable doubt as to the terms of the notice. Although the notice in this case was a contractual one, the Court of Appeal in *Garston v Scottish Widows' Fund and Life Assurance Society* [1998] 3 All ER 596 approved the *Mannai* test in the context of a statutory notice under the 1954 Act. The test before *Mannai* was very similar, namely whether 'the notice is quite clear to a reasonable tenant receiving it . . . . Is it plain enough that he cannot be misled by it?' (*per* Goulding J in *Carradine Properties Ltd v Aslam* [1976] 1 WLR 442). (The pre-*Mannai* test was subsequently approved by the Court of Appeal in *Germax Securities Ltd v Spiegal* (1978) 37 P & CR 204 and *Bridgers v Stanford* [1991] 2 EGLR 265.) Although each case will turn on its own facts, it may be useful to consider examples of where defects have and have not invalidated a notice.   **13.52**

Examples of defects which have invalidated a s 25 notice: **13.53**

• failure to name all joint landlords in the notice (see *Smith v Draper* [1990] 2 EGLR 69, CA; *Pearson v Alyo* [1990] 1 EGLR 261);

• naming the wrong person as landlord (see *Morrow v Nadeem* [1986] 1 WLR 1381, CA);

- an assignor serving a notice after the reversion had been assigned (see *Yamaha-Kemble Music (UK) Ltd v ARC Properties* [1990] 1 EGLR 261).

13.54   Examples of defects which have *not* invalidated a s 25 notice:

- the notice was not signed but the covering letter made it apparent that the notice was served on behalf of the landlord (see *Stidolph v American School in London Educational Trust* (1969) 20 P & CR 802, CA);
- the notice stated the wrong termination date but the covering letter made it apparent what date was intended (see *Germax Securities Ltd v Spiegal* (1978) 37 P & CR 204);
- failure to date the notice (see *Falcon Pipes Ltd v Stanhope Gate Property Co. Ltd* (1967) 204 EG 1243);
- failure to refer to a tiny part of the premises (see *Safeway Food Stores Ltd v Morris* [1980] 1 EGLR 59).

13.55   If the landlord discovers that a s 25 notice it has served is defective in some way (e.g. it contains an error or has been incorrectly served), best practice is to serve a fresh notice without prejudice to the validity of the original notice. Then if the original notice is subsequently held to be invalid, the second notice will become effective (see *Smith v Draper* [1990] 2 EGLR 69, CA; see also *Barclays Bank v Bee* [2001] EWCA Civ 1126, concerning a third notice held to be valid).

Time limits for service of s 25 notice

13.56   The notice must be given not more than 12 months or less than six months, before the date of termination specified in the notice (s 25(2)). Moreover, this date of termination cannot be earlier than the date on which the tenancy can be terminated at common law. There are thus different considerations for a normal fixed term, a fixed term with a break clause, and a periodic tenancy. These are considered in the following paragraphs. In computing time limits under the Act the corresponding date rule is used, and 'month' means calendar month (Interpretation Act 1975, ss 5 and 22(1) and Schedule 4, para 4(1)). This means that the relevant period will end on the corresponding date in the appropriate subsequent month. So, for example, two months starting on 2 May will end on 2 July; but two months starting on 31 July will end on 30 September, and two months starting on 31 December will end on 28 (or 29) February (see Lord Diplock's judgment in *Dodds v Walker* [1981] 1 WLR 1027, HL, at 1029). These time limits are strictly enforced by the courts and it is therefore vitally important for practitioners to abide by them.

13.57   **Normal fixed-term tenancies without a break clause**   In the usual case of a fixed-term lease, the earliest time a landlord can serve the notice is one year before the end of the contractual term. For example, if the lease is due to end on 30 September 2019, the landlord cannot serve the notice earlier than 30 September 2018 (and for the avoidance of doubt it is probably safer to wait until the next day, 1 October 2018).

13.58   If the landlord delays serving notice until less than six months remain of the fixed term, it must still give the tenant at least six months' notice. In this situation the landlord would have to specify a termination date in the notice later than the contractual expiry date. In the example at 13.57, the lease is due to expire on 30 September 2019. If the landlord delays giving notice until after 30 March 2019, the termination date he specifies in the notice will inevitably need to be later than the contractual expiry date (30 September 2019). Even if the landlord delays serving notice until after the contractual expiry date has passed (i.e. when the lease is continuing under s 24), the tenant must still be given a minimum of six months' notice.

Fixed-term tenancies with a break clause   Landlords' advisers must take great care when   **13.59**
exercising a break option to end a lease before the contractual expiry date. How many
notices must be served? One under the contract, and one under the Act, or just one covering both contract and Act? The answer is that a single notice will suffice provided it fulfils
both the statutory requirements and the requirements of the break clause (see *Scholl Manufacturing Co. Ltd v Clifton (Slim-Line) Ltd* [1967] Ch 41). If the notice fails to fulfil the
requirements of s 25, the tenancy will not end but will continue under s 24. If the notice
fails to fulfil the requirements of the contractual break clause, the lease will not 'break' and
the opportunity for the landlord to break at this stage will have been lost. To be sure, it is
recommended that landlords should serve both notices.

Periodic tenancies   The notice required to end a periodic tenancy at common law is at   **13.60**
least one full period of the lease expiring on the last day of a completed period of the tenancy (i.e. on a rent day). The landlord serving a s 25 notice must ensure that the date of
termination specified in the notice is not earlier than the date at which the tenancy could
have been terminated by notice to quit (see *Commercial Properties Ltd v Wood* [1968]
1 QB 15, CA). However, the s 25 notice must be given not more than 12 months, or less
than six months, before the date of termination specified in the notice (s 25(2)).

The following examples show how this works with both a monthly and a yearly tenancy: **13.61**

- *Monthly tenancy*: assume that a tenant has a monthly periodic tenancy running from the
twentieth of each month. To end the tenancy at common law the landlord would need to
serve notice to quit on, say, 19 April to expire on 20 May. But to comply with the requirements of the Act the landlord would need to give at least six months' notice. The notice
served on 19 April could not therefore specify a termination date earlier than 20 October.
- *Yearly tenancy*: if the periodic tenancy were yearly from, say, 20 May, the minimum notice
period at common law would be at least *six* months ending on the last day of a completed
period, i.e. 19 May. Thus if the landlord were to serve notice, say, on 10 August, he would
have to specify a termination date between 19 May and 10 August of the following year.

If the periodic tenancy requires more than six months' notice (e.g. contractually), s 25(3)(b)   **13.62**
of the Act provides that the maximum period in the s 25 notice shall be six months longer
than the length of notice required under the tenancy agreement. This circumvents the difficulty of a contractual notice period of more than 12 months. Without the assistance of
s 25(3)(b) a landlord could never comply with the general statutory rule that notice must
be given not more than 12 months before the termination date specified in the notice.

The tenant's counter-notice

The requirement for the tenant to serve a counter-notice is abolished in relation to s 25   **13.63**
notices given on or after 1 June 2004.

Tenant's and landlord's applications to the court for a new tenancy

Before 1 June 2004 only the tenant could apply to the court for an order for the grant of   **13.64**
a new tenancy. As from 1 June 2004 three important statutory changes were made. First,
both the tenant and the landlord can now apply to the court for a new tenancy; second, the
time limit for making the court application is extended; and third, the landlord and tenant
may agree to extend that time limit. These procedures are now considered.

Section 24(1) of the Act, as amended, enables either the tenant or the landlord to apply to the   **13.65**
court for an order for the grant of a new tenancy. The application can be made only after the
service of a landlord's s 25 notice or a tenant's s 26 request (the latter is considered at 13.69)
and must be made within the time limits referred to at 13.66. Neither party may make an

application if the other has already made an application under s 24(1) and the application has been served. Nor can either party make an application under s 24(1) if the landlord has already made an application under the new s 29(2) for an order for the termination of the current tenancy and the application has been served (see 13.77 regarding such applications).

13.66   **Time limits**   Section 29A provides that an application to the court by either party under s 24(1) must be made on or before the date specified in the landlord's s 25 notice or immediately before the date specified in the tenant's s 26 request. These are the latest dates by which the application can be made (unless there is an agreement to extend, see 13.68). The deadline is strictly enforced and so, for example, if the tenant fails to apply within the required time the tenancy will come to an end on the date specified in the s 25 notice or immediately before the date specified in the s 26 request, as the case may be. As such the tenant's right to apply for a new tenancy will be lost and the tenant's solicitor is likely to be sued in negligence. A fail-safe diary system is therefore essential. Even if the landlord has indicated that he is willing to grant a new tenancy and terms are nearly agreed, the tenant must still apply to the court as a 'fall-back'. Without the back-up of the court application, the landlord could simply change his mind and there would be nothing the tenant could do about it (save possibly a claim in estoppel (see *Bristol Cars Ltd v RKH Hotels Ltd* (1979) 38 P & CR 411) or that the landlord has waived its rights (see *Kammins Ballrooms Co. Ltd v Zenith Investments (Torquay) Ltd* [1971] AC 850)).

13.67   Where the tenant has made a s 26 request, the landlord or the tenant may not apply to the court until the landlord has served the required counter-notice, or the two-month period for service of the counter-notice has expired, whichever occurs first (s 29A(3)). Without this provision, a court application might be made at a time when it was not known whether the landlord opposed renewal and, if so, on what grounds. Once the landlord's counter-notice has been served, either party may apply to the court without waiting for the two months to elapse. The position in respect of a s 25 notice is much simpler. If the landlord has served a s 25 notice, there is no two-month waiting period and either party may apply to the court immediately.

13.68   **Agreement to extend time limit**   Section 29B allows the parties to agree to extend the latest time for applying to the court, provided they do so before the current time limit expires. The agreement must be made in writing. The parties may agree further postponements from time to time provided the agreement is made before the end of the period of postponement specified in the current agreement (s 29B(2)). The effect of such an agreement is that the s 25 notice or s 26 request is treated as terminating the tenancy at the end of the period specified in the agreement (s 29B(4)). This provision, introduced in the 2004 reforms, has assisted in reducing the number of court applications.

Tenant's request under s 26

13.69   This method of termination is not available to periodic tenants and those with fixed terms of one year or less. However, such tenants still have security of tenure and can apply for a new tenancy if the landlord has served them with a s 25 notice. Accordingly, to be able to serve a s 26 request the tenant must have been granted a term of years certain exceeding one year (whether or not continued by s 24), or a term of years certain and thereafter from year to year (s 26(1)).

13.70   A s 26 request must be served on the tenant's 'competent' landlord, or its agent, otherwise it will be invalid (see *Railtrack plc v Gojra* [1998] 1 EGLR 63, CA). The tenant's competent landlord may not necessarily be the same as the tenant's immediate landlord (see 13.84–13.91 for a discussion of competent landlord). A s 26 request cannot be served if the landlord has already served a s 25 notice, or the tenant has already served a s 27 notice (see 13.37). Once the tenant has served a valid s 26 request it cannot later withdraw it and serve another amended one (see *Polyviou v Seeley* [1980] 1 WLR 55).

Situations in which a tenant would be advised to serve a s 26 request

If a tenant has security of tenure, then the tenancy will continue under s 24 until it is termin-   **13.71** ated by one of the ways under the Act. This gives rise to the question, why, if the tenant can continue in occupation under s 24, paying the existing rent, should it want to end the lease by serving a s 26 request? Why not wait until the landlord serves a s 25 notice, and in the meantime carry on paying rent that is probably less than the market rent under any new lease? The following are situations in which a tenant would be advised to serve a s 26 request:

(a) **Tenant's tactical pre-emptive strike**   In a normal rising market, the tenant will wish to pay the current rent as long as possible because it will be lower than the market rent. In these circumstances, a prudent landlord would end the lease as early as possible by serving a s 25 notice one year before the expiry date (the termination date in the notice would be the expiry date of the contractual term, i.e. 12 months hence). However, if the landlord is dilatory and forgets to serve a s 25 notice, the tenant could serve a s 26 request, say, six months before the expiry date, in which the tenant specifies a date which is 12 months ahead as the commencement date of the new tenancy. In this way the tenant would get six months longer paying the old rent. As an example, assume a lease has a contractual expiry date of 31 December. If by the middle of the previous June the landlord has not served a s 25 notice, the tenant could serve a s 26 request specifying a commencement date which is 12 months ahead, i.e. in June of the following year. That would be six months after the earliest date the landlord could have ended the lease.

    Interim rent   As a consequence of the 2004 reforms, tenants should be aware that interim rent is now payable from the earliest date that *could have been* specified for commencement of the new tenancy in the s 26 request. Thus a tenant who serves a s 26 request but states a commencement date for the new tenancy 12 months after service when the contractual termination date is only six months away (and so he could have served six months' notice) will find that the interim rent will be payable from the earliest date that he could have specified. In a rising market, a well-advised landlord could therefore reduce the effectiveness of the tenant's pre-emptive strike by applying for an interim rent payable from this earlier date (see 13.103).

(b) **Proposed improvements**   If the tenant intends to spend money improving the premises, they may prefer the certainty of a new fixed-term lease before doing so.

(c) **Proposed sale**   If the tenant intends to assign the lease, a prospective buyer will probably want the certainty of a new fixed-term lease being in place.

(d) **Fall in market rent**   If the market rent has fallen (e.g. during a recession) and is less than the existing rent under the lease, the tenant will want a new lease with a lower market rent in place as soon as possible. The landlord, of course, will be happy for the old (higher) rent to continue.

Prescribed form and content of s 26 request

The current prescribed form for a s 26 request is set out on the Online Resource Centre   **13.72** accompanying this book. A form 'substantially to the like effect' can be used, but this is not to be recommended. For cases on defects in notices and whether they invalidate them, see 13.52, in particular *Mannai Investment Co. Ltd v Eagle Star Life Assurance Ltd* [1997] 3 All ER 352. To ensure that the most current form is used, the safest practice is to use a printed form from law stationers or a computer software form. If firms use their own word-processed forms there is always a danger that errors could occur, leading to possible negligence claims. Forms available before 1 June 2004 should not be used.

13.73   The s 26 request must:

(a) specify a date for the commencement of the new tenancy (the existing tenancy will end immediately before this date). This commencement date must not be more than 12 months or less than six months after the making of the request. Nor must it be until after the date on which the tenancy could have been terminated at common law. Thus for a normal fixed term without a break clause, the specified commencement date cannot be until after the lease expiry date. And for a fixed-term lease with a break clause, the specified commencement date cannot be until after the date upon which the tenant could have ended the tenancy by common law notice. In *Garston v Scottish Widows Fund and Life Assurance Society* [1998] 3 All ER 596, CA, the tenant effectively tried to engineer a downwards rent review by serving a break notice as permitted by the lease, and at the same time serving a s 26 request. The court disallowed this practice as being contrary to the spirit and purpose of the Act;

(b) set out the tenant's proposals for the new lease, namely:

   (i)   the property to be comprised in the new tenancy. This can be either the whole or part of the property in the current tenancy (compare this with a s 25 notice in which the whole of the property must be specified);

   (ii) the new rent (valuation advice should be taken before doing so);

   (iii) the other terms of the new tenancy.

These proposals must be genuine and the tenant must have a real intention of taking up the new tenancy. Thus a request served merely as a precautionary measure will be invalid (see *Sun Life Assurance plc v Racal Tracs Ltd* [2000] 1 EGLR 138);

(c) be given and signed by, or on behalf of, the tenant. If there is more than one tenant, all their names must be given (see *Jacobs v Chaudhuri* [1968] 1 QB 470, CA) unless the joint tenancy is held by a partnership. In this case, s 41A of the Act allows only those tenants who are partners carrying on the business to be named in the request. If there are joint landlords the notice must be served on all of them.

Time limits for service of s 26 request

13.74   As mentioned at 13.73, the date specified in the s 26 request as the date for the commencement of the new tenancy must not be more than 12 months or less than six months after the request is served on the landlord. Accordingly, the earliest time a tenant can serve a request is one year before the date the tenant wants the new tenancy to begin. In the case of a 'tenant's pre-emptive strike' (see 13.71) the tenant will often specify a commencement date which is 12 months ahead, having given the request between 12 and six months before the date the tenant wants the new tenancy to begin.

The landlord's counter-notice

13.75   Upon receiving a tenant's s 26 request the landlord has two months in which to notify the tenant if he intends to oppose the tenant's application to the court for a new tenancy (s 26(6)). There is no prescribed form of 'counter-notice' so a clear letter will suffice, but the landlord must state on which grounds in s 30 of the Act the landlord opposes the application (see 13.117). The landlord should be certain of his grounds because they cannot be amended later. If the landlord fails to serve a counter-notice within the two months he will lose his right to oppose the new tenancy. If the reversion is assigned after the counter-notice has been given, the incoming landlord steps into the shoes of the outgoing landlord and can rely on the grounds specified in the counter-notice (see *Morris Marks v British Waterways Board* [1963] 1 WLR 1008). Needless to say, there have been many cases of negligence against landlords' solicitors who have overlooked this two-month deadline.

A typical form of counter-notice might read as follows: **13.76**

> To [name of tenant]
> of [address of tenant]
>
> I [name of landlord] of [address of landlord] received on [date of receipt] your request under s 26 of the Landlord and Tenant Act 1954 Part II ('the Act') for a new tenancy of [description of property] ('the Property').
>
> I hereby give you notice that I will oppose your application to the court for a new tenancy of the Property on the following ground(s) contained in s 30(1) of the Act, namely paragraph(s) [insert paragraph letter(s)].
>
> Dated:
>
> Signed:
>
> [signature of landlord, or on behalf of landlord]

Landlord's application to the court for an order for the termination of the current tenancy without the grant of a new tenancy

A provision, introduced on 1 June 2004, enables the landlord to apply to the court for   **13.77**
an order for the termination of the current tenancy without the grant of a new tenancy (s 29(2)). This is permitted either:

(a) where the landlord has given notice under s 25 that he is opposed to the grant of a new tenancy; or
(b) where the tenant has made a s 26 request and the landlord indicated in his counter-notice that he will oppose an application for a new tenancy, stating the ground(s) on which he will do so.

The landlord is not permitted to make an application for termination of the current ten-   **13.78**
ancy if the tenant or the landlord has already made an application (albeit not served) for the grant of a new tenancy under s 24(1).

Accordingly, if the landlord opposes the grant of a new tenancy on one or more of the   **13.79**
grounds in s 30(1), the landlord has two options. He can either make his own application for termination of the current tenancy without the grant of a new tenancy under s 29(2) or he can defend the tenant's application under s 24(1) for the grant of a new tenancy.

Where the landlord has made and served his application for an order for the termination   **13.80**
of the tenancy, the tenant is not permitted to make an application for an order for a new tenancy (s 24(2B)). But if the landlord fails to establish any of the s 30(1) grounds of opposition, how does the tenant get his new tenancy? The answer lies in the new s 29(4)(b), which provides that the court 'shall make an order for the grant of a new tenancy and accordingly for the termination of the current tenancy immediately before the commencement of the new tenancy'. The clever landlord might try to defeat such an order by withdrawing his application. However, s 29(6) prevents this by providing that the landlord may not withdraw his application for an order for termination unless the tenant consents. If the tenant wants a new tenancy he should not simply consent to the withdrawal of the landlord's application. In doing so, he would lose his right to an order for a new tenancy!

DEFINITION OF 'THE HOLDING'

On an application for a renewal of the lease the tenant will only be entitled to a renewal of   **13.81**
'the holding' as defined by the Act in s 23(3). The holding is defined as:

the property comprised in the tenancy, there being excluded any part thereof which is occupied neither by the tenant nor by a person employed by the tenant and so employed for the purposes of a business by reason of which the tenancy is one to which this Part of this Act applies.

13.82 It follows that the holding will not include the following, in respect of which the tenant cannot claim a new lease:

(a) any part of the premises presently sub-let by the tenant will generally not form part of the holding unless the tenant can show that it remains in occupation of that part for business purposes (see 13.31 and *Graysim Holdings Ltd v P&O Property Holdings Ltd* [1995] 3 WLR 854);

(b) any part of the premises occupied by a third party;

(c) any part of the premises that is unoccupied;

(d) any part of the premises occupied by the tenant's employees in connection with another of the tenant's businesses.

13.83 It should be noted, however, that as long as the tenant occupies part of the premises for business purposes the holding will include other parts of the premises that the tenant occupies for other purposes, e.g. residential use. The extent of the holding is determined on the date on which the order for the grant of the new tenancy is made (s 32(1)). Some of the landlord's statutory grounds of opposition also refer to 'the holding'.

DEFINITION OF 'COMPETENT LANDLORD'

13.84 A tenant's request for a new tenancy under s 26 must be served on the 'competent landlord' as defined by s 44(1) of the Act. Similarly, the 'competent landlord' must serve a landlord's s 25 notice. There can only be one competent landlord at any given time, and his or her identity may change during the course of the renewal procedure. If this occurs, the new competent landlord must be made party to any proceedings under the Act (see *Piper v Muggleton* [1956] 2 All ER 875, CA). The time for determining the competent landlord is the date of service of the s 25 notice or s 26 request.

Sub-leases

13.85 Where the tenant's immediate landlord is the freeholder, establishing the identity of the competent landlord will be easy (as it will obviously be the freeholder). However, in the case of sub-leases it is necessary to consider s 44(1) of the Act. This provides that where a landlord is a tenant himself, he will be the competent landlord to his immediate tenant only if his own tenancy will *not* come to an end within 14 months. If it will end within 14 months, the competent landlord will be the next landlord up the chain of tenancies whose tenancy satisfies this criterion (or the freeholder if you reach the top). This may be illustrated by the examples of sub-leases at Figure 13.1 below. In each case, consider who is the sub-tenant's competent landlord.

Figure 13.1 Examples of sub-leases

EXAMPLE 1	EXAMPLE 2
L	L
⬇ Fixed-term headlease	⬇ Fixed-term headlease
T	T
⬇ Sub-lease of *whole*	⬇ Sub-lease of *part*
ST	ST
Example 1: L (freeholder) lets premises to T on fixed term; T sub-lets *whole* of premises to ST.	Example 2: L (freeholder) lets premises to T on fixed term; T sub-lets *part* of premises to ST.

In Example 1, because T has sub-let the whole, T is not 'in occupation', will not have the pro-   **13.86**
tection of the Act, and T's lease will not continue under s 24 (i.e. it ends on the contractual
expiry date). Thus, once T's lease (L–T) has less than 14 months to run, it will certainly come
to an end within 14 months. ST's competent landlord will be L (freeholder) in any event.

In Example 2, T occupies that part of the premises he has not sub-let to ST. Accordingly,   **13.87**
T is protected by the Act ('in occupation') and T's lease (L–T) will continue under the Act
(s 24). Thus, even during the last 14 months of T's lease, it will *not* come to an end within
14 months because it continues under the Act (see *Bowes-Lyon v Green* [1963] AC 420).
ST's competent landlord will be T.

Importantly, however, the situation in Example 2 is reversed if L serves T with a s 25 notice,   **13.88**
or T serves L with a s 26 request or s 27 notice. In this case T's lease *will* come to an end
within 14 months because it is being terminated by one of the ways prescribed by the Act.
In this case, ST's competent landlord will be L (freeholder).

In Example 2, for ST of part where T remains in occupation of the remainder, it is crucial   **13.89**
for ST to know, in respect of T's lease (L–T), whether T has been served with a s 25 notice
(by L), or whether T has himself served a s 27 notice or s 26 request (on L). To establish
the position, ST can serve a notice on T under s 40 of the Act. Section 40 notices are considered at 13.92.

The following should also be considered where there is a sub-lease or sub-leases. If the   **13.90**
immediate landlord is the competent landlord and the immediate landlord's own lease has
less than 16 months to run from the date of service or receipt, he is obliged to send a copy
of the s 25 notice or s 26 request to his own landlord (1954 Act, Schedule 6, para 7). The superior landlord, if he becomes the competent landlord within two months of service of the
s 25 notice, may serve notice withdrawing the s 25 notice (1954 Act, Schedule 6, para 6). The
superior landlord may then choose whether to serve his own s 25 notice on the sub-tenant.

Similarly, where the superior landlord is not himself the freeholder, he must send a copy   **13.91**
to his landlord, who has the same rights as described above. The superior/competent landlord will bind the intermediate landlord(s) in relation to s 25 notices that he gives to the
sub-tenant. Moreover, the terms of any new tenancy that the superior/competent landlord
agrees with the sub-tenant are binding on the intermediate landlord(s). However, the latter
must give its/their consent (such consent not to be unreasonably withheld), failing which
the superior/competent landlord will be liable to pay compensation for any loss arising
from the making of the agreement (1954 Act, Schedule 6, para 4).

SECTION 40 NOTICES

Rationale

The identity of the competent landlord can change more than once during the course of   **13.92**
the litigation and renewal procedure. In Example 2 in 13.85, the identity of the competent
landlord will depend on whether notices or requests have been given to terminate T's lease
(L–T) under the Act. To request information about superior leases and sub-leases, and
whether notices or requests have been given, landlords and tenants can serve on each other
a notice under s 40 of the Act. The 2004 reforms have increased the amount of information
required to be given. Ideally, the s 40 notice should be served before or simultaneously with
the notices or requests under ss 25, 26, and 27. For the consequences of a tenant serving
the wrong person, see *Re 55 and 57 Holmes Road, Kentish Town, Beardmore Motors Ltd*

v Birch Bros (Properties) Ltd [1959] Ch 298. A tenant can also serve a s 40 notice on any person being a mortgagee in possession. A s 40 notice may not be served earlier than two years before the date on which, apart from the Act, the tenancy would end by effluxion of time, or could be brought to an end by notice to quit given by the landlord (s 40(6)).

Good practice

13.93   As a matter of good practice, the only time one can safely dispense with a s 40 notice is where one is certain that the landlord is the freeholder and the tenant occupies the whole of the premises. (Perhaps a tenant should also resist serving a s 40 notice where he intends to serve a s 26 request and does not wish to prompt his landlord into serving a s 25 notice.) Only a tenant who is entitled to serve a s 26 request may serve a s 40 notice; thus, a periodic tenant cannot serve one.

ACTION BY RECIPIENT OF s 40 NOTICE

13.94   A tenant who receives a s 40 notice must indicate within one month whether he occupies the premises or any part of them wholly or partly for business purposes. The tenant must also indicate whether he has sub-let; and if so, must provide information about the sub-letting, including whether there has been a contracting-out and whether a s 25 notice has been served or a s 26 request made. The tenant must state the identity of any known reversioner. Conversely, a landlord who receives a s 40 notice must indicate within one month whether he owns the freehold; and if not, must give the identity of his immediate landlord and when his own tenancy will expire. A landlord must also state whether there is a mortgagee in possession and, if so, its name and address. Where there is a superior lease the landlord must state whether a s 25 notice has been served or a s 26 request has been made. The landlord must also state the identity of any known reversioner. There is a statutory duty on both landlord and tenant to update the information given for a period of six months from the date of service of the s 40 notice, where it ceases to be correct (s 40(5)).

13.95   A landlord may learn from a tenant in response to a s 40 notice that the premises have been sub-let. If the landlord has served a s 25 notice on the tenant, the landlord will now be the competent landlord of the sub-tenant. In these circumstances, generally it will be good practice for the landlord to serve a s 25 notice on the sub-tenant to prevent the sub-tenant making a s 26 request.

Subsequent transfer of interest by recipient of s 40 notice

13.96   Section 40A, introduced on 1 June 2004, deals with cases concerning the transfer of an interest following the service of a s 40 notice. Section 40A(1) deals with the case of a recipient of a s 40 notice (either landlord or tenant) who subsequently transfers his interest in the property. Provided notice in writing of the transfer and of the name and address of the transferee is given to the server of the s 40 notice, the recipient of the s 40 notice ceases to be under a duty to comply with the original s 40 notice. This includes the duty to update any information already given. It follows that the server of the s 40 notice must serve a fresh s 40 notice on the transferee of the interest if they wish to receive up-to-date information.

Subsequent transfer of interest by server of s 40 notice

13.97   Likewise, s 40A(2) deals with the case of the server of a s 40 notice who subsequently transfers his interest in the property. Here, the server (or his transferee) must give the recipient of the s 40 notice a notice in writing of the transfer and the name and address of the transferee. Once this is done, the duty to provide information becomes owed to the transferee of the interest. Where there has been no notice given of the transfer of an interest by the server of the s 40 notice, the recipient of the s 40 notice can perform his duty by providing the information either to the server of the s 40 notice or to the transferee of the interest (s 40A(3)).

Dangers of non-compliance

Failure to comply with any of the s 40 requirements may result in civil proceedings in tort **13.98** for breach of statutory duty. This is expressly laid down in s 40B. The court may make an order requiring compliance and make an award of damages. This provision, introduced by the 2004 reforms, will mean that many landlords and tenants will need to take a far more serious attitude to their responses to s 40 notices than they have done in the past.

RULES FOR SERVICE OF NOTICES

Section 66(4) of the Act provides that the service of notices under the Act is governed by **13.99** s 23 of the Landlord and Tenant Act 1927. The prescribed methods of service are:

(a) personal service;
(b) leaving at the last known place of abode in England and Wales (or place of business: *Price v West London Investment Building Society* [1964] 2 All ER 318);
(c) sending by registered post or recorded delivery to the last known place of abode in England and Wales (or business). The benefit of using registered post or recorded delivery is that, even if the notice is not received, service is presumed (although it can be rebutted; see *Lex Service plc v Johns* [1990] 1 EGLR 92, CA, and *Italica Holdings SA v Bayadea* [1985] 1 EGLR 70). Another benefit is that the notice or request is deemed to have been served on the day it was posted (see *Railtrack plc v Gojra* [1998] 08 EG 158). This makes calculating dates easier, e.g. the termination date in a s 25 notice. If the notice is sent by recorded delivery but there is no one in the recipient's office when the post office attempts delivery, delivery is still deemed to have taken place (see *WX Investments v Begg* [2002] EWHC 925, Ch).

Ordinary post

Service by ordinary post is also effective, provided the sender can prove that the posted **13.100** item was received. This allows the obvious risk that the notice could get lost in the post (see *Chiswell v Griffon Land and Estates Ltd* [1975] 2 All ER 665). Unlike registered post or recorded delivery, when service is effected by ordinary post the date of service is deemed to be the date of actual receipt. For companies, service can be effected at their registered offices (Companies Act 1985, s 725; *National Westminster Bank v Betchworth Investments* [1975] 1 EGLR 57, CA). Service by fax is permitted provided the facsimile copy received is in a complete and legible state (see *Hastie & Jenkerson v McMahon* [1990] RVR 172, CA). Service by fax is not recommended, because the recipient's fax machine may not be operating correctly, or it may be using poor quality paper.

Residency abroad

What if the person carrying on the business is resident abroad? In this case, if the property **13.101** contained in the tenancy is the only territorial link that person has in England and Wales then the tenanted property may be used as the place of abode (see *Italica Holdings SA v Bayadea* [1985] 1 EGLR 70). Notice may be served on the landlord's agent where the agent has been duly authorized to receive notice (1927 Act, 23(1)).

KEY POINTS SUMMARY

S 25 NOTICES AND S 26 REQUESTS

Landlord

13.102
- If you want the tenant to leave at the end of the lease, serve a hostile s 25 notice and be sure of your statutory grounds for opposing a new lease.

- Be sure you are the 'competent' landlord for the tenant in question (see 13.84). It may be necessary to serve a notice under s 40 to be sure (see 13.92).

- The s 25 notice must be given not more than 12 months or less than six months before the date of termination specified in the notice; this termination date must not be earlier than the date on which the tenancy could have been terminated at common law (e.g. the contractual expiry date of a fixed term).

- If you are happy for the tenant to continue in occupation under a new lease and wish the new lease to be in place as soon as possible, serve a non-hostile s 25 notice one year before the contractual expiry date specifying the contractual expiry date as the termination date in the notice.

- Ensure that any s 25 notice is in the prescribed form and contains the prescribed content.

- If you receive a tenant's s 26 request and you want the tenant to leave, you must serve a counter-notice within two months specifying your statutory grounds for opposing a new lease.

- Serve by registered post or recorded delivery (in which case service is deemed to be the date of postage).

Tenant

- If you receive a landlord's s 25 notice and you want to renew your lease, ensure that you apply to the court for a new lease on or before the date specified in the s 25 notice.

- If you have not received a s 25 notice by the time there is less than 12 months to go on the lease, consider a 'pre-emptive strike' by serving a s 26 request and specifying a commencement date for the new lease 12 months hence.

- Serve the s 26 notice on your 'competent' landlord (see 13.84). It may be necessary to serve a notice under s 40 to be sure (see 13.92).

- Ensure that your s 26 request is in the prescribed form and contains the prescribed content.

- If you serve a s 26 request, be sure to apply to the court for a new lease before the date specified in the s 26 request.

- Serve by registered post or recorded delivery (in which case service is deemed to be the date of postage).

INTERIM RENT APPLICATIONS

Landlord's application

13.103   After an application to the court for a new lease, the current tenancy continues at the old contractual rent until three months after the conclusion of the proceedings (s 64). This is clearly disadvantageous to a landlord seeking a higher market rent under the new lease, and it is also an incentive for the tenant to extend the proceedings for as long as possible. To remedy this unreasonable state of affairs the Law of Property Act 1969 inserted a new s 24A into the Act to allow the competent landlord to apply to the court for an interim rent to be fixed until the current tenancy comes to an end. In the case of a sub-tenancy where the head tenancy is also being continued under s 24, the competent landlord will be the head landlord. Thus, rather curiously, the head landlord will be applying for an interim rent which is payable to the intermediate landlord.

Tenant's application

Under the 2004 reforms both landlords and tenants now have the right to make applica- **13.104**
tions for interim rent. The reason for allowing the tenant to apply as well is because there may be market conditions under which rents are falling and, in this situation, it is only fair to allow tenants to benefit from such market conditions.

A new s 24A was introduced on 1 June 2004. It states that provided either a s 25 notice **13.105**
has been served or a s 26 request has been made, both landlords and tenants may apply for an interim rent while the tenancy is continuing under s 24. However, no application may be made later than six months after the termination of the contractual tenancy. To avoid duplication of proceedings, neither party may apply if the other party has already done so, unless that application has been withdrawn.

Under s 24B the interim rent is payable from: **13.106**

(a) the earliest date that could have been specified for termination of the tenancy, where a s 25 notice has been served (s 24B(2)); or
(b) the earliest date that could have been specified for commencement of the new tenancy, where a s 26 request has been made (s 24B(3)).

This is intended to rule out the tactical use of s 25 notices and s 26 requests (e.g. the **13.107**
tenant's pre-emptive strike: see 13.71(a)).

The basis for valuation of interim rent

The court is given a discretion to determine an interim rent which the tenant is to pay while **13.108**
the current tenancy continues under s 24. There are two different methods for determining the amount of the interim rent. These are contained in ss 24C and 24D, respectively, and are now considered.

Section 24C valuation

The method of valuation contained in s 24C applies where the landlord grants a new ten- **13.109**
ancy of the whole of the property previously let to the tenant, whether pursuant to a court order or otherwise, and three conditions are met. They are:

(a) that the landlord's s 25 notice or the tenant's s 26 request applies to the whole of the property let; and
(b) that the tenant is in business occupation of the whole of that property; and
(c) that the landlord does not oppose the grant of a new tenancy.

Subject to the two exceptions referred to at 13.111, under s 24C the market rent payable **13.110**
at the commencement of the new tenancy shall also be the interim rent. Significantly there-fore, unlike the position before 1 June 2004, the landlord should receive the full market rent as interim rent and, as such, the interim rent will have no 'cushioning effect' on the tenant (explained at 13.113).

Exceptions

13.111 The two exceptions to this basis of valuation are as follows:

(a) a substantial change in the market rent since the date when the interim rent became payable. Where either party is able to establish that the rent for the new tenancy differs substantially from the rent (determined on the same basis) that the court would have ordered had it been fixed to run from the date at which interim rent became payable, the latter becomes the interim rent;

(b) a substantial change in rent caused by a change in terms of the new tenancy. Where either party is able to establish that the occupational terms of the new tenancy are so different from those of the old one that they would affect the rent for the new tenancy, had it been granted on the same occupational terms as the old one, the interim rent becomes the rent it would be reasonable for the tenant to pay.

13.112 Where either of these exceptions apply, the court can use its discretion to fix a rent that it would be reasonable for the tenant to pay.

Section 24D valuation

13.113 The second method of valuation is contained in s 24D and applies in every other case, for example where the landlord opposes the renewal. Essentially this is the same as the method used before 1 June 2004. The interim rent is 'the rent which is reasonable for the tenant to pay while the relevant tenancy continues by virtue of s 24' (s 24D(1)). It is assessed on the basis of a yearly tenancy and will generally be 10–15 per cent lower than the market rent for a fixed-term lease (see *Janes (Gowns) Ltd v Harlow Development Corporation* (1979) 253 EG 799). The interim rent thus acts as a 'cushion' protecting the tenant from the blow of moving to a much higher market rent (see generally *English Exporters (London) Ltd v Eldonwall Ltd* [1973] Ch 415, and *Baptist v Masters of the Bench and Trustees of the Honourable Society of Gray's Inn* [1993] 2 EGLR 159).

13.114 However, the level of interim rent is entirely at the court's discretion. In *Department of the Environment v Allied Freehold Property Trust Ltd* [1992] 45 EG 156, the court fixed a full market rent because the tenant had been paying a low contractual rent for a long period. In *Fawkes v Viscount Chelsea* [1980] QB 441, the court ordered a much lower rent until the landlord remedied breach of his repairing obligations. Additionally, and introduced by the 2004 reforms, the court must also have regard to the rent payable under any sub-tenancy of part of the property.

Good practice

13.115 In a normal rising market the landlord will generally apply for an interim rent as early as possible, namely as soon as the s 25 notice or s 26 request has been given or received. Conversely, in a falling market the landlord will have no need for an interim rent if the contractual rent is higher than the prevailing market rent. Here, it is the tenant who would be advised to apply for an interim rent. Another instance when it should be unnecessary for a landlord to apply for an interim rent will be where the rent was reviewed immediately before the contractual expiry date (a 'penultimate day rent review'); in this case the tenant should already be paying the market rent.

13.116 The tenant will be required to start paying interim rent as soon as the court determines it. Interest will also be payable from this date, unless the lease provides that interest will be payable from a period after the rent becomes due, for example 14 days. Interim rent continues to be payable until the date on which the current tenancy comes to an end.

LANDLORD'S STATUTORY GROUNDS OF OPPOSITION

There are seven statutory grounds in s 30(1) of the 1954 Act which entitle a landlord to resist **13.117** a tenant's application for a new lease. If the landlord is successful in proving one or more of those grounds then the tenant's application should fail. It should be noted that some grounds are subject to the court's discretion. The landlord must state the relevant ground(s) in its s 25 notice or counter-notice to the tenant's s 26 request. No later amendments or additions to the grounds are allowed, so it is important that the landlord specifies the correct grounds at this early stage. In *Waterstones Booksellers Ltd v Notting Hill Gate KCS Ltd* (2016, unreported), a landlord who initially opposed renewal under paragraph (f) (redevelopment) later withdrew its opposition but was subsequently permitted to resurrect it and oppose the renewal, relying on the Consumer Protection Regulations (CPR), Part 17 (amendment of pleadings) and CPR, r 14.1 (withdrawal of an admission). Hammersmith County Court found that the correct balance between the respective prejudice to the two parties favoured permitting the landlord to amend and revert to its original position. However, the landlord's stated grounds must be genuine; if the grounds are false and made fraudulently, the notice may be rendered invalid and unenforceable (see *Rous v Mitchell* [1991] 1 All ER 676, CA). A subsequent purchaser of the landlord's interest will also be bound by the original landlord's choice of ground(s) (see *Morris Marks v British Waterways Board* [1963] 3 All ER 28, CA).

In summary, the grounds of opposition are: **13.118**

(a) the tenant's failure to carry out repairing obligations;
(b) the tenant's persistent delay in paying rent;
(c) the tenant's substantial breaches of other obligations;
(d) suitable alternative accommodation is available for the tenant;
(e) on sub-letting of part, the landlord requires the whole property for subsequent letting;
(f) the landlord intends to demolish or reconstruct the premises;
(g) the landlord intends to occupy the holding.

Discretionary grounds

Grounds (a), (b), (c), and (e) are discretionary. Thus even if the landlord establishes the **13.119** ground, the court may decide to order a new tenancy in any event, for example because of the tenant's good conduct. Examples of situations where the court may decide to use its discretion are considered in the following paragraphs under the individual grounds. The remaining grounds—(d), (f), and (g)—are mandatory, so that if the landlord establishes the ground the court must refuse to order a new tenancy.

The specific grounds are now considered; and to assist in interpretation, the precise word- **13.120** ing of the grounds is set out followed by commentary and reference to cases.

Ground (a): tenant's failure to carry out repairing obligations

(a) where under the current tenancy the tenant has any obligations as respects the repair and maintenance of the holding, that the tenant ought not to be granted a new tenancy in view of the state of repair of the holding, being a state resulting from the tenant's failure to comply with the said obligations . . .

Ground (a) only applies to failure to repair the tenant's 'holding' as defined by the Act **13.121** (see 13.81). Thus it would not apply to a part of the demised premises in disrepair which is occupied by a sub-tenant. Moreover, a substantial breach of covenant on the tenant's part may on its own be insufficient to establish the ground. The landlord must go further and show that the breach is serious enough that the 'tenant ought not to be granted a new tenancy'. Because of the ground's discretionary nature, the court may grant a new tenancy despite the breach (see *Nihad v Chain* (1956) 167 EG 139). The grant could be on the basis of an undertaking by the tenant to remedy the breach (see *Lyons v Central Commercial Properties Ltd* [1958] 2 All ER 767, CA at 775; although a grant was actually refused in this case). In exercising its discretion, the court will consider whether a new tenancy would be unfair to the landlord, having regard to the tenant's past performances and conduct. It will also consider the reasons for the tenant's breach of covenant to repair (see generally *Lyons v Central Commercial Properties Ltd*, applied subsequently in *Eichner v Midland Bank Executor & Trustee Co. Ltd* [1970] 2 All ER 597, CA).

13.122 If the landlord intends to rely on this ground, it (or its surveyor) should first serve on the tenant a schedule of dilapidations with a request that the repairs be carried out (on the assumption that there is a lease-repairing covenant). The landlord may also consider forfeiture of the lease as an alternative to ground (a). A tenant faced with opposition under ground (a) should consider giving the landlord an undertaking to carry out the repairs within a set time. A court may take such an undertaking into account when exercising its discretion but may also seek evidence that the tenant has sufficient funds to carry out the works. If the tenant is refused a new lease under ground (a), the tenant is not entitled to compensation.

Ground (b): tenant's persistent delay in paying rent

(b) that the tenant ought not to be granted a new tenancy in view of his persistent delay in paying rent which has become due . . .

13.123 The word 'persistent' is significant as it clearly means more than one incident of delay. The court will consider the frequency and extent of the delays (see *Hopcutt v Carver* (1969) 209 EG 1069, CA), the steps the landlord had to take to secure payment, and how the landlord may be protected against delay in any future tenancy (see *Rawashdeh v Lane* [1988] 2 EGLR 109, CA). In *Hazel v Akhtar* [2001] EWCA Civ 1883, the Court of Appeal held, interestingly, that the longer the practice of late payment continued, the easier it was for the tenant to argue that the landlord had accepted the tenant's conduct and was estopped from using ground (b). The ground is discretionary, so that even if persistent delay is proven the court may decide to order a new tenancy if the tenant can offer a satisfactory explanation for the delay. This occurred in *Hurstfell Ltd v Leicester Square Property Co. Ltd* [1988] 2 EGLR 105, where the Court of Appeal declined to interfere with a decision of the county court judge, who accepted the tenant's reasons for persistent delays over a period of more than two-and-a-half years.

13.124 The word 'rent' may include other payments due under the lease if these are reserved as rent, e.g. service charges. The landlord should prepare a full schedule of arrears which, if possible, should be agreed with the tenant. In the absence of agreement, the landlord should serve it on the tenant with a 'Notice to Admit Facts' under CPR, r 32.18. The tenant seeking to resist an opposition under ground (b) should ensure that no further arrears accrue and, if appropriate, suggest means of guaranteeing future payments (e.g. a rent deposit or guarantor). If the tenant is refused a new lease under ground (b), the tenant is not entitled to compensation.

Ground (c): tenant's substantial breaches of other obligations

(c) that the tenant ought not to be granted a new tenancy in view of other substantial breaches by him of his obligations under the current tenancy, or for any other reason connected with the tenant's use or management of the holding . . .

This is another discretionary ground. It concerns the tenant's substantial breaches (note the **13.125** use of the word 'substantial') of *other* obligations in the lease (i.e. other than repair or rent), and it also extends to reasons linked generally with the tenant's use or management of the holding. Thus a court can refuse to grant a new lease if the tenant is at fault in some way even though the tenant has performed all his obligations under the lease. This occurred in *Turner & Bell v Searles (Stanford-le-Hope) Ltd* (1977) 33 P & CR 208, where the Court of Appeal allowed the landlord to succeed on this ground because the tenant's use of the premises contravened a planning enforcement notice. For a more recent case on similar facts, see *Fowles v Heathrow Airport* [2008] EWCA Civ 757. The court must have regard to all relevant circumstances, including whether the landlord's interest has been prejudiced, the general conduct of the tenant, and any proposals for remedying the breach (see *Eichner v Midland Bank Executor & Trustee Co. Ltd* [1970] 2 All ER 597 and *Beard v Williams* [1986] 1 EGLR 148).

Whether a breach is 'substantial' is a question of fact in each case. In *Youssefi v Mussell-* **13.126** *white* [2014] EWCA Civ 885 the tenant's failure to allow access to the property and its failure to open a business were found to be substantial breaches of the lease. In addition, the reference to 'breaches' would not preclude a single substantial breach. This is because in an Act of Parliament, unless a contrary intention appears, words in the singular include the plural and *vice versa* (Interpretation Act 1978, s 6)). It is not necessary for the breaches to relate to 'the holding' and so substantial breaches relating to any sub-let part of the premises may be included. If the tenant is refused a new lease under ground (c), the tenant is not entitled to compensation.

Ground (d): suitable alternative accommodation is available for tenant

(d) that the landlord has offered and is willing to provide or secure the provision of alternative accommodation for the tenant, that the terms on which the alternative accommodation is available are reasonable having regard to the terms of the current tenancy and to all other relevant circumstances, and that the accommodation and the time at which it will be available are suitable for the tenant's requirements (including the requirement to preserve goodwill) having regard to the nature and class of his business and to the situation and extent of, and facilities afforded by, the holding . . .

This ground is not discretionary, so if the landlord can provide suitable alternative accom- **13.127** modation based on the above criteria the court must dismiss the tenant's application for a new tenancy (see *Betty's Cafes Ltd v Phillips Furnishing Stores Ltd* [1957] Ch 67 at 84). The relevant date to assess the reasonableness of the terms and the suitability of the alternative accommodation is the date of the hearing. Interestingly, the landlord may offer part of the tenant's existing premises as alternative accommodation (as is the case under the Rent Act 1977). The landlord must show, however, that the part in question is sufficient for the tenant's business purposes as at the date of the hearing (see *Mykolyshyn v Noah* [1971] 1 All ER 48).

Alternative accommodation in the future may also be sufficient for the landlord. If he can **13.128** establish that it will be available at a later date (i.e. even after the termination date in the s 25 notice or s 26 request), he may still be able to succeed on ground (d) (see s 31(2) of the Act; see also 'near miss' cases at 13.152). If the tenant is refused a new lease under ground (d), the tenant is not entitled to compensation.

Ground (e): on sub-letting of part, landlord requires the whole property for subsequent letting

(e) where the current tenancy was created by the sub-letting of part only of the property comprised in a superior tenancy and the landlord is the owner of an interest in reversion expectant on the termination of that superior tenancy, that the aggregate of the rents reasonably obtainable on separate lettings of the holding and the remainder of that property would be substantially less than the rent reasonably obtainable on a letting of that property as a whole, that on the termination of the current tenancy the landlord requires possession of the holding for the purpose of letting or otherwise disposing of the said property as a whole, and that in view thereof the tenant ought not to be granted a new tenancy.

13.129 Ground (e) is another discretionary ground and is the least used of all the grounds (indeed, there are no reported cases on how the discretion is to be exercised). It applies only where there is a sub-letting of part and the 'competent' landlord of the sub-tenant is the superior landlord, i.e. not the sub-tenant's immediate landlord. As previously explained at 13.85, the intermediate lease will, in these circumstances, have less than 14 months to run.

13.130 The landlord must show two things:

(a) the rent obtainable on separate lettings of the whole building would be substantially less than the rent obtainable on a letting of the whole. It should be noted that the rent has to be substantially less, not merely less (see *Greaves Organization Ltd v Stanhope Gate Property Co. Ltd* (1973) 228 EG 725); and

(b) on the termination of the sub-tenancy the landlord requires possession of the sub-let part to let or otherwise dispose of the property as a whole. The landlord may have difficulty in establishing this unless the intermediate lease is due to end before the sub-tenancy is terminated (on the basis that he cannot re-let the whole if the intermediate tenant is still in occupation).

13.131 In exercising its discretion a court would have regard to whether the landlord originally consented to the sub-letting. Section 31(2) of the Act also applies to ground (e), i.e. if the landlord can establish the ground at a later date (see 'near miss' cases at 13.152). If the tenant is refused a new lease under ground (e), the tenant is entitled to compensation (see 13.155).

Ground (f): the landlord intends to demolish or reconstruct premises

(f) that on the termination of the current tenancy the landlord intends to demolish or reconstruct the premises comprised in the holding or a substantial part of those premises or to carry out substantial work of construction on the holding or part thereof and that he could not reasonably do so without obtaining possession of the holding . . .

13.132 This is the most frequently used ground. To rely on it the landlord must show on the termination of the tenancy the following three elements:

(a) the landlord's intention;

(b) to demolish or reconstruct the premises in the holding (or a substantial part thereof), or to carry out substantial work of construction on the holding (or part thereof); and

(c) that he could not reasonably do so without obtaining possession of the holding.

13.133 Each of these three elements is now considered.

Landlord's intention

13.134 The landlord's intention to carry out the work must be more than a simple desire to bring it about. The intention must be firm and settled. It must have 'moved out of the zone of contemplation—out of the sphere of the tentative, the provisional and the exploratory—into the valley of decision' (*per* Asquith LJ in *Cunliffe v Goodman* [1950] 2 KB 237, and subsequently approved by Viscount Simonds in *Betty's Cafes Ltd v Phillips Furnishing Stores Ltd* [1959] AC 20, HL). Further, as a question of fact, there must be a reasonable prospect that the landlord's plan will succeed, although he does not need to prove that it will be a commercial success (see *Dolgellau Golf Club v Hett* [1998] 2 EGLR 75, CA). As long as the landlord can show the requisite intention to carry out the works, any ulterior motive of the landlord is likely to be ignored (see *S Franses Ltd v The Cavendish Hotel (London) Ltd* [2017] EWHC 1670 (QB), where the proposed works appeared to be devised for the sole purpose of evicting the tenant, with no other benefit for the landlord).

The time when the landlord's intention must be established is the date of the court hearing **13.135** (see *Betty's Cafes Ltd v Phillips Furnishing Stores Ltd*). The fact that the landlord (or his predecessor) had no such intention at the time of serving the s 25 notice (or counter-notice to s 26 request) is irrelevant (see *Marks v British Waterways Board* [1963] 3 All ER 28). Provided the landlord can prove the ground as a matter of fact, the court will not examine the landlord's motives for using the ground. Thus in *Fisher v Taylors Furnishing Stores Ltd* [1956] 2 QB 78, it did not matter that the landlord's primary object was to occupy the reconstructed premises himself.

The necessary intention is a question of fact in each case, but the landlord's position will **13.136** be strengthened if, by the time of the hearing, he has taken appropriate steps. These would include: instructing professionals, obtaining quotations, preparing plans and drawings, securing any necessary planning permissions, arranging finance, and, for a company land-lord, passing a board resolution. The less the landlord has to do by the time he gets to court, the better (see *Gregson v Cyril Lord* [1962] 3 All ER 907). Where planning permission has been applied for but not obtained by the date of the hearing, the test the court will use is whether there is a reasonable prospect that permission will be granted (see *Westminster City Council v British Waterways Board* [1984] 3 WLR 1047, HL). This 'reasonable prospect' test was applied in *Aberdeen Steak Houses Group Ltd v Crown Estates Commissioners* [1997] 31 EG 101, *Coppin v Bruce-Smith* [1998] EGCS 55, CA, and *Gatwick Parking Service Ltd v Sargent* [2000] 25 EG 141, CA.

The works must be carried out 'on the termination of the current tenancy'. The Court of **13.137** Appeal has held this to include within a reasonable time from the date of the termination of the tenancy (see *London Hilton Jewellers Ltd v Hilton International Hotels Ltd* [1990] 1 EGLR 112). For practical purposes, 'termination of the current tenancy' would include any continuation tenancy under s 64 of the Act, as the landlord would clearly be entitled to possession before the works were carried out. A reasonable time will, of course, be a question of fact in each case.

Demolish, reconstruct, or carry out substantial work of construction

In addition to establishing an intention, the landlord must also show that the proposed works **13.138** fall within the express wording of ground (f). This will depend on the nature and extent of the works and is a question of fact in each case. The key words used are 'demolish', 'reconstruct', and 'substantial work of construction'. 'Demolish' is easily understood and there must be some property on the holding which is capable of being demolished, for example a building or wall (see *Housleys Ltd v Bloomer-Holt Ltd* [1966] 2 All ER 966, CA, involving a wall and garage). If part of the premises are to be demolished, then they must be 'substantial', which is a question of fact (see *Atkinson v Bettison* [1953] 3 All ER 340, CA). 'Reconstruct' has been held to involve rebuilding and a substantial interference with the structure of the building. The work need not be confined necessarily to the outside of the premises or to load-bearing walls (see *Percy E Cadle & Co. Ltd v Jacmarch Properties Ltd* [1957] 1 QB 323, CA and *Romulus Trading Co. Ltd v Henry Smith's Charity Trustees* [1990] 2 EGLR 75, CA).

'Substantial work of construction' implies a new building or adding to what was already **13.139** there (see *per* Ormerod LJ in *Cook v Mott* (1961) 178 EG 637). It connotes more than mere refurbishment or improvement. In *Barth v Pritchard* [1990] 1 EGLR 109, CA, an intention to rewire, re-roof, redecorate, install central heating, and reposition a staircase was held to be insufficient. Yet in *Joel v Swaddle* [1957] 1 WLR 1094, a proposal to convert a shop with two storage rooms into part of a large amusement arcade came within the ground. Other successful works of 'construction' have been the laying of pipes, wires, cables, and drains, and the laying of a road (see *Housleys v Bloomer-Holt Ltd*).

13.140 On the question of what amounts to a reconstruction of a substantial part of the holding, the court in *Joel v Swaddle* said the proper approach was to look at the position as a whole. One should compare the result after carrying out the proposed work with the condition and state of the premises before the work was begun.

Landlord could not reasonably carry out the work without obtaining possession of the holding

13.141 The landlord must show that he needs legal possession of the holding, not merely physical possession. In other words, he must show that he needs to terminate the tenancy in order to carry out the work. If the landlord can do the work simply by exercising his right of entry under the terms of the lease, ground (f) will not be established (this right is often reserved by landlords to enable them to execute improvements and alterations; see *Heath v Drown* [1973] AC 496, HL).

Tenant's defences under s 31A

13.142 Even if the landlord can show that he requires possession to carry out work, the tenant may be assisted by s 31A of the Act (inserted by the Law of Property Act 1925, s 7(1)). This effectively prevents the landlord from using ground (f) in circumstances where the proposed work would be over quickly, or where the work will affect only part of the premises. Section 31A provides that a court cannot hold that the landlord could not reasonably carry out the demolition or other work without obtaining possession if either of the following occurs:

(a) The tenant agrees to the inclusion in the terms of the new tenancy of terms giving the landlord access and other facilities for carrying out the work intended and, given that access and those facilities, the landlord could reasonably carry out the work without obtaining possession of the holding and without interfering to a substantial extent or for a substantial time with the use of the holding for the purposes of the business carried on by the tenant.

  The tenant may decide to rely on this defence where the landlord has failed to reserve adequate rights in the lease to allow him to carry out the work (*Heath v Drown* [1973] AC 496, HL). 'The work' means the landlord's intended works and the court has no power to consider whether the landlord should be carrying out different works (see *The Decca Navigator Co. Ltd v Greater London Council* [1974] 1 All ER 1178). The word 'interfering' refers to interference with the tenant's use of the holding for its business purposes, not the business itself or the goodwill. Thus a tenant intending to leave while the works are being carried out and then return with its goodwill unaffected cannot use s 31A (see *Redfern v Reeves* [1978] 2 EGLR 52, CA).

(b) The tenant is willing to accept a tenancy of an economically separable part of the holding and either paragraph (a) above is satisfied with respect to that part, or possession of the remainder of the holding would be reasonably sufficient to enable the landlord to carry out the intended work.

Here, a part of the holding will be an economically separable part if, and only if, the aggregate of the rents which, after completion of the intended work, would be reasonably obtainable on separate lettings of that part and the remainder of the premises affected by or resulting from the work would not be substantially less than the rent which would then be reasonably obtainable on a letting of those premises as a whole (s 31A(2)). If the tenant establishes defence (b), the order for the new tenancy will be only of the economically separable part (s 32(1A)).

Section 31(2) of the Act applies to ground (f), i.e. the landlord has a second chance if he **13.143** can establish the ground at a later date (see 'near miss' cases at 13.152). However, ground (f) must be established within one year of the termination date specified in the s 25 notice or s 26 request. If the tenant is refused a new lease under ground (f), the tenant is entitled to compensation (see 13.155).

Ground (g): the landlord intends to occupy the holding

> (g) . . . that on the termination of the current tenancy the landlord intends to occupy the holding for the purposes, or partly for the purposes, of a business to be carried on by him therein, or as his residence.

This is another frequently used ground which has three important elements: the five-year **13.144** rule; the landlord's intention; and the occupation of the holding. These are now considered.

The five-year rule

The five-year rule is an integral part of ground (g) and is set out in s 30(2) of the Act. **13.145** It provides that the landlord cannot rely on ground (g) if the landlord's interest 'was purchased or created after the beginning of the period of five years which ends with the termination of the current tenancy'. So to rely on ground (g) the landlord effectively must have owned the reversion for at least five years before the termination date specified in the s 25 notice or s 26 request. The word 'purchased' means 'bought for money', and the time at which the purchase occurs is the date of exchange of contracts (see *HL Bolton (Engineering) Co. Ltd v TJ Graham & Sons Ltd* [1957] 1 QB 159, CA). Where the landlord has a leasehold interest, it is 'created' when the lease is executed, not when the term begins or the lease is registered (see *Northcote Laundry Ltd v Frederick Donnelly Ltd* [1968] 1 WLR 562, CA). The landlord must have been the 'competent' landlord for the five years prior to the end of the tenancy. This means that the landlord must either have owned the freehold, or had a leasehold interest with at least 14 months to run (see *Frozen Value Ltd v Heron Foods Ltd* [2012] EWCA Civ 473).

Purpose of rule   The purpose of this rule is to prevent persons from buying the landlord's **13.146** interest towards the end of the tenancy simply in order to gain possession for themselves. The rule applies only where the premises have been let on a tenancy or series of tenancies within the Act's protection throughout the five-year period. So for example, if three years before the end of a tenancy a purchaser buys the reversion (subject to the tenancy), the five-year restriction would prevent him from using ground (g). However, if the same purchaser bought the freehold with vacant possession and then subsequently granted a lease, the five-year restriction would not apply.

Circumventing rule   A landlord requiring possession can circumvent the five-year rule if he **13.147** can prove ground (f) instead, i.e. an intention to demolish or reconstruct the premises (see 13.132). The court will not examine the landlord's motives for using ground (f), so he could lawfully move in after the construction works have been completed. In addition, the future application of the five-year rule can be avoided if the current landlord is a company. Here, if the purchaser acquires the company by share acquisition it will not be purchasing the 'landlord's interest' (see *Wates Estate Agency Services Ltd v Bartleys Ltd* [1989] 2 EGLR 87).

Landlord's intention

The landlord must intend to occupy the premises either for business purposes, or as his **13.148** residence. As with ground (f), the landlord must be able to show by the date of the hearing a firm and settled intention. The matters considered at 13.134 are therefore equally applicable here. One relevant factor will be the likely prospect of the landlord succeeding in his plans to occupy. For example, if planning permission were to be refused for the landlord's intended business use, this could make the necessary intention harder to establish (see *Westminster City Council v British Waterways Board* [1985] AC 676, HL and *Gatwick Parking Service Ltd v Sargent* [2000] 25 EG 141, CA). However, the likely failure of the landlord's proposed business is not a relevant consideration (see *Cox v Binfield* [1989] 1 EGLR 97, CA), nor whether it is commercially sensible (see *Humber Oil v ABP* [2011] EWHC 2043 (Ch)).

The occupation of the holding

13.149   The landlord must intend to occupy the holding for the purposes, or partly for the purposes, of a business to be carried on by him in the premises, or as his residence. The words 'carried on by him' enable occupation through the landlord's manager (see *Skeet v Powell-Sheddon* [1988] 2 EGLR 112) or agent (see *Parkes v Westminster Roman Catholic Diocese Trustee* (1978) 36 P & CR 22, where trustees occupied through the agency of a parish priest). The landlord may also occupy in partnership with others (see *Re Crowhurst Park, Sims-Hilditch v Simmons* [1974] 1 All ER 991).

13.150   Section 42(3) enables a landlord which is a company in a group of companies to rely on ground (g) where another member of the group is to occupy the premises. Section 41(2) enables a landlord who is a trustee to rely on ground (g) where there is an intention to occupy by a beneficiary under the trust. Under the 2004 reforms, ground (g) is extended to a wider category of landlords. Section 30(1A) provides that where a landlord has a controlling interest in a company, then a reference in ground (g) to the landlord is a reference either to the landlord or to the company. Similarly, s 30(1B) provides that where the landlord is a company, and a person has a controlling interest in that company, then a reference in ground (g) to the landlord is a reference either to the landlord or that person.

13.151   If the tenant is refused a new lease under ground (g), the tenant is entitled to compensation (see 13.155).

'Near miss' cases

13.152   If the landlord fails to establish grounds (d), (e), or (f) (alternative accommodation, uneconomic sub-lease, or intention to demolish or reconstruct) at the date of the hearing, he may still be saved by s 31(2) of the Act. If the landlord can show that he would have been able to establish one of these grounds had the termination date in the s 25 notice or s 26 request been up to 12 months later, the court must refuse the tenant's application for a new tenancy. In this case the tenant can ask the court to substitute that later date for the original termination date in the s 25 notice or s 26 request and the tenancy will continue until the later date. For a case involving the application of s 31(2), see *Accountancy Personnel Ltd v Worshipful Co. of Salters* (1972) 222 EG 1589, CA.

Compensation for misrepresentation

13.153   Where a misrepresentation has been made to the court or there has been concealment of material facts, the court may order compensation to be paid by the landlord to the tenant or *vice versa*. The tenant can claim compensation if he is induced not to apply to court, or to withdraw an application for renewal, because of a misrepresentation. The detailed provisions are contained in s 37A, which was introduced in the 2004 reforms. For an example of a successful claim for compensation under s 37A, see *Inclusive Technology v Williamson* [2009] EWCA Civ 718.

KEY POINTS SUMMARY

STATUTORY GROUNDS UNDER S 30(1)

- Four of the seven grounds are discretionary. They are the tenant's 'fault' grounds—(a) tenant's failure to repair; (b) tenant's delay in paying rent; and (c) tenant's breaches of other obligations—and ground (e) on sub-letting of part, where the superior landlord requires the whole property for subsequent letting. **13.154**

- You cannot amend your grounds at a later date, so be sure of them when the notices are served.

- Grounds (f) (demolish/reconstruct) and (g) (landlord's occupation) are the most frequently used grounds. They require a firm and settled intention on the landlord's part, to be established at the date of the hearing.

- Ground (f) (demolish/reconstruct) will not be established if the tenant is willing to accept a new tenancy of part of the holding, or under the new lease the landlord is allowed access to carry out the works.

- Ground (g) (landlord's occupation) will not be established if the landlord acquired the reversion less than five years before the end of the current tenancy.

- Grounds (d), (e), or (f) may be proven under the 'near miss' rule if the landlord can show he could have established them within 12 months.

TENANT'S RIGHT TO COMPENSATION FOR FAILURE TO OBTAIN A NEW TENANCY

The tenant can claim financial compensation from the landlord if the landlord succeeds in establishing one or more of the 'non-fault' grounds (e), (f), or (g). This is often referred to as 'compensation for disturbance'. The tenant's right to compensation on quitting the premises is contained in s 37(1) of the Act. The basis for compensation is that the tenant is being denied a new tenancy through no fault of their own. Conversely, if one of the 'fault' grounds (a), (b), or (c) is established, then the tenant properly will have no right to compensation. Similarly, there will be no right to compensation if the landlord can provide suitable alternative accommodation under ground (d) (on the basis that the tenant has suffered no loss). **13.155**

It should be noted that s 37(1) allows the tenant compensation on quitting the holding where the landlord in his s 25 notice (or counter-notice to a s 26 request) has specified grounds (e), (f), or (g) in the notice and the tenant has either: **13.156**

(a) not applied to the court for a new tenancy (see *Re 14 Grafton Street London W1, De Havilland (Antiques) Ltd v Centrovincial Estates (Mayfair) Ltd* [1971] 2 All ER 1); or
(b) made and then withdrawn an application for a new tenancy; or
(c) applied to the court for a new tenancy but has been defeated on one or more of grounds (e), (f), or (g).

Where the landlord has opposed on both fault and non-fault grounds and has been successful, the tenant must, in order to claim compensation, apply to the court for a certificate confirming that the landlord was successful only on grounds (e), (f), or (g) and on no other ground (s 37(4)). This is normally done at the hearing of the application for the new lease and the certificate is then incorporated into the court order. The landlord's stated grounds must be genuine; if the grounds are false and made fraudulently, for example by stating a false ground in an attempt to avoid paying compensation, the notice may be rendered invalid and unenforceable (see *Rous v Mitchell* [1991] 1 All ER 676, CA). **13.157**

Amount of compensation

13.158   The amount of compensation is calculated by multiplying the rateable value of the holding (as at the date of service of the s 25 notice or s 26 request) by the 'appropriate multiplier' set from time to time by the Secretary of State. The current multiplier at the time of writing is 1, as prescribed by the Landlord and Tenant Act 1954 (Appropriate Multiplier) Order 1990 (SI 1990/363) which came into force on 1 April 1990 (before that date the multiplier was 3). The rateable value to be used is taken from the valuation list in force at the date of service of the landlord's s 25 notice or s 26(6) counter-notice (s 37(5)(a); see *Plessey & Co. Ltd v Eagle Pension Funds Ltd* [1989] EGCS 149). Any disputes over rateable value are determined by a valuation officer appointed by HM Revenue & Customs under the Landlord and Tenant (Determination of Rateable Value Procedure) Rules 1954 (SI 1954/1255). A right of appeal against the decision of the valuation officer lies to the Lands Chamber.

Double compensation

13.159   Double compensation is payable where the tenant or his predecessors in the same business have been in occupation for at least 14 years prior to the termination of the current tenancy (s 37(3)). The date of termination is either the date of termination specified in the s 25 notice, or the date specified in the s 26 request as being the date from which the new tenancy is to start (s 37(7)). In these circumstances, double compensation is calculated by multiplying twice the rateable value by the appropriate multiplier (presently 1). If the tenant vacates for a short period (e.g. before the end of the tenancy) it should not lose its right to double compensation, provided, during the vacation period, the premises were not being used by another business or for non-business purposes (see *Bacchiocchi v Academic Agency Ltd* [1998] 2 All ER 241, CA, where the tenant closed down 12 days early). Notwithstanding the decision in *Bacchiochi*, best practice for tenants wishing to secure double compensation is not to vacate until the date specified in the s 25 notice or s 26 request has passed.

13.160   Importantly, double compensation can still be claimed even if only part of the holding has been occupied for 14 years for the purposes of the business (see *Edicron Ltd v William Whiteley Ltd* [1984] 1 All ER 219, CA). An example of this might occur where the tenant surrenders its lease and takes a new lease of the same premises together with other premises in the same building. Here the tenant will be entitled to double compensation in respect of the entire holding even though it has not been in occupation of all of it for 14 years. The tenant may wish to consider moving back into part of the premises it has vacated in order to secure increased compensation. Moreover, where the tenant has occupied for nearly 14 years, the timing of a s 26 request or s 25 notice may be crucial in determining whether double compensation is payable.

Excluding compensation by agreement

13.161   The landlord and tenant may agree (e.g. in the lease) to exclude or modify the tenant's right to compensation for failure to obtain a new tenancy (s 38(3)). However, s 38(2) provides that such agreement will be void where the tenant or his predecessors in the same business have been in occupation for five years or more prior to the date the tenant quits the premises. A prospective tenant would be wise to resist attempts by the landlord to 'contract out' of compensation, as such a provision may adversely affect the marketability of the lease during the last five years of the term.

13.162   Compensation is also available in special circumstances, for example a failure to be granted a new tenancy on the grounds of public interest or national security (see ss 57–60 of the Act).

THE TERMS OF THE NEW TENANCY

If the tenant properly applies to the court after following all the correct procedures, the court **13.163** will order a new lease where: (i) the landlord fails to establish an opposition ground under s 30; or (ii) the landlord has not opposed the tenant's application. In (ii), it is rare for the matter to get to court, as the parties' solicitors, after a period of negotiation, will normally be able to agree on the terms of the new lease. The tenant's application in this situation is simply a backup in case the negotiations break down, and if the parties reach agreement on the terms of the new lease the tenant can simply instruct the court to close its file on the matter.

When conducting negotiations it is important to know the powers of the court, and in par- **13.164** ticular the lease terms that the court would be likely to impose. Practitioners are clearly in a far stronger position if they can argue for the inclusion of a particular clause on the basis that the court would agree with them. Accordingly, this section will concentrate on the terms a court would be likely to impose in a renewed tenancy. If the parties agree some terms but not others, the court will rule on the unresolved matters, leaving the agreed terms to stand.

The premises

Generally the new lease will be of 'the holding' (s 32), which is all the property comprised **13.165** in the existing tenancy, excluding any part not occupied by the tenant (e.g. a sub-let part). The parties may agree as to the extent of the premises to be comprised in the new lease.

In the following situations the premises in the new lease may be more or less than 'the **13.166** holding':

(a) **More than the holding**   Under s 32(2), the landlord (but not the tenant) can require the new tenancy to be of the whole of the premises in the current tenancy. A landlord may wish to do this where the tenant has sub-let part of the premises but the landlord has no interest in recovering possession of the sub-let part (e.g. a flat over an office). The landlord would prefer instead to grant a new tenancy of the whole.

(b) **Less than the holding**   Where the landlord has succeeded under ground (f) (demolition or reconstruction; see 13.132) and the tenant has agreed to accept a tenancy of an 'economically separable part' of the holding (see s 31A).

If the current lease includes rights enjoyed by the tenant in connection with the hold- **13.167** ing, those rights will be included in the new lease unless the parties agree to the contrary (s 32(3)). If the parties fail to agree, the court will decide which rights should be included. In *Re No 1 Albemarle Street W1* [1959] Ch 531, the court included in the new tenancy the tenant's existing 'right' to display advertising signs on the outside of the property. However, this was not by virtue of s 32(3) as it was merely personal in nature. Instead the court allowed the right to be included as one of the 'other terms' by virtue of s 35 (see 13.178). Only existing legal rights will be permitted under s 32(3), not equitable rights. In *G Orlik (Meat Products) Ltd v Hastings and Thanet Building Society* [1974] 29 P & CR 126, an informal right to park delivery vans on adjoining land was not granted in the new lease.

Duration

The parties are free to agree whatever length of term they like, but in default of agreement, **13.168** the maximum fixed term that the court can order is 15 years (s 33). The court has a wide discretion and may order such term as it considers reasonable in all the circumstances (subject to the 15-year maximum). The court also has the power to order a periodic tenancy (although this is rare). In the absence of agreement between the parties the new tenancy will commence when the current tenancy ends under s 64, i.e. three months after the application has finally been disposed of. The court should also specify an end date for the new tenancy.

13.169 The court will consider such matters as:

- duration of current tenancy (see *Betty's Cafes Ltd v Phillips Furnishing Stores Ltd* [1959] AC 20);
- length of time tenant has held over under the current tenancy (see *London and Provincial Millinery Stores Ltd v Barclays Bank Ltd* [1962] 2 All ER 163);
- comparative hardship caused to either party (see *Amika Motors Ltd v Colebrook Holdings Ltd* (1981) 259 EG 243);
- landlord's future plans for the property. The court may decide to order a short term where although the landlord at the date of the hearing is unable to show sufficient intention under ground (f) (demolition/reconstruction), the court is satisfied that he will do so in the near future (see *Roehorn v Barry Corporation* [1956] 2 All ER 742, CA). Similarly, the court may order a short term if the landlord narrowly missed being able to rely on ground (g) (own occupation; see 13.144) because of the five-year rule in s 30(2) (see *Upsons Ltd v E Robins Ltd* [1956] 1 QB 131). The court may include a break clause in the lease, which would allow the landlord to end the lease early to carry out future development plans (see *National Car Parks Ltd v The Paternoster Consortium Ltd* [1990] 2 EGLR 99);
- any other factors relevant to the particular case (see *Becker v Hill Street Properties Ltd* [1990] 2 EGLR 78).

Rent

13.170 Rent is usually the most contentious matter between the parties. Section 34(1) provides that the rent shall be that at which 'having regard to the terms of the tenancy (other than those relating to rent), the holding might reasonably be expected to be let in the open market by a willing lessor'. In assessing the rent, the court will usually hear evidence from surveyors or valuers and consider comparable rents in the area ('comparables'). If relevant comparables are not available, the court will consider generally any increases of rent in the locality (see *National Car Parks Ltd v Colebrook Estates Ltd* [1983] 1 EGLR 78). For a more recent case, see *Flanders Community Centre Ltd v Newham LBC* [2016] EWHC 1089 (Ch) on the importance of having reliable and credible expert evidence as to market rent.

13.171 As the other terms of the tenancy will have a bearing on the rent, such other terms are normally agreed before the rent. The courts have approved this as being the most sensible approach (see *Cardshops Ltd v Davies* [1971] 2 All ER 721, CA). The tenant's user covenant in the new lease will be especially relevant when determining the new rent. Landlords often seek a wider use clause so as to command a higher rent (on the basis that a wider use is more attractive to a tenant, thus increasing the rent a tenant in the open market would be willing to pay). In general the courts have been reluctant to permit a relaxation of the user covenant for this purpose (see *Gorleston Golf Club Ltd v Links Estates (Gorleston) Ltd* [1959] CLY 1830 and *Charles Clements (London) Ltd v Rank City Wall Ltd* [1978] 1 EGLR 47).

Disregards when assessing rent

13.172 Under s 34(1), the court when assessing the rent must disregard certain factors which would otherwise work against the tenant. These 'disregards' are similar to those found in a typical rent review clause in a business lease. For further reference on rent review and cases interpreting these disregards, see Chapter 2 of our companion volume, *A Practical Approach to Commercial Conveyancing and Property* (5th edn, OUP, 2016).

The 'disregards' in s 34(1) are: **13.173**

(a) Occupation: *'any effect on rent of the fact that the tenant has or his predecessors in title have been in occupation of the holding'*. Thus the landlord cannot argue for a higher rent on the basis that a tenant in occupation would pay more rent to avoid the expense of moving elsewhere.

(b) Goodwill: *'any goodwill attached to the holding by reason of the carrying on thereat of the business of the tenant (whether by him or by a predecessor of his in that business)'*. If the tenant has through his own efforts generated goodwill in his business, then he should not be penalized for it by having to pay a higher rent.

(c) Improvements: *'any effect on rent of an improvement . . . carried out by a person who at the time it was carried out was the tenant . . . otherwise than in pursuance of an obligation to his immediate landlord'*. This effectively avoids the tenant paying for the improvements twice over; once when the tenant carries them out and again through a consequential uplift in the rent. The words 'otherwise than in pursuance of an obligation to his immediate landlord' (s 34(2)), mean that improvements to the premises that the tenant was obliged to carry out (e.g. under the terms of the lease) will not be disregarded. In other words, such obligatory improvements will be taken into account when assessing the rent.

   In addition under s 34(2), a voluntary improvement will be disregarded only if it has been carried out during the current tenancy, or:

   (i) it was completed not more than 21 years before the application for the new tenancy was made; and

   (ii) the holding or any part of it affected by the improvement has at all times since been comprised in tenancies to which the Act applies; and

   (iii) at the termination of each of those tenancies the tenant did not quit the premises.

(d) For licensed premises only, e.g. a public house, any addition to the value of the premises attributable to the tenant's licence is disregarded (s 34(1)(d)). This includes betting shops licensed under the Betting, Gaming and Lotteries Act 1963 (see *Ganton House Investments v Crossman Investments* [1995] 1 EGLR 239).

Effect on rent of premises in disrepair

If the premises are in disrepair due to the tenant's breach of repairing covenant, should the court disregard the disrepair in assessing the new rent? The courts have supported conflicting approaches to the problem.   **13.174**

The tenant would argue that the disrepair should be taken into account to reflect the actual condition of the premises (thus resulting in a lower rent). The tenant would say that the landlord could always sue him for breach and in that way recover any diminution in the value of the reversion. The tenant would further argue that there is nothing in s 34 directing the court to assume that the premises are in good repair. The tenant's approach was supported by the Court of Appeal in *Fawkes v Viscount Chelsea* [1980] QB 441, where the Court accepted that the rent should be assessed having regard to the actual state of repair of the property. (This case actually concerned a landlord's failure to repair.)   **13.175**

Conversely, the landlord would argue that the disrepair should be disregarded so as to prevent the tenant from prospering from his own wrongdoing. In other words, there should be an assumption that the tenant has performed his repairing obligations. Such an approach was supported by the Court of Appeal in *Family Management v Gray* (1979) 253 EG 369, and later in *Crown Estate Commissioners v Town Investments Ltd* [1992] 1 EGLR 61.   **13.176**

Rent review in new tenancy

13.177 The court is permitted, if it thinks fit, to include a provision in the new lease for varying the rent, i.e. a rent review clause (s 34(3)). This applies irrespective of whether a rent review clause was included in the current lease. However, a court will normally include a review clause if one is present in the current lease. The scope and frequency of the rent review is entirely at the court's discretion. Upward-only reviews are common, but tenants have successfully argued for the inclusion of downward reviews if market rents have fallen (see *Forbouys plc v Newport Borough Council* [1994] 1 EGLR 138).

Other terms of the new tenancy

13.178 In default of agreement the other terms of the lease 'may be determined by the court; and in determining those terms the court shall have regard to the terms of the current tenancy and to all relevant circumstances' (s 35(1)). This includes the operation of the provisions of the Landlord and Tenant (Covenants) Act 1995 (see 13.183). Accordingly, if either party wishes to introduce terms that were not included in the current lease, they must justify this by showing that it is fair and reasonable in all the circumstances.

Help for tenant in the case of O'May

13.179 It is usually the landlord who seeks to introduce new terms under the guise of 'modernizing' the lease. Predictably, these new terms are usually more onerous on the tenant. Such modernization provisions should be resisted by the tenant, who is assisted by the House of Lords' decision in *O'May v City of London Real Property Co. Ltd* [1983] 2 AC 726. In *O'May*, Lord Hailsham gave the following guidance:

> . . . the court must begin by considering the terms of the current tenancy, that the burden of persuading the court to impose a change in those terms against the will of either party must rest on the party proposing the change and the change proposed must in the circumstances of the case be fair and reasonable and should take into account, amongst other things, the comparatively weak negotiating position of a sitting tenant requiring renewal, particularly in conditions of scarcity, and the general purpose of the Act which is to protect the business interests of the tenant so far as they are affected by the approaching termination of the current lease, in particular as regards his security of tenure.

13.180 The landlord in *O'May* failed to show that a proposed new term requiring the tenant to pay a service charge was reasonable, even though the tenant was offered a reduction in rent. The court could see that the landlord's true intention was to shift the burden of maintenance and repair of the building onto the tenant, and this was unjustified.

13.181 Landlords have understandably been critical of *O'May* and maintain that the courts should not shield tenants from commercial reality. They argue that if tenants were taking alternative premises in the area, they would probably have to accept modern provisions in a *new* lease, so why should they not do so in a renewed lease? The landlord is naturally concerned to maintain the value of his reversion, and the acceptability of lease terms to institutional investors is a crucial factor in this. Yet the tenant must not be unfairly disadvantaged in carrying on his business; this is a general purpose of the Act (see the judgment of Denning LJ in *Gold v Brighton Corporation* [1956] 3 All ER 442). Ultimately it is a question of general policy towards commercial property and balancing the respective interests of the landlord and tenant. See also *Edwards & Walkden (Norfolk) Ltd v The Mayor and Commonality and Citizens of the City of London* [2012] EWHC 2527 (Ch).

Guarantors

13.182 The court is able to require the tenant to provide guarantors for the new tenancy (see *Cairnplace Ltd v CBL (Property Investment) Co. Ltd* [1984] 1 All ER 315). This is likely to occur where the tenant has a poor record of paying rent or performing other covenants, or where the tenant is a recent assignee or newly formed company.

Effect of the Landlord and Tenant (Covenants) Act 1995

Alienation covenant in new lease

One area in which the courts may be sympathetic to a landlord seeking to introduce new   **13.183** terms is with regard to the tenant's alienation covenant. If the current lease was granted before 1 January 1996, the old privity of contract rules meant that the original tenant was bound for the entire duration of the lease even after he had assigned it. The change to the privity of contract rule introduced by the Landlord and Tenant (Covenants) Act 1995 ('the 1995 Act') benefited tenants, in that for leases granted on or after 1 January 1996 the tenant was released from liability after assignment. A renewed lease today is therefore a 'new lease' under the 1995 Act, and the landlord's position will be worse than it was under the current lease (assuming the current lease was granted before 1 January 1996).

Authorized guarantee agreements (AGAs)   To reflect the changes introduced by the 1995   **13.184** Act, new leases generally contain more restrictive alienation obligations on the tenant, for example preconditions to be satisfied before assignment and the use of AGAs. Accordingly, to counteract the landlord's loss of privity, the courts will generally permit a modernization of the alienation covenant in the renewed lease to reflect current practice on the grant of new leases. This is reinforced by Schedule 1, para 4 to the 1995 Act, which amends s 35 of the 1954 Act to provide that the reference to 'all relevant circumstances' includes the operation of the provisions of the 1995 Act (s 35(2)). In *Wallis Fashion Group Ltd v CGU Life Assurance Ltd* [2000] 27 EG 145, the landlord argued that the renewal lease should entitle the landlord to an automatic AGA from the assigning tenant. However, Neuberger J held that although there could be an AGA condition, it should be qualified by the words 'where reasonable'. This decision is important for tenants, who can now properly resist any claim by the landlord for an automatic AGA. An AGA is appropriate only if it is reasonable in all the circumstances.

Alternatively, the landlord's loss of privity under the 1995 Act may be counterbalanced by   **13.185** changes to other terms in the lease, including the level of rent. To underline the point, the 1995 Act amends s 34 of the 1954 Act by inserting a new s 34(4) as follows:

> It is hereby declared that the matters which are to be taken into account by the court in determining the rent include any effect on rent of the operation of the provisions of the Landlord and Tenant (Covenants) Act 1995.

Costs of the new tenancy

The question of whether the tenant agrees to pay the landlord's costs in connection with   **13.186** the new lease will depend on the parties' relative bargaining strengths. However, the tenant should endeavour to resist this as it is highly unlikely that the tenant will be forced to do so by the court (see *Cairnplace Ltd v CBL (Property Investment) Co. Ltd* [1984] 1 All ER 315). Section 1 of the Costs of Leases Act 1958 provides that, unless the parties otherwise agree in writing, each party should be responsible for its own costs.

Professional arbitration on court terms (PACT)

To resolve lease renewal disputes, rather than go to court the parties may find it cheaper   **13.187** and more efficient to use an alternative dispute resolution scheme offered jointly by the Law Society and the Royal Institution of Chartered Surveyors (RICS). The PACT scheme (Professional Arbitration on Court Terms) provides an opportunity for landlords and tenants to have the rent and other lease terms decided by a surveyor or solicitor acting as either an independent expert or arbitrator. The professionals appointed are experienced specialists who have been specifically trained under the PACT scheme.

KEY POINTS SUMMARY

TERMS OF THE NEW LEASE

13.188
- The parties' advisers should appreciate the terms a court is likely to order in the lease. This puts them in a stronger negotiating position. In particular:

  - The court will order a new lease of 'the holding' which generally excludes sub-let parts.

  - The maximum fixed term the court can order is 15 years. The duration of the current tenancy will be an important consideration, but there are other factors (see 13.168).

  - In assessing the rent the court will consider comparable rents in the area and disregard the matters in s 34 of the 1954 Act.

  - The court will take into account the effect of the Landlord and Tenant (Covenants) Act 1995 (i.e. landlord's loss of privity) when fixing the rent and other terms (e.g. alienation provisions).

  - Tenants are within their rights to resist a landlord's demand for an automatic AGA; accept an AGA only 'where reasonable'.

COURT ORDER FOR NEW TENANCY

13.189 If the court orders a new tenancy it will not commence until three months after the proceedings are 'finally disposed of' (s 64). The landlord and tenant should execute a lease and counterpart lease respectively (s 36(1)). The parties may agree not to act on the order if they so wish, but such an agreement should be in writing (s 69(2)) and comply with the ordinary principles of contract law.

Revocation of court order

13.190 If the tenant is not satisfied with the terms of the new lease as ordered by the court, it has a last chance to apply to the court within 14 days for the order to be revoked (s 36(2)). In this case the current tenancy will continue for such period as the parties agree, or the court determines, to enable the landlord to re-let or otherwise dispose of the property (s 36(2)). A tenancy which continues under s 36(2) will not be a tenancy to which the 1954 Act applies. Where an order for a new tenancy is revoked, the court may also vary, revoke, or award an order for costs (s 36(3)).

PRACTICAL CHECKLISTS

SUMMARY OF THE 1954 ACT

13.191
- The Act affords statutory protection to 'a tenant who occupies premises for the purposes of a business'.

  - The tenant's statutory protection is twofold: the tenancy automatically continues at the end of the contractual tenancy; and the tenant can apply to the court for a statutory renewal of the tenancy.

- Certain tenancies are excluded from statutory protection, for example fixed-term tenancies not exceeding six months and contracted out tenancies.
- For an agreement to contract out of the security-of-tenure provisions to be valid, the landlord must first serve a 'health warning' on the tenant who, in turn, must sign a declaration that he has received it.
- Tenancies protected by the Act can be terminated only by one of the methods prescribed by the Act.
- The most common methods of termination are by landlord's s 25 notice or tenant's s 26 request.
- The landlord can oppose the tenant's application for a new lease by relying on one or more of the statutory grounds for opposition in s 30. Some of these grounds are at the discretion of the court.
- Section 25 notices and s 26 requests must be in prescribed form and contain prescribed information. There are strict deadlines for service (see 13.102).
- The s 25 notice/s 26 request must be served by/on the 'competent landlord'. Consider serving a s 40 notice to establish the identity of the competent landlord.
- The competent landlord should consider applying to the court for an interim rent to be assessed. If market rents have fallen, the tenant should consider doing so.
- If the landlord successfully opposes a new tenancy under grounds (e), (f), or (g), the landlord will have to pay the tenant compensation for disturbance.
- In default of agreement the court will determine the terms of the new lease.
- In assessing the new rent the court will disregard certain matters such as tenant's occupation, goodwill, and voluntary improvements (s 34).
- If the landlord wishes to impose new terms in the renewed tenancy, the landlord will have to show that it is fair and reasonable in all the circumstances (see *O'May v City of London Real Property Co. Ltd* [1983] 2 AC 726).

ACTING FOR THE LANDLORD

Serving a s 25 notice

- If you want the tenant to leave at the end of the lease, serve a hostile s 25 notice and be sure of your statutory grounds for opposing a new lease.   **13.192**
- Be sure you are the 'competent' landlord for the tenant in question (see 13.84). It may be necessary to serve a notice under s 40 to be sure.
- The s 25 notice must be given not more than 12 months or less than six months before the date of termination specified in the notice; this termination date must not be earlier than the date on which the tenancy could have been terminated at common law (e.g. the contractual expiry date of a fixed term).
- If you are happy for the tenant to continue in occupation under a new lease and wish the new lease to be in place as soon as possible, serve a non-hostile s 25 notice one year before the contractual expiry date specifying the contractual expiry date as the termination date in the notice.
- Ensure that the s 25 notice is in the prescribed form and contains the prescribed content.
- If you receive a tenant's s 26 request and you want the tenant to leave, you must serve a counter-notice within two months specifying your statutory grounds for opposing a new lease.

- Serve by registered post or recorded delivery (in which case service is deemed to be the date of postage).

Landlord's statutory grounds under s 30(1)

Four of the seven grounds are discretionary. They are the tenant's 'fault' grounds—(a) tenant's failure to repair; (b) tenant's delay in paying rent; and (c) tenant's breaches of other obligations—and ground (e) on sub-letting of part where the superior landlord requires the whole property for subsequent letting.

- You cannot amend your grounds at a later date, so be sure of them when the notices are served.
- Grounds (f) (demolish/reconstruct) and (g) (landlord's occupation) are the most frequently used grounds. They require a firm and settled intention on the landlord's part, to be established at the date of the hearing.
- Ground (f) (demolish/reconstruct) will not be established if the tenant is willing to accept a new tenancy of part of the holding, or under the new lease the landlord is allowed access to do the works.
- Ground (g) (landlord's occupation) will not be established if the landlord acquired the reversion less than five years before the end of the current tenancy.
- Grounds (d), (e), or (f) may be proven under the 'near miss' rule if the landlord can show he could have established them within 12 months.

Landlord's obligation to pay compensation

- The landlord must pay the tenant compensation for disturbance if he establishes one or more of the 'non fault' grounds ((e), (f), or (g)).
- The amount of compensation is the rateable value of the holding x 1. However, the landlord must pay double compensation if the tenant or predecessors in the same business have occupied for at least 14 years.
- The parties may exclude compensation by agreement, unless the tenant or predecessor in the same business has been in occupation for five years or more.

ACTING FOR THE TENANT

Responding to a s 25 notice

13.193
- If you receive a landlord's s 25 notice and you want to renew your lease, ensure that you apply to the court for a new lease on or before the date specified in the s 25 notice.
- If you have not received a s 25 notice by the time there is less than 12 months to go on the lease, consider a 'pre-emptive strike' by serving a s 26 request and specifying a commencement date for the new lease 12 months hence.

Serving a s 26 request

- Serve the s 26 request on your 'competent' landlord (see 13.84). It may be necessary to serve a notice under s 40 to be sure.
- Ensure that your s 26 request is in the prescribed form and contains the prescribed content.
- If you serve a s 26 request, be sure to apply to the court for a new lease before the date specified in the s 26 request.

- Serve by registered post or recorded delivery (in which case service is deemed to be the date of postage).

Tenant's right to compensation for failure to secure new lease

- The landlord must pay the tenant compensation for disturbance if he establishes one or more of the 'non-fault' grounds ((e), (f), or (g)).
- The current amount of compensation is the rateable value of the holding x 1. However, the landlord must pay double compensation if the tenant or predecessors in the same business have occupied for at least 14 years.
- The parties may exclude compensation by agreement, unless the tenant or predecessor in the same business has been in occupation for five years or more.

NEGOTIATING THE TERMS OF THE RENEWED LEASE

Appreciate what terms a court would be likely to order in the lease. This puts you in a stronger **13.194** negotiating position. In particular:

- The court will order a new lease of 'the holding', which generally excludes sub-let parts.
- The maximum fixed term the court can order is 15 years. The duration of the current tenancy will be an important consideration, but there are other factors too.
- In assessing the rent the court will consider comparable rents in the area and disregard the matters in s 34 of the 1954 Act.
- The court will take into account the effect of the Landlord and Tenant (Covenants) Act 1995 (i.e. landlord's loss of privity) when fixing the rent and other terms (e.g. alienation provisions).
- Consider the case of *O'May v City of London Real Property Co. Ltd* [1983] 2 AC 726. Any variations from the current lease must be fair and reasonable in all the circumstances. This will prevent the landlord from 'modernizing' the lease unfairly.
- Consider using professional arbitration on court terms (PACT) as a means of resolving lease renewal disputes; it is likely to be quicker, cheaper, and more efficient than going to court.

KEY REFORMS INTRODUCED ON 1 JUNE 2004

Contracting out   **13.195**

It is no longer necessary to apply to the court for an order approving an agreement to contract out of the security of tenure provisions of the Act. The landlord must serve a prior 'health warning' notice on the tenant. The tenant must sign a declaration that he has received and accepted the consequences of the notice.

- The prescribed form of s 25 notice and s 26 request has changed. Use the up-to-date forms.
- The requirement for the tenant to serve a counter-notice to a landlord's s 25 notice is abolished.
- When serving a 'non-hostile' s 25 notice, the landlord must include in the notice the key terms of the proposed new tenancy.
- Following service of a s 40 notice, the recipient has a duty to revise the information supplied if circumstances change.
- Both landlords and tenants are now permitted to apply to the court for the terms of a new tenancy to be settled.

- There are new time limits for applications to the court to renew tenancies and the parties can agree to extend these.

- Landlords are permitted to apply for an order that the tenancy be terminated without renewal if they can make out one of the statutory grounds for opposition.

- Ownership and control of businesses. The circumstances in which landlords and tenants can operate the procedures under the Act are widened. In particular, an individual and any company he controls should be treated as one and the same and companies controlled by one individual should be treated as members of a group of companies.

- Interim rent. Tenants as well as landlords can apply to the court for an interim rent. The date from which interim rent is payable becomes the earliest date for renewal of the tenancy which could have been specified in the s 25 notice or s 26 request. Where the landlord does not oppose the renewal, the interim rent is likely to be set at the same level as the rent for the new tenancy, i.e. the market rent.

APPENDIX 1

Additional Chapter

An additional chapter to accompany this text can be found at the following location: www.oxfordtextbooks.co.uk/orc/apaconveyancing20e/.

COMMONHOLDS

It has been the law for many years that positive obligations cannot be enforced in freehold land. In essence a burden of a positive covenant does not run with the land; see *Auterberry v Oldham Corporation* (1885) 29 ChD 750. To deal with this problem, the legislatures introduced commonhold land. This is defined in the Commonhold and Leasehold Reform Act 2002 (CLRA) as the land specified in the memorandum of association in relation to which a commonhold association exercises functions (see s 1(1)). It is in effect the name for the special way freehold land will be held by a community of freeholders entitled to participate in the association. Each separate property in a commonhold development will be termed a unit. A unit can be either residential or commercial and the owner will be the unit-holder. There will be a commonhold association that will own and manage the common parts. It will be a company limited by guarantee, where all the members will be the unit-holders. Thus unit owners will have a duality of ownership. First they will own their units and, second, they will own a share of the commonhold association and thus indirectly the common parts.

All commonhold will be registrable at Land Registry, which will require on registration a Commonhold Community Statement (CCS) and the memorandum and articles of association. The CCS will contain the rules and regulations for the commonhold. It will be possible for owners of existing non-commonhold property to seek to convert their title to a commonhold arrangement, but 100 per cent of all owners will have to agree to the conversion. The freeholder must consent to the conversion, without which it cannot proceed.

In summary, the unit-holder will in effect own, freehold-style, his or her flat or property instead of being a leaseholder. The unit-holder will share in the running of the commonhold-held common parts and be required to pay a management or service charge. Unlike leaseholds, the units will not be wasting assets; neither will they be at the whim of a freeholder and/or the freeholder's management policies.

APPENDIX 2

List of Useful Websites

The Internet websites are listed alphabetically. If you wish to access Internet sites, please note that to save time when using most of the leading web browsers, you can leave out the prefix **http://** when inputting site addresses. Website addresses change frequently. If you have difficulty in locating any of these sites, try searching for them using a web search site such as **http://search.yahoo.com**, **https://www.bing.com**, or **http://www.google.co.uk** and by searching against the main title of the site itself. This should produce a search result that will take you to the correct location.

1. Acts of Parliament: **www.legislation.gov.uk/ukpga**
2. Association of British Insurers: **www.abi.org.uk**
3. Bank of England: **www.bankofengland.co.uk**
4. Building Societies Association: **www.bsa.org.uk**
5. Canal & River Trust: **www.canalrivertrust.org.uk**
6. Chancelcheck, for chancel repairs liability checks: **www.clsl.co.uk**
7. Chartered Institute of Arbitrators: **www.ciarb.org**
8. Chartered Surveyors, the Royal Institution of Chartered Surveyors: **www.rics.org**
9. Coal Mining Report Service: **https://www.groundstability.com/public/web/home.xhtml**
10. Companies House: **https://www.gov.uk/government/organisations/companies-house**
11. UK Finance formerly the Council of Mortgage Lenders: **https://www.ukfinance.org.uk**
12. Countrywide Legal Indemnities: **www.countrywidelegal.co.uk**
13. Energy Saving Trust: **www.energysavingtrust.org.uk**
14. Environment Agency: **https://www.gov.uk/government/organisations/environment-agency**
15. Estates Gazette: **https://www.egi.co.uk/Property/Home.aspx**
16. Financial Conduct Authority: **www.fca.org.uk**
17. First-tier Tribunal (Property Chamber): **https://www.gov.uk/courts-tribunals/first-tier-tribunal-property-chamber**
18. Solicitors' online conveyancing division: **www.legalmove.com**
19. Highways England, formerly Highways Agency: **https://www.gov.uk/government/organisations/highways-england**
20. HM L and Registry Internet register access: **https://www.gov.uk/government/organisations/land-registry**
21. HM Revenue & Customs: **https://www.gov.uk/government/organisations/hm-revenue-customs**
22. HM Treasury: **www.gov.uk/government/organisations/hm-treasury**
23. Homes England, formerly Home and Communities Agency: **https://www.gov.uk/government/organisations/homes-england**
24. Landmark, formerly Homecheck: **https://reportfinder.landmark.co.uk/?source=homecheck**
25. House of Lords' judgments: **www.publications.parliament.uk/pa/ld/ldjudgmt.htm**
26. An Islamic Bank of Britain, Sharia compliant: **http://www.alrayanbank.co.uk/**
27. Jordans Limited: **www.jordans.co.uk**
28. Land Registry: **https://www.gov.uk/government/organisations/land-registry**
29. Landmark Information group (property and environmental risk information): **www.landmark.co.uk**
30. Upper Tribunal (Lands Chamber): **https://www.gov.uk/courts-tribunals/upper-tribunal-lands-chamber**

31. Law Commission: **https://www.lawcom.gov.uk/**
32. Law Society: **www.lawsociety.org.uk**
33. *Law Society Gazette*: **www.lawgazette.co.uk**
34. Licensed Conveyancers (the Council for Licensed Conveyancers): **http://www.clc-uk.org/**
35. Location statistics: **www.zoopla.co.uk**
36. Ministry of Justice: **www.gov.uk/government/organisations/ministry-of-justice**
37. National Association of Estate Agents: **www.naea.co.uk**
38. National House Building Council: **www.nhbc.co.uk**
39. National Land Information Service: **www.nlis.org.uk**
40. Office for National Statistics: **www.statistics.gov.uk**
41. Online SDLT submissions: **www.sdlt.co.uk**
42. Ordnance Survey: **www.ordnancesurvey.co.uk**
43. Practical Law Company: **www.uk.practicallaw.com**
44. Public Record Office (The National Archives): **www.nationalarchives.gov.uk**
45. Registers of Scotland: **www.ros.gov.uk**
46. Royal Institute of British Architects: **www.architecture.com**
47. Royal Town Planning Institute: **www.rtpi.org.uk**
48. Searchflow: **www.searchflow.co.uk**
49. Sitecheck (Landmark Information Group): **https://www.landmark.co.uk/landmark-legal52**
50. Solicitors Regulation Authority: **www.sra.org.uk**
51. Streetmap anywhere in the UK: **www.streetmap.co.uk**
52. TM Property Service Limited: **www.tmgroup.co.uk**
53. UK Parliament: **www.parliament.uk**
54. Valuation Office Agency: **https://www.gov.uk/government/organisations/valuation-office-agency**
55. Verderers of the New Forest: **www.verderers.org.uk**
56. Water UK: **www.water.org.uk**

(All website addresses correct as at 01 March 2018.)

The Law Society Conveyancing Protocol

A specimen copy of the Law Society Conveyancing Protocol can be accessed online at http://www.lawsociety.org.uk/advice/articles/conveyancing-protocol/.

APPENDIX 4

Standard Conditions of Sale (5th edition) (National Conditions of Sale, 25th edition, Law Society's Conditions of Sale 2011)

1. GENERAL

1.1 Definitions

1.1.1 In these conditions:
- (a) 'accrued interest' means:
  - (i) if money has been placed on deposit or in a building society share account, the interest actually earned
  - (ii) otherwise, the interest which might reasonably have been earned by depositing the money at interest on seven days' notice of withdrawal with a clearing bank less, in either case, any proper charges for handling the money
- (b) 'clearing bank' means a bank which is a shareholder in CHAPS Clearing Co. Limited
- (c) 'completion date' has the meaning given in condition 6.1.1
- (d) 'contents price' means any separate amount payable for contents included in the contract
- (e) 'contract rate' means the Law Society's interest rate from time to time in force
- (f) 'conveyancer' means a solicitor, barrister, duly certified notary public, licensed conveyancer or recognised body under sections 9 or 23 of the Administration of Justice Act 1985
- (g) 'lease' includes sub-lease, tenancy and agreement for a lease or sub-lease
- (h) 'mortgage' means a mortgage or charge securing the repayment of money
- (i) 'notice to complete' means a notice requiring completion of the contract in accordance with condition 6.8
- (j) 'public requirement' means any notice, order or proposal given or made (whether before or after the date of the contract) by a body acting on statutory authority
- (k) 'requisition' includes objection
- (l) 'transfer' includes conveyance and assignment
- (m) 'working day' means any day from Monday to Friday (inclusive) which is not Christmas Day, Good Friday or a statutory Bank Holiday.

1.1.2 In these conditions the terms 'absolute title' and 'official copies' have the special meanings given to them by the Land Registration Act 2002.

1.1.3 A party is ready, able and willing to complete:
- (a) if he could be, but for the default of the other party, and
- (b) in the case of the seller, even though the property remains subject to a mortgage, if the amount to be paid on completion enables the property to be transferred freed of all mortgages (except any to which the sale is expressly subject).

1.1.4 These conditions apply except as varied or excluded by the contract.

1.2 Joint parties

If there is more than one seller or more than one buyer, the obligations which they undertake can be enforced against them all jointly or against each individually.

1.3   Notices and documents

1.3.1 A notice required or authorised by the contract must be in writing.

1.3.2 Giving a notice or delivering a document to a party's conveyancer has the same effect as giving or delivering it to that party.

1.3.3 Where delivery of the original document is not essential, a notice or document is validly given or sent if it is sent:

(a) by fax, or

(b) by e-mail to an e-mail address for the intended recipient given in the contract.

1.3.4 Subject to conditions 1.3.5 to 1.3.7, a notice is given and a document is delivered when it is received.

1.3.5 (a) A notice or document sent through a document exchange is received when it is available for collection.

(b) A notice or document which is received after 4.00pm on a working day, or on a day which is not a working day, is to be treated as having been received on the next working day.

(c) An automated response to a notice or document sent by e-mail that the intended recipient is out of the office is to be treated as proof that the notice or document was not received.

1.3.6 Condition 1.3.7 applies unless there is proof:

(a) that a notice or document has not been received, or

(b) of when it was received.

1.3.7 A notice or document sent by the following means is treated as having been received as follows:

(a)	by first-class post:	before 4.00pm on the second working day after posting
(b)	by second-class post:	before 4.00pm on the third working day after posting
(c)	through a document exchange:	before 4.00pm on the first working day after the day on which it would normally be available for collection by the addressee
(d)	by fax:	one hour after despatch
(e)	by e-mail:	before 4.00pm on the first working day after despatch.

1.4   VAT

1.4.1 The purchase price and the contents price are inclusive of any value added tax.

1.4.2 All other sums made payable by the contract are exclusive of any value added tax and where a supply is made which is chargeable to value added tax, the recipient of the supply is to pay the supplier (in addition to any other amounts payable under the contract) a sum equal to the value added tax chargeable on that supply.

1.5   Assignment and sub-sales

1.5.1 The buyer is not entitled to transfer the benefit of the contract.

1.5.2 The seller cannot be required to transfer the property in parts or to any person other than the buyer.

1.6   Third party rights

Unless otherwise expressly stated nothing in this contract will create rights pursuant to the Contracts (Rights of Third Parties) Act 1999 in favour of anyone other than the parties to the contract.

2. FORMATION

2.1 Date

2.1.1 If the parties intend to make a contract by exchanging duplicate copies by post or through a document exchange, the contract is made when the last copy is posted or deposited at the document exchange.

2.1.2 If the parties' conveyancers agree to treat exchange as taking place before duplicate copies are actually exchanged, the contract is made as so agreed.

2.2 Deposit

2.2.1 The buyer is to pay or send a deposit of 10 per cent of the purchase price no later than the date of the contract.

2.2.2 If a cheque tendered in payment of all or part of the deposit is dishonoured when first presented, the seller may, within seven working days of being notified that the cheque has been dishonoured, give notice to the buyer that the contract is discharged by the buyer's breach.

2.2.3 Conditions 2.2.4 to 2.2.6 do not apply on a sale by auction.

2.2.4 The deposit is to be paid:
  (a) by electronic means from an account held in the name of a conveyancer at a clearing bank to an account in the name of the seller's conveyancer or (in a case where condition 2.2.5 applies) a conveyancer nominated by him and maintained at a clearing bank, or
  (b) to the seller's conveyancer or (in a case where condition 2.2.5 applies) a conveyancer nominated by him by cheque drawn on a solicitor's or licensed conveyancer's client account.

2.2.5 If before completion date the seller agrees to buy another property in England and Wales for his residence, he may use all or any part of the deposit as a deposit in that transaction to be held on terms to the same effect as this condition and condition 2.2.6.

2.2.6 Any deposit or part of a deposit not being used in accordance with condition 2.2.5 is to be held by the seller's conveyancer as stakeholder on terms that on completion it is paid to the seller with accrued interest.

2.3 Auctions

2.3.1 On a sale by auction the following conditions apply to the property and, if it is sold in lots, to each lot.

2.3.2 The sale is subject to a reserve price.

2.3.3 The seller, or a person on his behalf, may bid up to the reserve price.

2.3.4 The auctioneer may refuse any bid.

2.3.5 If there is a dispute about a bid, the auctioneer may resolve the dispute or restart the auction at the last undisputed bid.

2.3.6 The deposit is to be paid to the auctioneer as agent for the seller.

3. MATTERS AFFECTING THE PROPERTY

3.1 Freedom from incumbrances

3.1.1 The seller is selling the property free from incumbrances, other than those mentioned in condition 3.1.2.

3.1.2 The incumbrances subject to which the property is sold are:
  (a) those specified in the contract
  (b) those discoverable by inspection of the property before the date of the contract
  (c) those the seller does not and could not reasonably know about
  (d) those, other than mortgages, which the buyer knows about
  (e) entries made before the date of the contract in any public register except those main-tained by the Land Registry or its Land Charges Department or by Companies House
  (f) public requirements.

3.1.3 After the contract is made, the seller is to give the buyer written details without delay of any new public requirement and of anything in writing which he learns about concerning a matter covered by condition 3.1.2.

3.1.4 The buyer is to bear the cost of complying with any outstanding public requirement and is to indemnify the seller against any liability resulting from a public requirement.

3.2 Physical state

3.2.1 The buyer accepts the property in the physical state it is in at the date of the contract unless the seller is building or converting it.

3.2.2 A leasehold property is sold subject to any subsisting breach of a condition or tenant's obligation relating to the physical state of the property which renders the lease liable to forfeiture.

3.2.3 A sub-lease is granted subject to any subsisting breach of a condition or tenant's obligation relating to the physical state of the property which renders the seller's own lease liable to forfeiture.

3.3 Leases affecting the property

3.3.1 The following provisions apply if any part of the property is sold subject to a lease.

3.3.2 (a) The seller having provided the buyer with full details of each lease or copies of the documents embodying the lease terms, the buyer is treated as entering into the contract knowing and fully accepting those terms.
  (b) The seller is to inform the buyer without delay if the lease ends or if the seller learns of any application by the tenant in connection with the lease; the seller is then to act as the buyer reasonably directs, and the buyer is to indemnify him against all consequent loss and expense.
  (c) Except with the buyer's consent, the seller is not to agree to any proposal to change the lease terms nor to take any step to end the lease.
  (d) The seller is to inform the buyer without delay of any change to the lease terms which may be proposed or agreed.
  (e) The buyer is to indemnify the seller against all claims arising from the lease after actual completion; this includes claims which are unenforceable against a buyer for want of registration.
  (f) The seller takes no responsibility for what rent is lawfully recoverable, nor for whether or how any legislation affects the lease.
  (g) If the let land is not wholly within the property, the seller may apportion the rent.

4. TITLE AND TRANSFER

4.1 Proof of title

4.1.1 Without cost to the buyer, the seller is to provide the buyer with proof of the title to the property and of his ability to transfer it, or to procure its transfer.

4.1.2 Where the property has a registered title the proof is to include official copies of the items referred to in rules 134(1)(a) and (b) and 135(1)(a) of the Land Registration Rules 2003, so far as they are not to be discharged or overridden at or before completion.

4.1.3 Where the property has an unregistered title, the proof is to include:
(a) an abstract of title or an epitome of title with photocopies of the documents, and
(b) production of every document or an abstract, epitome or copy of it with an original marking by a conveyancer either against the original or an examined abstract or an examined copy.

4.2 Requisitions

4.2.1 The buyer may not raise requisitions:
(a) on any title shown by the seller before the contract was made
(b) in relation to the matters covered by condition 3.1.2.

4.2.2 Notwithstanding condition 4.2.1, the buyer may, within six working days of a matter coming to his attention after the contract was made, raise written requisitions on that matter. In that event, steps 3 and 4 in condition 4.3.1 apply.

4.2.3 On the expiry of the relevant time limit under condition 4.2.2 or condition 4.3.1, the buyer loses his right to raise requisitions or to make observations.

4.3 Timetable

4.3.1 Subject to condition 4.2 and to the extent that the seller did not take the steps described in condition 4.1.1 before the contract was made, the following are the steps for deducing and investigating the title to the property to be taken within the following time limits:

Step	Time Limit
1. The seller is to comply with Condition 4.1.1	Immediately after making the contract
2. The buyer may raise written requisitions	Six working days after either the date of the contract or the date of delivery of the seller's evidence of title on which the requisitions are raised, whichever is the later
3. The seller is to reply in writing to any requisitions raised	Four working days after receiving the requisitions
4. The buyer may raise written observations on the seller's replies	Three working days after receiving the replies

The time limit on the buyer's right to raise requisitions applies even where the seller supplies incomplete evidence of his title, but the buyer may, within six working days from delivery of any further evidence, raise further requisitions resulting from that evidence.

4.3.2 The parties are to take the following steps to prepare and agree the transfer of the property within the following time limits:

Step	Time Limit
A. The buyer is to send the seller a draft transfer	At least twelve working days before completion date
B. The seller is to approve or revise that draft and either return it or retain it for use as the actual transfer	Four working days after delivery of the draft transfer
C. If the draft is returned the buyer is to send an engrossment to the seller	At least five working days before completion date

4.3.3 Periods of time under conditions 4.3.1 and 4.3.2 may run concurrently.

4.3.4 If the period between the date of the contract and completion date is less than 15 working days, the time limits in conditions 4.2.2, 4.3.1 and 4.3.2 are to be reduced by the same proportion as that period bears to the period of 15 working days. Fractions of a working day are to be rounded down except that the time limit to perform any step is not to be less than one working day.

4.4 Defining the property

The seller need not:

(a) prove the exact boundaries of the property
(b) prove who owns fences, ditches, hedges or walls
(c) separately identify parts of the property with different titles further than he may be able to do from information in his possession.

4.5 Rents and rentcharges

The fact that a rent or rentcharges, whether payable or receivable by the owner of the property, has been, or will on completion be, informally apportioned is not to be regarded as a defect in title.

4.6 Transfer

4.6.1 The buyer does not prejudice his right to raise requisitions, or to require replies to any raised, by taking any steps in relation to preparing or agreeing the transfer.

4.6.2 Subject to condition 4.6.3, the seller is to transfer the property with full title guarantee.

4.6.3 The transfer is to have effect as if the disposition is expressly made subject to all matters covered by condition 3.1.2 and, if the property is leasehold, is to contain a statement that the covenants set out in section 4 of the Law of Property (Miscellaneous Provisions) Act 1994 will not extend to any breach of the tenant's covenants in the lease relating to the physical state of the property.

4.6.4 If after completion the seller will remain bound by any obligation affecting the property which was disclosed to the buyer before the contract was made, but the law does not imply any covenant by the buyer to indemnify the seller against liability for future breaches of it:

(a) the buyer is to covenant in the transfer to indemnify the seller against liability for any future breach of the obligation and to perform it from then on, and
(b) if required by the seller, the buyer is to execute and deliver to the seller on completion a duplicate transfer prepared by the buyer.

4.6.5 The seller is to arrange at his expense that, in relation to every document of title which the buyer does not receive on completion, the buyer is to have the benefit of:

(a) a written acknowledgement of his right to its production, and
(b) a written undertaking for its safe custody (except while it is held by a mortgagee or by someone in a fiduciary capacity).

4.7 Membership of company

Where the seller is, or is required to be, a member of a company that has an interest in the property or has management responsibilities for the property or the surrounding areas, the seller is, without cost to the buyer, to provide such documents on completion as will enable the buyer to become a member of that company.

5. RISK, INSURANCE AND OCCUPATION PENDING COMPLETION

5.1.1 The property is at the risk of the buyer from the date of the contract.

5.1.2 The seller is under no obligation to the buyer to insure the property unless:

(a) the contract provides that a policy effected by or for the seller and insuring the property or any part of it against liability for loss or damage is to continue in force, or

(b) the property or any part of it is let on terms under which the seller (whether as landlord or as tenant) is obliged to insure against loss or damage.

5.1.3 If the seller is obliged to insure the property under condition 5.1.2, the seller is to:

(a) do everything necessary to maintain the policy

(b) permit the buyer to inspect the policy or evidence of its terms

(c) if before completion the property suffers loss or damage:

(i) pay to the buyer on completion the amount of the policy monies which the seller has received, so far as not applied in repairing or reinstating the property, and

(ii) if no final payment has then been received, assign to the buyer, at the buyer's expense, all rights to claim under the policy in such form as the buyer reasonably requires and pending execution of the assignment hold any policy monies received in trust for the buyer

(d) cancel the policy on completion.

5.1.4 Where the property is leasehold and the property, or any building containing it, is insured by a reversioner or other third party, the seller is to use reasonable efforts to ensure that the insurance is maintained until completion and if, before completion, the property or building suffers loss or damage the seller is to assign to the buyer on completion, at the buyer's expense, such rights as the seller may have in the policy monies, in such form as the buyer reasonably requires.

5.1.5 If payment under a policy effected by or for the buyer is reduced, because the property is covered against loss or damage by an insurance policy effected by or on behalf of the seller, then, unless the seller is obliged to insure the property under condition 5.1.2, the purchase price is to be abated by the amount of that reduction.

5.1.6 Section 47 of the Law of Property Act 1925 does not apply.

5.2 Occupation by buyer

5.2.1 If the buyer is not already lawfully in the property, and the seller agrees to let him into occupation, the buyer occupies on the following terms.

5.2.2 The buyer is a licensee and not a tenant. The terms of the licence are that the buyer:

(a) cannot transfer it

(b) may permit members of his household to occupy the property

(c) is to pay or indemnify the seller against all outgoings and other expenses in respect of the property

(d) is to pay the seller a fee calculated at the contract rate on a sum equal to the purchase price (less any deposit paid) for the period of the licence

(e) is entitled to any rents and profits from any part of the property which he does not occupy

(f) is to keep the property in as good a state of repair as it was in when he went in to occupation (except for fair wear and tear) and is not to alter it

(g) if the property is leasehold, is not to do anything which puts the seller in breach of his obligations in the lease, and

(h) is to quit the property when the licence ends.

5.2.3 The buyer is not in occupation for the purposes of this condition if he merely exercises rights of access given solely to do work agreed by the seller.

5.2.4 The buyer's licence ends on the earliest of: completion date, rescission of the contract or when five working days' notice given by one party to the other takes effect.

5.2.5 If the buyer is in occupation of the property after his licence has come to an end and the contract is subsequently completed he is to pay the seller compensation for his continued occupation calculated at the same rate as the fee mentioned in condition 5.2.2(d).

5.2.6 The buyer's right to raise requisitions is unaffected.

6. COMPLETION

6.1 Date

6.1.1 Completion date is twenty working days after the date of the contract but time is not of the essence of the contract unless a notice to complete has been served.

6.1.2 If the money due on completion is received after 2.00pm, completion is to be treated, for the purposes only of conditions 6.3 and 7.2, as taking place on the next working day as a result of the buyer's default.

6.1.3 Condition 6.1.2 does not apply and the seller is treated as in default if:
(a) the sale is with vacant possession of the property or any part of it, and
(b) the buyer is ready, able and willing to complete but does not pay the money due on completion until after 2.00pm because the seller has not vacated the property or that part by that time.

6.2 Arrangements and place

6.2.1 The buyer's conveyancer and the seller's conveyancer are to co-operate in agreeing arrangements for completing the contract.

6.2.2 Completion is to take place in England and Wales, either at the seller's conveyancer's office or at some other place which the seller reasonably specifies.

6.3 Apportionments

6.3.1 On evidence of proper payment being made, income and outgoings of the property are to be apportioned between the parties so far as the change of ownership on completion will affect entitlement to receive or liability to pay them.

6.3.2 If the whole property is sold with vacant possession or the seller exercises his option in condition 7.2.4, apportionment is to be made with effect from the date of actual completion; otherwise, it is to be made from completion date.

6.3.3 In apportioning any sum, it is to be assumed that the seller owns the property until the end of the day from which apportionment is made and that the sum accrues from day to day at the rate at which it is payable on that day.

6.3.4 For the purpose of apportioning income and outgoings, it is to be assumed that they accrue at an equal daily rate throughout the year.

6.3.5 When a sum to be apportioned is not known or easily ascertainable at completion, a provisional apportionment is to be made according to the best estimate available. As soon as the amount is known, a final apportionment is to be made and notified to the other party. Any resulting balance is to be paid no more than ten working days later, and if not then paid the balance is to bear interest at the contract rate from then until payment.

6.3.6 Compensation payable under condition 5.2.5 is not to be apportioned.

6.4 Amount payable

The amount payable by the buyer on completion is the purchase price and the contents price (less any deposit already paid to the seller or his agent) adjusted to take account of:

(a) apportionments made under condition 6.3

(b) any compensation to be paid or allowed under condition 7.2

(c) any sum payable under condition 5.1.3.

6.5 Title deeds

6.5.1 As soon as the buyer has complied with all his obligations under this contract on completion the seller must hand over the documents of title.

6.5.2 Condition 6.5.1 does not apply to any documents of title relating to land being retained by the seller after completion.

6.6 Rent receipts

The buyer is to assume that whoever gave any receipt for a payment of rent or service charge which the seller produces was the person or the agent of the person then entitled to that rent or service charge.

6.7 Means of payment

The buyer is to pay the money due on completion by a direct transfer of cleared funds from an account held in the name of a conveyancer at a clearing bank and, if appropriate, an unconditional release of a deposit held by a stakeholder.

6.8 Notice to complete

6.8.1 At any time after the time applicable under condition 6.1.2 on completion date, a party who is ready, able and willing to complete may give the other a notice to complete.

6.8.2 The parties are to complete the contract within ten working days of giving a notice to complete, excluding the day on which the notice is given. For this purpose, time is of the essence of the contract.

6.8.3 On receipt of a notice to complete:

(a) if the buyer paid no deposit, he is forthwith to pay a deposit of 10 per cent

(b) if the buyer paid a deposit of less than 10 per cent, he is forthwith to pay a further deposit equal to the balance of that 10 per cent.

7. REMEDIES

7.1 Errors and omissions

7.1.1 If any plan or statement in the contract, or in the negotiations leading to it, is or was misleading or inaccurate due to an error or omission by the seller, the remedies available to the buyer are as follows.

(a) When there is a material difference between the description or value of the property, or of any of the contents included in the contract, as represented and as it is, the buyer is entitled to damages.

(b) An error or omission only entitles the buyer to rescind the contract:

(i) where it results from fraud or recklessness, or

(ii) where he would be obliged, to his prejudice, to accept property differing substantially (in quantity, quality or tenure) from what the error or omission had led him to expect.

7.1.2 If either party rescinds the contract:

(a) unless the rescission is a result of the buyer's breach of contract the deposit is to be repaid to the buyer with accrued interest

(b) the buyer is to return any documents he received from the seller and is to cancel any registration of the contract.

7.2   Late completion

7.2.1 If there is default by either or both of the parties in performing their obligations under the contract and completion is delayed, the party whose total period of default is the greater is to pay compensation to the other party.

7.2.2 Compensation is calculated at the contract rate on an amount equal to the purchase price, less (where the buyer is the paying party) any deposit paid, for the period by which the paying party's default exceeds that of the receiving party, or, if shorter, the period between completion date and actual completion.

7.2.3 Any claim for loss resulting from delayed completion is to be reduced by any compensation paid under this contract.

7.2.4 Where the buyer holds the property as tenant of the seller and completion is delayed, the seller may give notice to the buyer, before the date of actual completion, that he intends to take the net income from the property until completion. If he does so, he cannot claim compensation under condition 7.2.1 as well.

7.3   After completion

Completion does not cancel liability to perform any outstanding obligation under this contract.

7.4   Buyer's failure to comply with notice to complete

7.4.1 If the buyer fails to complete in accordance with a notice to complete, the following terms apply.

7.4.2 The seller may rescind the contract, and if he does so:
   (a) he may:
      (i)   forfeit and keep any deposit and accrued interest
      (ii) resell the property and any contents included in the contract
      (iii) claim damages
   (b) the buyer is to return any documents he received from the seller and is to cancel any registration of the contract.

7.4.3 The seller retains his other rights and remedies.

7.5   Seller's failure to comply with notice to complete

7.5.1 If the seller fails to complete in accordance with a notice to complete, the following terms apply.

7.5.2 The buyer may rescind the contract, and if he does so:
   (a) the deposit is to be repaid to the buyer with accrued interest
   (b) the buyer is to return any documents he received from the seller and is, at the seller's expense, to cancel any registration of the contract.

7.5.3 The buyer retains his other rights and remedies.

8. LEASEHOLD PROPERTY

8.1   Existing leases

8.1.1 The following provisions apply to a sale of leasehold land.

8.1.2 The seller having provided the buyer with copies of the documents embodying the lease terms, the buyer is treated as entering into the contract knowing and fully accepting those terms.

8.2 New leases

8.2.1 The following provisions apply to a contract to grant a new lease.

8.2.2 The conditions apply so that:
'seller' means the proposed landlord
'buyer' means the proposed tenant
'purchase price' means the premium to be paid on the grant of a lease.

8.2.3 The lease is to be in the form of the draft attached to the contract.

8.2.4 If the term of the new lease will exceed seven years, the seller is to deduce a title which will enable the buyer to register the lease at the Land Registry with an absolute title.

8.2.5 The seller is to engross the lease and a counterpart of it and is to send the counterpart to the buyer at least five working days before completion date.

8.2.6 The buyer is to execute the counterpart and deliver it to the seller on completion.

8.3 Consent

8.3.1 (a) The following provisions apply if a consent to let, assign or sub-let is required to complete the contract.
 (b) In this condition 'consent' means consent in the form which satisfies the requirement to obtain it.

8.3.2 (a) The seller is to apply for the consent at his expense, and to use all reasonable efforts to obtain it.
 (b) The buyer is to provide all information and references reasonably required.

8.3.3 Unless he is in breach of his obligation under condition 8.3.2, either party may rescind the contract by notice to the other party if three working days before completion date (or before a later date on which the parties have agreed to complete the contract):
 (a) the consent has not been given, or
 (b) the consent has been given subject to a condition to which a party reasonably objects. In that case, neither party is to be treated as in breach of contract and condition 7.1.2 applies.

9. CONTENTS

9.1 The following provisions apply to any contents which are included in the contract, whether or not a separate price is to be paid for them.

9.2 The contract takes effect as a contract for sale of goods.

9.3 The buyer takes the contents in the physical state they are in at the date of the contract.

9.4 Ownership of the contents passes to the buyer on actual completion.

APPENDIX 5

The Law Society's Standard Form of Contract

Only pages 1 and 4 of the contract are reproduced here. Pages 2 and 3 are the Standard Conditions of Sale which are set out in Appendix 4. The contract has been drafted on the basis of a sale by Christopher Hunt of the registered title set out in Appendix 15.

CONTRACT

Incorporating the Standard Conditions of Sale (Fifth Edition)

Date	:
Seller	: Christopher Hunt of 14 Heather Close Waverley WY15 9PB
Buyer	: Emily Abigail Harriet Rush of Saxifrage Lady Jane Court Blakey Cornshire CL3 5EH
Property (freehold/leasehold)	: 14 Heather Close Waverley registered at Land Registry with Title Absolute
Title number/root of title	: DN64963
Specified incumbrances	: None
Title guarantee (full)	: Full title guarantee
Completion date	:
Contract rate	: 4% above the base rate of Barclays Bank plc for the time being in force
Purchase price	: £450,000.00
Deposit	: £45,000.00
Contents price (if separate)	:
Balance	: £405,000.00

The seller will sell and the buyer will buy the property for the purchase price.

WARNING	**Signed**
This is a formal document, designed to create legal rights and legal obligations. Take advice before using it.	
	Seller/Buyer

SCS1_2/1

SPECIAL CONDITIONS

1 (a) This contract incorporates the Standard Conditions of Sale (Fifth Edition).

   (b) The terms used in this contract have the same meaning when used in the Conditions.

2 Subject to the terms of this contract and to the Standard Conditions of Sale, the seller is to transfer the property with either full title guarantee or limited title guarantee, as specified on the front page.

3 (a) The sale includes those contents which are indicated on the attached list as included in the sale and the buyer is to pay the contents price for them.

   (b) The sale excludes those fixtures which are at the property and are indicated on the attached list as excluded from the sale

4 The property is sold with vacant possession.

   (or)

✱ ~~The property is sold subject to the following leases or tenancies~~

5 Conditions 6.1.2 and 6.1.3 shall take effect as if the time specified in them were
   rather than 2.00 p.m.

6 **Representations**
   Neither party can rely on any representation made by the other, unless made in writing by the other or his conveyancer, but this does not exclude liability for fraud or recklessness.

7 **Occupier's consent**
   Each occupier identified below agrees with the seller and the buyer, in consideration of their entering into this contract, that the occupier concurs in the sale of the property on the terms of this contract, undertakes to vacate the property on or before the completion date and releases the property and any included fixtures and contents from any right or interest that the occupier may have.

   Note: this condition does not apply to occupiers under leases or tenancies subject to which the property is sold.

Name(s) and signature(s) of the occupier(s) (if any):

Name

Signature

Notices may be sent to:

Seller's conveyancer's name: Abbey Richards & Co
                                    East Chamber, 4 High Street
                                    Blakey, Cornshire CL1 3EG

   E-mail address:*   abbeyrichards@aul.com

Buyer's conveyancer's name: Paul Stewart & Co
                                    45 Chrisham Place
                                    Blakey, Cornshire CL2 6TY

   E-mail address:*   p.stewart@aul.com

*Adding an e-mail address authorises service by e-mail see condition 1.3.3(b)

APPENDIX 6

Example of an Epitome of Title

EPITOME OF TITLE[a]

Relating to The Old Forge Ridgewood Industrial Estate Seatown Cornshire

which is a free hold property

NOTES FOR GUIDANCE

(a) Acceptable forms of abstracts are an Epitome with photocopies of the documents or abstracts in traditional form or photocopies of such abstracts.

(b) If any part of any document is not relevant, mark it as such on the copy.

(c) Give the names of persons against whom a search was made in the case of a search certificate.

(d) Photographic copies should be:-
- durable and legible even if subject to frequent use for more than thirty years
- of sufficient contrast and clarity to allow further photographic reproduction
- printed in black on good quality white paper
- capable of being marked at a later date
- carefully coloured to show every detail of the original, in the case of plans.

(e) Every document in the epitome should be numbered in sequence. New documents added to an existing epitome should continue the established numbering sequence.

Date	Nature of document or event [b]	Parties [c]	Whether abstract or photographic copy [d]	Document number [e]	Whether original document to be handed over on completion
2 April 1990	Power of Attorney	(1) Richard Tyler (2) Steven Cox	copy	1	no
8 June 1990	Land charges search certificate	against names of Richard Tyler and Mary Ann Jessop	copy	2	yes
12 June 1990	Conveyance	(1) Richard Tyler (2) Mary Ann Jessop	copy	3	yes
12 June 1990	Legal Charge	(1) Mary Ann Jessop (2) Cornshire Building Society (receipt endorsed dated 20/2/98)	copy	4	yes

Date	Nature of document or event [b]	Parties [c]	Whether abstract or photographic copy [d]	Document number [e]	Whether original document to be handed over on completion
11 February 1998	Examined copy grant of probate of estate of Mary Ann Jessop	granted to Guy Budd and Ann Budd	copy	5	no
7 March 1998	Land charges search certificate	against names of Mary Ann Jessop Guy Budd and Ann Budd	copy	6	yes
12 March 1998	Assent	(1) Guy Budd and Ann Budd (2) Philip Ross	copy	7	Yes

EPT Epitome of title   Laserform International 1/94

APPENDIX 7

Precedent for Conveyance of Part of Unregistered Land

THIS CONVEYANCE is made the   day of   20   BETWEEN (1) EMILY HANNAH RIDDLE of 24 Lady Jane Avenue Blakey Cornshire ('the Seller') and (2) JUSTIN JOSHUA BOYES and ABIGAIL HARRIET BOYES both of 18 Park Road Blakey Cornshire ('the Buyers')

WHEREAS

(1)   The Seller is seised of the property described in the First Schedule hereto ('the Property') for an estate in fee simple in possession subject as hereinafter mentioned but otherwise free from incumbrances

(2)   The Seller has agreed to sell the Property to the Buyers at the price of Fifty five thousand pounds (£55,000.00) and the Buyers have agreed to hold the Property as joint tenants in equity

NOW THIS DEED WITNESSETH as follows:

1.   IN consideration of the sum of Fifty five thousand pounds (£55,000.00) paid by the Buyers to the Seller (the receipt whereof the Seller hereby acknowledges) the Seller with full title guarantee HEREBY CONVEYS unto the Buyers ALL THAT the Property TOGETHER WITH the rights set out in the Second Schedule hereto EXCEPTING AND RESERVING to the Seller and her successors in title the owners and occupiers for the time being of the land retained by the Seller ('the Retained Land') described in the Third Schedule hereto the rights set out in the Fourth Schedule hereto TO HOLD the same unto the Buyers in fee simple SUBJECT TO the restrictive covenants ('the Covenants') contained or referred to in a conveyance dated 28 May 1957 and made between (1) Sarah Louise Mathysse and (2) David Jack Hobbs so far as the same affect the Property and are still subsisting and capable of being enforced

2.   IT IS HEREBY AGREED AND DECLARED that the Buyers shall not by implication or otherwise become entitled to any rights of light or air which would restrict or interfere with the free use of the Retained Land for building or other purposes

3.   THE Buyers (with the object of affording to the Seller a full indemnity in respect of any breach of the Covenants but not further or otherwise) HEREBY JOINTLY AND SEVERALLY COVENANT with the Seller that the Buyers and the persons deriving title under them will at all times hereafter observe and perform the Covenants and keep the Seller and her estate and effects indemnified against all future actions claims demands and liabilities in respect thereof so far as the same affect the Property and are still subsisting and capable of being enforced

4.   FOR the benefit and protection of the Retained Land or any part or parts thereof and so as to bind so far as may be the Property into whosesoever hands the same may come the Buyers HEREBY JOINTLY AND SEVERALLY COVENANT with the Seller that the Buyers and the persons deriving title under them will at all times hereafter observe and perform the restrictions and stipulations set out in the Fifth Schedule hereto

5.   THE Buyers shall stand possessed of the Property UPON TRUST to sell the same or any part thereof (with full power to postpone the sale) and to stand possessed of the net proceeds of sale and the net profits until sale in trust for themselves as joint tenants

6.   PENDING the sale of the whole of the Property the Buyers shall have the same full and unrestricted powers of mortgaging charging leasing or otherwise dealing with all or any part of the Property in all respects as if they were an absolute owner thereof

[*Note. Since 1 January 1997 this clause is no longer necessary as s 6(1) of the Trusts of Land and Appointment of Trustees Act 1996 gives trustees of land all the powers of an absolute owner.*]

7.   THE Seller hereby acknowledges the right of the Buyers to the production of the documents ('the Documents') specified in the Sixth Schedule hereto (the possession of which is retained by the Seller) and to delivery of copies thereof and hereby undertakes with the Buyers for the safe custody of the Documents

8.   IT IS HEREBY CERTIFIED that the transaction hereby effected does not form part of a larger transaction or of a series of transactions in respect of which the amount or value or the aggregate amount or value of the consideration exceeds £60,000.

[*Note. Since 1 December 2003 this clause is no longer necessary as stamp duty land tax has replaced stamp duty.*]

IN WITNESS whereof the parties hereto have executed this deed the day and year first before written

FIRST SCHEDULE

(The property)

ALL THAT piece or parcel of land adjoining the northeast side and formerly forming part of the garden of 24 Lady Jane Avenue Blakey Cornshire together with the dwellinghouse recently erected on part thereof and known as 24A Lady Jane Avenue Blakey all of which property is more particularly delineated and edged red on the plan annexed hereto (hereinafter called 'the Plan') [*The plan is not reproduced.*]

SECOND SCHEDULE

(Rights granted)

1.   The free and uninterrupted right of way at all times and for all purposes with or without vehicles over the Accessway shown coloured brown on the Plan leading across the Retained Land subject to the Buyers bearing a fair proportion according to user of the expense of repairing and maintaining the said Accessway

2.   The right to the free and uninterrupted passage of water soil gas electricity and other services through all drains channels sewers pipes cables watercourses and other conducting media ('the Conducting Media') laid or to be laid within a period of eighty years from the date hereof in on or under the Retained Land subject to the Buyers bearing a fair proportion according to user of the expense of repairing and maintaining the Conducting Media

3.   The right on giving reasonable notice and at reasonable times (except in the case of emergencies) to enter upon the Retained Land for the purpose of inspecting maintaining and repairing the Conducting Media the person exercising such right causing as little damage as possible and making good any damage caused

THIRD SCHEDULE

(The retained land)

ALL THAT piece or parcel of land known as 24 Lady Jane Avenue Blakey Cornshire more particularly delineated and edged blue on the Plan

FOURTH SCHEDULE

(Exceptions and reservations)

1. The right to the free and uninterrupted passage of water soil gas electricity and other services through the Conducting Media laid or to be laid within a period of eighty years from the date hereof in on or under the Property subject to the Seller bearing a fair proportion according to user of the expense of repairing and maintaining the Conducting Media
2. The right on giving reasonable notice and at reasonable times (except in the case of emergencies) to enter upon the Property for the purpose of inspecting maintaining and repairing the Conducting Media the person exercising such right causing as little damage as possible and making good any damage caused
3. Any easement or right of light air or otherwise which would restrict or interfere with the free use of the Retained Land for building or any other purpose

FIFTH SCHEDULE

(New covenants)

1. No building erected or to be erected on the Property shall be used otherwise than as a private dwelling house for the occupation of one family
2. Nothing shall be done or permitted on the Property that shall be a nuisance or annoyance to the owners or occupiers of the Retained Land
3. To maintain and repair the close boarded fence erected along the boundary between the Property and the Retained Land shown by a T mark on the Plan

SIXTH SCHEDULE

(The documents)

28th May 1957	Conveyance	(1) Sarah Louise Mathysse
		(2) David Jack Hobbs
23rd April 1971	Conveyance	(1) David Jack Hobbs
		(2) Andrew Hugh Ellins
12th March 1983	Conveyance	(1) Andrew Hugh Ellins
		(2) the Seller

SIGNED AS A DEED

by the said EMILY HANNAH RIDDLE
in the presence of:

SIGNED AS A DEED
by the said JUSTIN JOSHUA BOYES
and ABIGAIL HARRIET BOYES
in the presence of:

APPENDIX 8

Completion Information and Requisitions on Title

A specimen copy of the Completion Information and Undertakings form TA13 (2nd edition) can be accessed online at:

http://www.lawsociety.org.uk/support-services/documents/TA13-form-specimen/.

APPENDIX 9

Specimen Financial or Completion Statements

In general there are three principal forms of completion statement. They are:

(a) financial statement prepared by the seller's practitioner for the seller;
(b) completion statement prepared by the seller's practitioner for the buyer;
(c) financial statement prepared by the buyer's practitioner for the buyer.

We also set out at (D) a typical commercial property completion statement.

Representative examples are given below with supporting information. All figures quoted are for illustrative purposes only.

(A) A FINANCIAL STATEMENT PREPARED BY THE SELLER'S PRACTITIONER FOR THE SELLER

You act for Michael Fawn, the seller, who has contracted to sell his freehold shop and upper part at 69 Wycombe Road, Brighton with full vacant possession for £119,950 to Pauline Greene, the buyer. The property is registered. You have to prepare a completion statement for the buyer and a draft completion statement for the client.

You have looked at the file and have noted the following details:

(a) The selling agents, Browning & Co., hold a deposit of £495.
(b) A deposit was paid to the firm on exchange of £11,500.
(c) There is a first mortgage with the Megalopolis Bank for which the redemption figure is £62,356.55.
(d) There is a second charge with Hove Loans plc for which the redemption figure is £19,955.32.
(e) The estate agents' fees are £4,228.24 inclusive of VAT.
(f) Official copies cost £10.
(g) Our legal fees were originally quoted at £575 exclusive of VAT.
(h) The contract provides for the sale of chattels at a price of £775.

There is set out below a draft of the financial statement for the seller required for the above scenario. It is assumed that a detailed bill of costs will be prepared in addition to the documents set out below.

All fee levels and charges are imaginary and are simply provided for illustrative purposes.

FINANCIAL STATEMENT
69 WYCOMBE ROAD BRIGHTON
FAWN TO GREENE

Sale price		**£119,950.00**
ADD amount payable for chattels		£775.00
		£120,725.00
DEDUCT mortgage redemption monies		
Megalopolis Bank	£62,356.55	
Hove Loans plc	£19,955.32	
		£82,311.87
		£38,413.13
DEDUCT estate agents' charges		
(Browning & Co)		£4,228.24
		£34,184.89
DEDUCT Land Registry copy		
deeds fee		
		£10.00
		£34,174.89
DEDUCT legal fees		
Agreed costs	£575.00	
ADD VAT (20 per cent)	£115.00	
		£690.00
BALANCE DUE TO YOU		£33,484.89

(B) A COMPLETION STATEMENT PREPARED BY THE SELLER'S PRACTITIONER FOR THE BUYER

You act for the seller, Michael Fawn, who has contracted to sell his freehold shop and upper part at 69 Wycombe Road, Brighton with vacant possession for £119,950 to Pauline Greene, the buyer. The property is registered. You have to prepare a completion statement for the buyer and a draft completion statement for the client.

You have looked at the file and have noted the following details:

(a) The selling agents, Browning & Co., hold a preliminary deposit of £495.

(b) A deposit was paid to the firm on exchange of £11,500.

(c) There is a first mortgage with Megalopolis Bank for which the redemption figure is £62,356.55.

(d) There is a second charge with Hove Loans plc for which the redemption figure is £19,955.32.

(e) The estate agents' fees are £4,228.24 inclusive of VAT.

(f) Official copies cost £10.

(g) Our legal fees were originally quoted at £575 exclusive of VAT.

(h) The contract provides for the sale of chattels at a price of £775.

There is set out below a draft of the completion statement for the buyer required for the above scenario.

All fee levels and charges are imaginary and are simply provided for illustrative purposes:

COMPLETION STATEMENT
69 WYCOMBE ROAD BRIGHTON
FAWN TO GREENE

Purchase price		£119,950.00
DEDUCT deposits paid		
On exchange	£11,500.00	
To Agents	£495.00	
		£11,995.00
		£107,955.00
ADD amount payable for chattels		£775.00
TOTAL payable on completion		£108,730.00

(C) A FINANCIAL STATEMENT PREPARED BY THE BUYER'S PRACTITIONER FOR THE BUYERS

Your client is Anne Scott, who is due to complete her purchase of the freehold property at 21 Linden Lea, Brentwood in 10 days' time. The property is registered. The purchase price is £129,000. Your client paid a deposit of £1,250 on exchange and a preliminary deposit of £250 was paid to the estate agents acting for the seller, Nigel Smith. You have mortgage instructions from the Chestnut Building Society, for a proposed loan of £52,750, and you have noted from the special conditions of the loan terms the following:

(a) There is a repairs retention of £995.
(b) There is an indemnity policy premium charged of £575.
(c) There is a completion monies transfer fee charged of £23.
(d) There is a society minimum membership fee of £1.

The firm's fees will be £295 exclusive and the Land Registry fees are £180. You have checked the accounts ledger for the client in the accounts department and have noted the following debit entries in the office account:

Local search fee	£75
Coal search fee	£23.50
Commons search	£10
Land charges fee	£1
Land Registry search fee	£5

There is set out below a draft of the financial statement. Two points are not mentioned which have been incorporated in the drafts, namely VAT on the legal costs and Stamp Duty Land Tax of 2 per cent of the purchase price. (Remember that currently you will pay:

- nothing on the first £125,000 of the property price;
- 2% on the next £125,000;
- 5% on the next £675,000;
- 10% on the next £575,000;
- 12% on the rest (above £1.5 million).

Always adjust your completion statement accordingly to take into account this graduated level of charges for stamp duty purposes. There are differences to these details for non-residential property. See Chapter 9 for further details.)

All fee levels and charges are imaginary and are simply provided for illustrative purposes.

COMPLETION STATEMENT
21 Linden Lea Brentwood
Smith to Scott

Purchase price		£129,000.00
DEDUCT deposits paid		
On exchange	£1,250.00	
To Agents	£250.00	
		£1,500.00
		£127,500.00
DEDUCT net mortgage		
Gross advance	£52,750.00	
less retention	£995.00	
less indemnity fee	£575.00	
less transfer fee	£23.00	
less membership fee	£1.00	
NET advance		£51,156.00
		£76,344.00
ADD Stamp Duty Land Tax at 2 per cent		£80.00
		£76,424.00
ADD costs and other payments		
Legal fees	£295.00	
VAT thereon @ 20 per cent	£59.00	
Local search fee	£75.00	
Coal search fee	£23.50	
Commons search fee	£10.00	
Land charges fee	£1.00	
Land Registry fee	£180.00	
Land Registry search fee	£5.00	£648.50
REQUIRED from you to complete		£77,072.50

(D) A TYPICAL COMMERCIAL PROPERTY TRANSACTION COMPLETION STATEMENT

Megatens plc are selling a freehold property subject to two lettings to Rudens Ltd for £750,000. The tenancy details are:

1. Ground floor let to M. Patel on a lease of 15 years with 12 years remaining paying £75,000 per annum quarterly in advance.

2. First floor let to W. Okeku on a lease of 15 years with 12 years remaining paying £15,000 per annum quarterly in advance.

Although the landlord insures, the seller has agreed with the buyer to cancel cover on completion so that the buyer can put in place their own insurance. Accordingly the insurance arrangements will not arise until completion actually takes place so that any refund obtained by the seller will be returned to the tenants. Thereafter the tenants will be required to refund the buyer's insurance premium.

For the purpose of this statement completion is due on 1 December next and there are no rent arrears. The Standard Commercial Property Conditions apply to this transaction.

COMPLETION STATEMENT
121 BRIGHTON STREET LONDON WC1
MEGATENS TO RUDENS

Purchase price		£750,000.00
DEDUCT deposit paid		
on exchange	£75,000.00	
		£675,000.00
DEDUCT rent by Patel from 1–12 to 24–12 at £75,000 p.a. (24 days)	£4,931.51	
DEDUCT rent by Okeku from 1–12 to 24–12 at £15,000 p.a. (24 days)	£986.30	£5,917.81
TOTAL payable on completion		£669,082.19

The Law Society's Code for Completion by Post (2011 edition)

The version issued in 2011 can be found at the following address:

http://www.lawsociety.org.uk/support-services/documents/postal-completion/.

APPENDIX 11

Standard Commercial Property Conditions (3rd edition)

The third edition of The Law Society's Standard Commercial Property Conditions can be found at the following address:

http://www.oyezstore.co.uk/legal_form_6232/Standard_Commercial_Property_Conditions_(3rd.edition)_.htm.

APPENDIX 12

The *UK Finance Mortgage Lenders' Handbook for England and Wales:* PART 1

Part 1 of the *UK Finance Mortgage Lenders' Handbook* as at 1 July 2017 is reproduced in this appendix with the kind permission of the Council of Mortgage Lenders. Please note that it may be updated at any time; for current practice, readers should refer to the *Lenders' Handbook* section of the CML website at: **https://www.cml.org.uk/lenders-handbook/.**

Part 1 of the *Handbook* should be read in conjunction with the Disclosure of Incentives Form and Professional Consultant Certificate, which can be accessed at the following links:

Disclosure of Incentives Form: **http://www.cml.org.uk/cml/handbook/form**

Professional Consultant Certificate: **http://www.cml.org.uk/cml/handbook/certificates.**

UK FINANCE MORTGAGE LENDERS' HANDBOOK

Part 1: England and Wales

Last modified: 01/07/2017

Contents

1.   GENERAL

Part 1—Instructions and Guidance

Those lenders who instruct using the UK Finance Mortgage Lenders' Handbook certify that these instructions have been prepared to comply with the requirements of the Solicitors Regulation Authority (SRA's) Code of Conduct 2011 and the CLC Code of Conduct 2011.

1.1   The UK Finance Mortgage Lenders' Handbook is issued by UK Finance. Your instructions from an individual lender will indicate if you are being instructed in accordance with the Lenders' Handbook. If you are, the general provisions in part 1 and any **lender specific requirements in part 2** must be followed.

1.2   References to **"we"**, **"us"** and **"our"** mean the lender from whom you receive instructions.

1.3   The Lenders' Handbook does not affect any responsibilities you have to us under the general law or any practice rule or guidance issued by your professional body from time to time.

1.4   The standard of care which we expect of you is that of a reasonably competent solicitor or licensed conveyancer acting on behalf of a mortgagee.

1.5   If you are regulated by the Solicitors Regulation Authority (SRA) the limitations contained in the SRA's Code of Conduct 2011 apply to the instructions contained in the Lenders' Handbook and any separate instructions.

1.6   You must also comply with any separate instructions you receive for an individual loan.

1.7   If the borrower and the mortgagor are not one and the same person, all references to **"borrower"** shall include the mortgagor. Check **part 2** to see if we lend in circumstances where the borrower and the mortgagor are not one and the same.

1.8   References to **"borrower"** (and, if applicable, **"guarantor"** or, expressly or impliedly, the mortgagor) are to each borrower (and guarantor or mortgagor) named in the mortgage instructions/offer (if sent to the conveyancer). This applies to references in the Lenders' Handbook and in the certificate of title.

1.9   References to **"mortgage offer"** include any loan agreement, offer of mortgage or any other similar document.

1.10   If you are instructed in connection with any additional loan (including a further advance) then you should treat references to "mortgage" and "mortgage offer" as applying to such "additional loan" and "additional loan offer" respectively.

1.11   In any transaction during the lifetime of the mortgage when we instruct you, you must use our current standard documents in all cases and must not amend or generate them without our written consent. We will send you all the standard documents necessary to enable you to comply with our instructions, but please let us know if you need any other documents and we will send these to you. Check part 2 to see who you should contact. If you consider that any of the documentation is inappropriate to the particular facts of a transaction, you should write to us (see part 2) with full details and any suggested amendments.

1.12   In order to act on our behalf your firm must be a member of our conveyancing panel. You must also comply with any terms and conditions of your panel appointment.

1.12.1 Our instructions are personal to the firm to whom they are addressed and must be dealt with solely by that firm. You must not sub-contract or assign our instructions to another firm or body, nor may you accept instructions to act for us from another body, unless we confirm in writing otherwise.

1.13   If you or a member of your immediate family (that is to say, a spouse, civil partner, co-habitee, parent, sibling, child, step-parent, step-child, grandparent, grandchild, parent-in-law, or child-in-law) is the borrower and you are the sole practitioner, you must not act for us.

1.14   Your firm or company must not act for us if the partner or fee earner dealing with the transaction or a member of his immediate family is the seller, unless we say your firm may act (see **part 2**) and a separate fee earner of no less standing or a partner within the firm acts for us.

1.15   Your firm or company must not act for us if the partner or fee earner dealing with the transaction or a member of his immediate family is the borrower, unless we say your firm may act (see part 2) and a separate fee earner of no less standing or a partner within the firm acts for us.

1.16   If there is any conflict of interest, you must not act for us and must return our instructions.

1.17   Nothing in these instructions lessens your duties to the borrower. This does not apply if acting in accordance with Part 3—Separate Representation Standard Instructions.

1.18   In addition to these definitions any reference to any regulation, legislation or legislative provision shall be construed as a reference to that regulation, legislation or legislative provision as amended, re-enacted or ex-tended at the relevant time.

2.   COMMUNICATING WITH THE LENDER

2.1   All communication between you and us should be in writing quoting the mortgage account or roll number, the surname and initials of the borrower and the property address. You should keep copies of all written communication on your file as evidence of notification and authorisation. If you use PC fax or e-mail, you should retain a copy in readable form.

2.2   If you require deeds or information from us in respect of a borrower or a property then you must first of all have the borrower's authority for such a request. If there is more than one borrower, you must have the authority of all the borrowers. This does not apply if acting in accordance with Part 3—Separate Representation Standard Instructions.

2.3   If you need to report a matter to us, you must do so as soon as you become aware of it so as to avoid any delay. If you do not believe that a matter is adequately provided for in the Handbook, you should:
   - identify the relevant Handbook provision and the extent to which the issue is not covered by it
   - provide a concise summary of the legal risks
   - provide your recommendation on how we should protect our interest.

After reporting a matter you should not complete the mortgage until you have received our further written instructions. We recommend that you report such matters before exchange of contracts because we may have to withdraw or change the mortgage offer.

3.   SAFEGUARDS

3.1   Safeguards for solicitors

3.1.1   **This sub-section relates to solicitors and those working in practices regulated by the Solicitors Regulation Authority only.**

3.1.2   You must follow the rules and guidance of your professional body relating to money laundering and comply with the current money laundering regulations and the Proceeds of Crime Act 2002 to the extent that they apply and you must follow other relevant guidance, for example, the Law Society of England and Wales mortgage fraud practice note, the Council for Licensed Conveyancers' Acting for Lenders and Prevention of Mortgage Fraud Code and Guidance, and take account of relevant regulatory warning notices.

3.1.3   If you are not familiar with the seller's regulated legal representatives (as defined by the Legal Services Act 2007 Schedule 4 and Schedule 2 paragraph 5), you must verify that they are currently on record with the Solicitors Regulation Authority, Council for Licensed Conveyancers or other legal regulatory body as practising at the address they have provided to you. Check part 2 to see whether we require you to notify us of the name and address of the regulated legal representatives (as defined above) acting for the seller.

3.1.4   If the seller does not have legal representation you should check part 2 to see whether or not we need to be notified so that a decision can be made as to whether or not we are prepared to proceed.

3.1.5   Unless you personally know the signatory of a document, you must ask the signatory to provide evidence of identity, which you must carefully check. You should check the signatory's identity against one of the documents from list A or two of the documents in list B:

List A

- a valid full passport; or
- a valid HM Forces identity card with the signatory's photograph; or
- a valid UK Photo-card driving licence; or
- any other document listed in the additional list A in part 2.

List B

- a cheque guarantee card, credit card (bearing the Mastercard or Visa logo) American Express or Diners Club card, debit or multi-function card (bearing the Switch or Delta logo) issued in the United Kingdom with an original account statement less than three months old; or
- a firearm and shot gun certificate; or
- a receipted utility bill less than three months old; or
- a council tax bill less than three months old; or
- a council rent book showing the rent paid for the last three months; or
- a mortgage statement from another lender for the mortgage accounting year just ended; or
- any other document listed in the additional list B in part 2.

3.1.6   You should check that any document you use to verify a signatory's identity appears to be authentic and current, signed in the relevant place. You should take a copy of it and keep the copy on your file. You should also check that the signatory's signature on any document being used to verify identity matches the signatory's signature on the document we require the signatory to sign and that the address shown on any document used to verify identity is that of the signatory.

3.2   Safeguards for licensed conveyancers

3.2.1   This sub-section applies to licensed conveyancers practices only.

3.2.2   You must follow the professional guidance of the Council for Licensed Conveyancers relating to money laundering and comply with the current money laundering regulations and the Proceeds of Crime Act 2002 to the extent that they apply and you must follow all other relevant guidance issued by the Council for Licensed Conveyancers.

3.2.3   If you are not familiar with the seller's regulated legal representatives (as defined by the Legal Services Act 2007 Schedule 4 and Schedule 2 paragraph 5), you must verify that they are currently on record with the Law Society or Council for Licensed Conveyancers or other legal regulatory body as practising at the address they have provided to you. Check part 2 to see whether we require you to notify us of the name and address of the regulated legal representatives (as defined above) acting for the seller.

3.2.4   If the seller does not have legal representation you should check part 2 to see whether or not we need to be notified so that a decision can be made as to whether or not we are prepared to proceed.

3.2.5   Unless you personally know the signatory of a document, you must ask the signatory to provide evidence of identity, which you must carefully check. You must satisfy yourself that the person signing the document is the borrower, mortgagor or guarantor (as appropriate). If you have any concerns about the identity of the signatory you should notify us immediately.

3.2.6   You should check that any document you use to verify a signatory's identity appears to be authentic and current, signed in the relevant place. You should take a copy of it and keep the copy on your file. You should also check that the signatory's signature on any document being used to verify identity matches the signatory's signature on the document we require the signatory to sign and that the address shown on any document used to verify identity is that of the signatory.

4.   VALUATION OF THE PROPERTY

4.1   Check part 2 to see whether we send you a copy of the valuation report or if you must get it from the borrower. If you get a copy of the valuation report from the borrower, we do not expect you to check the content of that report matches the information we hold. For the avoidance of doubt, regardless of where the report is obtained from, you must carry out the checks detailed in sections 4.2 and 4.3.

4.2   You must take reasonable steps to verify that there are no discrepancies between the description of the property as valued and the title and other documents which a reasonably competent conveyancer should obtain, and, if there are, you must tell us immediately.

4.3   You should take reasonable steps to verify that the assumptions stated by the valuer about the title (for example, its tenure, easements, boundaries and restrictions on its use) in the valuation and as stated in the mortgage offer are correct. If they are not, please let us know as soon as possible (see part 2) as it will be necessary for us to check with the valuer whether the valuation needs to be revised. We are not expecting you to assume the role of valuer. We are simply trying to ensure that the valuer has valued the property based on correct information.

4.4   We recommend that you should advise the borrower that there may be defects in the property which are not revealed by the inspection carried out by our valuer and there may be omissions or inaccuracies in the report which do not matter to us but which would matter to the borrower. We recommend that, if we send a copy of a valuation report that we have obtained, you should also advise the borrower that the borrower should not rely on the report in deciding whether to proceed with the purchase and that he obtains his own more detailed report on the condition and value of the property, based on a fuller inspection, to enable him to decide whether the property is suitable for his purposes.

4.5   Where the mortgage offer states that a final inspection is needed, you must ask for the final inspection at least ten working days before the advance is required. Failure to do so may cause delay in the issue of the advance. Your certificate of title must be sent to us in the usual way.

5.   TITLE

5.1   Length of Ownership

5.1.1   Please report to us immediately if the owner or registered proprietor has been registered for less than six months.

5.2   Seller Not The Owner or Registered Proprietor

5.2.1   Please report to us immediately if the person selling to the borrower is not the owner or registered proprietor unless the seller is:
- a personal representative of the registered proprietor; or
- an institutional mortgagee exercising its power of sale; or
- a receiver, trustee-in-bankruptcy or liquidator; or
- a developer or builder selling a property acquired under a part-exchange scheme; or
- a Registered Housing Provider (Housing Association) exercising a power of sale.

5.3   Conflict of Interest

5.3.1   If any matter comes to your attention which you should reasonably expect us to consider important in deciding whether or not to lend to the borrower (such as whether the borrower has given misleading information to us or the information which you might reasonably expect to have been given to us is no longer true) and you are unable to disclose that information to us because of a conflict of interest, you must cease to act for us and return our instructions stating that you consider a conflict of interest has arisen. This does not apply if acting in accordance with Part 3—Separate Representation Standard Instructions.

5.4   Searches and Reports

5.4.1   In carrying out your investigation, you must ensure that all usual and necessary searches and enquiries have been carried out. You must report any adverse entry to us but we do not want to be sent the search itself. We must be named as the applicant in the Land Registry search.

5.4.2   In addition, you must ensure that any other searches which may be appropriate to the particular property, taking into account its locality and other features are carried out.

5.4.3   All searches except where there is a priority period must not be more than six months old at completion.

5.4.4   You must advise us of any contaminated land entries revealed in the local authority search. Check part 2 to see if we want to receive environmental or contaminated land reports (as opposed to contaminated land entries revealed in the local authority search). If we do not, you do not need to make these enquiries on our behalf.

5.4.5   Check part 2 to see if we accept personal searches.

5.4.6   Check part 2 to see if we accept search insurance.

5.4.7   If we accept personal searches or search insurance you must ensure that:
- a suitably qualified search agent carries out the personal search and has indemnity insurance that adequately protects us; or
- the search insurance policy adequately protects us.

5.4.8   Check you are satisfied that you will be able to certify that the title is good and marketable unless stated otherwise in our specific requirements listed in part 2.

5.5   Planning and Building Regulations

5.5.1   You must by making appropriate searches and enquiries take all reasonable steps (including any further enquiries to clarify any issues which may arise) to ensure:
- the property has the benefit of any necessary planning consents (including listed building consent) and building regulation approval for its construction and any subsequent change to the property and its current use; and
- there is no evidence of any breach of the conditions of that or any other consent or certificate affecting the property; and
- that no matter is revealed which would preclude the property from being used as a residential property or that the property may be the subject of enforcement action.

If there is evidence of such a breach or matter but in your professional judgement there is no reasonable prospect of enforcement action and, following reasonable enquiries, you are satisfied that the title is good and marketable and you can provide an unqualified certificate of title, we will not insist on indemnity insurance and you may proceed.

5.5.2   If there is such evidence and all outstanding conditions will not be satisfied by completion, where you are not able to provide an unqualified certificate of title, you should report this to us in accordance with 2.3.

5.5.3   Check part 2 to see if copies of planning permissions, building regulations and other consents or certificates should be sent to us.

5.5.4   If the property will be subject to any enforceable restrictions, for example under an agreement (such as an agreement under section 106 of the Town and Country Planning Act 1990) or in a planning permission, which, at the time of completion, might reasonably be expected materially to affect its value or its future marketability, you should report this to us (see part 2).

5.5.5   If different from 1.11, contact point if the property is subject to restrictions which may affect its value or marketability.

5.6   Good and Marketable Title

5.6.1   The title to the property must be good and marketable free of any restrictions, covenants, easements, charges or encumbrances which, at the time of completion, might reasonably be expected to materially adversely affect the value of the property or its future marketability (but excluding any matters covered by indemnity insurance) and which may be accepted by us for mortgage purposes. Our requirements in respect of indemnity insurance are set out in section 9. If, based on your professional judgement, you are able to provide an unqualified certificate of title, we will not require indemnity insurance. You must also take reasonable steps to ensure that, on completion, the property will be vested in the borrower.

5.6.2   Good leasehold title will be acceptable if:
- a marked abstract of the freehold and any intermediate leasehold title for the statutory period of 15 years before the grant of the lease is provided; or
- you are prepared to certify that the title is good and marketable when sending your certificate of title (because, for example, the landlord's title is generally accepted in the district where the property is situated); or
- you arrange indemnity insurance. Our requirements in respect of indemnity insurance are set out in section 9.

5.6.3   A title based on adverse possession or possessory title will be acceptable if the seller is or on completion the borrower will be registered at the Land Registry as registered proprietor of a possessory title. In the case of lost title deeds, the statutory declaration must explain the loss satisfactorily.

5.6.4   We will also require indemnity insurance where there are buildings on the part in question or where the land is essential for access or services.

5.6.5   We may not need indemnity insurance in cases where such title affects land on which no buildings are erected or which is not essential for access or services. In such cases, you must send a plan of the whole of the land to be mortgaged to us identifying the area of land having possessory title. We will refer the matter to our valuer so that an assessment can be made of the proposed security. We will then notify you of any additional requirements or if a revised mortgage offer is to be made.

5.7   Flying Freeholds and Freehold Flats

5.7.1   If any part of the property comprises or is affected by a flying freehold or the property is a freehold flat, check part 2 to see if we will accept it as security.

5.7.2   If we are prepared to accept a title falling within 5.7.1:
- the property must have all necessary rights of support, protection, and entry for repair as well as a scheme of enforceable covenants that are also such that subsequent buyers are required to enter into covenants in identical form; and
- you must be able to certify that the title is good and marketable; and
- in the case of flying freeholds, you must send us a plan of the property clearly showing the part affected by the flying freehold.

If our requirements in the first bullet under 5.7.2 are not satisfied, indemnity insurance must be in place at completion (see section 9).

5.8   Other Freehold Arrangements

5.8.1   Unless we indicate to the contrary (see part 2), we have no objection to a security which comprises a building converted into not more than four flats where the borrower occupies one of those flats and the borrower or another flat owner also owns the freehold of the building and the other flats are subject to long leases.

5.8.2   If the borrower occupying one of the flats also owns the freehold, we will require our security to be:
- the freehold of the whole building subject to the long leases of the other flats; and
- any leasehold interest the borrower will have in the flat the borrower is to occupy.

5.8.3   If another flat owner owns the freehold of the building, the borrower must have a leasehold interest in the flat the borrower is to occupy and our security must be the borrower's leasehold interest in such flat.

5.8.4   The leases of all the flats should contain appropriate covenants by the tenant of each flat to contribute towards the repair, maintenance and insurance of the building. The leases should also grant and reserve all necessary rights and easements. They should not contain any unduly onerous obligations on the landlord.

5.8.5   Where the security will comprise:
- one of a block of not more than four leasehold flats and the borrower will also own the freehold jointly with one or more of the other flat owners in the building; or
- one of two leasehold flats in a building where the borrower also owns the freehold reversion of the other flat and the other leaseholder owns the freehold reversion in the borrower's flat; check part 2 to see if we will accept it as security and if so, what our requirements will be.

5.9   Commonhold

5.9.1   If any part of the property comprises of commonhold, check part 2 to see if we will accept it as security.

5.9.2   If we are prepared to accept a title falling within 5.9.1, you must:
- ensure that the commonhold association has obtained insurance for the common parts which complies with our requirements (see 6.14);
- obtain a commonhold unit information certificate and ensure that all of the commonhold assessment in respect of the property has been paid up to the date of completion;
- ensure that the commonhold community statement does not include any material restrictions on occupation or use (see 5.6 and 5.10);
- ensure that the commonhold community statement provides that in the event of a voluntary termination of the commonhold the termination statement provides that the unit holders will ensure that any mortgage secured on their unit is repaid on termination;
- make a company search to verify that the commonhold association is in existence and remains registered, and that there is no registered indication that it is to be wound up; and
- within 14 days of completion, send the notice of transfer of a commonhold unit and notice of the mortgage to the commonhold association.

5.10   Restrictions on Use and Occupation

5.10.1   You must check whether there are any material restrictions on the occupation of the property as a private residence or as specified by us (for example, because of the occupier's employment, age or income), or any material restrictions on its use. If there are any restrictions, you must report details to us (see part 2). We may accept a restriction, particularly if this relates to sheltered housing or to first-time buyers.

5.11   Restrictive Covenants

5.11.1   You must enquire whether the property has been built, altered or is currently used in breach of a restrictive covenant. We rely on you to check that the covenant is not enforceable. If you are unable to provide an unqualified certificate of title as a result of the risk of enforceability you must ensure (subject to paragraph 5.11.2) that indemnity insurance is in place at completion of our mortgage (see section 9).

5.11.2   If there is evidence of a breach and, following reasonable enquiries, you are satisfied that the title is good and marketable; you can provide an unqualified certificate of title and the breach has continued for more than 20 years without challenge, then we will not insist on indemnity insurance.

5.12   First Legal Charge

5.12.1   On completion, we require a fully enforceable first charge by way of legal mortgage over the property executed by all owners of the legal estate. All existing charges must be redeemed on or before completion, unless we agree that an existing charge may be postponed to rank after our mortgage. Our standard deed or form of postponement must be used.

5.13   Balance of Purchase Price

5.13.1   You must ask the borrower how the balance of the purchase price is being provided. If you become aware that the borrower is not providing the balance of the purchase price from his own funds or is proposing to give a second charge over the property, you must report this to us if the borrower agrees (see part 2), failing which you must return our instructions and explain that you are unable to continue to act for us as there is a conflict of interest. You should also have regard to 6.3.1 with regard to any implications on the purchase price.

5.14   Leasehold Property

5.14.1   Our requirements on the unexpired term of a lease offered as security are set out in part 2.

5.14.2   There must be no provision for forfeiture on the insolvency of the tenant or any superior tenant.

5.14.3   The only situations where we will accept a restriction on the mortgage or assignment (whether by a tenant or a mortgagee) of the lease is where the person whose consent needs to be obtained cannot unreasonably withhold giving consent. The necessary consent for the particular transaction must be obtained before completion. If the lease requires consent to an assignment or mortgage to be obtained, you must obtain these on or before completion (this is particularly important if the lease is a shared ownership lease). You must not complete without them.

5.14.4   You must take reasonable steps to check that:
- there are satisfactory legal rights, particularly for access, services, support, shelter and protection; and
- there are also adequate covenants and arrangements in respect of the following matters: buildings insurance, maintenance and repair of the structure, foundations, main walls, roof, common parts, common services and grounds (the "common services").

5.14.5   You should ensure that responsibility for the insurance, maintenance, and repair of the common services is that of:
- the landlord; or
- one or more of the tenants in the building of which the property forms part; or
- the management company—see sub-section 5.15.

5.14.6   Where the responsibility for the insurance, maintenance and repair of the common services is that of one or more of the tenants the lease must contain adequate provisions for the enforcement of these obligations by the landlord or management company at the request of the tenant.

5.14.7   In the absence of a provision in the lease that all leases of other flats in the block are in, or will be granted in, substantially similar form, you should take reasonable steps to check that the leases of the other flats are in similar form. If you are unable to do so, you should effect indemnity insurance (see section 9). This is not essential if the landlord is responsible for the maintenance and repair of the main structure.

5.14.8   We do not require enforceability covenants mutual or otherwise for other tenant covenants.

5.14.9   We have no objection to a lease which contains provision for a periodic increase of the ground rent provided that the amount of the increased ground rent is fixed or can be readily established and is reasonable. If you consider any increase in the ground rent may materially affect the value of the property, you must report this to us (see part 2).

5.14.10 You should enquire whether the landlord or managing agent foresees any significant increase in the level of the service charge in the reasonably foreseeable future and, if there is, you must report to us (see part 2).

5.14.11 If the terms of the lease are unsatisfactory, you must obtain a suitable deed of variation to remedy the defect. We may accept indemnity insurance (see section 9). See part 2 for our requirements.

5.14.12 You must obtain on completion a clear receipt or other appropriate written confirmation for the last payment of ground rent and service charge from the landlord or managing agents on behalf of the landlord. Check part 2 to see if it must be sent to us after completion. If confirmation of payment from the landlord cannot be obtained, we are prepared to proceed provided that you are satisfied that the absence of the landlord is common practice in the district where the property is situated, the seller confirms there are no breaches of the terms of the lease, you are satisfied that our security will not be prejudiced by the absence of such a receipt and you provide us with a clear certificate of title.

5.14.13 Notice of the mortgage must be served on the landlord and any management company immediately following completion, whether or not the lease requires it. Please ensure that you can provide either suitable evidence of the service of notice on the landlord or management company or a receipt of notice. Check part 2 to see if a receipted copy of the notice or evidence of service must be sent to us after completion.

5.14.14 We will accept leases which require the property to be sold on the open market if re-building or re-instatement is frustrated provided the insurance proceeds and the proceeds of sale are shared between the landlord and tenant in proportion to their respective interests.

5.14.15 You must report to us (see part 2) if it becomes apparent that the landlord is either absent or insolvent. If we are to lend, we may require indemnity insurance (see section 9). See part 2 for our requirements.

5.14.16 You must check a certified or official copy of the original lease. In the case of a registered lease where the original lease is now lost, or destroyed by Land Registry, we are prepared to proceed provided you have checked an official copy of the lease from the Land Registry.

5.15   Management Company

5.15.1   In paragraphs 5.15.1 to 5.15.2 the following meanings shall apply:
  • "management company" means the company formed to carry out the maintenance and repair of the common parts;
  • "common parts" means the structure, main walls, roof, foundations, services, grounds and any other common areas serving the building or estate of which the property forms part.

If a management company is required to maintain or repair the common parts, the management company should have a legal right to enter the property; if the management company's right to so enter does not arise from a leasehold interest, then the tenants of the building should also be the members of the management company. If this is not the case, there should be a covenant by the landlord to carry out the obligations of the management company should it fail to do so. For leases granted before 1 September 2000, if the lease does not satisfy the requirements of paragraph 5.15.1 but you are nevertheless satisfied with the existing arrangements affecting the management company and the maintenance and repair of the common parts and you are able to provide a clear certificate of title, then we will rely on your professional judgement.

5.15.2   You should make a company search and verify that the company is in existence and registered at Companies House. You should also obtain the management company's last three years' published accounts (or the accounts from inception if the company has only been formed in the past three years). Any apparent problems with the company should be reported to us (see part 2). If the borrower is required to be a shareholder in the management company, check part 2 to see if you must arrange for the share certificate, a blank stock transfer form executed by the borrower and a copy of the memorandum and articles of association to be sent to us after completion (unless we tell you not to). If the management company is limited by guarantee, the borrower (or at least one of them if two or more) must follow the procedure necessary to become a member after completion.

5.16   Insolvency Considerations

5.16.1   You must obtain a clear bankruptcy search against each borrower (and each mortgagor or guarantor, if any) providing us with protection at the date of completion of the mortgage. You must fully investigate any entries revealed by your bankruptcy search against the borrower (or mortgagor or guarantor) to ensure that they do not relate to them.

5.16.2   Where an entry is revealed that may relate to the borrower (or the mortgagor or guarantor):
- you must be satisfied that the entry does not relate to the borrower (or the mortgagor or guarantor) if you are able to do so from your own knowledge or enquiries; or
- if, after obtaining office copy entries or making other enquiries of the Official Receiver, you are unable to satisfy yourself that the entry does not relate to the borrower (or the mortgagor or guarantor) you must report this to us (see part 2). We may as a consequence need to withdraw our mortgage offer.

5.16.3   If you are aware that the title to the property is subject to a deed of gift or a transaction at an apparent undervalue completed within five years of the proposed mortgage then you must be satisfied that we will acquire our interest in good faith and will be protected under the provisions of the Insolvency (No 2) Act 1994 against our security being set aside. If you are unable to give an unqualified certificate of title, you must arrange indemnity insurance (see section 9).

5.16.4   You must also obtain clear bankruptcy searches against all parties to any deed of gift or transaction at an apparent undervalue.

5.17   Powers of Attorney

5.17.1   If any document is being executed under power of attorney, you must ensure that the power of attorney is, on its face, properly drawn up, that it appears to be properly executed by the donor and that the attorney knows of no reason why such power of attorney will not be subsisting at completion.

5.17.2   Where there are joint borrowers the power should comply with section 25 of the Trustee Act 1925, as amended by section 7 of the Trustee Delegation Act 1999, or with section 1 of the Trustee Delegation Act 1999 with the attorney making an appropriate statement under section 2 of the 1999 Act.

5.17.3   In the case of joint borrowers, neither borrower may appoint the other as their attorney.

5.17.4   A power of attorney must not be used in connection with a regulated loan under the Consumer Credit Act 1974.

5.17.5   Check part 2 to see if:

- the original or a certified copy of the power of attorney must be sent to us after completion; and
- where the power of attorney is a general power of attorney and was completed more than 12 months before the completion of our mortgage, whether you must send us a statutory declaration confirming that it has not been revoked.

5.18   The Guarantee

5.18.1   Whilst we recommend that a borrower should try to obtain a full title guarantee from the seller, we do not insist on this. We, however, require the borrower to give us a full title guarantee in the mortgage deed. The mortgage deed must not be amended.

5.19   Affordable Housing: Shared Ownership and Shared Equity

5.19.1   Housing associations, other social landlords and developers sometimes provide schemes under which the borrower will not have 100% ownership of the property and a third party will also own a share or will be a taking a charge over the title. In these cases you must check with us to see if we will lend and what our requirements are unless we have already provided these (see part 2).

5.20   Energy Technologies Installed on Residential Properties

5.20.1   Where a property is subject to a registered lease of roof space for solar PV panels we require you to check that the lease meets the UK Finance minimum requirements. Where you consider it does not, check part 2 to see whether you must report this to us and for details of any additional requirements.

5.20.2   If, after completion, the borrower informs you of an intention to enter into a lease of roof space relating to energy technologies, you should advise the borrower that they, or the energy technology provider on their behalf, will need to seek consent from us.

5.20.3   UK Finance has issued a set of minimum requirements where a provider/homeowner is seeking lender consent for a lease of roof space for solar PV panels. See part 2 for our additional requirements relating to these leases.

5.20.4   Check part 2 to see whether we require you to disclose the details of any existing Green Deal Plan(s) on a property.

6.   THE PROPERTY

6.1   Mortgage Offer and Title Documents

6.1.1   The loan to the borrower will not be made until all relevant conditions of the mortgage offer which need to be satisfied before completion have been complied with and we have received your certificate of title.

6.1.2   You must check your instructions and ensure that there are no discrepancies between them and the title documents and other matters revealed by your investigations.

6.1.3   You should tell us (see part 2) as soon as possible if you have been told that the borrower has decided not to take up the mortgage offer.

6.2   Boundaries

6.2.1   These must be clearly defined by reference to a suitable plan or description. They must also accord with the information given in the valuation report, if this is provided to you. You should check with the borrower that the plan or the description accords with the borrower's understanding of the extent of the property to be mortgaged to us. You must report to us (see part 2) if there are any discrepancies.

6.3   Purchase Price

6.3.1   The purchase price for the property must be the same as set out in our instructions. If it is not, you must tell us (unless we say differently in part 2).

6.4   Incentives

6.4.1   You must obtain a completed copy of the UK Finance Disclosure of Incentives Form for any property that is yet to be occupied for the first time, or for the first time in its current form, for example, because of a renovation or conversion. You should only report incentives to the lender as instructed below.

6.4.2   You will not be able to send a completed Certificate of Title to the lender unless you have received the UK Finance Disclosure of Incentives Form. When you send a completed Certificate of Title you are confirming you are in receipt of a completed UK Finance Disclosure of Incentives Form from the developer/seller's conveyancer which complies with your instructions.

6.4.3   This does not override your duty to the lender via the instructions provided elsewhere in the Lenders' Handbook.

6.4.4   You must tell us (unless we say differently in part 2) if the contract provides for or you become aware of any arrangement in which there is:
- a cashback to the buyer; or
- part of the price is being satisfied by a non-cash incentive to the buyer; or
- any indirect incentive (cash or non-cash) or rental guarantee.

Any such arrangement may lead to the mortgage offer being withdrawn or amended.

6.4.5   You must report to us (see part 2) if you will not have control over the payment of all of the purchase money (for example, if it is proposed that the borrower pays money to the seller direct) other than a deposit held by an estate agent or a reservation fee of not more than £1,000 paid to a builder or developer.

6.5   Vacant Possession

6.5.1   Unless otherwise stated in your instructions, it is a term of the loan that vacant possession is obtained. The contract must provide for this. If you doubt that vacant possession will be given, you must not part with the advance and should report the position to us (see part 2).

6.6   Properties Let at Completion

6.6.1   Unless it is clear from the mortgage offer that the property is let or is to be let at completion then you must check with us whether we lend on "buy-to-let" properties and that the mortgage is for that purpose (see part 2).

6.6.2   Where the property, or part of it, is already let, or is to be let at completion, then the letting must comply with the details set out in the mortgage offer or any consent to let we issue. If the letting does not comply, or no such details are mentioned, you must report the position to us (see part 2).

6.6.3   Check part 2 for whether counterparts or certified copies of all tenancy agreements and leases in respect of existing tenancies must be sent to us after completion.

6.6.4   Where the property falls within the definition of a house in multiple occupation under the Housing Act 2004 see part 2 as to whether we will accept this as security and if so what our requirements are.

6.7   New Properties—Building Standards Indemnity Schemes

6.7.1   If the property has been built or converted within the past ten years, or is to be occupied for the first time, you must ensure that it was built or converted under a scheme acceptable to us (see part 2 for the list of schemes acceptable to us and our requirements).

6.7.2   Where the cover under a scheme referred to in clause 6.7.1 is not yet in place before you send us the certificate of title, you must obtain a copy of a new home warranty provider's cover note from the developer. The cover note must confirm that the property has received a satisfactory final inspection and that the new home warranty will be in place on or before legal completion. This does not apply to self-build schemes. Check part 2 to see what new home warranty documentation should be sent to us after completion.

6.7.3   We do not insist that notice of assignment of the benefit of the new home warranty agreement be given to the builder in the case of a second and subsequent purchase(s) during the period of the insurance cover. Check part 2 to see if any assignments of building standards indemnity schemes which are available should be sent to us after completion.

6.7.4   Where the property does not have the benefit of a scheme under 6.7.1 and has been built or converted within the past six years check part 2 to see if we will proceed and, if so, whether you must satisfy yourself that the building work is being monitored (or where the work is completed was monitored) by a professional consultant. If we do accept monitoring you should ensure that the professional consultant has provided the lender's Professional Consultant's Certificate which forms an appendix to this Handbook or such other form as we may provide. The professional consultant should also confirm to you that he has appropriate experience in the design or monitoring of the construction or conversion of residential buildings and has one or more of the following qualifications:
- fellow or member of the Royal Institution of Chartered Surveyors (FRICS or MRICS); or
- fellow or member of the Institution of Structural Engineers (F.I.Struct.E or M.I.Struct.E); or
- fellow or member of the Chartered Institute of Building (FCIOB or MCIOB); or
- fellow or member of the Architecture and Surveying Institute (FASI or MASI) (only if in conjunction with a FCIOB or MCIOB qualification); or
- fellow or member of the Chartered Association of Building Engineers (C.Build E MCABE and C.Build E FCABE); or
- member of the Chartered Institute of Architectural Technologists (formerly British Institute of Architectural Technologists) (MCIAT); or
- architect registered with the Architects Registration Board (ARB). An architect must be registered with the Architects Registration Board, even if also a member of another institution, for example the Royal Institute of British Architects (RIBA); or
- fellow or member of the Institution of Civil Engineers (FICE or MICE).

6.7.5   At the time he issues his certificate of practical completion, the consultant must have professional indemnity insurance in force for each claim for the greater of either:
- the value of the property once completed; or
- £250,000 if employed directly by the borrower or, in any other case, £500,000. If we require a collateral warranty from any professional adviser, this will be stated specifically in the mortgage instructions.

6.7.6   Check part 2 to see if the consultant's certificate must be sent to us after completion.

6.8   Roads and Sewers

6.8.1   If the roads or sewers immediately serving the property are not adopted or maintained at public expense, there must be an agreement and bond in existence or you must report to us (see part 2 for who you should report to).

6.8.2   If there is any such agreement, it should be secured by bond or deposit as required by the appropriate authority to cover the cost of making up the roads and sewers to adoptable standards, maintaining them thereafter and procuring adoption.

6.8.3   If there is an arrangement between the developer and the lender whereby the lender will not require a retention, you must obtain confirmation from the developer that the arrangement is still in force.

6.8.4   Where roads and sewers are not adopted or to be adopted but are maintained by local residents or a management company this is acceptable providing that in your reasonable opinion appropriate arrangements for maintenance repairs and costs are in place.

6.9   Easements

6.9.1   You must take all reasonable steps to check that the property has the benefit of all easements necessary for its full use and enjoyment. All such rights must be enforceable by the borrower and the borrower's successors in title. If they are not check part 2 for our requirements.

6.9.2   If the borrower owns adjoining land over which the borrower requires access to the property or in respect of which services are provided to the property, this land must also be mortgaged to us unless all relevant easements are granted in the title of the land to be mortgaged to us and those rights are and remain enforceable in accordance with section 6.9.1.

6.10   Release of Retentions

6.10.1   If we make a retention from an advance (for example, for repairs, improvements or road works) we are not obliged to release that retention, or any part of it, if the borrower is in breach of any of his obligations under the mortgage, or if a condition attached to the retention has not been met or if the loan has been repaid in full. You should, therefore not give an unqualified undertaking to pay the retention to a third party.

6.10.2   Check part 2 to see who we will release the retention to.

6.11   Neighbourhood Changes

6.11.1   The local search or the enquiries of the seller's conveyancer should not reveal that the property is in an area scheduled for redevelopment or in any way affected by road proposals. If it is please report to us (see part 2).

6.12   Rights of Pre-emption and Restriction on Resale

6.12.1   You must ensure that there are no rights of pre-emption, restrictions on resale, options or similar arrangements in existence at completion which will affect our security. If there are, please report this to us (see part 2).

6.13   Improvements and Repair Grants

6.13.1   Where the property is subject to an improvement or repair grant which will not be discharged or waived on completion, check part 2 to see whether you must report the matter to us.

6.14   Insurance

6.14.1   You must make reasonable enquiries to satisfy yourself that buildings insurance has been arranged for the property from no later than completion.
You should remind the borrower that they:
- must have buildings insurance in accordance with the requirements of the mortgage contract no later than completion; and
- must maintain such buildings insurance throughout the mortgage term.

7.   OTHER OCCUPIERS

7.1   Rights or interests of persons who are not a party to the mortgage and who are or will be in occupation of the property may affect our rights under the mortgage, for example as overriding interests.

7.2   If your instructions state the name of a person who is to live at the property, you should ask the borrower before completing the mortgage that the information given by us in our mortgage instructions or mortgage offer about occupants is correct and nobody else is to live at the property.

7.3   Unless we state otherwise (see part 2), you must obtain a signed deed or form of consent from all occupants aged 17 or over of whom you are aware who are not a party to the mortgage before completion of the mortgage. If you are acting in accordance with part 3—Separate Representation Standard Instructions you should refer to section 7 ("Other occupiers") of part 3.

7.4   We recognise that in some cases the information given to us or you by a borrower may be incorrect or misleading. If you have any reason to doubt the accuracy of any information disclosed, you should report it to us (see part 2) provided the borrower agrees; if the borrower does not agree, you should return our instructions.

8.   CIRCUMSTANCES REQUIRING INDEPENDENT LEGAL ADVICE

8.1   Unless we otherwise state (see part 2), you must not advise:
- any borrower who does not personally benefit from the loan; or
- any guarantor; or
- anyone intending to occupy the property who is to execute a consent to the mortgage and you must arrange for them to seek independent legal advice.

If you are acting in accordance with part 3—Separate Representation Standard Instructions you should refer to section 8 (Circumstances Requiring Independent Legal Advice) of part 3.

8.2   If we do allow you to advise any of these people, you must only do so after recommending in the absence of any other person interested in the transaction that such person obtains independent legal advice. Any advice that you give any of these people must also be given in the absence of any other person interested in the transaction. You should be particularly careful if the matrimonial home or family home is being charged to secure a business debt. Any consent should be signed by the person concerned. A power of attorney is not acceptable.

9.   INDEMNITY INSURANCE

9.1   You must effect an indemnity insurance policy whenever the Lenders' Handbook identifies that this is an acceptable or required course to us to ensure that the property has a good and marketable title at completion. This paragraph does not relate to mortgage indemnity insurance. The draft policy should not be sent to us unless we ask for it. Check part 2 to see if the policy must be sent to us after completion.

9.2   Where indemnity insurance is effected:
- you must approve the terms of the policy on our behalf; and
- the limit of indemnity must meet our requirements (see part 2); and
- the policy must be effected without cost to us; and

- you must disclose to the insurer all relevant information which you have obtained; and
- the policy must not contain conditions which you know would make it void or prejudice our interests; and
- you must provide a copy of the policy to the borrower and explain to the borrower why the policy was effected and that a further policy may be required if there is further lending against the security of the property; and
- you must explain to the borrower that the borrower will need to comply with any conditions of the policy and that the borrower should notify us of any notice or potential claim in respect of the policy; and
- the policy should always be for our benefit and, if possible, for the benefit of the borrower and any subsequent owner or mortgagee. If the borrower will not be covered by the policy, you must advise the borrower of this.

10.   THE LOAN AND CERTIFICATE OF TITLE

10.1   You should not submit your certificate of title unless it is unqualified or we have authorised you in writing to proceed notwithstanding any issues you have raised with us.

10.2   We shall treat the submission by you of the certificate of title as confirmation that the borrower has chosen to proceed with our mortgage offer and as a request for us to release the mortgage advance to you. Check part 2 to see if the mortgage advance will be paid electronically or by cheque and the minimum number of days notice we require.

10.3   See part 2 for any standard deductions which may be made from the mortgage advance.

10.4   You are only authorised to release the loan when you hold sufficient funds to complete the purchase of the property and pay all stamp duty land tax and registration fees to perfect the security as a first legal mortgage or, if you do not have them, you accept responsibility to pay them yourself. This does not apply if acting in accordance with Part 3—Separate Representation Standard Instructions.

10.5   Before releasing the loan when the borrower is purchasing the property you must either hold a properly completed and executed stamp duty land tax form or you must hold an appropriate authority from the borrower allowing you to file the necessary stamp duty land tax return(s) on completion.

10.6   You must ensure that all stamp duty land tax returns are completed and submitted to allow registration of the charge to take place in the priority period afforded by the search.

10.7   You must hold the loan on trust for us until completion. If completion is delayed, you must return it to us when and how we tell you (see part 2).

10.8   You should note that although your certificate of title will be addressed to us, we may at some time transfer our interest in the mortgage. In those circumstances, our successors in title to the mortgage and persons deriving title under or through the mortgage will also rely on your certificate.

10.9   If, after you have requested the mortgage advance, completion is delayed you must contact us immediately after you are aware of the delay and you must inform us of the new date for completion (see part 2).

10.10 See part 2 for details of how long you can hold the mortgage advance before returning it to us. If completion is delayed for longer than that period, you must return the mortgage advance to us. If you do not, we reserve the right to require you to pay interest on the amount of the mortgage advance (see part 2).

10.11   If the mortgage advance is not returned within the period set out in part 2, we will assume that the mortgage has been completed, and we will charge the borrower interest under the mortgage.

11.   THE DOCUMENTATION

11.1   The Mortgage

11.1.1   The mortgage incorporates our current mortgage conditions and, where applicable, loan conditions. If the mortgage conditions booklet is supplied to you with your instructions you must give it to the borrower before completion of the mortgage.

11.1.2   You should explain to each borrower (and any other person signing or executing a document) his responsibilities and liabilites under the documents referred to in paragraph 11.1.1 and any documents he is required to sign.

11.2   Signing and Witnessing of Documents

11.2.1   Except where we specify otherwise in our individual instructions, the signature of a document that needs to be witnessed must be witnessed by an independent person. The witness's signature must clearly record the witnessing of the signing of the document by the individual concerned, and the name and address of the witness must appear in legible form. All documents required at completion must be dated with the date of completion of the loan.

12.   INSTALMENT MERTGAGES AND MORTGAGE ADVANCES RELEASED IN IINSTALMENTS

12. 1   Introduction

12.1.2   The borrower is expected to pay for as much work as possible from his own resources before applying to us for the first instalment. However, we may, if required, consider advancing a nominal sum on receipt of the certificate of title to enable the mortgage to be completed so long as the legal estate in the property is vested in the borrower.

12.1.3   The borrower is responsible for our valuer's fees for interim valuations as well as the first and final valuations.

12.2   Applications for Part of the Advance

12.2.1   As in the case of a normal mortgage account, funds for instalment mortgages may be sent to you. However, instalments (apart from the first which will be sent to you to enable you to complete the mortgage) can be sent directly to the borrower on request. We may make further payments and advances without reference to you.

12.3   Requests for Intermediate Funds

12.3.1   To allow time for a valuation to be carried out, your request should be sent to us (see part 2) at least 10 days before the funds are required.

12.4   Building Contract as Security

12.4.1   We will not lend on the security of a building contract unless we tell you to the contrary. As a result the mortgage must not be completed and no part of the advance released until the title to the legal estate in the property has been vested by the borrower.

13.   MORTGAGE INDEMNITY INSURANCE OR HIGHER LENDING CHARGE

13.1   You are reminded to tell the borrower that we (and not the borrower) are the insured under any mortgage indemnity or similar form of insurance policy and that the insurer will have a subrogated right to claim against the borrower if it pays us under the policy. Different lenders call the various schemes of this type by different names. They may not involve an insurance policy.

14.   AFTER COMPLETION

14.1   Registration

14.1.1   You must register our mortgage as a first legal charge at the Land Registry.

14.1.2   Where the borrower or mortgagor is a company an application to register the charge must be lodged at Companies House within the required time period.

14.1.3   Our mortgage conditions and mortgage deed have been deposited at the Land Registry and it is therefore unnecessary to submit a copy of the mortgage conditions on an application for registration.

14.1.4   Where the loan is to be made in instalments or there is any deferred interest retention or stage release, check part 2 to see whether you must apply to Land Registry on form CH2 for entry of a notice on the register that we are under an obligation to make further advances. If the mortgage deed states that it secures further advances, and that the lender is under an obligation to make them, there is no need to submit a form CH2 provided the mortgage deed also states that application is made to the Registrar for a note to be entered on the register to that effect and the mortgage deed bears a Land Registry MD reference at its foot.

14.1.5   The application for registration must be received by the Land Registry during the priority period afforded by the subsisting Land Registry or Land Charges search at the time of completion. Please check part 2 to see if we require the original mortgage deed and/or any other original title documents to be returned to us. You may use any available Land Registry process for registration including electronic registration. You should retain any original documents until you are satisfied that the registration is completed. You are not otherwise required by us to retain any original documents.

14.2   Title Deeds

14.2.1   All title deeds, official copies of the register (where these are issued by the Land Registry after registration), searches, enquiries, consents, requisitions and documents relating to the property in your possession must be held to our order pending completion of the retainer and you must not create or exercise any lien over them. Check part 2 for our requirements on what you should do with these documents following registration. If registration at the Land Registry has not been completed within three months from completion you must advise us in writing with a copy of any correspondence with the Land Registry explaining the delay.

14.2.2   You must only send us documents we tell you to (see part 2). You should obtain the borrower's instructions concerning the retention of documents we tell you not to send us.

14.3   Your Mortgage File

14.3.1   For evidential purposes you must keep your file for at least six years from the date of the mortgage before destroying it. You should retain on file those documents as specified in these instructions, and/or our individual instructions, and any other documents which a reasonably competent solicitor/conveyancer would keep. Microfiching, data imaging or material held electronically consititutes suitable compliance with this requirement. It is the practice of some fraudsters to demand the conveyancing file on completion in order to destroy evidence that may later be used against them. It is important to retain these documents to protect our interests.

14.3.2   Where you are processing personal data (as defined in the Data Protection Act 1998) on our behalf, you must;

- take such security measures as are required to enable you to comply with obligations equivalent to those imposed on us by the seventh data protection principle in the 1998 Act; and

- process such personal data only in accordance with our instructions. In addition, you must allow us to conduct such reasonable audit of your information security measures as we require to ensure your compliance with your obligations in this paragraph.

14.3.3   Subject to any right of lien or any overriding duty of confidentiality, you should treat documents comprising your file as if they are jointly owned by the borrower and us and you should not part with them without the consent of both parties. You should on request supply certified copies of documents on the file or a certified copy of the microfiche to either the borrower or us, and may make a reasonable charge for copying and certification. This does not apply if acting in accordance with Part 3—Separate Representation Standard Instructions.

15.   LEGAL COSTS

15.1   Your charges and disbursements are payable by the borrower and should be collected from the borrower on or before completion. You must not allow non-payment of fees or disbursements to delay the payment of stamp duty land tax, the lodging of any stamp duty land tax return and registration of documents.

16.   TRANSACTIONS DURING THE LIFE OF THE MORTGAGE

16.1   Request for Title Documents

16.1.1   All requests for title documents should be made in writing and sent to us (see part 2). In making such a request you must have the consent of all of the borrowers to apply for the title documents.

16.2   Further Advances

16.2.1   Our mortgage secures further advances. Consequently, when a further advance is required for alterations or improvements to the property we will not normally instruct a member of our conveyancing panel but if you are instructed the appropriate provisions of this Handbook will apply.

16.3   Transfers of Equity

16.3.1   You must approve the transfer (which should be in the Land Registry's standard form) and, if we require, the deed of covenant on our behalf. Check part 2 to see if we have standard forms of transfer and deed of covenant.

16.3.2   When drafting or approving a transfer, you should bear in mind that:

- although the transfer should state that it is subject to the mortgage (identified by date and parties), it need give no details of the terms of the mortgage;

- the transfer need not state the amount of the mortgage debt. If it does, the figure should include both principal and interest at the date of completion, which you must check (see part 2 for where to obtain this);
- there should be no statement that all interest has been paid to date.

16.3.3 You must ensure that every person who will be a borrower after the transfer covenants with us to pay the money secured by the mortgage, except in the case of:
- an original party to the mortgage (unless the mortgage conditions are being varied); or
- a person who has previously covenanted to that effect.

16.3.4 Any such covenant will either be in the transfer or in a separate deed of covenant. In a transfer, the wording of the covenant should be as follows, or as close as circumstances permit: "The new borrower agrees to pay the lender all the money due under the mortgage and will keep to all the terms of the mortgage." If it is in the transfer, you must place a certified copy of the transfer with the deeds (unless we tell you not to in part 2).

16.3.5 If we have agreed to release a borrower or a guarantor and our standard transfer form (if any) includes no appropriate clause, you must add a simple form of release. The release clause should be as follows, or as close as circumstances permit: "The lender releases . . . from [his/her/their] obligations under the mortgage." You should check whether a guarantor who is to be released was a party to the mortgage or to a separate guarantee.

16.3.6 You must obtain the consent of every guarantor of whom you are aware to the release of a borrower or, as the case may be, any other guarantor.

16.3.7 You must only submit the transfer to us for execution if it releases a party. All other parties must execute the transfer before it is sent to us. See part 2 for where the transfer should be sent for sealing. Part 2 also gives our approved form of attestation clause.

16.4   Properties to be Let after Completion (other than "Buy-to-Let")

16.4.1 If prior to completion of the retainer, the Borrower informs you of an intention to let the property you should advise the borrower that any letting of the property is prohibited without our prior consent. If the borrower wishes to let the property after completion then an application for consent should be made to us by the borrower (see part 2).

16.4.2 Check part 2 to see whether it is necessary to send to us a copy of the proposed tenancy when making the application.

16.4.3 If the application for our consent is approved and we instruct you to act for us, you must approve the form of tenancy agreement on our behalf in accordance with our instructions.

16.5   Deeds of Variation etc

16.5.1 If we consent to any proposal for a deed of variation, rectification, easement or option agreement, we will rely on you to approve the documents on our behalf.

16.5.2 Our consent will usually be forthcoming provided that you first of all confirm in writing to us (see part 2) that our security will not be adversely affected in any way by entering into the deed. If you are able to provide this confirmation then we will not normally need to see a draft of the deed. If you cannot provide confirmation and we need to consider the matter in detail then an additional administration fee is likely to be charged.

16.5.3 Whether we are a party to the deed or give a separate deed or form of consent is a matter for your discretion. It should be sent to us (see part 2) for sealing or signing with a brief explanation of the reason for the document and its effect together with your confirmation that it will not adversely affect our security.

16.6   Deeds of Postponement or Substitution

16.6. 1 If we agree to enter into an arrangement with other lenders concerning the order of priority of their mortgages, you will be supplied with our standard form of deed or form of postponement or substitution. We will normally not agree to any amendments to the form. In no cases will we postpone our first charge over the property.

17. REDEMPTION

17.1   Redemption Statement

17.1.1   When requesting a redemption statement (see part 2) you should quote the expected repayment date and whether you are acting for the borrower or have the borrower's authority to request the redemption statement in addition to the information mentioned in paragraph 2.1. You should request this at least five working days before the expected redemption date. You must quote all the borrower's mortgage account or roll numbers of which you are aware when requesting the repayment figure. You must only request a redemption statement if you are acting for the borrower or have the borrower's written authority to request a redemption statement.

17.1.2   To guard against fraud please ensure that if payment is made by cheque then the redemption cheque is made payable to us and you quote the mortgage account number or roll number and name of the borrower.

17.2   Discharge

17.2.1   On the day of completion you should send the discharge (if required) and your remittance for the repayment to us (see part 2). Check part 2 to see if we discharge via a DS1 form or direct notification to the Land Registry.

APPENDIX 13

Mortgage Deed

MORTGAGE DEED

Account number: 38877863637/KHY
Date: 20 July 2018
The Lender: Wiltshire Building Society of Balmour House Swindon SN38 3FN
The Mortgage Conditions: The Lender's mortgage conditions 2009 filed at Land Registry under reference DHSJD/556
The Borrower: Adam William Federici of 27 Winton Road Reading RG3 1PW
The Guarantor: Not applicable
The Property: 27 Winton Road Reading RG3 1PW
Title number: BK284674

1. This mortgage deed incorporates the Mortgage Conditions a copy of which has been received by the Borrower.
2. The Borrower with full title guarantee charges the Property by way of legal mortgage with the payment of all money payable by the Borrower to the Lender under the Mortgage Conditions.
3. The mortgage secures further advances but does not oblige the Lender to make further loans.
4. The Guarantor (if any) confirms receipt of the Mortgage Conditions and gives the guarantee set out in them.

SIGNED AS A DEED as under in the presence of the witness

Signature of the Borrower and Guarantor (if any) Signature, name and address of each witness

NOTE TO GUARANTOR: By signing this deed you may become liable instead of or as well as the Borrower for all the money owing under this deed. You should take independent advice before signing.

Note: For an example of mortgage instructions to a solicitor see Figure 6.1 in Chapter 6.

APPENDIX 14

Guide to Completing Prescribed Clauses: Text that Must be Included

Please note that guidance regarding prescribed clauses will appear within brackets.

LR1. Date of lease

LR2. Title number(s)

LR2.1 Landlord's title number(s)

(Title number out of which the lease is granted. Leave blank if not registered.)

LR2.2 Other title numbers

(Existing title number(s) against which entries of matters referred to in LR9, LR10, LR11 and LR13 are to be made.)

LR3. Parties to this lease

Landlord, Tenant

(Give full names, addresses and company's registered number, if any, of each of the parties. For Scottish companies use a SC prefix and for limited liability partnerships use an OC prefix. For foreign companies give territory in which incorporated.)

Other parties

(Specify capacity of each party, for example 'management company', 'guarantor', etc.)

LR4. Property

In the case of a conflict between this clause and the remainder of this lease then, for the purposes of registration, this clause shall prevail.

(Insert a full description of the land being leased, or refer to the clause, schedule or paragraph of a schedule in this lease in which the land being leased is more fully described. Where there is a letting of part of a registered title, a plan must be attached to this lease and any floor levels must be specified.)

LR5. Prescribed statements, etc.

(If the lease includes a statement falling within LR5.1, insert under that sub-clause the relevant statement or refer to the clause, schedule or paragraph of a schedule in this lease which contains the statement. In LR5.2, omit or delete those Acts which do not apply to this lease. LR5.1 Statements prescribed under rules 179 (dispositions in favour of a charity), 180 (dispositions by a charity) or 196 (leases under the Leasehold Reform, Housing and Urban Development Act 1993) of the Land Registration Rules 2003.

LR5.2 This lease is made under, or by reference to, provisions of: Leasehold Reform Act 1967, Housing Act 1985, Housing Act 1988, Housing Act 1996.)

LR6. Term for which the Property is leased

(Include only the appropriate statement (duly completed) from the three options. NOTE: the information you provide, or refer to here, will be used as part of the particulars to identify the lease under rule 6 of the Land Registration Rules 2003.)

From and including /To and including (or)

The term as specified in this lease at clause/schedule/paragraph (or)

The term is as follows:

LR7. Premium

(Specify the total premium, inclusive of any VAT where payable.)

LR8. Prohibitions or restrictions on disposing of this lease

(Include whichever of the two statements is appropriate. Do not set out here the wording of the provision.)

This lease does not contain a provision that prohibits or restricts dispositions. (Or) This lease contains a provision that prohibits or restricts dispositions.

LR9. Rights of acquisition, etc.

(Insert the relevant provisions in the sub-clauses or refer to the clause, schedule or paragraph of a schedule in this lease which contains the provisions.)

LR9.1 Tenant's contractual rights to renew this lease, to acquire the reversion or another lease of the Property, or to acquire an interest in other land

LR9.2 Tenant's covenant to (or offer to) surrender this lease

LR9.3 Landlord's contractual rights to acquire this lease

LR10. Restrictive covenants given in this lease by the Landlord in respect of land other than the Property

(Insert the relevant provisions or refer to the clause, schedule or paragraph of a schedule in this lease which contains the provisions.)

LR11. Easements

(Refer here only to the clause, schedule or paragraph of a schedule in this lease which sets out the easements.)

LR11.1 Easements granted by this lease for the benefit of the Property

LR11.2 Easements granted or reserved by this lease over the Property for the benefit of other property

LR12. Estate rentcharge burdening the Property

(Refer here only to the clause, schedule or paragraph of a schedule in this lease which sets out the rentcharge.)

LR13. Application for standard form of restriction

(Set out the full text of the standard form of restriction and the title against which it is to be entered. If you wish to apply for more than one standard form of restriction use this clause to apply for each of them, tell us who is applying against which title and set out the full text of the restriction you are applying for. Standard forms of restriction are set out in Schedule 4 to the Land Registration Rules 2003.)

The Parties to this lease apply to enter the following standard form of restriction (against the title of the Property or against title number.)

LR14. Declaration of trust where there is more than one person comprising the Tenant

(If the Tenant is one person, omit or delete all the alternative statements. If the Tenant is more than one person, complete this clause by omitting or deleting all inapplicable alternative statements.)

The Tenant is more than one person. They are to hold the Property on trust for themselves as joint tenants. (Or)

The Tenant is more than one person. They are to hold the Property on trust for themselves as tenants in common in equal shares. (Or)

The Tenant is more than one person. They are to hold the Property on trust (complete as necessary).

APPENDIX 15

Specimen Land Registry Official Copy Entries and Title Plan

Land Registry

Official copy of register of title	Title number DN649563	Edition date 28.02.2018

— This official copy shows the entries in the register of title on 28 February 2018 at 11:50:13.
— This date must be quoted as the "search from date" in any official search application based on this copy.
— The date at the beginning of an entry is the date on which the entry was made in the register.
— Issued on 28 February 2018.
— Under s.67 of the Land Registration Act 2002, this copy is admissible in evidence to the same extent as the original.
— For information about the register of title see Land Registry website www.landregistry.gov.uk or Land Registry Public Guide1 - *A guide to the information we keep and how you can obtain it.*
— This title is dealt with by Land Registry Plymouth Office.

A: Property register
This register describes the land and estate comprised in the title.

```
DEVON : SOUTH HAMS
DEVON : EXETER
CITY OF PLYMOUTH
```

1   (28.02.2018) The Freehold land shown edged with red on the plan of the above Title filed at the Registry and being 14 Heather Close, Waverley (WY15 9PB).

B: Proprietorship register
This register specifies the class of title and identifies the owner. It contains any entries that affect the right of disposal.

Title absolute

1   (28.02.2018) PROPRIETOR: Christopher Hunt of 14 Heather Close, Waverley (WY15 9PB).

2   (28.02.2018) The price stated to have been paid on 12 February 2018 was £125,000.

3   (28.02.2018) RESTRICTION: No disposition of the registered estate by the proprietor of the registered estate is to be registered without a written consent signed by the proprietor for the time being of the Charge dated 12 February 2018 in favour of Limitless Mortgages UK Ltd referred to in the Charges Register.

C: Charges register
This register contains any charges and other matters that affect the land.

1   (28.02.2018) REGISTERED CHARGE dated 12 February 2018.

2   (28.02.2018) Proprietor: LIMITLESS MORTGAGES UK LTD (Co. Regn. No.
     7654321) of Poplar House, 104 Barge Street, Leatherhead, Surrey KT23 8BZ.

End of register

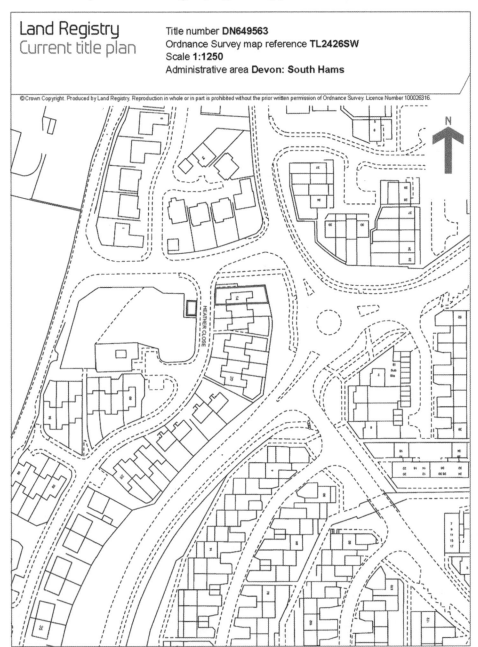

Land Registry
Current title plan

Title number **DN649563**
Ordnance Survey map reference **TL2426SW**
Scale **1:1250**
Administrative area **Devon: South Hams**

© Crown Copyright. Produced by Land Registry. Reproduction in whole or in part is prohibited without the prior written permission of Ordnance Survey. Licence Number 100026316.

This official copy issued on 28 February 2018 shows the state of this title plan, on 28 February 2018 at 11:50:13 admissible in evidence to the same extent as the original (s.67 Land Registration Act 2002).
This title plan shows the general position, not the exact line, of the boundaries. It may be subject to distortions in scale. Measurements scaled from this plan may not match measurements between the same points on the ground. See Land Registry Public Guide 7 – Title Plans.
This title is dealt with by Land Registry Plymouth Office

INDEX